TARP AND OTHER BANK BAILOUTS AND BAIL-INS AROUND THE WORLD

TARP AND OTHER BANK BAILOUTS AND BAIL-INS AROUND THE WORLD

Connecting Wall Street, Main Street, and the Financial System

ALLEN N. BERGER
Moore School of Business
University of South Carolina
Columbia, SC, United States
Wharton Financial Institutions Center, United States
European Banking Center, the Netherlands

RALUCA A. ROMAN
Federal Reserve Bank of Philadelphia
Philadelphia, PA, United States

ACADEMIC PRESS
An imprint of Elsevier

Academic Press is an imprint of Elsevier
125 London Wall, London EC2Y 5AS, United Kingdom
525 B Street, Suite 1650, San Diego, CA 92101, United States
50 Hampshire Street, 5th Floor, Cambridge, MA 02139, United States
The Boulevard, Langford Lane, Kidlington, Oxford OX5 1GB, United Kingdom

Notices
Knowledge and best practice in this field are constantly changing. As new research and
experience broaden our understanding, changes in research methods, professional
practices, or medical treatment may become necessary.

Practitioners and researchers must always rely on their own experience and knowledge
in evaluating and using any information, methods, compounds, or experiments
described herein. In using such information or methods they should be mindful of
their own safety and the safety of others, including parties for whom they have a
professional responsibility.

To the fullest extent of the law, neither the Publisher nor the authors, contributors, or
editors, assume any liability for any injury and/or damage to persons or property as a
matter of products liability, negligence or otherwise, or from any use or operation of
any methods, products, instructions, or ideas contained in the material herein.

Library of Congress Cataloging-in-Publication Data
A catalog record for this book is available from the Library of Congress

British Library Cataloguing-in-Publication Data
A catalogue record for this book is available from the British Library

ISBN: 978-0-12-813864-9

For information on all Academic Press publications visit our website at
https://www.elsevier.com/books-and-journals

Publisher: Brian Romer
Editorial Project Manager: Lindsay Lawrence
Production Project Manager: Niranjan Bhaskaran
Cover Designer: Christian J. Bilbow

Typeset by TNQ Technologies

Working together
to grow libraries in
developing countries

www.elsevier.com • www.bookaid.org

Dedication

Allen N. Berger
To my wife, Mindy Ring

Raluca A. Roman
To my son Oliver, my husband Catalin, and my parents Rodica and Mihai

Contents

I

Introductory materials 1

II

Empirical research on TARP 173

5. Methodologies used in most of the TARP empirical studies

6. Determinants of applying for and receiving TARP funds and exiting early from the program

7. Effects of TARP on recipient banks' valuations

8. Effects of TARP on market discipline

9. Effects of TARP on bank leverage risk

10. Effects of TARP on bank competition

11. Effects of TARP on bank credit supply

12. Effects of TARP on bank portfolio risk

13. Effects of TARP on recipient banks' credit customers

14. Effects of TARP on the real economy

15. Effects of TARP on systemic risk

III

Empirical evidence on bank bailouts other than TARP, bail-ins, and other resolution approaches 257

16. Empirical research on bailouts other than TARP

17. Empirical research on bail-ins

18. Empirical research on other resolution approaches

IV

First lines of defense to help avoid bailouts, bail-ins, and other resolutions 303

19. Mechanisms for the first lines of defense

25. Deposit insurance

26. Direct government ownership of banks

V

Looking toward the future   399

27. Social costs and benefits

28. Implications for bank policymakers and bank managers

29. Open research questions to be addressed by future research

Author Biographies

Allen N. Berger is the H. Montague Osteen, Jr., Professor in Banking and Finance in the Finance Department, Darla Moore School of Business, University of South Carolina, since 2008. He is also a PhD coordinator of the Finance Department and Carolina Distinguished Professor of the University. Outside the University, he is currently Vice President of the Financial Intermediation Research Society (FIRS), and will be its 2021 Conference Coordinator, and 2022 Program Chair and President. He is also a Senior Fellow at the Wharton Financial Institutions Center and Fellow of the European Banking Center, and serves on the editorial boards of eight profes-

Allen N. Berger

sional finance and economics journals. Professor Berger was an editor of the *Journal of Money, Credit, and Banking* from 1994 to 2001, has coedited seven special issues of various professional journals, and has coorganized a number of professional research conferences. He also coedited all three editions of the *The Oxford Handbook of Banking*, 2010, 2015, and 2019. His research covers a variety of topics related to financial institutions. He is a coauthor of *Bank Liquidity Creation and Financial Crises* (2016, Elsevier) as well as *TARP and other Bank Bailouts and Bail-Ins around the World: Connecting Wall Street, Main Street, and the Financial System* (2020, Elsevier).

He has published over 150 professional articles, including well over 100 in refereed journals. These include papers in top finance journals, *Journal of Finance, Journal of Financial Economics, Review of Financial Studies, Journal of Financial and Quantitative Analysis, Review of Finance,* and *Journal of Financial Intermediation*; top economics journals, *Journal of Political Economy, American Economic Review, Review of Economics and Statistics,* and *Journal of Monetary Economics*; and other top professional business journals, *Management Science, Journal of Business,* and *European Journal of Operational Research*. His research has been cited over 80,000 times according to Google Scholar, including 27 different articles with over 1000 citations. He has given invited keynote addresses on five continents and has been a visiting scholar at several Federal Reserve Banks and central banks of other nations.

Professor Berger received the University of South Carolina Educational Foundation Award for Research in Professional Schools for 2018 and was named Professor of the Year for 2015–2016 by the Darla Moore School of Business Doctoral Students Association. He also has won a number of best paper awards from different journals and finance conferences. He was a Secretary/Treasurer of Financial Intermediation Research Society (FIRS) from 2008 to 2016; and Senior Economist from 1989 to 2008 and Economist from 1982 to 1989 at the Board of Governors of the Federal Reserve System. He received a PhD in Economics from the University of California, Berkeley in 1983 and a BA in Economics from Northwestern University in 1976.

Raluca A. Roman

Raluca A. Roman is Senior Economist at the Federal Reserve Bank of Philadelphia since July 2018. From 2015 to 2018, she was Research Economist at Federal Reserve Bank of Kansas City. She holds a PhD in Finance from University of South Carolina. Raluca also holds an MBA with concentration in Finance from University of Bridgeport and a BA in Economics from Alexandru Ioan Cuza University (Romania). Raluca's research areas include a variety of topics related to banking and financial institutions (including bank government bailouts and bail-ins, bank stress tests, internationalization, and corporate governance), consumer finance (including retail credit, consumer behavior, and consumer market trends), corporate finance, and international finance. She has published three articles in the *Journal of Financial and Quantitative Analysis,* one in *Management Science,* two in the *Journal of Financial Intermediation,* one in *Journal of Money, Credit, and Banking,* one in *Financial Management,* one in *Journal of Corporate Finance,* one in *Journal of Banking and Finance,* one book chapter in the *Handbook of Finance and Development* and one book chapter in the *The Oxford Handbook of Banking,* and has received four awards for her papers at conferences. She is also currently coauthoring the book *TARP and other Bank Bailouts and Bail-Ins around the World: Connecting Wall Street, Main Street, and the Financial System* (2020, Elsevier). Raluca has presented her research and discussed the research of others at numerous finance and regulatory conferences. She also has over 7 years of professional experience in banking and corporate finance and worked for top international organizations like UBS Investment Bank and MasterCard International, where she won various awards.

Foreword

This is an impressive book on perhaps the most enduring and important regulatory policy response to financial crises: bank bailouts. This regulatory response that has elicited much discussion and controversy because it solves a vexing problem in the midst of a crisis while raising the specter of moral hazard in future behavior. Allen N. Berger and Raluca A. Roman—who have together published a number of influential research papers on bailouts and other banking topics—have put together an extraordinarily comprehensive research-based discussion of the core issues involved in bailouts and bail-in measures for banks. Their deep knowledge of these issues and prescriptions for regulators lead to a book that is rich in insights and extensive in its coverage.

The book takes the reader through a careful discussion of what these measures really are, why they are used, how they are used, and what their economic effects are. The reader not only gets a good understanding of the economic circumstances in which these measures are used, but also an understanding of complementary regulatory initiatives like regulatory supervision, bank activity restrictions, deposit insurance, government ownership, capital and liquidity requirements. Why do we need so many intervention tools? How are they related? How do they differ? How do they work in concert? Read this book to find out!

The book contains an extensive discussion of TARP (Troubled Asset Relief Program) that the US government used to resolve the 2007—09 crisis. If you ever wondered what this program was all about, how it was executed, and what its consequences were, this book has all the answers.

A good book on any topic helps the novice understand the core issues, but is also informative for the expert. That is exactly what this book achieves. It is a must-read for all interested in financial crises and policy measures to deal with crises, including bailouts and bail-ins.

Anjan V. Thakor
John E. Simon, Professor of Finance,
Director of the PhD Program, and Director of the WFA
Center for Finance and Accounting Research
Olin School of Business, Washington University in St. Louis

Preface

We met in August 2010 when Raluca was a starting PhD student in Finance in the Darla Moore Business School at the University of South Carolina and Allen was H. Montague Osteen, Jr., Professor in Banking and Finance in the same Finance Department. We had no idea at that time what lay ahead in terms of an extremely productive research relationship as well as a warm personal friendship.

Prior to then, Raluca had earned her MBA with concentration in Finance at University of Bridgeport, Bridgeport, Connecticut, and a BA in Economics at Alexandru Ioan Cuza University in her home nation of Romania, and worked several years in the banking industry. Allen had earned his PhD and MA degrees in Economics at University of California, Berkeley and his BA in Economics at Northwestern University. He worked at the Federal Reserve Board in Washington prior to joining the Finance faculty at University of South Carolina.

During her years of PhD study, Raluca served as research assistant, teaching assistant, and co-author to Allen. After finishing her PhD in May 2015, Raluca has worked at the Federal Reserve Bank of Kansas City, and now at the Federal Reserve Bank of Philadelphia. Allen has been promoted to Carolina Distinguished Professor at the University of South Carolina.

As with any research relationship, ours started off slowly and accelerated over time. Our first project together was "Did TARP Banks Get Competitive Advantages?" published in the *Journal of Financial and Quantitative Analysis* in 2015. Since then, we have published together several other TARP papers, and additional finance papers in quality finance and management journals, as well as a book chapter. We also have a number of working papers in various states of progress toward publication, including more TARP papers. Importantly, each of us also has publications independent of one another. All of our research is banking related.

We believe that this research has paved the way nicely for this book, and we are delighted that Elsevier has agreed to publish it. We hope that the readers both enjoy and are informed by it.

Finally, we want to thank again the students noted in the acknowledgments that assisted us in this endeavor. We could not have done it without you!

Acknowledgments

The views expressed herein are those of the authors and do not necessarily reflect the views of the Federal Reserve Bank of Philadelphia or the Federal Reserve System. The authors thank Arnoud Boot, John Hackney, Chuck Morris, John Sedunov, Anjan Thakor, Sergey Tsyplakov, and Teng Wang for useful comments, and students Jin Cai, Yamaisi Errasti, Jiarui (Jerry) Guo, Andrew (Drew) Jurs, Destan Kirimhan, Kornelia (Kora) Kostka, Xinming Li, Xiaonan (Flora) Ma, Virginia Traweek, and Hyo Jin Yoon for both useful comments and excellent research assistance.

PART I

Introductory materials

Introduction to Part I

This book reviews and critically assesses the theoretical and empirical research evidence on the Troubled Asset Relief Program (TARP) in the United States (US) and other bank bailouts and bail-ins in the US and around the world. Bank bailouts generally involve putting taxpayer funds at risk to rescue banks, while bail-ins require private sector agents to provide the capital. We assess the important costs and benefits of these programs, and suggest potential policy implications for prospective future bailouts and bail-ins.

We take a holistic approach in this book with much broader goals than just evaluating bailouts and bail-ins, which are not the only policy choices. We also consider other resolution options, including bankruptcy/failure, in which the bank holding company (BHC) that owns the bank goes bankrupt and the bank fails; living wills, in which the bank is saved by reorganizing and/or selling off less important subsidiaries of the BHC; forbearance, in which banks continue operations with little or no capital; and breaking up large and complex institutions into either smaller banks or separate commercial and investment banks.

We also evaluate other options for policymakers to help prevent the needs for bailouts, bail-ins, or other resolution methods in the first place. We call one set of such policies "first lines of defense," which help avoid the need for bank resolution by keeping the banks out of individual financial distress. We discuss and evaluate the research on seven such policies in the book, capital requirements, liquidity requirements, stress tests, prudential regulatory activity restrictions, prudential supervision, deposit insurance, and direct government bank ownership.

We also describe in the book research on a second set of policies designed to lessen the incidence of financial distress on an aggregate level. This involves reducing the likelihood and severity of financial crises through countercyclical prudential policy actions that lean against lending booms and excessive aggregate bank liquidity creation. In addition, countercyclical conventional monetary policy can also help lessen the financial and economic excesses that might otherwise increase the probability and intensity of financial crises.

Finally, we evaluate the social costs and benefits of all of these 16 different policy tools, draw policy implications, and provide suggestions for future research to help with understanding bailouts, bail-ins, and other resolution methods, first lines of defense, and countercyclical prudential and monetary policies.

There are five parts to the book, each containing a different number of chapters. For each of the five parts, we provide an introduction that briefly describes that part and includes a virtual "tree of knowledge." The leaves of the trees show the topics of the chapters in that part of the book, as well as the "fruits of knowledge," the key references that supplied the knowledge in these chapters. Without these "fruits" provided by the many authors cited in the book, there would be no body of knowledge about the topics covered by the book and no book itself. We thank these authors for their contributions.

Part I contains introductory materials and includes four chapters. Chapter 1 provides an introduction to bank bailouts, bail-ins, and the related topics covered in the book. It also briefly summarizes Parts II, III, IV, and V, and includes brief summaries of the chapters in all five parts of the book. Chapter 2 discusses the conditions that generally bring about bank bailouts, bail-ins, and other types of bank resolution. These conditions usually involve financial crises and/or the financial distress of certain banks that are considered too important to the economy and/or financial system to be allowed to fail. The chapter also analyzes some research on the underlying causes of financial crises and the distress of these important banks. Chapter 3 describes the TARP program, other bank bailouts and bail-ins in the US and around the world, as well as the other resolution methods. Chapter 4 completes the introductory materials by giving the theoretical background on bank bailouts, bail-ins, and these other resolution approaches.

Part II discusses the relatively large extant empirical research literature on TARP and may serve as a primer or mini-textbook on TARP bailouts. The 11 chapters of Part II each describe a different aspect of the research, most of them focusing on a particular consequence of the program. Part III provides three chapters that review the empirical research on bailouts other than TARP, bail-ins, and other resolution approaches, respectively. Part IV describes first lines of defense to help avoid the need for bank resolutions. The seven chapters in Part IV provide a relatively comprehensive review of prudential banking policies around the world and may also serve as a primer or mini-textbook on this topic for interested readers. Part V looks to the future with three final chapters that discuss the net social costs and benefits of the various resolution approaches, lines of defense, and countercyclical policy implications of the research, the policy implications from this research, and the research questions that remain open, respectively.

Part I: Introductory materials

1. Introduction to bank bailout and bail-ins and the rest of the book

Atkinson Luttrell, and Rosenblum, 2013; Avgouleas, Goodhart, and Schoenmaker, 2013; Bernanke, 1983; Claessens, Herring, Schoenmaker, and Summer, 2010; Friedman and Schwartz, 1963; García, 2015; U.S. Government Accountability Office Report, 2013.

2. Conditions that bring about bailouts and bail-ins

Acharya, 2009; Acharya and Naqvi, 2012; Acharya and Yorulmazer, 2007, 2008; Acharya, Mehran, and Thakor, 2016; Adnani, DeMarzo, Hellwig, and Pfleiderer, 2013; Assaf, Berger, Roman, and Tsionas, 2019; Barth and Wihlborg, 2015; Beltratti and Stulz, 2012; Berger and Bouwman, 2009, 2013, 2016, 2017; Berger and Udell, 2004; Berger, Imbierowicz, and Rauch, 2016; Book and Thakor, 1993; Brown and Dinc, 2011; Brunnermeier, Gorton, and Krishnamurthy, 2011; Cai, 2019; Calomiris and Carlson, 2017; Calomiris and Mason, 1997, 2003; Cetorelli and Traina, 2018; Choi, 2014; Cole and Fenn, 2008; Cole and Gunther, 1995, 1998; Cole and White, 2012; Dell'Ariccia, Igan, and Laeven, 2012; Demirguc-Kunt and Detragiache, 1998; DeYoung and Torna, 2013; Elsinger, Lehar, and Summer, 2006; Fahlenbrach and Stulz, 2011; Farhi and Tirole, 2012; Federal Deposit Insurance Corporation, 1997; Greenspan, 2001; Kane, 1989, 1991; Knaup and Wagner, 2012; Laeven and Valencia, 2018; Lane, Looney, and Wansley, 1986; Lui, Quiet, and Roth, 2015; Miskhin, 2006; Pagano and Sedunov, 2016; Rajan, 1994; Reinhart and Rogoff, 2009; Schaeck, 2008; Stern and Feldman, 2004; Thakor, 2005, 2015a,b, 2016; Von Hagen and Ho, 2007; Wheelock and Wilson, 1995, 2000.

4. Theory on bailouts, bail-ins, and other approaches

Acharya and Yorulmazer, 2007, 2008; Acharya, Mehran, and Thakor, 2016; Acharya and Thakor, 2016; Adnani, DeMarzo, Hellwig, and Pfleiderer, 2013; Allen, Carletti, Goldstein, and Leonello, 2018; Allen and Tang, 2016; Ammann, Blickle, and Ehmann, 2017; Avdjiev, Bogdanova, Bolton, Jiang, and Kartasheva, 2017; Avgouleas and Goodhart, 2016; Berger, 2018; Berger and Bouwman, 2013; Berger, Himmelberg, Roman, and Tsyplakov, 2019; Berger, Makaew, and Roman, 2019; Berger and Roman, 2015, 2017; Berger, Roman, and Sedunov, 2020; Besanko and Kanatas, 1996; Bindal, Bouwman, Hu, and Johnson, 2020; Black and Hazelwood, 2013; Bleck, 2014; Bouwman, Hu, and Johnson, 2018; Brown and Dinc, 2011; Calem and Rob, 1999; Calomiris and Herring, 2011, 2013; Carmassi and Herring, 2015; Cetorelli and Traina, 2018; Chan and Van Wijnbergen, 2014; Choi, 2014; Clayton and Schaab, 2019; Cordella and Yeyati, 2003; De Spiegeleer, Höcht and Schoutens, 2015; Dewatripont and Tirole, 2018; Duchin and Sosyura, 2014; Farhi and Tirole, 2012; Flannery, 2017; Fudenberg and Tirole, 1986; Grauwe, 2013; Gropp, Hakenes, and Schnabel, 2011; Hakimmanaul, 2016; Hart and Zingales, 2011; Hicks, 1935; Himmelberg and Tsyplakov, 2017; Hoshi and Kashyap, 2010; Huser, Halaj, Kok, Perales, and Van der Kraaij, 2018; Kane, 2003; Kashyap, Rajan, and Stein, 2008; Keeley, 1990; Keister and Mirkov, 2017; Keister and Narasiman, 2016; Kim and Santomero, 1988; Klimek, Poledna, Farmer, and Thurner, 2015; Koehn and Santomero, 1980; Kormendi, Bernard, Pirrong, and Snyder, 1989; Leanza, Sbuelz, and Tarelli, 2019; Li, 2013; Lupo-Pasini and Buckley, 2015; Merton and Thakor, 2019; Mitts, 2015; Nosal and Ordonez, 2016; Pandolfi, 2018; Persaud, 2014; Philippon and Schnabl, 2013; Roman, 2020; Teker, 1966; Walther and White, 2018; Zenios, 2016; Zombirt, 2015.

3. Descriptions of TARP, other bailouts, bail-ins, and other approaches

Anderson, Barth, Choi, 2018; Barofski, 2013; Bayazitova and Shivdasani, 2011; Berger and Bouwman, 2016; Berger, Black, Bouwman, and Dlugosz, 2017; Berger, Bouwman, Kick, and Schaeck, 2016; Bernanke, 2017; Brunner, Decressin, Hardy, and Kudela, 2004; Bush, 2008; Calomiris and Herring, 2011, 2013; Cetorelli and Traina, 2018; Congressional Oversight Panel, 2009, 2010; Cortés and Millington, 2014; Dam and Koetter, 2012; Duchin and Sosyura, 2011; Federal Reserve Bank of Minneapolis Plan, 2017; Federal Reserve Board of Governors, 2013; Flannery, 2014, 2016; Flannery and Bliss, 2019; Gropp and Tonzer, 2016; Hendrickson, 2014; Hinsenrath, Solomon, and Paletra, 2008; Hoenig, Morris, and Spong, 2009; Issac, 2010; Jackson, 2009, 2015; Leijonhufvud, 2010; Macey and Miller, 1992; Massad, 2011; Mukherjee and Pana, 2018; Ongena and Nistor-Mutu, 2019; Paulson, 2013; Pisani-Ferry and Sapir, 2010; Salter, Veetil, and White, 2017; Solomon and Enrich, 2008; Zingales, 2011.

1

Introduction to bank bailouts, bail-ins and related topics covered in the book

Bank bailouts occur when governments, central banks, or other public national or international organizations supported by governments—such as the International Monetary Fund (IMF), the European Commission, and the European Stability Mechanism (ESM)—provide assistance to banks during times of financial distress beyond the support given in normal circumstances. The assistance may be broadly distributed during financial crises or narrowly focused during other times to banks that are in significant financial distress or in danger of failing. As discussed in more detail below, these bailouts may take many different forms. Bank bail-ins differ from bailouts in that private-sector agents, such as shareholders, creditors, or other banking organizations, provide the aid. The agents providing this bail-in aid mostly agree to give support in advance, whereas bailouts are more often arranged on an *ad hoc* basis shortly before the support is provided.

Many of the bailouts and bail-ins, including the Troubled Asset Relief Program (TARP) prominently featured in this book, are primarily of the BHCs that own banks, rather than the banks themselves. For expositional convenience, we generally use the term "bank" to mean either a bank or a BHC, except in circumstances for which this would create confusion or misrepresent the facts. Importantly, this book is only about bailouts, bail-ins, and other resolutions of banks, and not the rescue methods of other financial institutions and markets that took place during recent financial crises, such as the Global Financial Crisis and the European Sovereign Debt Crisis.

1.1 The focus of the book

There are many different types of bank bailouts and bail-ins. For the purposes of this book, we take the broadest possible view of what

5

constitutes a bailout or bail-in in order to ensure that we leave no stone unturned. Bailouts may take the form of capital injections as in the TARP case, as well as liquidity provisions, guarantees of bank liabilities, government takeovers of banks or other institutions that are interconnected to banks, asset relief programs such as purchases of securities for which banks have large inventories, and public certifications of the safety of the banks. As shown below, all of these types of bank bailouts occurred in the United States (US) in response to the Global Financial Crisis of the late 2000s that started in the US and its aftermath. Many of these types of bailouts also took place in Europe and other places around the world in response to the spread of the Global Financial Crisis from the United States to other countries, as well as the European Sovereign Debt Crisis that followed.

Bank bail-ins often take the form of converting one or more different debt instruments to equity. These instruments include, but are not limited to subordinated debt, senior unsecured debt, contingent convertible bonds (CoCos), and uninsured deposits. Other forms of bail-ins include requiring equity holders to provide extra capital (e.g., double liability), whole or partial sale of a distressed or about-to-fail bank to another institution to provide capital, and capital provision by other nongovernment organizations. Bail-ins may also include good bank—bad bank separations. These can involve the formation of a bridge institution that holds the "good" or relatively safe assets of a distressed organization temporarily until sale to recover value, while "bad" or relatively risky assets are isolated or transferred to an asset management vehicle for orderly winding down.

Many of these types of bank bail-ins were implemented in the US and Europe during and after the financial crises of the late 2000s and early 2010s. Two very broad bail-in mechanisms deserve special attention. In the US, the Orderly Liquidation Authority (OLA) bail-in regime was put into effect for some large banking organizations in the US by the Dodd—Frank Act of 2010. OLA converts subordinated debt and possibly some other uninsured credits into equity in the event of distress and impending failure of one or more of these organizations. In the European Union (EU), the Bank Recovery and Resolution Directive (BRRD) and the Single Resolution Mechanism (SRM) were introduced in 2014 and formally implemented in 2016. Under the BRRD, equity holders and a number of uninsured creditors must suffer losses and contribute to the recapitalization of the bank similar to OLA. A number of other resolution tools, such as sale of business tool, are also put into place to deal with the resolution of failing institutions.[1] After the full BRRD implementation, the

---

[1] Under BRRD Article 2(1) (57), bail-in is defined as "the mechanism for effecting the exercise by a resolution authority of the write-down and conversion powers in relation to liabilities of an institution under resolution."

first resolution carried out was Banco Popular in June 2017, which entailed the write-down of the institution's own funds, bail-in of subordinated debtholders, as well as the sale of the institution to Banco Santander.[2] However, a number of bail-in cases occured in EU prior to the full implementation of the BRRD bail-in provisions, including the resolution of two Cypriot large banks in 2013, resolution of four Greek banks in 2014, and the resolution of four small Italian banks in 2015. Please see Box 1.5 below for brief summaries of these cases.

All of these types of bailouts and bail-ins are discussed in this book, and real-world examples of them are provided. Bank bailouts and bail-ins usually, but not always, occur in response to financial crises, or are undertaken to prevent idiosyncratic events from evolving into such crises. Bailouts and bail-ins in response to financial crises are designed to temporarily stabilize the financial system and mitigate the real economic consequences of these systemic problems, including recessions that may stem from widespread bank distress and failures. In some cases, bailouts and bail-ins are also used in nonfinancial crisis times for individual distressed banks that are considered too-big-to-fail (TBTF) or too-interconnected-to-fail (TITF), or groups of banks in similar conditions that are considered too-many-to-fail (TMTF). The goals of these latter sets of bailouts and bail-ins are to prevent the emergence of financial crises and their consequences and/or to avoid the large economic losses associated with the failures of these banks.

1.1.1 Descriptions of bailouts

Prior to and during the Global Financial Crisis and European Sovereign Debt Crisis, bank bailouts were the most frequent responses by governments to financial crises, as well as to TBTF, TITF, or TMTF problems. Boxes 1.1 and 1.2 provide lists of bank bailouts during these financial crises in the US and EU, respectively. We are unable to discuss the actions taken during the global Coronavirus financial crisis, which was beginning as this book was going to press.

As shown in Box 1.1, there were many large programs to aid the banks in the US during and after the Global Financial Crisis. Many consider the Capital Purchase Program (CPP) component of TARP as "the" bank bailout in the US. Under the CPP, the US Treasury Department injected $204.9 billion of preferred equity into 709 banking organizations. Another $40 billion was distributed to two large banking organizations through the Targeted Investment Program (TIP), and $0.57 billion was disbursed to 84 institutions under the Community Development Capital Initiative

---

[2] In contrast to OLA, bail-in provisions under BRRD allow access to external financial support after writing down and conversion of shares and eligible liabilities up to a minimum of 8% of the bank's total liabilities.

BOX 1.1

SELECTED BAILOUT PROGRAMS IN THE U.S. FOR BANKING ORGANIZATIONS DURING THE GLOBAL FINANCIAL CRISIS

Bailout Program	Time Period	Amount ($Bill)	Purpose
TARP Capital Purchase Program (CPP), the main component of the U.S. Treasury Troubled Asset Relief Program.	Oct. 28, 2008–Dec. 29, 2009	$204.9 billion in 709 depository institutions	The largest program under Treasury's Troubled Asset Relief Program, which provided capital to eligible depository institutions by purchasing preferred shares and in some cases also subordinated debt.
TARP Targeted Investment Program (TIP) Assistance to Bank of America Corporation and Citigroup, Inc.	Dec. 2008	$40 billion in additional capital ($20 billion for each institution)	Capital injection and agreements with regulators to protect institutions against larger-than-expected losses on asset portfolios.
TARP Community Development Capital Initiative (CDCI) Assistance	Feb. – Sep. 2010	$0.57 billion into 84 institutions	To help viable certified community development institutions and their underserved communities to cope with the financial crisis.
Term Discount Window Program (TDW)	Aug. 17, 2007-Mar. 18, 2010	Dollar amounts of borrowing during the program period were not made publicly available.	TDW provided discount window funds with maturities beyond overnight, funds being initially made available for up to 30 days, and later extended to 90 days.
Federal Reserve System Term Auction Facilities (TAF)	Dec. 12, 2007–Mar. 8, 2010	$493 billion at the height of the program, and about $3,818 billion in total over the period	Auctioned 1- and 3-month discount window loans to depository institutions to address strains in term interbank lending markets.

Continued

—cont'd

Bailout Program	Time Period	Amount ($Bill)	Purpose
FDIC Temporary Liquidity Guarantee Program (TLGP) • *Temporary Debt Guarantee Program (TDGP)* • *Transaction Account Guarantee Program (TAGP)*	Oct. 14, 2008 - Dec. 31, 2012 for TDGP and Oct. 14, 2008 - Dec. 31, 2010 for TAGP	Approximately $346 billion debt and approximately $835 billion deposits	TDGP guaranteed certain newly-issued unsecured senior debt of eligible institutions to improve liquidity in term funding markets. TAGP temporarily extended an unlimited deposit guarantee to domestic noninterest-bearing transaction accounts at participating insured depository institutions to limit further outflows of these deposits.
U.S. Treasury Small Business Lending Fund (SBLF)	Established by the Small Business Jobs Act of 2010.	Over $4 billion in 332 institutions	SBLF provided preferred capital injections to qualified community banks (assets < $10 billion) in order to encourage small business lending.
Federal Home Loan Bank (FHLB) System	In effect before, during, and after the financial crisis.	Approximately 80% of U.S. lending institutions rely on the FHLB banks	FHLB system provided loans to member banks to support mortgage lending and related community investment.
American International Group, Inc. (AIG) Loan and Equity Injection by US Treasury and Federal Reserve System	Sep. 16, 2008	$182 billion peak commitment by US Treasury and Federal Reserve Bank of New York (FRBNY)	Combination of loans and stock investments in AIG.

Continued

—cont'd

Bailout Program	Time Period	Amount ($Bill)	Purpose
Quantitative Easing (QE) Programs	Policy pursued by the Federal Reserve Board between 2008 and 2014. QE1: announced in Nov. 2008, and took place between December 2008 to June 2010. QE2 was implemented from Nov. 2010 to June 2011. Operation Twist, similar to QE2 occurred between September 2011 to December 2012 to support the sluggish housing market by buying long-term notes and stepping up purchases of MBS. QE3 was largely unanticipated, and took place between September 2012 and December 2012. Finally, QE4, occurred between January 2013 and October 2014. On June 14, 2017, FOMC announced its beginning efforts to reduce the QE holdings.	QE1: $800 billion in bank debt, MBS, and Treasuries from member banks. It bought $175 billion in MBS originated by Fannie and Freddie and the Federal Home Loan Banks and also bought $1.25 trillion MBS guaranteed by the mortgage giants and $300 billion long-term Treasuries. QE2: $600 billion of Treasury securities. Operation Twist: $400 billion in long-term Treasuries and new MBSs. QE3: $40 billion in MBS and continue Operation Twist. QE4: $85 billion in MBS and long-term Treasuries and ended Operation Twist.	In QE1, QE3, QE4, and Operation Twist, the Federal Reserve bought MBS and Treasuries. In QE2, it bought primarily Treasuries.

Notes: Dollar amounts for the programs are sourced from GAO Report (2013), GAO-14-18 available at: https://www.gao.gov/assets/660/659004.pdf U.S. Treasury website https://www.treasury.gov/resource-center/sb-programs/Pages/Small-Business-Lending-Fund.aspx, and other sources https://www.thebalance.com/what-is-quantitative-easing-definition-and-explanation-3305881; https://www.thebalance.com/federal-reserve-s-operation-twist-3305529.

BOX 1.2

EU BANK BAILOUTS INITIATIVES (28 MEMBER STATES)

European Commission Aid Instrument (Approved)	EU Bank Bailouts (Billion Euros)									
	2008	2009	2010	2011	2012	2013	2014	2015	2016	Max or Total
1. Recapitalizations	269.9	110.0	184.0	37.5	150.8	29.6	20.3	18.8	8.5	829.4
2. Impaired Asset Measures	4.8	338.5	78.0	6.3	157.5	14.7	3.5	1.0	0.0	604.3
3. Guarantees	3097.3	87.6	54.8	179.7	266.8	37.9	0.4	156.4	303.3	3381.6
4. Other Liquidity Measures	85.5	5.5	66.8	50.2	37.5	9.7	1.7	0.0	0.0	229.7
Total	3457.5	541.6	383.6	273.7	612.6	91.8	26.0	176.2	311.8	5045.0
European Commission Aid Instrument (Used)	2008	2009	2010	2011	2012	2013	2014	2015	2016	Max or Total
1. Recapitalizations	115.2	90.7	93.5	35.0	90.8	20.5	7.6	11.3	0.0	464.6
2. Impaired Asset Measures	9.8	79.5	54.0	0.0	35.4	9.5	0.3	0.3	0.5	189.2
3. Guarantees	400.4	835.8	799.8	589.0	492.1	352.3	204.5	167.8	121.9	1188.1
4. Other Liquidity Measures	22.2	70.1	62.6	60.6	44.3	34.6	31.6	4.6	1.4	105.0
Total	547.6	1076.2	1009.9	684.5	662.6	416.9	244.0	183.9	123.7	1946.9

Source: European Commission

(CDCI) of TARP. The original plan for TARP was to purchase "toxic" mortgage-backed securities (MBS), but this role later fell to Federal Reserve in its Quantitative Easing (QE) programs, as discussed below. Also shown in Box 1.1, the Federal Reserve greatly expanded its Discount Window program to provide funds with maturities beyond overnight, which we refer to as the Term Discount Window (TDW) program. The Federal Reserve also created the Term Auction Facilities (TAF) to address the potential stigma associated with borrowing from the lender of last resort through the discount window, encourage bank participation, and provide additional liquidity to the banks. The Federal Deposit Insurance Corporation (FDIC) enacted the Temporary Liquidity Guarantee Program (TLGP), which guaranteed some otherwise uninsured bank creditors through the Transaction Account Guarantee Program (TAGP) and the Debt Guarantee Program (DGP), preventing possible liquidity drains from the banks. The Federal Home Loan Bank (FHLB) system provided low-cost funding to local banks to support mortgage lending.

The Federal Reserve additionally engaged in unconventional monetary policy, including massive purchases of MBS, well beyond the $700 billion originally planned for TARP, as well as trillions of dollars more of long-term treasuries under the QE programs. QE was implemented in four phases, QE1, QE2, QE3, and QE4, with pauses in between them. The US Treasury and Federal Reserve also bailed out an insurance company, American International Group (AIG), using a combination of loans and capital injections. Although AIG is not a bank, we consider this as a type of bank bailout because the company owed significant amount of funds to a number of large banks and this helped avoid large losses for these banks.

The reader needs not agree with our characterization of all of these US government, Federal Reserve, and other agency actions as bank bailouts to gain something from this book. Whether the reader (1) thinks of TARP or CPP as "the" US bank bailout, (2) agrees that all of the actions described above are bailouts, or (3) lands somewhere in between, there should be plenty of information to inform the reader.

Bailouts in Europe were originally initiated by individual country governments or small groups of governments as large banks in their countries were affected by the financial crises. For example, in August 2008, Northern Rock Bank was bailed out by the Bank of England and was later nationalized. Shortly thereafter, Fortis, and later Dexia, both of which operated in multiple nations, were bailed out by the governments of Belgium, Luxembourg, and Netherlands. The government of Ireland announced its decision to guarantee all deposits and debts of six Irish banks and all their subsidiaries abroad. Many other banks in other EU countries were bailed out by their own governments or nationalized.

As the financial crises became aggravated, an EU-level bailout approach was considered necessary to handle the situation, as shown in Box 1.2. Between 2008 and 2016, the European Commission approved a total of about €5.0 trillion of state aid to be granted to 28 EU countries, of which about €1.9 trillion was effectively implemented.[3] The total implemented measures accounted for about 13.1% of 2016 EU Gross Domestic Product (GDP), with considerable variation across countries. Four different types of bailout support were used: guarantees on bank liabilities (61% of the total support), capital injections or recapitalizations (24% of the total support), asset relief interventions (10% of the total support), and bank liquidity support (5% of the total support) (Fig. 1.1 below). In all, EU states made extensive use of various forms of government support to stabilize the banking sector. Guarantees, rather than capital injections, were the most frequently used bailout instrument.

1.1.2 Consequences of bailouts

Bailouts are often very attractive to government officials because they can usually be put together relatively quickly and do not require the advance cooperation of private-sector agents that bail-ins often do. Bailouts help avoid or mitigate short-term financial system problems, increase stability, reduce systemic risk, and reduce the likelihood and severity of recessions which are often the consequences of banks' financial distress and failures. As discussed in later chapters, bailouts are also generally found to increase credit supply and improve economic

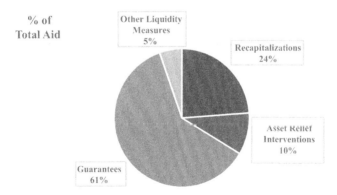

FIGURE 1.1   Different government aid measures in the European Union (EU). *Source: Compiled based on data from the European Commission.*

---

[3] See European Commission website at http://ec.europa.eu/competition/state_aid/ scoreboard/index_en.html.

conditions by increasing employment and reducing firm and consumer bankruptcies.

However, bailouts also come with social costs. They may create long-run moral hazard incentives for banks to take on excessive risks because bailouts may raise expectations of future bailouts that may weaken market discipline. Bailouts may also impose costs on taxpayers that may not be adequately compensated for the risks taken. Bailouts of some banks and not others could create distortions in bank competition as well. Bailouts may additionally distort funds allocation to the extent that they may be distributed partially according to the banks' political and regulatory connections. Thus, bailouts have a multitude of effects, and as discussed further below, the theory does not provide a clear answer *ex ante* as to whether the net effect of bailouts are considered beneficial.

The bank bailouts during the Global Financial Crisis and European Sovereign Debt Crisis were largely unpopular. Fig. 1.2, the *Chicago Booth / Kellogg School Financial Trust Index Survey*, demonstrates some of this disapproval for US. It suggests that US respondents have the least trust in bailed-out banks over the period 2009-2015. Similarly, a poll by Gallup about confidence in banks for selected EU countries with bailouts, shows that confidence in these banks has been very slow to return to pre-crisis levels[4]. Some major reasons behind this unpopularity are the perceived unfairness of bailing out wealthy banks and that bailouts are often quite

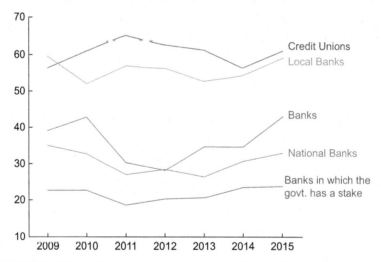

FIGURE 1.2   Financial trust survey. *Source: Financial Trust Index, Wave 24 (University of Chicago Booth School of Business/Northwestern University Kellogg School of Management).*

[4] https://news.gallup.com/poll/175700/confidence-banks-slow-return-bailout-countries. aspx

expensive for governments and taxpayers, and sometimes led to sovereign debt problems (e.g., Spain).

1.1.3 Descriptions of bail-ins

In part as a result of the general dissatisfaction with the bailouts implemented during the Global Financial Crisis and European Sovereign Debt Crisis, governments established bail-in regimes, in which private stakeholders provide much of the capital, liquidity, guarantees, or other support. Boxes 1.3 and 1.4 show the bail-in programs in the US and the EU, respectively, after these financial crises. Currently, large banks in both

---

BOX 1.3

BAIL-IN PROGRAM IN THE U.S.

Emergency Program	Time Period	Purpose
Orderly Liquidation Authority (OLA)	Became effective after the implementation of the Dodd Frank Act in 2010:Q3.	Bail-in is applied to large systemically important institutions in default or danger of default whose failure would have adverse effects on the financial system and the real economy.

BOX 1.4

BAIL-IN PROGRAMS IN THE EU

Emergency Program	Time Period	Purpose
The Bank Recovery and Resolution Directive (BRRD) and the Single Resolution Mechanism (SRM)	Became mandatory on Jan. 1, 2016.	Bail-in applied to 8% of banks' liabilities and own funds before any state aid can be used for distressed institutions.

---

the US and the EU are under bail-in regimes via the OLA and the BRRD, respectively.

OLA was established by the Dodd–Frank Act of 2010. An OLA event is triggered when a very large BHC is in default or danger of default, and its failure would have serious adverse financial stability consequences. The FDIC temporarily takes over the BHC and fires its management, while the banks and other holding company subsidiaries it owns continue to operate. Existing shareholders are wiped out and subordinated debt-holders and possibly other uninsured creditors have part of their debt claims turned into equity capital, so that the BHC becomes well capitalized. The BHC is then returned to private hands with new management.

Importantly, while no OLA bail-in event has been triggered for any BHC as of this writing, this does not mean that OLA has not had an impact on BHC behavior or the stability of the financial system. To the contrary, we review some research below that suggests that the incentives created by the OLA regime have already had significant effects in terms of encouraging banks to hold higher capital ratios and respond to distress by increasing these ratios more quickly. Of course, more evidence will be revealed about the effectiveness of OLA if and when it is triggered in the future, possibly during forthcoming financial crises.

In the EU, the BRRD and the SRM became effective in January 2016. The goal was to create a common framework for bank resolution across all EU member states to deal with resolving potential failure of large financial institutions. The BRRD is the set of rules for bail-ins, while the SRM is the organization that implements these rules. Once an institution reaches the point of nonviability and is declared as "failing or likely to fail," a bail-in tool allows regulators to conduct a fast recapitalization of a troubled institution prior to default by either writing-off or converting liabilities to equity and requiring creditors to take losses on holdings according to a certain hierarchy. Particularly, BRRD establishes the hierarchy such that the bail-in will affect equity holders first, followed by subordinated debt holders, senior unsecured debt holders, and uninsured depositors. This is intended to minimize the costs for taxpayers and real economy. There is some experience with and research on these bail-in regimes as shown by the individual EU country bail-in examples in Box 1.5. Similar to OLA, more evidence about the effectiveness of BRRD will be revealed if and when the system is more thoroughly tested during future financial crises.

As shown in Box 1.6 and discussed below, bail-in regimes may have advantages over bailout regimes in terms of better safeguarding taxpayer funds and lessening unfair competitive advantages that bailouts may provide to the recipient banks. They may also induce more prudent bank management behavior in terms of holding preemptively adequate capital to avoid bail-ins. In addition, the market participants provision of increased market discipline from bail-ins may be nimbler than

---

BOX 1.5

BAIL-IN CASES IN THE EU

Selected Country-Level Bank Bail-Ins			
Country	Bailout	Period	Details
Cyprus	Bank of Cyprus (the largest bank) and Cyprus Popular Bank (also known as Laiki Bank, the second largest bank)	2013	Uninsured depositors lost everything in Cyprus Popular Bank while about 48% of uninsured depositors suffered losses in Bank of Cyprus.
Greece	Panellinia Bank, Cooperative Bank of Peloponnese, National Bank of Greece, and Piraeus Bank	2015	Panellinia Bank was resolved by transferring selected assets and liabilities to Piraeus Bank, through a tender process. The common and preferred shares remained in the entity in liquidation and were bailed-in. Cooperative Bank of Peloponnese was put in resolution, deposits were transferred to National Bank of Greece following a tender process, while all other assets and remaining liabilities, as well as shareholders, were bailed-in. Two of the four main Greek banks (National Bank of Greece and Piraeus Bank) were partially recapitalized but most bondholders and shareholders were bailed-in and did incur losses.
Italy	Four small banks (Banca Marche, Banca Popolare dell'Etruria, Cassa di Risparmio di Ferrara, and Cassa di Risparmio della Provincia di Chieti) and 3 large banks (Banca Monte dei Paschi di Siena SpA (BMPS) (4th largest), Vicenza (10th largest) and Veneto Banca (11th largest))	2015	Four small Italian banks (Banca Marche, Banca Popolare dell'Etruria, Cassa di Risparmio di Ferrara, and Cassa di Risparmio della Provincia di Chieti, with aggregate total assets of €47 billion) were bailed-in and all assets and liabilities were transferred to bridge banks, and senior bondholders were spared, but equity holders and subordinated debtholders incurred losses. Banca Popolare di Vicenza (10th largest) and Veneto Banca (11th largest) are two banks that were declared by the European Central Bank (ECB) as "failing or likely to fail" and their good assets were sold to Intesa Sanpaolo, Italy's 2nd largest bank by assets for €1, and their bad assets were put into a "bad bank". Banca Monte dei Paschi di Siena SpA (BMPS) - Italy's 4th largest bank, faced a precautionary recapitalization with bail-in. The Italian government received approval from the EU to bail out the bank, injecting €5.4 billion (giving it a 70% stake) into the bank, while bank's shareholders and junior creditors took losses first for an estimated €4.3 billion to minimize the bill for the government.

Continued

supervisory authorities exerting supervisory discipline in reducing long-term moral hazard incentives for banks to allow capital to fall too low or shift into riskier portfolios.

There are also some potential disadvantages of bail-ins. These include possibly more delays and high financial costs in implementation compared to bailouts; credibility problems that the governments may bail

—cont'd

Selected Country-Level Bank Bail-Ins			
Country	Bailout	Period	Details
Portugal	Banco Espirito Santo (BES) and Banco Internacional do Funchal (BANIF, 7th largest bank)	2014-2015	Banco Espirito Santo (BES) was resolved via a bail-in. Portuguese authorities used a bridge bank strategy to put the bank's good assets and liabilities, together with an equity injection from the Portugal resolution fund. Equity holders and subordinated debtholders were left in the legacy bank and faced severe losses. Banco Internacional do Funchal (BANIF, 7th largest bank) was resolved using the same good bank/bad bank split, where the good assets were sold to Santander with state aid help, while another entity was created to house some of the bad assets. Equity holders and subordinated bondholders were left behind in the legacy bank, incurring losses.
Spain	Banco Popular (6th largest bank)	2017	ECB declared the bank as "failing or likely to fail" and immediately after Banco Santander (Spain's largest bank) announced that it would buy Popular for a nominal €1 and carry out a capital increase of €7 billion to cover the capital and provisions required to boost Banco Popular's finances. The deal caused shareholders and some bondholders to be wiped out (including owners of contingent convertible debt which had their debt turned into equity).

out the banks instead; difficulties in handling systemic events that may include distress of many large institutions at the same time; contagion and run-off by creditors; potentially transferring risks to private-sector agents that do not understand these risks; and transmitting financial problems to other parts of the financial system which may also be fragile at the same time as banks. Last but not least, bail-ins may also lead to worse outcomes in credit supply and economic conditions for the connected borrowers of the bailed-in institutions compared to bailouts. We refer the reader to Chapter 27 for a more in-depth analysis of the benefits and costs of bailouts, bail-ins, and other approaches for dealing with the financial distress of important financial institutions.

As discussed below, some theoretical research finds similar social welfare values for bailouts and bail-ins, measured by the expected value of the recipient bank minus the expected external costs on society from its default. However, the research also shows a key advantage of bail-ins over bailouts in that bail-ins provide superior *ex ante* incentives for banks to rebuild capital preemptively during financial distress. This advantage is confirmed by empirical analysis. Bail-ins may also be

BOX 1.6

PROS AND CONS OF BAILOUTS AND BAIL-INS

	Pros	Cons
Bailouts	Easy to put together to capitalize banks	Increase costs to taxpayers
	Increase financial stability/reduce systemic risk in the short-term	Provide banks with an implicit bailout protection: increase the perception that banks can be too big to fail (TBTF), too-important-to-fail (TITF), or too-many-to-fail (TMTF)
	Increase credit supply	Increase moral hazard incentives of banks
	Can improve economic conditions	Uncertain effects on market discipline
	Increase market returns for the treated banks and their connected customers	Cause competitive distortions
		Reduce bank efficiency
		Selection may be based on non-economic or political connections rather than merit
Bail-Ins	Reduce costs to taxpayers	Slow and expensive to reestablish market confidence in the bailed-in institution
	Reduce moral hazard incentives of banks	Likely increase contagious effects and cause run of creditors on affiliated entities/subsidiaries
	Improve market discipline	Likely worsen credit supply for connected borrowers
	Effective to resolve idiosyncratic failure	Likely worsen economic conditions for connected borrowers
	Reduce competitive advantages for TBTF	Not so effective to resolve systemic failures
	Improve bank capital structure incentives	Level of international cooperation required is unprecedented in some cases
		Can lead to severe social costs for unsophisticated creditors
		Transfer risks to other parts of the financial system that may also be fragile

superior to bailouts in terms of reducing banks' moral hazard incentives to shift into riskier portfolios.

1.1.4 Descriptions of bank resolution approaches other than bailouts and bail-ins

1.1.4.1 Bankruptcy/Failure

An alternative response to financial crises and/or the distress of TBTF, TITF, or TMTF banks is what we refer to as bankruptcy/failure. This is one case in which we must distinguish between banks and BHCs. By bankruptcy/failure, we mean that the BHC declares bankruptcy and bank or banks it owns are allowed to fail.

This approach may have social advantages in terms of reduced long-term moral hazard incentives and improved market discipline. That is, reduced expectations of government interventions may encourage banks and BHCs to hold higher capital ratios to protect themselves against this outcome and may increase debtholders' incentives to monitor and react to risks to preserve the value of their claims. As discussed below, some theoretical research supports the notion that bankruptcy/failure would result in higher capital ratios.

However, bankruptcy/failure may also pose very substantial short-term risks to the financial system and real economy. The bankruptcy of the BHC results in its stock market value being wiped out and losses imposed on all of its creditor financial institutions, which may greatly harm the financial system. These creditor institutions may, in turn, become distressed, which further weakens the financial system and may result in reduced credit to the public, also harming the real economy. The failure of the bank itself results in a cutoff of credit to all of its borrowers, which may also have a first-order effect in damaging the real economy.

These dangers to the financial system and the real economy may be exacerbated by two factors. First, these financial and economic problems may be exacerbated during a financial crisis, when many BHCs may become bankrupt and many banks may fail. Second, the judicial system for handling the bankruptcy process may have difficulties in terms of the financial expertise and speed needed to resolve complex financial institutions, particularly during a financial crisis.

The theoretical research discussed below suggests that at least under some assumptions, bankruptcy/failure is strictly dominated by bailouts and bail-ins in terms of both social welfare and the private welfare of shareholders. It is also dominated by bail-ins in terms of providing incentives for banks to recapitalize to avoid financial distress.

During the Global Financial Crisis, very few large financial institutions were allowed to fail. In the US, one large, very interconnected investment bank, Lehman Brothers, and two large, relatively unconnected thrift institutions, Washington Mutual and IndyMac Bank, failed. There is virtual consensus that the Lehman Brothers failure caused significant harm to both the financial system and the real economy, although it is difficult to determine how much of the trillions of dollars of costs to the US economy of the crisis can be attributed to the effects of this one failure.

Strategies such as allowing significant numbers of failures during financial crises or letting TBTF, TITF, or TMTF banks fail have not been widely implemented in developed economies since the Great Depression. Bernanke (1983) suggests that the widespread bank failures during the Great Depression reduced lending, which made the economy much worse. Friedman and Schwartz (1963) find that the reduction of money supply caused by these bank failures also significantly harmed the economy.

Nonetheless, widespread implementation of bankruptcy/failure is important to address because it is a future possibility. It was advocated in the Financial CHOICE Act, which passed the US House of Representatives in 2017, although it was not enacted. The Act would expand the role of bankruptcy for large banking organizations and allow failures of large banks by repealing OLA and establishing a new section of the US bankruptcy code (Chapter 14) to resolve failed complex financial institutions. Resolutions would be conducted under the auspices of a bankruptcy court and would not include regulatory intervention.

1.1.4.2 Reorganizing large, complex banking organizations using living wills

An alternative way to resolve the distress and impending failure of large, complex banking organizations is to reorganize them using living wills, or resolution plans that are designed *ex ante* by these organizations to restore financial strength and viability. In the US, Section 165(d) of the Dodd−Frank Act requires banking organizations with total assets of $50 billion or more to report annually to the Federal Reserve and the FDIC their plans for rapid and orderly resolution under the US Bankruptcy Code in the event of material distress or failure. The G20 countries have also requested living wills from the top 24 global banks and six insurance companies (Claessens, Herring, Schoenmaker, and Summe, 2010). For example, under the living will, the banks may develop scenarios under which certain, less important, parts can be sold, or put into liquidation while the systemically important parts may then be rescued (e.g., Avgouleas, Goodhart, and Schoenmaker, 2013). Chapter 4 gives more details about these resolution tools, provides excerpts from two actual living wills posted by large US BHCs, and discusses implications of these plans for complex domestic and international organizations.

From a theoretical viewpoint, living wills are much like the bankruptcy/failure option discussed above, except that they are designed to be more orderly and preserve more of the financially viable parts of the organization. It is also noteworthy that in the US, OLA bail-in resolution method and living wills are both products of the Dodd—Frank Act, despite the fact that they appear to be substitute resolution approaches that may not be executed simultaneously on the same banking organization.

1.1.4.3 Regulatory forbearance

Another alternative response to bank financial distress, known as either "regulatory forbearance" or "capital forbearance," involves allowing banks with very low or negative capital ratios to continue operating without significant regulatory intervention or failure. This approach is sometimes used to save on closure costs, postpone dealing with problems until another regulator is in charge, or in the hope that the problems will be reversed on their own. However, it may create more losses in the long run.

As discussed below in Part III of the book, allowing significant numbers of problematic financial institutions to go unresolved was applied widely in the 1980s to savings and loans (S&Ls) and to a lesser extent to banks at that time. Many S&Ls suffered significant interest rate risk losses that devastated their equity capital as all of their mortgages were required to be fixed-rate, while short-term interest rates rose as a result of very restrictive monetary policy. They borrowed at high rates in the short-term and were locked in low rates on their loans in the long-term and as a consequence, they lost most or all of their market values.

Regulators largely let these "zombie thrifts" with low or negative capital stay open, and Congress actually expanded their investment powers in the 1980 Depository Institutions Deregulation and Monetary Control Act (DIDMCA) and 1982 Garn—St. Germain Act. In some cases, moral hazard incentives from the lack of capital resulted in additional credit risk and other problems. The results of these problems were massive losses to taxpayers in the long run until the situation was somewhat resolved by the passage of the Financial Institutions Reform, Recovery, and Enforcement Act (FIRREA) in 1989.

1.2 Other introductory materials

1.2.1 Conditions that generally bring about bailouts, bail-ins, and other resolution methods

Chapter 2 discusses the conditions that typically result in bailouts, bail-ins, and other resolutions. These conditions are usually financial crises and/or the distress of TBTF, TITF, or TMTF banks. We also discuss some research on what tends to bring about financial crises and bank distress. In particular, we focus on excessive lending booms and liquidity buildups as determinants of financial crises. We also review the literature on bank performance and failure to inform the reader about what brings about the distress and potential failure of TBTF, TITF, and TMTF banks.

1.2.2 Descriptions of TARP and other bank bailouts, bail-ins, and other resolutions in the US and around the world

Chapter 3 describes bailouts and bail-ins around the world, as well as alternatives such as bankruptcy/failure, living wills, regulatory forbearance, and breaking up large complex banking organizations according to size or activities. We pay particular attention to TARP and the other bailouts during the Global Financial Crisis and European Sovereign Debt Crisis. We also focus on OLA and BRRD and other bail-in programs that were implemented following these crises.

1.2.3 Theoretical background on bank bailouts, bail-ins, and other resolution approaches

Chapter 4 reviews the theories of bank bailouts, bail-ins, and other resolution approaches, including bankruptcy/failure, reorganization using living wills, and regulatory forbearance. In doing so, we discuss the advantages and disadvantages of the different resolution approaches.

Most of the chapter follows the theoretical pathways through which bailouts and bail-ins may or may not achieve their ultimate goals or outcomes of reducing systemic risk and improving the real economy. To succeed in these ultimate goals, bailouts and bail-ins must first achieve certain intermediate financial and economic outcomes by affecting the behavior of the banks, markets, and stakeholders. These intermediate outcomes may then affect the ultimate outcomes for systemic risk and the real economy. Finally, the interactions between systemic risk and the real economy must be taken into account. Thus, the effects of bailouts and bail-ins on systemic risk and the real economy are traced through the direct channels that affect the intermediate financial and economic outcomes to the effects on these ultimate outcomes and their interactions.

The chapter also reviews further theoretical research covering bailouts, bail-ins, and other resolution approaches, and comparisons among these methods.

1.3 Empirical research on TARP

Part II contains 11 chapters that review the empirical research on the determinants and effects of the TARP bailout, which took place in the US during the Global Financial Crisis. TARP was mainly designed to reduce risks to the financial system due to the crisis and to improve the real economy relative to what its condition would otherwise be in the absence of the bailout.

As indicated above, there is more research on TARP than on any bailout or bail-in program. Notably, the empirical methods employed in most of the TARP studies are quite good because TARP may be considered a rare quasi-natural experiment in the research literature that is reasonably exogenous because it was largely unexpected. Most of the studies use the difference-in-difference (DID) methods with relatively clean instrumental variables for identification.

There are several reasons for our extra emphasis on TARP. First, TARP was a key response to the biggest financial crisis in modern times. The costs to the US economy alone of the Global Financial Crisis are estimated to be in the range of $12 trillion–$22 trillion in terms of lost output and destruction of financial assets (e.g., Atkinson, Luttrell, and Rosenblum, 2013; U.S. Government Accountability Office Report, 2013; Garcia, 2015).

Second, TARP was a very large and widespread bailout. The US Treasury injected over $200 billion in preferred equity capital into over 700 banks and other depository financial institutions in a relatively short time period.

Third, TARP has by far had the most public and media attention, and it likely sparked many of the regulatory changes that followed the subprime crisis, including the Dodd–Frank Act that substantially increased bank regulation and created the OLA bail-in regime discussed above. As noted above, it is often considered to be "the" bank bailout in the press, with much less recognition of the other bailouts or even disagreement that the liquidity injections, guarantees, and the other actions discussed above are bank bailouts. Currently, there is much disagreement over the short-run and long-run effectiveness of TARP, with most of the initial advocates and opponents of the program sticking to their original positions in spite of the substantial research on TARP, discussed next.

Fourth, there is much more research on TARP than any other bank bailout or bail-in program. Researchers have studied the determinants of which banks were bailed out and repaid the funds early; the effects of TARP on the market valuations of the bailed-out banks; its impacts on bank market discipline, leverage risk, competition, credit supply, and portfolio risk, as well as the bearing of the program on bank credit customers. Importantly, there is also research conducted to determine whether TARP was effective in achieving its two main goals of boosting the real economy and reducing systemic risk.

Part II of the book has chapters devoted to each of these topics. We acknowledge in Part II that these topics are highly interrelated, although the individual research papers do not necessarily draw out all of the implications of TARP. For example, the papers that focus on the direct impact of TARP on bank credit supply do not always discuss fully the indirect effects of this credit on bank portfolio risks, the welfare of credit customers, the real economy, and systemic risk. To the best of our abilities, we try to tie together the results of the papers on seemingly different TARP research topics. To keep things manageable and avoid repetition, we discuss each direct research result only in the chapter on that topic, leaving the indirect effects for later chapters.

1.3.1 Methodologies used in most of the TARP empirical studies

Chapter 5 discusses the main empirical methodologies employed in the empirical TARP studies to help with the understanding of the research. The chapter describes difference-in-difference (DID), instrumental variables (IV), propensity score matching (PSM), Heckman sample selection models, and placebo tests.

1.3.2 Determinants of applying for and receiving TARP funds and exiting early from the program

Chapter 6 discusses research on which banks received the TARP injections and the determinants of early exit from TARP. As discussed there, larger and healthier banks were more likely to receive the funds and to repay early. Political and regulatory influence also played important roles for some of the banks' funds allocations. Banks that were constrained by the executive pay restrictions tended to choose to exit early.

1.3.3 Effects of TARP on recipient banks' valuations

Chapter 7 explains the research on the effects of TARP on recipient banks' valuations. The research appears to suggest that TARP led to different effects on bank valuations depending on the events analyzed. Bank valuations generally increased around TARP program announcements, but valuations around individual capital injections were mostly either insignificant or significantly negative, consistent with various concerns about program or bank condition. Bank valuations around repayments were unanimously positive, consistent with the recognition of repaying TARP banks being healthy and viable, and other reasons including removal of compensation restrictions associated with the bailouts.

1.3.4 Effects of TARP on market discipline

Chapter 8 discusses research findings on the effects of TARP on market discipline by bank shareholders, creditors other than depositors, and depositors. Theoretically, bailouts such as TARP may either decrease or increase the extent to which these market participants act against banks that are taking more risks. For example, TARP could signal an increase in the likelihood of future bailouts for TARP banks, reducing market discipline. Alternatively, TARP could signal bank weakness and increase market discipline. The empirical research on discipline by the different groups of market stakeholders is mixed.

1.3.5 Effects of TARP on bank leverage risk

Chapter 9 describes research findings on the impacts of TARP on leverage risk. As discussed above, the TARP capital injections were in the form of preferred equity, which counts toward capital ratios based on Tier 1 capital. Although it is found that Tier 1 capital rose relative to assets for TARP banks, such ratios are mechanically affected by TARP, even if no further actions are taken by the TARP banks or market participants. There is no mechanical effect of TARP on standard accounting-based or market-based leverage ratios, which are based on common equity, measured using either accounting or market data.

As discussed in more detail in Chapter 9, leverage risk measured using either accounting or market data may either be decreased or increased by TARP preferred equity injections. For example, common equity may be increased because of boosted confidence in the bank, which may make it easier to raise common equity or increase the market value of existing equity. In contrast, to the extent that TARP stigmatizes the bank, the opposite effects may occur.

The relatively small amount of empirical research on this topic suggests that leverage risk is reduced. One paper finds that the common equity to assets accounting ratio is increased, implying a decrease in accounting-based leverage, and one paper finds that market leverage is also decreased.

1.3.6 Effects of TARP on bank competition

Chapter 10 discusses research findings on the competitive effects of TARP. Two empirical studies using the DID methodology suggest that TARP banks very significantly increased both their market shares and market power relative to non-TARP banks and are able to identify some of the channels through which this occurs. A third empirical study of the competitive effects of TARP also finds competitive distortions for sound non-TARP peers that did not receive bailout funds.

The results of the last study suggest that the competitive distortions implied by the first two studies may be understated. The DID methodology of the first two studies only measures the effects of TARP on TARP banks relative to non-TARP banks, and the third study suggests that some of these non-TARP banks also achieved higher market power from TARP, so the competitive distortions created by the program may be very large. Further research to clarify this is obviously needed.

1.3.7 Effects of TARP on bank credit supply

Chapter 11 gives a summary of the research findings about the effects of the program on the credit supply of the recipient banks relative to others, generally using the DID framework. Most, but not all of the studies find increased credit supply at the *extensive margin*—more dollars of loans and loan commitments—for TARP banks relative to non-TARP banks. There is also evidence of improved credit supply to large firms at the *intensive margin*—lower interest rate spreads, larger amounts, longer maturities, less frequency of collateral, and less restrictive covenants.

Importantly, as discussed in Chapter 11, this evidence is not fully conclusive on whether TARP increased *total* bank credit supply because the DID framework measures only the change in credit supply of TARP banks relative to non-TARP banks. The total change in lending would include the effects of TARP on the lending by non-TARP banks, which may have also been affected by the program. As discussed in Chapter 11, non-TARP banks may have either decreased or increased their credit supplies as results of TARP.

1.3.8 Effects of TARP on recipient bank portfolio risk

Chapter 12 reviews research on the effects of TARP on the individual recipient banks' portfolio risk. It is documented that TARP banks seem to have increased the portfolio risk of TARP banks in at least three ways—shifting into riskier assets, easing the terms of issued loans, and easing these terms relatively more for riskier borrowers. The results in Chapter 11 suggesting that lending increased also contributes to additional portfolio risk.

Similar to the arguments above about lending, this evidence on increased portfolio risk is not conclusive on the effects of TARP on the risk of the financial system. The DID framework measures only the change in the portfolio risk of TARP banks relative to non-TARP banks and excludes the effects of TARP on the risk of non-TARP banks. It also neglects other factors that affect systemic risk, including individual banks' size and capital or leverage risk, as well as interconnections among the banks.

1.3.9 Effects of TARP on recipient banks' credit customers

The research on the effects of TARP on bank competition in Chapter 10 and bank credit supply in Chapter 11 suggests that TARP affected bank borrowers as well. As discussed in Chapter 13, the greater market power for TARP banks may help or hurt their credit customers, depending on whether these borrowers are primarily served using transactional versus relationship lending technologies, and which of different theories dominates. The greater credit supply of TARP banks—to the extent that it is not offset by any reduced lending of non-TARP banks—would generally benefit borrowers.

The additional research discussed in Chapter 13 is about the measurement of the net effects. Two studies of the effects of TARP on the market values of TARP banks' relationship corporate borrowers have opposing results, but a third study finds that corporate borrowers of TARP banks increased their supplies of trade credit, while non-TARP banks did not. Thus, most of the limited evidence suggests that corporate borrowers were better off.

We are not aware of any direct evidence for unlisted small business borrowers, but some evidence summarized in Chapter 14 on the real economic effects of TARP is suggestive that small businesses may have been helped by TARP. That evidence suggests that TARP increased net job creation and net hiring establishments and decreased business and personal bankruptcies. Given that most job creation, hiring establishments, and bankruptcies are related to small businesses, it seems likely that small businesses were positively affected.

1.3.10 Effects of TARP on the real economy

Chapter 14 focuses on the research findings about the effects of TARP on the real economy. The findings of research in Chapter 11 that TARP likely increased credit supply and in Chapter 13 that corporate borrowers were likely better off are suggestive of benefits to the real economy.

However, these findings are not fully conclusive because they do not take the final step of showing that the lending increases or borrower benefits had beneficial effects on the real economy. Any increase in lending might not have resulted in increased spending (such as investment, hiring, or purchases of homes or other consumption goods) by borrowers that would boost the real economy. Instead, the borrowed funds might have been saved or replaced other sources of funding. Determination of the effects on the real economy requires study of the real effects.

We are able to find only two such studies of real economic effects. The research study alluded to above shows significant positive real economic benefits of TARP in terms of increased net job creation, increased net hiring establishments and decreased business and personal bankruptcies in the states with more TARP recipients. The second study examines the negative impacts of bank failures on business formation and net job creation at the local level, and finds that TARP is effective in reducing these negative consequences. Importantly, the benefits in these studies may be understated because they exclude the favorable effects of TARP of potentially saving the financial system from a bigger collapse. For the complete picture, we also need to know the effects of TARP on systemic risk. If TARP saved the financial system, even only partially, then the real economic effects may be much larger than the measured state-level effects. In other words, TARP may have helped both TARP and non-TARP banks, so the differences between them may understate the total effects on the real economy.

1.3.11 Effects of TARP on systemic risk

Chapter 15 completes the research on the empirical effects of TARP by examining the research findings on the direct measurement of the effects of TARP on systemic risk. The one research paper of which we are aware on this topic applies the DID approach to the latest indicators of systemic risk contributions. The study finds that TARP banks contributed significantly less to systemic risk after receiving TARP funds than non-TARP banks. This seems to happen almost exclusively by increasing the common equity values of TARP banks through share price increases, reducing the market leverage measure, *LVG*. As indicated above, this is not a mechanical effect, given that the common equity values are distinctly different from the preferred equity that was injected by the US Treasury under TARP.

Analogous to the arguments above, the DID framework measures only reduced contributions to systemic risk of the TARP banks relative to non-TARP banks. This may understate the overall reduction in systemic risk because the non-TARP banks were almost surely made safer as well.

Importantly, reducing contributions to systemic risk undoubtedly have strong, but difficult to measure, positive effects on the real economy by keeping business and consumer confidence and bank credit higher than it otherwise would be. Historically, financial crises imperil the real economy as financing for real investments and hiring are withdrawn and recessions often result. Thus, had TARP not reduced contributions to systemic risk, the Global Financial Crisis would likely been worse, and an even greater recession would likely have ensued.

1.4 Empirical research on bank bailouts other than TARP, bail-ins, and other resolution approaches

Part III of the book has three chapters on empirical research. One is on bank bailouts other than TARP, some of which are summarized in Box 1.1, the second discusses bail-ins, some of which are summarized in Boxes 1.3–1.5, and the third covers the other resolution approaches of bankruptcy/failure, reorganization using living wills, regulatory forbearance, and breakups of large complex financial institutions either into smaller institutions that are less systemically important or into institutions with different activities, which are summarized in Box 1.7 below.

1.4.1 Empirical research on bank bailouts other than TARP

Chapter 16 focuses on bailouts other than TARP, primarily those in the US and Europe during and after the Global Financial Crisis and European Sovereign Debt Crisis. As noted earlier and shown in Box 1.1 above, bailouts other than TARP in the US during the Global Financial Crisis include other actions by the Federal Reserve, FDIC, Treasury, and Federal Home Loan Bank (FHLB) System discussed above.

European bailouts include some country-level and several countries' collective responses in the early times of the Global Financial Crisis. These include the bailouts of Fortis and Dexia by the Benelux nations, Belgium, the Netherlands, and Luxembourg; the bailouts of six large banks in Ireland; the bailout of Northern Rock by the UK government, and among many others.

Later on, it was agreed that the economic situation was rather dire, so the European Commission executed a coordinated response at the EU level by authorizing national governments to provide state aid and guarantees to financial institutions in several forms ranging from guarantees on bank liabilities to capital injections, and from asset relief interventions to bank liquidity support, summarized in Box 1.2 above. A number of EU countries, including Greece, Portugal, Ireland, Spain, and Cyprus, increased their government debt to significant ratios, which in turn led to the sovereign crisis that would require assistance from the other EU countries, ECB, and the IMF. More details on the crises in Europe are given in Chapter 2, and additional information on the aid measures is covered in Chapter 3.

BOX 1.7

ALTERNATIVE RESOLUTION METHODS

No.	First Line of Defense	Description
1	**Bankruptcy/Failure**	Allowing institutions to fail under a U.S. Bankruptcy Code for BHCs and/or be closed by a federal or state banking regulatory agency for commercial banks
2	**Living Wills (Reorganizing Large Banking Organizations)**	Resolution plans that are designed *ex ante* by the organizations to restore financial strength and viability in cases of material distress and failure.
3	**Regulatory Forbearance**	Allowing undercapitalized banks to continue operations without significant regulatory intervention or failure.
4	**Breaking Up TBTF Banking Organizations**	Breaking up large institutions into smaller non-systemically important ones that can be easier to manage when they pose "grave" systemic threats.
5	**Breaking Up Types of Activities**	Breaking up different types of activities of banks or repealing the Gramm-Leach-Bliley Act of 1999 and going back to Glass Steagall Act restrictions on combining commercial and investment banks.

The bailout research in nations other than US covered in Chapter 16 discusses political determinants, as well as effects of these bailouts on competition, credit supply, bank risk, real economy, and systemic risk.

While a large number of research papers are summarized in Chapter 16, the empirical research regarding non-TARP bailouts in this chapter is much less comprehensive than the empirical research on TARP discussed in the 11 chapters of Part II. The research on these other bailouts have a number of results in common with the TARP research, including that most of the bailouts appear to have increased bank lending, to have increased bank portfolio risks in response to moral hazard incentives, and to have distorted bank competition in favor of the bailed-out banks. Some of the findings also suggest stigma effects on the recipient banks, and awarding of bailouts based on political connections. The findings with regard to the two ultimate goals of bailouts of improving the real economy and reducing systemic risk are considerably less favorable than the TARP research results. For the non-TARP U.S. bailouts, there is little research on these issues and the systemic risk results are mixed. For the European bailouts, the long-run effects on the real economy and financial system may be negative according to some of the research. The increased lending in some cases was socially-unproductive negative net present value "zombie" credits. In some cases, the bank bailouts burdened the national governments and led to distressed sovereign debt.

1.4.2 Empirical research on the consequences of bail-ins

Chapter 17 summarizes the empirical research findings on bail-ins, including OLA in the US and BRRD in Europe. We also elaborate on research on contingent convertibles (Cocos), a form of bail-in that is used in some European nations. The chapter also discusses briefly other historical bail-in-like tools or episodes such as the double liability on shareholders, used by the regulators prior to the Great Depression. This caused shareholders of failing institutions to lose their initial investments and required them to come up with additional equity to compensate depositors.

We also briefly discuss one significant earlier episode of the US government dealing with a large, distressed financial institution. The case of the hedge fund Long-Term Capital Management (LTCM) in 1998 was a combination of a bailout and bail-in in which the Federal Reserve Bank of New York helped arrange financing by a group of private-sector financial institutions.

The bail-in research is significantly underdeveloped relative to the bailout literature because most of the bail-in programs, events, and instruments are relatively recent, yielding few observations to study. Nonetheless, the research strongly suggests that bail-ins appear to promote market discipline by stakeholders including depositors, bondholders, stockholders, and CDS holders. Bail-in regimes may also provide much better incentives for banks to build capital than bailouts. The research yields no strong conclusions about the efficacy of bail-ins on individual institution risk or systemic risk, and the findings are quite limited on the effects of bail-ins on the real economy.

1.4.3 Empirical research on the consequences of other resolution approaches

Chapter 18 reviews empirical research findings on several resolution approaches other than bailouts and bail-ins. These are: 1) Bankruptcy/failure (the BHC goes bankrupt and the systemically important bank fails); 2) Reorganization using living wills as directed by the Dodd-Frank Act; 3) Regulatory forbearance (keeping the banks operating with little or no capital); 4) Breakups of large complex financial organizations in small institutions; and 5) Breakups of bank activities into specialized commercial banks and investment banks.

The research reviewed in Chapter 18 does not provide significant support for any of these alternatives to bailouts and bail-ins. The findings often suggest that bankruptcy/failure, regulatory forbearance, and breaking up large institutions may more often cause more harm than good. Bankruptcy/failure may drag down other financial institutions and exacerbate systemic risk. Regulatory forbearance may exacerbate moral hazard incentives for banks to take on excess risk. Breaking up large banks into smaller institutions can create bank inefficiencies that increase financial distress and failures in future crises. Separating investment banks from commercial banks may create institutions that cannot easily survive severe liquidity crises. The existing findings are more favorable for living wills, but the research is too thin to draw strong conclusions.

1.5 First lines of defense to help avoid bailouts, bail-ins, and other resolution methods

Part IV contains eight chapters on "first lines of defense," tools that governments use to help reduce the likelihood of banks' financial distress that might otherwise result in bailouts, bail-ins, or other resolution methods. Chapter 19 explains the three mechanisms through which the first lines of defense may operate—the *Prudential, Certification,* and *Subsidy Mechanisms.* Chapters 20 to 26 describe the seven individual first lines of defense, capital requirements (Chapter 20), liquidity requirements (Chapter 21), stress tests (Chapter 22), regulatory activity restrictions (Chapter 23), prudential supervision (Chapter 24), deposit insurance (Chapter 25), and government ownership of banks (Chapter 26). Each of these chapters also gives details on which of the three mechanisms through which the respective first line of defense operates, how that first line is implemented in different countries, and discusses empirical research on how well it works through the mechanisms. Box 1.8 shows each of the seven first lines of defense. As discussed in these chapters, the theory often provides conflicting predictions about whether the first lines

BOX 1.8

FIRST LINES OF DEFENSE

	First Line of Defense	Description
1	Capital Requirements	Capital requirements prescribe the amount of capital a bank or other financial institution has to hold as required by its financial regulator. Basel Accord minimum capital requirements are key regulatory tools for ensuring resilience of banks in many nations.
2	Liquidity Requirements	Liquidity requirements were introduced as part of Basel III and are designed to ensure banks maintain an adequate level of high-quality liquid assets to meet their liquidity needs. Liquidity Coverage Ratio (LCR) is designed to improve the short-term resilience of banks against liquidity shocks, while net stable funding ratio (NSFR) requires banks to fund illiquid assets with a minimum amount of stable liabilities over a horizon of one year.
3	Stress Tests	Stress tests applied to banking organizations estimate the degree to which they would be able to lend and perform other normal banking functions in simulated adverse scenarios that emulate possible future financial crises or difficult periods. Stress tests are essentially forward-looking capital requirements that require large banks to hold sufficient capital during hypothetical future adverse scenarios.
4	Prudential Regulatory Activity Restrictions	Regulatory activity restrictions include limits on how much banks may engage in some activities, such as lending limits on credit exposures to a single counterparty and the 2010 Dodd-Frank Act's Volcker Rule limits on BHC investments in private equity and hedge funds, outright bans on some activities considered to be too risky for banks such as proprietary trading under the Volcker Rule, and prohibitions on investment banking and nonfinancial activities in commercial banks.

Continued

—cont'd

	First Line of Defense	Description
5	**Prudential Supervision**	Prudential regulation measures are designed to keep banks safe and sound, and include supervisory examinations to identify bank risks and management problems, and the informal and formal actions that come about as results of these examinations that try to tamp down some of these risks and management problems before they result in financial distress.
6	**Deposit Insurance**	Government-backed deposit insurance provides protections for the claims of a subset of depositors against bank failure and pays them if the bank is unable to do so.
7	**Direct Government Ownership of Banks**	Direct government ownership can be regarded as the ultimate deposit insurance as bank losses may be backstopped by the government's deep pockets.

of defense are effective through the three mechanisms, but the empirical research is often clearer on their efficacy.

1.5.1 The three mechanisms through which the first lines of defense operate

As discussed in Chapter 19, the *Prudential Mechanism* prudential mechanism involves mitigating risks that are primarily under the bank's control, such as leverage risk, credit risk, or liquidity risk. As a result, banks are less likely to experience financial distress. An example of a line of defense that may operate through the *Prudential Mechanism* is capital requirements, which directly decrease leverage risk and may also reduce other types of risk by mitigating moral hazard incentives to take on excessive risks. As discussed in Chapter 20, while some theories yield opposing predictions, the empirical research is strongly consistent with the *Prudential Mechanism* for capital requirements.

The *Certification Mechanism* assures the public about the safety of their investments in the banks. This reduces banks' risks from runs by depositors or other liability holders that might create liquidity problems or make it difficult for banks to raise funds. The assurances of safety may also reduce the likelihood of rapid sales by shareholders or short sales by others that might reduce the market values of the banks and/or make it difficult for them to raise equity capital during distress. To illustrate, a line of defense that may operate through the certification mechanism is stress tests—a passing grade on a stress test may raise the public's perception of the safety of the bank, although a failing grade may have the opposite effect.

The *Subsidy Mechanism* involves providing banks with subsidies that may prop up the bank, increase its capital, and reduce its leverage risk to make it less likely to experience financial distress. One of the lines of defense that operates through the *Subsidy Mechanism* is deposit insurance, which enriches the banks by allowing them to borrow at close to the risk-free rate due to the government protection.

1.5.2 Using capital requirements as a first line of defense

Chapter 20 discusses capital requirements, which are employed by regulators around the world to keep banks from falling into financial distress that might otherwise result in bank bailouts, bail-ins, or other resolutions. The chapter describes the concepts and theories behind these requirements, how these requirements may or may not function through the three mechanisms for avoiding bank financial distress. Both international and US capital requirements are explained, and the empirical evidence on the mechanisms is reviewed. While the theory is equivocal about the *Prudential* and *Certification Mechanisms*, the empirical evidence overwhelmingly suggests that capital requirements are effective through these mechanisms. The *Subsidy Mechanism* is not relevant for capital requirements. The chapter also reviews the evidence on the controversial issues regarding the effects of capital requirements on bank liquidity creation and profitability, suggesting mixed results for liquidity creation, but mostly positive effects on profitability.

1.5.3 Using liquidity requirements as a first line of defense

Chapter 21 reviews liquidity requirements, a first line of defense to reduce liquidity risk to avoid bank distress and reduce the likelihoods of bailouts, bail-ins, or other bank resolutions. Liquidity requirements are explained, and the mechanisms through which they may operate are analyzed. The chapter also describes international and country-specific liquidity requirements, and summarizes the empirical evidence on the mechanisms. The theory is mixed as to whether liquidity requirements work through the *Prudential* and *Certification Mechanisms*. Most of the empirical evidence supports that liquidity requirements generally operate through the *Prudential Mechanism*, albeit with some room for improvement. There is no empirical evidence to our knowledge on the *Certification Mechanism* for liquidity requirements. The *Subsidy Mechanism* is not applicable for this line of defense.

We also discuss in Chapter 21 the issue of whether it is appropriate to have liquidity requirements that guard against large aggregate liquidity shocks, when such shock may be alternatively dealt with by central banks' lender of last resort (LOLR) function. Research discussed in Chapter 16 suggests that the expansion of the Federal Reserve's use of LOLR was highly successful in boosting bank lending during the Global Financial Crisis.

1.5.4 Using stress tests as a first line of defense

Chapter 22 discusses stress tests, which have been employed by regulators since the Global Financial Crisis to make large banking organizations resistant to future crises and other problematic situations. They are essentially forward-looking capital requirements that mandate that these organizations hold sufficient capital so they would be able to continue to operate and lend during hypothetical future adverse scenarios like financial crises. As is the case for the other chapters in Part IV, the theory, practice, and empirical research results are reviewed and analyzed. Analogous to capital requirements, the theory is ambiguous about the *Prudential* and *Certification Mechanisms* for stress tests, but the empirical evidence suggests that stress tests are operative through both of these mechanisms. The *Subsidy Mechanism* does not apply to stress tests. The chapter also discusses the potential downsides of stress tests. They may confer TBTF status to the stress-tested banks and appear to reduce their credit supplies to large and small businesses.

1.5.5 Using prudential regulatory activity restrictions as a first line of defense

Chapter 23 provides information and research findings for prudential regulatory activity restrictions. These are limits or outright bans on what are considered risky bank activities, and are imposed by regulators to reduce the incidence of financial distress and reduce the likelihood that bailouts, bail-ins, or other resolutions are needed. The chapter describes several important prudential regulatory activity restrictions that have been imposed in the US and EU. Similar to the other first lines of defense that are explicitly designed to limit bank risk taking, the theory is ambiguous about whether these restrictions operate through the *Prudential* and *Certification Mechanisms*. The empirical evidence is also unclear regarding these two mechanisms. The *Subsidy Mechanism* is not applicable for prudential regulatory activity restrictions.

1.5.6 Using prudential supervision as a first line of defense

Chapter 24 gives background information and reviews the theory as well as empirical research findings regarding prudential supervision. This first line of defense aims to contain and reduce risks at both the bank and system levels, referred to as microprudential and macroprudential supervision, respectively. Prudential supervisors check if banks are in compliance with safety and soundness rules and regulations, monitor banks for excessive bank risk taking, and take actions against banks that do not follow the rules or regulations or are found to be excessively risky, preventing if possible, bailouts, bail-ins, or other resolutions. As is the case for the other policies to designed to reduce bank risk, the theory is ambiguous about whether prudential supervision makes banks safer versus riskier through the *Prudential* and *Certification Mechanisms*. However, the empirical evidence is consistent with this supervision operating through these two mechanisms. The *Subsidy Mechanism* is reversed for prudential supervision, as supervisors impose costs on and collect funds from the banks, acting more as a tax than a subsidy.

1.5.7 Using deposit insurance as a first line of defense

Chapter 25 describes deposit insurance, discusses the theory and practice of this first line of defense around the world, and evaluates how well it operates or fails to operate through the three mechanisms to prevent and/or deter financial distress and avoid resolution. Importantly, some deposit insurance schemes are explicit or *de jure*, some are implicit or *de facto*, and most countries have a combination of both. *De facto* insurance often protects depositors broadly during financial crises, and also covers banks that are TBTF, TITF, or groups of banks that are considered TMTF at other times, and could be considered a form of preemptive bailout. The theory and empirical research both suggest that deposit insurance makes banks safer through the *Certification* and *Subsidy Mechanisms*. The insurance deters runs by depositors and other liability holders (*Certification Mechanism*), and bolsters bank capital by allowing them to borrow at close to the risk-free rate because of the government protection (*Subsidy Mechanism*). The theory suggests that the moral hazard incentives engendered by deposit insurance make individual banks riskier rather than safer through the *Prudential Mechanism*. However, the continued lending and other services provided by these banks during recessions — which often coincide with financial crises — may support the real economy at these times and reduce risk at the system level. The empirical literature has mixed results for the *Prudential Mechanism* for deposit insurance.

1.5.8 Using direct government ownership as a first line of defense

Chapter 26 gives background information and reviews theory and empirical research findings for direct government ownership of banks. This is a common practice in many nations around the world, including some developed nations other than the US. There are several motivations for this ownership, including the safety of the financial system. The chapter investigates the extent to which this first line of defense accomplishes this goal through the three mechanisms. From a theoretical standpoint, the direct ownership of banks operates through these mechanisms in a very similar fashion to deposit insurance. The incentives generated by this ownership is predicted to make individual institutions behave relatively poorly in terms of efficiency and performance at virtually all times. However, their continued lending and support for the real economy during recessions − which often coincide with financial crises − may reduce systemic risk and improve financial stability at stressful times. The empirical literature finds split results for the *Prudential Mechanism* that essentially follow the theoretical predictions. The findings from the data suggest that direct government ownership may make the individual banks riskier, but the financial system safer. The empirical research also suggests that government ownership makes banks safer through the *Certification* and *Subsidy Mechanisms*.

1.6 Looking toward the future

The final part of the book, Part V, looks to the future and contains three chapters on social costs and benefits, policy implications, and open research questions.

1.6.1 Social costs and benefits

Chapter 27 weighs the net social costs and benefits of bailouts, bail-ins, other resolution methods, first lines of defense, and countercyclical policies. This chapter also reviews some additional research on TARP and countercyclical prudential and monetary policies that is relevant for drawing conclusions, but does not neatly fit the topics of the earlier chapters. Any conclusions as to whether social benefits versus social costs dominate depend on the financial circumstances and the short- versus long-run orientation for evaluation. The chapter therefore discusses conclusions for different financial stability conditions (severe financial crises and TMTF versus other financial conditions) and effects for short- versus long-term orientations. Table 19.1 displays these conclusions for all 16 of the policies for addressing the financial distress and potential failure of financial institutions analyzed in the book under these different circumstances.

1.6.2 Implications for bank policymakers and bank managers

Chapter 28 offers logical implications of the research findings in the book for both bank policymakers and bank managers. The suggestions reflect both short- and long-term orientations and are tailored to the stability conditions of the financial system. We also tailor our suggestions for bank managers to the individual financial conditions of their banks. For a number of the policies, the implications of the research are quite clear. During difficult financial conditions of severe financial crises and TMTF circumstances, bailouts may be a better policy choice than bail-ins, at least in the short run because bail-ins risk bringing down other financial institutions at precisely the wrong time. However, under more tranquil financial conditions, bail-ins may be preferred over bailouts because of the superior incentives provided by bail-ins. Some of the other resolutions, such as bankruptcy/failure and regulatory forbearance, are not supported by the research under any circumstances. Other policies, such as prudential supervision, deposit insurance, and countercyclical prudential policy are found to be generally favored, while support for strict enforcement of other policies, such as capital requirements and stress tests, depend on financial conditions.

1.6.3 Open research questions

Chapter 29 concludes the book by identifying the important unresearched and underresearched questions that need the most attention, and suggesting how future researchers might address them. The chapter gives five general suggestions for future research to help keep the financial system and real economy safe. These include: 1) A focus on reducing the likelihood and severity of financial crises; 2) Comparing multiple policy tools in the same study; 3) Measuring the indirect effects of policies on non-treated banks; 4) Comparing long-term and short-term program outcomes; and 5) Investigating policy tools in developing as well as developed nations. The chapter also points researchers toward key unanswered questions regarding each of the policy approaches for dealing with the financial distress of the banking industry — bailouts, bail-ins, and other resolution approaches; first lines of defense; and counter-cyclical policies.

References

Atkinson, T., Luttrell, D., & Rosenblum, H. (2013). How bad was it? The costs and consequences of the 2007—09 financial crisis. *Staff Papers*, (Jul).

Avgouleas, E., Goodhart, C., & Schoenmaker, D. (2013). Bank resolution plans as a catalyst for global financial reform. *Journal of Financial Stability, 9*(2), 210—18.

Bernanke, B. S. (1983). *Non-monetary effects of the financial crisis in the propagation of the Great Depression*. National Bureau of Economic Research.

Claessens, S., Herring, R., Schoenmaker, D., & Summe, K. A. (2010). *A safer world financial system: Improving the resolution of systemic institutions*. Geneva Reports on the World Economy.

Friedman, M., & Schwartz, A. J. (1963). *A monetary history of the US 1867—1960*. Princeton: Princeton University Press.

Garcia, G. G. H. (2015). *The U.S. financial crisis and the Great Recession: Counting the costs*. World scientific-NOW publishers series.

U.S. Government Accountability Office Report. (January 16, 2013). *Financial crisis losses and potential impacts of the Dodd-Frank Act*. report to congressional requesters. Available at www.gao.gov/products/GAO-13-180.

Conditions that generally bring about bank bailouts, bail-ins, and other resolution methods

This chapter discusses the conditions that typically bring about bailouts, bail-ins, and other types of bank resolution. As noted in the Introduction, bailouts and bail-ins are usually triggered by financial crises, but may also occur during normal times in response to the distress of too-big-to-fail (TBTF), too-interconnected-to-fail (TITF), or too-many-to-fail (TMTF) banks.

In the interest of brevity, Section 2.1 describes just two recent financial crises, the Global Financial Crisis and European Sovereign Debt Crisis, and the links between them, and refers the reader to some literature on other financial crises. The two recent crises are the most relevant here because they triggered most of the bailouts covered in this book and also helped in the creation of most of the bail-in regimes described in the book. We are not able to detail the Global Coronavirus Financial Crisis, which just began as this book was going to press. Section 2.2 reviews some research on the lending booms and liquidity buildups that tend to bring about financial crises. Section 2.3 discusses the theory of how the distress of TBTF, TITF, or TMTF banks may also trigger bailouts and bail-ins, and Section 2.4 examines the empirical research on factors that tend to bring about distress or failure of TBTF, TITF, and/or TMTF banks.

Note that in later chapters in Part V, we also discuss countercyclical prudential and conventional monetary policies that may reduce the likelihood and severity of financial crises that precipitate most of the needs for bailouts, bail-ins, and other resolutions. We also include an entire book part, Part IV, on the first lines of defense. These help avoid bank distress and the need for resolution for all types of banks during financial crises and TBTF, TITF, and/or TMTF banks at other times as well.

43

2.1 Financial crises

2.1.1 Links between recent financial crises

As noted above, we focus on the two recent crises—the Global Financial Crisis and European Sovereign Debt Crisis—that brought about most of the bailouts and bail-ins discussed in the book. These two crises are inexorably linked, and so any separate discussions of them are inevitably flawed. The Global Financial Crisis began in the US as the US Subprime Financial Crisis and spread through many linkages to Europe and the rest of the world, and so it is an integral part of the European Sovereign Debt Crisis. The distresses of banks and governments during the European Sovereign Debt Crisis are also inescapably linked. In some cases, government finances came under pressure because of the economic damages caused by the bank distress and the costs of the bank bailouts. In other cases, bank distress was exacerbated by sovereign debt problems because the banks invested substantially in sovereign debt, particularly the debt of their home countries. Despite these links, we briefly describe these two different crises separately.

2.1.2 The Global Financial Crisis

The Global Financial Crisis began as the US Subprime Financial Crisis in 2007:Q3 when losses on US Mortgage-Backed Securities (MBS) backed by subprime mortgages started to spread to other markets, including the syndicated loan market, the interbank lending market, and the commercial paper market. In some cases, these other markets at least partially froze up. Many banks experienced substantial capital losses and at least partially withdrew from these markets. A number of large financial institutions, especially thrifts that were heavily involved in subprime lending (e.g., Countrywide, Washington Mutual, IndyMac Bank), investment banks that purchased and/or packaged subprime MBS (e.g., Bear Stearns, Merrill Lynch, Lehman Brothers), and a large insurance company that sold many credit default swaps (CDSs) on subprime MBS (American International Group (AIG)) suffered capital, liquidity, and public confidence problems and either failed, were taken over, or were individually bailed out.

As the crisis spread to many commercial banks, the TARP program, expansion of the discount window and Term Auction Facilities (TAFs), and many other bank bailouts shown in the Introduction and described in more detail in Chapter 3 occurred. It is also notable that bank and thrift failures became so widespread that the FDIC Deposit Insurance Fund fell into a deficit position and assessed banks for 3 years of deposit insurance premiums in advance to try to fill this hole. US stock market values also plunged significantly, with the Dow Jones Industrial Average falling by more than half.

As a result of these financial problems, the US economy also suffered the most severe recession since the Great Depression. The recession resulted in a number of government programs to stimulate the economy, including a massive stimulus government spending package and expansive conventional and unconventional monetary policy stimulus by the Federal Reserve.

Despite all the bailouts of financial institutions and government stimulus programs, economic losses in the US totaled in tens of trillions of dollars, as noted in the Introduction. The US recession officially ended in mid-2009, but economic growth remained slow for many years afterward. The financial crisis in the US was more or less concluded by the end of 2009, by which point much of the TARP funds invested in financial institutions had been repaid, order had been restored to most of the financial markets, and the Federal Reserve shortly thereafter began rolling back expansions to the discount window and concluded the TAF auctions (Berger and Bouwman, 2016).

However, the financial issues continued in other nations. The US Subprime Financial Crisis became the Global Financial Crisis as financial losses spread to other countries through financial linkages. There are too many such linkages to discuss here, but we simply mention one. The Basel II capital requirements, which had been earlier adopted in Europe, gave very low capital weights to AAA-rated tranches of US subprime mortgage-backed securities (MBS). This encouraged their purchases by European banks, helping to spread the problems created by these securities across the Atlantic.

2.1.3 The European Sovereign Debt Crisis

The European Sovereign Debt Crisis began in 2008, with the collapse of Iceland's banking system, and then spread to the GIIPS countries, Greece, Italy, Ireland, Portugal, and Spain. The crisis was significant through 2012, and some might argue that remnants still exist as of this writing. Some government debt remains on shaky grounds, European authorities, such as the ECB, are still engaging in stimulus, and interest rates in a number of nations are negative. As indicated above, this crisis was precipitated in significant part by the Global Financial Crisis, and it involved sovereigns as well as banks, which are also linked (Pagano and Sedunov, 2016). Other contributing factors include the recessions that covered a number of countries, the real estate market crisis and property bubbles in several countries, and fiscal policies in some nations.

Regarding the latter point, Greece revealed in 2009 that its previous government had underreported its budget deficit, a violation of EU policy, prompting fears of a Eurozone collapse via political and financial contagion. In 2010, with the growing fear of excessive sovereign debt, lenders demanded higher interest rates from Eurozone states with high debt and deficit levels, aggravating their fiscal problems. Some affected countries raised taxes and cut expenditures to battle the crisis, which added to social unrest and confidence problems in their governments. During this crisis, several of these countries, including Greece, Portugal, and Ireland had their sovereign debt downgraded to junk by international credit rating agencies, augmenting investor fears.

Greece, Spain, Ireland, Portugal, and Cyprus were incapable of repaying or refinancing their government debt or bailing out their struggling banks without the help from third-party institutions such as the European Central Bank (ECB), the International Monetary Fund (IMF), and the European Financial Stability Facility (EFSF). Seventeen Eurozone countries voted to create the EFSF in 2010, specifically to resolve the European Sovereign Debt Crisis. These other Eurozone countries were partially driven by desires to preserve the Eurozone and/or EU, and partly driven by worries related to large investments by the banks in these healthier nations in the sovereign debt of the weaker nations. Some of these bank investments in risky sovereign debt were brought about in part by the low risk weights on this debt assigned by the Basel II capital requirements.

2.1.4 Blame for the recent financial crises

A number of parties are blamed for creating or exacerbating the effects of the Global Financial Crisis, and by implication, the European Sovereign Debt Crisis that followed. In some cases, the blame is not fully deserved either because the reasoning is incorrect or because the *ex post* consequences of some of the pre-crisis period actions could not be reasonably anticipated *ex ante*.

The Federal Reserve and its leaders receive blame for (1) keeping interest rates too low for too long in the pre-crisis period, encouraging risky lending; (2) not recognizing the dangers of the build-up of correlated risks in real estate lending; (3) not devoting sufficient resources to their financial stability mission to identify future stability and systemic risk threats; (4) pushing for Basel II capital standards, which lowered requirements for large, systemically important banking organizations and encouraged risky investments by European banks by putting low capital weights on AAA-rated tranches of MBS backed by subprime mortgages and sovereign debt of risky national governments; (5) not regulating the new complex and opaque instruments of finance, which were built on faulty models that underweighted the probability of housing price declines; and (6) not applying safety and soundness and consumer protection regulations consistently across intermediaries which gave rise to regulatory arbitrage; and (7) not pursuing accusations of consumer predatory lending.

Blame is also often assigned to Government Sponsored Enterprises (GSEs) Fannie Mae and Freddie Mac, which were undiversified entities that operated with very little capital and were able to borrow cheaply due to implicit government guarantees, which were realized during the crisis.

With the backing of the US President George W. Bush and Congress, the GSEs began investing in subprime MBS during the pre-crisis period, encouraging lenders to make more such loans.

In addition, the Securities and Exchange Commission (SEC) is blamed for allowing the investment banks to operate with very low capital ratios, despite very high portfolio risks in packaging and holding opaque MBS. The investment banks that engaged in these risky activities are also held responsible for their behavior. Rating agencies are blamed for faulty ratings on mortgage-related securities in which additional AAA-ratings were assigned to riskier and more opaquetranches. Accounting firms are criticized for unrealistic values placed on opaque MBS. Mortgage bankers and underwriters are charged with overlooking unfavorable credit information and in some cases, complicity in creating false favorable information.

Finally, a prior President and Congress were blamed for allowing combinations of commercial and investment banks under the Financial Services Modernization Act of 1999, aka the Gramm–Leach–Bliley Act. We argue that this blame is misplaced, given that the main financial institutions that created the crisis were not combined commercial banks and investment banks. To the contrary, one of the solutions to the crisis was to encourage such combinations because the stand-alone investment banks had significant liquidity problems during the crisis.

2.1.5 Literature on other financial crises

There are many other financial crises that are not discussed in this section in the interest of brevity. We refer readers to literature that discusses these crises in detail for the US by Berger and Bouwman (2013, 2016, 2017); and worldwide by Demirgüç-Kuntand Detragiache (1998), Von Hagen and Ho (2007), Reinhart and Rogoff (2009), and Laeven and Valencia (2018).

2.2 Research on lending booms and liquidity buildups that tend to bring about financial crises

There are as many causes as there are financial crises, and each one is different (Reinhart and Rogoff, 2009), so it is not possible to review all of the causes. In the interest of brevity, we focus here on just two recurring causes—lending booms and liquidity buildups. These two causes are not entirely independent, as bank credit also creates liquidity for the economy. It is often argued that unusually high quantities of bank lending and bank loan commitments may help result in financial crises. Loans are a form of on-balance sheet bank liquidity creation and loan commitments are a type of off-balance sheet bank liquidity creation (Berger and

Bouwman, 2009). Excessive credit of either type can result in asset price bubbles that burst and result in financial crises (Rajan, 1994; Acharya and Naqvi, 2012). Brunnermeier, Gorton, and Krishnamurthy (2011) also argue that liquidity build-ups in the financial sector can create systemic risk.

The quality of credit issued may also significantly deteriorate during lending and liquidity booms because of an institutional memory problem in banks. Veteran loan officers may have difficulty remembering how to deal with problem loans when it has been a long time since they dealt with significant problems, and turnover results in newer loan officers who have not previously faced such problems (Berger and Udell, 2004). In a theoretical setting, Thakor (2015a, 2016) show that good times corrupt risk management in banks and also lead to an "underpricing" of risk from an *ex post* perspective. This is because an extended period of profitable bank growth may also create a false sense of security among bankers and regulators that banks can withstand significant shocks (Thakor, 2015b). Excessive risk-taking may also occur off the balance sheet during economic booms, as banks shy away from exercising material adverse change (MAC) clauses on loan commitments[1] due to reputational concerns during such booms (Thakor, 2005). Consistent with these views, former Federal Reserve Chairman, Alan Greenspan argues that "the worst loans are made at the top of the business cycle." (Alan Greenspan, Chicago Bank Structure Conference, May 10, 2001). Both excessive credit and poor quality of credit were evident in the US in the buildup to the Global Financial Crisis. Subprime mortgages in great numbers were issued to overlevered consumers. In some cases, these mortgages were issued based on the optimistic assumption that housing prices would continue to rise, given that many of the subprime borrowers would be unable to make the future payments without refinancing at higher home prices. In addition, Fannie Mae and Freddie Mac lowered their credit standards by buying subprime mortgages in the mid-2000s, further encouraging banks to make such loans. Finally, another reason for bank failures and crises is that regulatory career concerns may lead bank regulators to pursue self-interest and delay closures of financial institutions until things get really bad (e.g., Boot and Thakor, 1993).

For the interest of brevity, we review one empirical paper on lending booms and one on liquidity buildups, both using US data. Dell'Ariccia, Igan, and Laeven (2012) examine factors related to the rapid expansion of the US mortgage market prior to the Global Financial Crisis. Using a large data set of loan applications, they find that the denial rates were lower in

---

[1] MAC clauses are intended to protect the lender against gaps in due diligence or unforeseen "material" changes to the borrower's financial condition and assets that could affect the borrower's ability to repay the loan. If a change is deemed material enough, the lender can modify terms or terminate its agreement with the borrower.

areas that experienced faster credit demand growth, and that lenders in these high-growth areas put less weight on applicants' loan-to-income ratios, after controlling for other economic fundamentals.

The other study explicitly tests the propositions that excessive on-balance sheet and off-balance sheet liquidity creation increase the likelihood of future financial crises. Berger and Bouwman (2017) use data on five financial crises in the US. They essentially use empirical models to predict when the fifth crisis (the subprime crisis) would occur, controlling for a number of other aggregate factors that might cause financial crises. They find that lagged detrended aggregate liquidity creation has a statistically and economically significantly positive effect on the probability of a future crisis, supporting the theories discussed above. They also find that the effects are primarily driven by off-balance sheet liquidity creation, which is mostly composed of loan commitments.

2.3 The theory of too-big-to-fail (TBTF), too-interconnected-to-fail (TITF), and too-many-to-fail (TMTF) banks

As discussed above, the distress of TBTF, TITF, and/or TMTF banks may trigger bailouts or bail-ins outside of crisis times. The TBTF term was introduced in 1984 by the bailouts of Continental Illinois National Bank and Trust Company, which failed at that time, but was not closed. It was propped up by government bailouts for a number of years, and was eventually bought by Bank of America. The Chicago bank was the seventh largest bank in the US, with about $40 billion in assets (FDIC, 1997), and its failure was the largest in US history as of that time.[2] After Continental Illinois, investors had reasons to believe that the creditors of large banks were likely to be protected. In addition, in congressional hearings after the event, Comptroller of the Currency, C. Todd Conover, the primary supervisor for national banks, explicitly stated that regulators were unlikely to allow the nation's 11 largest banks to fail.[3] Congressman

---

[2] https://www.federalreservehistory.org/essays/failure_of_continental_illinois.

[3] Although Conover did not name the banks, Barth and Wihlborg (2015) collected information from the *Wall Street Journal*, The Banker, Federal Reserve, and Milken Institute and identified the 11 largest banks and their associated BHCs in 1983 as: Citibank; Bank of America, San Francisco; Chase Manhattan Bank; Morgan Guaranty Trust, New York; Manufacturers Hanover Trust, New York; Chemical Bank, New York; Continental Illinois National Bank and Trust, Chicago; Security Pacific National Bank, Los Angeles; First National Bank of Chicago; Bankers Trust New York; and Wells Fargo Bank. The authors follow these banks through time and note that many of them got integrated into larger organizations, while two of the original BHCs remain, and all became much bigger over the past three decades.

Stewart McKinney responded, "let us not bandy words. We have [created] a new kind of bank. It is called too-big-to-fail, TBTF, and it is a wonderful bank." This was the first time that government officials confirmed the existence of such a government policy.

TBTF theory describes the motivations of the regulators in bailing out TBTF banks and the incentives that the expectations of such bailouts create for the banks and their stakeholders. Regulators' bailout decisions may be motivated by the desires to reduce damages to the financial system and the real economy. The failure of a large bank may spill over to other financial institutions and increase the likelihood of future financial crises. Supporting this, Acharya (2009) finds that the limited liability of banks and the presence of a negative externality of one bank's failure on the health of other banks give rise to a systemic risk-shifting incentive where all banks undertake correlated investments, thereby increasing economy-wide aggregate risk. The loss of credit and other banking services of a single large bank may also cause significant economic losses. In addition, they may bail out large banks to avoid personal embarrassment about failures on their watches or to direct credit according to their preferences (e.g., Kane, 1989, 1991; Stern and Feldman, 2004; Mishkin, 2006). The expectation that the largest banks are likely to be bailed out in the event of their distress from TBTF policies is a subsidy to large banks in conditions of financial distress and good financial health as well because the lessened probability of failure allows the large banks to raise equity and debt capital more cheaply. This motivates the banks to become larger to be able to raise capital more cheaply, and motivates shareholders, creditors, and other counterparties to do business with them (e.g., Cetorelli and Traina, 2018).

Table 2.1 provides some data indicating how large banks have grown since the TBTF policy was introduced in 1984. The number of FDIC insured banks has fallen by about 70% as of 2019:Q1, while the number of banks with at least $10 billion in assets has increased by about 340%, and their share of industry assets has more than tripled. Of course, both inflation and real growth of banks play roles in these figures, but it seems likely that TBTF be responsible for some of the growth of the large banks.

The theoretical motivations behind TITF and TMTF mostly follow those of TBTF. They also involve regulators avoiding risks to the financial system and the economy, circumventing personal embarrassment, and/or maintaining the ability to direct credit, and banks and their stakeholders taking actions to gain the subsidies of bailout expectations. TITF theory differs from TBTF theory in that it takes into account the highly interconnected network among banks, rather than the size of these institutions. Banks may be interconnected either directly or indirectly. Direct interconnectedness arises from bilateral transactions or relationships between banks, such as interbank deposits, loans, or derivatives (e.g., interest rate swaps). If the bank that owes money or is out-of-the-

TABLE 2.1 US bank numbers and asset concentration by size class, 1984:Q4 versus 2019:Q1.

Report period	1984:Q4						2019:Q1					
	Number		Assets				Number		Assets			
Bank size classes	Number	% of Total	Total assets	% of Total			Number	% of Total	Total assets	% of Total		
Assets ≥ $10 billion	32	0.2%	1004.6	27.5%			141	2.6%	15,208.2	84.1%		
Assets $1 billion–$10 billion	468	2.6%	1231.1	33.7%			648	12.1%	1718.5	9.5%		
Assets $100 million–$1 billion	3594	20.1%	934.8	25.6%			3306	61.7%	1096.3	6.1%		
Assets < $100 million	13,807	77.1%	484.0	13.3%			1267	23.6%	76.0	0.4%		
All FDIC insured commercial banks	17,901		3653.1				5362		18,090.0			

This table shows the numbers and asset concentration by bank size classes for all FDIC insured commercial banks in the US.
Source: Adapted based on FDIC quarterly banking profile, https://www.fdic.gov/bank/analytical/qbp/

money on derivative contracts becomes financial distressed or fails, the banks with direct interconnections to it suffer losses on the values of their claims, losing all of the values in the event of failure. Indirect interconnectedness—in which the financial distress or failure of a bank may spread losses to banks without direct bilateral exposures to it—stems from many potential sources. These include mark-to-market losses on similar assets, margin calls, and/or increased haircuts on posted collateral triggered by fire sales by other banks, or information spillovers from other banks that result in runs (e.g., Lui, Quiet, and Roth, 2015). Under TITF theory, the financial distress or failure of more interconnected banks causes more damage to the financial system than problems of less interconnected institutions. Thus, regulators are more likely to bail out more interconnected banks and banks have incentives to become more interconnected to increase their likelihoods of receiving such bailouts. The theoretical arguments in Choi (2014) suggest that bailouts be allocated to the stronger of the interconnected banks, who are in better positions to reduce systemic risk than the weaker banks.

TMTF theory posits a more dynamic view that includes multiple banks. Holding the total number of banks constant for a period of time, when the number of failed banks increases and the number of surviving banks decreases, the investment opportunity set for surviving financial institutions grows large, but the total investment capacity of surviving banks decreases (Acharya and Yorulmazer, 2007). To prevent widespread damage, the optimal choice for regulator is to bail out when the number of failures is large. The expectations of such widespread bailouts may encourage banks to engage in herding behavior that results in highly correlated portfolios to be able to benefit from future bailouts (e.g., Acharya and Yorulmazer, 2007, 2008; Brown and Dinc, 2011; Farhi and Tirole, 2012; Acharya, Mehran, and Thakor, 2016). Perhaps surprisingly, some empirical research suggests that the asset similarity created by TMTF may actually reduce systemic risk because the market expects banks with greater similarities to be more likely to survive during financial crises (Cai, 2019).

2.4 Empirical research on factors that tend to bring about distress or failure of TBTF, TITF, and/or TMTF banks

In this section, we focus on what might cause TBTF, TITF, and/or TMTF banks to become financially distressed and potentially fail that would result in bailouts or bail-ins. Most of the studies on the determinants of bank problems focus on bank failure, rather than financial distress, and so we review the bank failure literature. Presumably, the factors that bring about financial distress are largely in common with those that cause failure, given that banks usually fail before a period of financial distress.

Most of the literature on bank failure concentrates on accounting variables. Virtually all such studies find that low capital ratios raise the probability of bank failure. Other weak accounting performance measures such as low profitability and poor loan quality raise the probability of failure, as do certain activities, commercial real estate credit, particularly construction and development loans, and nontraditional activities (e.g., Lane, Looney, and Wansley, 1986; Cole and Gunther, 1995, 1998; Wheelock and Wilson, 1995, 2000; Calomiris and Mason, 1997, 2003; Elsinger, Lehar, and Summer, 2006; Schaeck, 2008, Cole and White, 2012; Knaup and Wagner, 2012; Admati, DeMarzo, Hellwig, and Pfleiderer, 2013; Berger and Bouwman, 2013; DeYoung and Torna, 2013; Berger, Imbierowicz, and Rauch, 2016).

Sampling a few of these studies, Cole and Gunther (1995) find that capital, troubled assets, and net income are key indicators in explaining bank failure. Berger and Bouwman (2013) find that low capital ratios reduce the probability of survival for small banks under all general economic conditions—banking crises, market crises, and normal times—while low capital hurts medium and large banks primarily during the banking crises. Schaeck (2008) finds that liability structure affects a bank's time to failure. Fee-based nontraditional activities (e.g., securities brokerage and insurance sales) decrease and asset-based nontraditional activities (e.g., venture capital, investment banking, and asset securitization) increase the probability of distressed bank failure (DeYoung and Torna, 2013). Some also find that commercial real estate loans, particularly real estate construction and development loans, play important recurring roles in explaining bank failure (e.g., Cole and Fenn, 2008; Cole and White, 2012). In addition, some composite measures of bank soundness or risks forecast bank failure, including the traditional measure of bank soundness, CAMELS components (Cole and White, 2012), and a market-based measure of credit portfolio quality and bank performance, Credit Risk Indicator (CRI) (Knaup and Wagner, 2012).

Others focus on corporate governance with mixed results on both bank performance and failure (e.g., Fahlenbrach and Stulz, 2011; Beltratti and Stulz, 2012; Berger and Bouwman, 2013; Berger, Imbierowicz, and Rauch, 2016; Calomiris and Carlson, 2016). One study also finds that bank cost inefficiency during normal times, a signal of poor management, predicts both performance problems and failure during subsequent financial crises (Assaf, Berger, Roman, and Tsonias, 2019).

References

Acharya, V. V. (2009). A theory of systemic risk and design of prudential bank regulation. *Journal of Financial Stability, 5*(3), 224–255.

Acharya, V. V., Mehran, H., & Thakor, A. V. (2016). Caught between Scylla and charybdis? Regulating bank leverage when there is rent seeking and risk shifting. *The Review of Corporate Finance Studies, 5*(1), 36–75.

Acharya, V. V., & Naqvi, H. (2012). The seeds of a crisis: A theory of bank liquidity and risk taking over the business cycle. *Journal of Financial Economics, 106*(2), 349–366.

Acharya, V. V., & Yorulmazer, T. (2007). Too many to fail—An analysis of time-inconsistency in bank closure policies. *Journal of Financial Intermediation, 16*(1), 1–31.

Acharya, V. V., & Yorulmazer, T. (2008). Cash-in-the-market pricing and optimal resolution of bank failures. *The Review of Financial Studies, 21*(6), 2705–2742.

Admati, A. R., DeMarzo, P. M., Hellwig, M. F., & Pfleiderer, P. C. (2013). Fallacies, irrelevant facts, and myths in the discussion of capital regulation, why bank equity is not socially expensive (Working Paper).

Assaf, A. G., Berger, A. N., Roman, R. A., & Tsionas, M. G. (2019). Does efficiency help banks survive and thrive during financial crises? *Journal of Banking and Finance, 106,* 445–470.

Barth, J. R., & Wihlborg, C. (2015). Too big to fail and too big to save: Dilemmas for banking reform. *National Institute Economic Review, 235*(1), R27–R39.

Beltratti, A., & Stulz, R. M. (2012). The credit crisis around the globe: Why did some banks perform better? *Journal of Financial Economics, 105*(1), 1–17.

Berger, A. N., & Bouwman, C. H. S. (2009). Bank liquidity creation. *The Review of Financial Studies, 22*(9), 3779–3837.

Berger, A. N., & Bouwman, C. H. S. (2013). How does capital affect bank performance during financial crises? *Journal of Financial Economics, 109*(1), 146–176.

Berger, A. N., & Bouwman, C. H. S. (2016). *Bank liquidity creation and financial crises.* North Holland: Elsevier.

Berger, A. N., & Bouwman, C. H. S. (2017). Bank liquidity creation, monetary policy, and financial crises. *Journal of Financial Stability, 30,* 139–155.

Berger, A. N., Imbierowicz, B., & Rauch, C. (2016). The roles of corporate governance in bank failures during the recent financial crisis. *Journal of Money, Credit, and Banking, 48*(4), 729–770.

Berger, A. N., & Udell, G. F. (2004). The institutional memory hypothesis and the procyclicality of bank lending behavior. *Journal of Financial Intermediation, 13*(4), 458–495.

Boot, A. W., & Thakor, A. V. (1993). Self-interested bank regulation. *The American Economic Review, 83*(2), 206–212.

Brown, C. O., & Dinç, I. S. (2011). Too many to fail? Evidence of regulatory forbearance when the banking sector is weak. *The Review of Financial Studies, 24*(4), 1378–1405.

Brunnermeier, M. K., Gorton, G., & Krishnamurthy, A. (2011). Risk topography. In D. Acemoglu, & M. Woodford (Eds.), *vol. 26. NBER Macroeconomics Annual 2011.*

Cai, J. (2019). *Bank herding and systemic risk* (Working Paper).

Calomiris, C. W., & Carlson, M. (2016). Corporate governance and risk management at unprotected banks, national banks in the 1890s. *Journal of Financial Economics, 119*(3), 512–532.

Calomiris, C. W., & Mason, J. R. (1997). Contagion and bank failures during the great depression: The June 1932 Chicago banking panic. *The American Economic Review, 87,* 863–883.

Calomiris, C. W., & Mason, J. R. (2003). Fundamentals, panics, and bank distress during the depression. *The American Economic Review, 93*(5), 1615–1647.

Cetorelli, N., & Traina, J. (2018). *Resolving 'too big to fail'* (Working Paper).

Choi, D. B. (2014). Heterogeneity and stability: Bolster the strong, not the weak. *The Review of Financial Studies, 27*(6), 1830–1867.

Cole, R. A., & Fenn, G. W. (2008). *The role of commercial real estate investments in the banking crisis of 1985-92* (Working Paper).

Cole, R. A., & Gunther, J. W. (1995). Separating the likelihood and timing of bank failure. *Journal of Banking and Finance, 19*(6), 1073–1089.

Cole, R. A., & Gunther, J. W. (1998). Predicting bank failures : A comparison of on-and off-site monitoring systems. *Journal of Financial Services Research, 13*(2), 103–117.

Cole, R. A., & White, L. J. (2012). Déjà vu all over again: The causes of US commercial bank failures this time around. *Journal of Financial Services Research, 42*(1–2), 5–29.

Dell'Ariccia, G., Igan, D., & Laeven, L. U. C. (2012). Credit booms and lending standards: Evidence from the subprime mortgage market. *Journal of Money, Credit, and Banking, 44*(2-3), 367–384.

Demirgüç-Kunt, A., & Detragiache, E. (1998). The determinants of banking crises in developing and developed countries. *Staff Papers, 45*(1), 81–109.

DeYoung, R., & Torna, G. (2013). Nontraditional banking activities and bank failures during the financial crisis. *Journal of Financial Intermediation, 22*(3), 397–421.

Elsinger, H., Lehar, A., & Summer, M. (2006). Risk assessment for banking systems. *Management Science, 52*(9), 1301–1314.

Fahlenbrach, R., & Stulz, R. M. (2011). Bank CEO incentives and the credit crisis. *Journal of Financial Economics, 99*(1), 11–26.

Farhi, E., & Tirole, J. (2012). Collective moral hazard, maturity mismatch, and systemic bailouts. *The American Economic Review, 102*(1), 60–93.

Federal Deposit Insurance Corporation. (1997). *History of the eighties, lessons for the future* (Vol. 1) (Washington, D.C).

Greenspan, A. (2001). The financial safety net. In *Speech at the 37th annual conference on bank structure and competition of the Federal Reserve Bank of Chicago, Chicago, Illinois. May 10, 2001.* Available at https://www.federalreserve.gov/boarddocs/speeches/2001/20010510/default.htm.

Kane, E. J. (1989). *The S and L insurance mess, how did it happen?* The Urban Insitute.

Kane, E. J. (1991). Principal-Agent Problems in S&L Salvage. *Journal of Finance, 45*(3), 755–764.

Knaup, M., & Wagner, W. (2012). A market-based measure of credit portfolio quality and banks' performance during the subprime crisis. *Management Science, 58*(8), 1423–1437.

Laeven, L., & Valencia, F. (2018). *Systemic banking crises revisited*. International Monetary Fund.

Lane, W. R., Looney, S. W., & Wansley, J. W. (1986). An application of the cox proportional hazards model to bank failure. *Journal of Banking and Finance, 10*(4), 511–531.

Liu, Z., Quiet, S., & Roth, B. (2015). *Banking sector interconnectedness, what is it, how can we measure it and why does it matter?* Bank of England Quarterly Bulletin, Q2.

Mishkin, F. S., & Eakins, S. G. (2006). *Financial markets and institutions*. Pearson Education India.

Pagano, M. S., & Sedunov, J. (2016). A comprehensive approach to measuring the relation between systemic risk exposure and sovereign debt. *Journal of Financial Stability, 23*, 62–78.

Rajan, R. G. (1994). Why bank credit policies fluctuate: A theory and some evidence. *The Quarterly Journal of Economics, 109*(2), 399–441.

Reinhart, C. M., & Rogoff, K. S. (2009). *This time is different: Eight centuries of financial folly.* Princeton University Press.

Schaeck, K. (2008). Bank liability structure, FDIC loss, and time to failure, a quantile regression approach. *Journal of Financial Services Research, 33*(3), 163–179.

Stern, G. H., & Feldman, R. J. (2004). *Too big to fail, the hazards of bank bailouts.* Brookings Institution Press.

Thakor, A. V. (2005). Do loan commitments cause overlending? *Journal of Money, Credit, and Banking, 37*, 1067–1099.

Thakor, A. V. (2015a). The financial crisis of 2007—2009: Why did it happen and what did we learn? *The Review of Corporate Finance Studies, 4*(2), 155—205.

Thakor, A. V. (2015b). Lending booms, smart bankers, and financial crises. *American Economic Review, 105*(5), 305—309.

Thakor, A. V. (2016). The highs and the lows: A theory of credit risk assessment and pricing through the business cycle. *Journal of Financial Intermediation, 25*, 1—29.

Von Hagen, J. V., & Ho, T.-kuang (2007). Money market pressure and the determinants of banking crises. *Journal of Money, Credit, and Banking, 39*(5), 1037—1066.

Wheelock, D. C., & Wilson, P. W. (1995). Explaining bank failures, deposit insurance, regulation, and efficiency. *The Review of Economics and Statistics*, 689—700.

Wheelock, D. C., & Wilson, P. W. (2000). Why do banks disappear? The determinants of US bank failures and acquisitions. *The Review of Economics and Statistics, 82*(1), 127—138.

CHAPTER

3

Descriptions of TARP, other bank bailouts and bail-ins, and other resolution approaches in the US and around the world

This chapter describes bailouts and bail-ins around the world as well as the alternatives of bankruptcy/failure (the BHC goes bankrupt and the systemically important bank fails); reorganization of the BHC using living wills; forbearance; keeping the banks operating with little or no capital; and breaking up large, systemically important institutions either by size into smaller institutions or by activity into separate commercial and investment banks.

First, we pay particular attention to the US Troubled Asset Relief Program (TARP) and the other bailouts during the Global Financial Crisis and European Sovereign Debt Crisis. Second, we focus on the US Orderly Liquidation Authority (OLA) and the European Union (EU) Bank Recovery and Resolution Directive (BRRD) and other bail-in programs that were implemented following these crises. Third, we discuss bankruptcy/failure as described under the Financial CHOICE Act that was under US Congressional consideration. Fourth, we discuss living wills directed by the Dodd–Frank Act as another potential way to resolve the financial distress an potential failure of large institutions. Fifth, we discuss regulatory forbearance or allowing institutions to operate unresolved, focusing on the US S&L financial crisis.Lastly, we discuss breaking up systemically important institutions, either by size or by financial activity, as two additional alternative resolution approaches.

3.1 The Troubled Asset Relief Program (TARP) in the US

This section discusses the legislation that created TARP and the US Treasury's implementation of the program.

3.1.1 The original intent of TARP and how the implementation differed

During the Global Financial Crisis, the US Department of the Treasury, the federal regulatory agencies, and the US Congress took broad assistance actions and some of the most aggressive fiscal and monetary policies in history to address the crisis and the severe volatility in the US banking system and financial markets. TARP was created as part of the Emergency Economic Stabilization Act (EESA) enacted in October 2008.

The original version of EESA was proposed as a plan by the US Treasury Secretary Henry Paulson in early 2008 to recapitalize the US banking system by purchasing a large amount of distressed assets (mortgages, mortgage-based securities, and other financial instruments) issued by financial institutions and their holding companies to reduce uncertainty about these assets' worth and restore market confidence. The EESA plan was structured as an amendment to H.R. 3997, but was rejected by the House of Representatives on September 29, 2008, which voted 205 in favor versus 228 against. Reasons for the rejection included the plan's cost and haste, little support by the public for "bailing out" Wall Street banks, and a need for considering alternatives. The same day, the stock market reacted significantly negatively to the defeat, with the Dow Jones Industrial Average (DJIA) Index falling by 777 points.[1]

A few days after this defeat, the Senate decided to amend an existing bill from the House, H.R. 1424, sponsored by US House Representative Patrick J. Kennedy, to incorporate the Senate version of the EESA of 2008. On October 1, 2008, the entire amended bill about the economic rescue plan was approved by a Senate vote of 74 to 25, and was returned to the House for consideration. On October 3, 2008, the bill passed by the Senate was accepted by a vote of 263–171 in the House. Finally, President George W. Bush signed the bill into law (Public Law 110-343, 122 Stat. 3765) after its congressional enactment on October 3, 2008. This also created the $700 billion TARP known as "the bank rescue package" under the EESA of 2008 (Division A). TARP's primary purpose was to mitigate the financial crisis by "providing authority for the Federal Government to purchase and insure certain types of troubled assets" from the financial institutions.

---

[1] See https://www.cnbc.com/id/26945972/ and https://nypost.com/2008/09/29/dow-drops-record-777-points/.

However, no "troubled assets" purchases on the secondary market were eventually made by the US Treasury. Instead, the US Treasury announced on October 13, 2008 that it would invest directly in the preferred equity of financial institutions to stabilize their capital ratios. On October 14, 2018, the Capital Purchase Program (CPP) was announced, allocating $250 billion for the US Treasury to purchase bank preferred equity or debt securities and equity warrants from 709 participating banking institutions. To protect certain institutions against larger-than-expected losses on asset portfolios, another $40 billion was distributed to Bank of America Corporation and Citigroup Inc. through the TARP Targeted Investment Program (TIP). Finally, to help community development institutions and their underserved communities cope with the financial crisis, another $0.57 billion was disbursed to 84 institutions under the TARP Community Development Capital Initiative (CDCI).

Table 3.1 shows a complete timeline of events surrounding TARP. As noted in the Introduction, we generally use the name TARP to refer to CPP, a practice widely used in the press and academic literature.

3.1.2 How the largest financial institutions were "forced" to take the bailouts

On October 28, eight large BHCs received capital injections totaling $125 billion without a formal evaluation process. The US Treasury bought $25 billion each in preferred equity from Bank of America Corporation (including soon-to-be acquired Merrill Lynch), JPMorgan Chase & Company, Citigroup Inc., and Wells Fargo & Company; $10 billion each from the Goldman Sachs Group Inc. and Morgan Stanley, $3 billion from The Bank of New York Mellon, and about $2 billion from State Street Corporation.[2] The remainder of the funds was to be made available to the rest of the banking institutions that applied for the program. Various press articles argued that the first recipients received funding regardless of their financial status or other connections considerations, but rather due to being "too-big-to-fail" banking organizations that are crucial for the financial system stability. Several Wall Street Journal articles provided anecdotal evidence, and research articles discussed that while TARP was voluntary, the US Treasury may have "forced" the eight major BHCs to agree to take the capital from the federal government to provide a confidence signal to the market at the start of the program and likely mask which banks were in less favorable financial conditions (see Solomon and Enrich, 2008; Hilsenrath, Solomon, and Paletta, 2008; Duchin and Sosyura, 2012). Excerpts from company press releases and 10-K and 8-K financial

---

[2] https://www.wsj.com/articles/SB122398468353632299.

TABLE 3.1 Timetable of events around TARP[a].

September 15, 2008: After failed discussions with the Federal Reserve Bank and possible buyers, Lehman Brothers (4th largest U.S. investment bank, $639 billion in total assets and $619 billion in debt) filed for bankruptcy, being recorded as the largest bankruptcy in history at that time. This filing for bankruptcy resulted in more than $46 billion of its market value being wiped out and led to a large global panic. In the same day, Bank of America made announcement that it will purchase the struggling Merrill Lynch for $50 billion.

September 16, 2008: AIG (which insured trillions of dollars of mortgages at the time) asked the Federal Reserve for emergency funding. Dreading a financial crisis extending globally, the Federal Reserve convened to a $85 billion bailout, which provides the government control of the insurance giant. Due to losses from Lehman's bankruptcy, investors ran away from the money market mutual funds. The very same day, the Reserve Primary Fund "broke the buck," because it did not have enough liquidity on hand to pay out all the redemptions that were occurring.

September 17, 2008: Investors withdrew a record $144.5 billion from their money market accounts, surpassing with much a typical week, withdrawal of only $7 billion and spreading the market panic. Should this have continued, businesses could not obtain money to fund their day-to-day operations. The US economy was near a complete collapse.

September 18, 2018: Paulson and Bernanke met with Congressional leaders to discuss the crisis. Both Republicans and Democrats leaders were taken by surprise by the dark situation and warnings, comprehending that credit markets were only a few days away from a meltdown. They agreed to collaborate in a bipartisan manner to find a solution.

September 19, 2008: The Federal Reserve made announcement that it would lend the money required by banks and businesses to keep operating so they would not have to take the cash in money market funds out. They also established the Asset-Backed Commercial Paper Money Market Fund Liquidity Facility to insure the money market accounts.

September 20, 2008: The US Treasury submitted a document asking Congress to approve a $700 billion bailout. They announced that they would use the money to purchase MBSs on the verge to default to take these off the books of banks and other intermediaries.

September 21, 2008: Goldman Sachs and Morgan Stanley, two large investment banks on Wall Street, applied to become regular BHCs to benefit from the Federal Reserve's protection and strengthen their capital and liquidity positions.

September 26, 2008: Washington Mutual Bank went bankrupt as depositors withdrew $16.7 billion in 10 days. Subsequently, the FDIC took it over and sold it to J.P. Morgan for $1.9 billion.

Table 3.1 Timetable of events around TARP[a].—cont'd

September 29, 2008: The grounds that the bill was bailing out Wall Street at the expense of taxpayers. The US DJIA fell 770 points, the most in any single day in its history. The global markets also entered in panic, with the Morgan Stanley Capital International World Index falling 6% in 1 day, the most since its establishment in 1970.

October 3, 2008: President Bush signed into law the EESA of 2008 which established the $700 billion TARP. This program would allow the US Treasury to inject capital promptly into the financial system, by helping the financially stressed banks, AIG, and auto companies.

October 14, 2008: The US Treasury announced the CPP that allowed US financial institutions to apply for preferred stock capital injections by the US Treasury. The nine largest BHCs announced they will apply for TARP for an aggregate amount of $125 billion. On the same day, the FDIC established the TLGP to guarantee the deposits and senior debt of all FDIC-insured institutions up to June 30, 2009.

November 14, 2008: This date is the deadline for publicly traded financial institutions to apply for CPP preferred stock investment by the US Treasury.

February 4, 2009: The US Treasury modified restrictions on executive compensation for TARP participants. The total annual compensation for senior executive officers was capped to $500,000 except for long-term restricted stock awards. Golden parachutes were also prohibited for the top 10 senior executives and the next 25 executives were prohibited from receiving golden parachute payments higher than 1 year's compensation severance. Bonus claw-back provisions were also extended from the top five executives to the next 25 executives.

February 10, 2009: US Treasury Secretary Timothy Geithner announced the Financial Stability Plan entailing forward-looking stress tests loss assessments for the 19 largest US banking organizations with assets more than $100 billion, the Supervisory Capital Assessment Program (SCAP), the creation of an Investment Fund to buy troubled loans and assets from financial institutions, as well as other programs to stalk residential mortgage foreclosures and to promote small business lending.

February 17, 2009: President Obama signed into law the American Recovery and Reinvestment Act (ARRA) of 2009 which included spending measures and tax cuts to induce economic recovery. It also included most of the executive compensation restrictions for TARP announced on February 4, 2009. It also included additional compensation limits for TARP participants such as prohibition on bonuses, retention awards, or incentive compensation exclusive of long-term restricted stock awards that did not surpass 1/3 of the annual compensation.

February 23, 2009: The US Treasury and Federal bank regulatory agencies issued a joint statement in which they restated that under the SCAP stress test, the capital needed will be provided in the form of compulsory convertible preferred stocks and any prior capital injections under TARP will also be qualified to be exchanged for these shares.

Continued

I. Introductory materials

Table 3.1 Timetable of events around TARP[a].—cont'd

February 24, 2009: Federal Reserve Chairman Ben Bernanke elucidated to Congress that the bank stress tests do not represent a forerunner to bank nationalization.

February 25, 2009: The US Treasury published details on the SCAP stress test program.

March 19, 2009: The US Congress proposed and passed H.R. 1586 in less than 24 h with a crushing margin. The bill imposed a castigatory exercise tax of 90% on all employee bonus payments made, backdated to January 1, 2009, by institutions that received $5 billion or more in TARP injections.

March 31, 2009: Four BHCs—Marin Bancorp, IberiaBank Corporation, Old National Bancorp, and Signature Bank—announced that they redeemed all of the preferred shares issued to the US Treasury under TARP.

April 24, 2009: The Federal Reserve Board published details on the process and methodology employed by federal banking regulators in their forward-looking assessment SCAP stress test for the 19 large US financial institutions.

May 6, 2009: The *Wall Street Journal* reported the SCAP stress tests results for several banks which were leaked to the media. It reported that American Express, Bank of New York Mellon, Capital One Financial, Goldman Sachs, MetLife and JPMorgan Chase would not need to raise additional capital, while Bank of America needed $34 billion, Wells Fargo needed $15 billion, and GMAC needed $11.5 billion. It also reported that Citigroup, State Street, Morgan Stanley and Regions Financial also needed supplementary capital.

May 7, 2009: The Federal Reserve released the results of the SCAP for the 19 largest US BHCs. It found that 10 firms needed to raise $185 billion in capital but that transactions and revenues since the 2008:Q4 reduced their capital shortfall to $75 billion. BHCs needing to raise capital were required to provide to their primary regulator a detailed plan within 30 days and raise the extra capital by November 2009.

June 10, 2009: The US Treasury Department issued detailed rules regarding the limits on executive and employee compensation under the ARRA of 2009 for companies receiving capital injections under TARP. The US Treasury Secretary Timothy Geithner also issued a press release about these compensation rules.

December 31, 2009: The authority of the US Treasury to purchase preferred capital in financial institutions under TARP was ended, as required by the EESA of 2008.

[a]*This list of events is compiled based on several sources including Bayazitova and Shivdasani (2012); https://www.reuters.com/article/us-usa-fed-lending-timeline/timeline-most-impactful-events-of-the-u-s-financial-crisis-idUSTRE72U4E720110331; and https://www.thebalance.com/2008-financial-crisis-timeline-3305540.*

statements showing banks' involuntary participants' opinions about TARP are shown in Table 3.2.

3.1.3 The method through which the other over 700 banks applied for and received TARP funds

All banks other than the initial involuntary participants had to apply for TARP funds from the US Treasury until the deadline of November 14, 2008.[3] In general, the financial institutions eligible to participate in TARP included domestic banks, BHCs, savings associations, and savings and loan holding companies. However, for all banks and savings associations controlled by a BHC, TARP investments were made at the BHC level. Applying institutions had to undergo a formal rigorous approval process analyzing their health and viability. The approval to receive TARP funds took into account the health of the banking organizations—healthy and viable ones were more likely to receive capital. An example of a blank application for TARP funds is shown in Table 3.4 and excerpts from company press releases and 10-K and 8-K financial statements indicating approval for TARP and other decisions are shown in Table 3.2.

3.1.4 The strings attached and why so many banks tried to repay the funds early

The capital injections came with restrictions on dividends, repurchases, and executive compensation which were further refined on February 17, 2009. For the first 3 years of the Treasury's ownership of preferred stock or warrants, participating banks could not increase dividends on their common shares or repurchase common stock or preferred shares junior to the Treasury's investment. In addition, there were restrictions on participating institutions' executive compensation. Banks were restricted from making golden parachute payments, and senior executives had limits on their total annual compensation and tax deductibility to $500,000, and employing incentive compensation schemes that encourage "unnecessary and excessive risks" to the value of the institution. There were also requirements to claw back any incentive compensation paid to executives based on earnings that were subsequently restated.

---

[3] See for example https://www.fdic.gov/news/news/inactivefinancial/2008/fil08109.html and https://www.fdic.gov/news/news/inactivefinancial/2008/fil08109.pdf and http://www.mondaq.com/unitedstates/x/68778/Credit+Crisis+Emergency+Economic+Stabilization+Act/Update+On+The+TARP+Capital+Purchase+Program+Action+Due+By+November+14+2008.

TABLE 3.2 Excerpts from companies' SEC public reports 8-Ks and 10-Ks about the TARP program.

Panel A: Involuntary participants

Example 1: Citigroup Inc ($25 Billion)

10/30/08 8-K

"On October 26, 2008, Citigroup Inc. ("Citigroup"), one of the initial nine institutions participating in the U.S. Department of the Treasury's previously announced TARP Capital Purchase Program, signed an agreement to issue to the Treasury $25 billion of its perpetual preferred stock and a warrant to purchase common stock. The transaction settled on October 28, 2008."

12/31/08 10-K

"The Committee has established specific guidelines, which are consistent with the objectives and spirit of the program. Pursuant to these guidelines, Citi will use TARP capital only for those purposes expressly approved by the Committee. TARP capital will not be used for compensation and bonuses, dividend payments, lobbying or government relations activities, or any activities related to marketing, advertising and corporate sponsorship. TARP capital will be used exclusively to support assets and not for expenses.

On February 3, 2009, Citi published a public report summarizing its TARP spending initiatives for the 2008 fourth quarter and made this report available at https://www.citigroup.com/. The report indicated that the Committee had authorized $36.5 billion in initiatives backed by TARP capital, spanning five major areas, as follows:

- *U.S. residential mortgage activities*—$25.7 billion (Citigroup is making mortgage loans directly to homebuyers and supporting the housing market through the purchase of prime residential mortgages and mortgage-backed securities in the secondary market).
- *Personal and business loans*—$2.5 billion (This includes $1.5 billion of consumer lending and $1.0 billion for tailored loans to people and businesses facing liquidity problems).
- *Student loans*—$1 billion (Citigroup is originating student loans through the Federal Family Education Loan Program).
- *Credit card lending*—$5.8 billion (Citigroup is offering special credit card programs that include expanded eligibility for balance-consolidation offers, targeted increases in credit lines and targeted new account originations).
- *Corporate loan activity*—$1.5 billion (The Company is investing $1.5 billion in commercial loan securitizations, which will inject liquidity into the U.S. corporate loan market).

Separately from the Company's initiatives under TARP, the report also describes Citigroup's other efforts to help U.S. homeowners remain in their homes, assist distressed borrowers and support U.S consumers and businesses."

Example 2: Wells Fargo Corporation ($25 Billion)

12/11/08—SEC Rule 425 prospectus or communication: transcript of an investor presentation given by Wells Fargo & Company on December 10, 2008.[a]

Table 3.2 Excerpts from companies' SEC public reports 8-Ks and 10-Ks about the TARP program.—cont'd

"Richard Ramsden - Goldman Sachs—Analyst:

Can you spend a couple of minutes on capital, in particular TARP capital? I guess the questions that we are giving the most frequently is that capital fully fungible with existing capital? Are you concerned about I guess political interference for want of a better expression in terms of how you redeployed that capital? And are you viewing this as cheap capital or is your intention to try and pay it back as quickly as you can?

John Stumpf - Wells Fargo Company - President and CEO:

Well, let me answer the pay it back as quickly as you can and then I'll turn to the guy who knows more about not only capital –but he can name all the capitals of all the states. Okay, not that kind of capital. That's what I brought Howard along for. He said I have them all memorized.

As far as the five-year deal, since the $25 billion that we got has a 5% preferred, has a 5% coupon or rate on it, and you can't pay it back before year three unless you raise capital equal. But then from year three to year five, I don't see why there's an incentive to pay it back, because it's 5% or less. Capital is really cheap capital. But then on the first day of year six, it goes to 9%, but you already have your embedded cost of the warrants day one. So unless you – there's no incentive to pay it between year three and year five.

But again, that all depends on rates and needs and so for the time. But those are things for the future. Capital is here right now. We're going to deploy it. We've been lending money. We're going to do the things that it was intended to do, not stupid. We've never done that, but it allows – provides more strength. I think it was good for the system and we are part of the system. We benefit from being part of the system and that's why we participated in it. Howard, maybe (multiple speakers)

Howard Atkins - Wells Fargo Company—CFO:

I think the main distinction between us and most other big banks around the country is that for the last year and a half we really never stopped lending. So we really have been growing our Company for the last year and a half at a time when everybody else has been shrinking. Assets were up 15% in the last year. And so we are conceiving of a TARP capital merely as fungible part of the capital base of the Company and it will allow us to continue to do what we've been doing for the last year and a half. We are open for business. We are doing commercial loans. We are doing consumer loans. They are good customers and good spreads. In fact better spreads today than a year and a half, and that's what we will continue to do."

Mark Calvey, San Francisco Business Times, June 13, 2012, "Former Wells Fargo CEO Dick Kovacevich blasts TARP: An 'unmitigated disaster'" [b]

"Former Wells Fargo Chairman and CEO Dick Kovacevich says the federal government's bank bailout during the depths of the financial crisis was an "unmitigated disaster" and laid much of the blame for the financial crisis on ineffective regulators."

The decision by the U.S. Treasury and the Federal Reserve in October 2008 to make banks take TARP money even if they didn't want it or need it was one of the worst economic decisions in the history of the United States,"Kovacevich told about 100 people attending a Stanford Institute for Economic Policy Research event Tuesday evening."

"TARP contributed to an unnecessary panic in the marketplace that still hasn't been fully restored…The government's bank bailout was designed to give billions to the nation's largest banks, whether they needed the money, in an effort to lift all boats, Kovacevich said. Wells took $25 billion, over its objections, then repaid it as soon as allowed…By giving capital to all banks, even the sound ones that didn't want it, would be seen as a sign that even healthy banks were in trouble and that confidence levels would decline," he said. "All boats would fall."

Continued

I. Introductory materials

Table 3.2 Excerpts from companies' SEC public reports 8-Ks and 10-Ks about the TARP program.—cont'd

5/11/09–8-K

"The recent economic stimulus legislation imposes new compensation restrictions that could adversely affect our ability to recruit and retain key employees. The American Recovery and Reinvestment Act of 2009 includes extensive new restrictions on our ability to pay retention awards, bonuses and other incentive compensation during the period in which we have any outstanding obligation arising from financial assistance provided to us under the TARP. Many of the restrictions are not limited to our senior executives and cover other employees whose contributions to revenue and performance can be significant. The limitations may adversely affect our ability to recruit and retain these key employees, especially if we are competing for management talent against U.S. and non-U.S. institutions that are not subject to the same restrictions. For more information, refer to the 'Regulation and Supervision' section in our 2008 Form 10-K"

Example 3: State Street Corporation ($2 Billion)

10/15/2008 8-K

Ronald E. Logue, State Street's chairman and chief executive officer, said, "We are pleased to be one of the nine financial institutions key to the infrastructure of the global financial markets, selected by the U.S. Treasury to initiate the TARP Capital Purchase Program, a program aimed at addressing the financial turmoil and restoring confidence in the markets. Our selection demonstrates the important role that State Street plays for its customers and in the global markets and reflects our core financial strengths. Although we have always been and remain well capitalized, the program adds additional capital and affords us additional flexibility to continue our leadership role in meeting the challenges and opportunities in current markets. It's my belief that the companies that will emerge from this turmoil are those, like State Street, with the right mix of businesses, a focus on customer service, and a prudent plan for this environment. As part of this program, State Street will issue $2 billion of senior preferred shares to the U.S. Treasury along with warrants to purchase common stock with a total market price equal to about $300 million at the time of issuance, which we anticipate will be minimally dilutive to our shareholders."

1/16/2009 8-K

"Our participation in the U.S. Treasury's TARP capital purchase program restricts our ability to increase dividends on our common stock, undertake stock repurchase programs and compensate our key executives. In October 2008, the U.S. Treasury invested $2 billion in State Street pursuant to the TARP capital purchase program. The terms of the TARP capital purchase program require us to pay preferred cumulative dividends to Treasury and restrict our ability to increase dividends on our common stock, redeem Treasury's investment without receiving high-quality replacement capital, undertake stock repurchase programs and pay executive compensation. Additional restrictions may be imposed by Treasury or Congress on us at a later date, and these restrictions may apply to us retroactively. These restrictions may have a material adverse effect on our operations, revenue and financial condition, on our ability to pay dividends, or on our ability to attract and retain executive talent."

Example 4: Goldman Sachs ($10 Billion)

10/17/08–8–K

"On October 13, 2008, The Goldman Sachs Group, Inc. (the 'Company') agreed to participate in the U.S. Treasury's TARP Capital Purchase Program. The Company has agreed to issue and sell to the U.S. Treasury preferred stock and warrants to purchase shares of common stock of the Company in accordance with the terms of the Capital Purchase Program for an aggregate purchase price of $10 billion."

Table 3.2 Excerpts from companies' SEC public reports 8-Ks and 10-Ks about the TARP program.—cont'd

"In the fall of 2008, Goldman appealed to the federal government and accepted a $10 billion TARP loan to ensure its survival. Because corporations such as Goldman that accepted TARP dollars were subject to oversight by the federal government, were restricted on their ability to pay out generous compensation, and were required to provide shareholders with an advisory vote on compensation policies (so-called 'say-on-pay'), defendants announced the Company's intention to pay back the TARP loan as soon as it could do so."

Panel B: Other participants and applicants

Example 1: Capital One Corporation

2/26/2009 - 10-K

"Under the EESA the Company is subject to increased Congressional scrutiny, including participating in Congressional hearings and investigations and providing reports to the Treasury Department and the Government Accountability Office ('GAO') as well as other entities created under the EESA to provide additional oversight. Congress has shown a strong interest in directing how the monies and programs under the EESA are managed. To this end, the U.S. House of Representatives has passed legislation addressing a number of terms of the EESA and a number of hearings have been scheduled. Recently Congress passed, and the President signed into law, the American Recovery and Reinvestment Act ('ARRA'), which, among other things, includes additional restrictions for participants in programs under the EESA. Such restrictions include limitations on hiring workers under the H1–B visa program and compliance with new standards to be adopted by the U.S. Treasury relating to the executive compensation practices of participants in programs under the TARP."

"Compliance with New and Existing Laws and Regulations May Increase Our Costs, Limit Our Ability to Pursue Business Opportunities, and Increase Compliance Challenges

There has been increased legislation and regulation with respect to the financial services industry in recent months, and we expect that oversight of our business will continue to expand in scope and complexity. A wide array of banking, consumer lending, and deposit laws apply to almost every aspect of our business. Failure to comply with these laws and regulations could result in financial, structural and operational penalties, including receivership. In addition, establishing systems and processes to achieve compliance with these laws and regulations may increase our costs and/or limit our ability to pursue certain business opportunities.

Our participation in the TARP Capital Purchase Program (the 'CPP') subjects us to increased oversight by the Treasury Department, regulators and Congress under the Emergency Economic Stabilization Act of 2008 ('EESA'). Congress may adopt further legislation to refine EESA in addition to other efforts to change lending practices that legislators believe led to the current economic situation. Such legislation could increase governmental oversight of the Company, restrict the Company's lending or governance practices, or both, all of which could negatively impact our business and revenues."

Example 2: United Bancshares (approved but declined the funds)

2/26/2009–10-K

"On January 27, 2009, United announced that it decided not to participate in the U.S. Treasury's TARP Capital Purchase Program. United had received preliminary approval to receive up to $197.28 million of capital from the TARP Capital Purchase Program. United's management and Board of

Continued

Table 3.2 Excerpts from companies' SEC public reports 8-Ks and 10-Ks about the TARP program.—cont'd

Directors, after careful consideration, believed it was in the best interests of United's shareholders not to participate. The program's restrictions on possible future dividend increases, the dilution to earnings, and the uncertainty surrounding future requirements of the program outweighed the benefits of United's participation in the program."

Example 3: Cardinal Financial Corp (approved but declined the funds)

3/16/2009—10-K

"On December 12, 2008, the Company announced that its application for $41.2 million in capital under the CPP had received the U.S. Treasury's preliminary approval. Upon preliminary approval, our Board of Directors performed careful analysis and decided to decline to participate in the CPP concluding that the significant expense of the program and challenge to prudently and profitably deploy the capital were inconsistent with our long term strategic objectives, and that the participation in the CPP would not be in the best interest of Cardinal's shareholders."

Example 4: Ameriana Bancorp (approved but declined the funds)

3/30/2009—10-K

"We anticipate that we have adequate capital for the foreseeable future. Based on this determination and an assessment that the restrictions contained in the Troubled Asset Relief Program's Capital Purchase Program could adversely affect our ability to successfully operate our business, our board of directors determined not to participate in the Capital Purchase Program, even though it had been preliminarily approved."

Example 5: First National Bancshares (applied but not approved)

5/1/2009 - 10-K

"Our application for participation in the TARP Capital Purchase Program has not been accepted. Therefore, we have withdrawn our application. We are actively pursuing a variety of other capital raising efforts. However, at present, the market for new capital for banks is limited and uncertain. Accordingly, we cannot be certain of our ability to raise capital on terms that satisfy our goals with respect to our capital ratios. If we are able to raise additional capital, it would likely be on terms that are substantially dilutive to current common shareholders."

Example 6: First California Financial Group (applied, approved, and received the funds)

12/02/2008- Press release of First California Financial Group

"December 2008, First California Financial Group, Inc., today announced that it has received preliminary approval to participate in the U.S. Treasury Department's Capital Purchase Program (TARP), with a preliminary commitment for $25 million in additional preferred equity."

12/19/2008: 8-K

"On December 19, 2008 (the 'Closing Date'), First California Financial Group, Inc. (the 'Company') issued and sold, and the United States Department of the Treasury (the 'U.S. Treasury') purchased 25,000 shares (the 'Preferred Shares') of the Company's Fixed Rate Cumulative Perpetual Preferred Stock, Series B ..."

^ahttps://www.secinfo.com/drDX9.t16u.htm?Find=tarp&Line=239#Line239.
^bhttps://www.bizjournals.com/sanfrancisco/blog/2012/06/wells-fargo-dick-kovacevich-occupy-tarp.html.

TABLE 3.3 Opinions about TARP bailouts.

Panel A: Prominent Economic and Political Figures

Name	Picture	Relevant Materials	Details
Neil Barofsky, Special Inspector General for TARP	©Sorel: Courtesy of NYU Photo Bureau	"How Washington Abandoned Main Street While Rescuing Wall Street," 2013	"To declare TARP a success is revisionist history … TARP was supposed to restore lending, and that didn't happen."[2]
Bill Issac, Former FDIC Chairman (having served during the Reagan Administration from 1981 through 1985)	Used with permission from William M. Isaac. http://www.williamisaac.com/	"Senseless Panic: How Washington Failed America," 2010	"Any objective analysis would conclude that the TARP legislation did nothing to stabilize the financial system that could not have been done without it. Moreover, the negative aspects of the TARP legislation far outweighed any possible benefit."[3]

Continued

I. Introductory materials

Table 3.3 Opinions about TARP bailouts.—cont'd

Name	Picture	Relevant Materials	Details
Ben Bernanke, Former Chairman of the Federal Reserve (having served from 2006 to 2014)	From https://www.federalreservehistory.org/people/ben_s_bernanke	"The Courage to Act: A Memoir of a Crisis and Its Aftermath," 2015	"The TARP, together with all the other measures, had prevented a financial meltdown that would have plunged the economy into an extraordinarily severe and protracted recession, or even a depression."[4]

Table 3.3 Opinions about TARP bailouts.—cont'd

Name	Picture	Relevant Materials	Details
Hank Paulson, Former U.S. Treasury Secretary (having served from July 10, 2006, to January 20, 2009)	From https://georgewbush-whitehouse.archives.gov/government/paulson-bio.html	"On the Brink, Inside the Race to Stop the Collapse of the Global Financial System," 2013	"I was never able to convince the American people that what we did with TARP was not for the banks. It was for them. It was to save Main Street. It was to save our economy from a catastrophe." [5]
Timothy G. Massad, U.S. Department of the Treasury Former Assistant Secretary for Financial Stability	https://www.cftc.gov/sites/default/files/reports/presbudget/2017/index.htm	**Testimony Before the Senate Committee on Banking, Housing and Urban Affairs** , 2011	"… we can safely say that this program has been remarkably effective by any objective measure" and, "We have helped bring stability to the financial system and the economy at a fraction of the expected costs.[6]" Massad added that TARP was integral to the economic recovery and that, because of TARP, banks are better capitalized and the public is less afraid that major financial institutions will fail.

Continued

I. Introductory materials

Table 3.3 Opinions about TARP bailouts.—cont'd

Name	Picture	Relevant Materials	Details
Luigi Zingales, Professor of Finance at the University of Chicago Booth School of Business	Used with permission from Luigi Zingales, https://faculty.chicagobooth.edu/luigi.zingales/index.html	Testimony before the Congressional Oversight Panel, 2011	"In providing an opinion on the impact of the Troubled Asset Relief Program (TARP) on the US financial sector and the US economy it is important to establish what is the counter factual: what would have happened in the absence of TARP. Chairman Bernanke and then Treasury Secretary Paulson repeatedly presented their choice as an alternative between TARP and a collapse of the entire financial system. If the alternative was indeed the abyss, TARP is clearly an unqualified success: we have escaped the abyss. Even if the alternative was between TARP and some chance of falling into the abyss, we have to conclude that TARP was a success. The cost of TARP, however big, is small with comparison to the possibility of a Second Great Depression."[7]

Table 3.3 Opinions about TARP bailouts.—cont'd

Name	Picture	Relevant Materials	Details
Elizabeth Warren, head of the Congressional Oversight Panel and fierce critic of Wall Street and the bailouts	From https://www.congress.gov/member/elizabeth-warren/W000817?searchResultViewType=expanded&K40CView=false	"Taking Stock: What Has the Troubled Asset Relief Program Achieved," Congressional Oversight Panel 2009 and "Assessing TARP on the Eve of Its Expiration," 2010[8]	The Congressional Oversight Group, chaired by Elizabeth Warren, suggested that TARP worked for the most part and was a critical part of the government strategy to stabilize the financial system. "In our view, the TARP—acting as the financial equivalent of a hospital ER—was helpful in returning financial stability to the markets during the last quarter of 2008 when properly considered along with the substantial and aggressive interventions of the Federal Reserve, Treasury, and the FDIC as well as the actions of the markets themselves."

Continued

I. Introductory materials

Table 3.3 Opinions about TARP bailouts.—cont'd

Name	Picture	Relevant Materials	Details
George W. Bush, Former U.S. President of the United States	 From https://georgewbush-whitehouse.archives.gov/news/releases/2008/10/20081003-11.html	President Bush Discusses Emergency Economic Stabilization Act of 2008, 2008[9]	"I know some Americans have concerns about this legislation, especially about the government's role and the bill's cost. As a strong supporter of free enterprise, I believe government intervention should occur only when necessary. In this situation, action is clearly necessary. And ultimately, the cost - ultimately, the cost to taxpayers will be far less than the initial outlay. See, the government will purchase troubled assets and once the market recovers, it is likely that many of the assets will go up in value. And over time, Americans should expect that much -- if not all - of the tax dollars we invest will be paid back."

Table 3.3 Opinions about TARP bailouts.—cont'd

Panel B : Opinions of the U.S. Public about the TARP Bailouts (Source: *Ballotpedia*)[16]

Poll Source	Poll Question	Support	Oppose
Pew Research Center	"As you may know, the government is potentially investing billions to try and keep financial institutions and markets secure. Do you think this is the right thing or the wrong thing for the government to be doing?"	57%	30%
Bloomberg	"Do you think the government should use taxpayers' dollars to rescue ailing private financial firms whose collapse could have adverse effects on the economy and market, or is it not the government's responsibility to bail out private companies with taxpayers' dollars?"	31%	55%
USA Today/Gallup	"As you may know, the Bush administration has proposed a plan that would allow the Treasury Department to buy and re-sell up to $700 billion of distressed assets from financial companies. What would you like to see Congress do?"	22%*	67%*
ABC	"Do you approve or disapprove of the steps the Federal Reserve and the Treasury Department have taken to try to deal with the current situation involving the stock market and major financial institutions?"	44%	42%

From Emergency Economic Stabilization Act of 2008,
https://ballotpedia.org/Emergency_Economic_Stabilization_Act_of_2008

[b]*https://www.amazon.com/Bailout-Account-Washington-Abandoned-Rescuing/dp/145168432.*

[c]*https://www.amazon.com.au/Senseless-Panic-Washington-Failed-America-ebook/dp/B008FCV11W.*

[d]*https://www.amazon.com/Courage-Act-Memoir-Crisis-Aftermath/dp/0393353990.*

[e]*http://blog.ceo.ca/2013/09/13/hank-five-years-from-the-brink-the-interview/ and https://www.bloomberg.com/news/articles/2013-09-12/hank-paulson-this-is-what-it-was-like-to-face-the-financial-crisis and https://www.amazon.com/Brink-Collapse-Financial-Original-Anniversary/dp/1455551902/ref=sr_1_1?keywords=five+years+from+the+brink+paulson+book8 qid=1563653896&s=movies-to&sr=1-1-catcorr.*

[f]*https://www.treasury.gov/press-center/press-releases/Pages/tg1091.aspx.*

[g]*https://faculty.chicagobooth.edu/luigi.zingales/papers/testimony/COP_Testimony_3-4-2011.pdf.*

[h]*https://fraser.stlouisfed.org/files/docs/historical/fct/cop_report_20091209.pdf; https://fraser.stlouisfed.org/files/docs/historical/fct/cop_report_20100916.pdf.*

[i]*https://georgewbush-whitehouse.archives.gov/news/releases/2008/10/20081003-11.html.*

TABLE 3.4   TARP application form[a].

Application for TARP Capital Purchase Program (CPP)

Please complete the following information and follow the submission instructions as described on your Federal banking agency's website. In addition to completing the information on this form, please provide a description of any mergers, acquisitions, or other capital raisings that are currently pending or are under negotiation and the expected consummation date (no longer than 1 page).

In the event the applicant files an application with the appropriate Federal banking agency prior to the availability of the investment agreement, the applicant must file an amended application which includes updated responses to any items in the application that required prior review of the investment agreement.

Institution Name: _____

Address of Institution: _____

_____

Primary Contact Name: _____

Primary Contact Phone Number: _____

Primary Contact Fax Number: _____

Primary Contact Email Address: _____

Secondary Contact Name: _____

Secondary Contact Phone Number: _____

Secondary Contact Fax Number: _____

Secondary Contact Email Address: _____

TABLE 3.4   TARP application form[a].—cont'd

RSSD, Holding Company Docket
Number and / or FDIC Certificate
Number, As Relevant: _____

Amount of Preferred Shares
Requested: _____

Amount Of Institution's Authorized
But Unissued Preferred Stock
Available For Purchase: _____

Amount Of Institution's Authorized
But Unissued Common Stock: _____

Amount Of Total Risk-Weighted
Assets As Reported On The
Holding Company's Or Applicable
Institution's Most Recent FR-Y9,
Call Report, Or TFR, As Relevant: _____

Institution Has Reviewed The
Investment Agreements And
Related Documentation On
Treasury's Website (Yes/No):   _____

Describe Any Condition, Including   _____
A Representation Or Warranty,
Contained In The Investment
Agreements And Related   _____
Documentation, The Institution
Believes it Cannot Comply With By
November 14, 2008 And Provide A   _____
Timeline For Reaching
Compliance[1]:   _____

Type of Company[2]:   _____

Signature of Chief Executive
Officer (or Authorized Designee):   _____

Date of Signature: _____

---

[1] May be provided as an attachment, no longer than 1 page
[2] Publicly Traded Stock Company; Stock Company Without Publicly Traded Shares; Other (please specify)

---

[a]https://www.treasury.gov/initiatives/financial-stability/TARP-Programs/bank-investment-programs/cap/Documents/application-guidelines.pdf.

I. Introductory materials

As Citigroup mentions in their 10-K filings on dividends "In accordance with various TARP programs, commencing in 2009, Citigroup has agreed not to pay common stock dividends in excess of $0.01 per share per quarter for 3 years without the consent of the US Treasury Department, FDIC, and the Federal Reserve Bank of New York." In regards to compensation restrictions, Citigroup mentions that: "The American Recovery and Reinvestment Act of 2009 includes extensive new restrictions on our ability to pay retention awards, bonuses and other incentive compensation during the period in which we have any outstanding obligation arising from financial assistance provided to us under the TARP. Many of the restrictions are not limited to our senior executives and cover other employees whose contributions to revenue and performance can be significant. The limitations may adversely affect our ability to recruit and retain these key employees, especially if we are competing for management talent against US and non-US institutions that are not subject to the same restrictions."

Wells Fargo also mentions in their 10-K that "In fourth quarter 2009, we fully repaid the US Treasury's $25 billion Troubled Asset Relief Program (TARP) Capital Purchase Program (CPP) preferred stock investment, including related preferred dividends…During 2009 the Board of Directors approved salary increases for certain executive officers that were paid, after taxes and other withholdings, in our common stock. About 245,000 shares were issued in 2009 for salary increases. There are no longer restrictions on these shares because we repaid the TARP investment in Wells Fargo in December 2009."

3.1.5 The goals of the program

TARP had several main objectives, which were not independent of one another. These included restoring the confidence and overall stability of the US financial system, preventing the disruption in the US economy and improving real economic conditions for average Americans by encouraging the participant financial institutions to increase their availability of credit to customers and to each other, and ultimately protect US taxpayers.

3.1.6 The controversy and opinions about TARP

More than 10 years later, TARP still spurs much controversy and debate on whether it succeeded in its goals and whether TARP was a worthwhile program. Table 3.3 shows divided opinions from prominent figures and also from the public regarding whether TARP was a successful program. Some opinions are against or pessimistic about TARP success. This includes Neil Barofsky, Special Inspector General for TARP, who said in his 2013 book on Bailout: "How Washington Abandoned

Main Street while Rescuing Wall Street" that "To declare TARP a success is revisionist history … TARP was supposed to restore lending, and that didn't happen." Similarly, Bill Isaac in his 2010 book, "Senseless Panic: How Washington Failed America" said that "Any objective analysis would conclude that the TARP legislation did nothing to stabilize the financial system that could not have been done without it. Moreover, the negative aspects of the TARP legislation far outweighed any possible benefit."

However, others viewed the program more favorable and/or a success. This includes Ben Bernanke who mentioned in 2015 in his book "The Courage to Act: A Memoir of the Crisis and its Aftermath" that "The TARP, together with all the other measures, had prevented a financial meltdown that would have plunged the economy into an extraordinarily severe and protracted recession, or even a depression." Luigi Zingales, in his "Testimony before the Congressional Oversight Panel" in 2011, also provided some positive views: "In providing an opinion on the impact of the Troubled Asset Relief Program (TARP) on the financial sector and the US economy, it is important to establish what is the counter factual: what would have happened in the absence of TARP. Chairman Bernanke and then Treasury Secretary Paulson repeatedly presented their choice as an alternative between TARP and a collapse of the entire financial system. If the alternative was indeed the abyss, TARP is clearly an unqualified success: we have escaped the abyss. Even if the alternative was between TARP and some chance of falling into the abyss, we have to conclude that TARP was a success. The cost of TARP, however big, is small with comparison to the possibility of a Second Great Depression."(Zingales, 2011, Testimony before the Congressional Oversight Panel). Former President George W. Bush also provided some positive arguments about TARP as follows: "I know some Americans have concerns about this legislation, especially about the government's role and the bill's cost. As a strong supporter of free enterprise, I believe government intervention should occur only when necessary. In this situation, action is clearly necessary. And ultimately, the cost—ultimately, the cost to taxpayers will be far less than the initial outlay. See, the government will purchase troubled assets and once the market recovers, it is likely that many of the assets will go up in value. And over time, Americans should expect that much—if not all—of the tax dollars we invest will be paid back." Others also with favorable views showed in Table 3.3 are Hank Paulson, Timothy G. Massad, and Elizabeth Warren. Finally, the public polls taken in 2008 about TARP also showed the divide, with Bloomberg and *USA Today*/Gallup polls showing 55% and 67% of the respondents being against TARP, while Pew Research Center and ABC showing 57% and 44% favoring TARP. Further details are shown in Table 3.3.

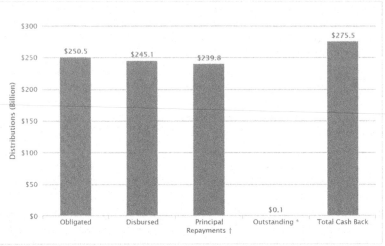

FIGURE 3.1   TARP capital injections to banks. *Source: Department of the US Treasury.* *https://www.treasury.gov/initiatives/financial-stability/reports/Pages/TARP-Tracker.aspx#Bank.*

3.1.7 TARP in numbers

The US Treasury report shows that banking organizations (both public and private) received TARP injections totaling $204.9 billion. Another $40.6 billion in was distributed through the TIP and the CDCI. Overall, these programs totaled $245.1 billion bank support (see Fig. 3.1). Taxpayers have already earned a positive return of about 12.7% from their investment in banks through the TARP. The program proceeds consisted of bank repayments, dividends, interest, warrant income, auctions, and other income.

The TARP injections ranged from 1% to 3% of a firm's risk-weighted assets or $25 billion, whichever was smaller. Many BHCs that received TARP preferred stock downstreamed some of the funds to their commercial banks (Mukherjee and Pana, 2018). The US Treasury purchased nonvoting preferred stock that paid quarterly dividends of 5% for the first 5 years and 9% afterward or subordinated debt for a selected number of private institutions. Together with the preferred equity or subordinated debt, the US Treasury also received warrants for an additional 5% of the banks' stock or subordinated debt.

Our analysis matching the names of the institutions in the US Treasury report to their RSSDIDs finds that the preponderance of the recipients are BHCs (572 or 81% of total), while a handful are commercial banks (87 or 12% of total) and thrifts or S&Ls (50 or 7% of total) as shown in Table 3.5 below. The top and bottom 10 participants in terms of size and age are shown in Table 3.6, a full list of all participants in the TARP

TABLE 3.5   TARP bailouts—institution types.

Criteria	Number of Institutions	% of Total
Institution Type		
BHC	572	81%
Commercial Bank	87	12%
S&L & Thrift	50	7%
Size		
Large	102	14%
Medium	119	17%
Small	488	69%
Age (groups split by mean)		
Old (Oldest Bank in Structure)	354	50%
Young (Youngest Bank in Structure)	355	50%
Payment		
Repaid early	140	20%
Did Not Repay Early	569	80%
Missed Payments	99	14%
Did Not Miss Payments	610	86%

The table above shows types of banks that received TARP capital injections. The data is compiled by the authors based on the Call Reports and SNL Financial and National Information Center where data for the institutions is not available in the Call Reports.

program is shown in Table 3.7, and those that repaid early no later than 2010:Q4 are shown in Table 3.8.

We also collect financial and geographic information from the Call Reports aggregated to the BHC level and fill in with data from SNL Financial for institutions not covered in the Call Reports. We find that TARP money went to institutions of all sizes, 102 large banks (gross total assets (GTA) exceeding $3 billion) or 14%, 119 medium-size banks (GTA exceeding $1 billion and up to $3 billion) or 17%, and 488 small banks (GTA up to $1 billion) or 69% of all institutions.

We also differentiate TARP recipients based on age. Looking at the age of the oldest bank in the recipient organization structure, we see that TARP went to 355 institutions with older banks (50%) and 354 younger banks (50%), based on the median age of 39.[4]

We next analyze repayment of the TARP funds. We find that 140 (20%) of the original recipients repaid all of the funds early by the end of 2010, including all of the involuntary recipients, while 569 did not repay early (80%). A total of 99 institutions missed dividend payments at least once (14%), while 610 never missed a dividend payment (86%).

---

[4] We are unable to identify age for the banks of two institutions so we leave them out for this analysis.

TABLE 3.6 Top and Bottom 10 TARP Participants by Size and Age

The table below shows top 10 and bottom 10 TARP participants for bank size in terms of total assets (large, medium, and small) and bank maximum age for the banks in the institution structure (above and below the median for the group of 39) for the banks that received TARP capital injections along with a set of financial characteristics in 2008:Q4, when the TARP program started. The data is compiled by the authors based on the Call Reports and SNL Financial and National Information Center where data for the institutions is not available in the Call Reports.

Panel A Large Banks - Top 10 in Terms of Bailout Amount

Rank	Name of Participating Institution	City	State	(1) Bailout ($thousands)	(2) Bailout /Equity	(3) Repaid Early	(4) Missed Pay	(5) Log (Total Assets)	(6) Equity/ Assets	(7) RWA Ratio
1	Bank of America Corporation	Charlotte	NC	$25,000,000	13.01%	Yes	No	9.24	11.05%	69.72%
2	Citigroup Inc.	New York	NY	$25,000,000	16.84%	No	No	9.25	8.42%	44.75%
3	JPMorgan Chase & Co.	New York	NY	$25,000,000	9.45%	Yes	No	9.38	10.90%	52.29%
4	Wells Fargo & Company	San Francisco	CA	$25,000,000	23.42%	Yes	No	9.09	8.61%	81.60%
5	Morgan Stanley	New York	NY	$10,000,000	172.11%	Yes	No	7.76	10.00%	77.31%
6	The Goldman Sachs Group, Inc.	New York	NY	$10,000,000	73.21%	Yes	No	8.21	8.37%	92.94%
7	The PNC Financial Services Group Inc.	Pittsburgh	PA	$7,579,200	30.01%	Yes	No	8.46	8.71%	84.46%
8	U.S. Bancorp	Minneapolis	MN	$6,599,000	28.62%	Yes	No	8.43	8.59%	84.40%
9	SunTrust Banks, Inc.	Atlanta	GA	$4,850,000	24.87%	No	No	8.27	10.54%	86.14%
10	Capital One Financial Corporation	McLean	VA	$3,555,199	14.62%	Yes	No	8.19	15.59%	71.85%

Rank	Name of Participating Institution	City	State	(8) Liquidity Ratio	(9) Loans/ Assets	(10) Deposits/ Assets	(11) NPL Ratio	(12) Charge-Offs Ratio	(13) Provisions/ Loans	(14) ROA	(15) Overhead Costs/Assets
1	Bank of America Corporation	Charlotte	NC	3.28%	52.10%	55.51%	3.19%	1.79%	2.89%	0.52%	3.98%
2	Citigroup Inc.	New York	NY	10.29%	43.06%	55.46%	3.41%	1.83%	4.07%	0.16%	5.90%
3	JPMorgan Chase & Co.	New York	NY	7.19%	30.74%	47.10%	3.33%	1.32%	2.84%	0.99%	3.74%
4	Wells Fargo & Company	San Francisco	CA	5.37%	64.04%	64.05%	2.93%	0.86%	1.72%	0.29%	2.22%
5	Morgan Stanley	New York	NY	51.81%	25.57%	79.98%	2.32%	0.25%	0.35%	-0.92%	1.62%
6	The Goldman Sachs Group, Inc.	New York	NY	7.53%	2.62%	27.62%	0.00%	0.00%	0.05%	-0.15%	0.68%
7	The PNC Financial Services Group Inc.	Pittsburgh	PA	6.54%	62.17%	69.38%	2.80%	0.30%	0.76%	0.17%	2.10%
8	U.S. Bancorp	Minneapolis	MN	3.28%	70.14%	64.10%	2.57%	0.97%	1.68%	1.28%	4.50%
9	SunTrust Banks, Inc.	Atlanta	GA	3.03%	70.80%	64.89%	3.79%	1.19%	1.89%	0.53%	4.70%
10	Capital One Financial Corporation	McLean	VA	5.63%	59.86%	75.21%	1.67%	3.08%	4.92%	0.10%	7.31%

Table 3.6 Top and Bottom 10 TARP Participants by Size and Age

The table below shows top 10 and bottom 10 TARP participants for bank size in terms of total assets (large, medium, and small) and bank maximum age for the banks in the institution structure (above and below the median for the group of 39) for the banks that received TARP capital injections along with a set of financial characteristics in 2008:Q4, when the TARP program started. The data is compiled by the authors based on the Call Reports and SNL Financial and National Information Center where data for the institutions is not available in the Call Reports.—cont'd

Panel B Large Banks – Bottom 10 in Terms of Bailout Amount

Rank	Name of Participating Institution	City	State	(1) Bailout ($thousands)	(2) Bailout /Equity	(3) Repaid Early	(4) Missed Pay	(5) Log (Total Assets)	(6) Equity/ Assets	(7) RWA Ratio
1	WSFS Financial Corporation	Wilmington	DE	$52,625	19.14%	No	No	6.54	8.01%	80.65%
2	First Financial Holdings Inc.	Charleston	SC	$65,000	36.60%	No	No	6.48	5.90%	74.75%
3	First BanCorp	San Juan	PR	$65,000	4.13%	No	No	7.27	8.52%	70.84%
4	First Place Financial Corp.	Warren	OH	$72,927	28.06%	No	No	6.52	7.85%	73.41%
5	Bank of the Ozarks, Inc.	Little Rock	AR	$75,000	20.43%	Yes	No	6.51	11.37%	79.69%
6	WesBanco, Inc.	Wheeling	WV	$75,000	10.46%	Yes	No	6.72	13.80%	73.34%
7	Texas Capital Bancshares, Inc.	Dallas	TX	$75,000	16.09%	Yes	No	6.71	9.08%	95.16%
8	TowneBank	Portsmouth	VA	$76,458	18.22%	No	No	6.50	13.39%	85.22%
9	Columbia Banking System, Inc.	Tacoma	WA	$76,898	21.23%	Yes	No	6.49	11.72%	82.96%
10	Independent Bank Corp.	Rockland	MA	$78,158	21.35%	Yes	No	6.56	10.22%	75.57%

Rank	Name of Participating Institution	City	State	(8) Liquidity Ratio	(9) Loans/ Assets	(10) Deposits/ Assets	(11) NPL Ratio	(12) Charge- Offs Ratio	(13) Provisions/ Loans	(14) ROA	(15) Overhead Costs/Assets
1	WSFS Financial Corporation	Wilmington	DE	7.24%	72.06%	61.92%	1.38%	0.12%	0.59%	-0.09%	1.14%
2	First Financial Holdings Inc.	Charleston	SC	2.00%	79.10%	66.93%	1.69%	0.12%	0.95%	-0.17%	1.27%
3	First BanCorp	San Juan	PR	1.88%	66.03%	67.91%	7.75%	1.17%	1.44%	0.70%	4.87%
4	First Place Financial Corp.	Warren	OH	3.33%	81.58%	77.86%	3.95%	0.26%	0.34%	-2.61%	3.84%
5	Bank of the Ozarks, Inc.	Little Rock	AR	1.27%	62.44%	72.83%	0.76%	0.45%	0.94%	1.18%	4.11%
6	WesBanco, Inc.	Wheeling	WV	2.75%	69.51%	67.43%	1.40%	0.55%	0.90%	0.83%	4.86%
7	Texas Capital Bancshares, Inc.	Dallas	TX	1.52%	88.18%	66.42%	1.14%	0.28%	0.59%	0.60%	3.85%
8	TowneBank	Portsmouth	VA	2.23%	75.83%	71.66%	0.15%	0.04%	0.30%	0.76%	5.42%
9	Columbia Banking System, Inc.	Tacoma	WA	2.74%	72.26%	79.41%	4.75%	1.12%	1.84%	0.25%	4.59%
10	Independent Bank Corp.	Rockland	MA	1.38%	73.18%	71.08%	0.99%	0.23%	0.41%	0.74%	4.61%

Continued

Table 3.6 Top and Bottom 10 TARP Participants by Size and Age

The table below shows top 10 and bottom 10 TARP participants for bank size in terms of total assets (large, medium, and small) and bank maximum age for the banks in the institution structure (above and below the median for the group of 39) for the banks that received TARP capital injections along with a set of financial characteristics in 2008:Q4, when the TARP program started. The data is compiled by the authors based on the Call Reports and SNL Financial and National Information Center where data for the institutions is not available in the Call Reports.—cont'd

Panel C Medium Banks - Top 10 in Terms of Bailout Amount

Rank	Name of Participating Institution	City	State	(1) Bailout ($thousands)	(2) Bailout /Equity	(3) Repaid Early	(4) Missed Pay	(5) Log (Total Assets)	(6) Equity/ Assets	(7) RWA Ratio
1	Metropolitan Bank Group, Inc.	Chicago	IL	$74,706	26.94%	No	Yes	6.44	10.06%	80.96%
2	Independent Bank Corporation	Ionia	MI	$74,426	28.71%	No	No	6.47	8.78%	79.91%
3	Old Second Bancorp, Inc.	Aurora	IL	$73,000	23.27%	No	Yes	6.47	10.52%	81.97%
4	Green Bankshares, Inc.	Greeneville	TN	$72,278	15.75%	No	No	6.47	15.62%	78.53%
5	Virginia Commerce Bancorp	Arlington	VA	$71,000	22.46%	No	No	6.43	11.65%	88.71%
6	Alpine Banks of Colorado	Glenwood Springs	CO	$70,000	26.25%	No	No	6.43	9.94%	87.28%
7	Southwest Bancorp, Inc.	Stillwater	OK	$70,000	21.64%	No	No	6.45	11.39%	97.99%
8	Nara Bancorp, Inc.	Los Angeles	CA	$67,000	20.78%	No	No	6.43	12.08%	85.00%
9	First Bancorp	Troy	NC	$65,000	22.78%	No	No	6.44	10.36%	79.31%
10	SCBT Financial Corporation	Columbia	SC	$64,779	22.87%	Yes	No	6.44	10.25%	80.10%

Rank	Name of Participating Institution	City	State	(8) Liquidity Ratio	(9) Loans/ Assets	(10) Deposits/ Assets	(11) NPL Ratio	(12) Charge-Offs Ratio	(13) Provisions/ Loans	(14) ROA	(15) Overhead Costs/Assets
1	Metropolitan Bank Group, Inc.	Chicago	IL	2.65%	74.99%	84.60%	4.94%	0.38%	0.39%	1.16%	5.16%
2	Independent Bank Corporation	Ionia	MI	1.94%	84.30%	71.05%	5.03%	2.39%	2.90%	-2.77%	8.00%
3	Old Second Bancorp, Inc.	Aurora	IL	2.24%	76.95%	80.07%	4.73%	0.39%	1.32%	0.60%	4.65%
4	Green Bankshares, Inc.	Greeneville	TN	6.57%	75.67%	74.83%	1.41%	1.71%	2.37%	-0.05%	5.06%
5	Virginia Commerce Bancorp	Arlington	VA	1.24%	85.34%	80.06%	5.07%	0.48%	1.10%	0.57%	4.38%
6	Alpine Banks of Colorado	Glenwood Springs	CO	2.37%	78.48%	87.61%	1.60%	0.07%	0.40%	1.30%	4.62%
7	Southwest Bancorp, Inc.	Stillwater	OK	0.94%	88.01%	76.14%	2.54%	0.35%	0.75%	0.63%	4.49%
8	Nara Bancorp, Inc.	Los Angeles	CA	1.13%	78.99%	72.70%	1.78%	1.21%	2.32%	0.20%	4.62%
9	First Bancorp	Troy	NC	5.48%	80.35%	75.49%	1.20%	0.21%	0.45%	0.90%	4.35%
10	SCBT Financial Corporation	Columbia	SC	1.75%	84.39%	78.02%	0.64%	0.25%	0.46%	0.64%	4.93%

The table below shows top 10 and bottom 10 TARP participants for bank size in terms of total assets (large, medium, and small) and bank maximum age for the banks in the institution structure (above and below the median for the group of 39) for the banks that received TARP capital injections along with a set of financial characteristics in 2008:Q4, when the TARP program started. The data is compiled by the authors based on the Call Reports and SNL Financial and National Information Center where data for the institutions is not available in the Call Reports.—cont'd

Panel D Medium Banks – Bottom 10 in Terms of Bailout Amount

Rank	Name of Participating Institution	City	State	(1) Bailout ($thousands)	(2) Bailout /Equity	(3) Repaid Early	(4) Missed Pay	(5) Log (Total Assets)	(6) Equity/ Assets	(7) RWA Ratio
1	Center Bancorp, Inc.	Union	NJ	$10,000	11.73%	No	No	6.01	8.33%	74.97%
2	The Landrum Company	Columbia	MO	$15,000	14.54%	No	No	6.12	7.74%	81.14%
3	Centra Financial Holdings, Inc.	Morgantown	WV	$15,000	13.37%	Yes	No	6.08	9.25%	79.62%
4	MidWestOne Financial Group, Inc.	Iowa City	IA	$16,000	12.46%	No	No	6.17	8.59%	84.72%
5	Community Bankers Trust Corporation	Glen Allen	VA	$17,680	16.37%	No	No	6.01	10.49%	58.95%
6	Peoples Bancorp	Lynden	WA	$18,000	21.43%	No	No	6.02	8.07%	91.28%
7	Community First Bancshares Inc.	Union City	TN	$20,000	19.81%	No	No	6.13	7.50%	81.44%
8	First Financial Service Corporation	Elizabethtown	KY	$20,000	22.39%	No	Yes	6.01	8.81%	88.08%
9	The ANB Corporation	Terrell	TX	$20,000	11.52%	No	No	6.31	8.57%	68.78%
10	Mercantile Bank Corporation	Grand Rapids	MI	$21,000	10.34%	No	No	6.34	9.22%	94.93%

Rank	Name of Participating Institution	City	State	(8) Liquidity Ratio	(9) Loans/ Assets	(10) Deposits/ Assets	(11) NPL Ratio	(12) Charge-Offs Ratio	(13) Provisions/ Loans	(14) ROA	(15) Overhead Costs/Assets
1	Center Bancorp, Inc.	Union	NJ	1.47%	66.12%	64.58%	0.10%	0.07%	0.23%	0.64%	4.19%
2	The Landrum Company	Columbia	MO	3.45%	81.20%	86.47%	0.87%	0.47%	0.63%	0.65%	6.38%
3	Centra Financial Holdings, Inc.	Morgantown	WV	1.67%	84.70%	83.65%	0.66%	0.23%	0.50%	0.59%	5.03%
4	MidWestOne Financial Group, Inc.	Iowa City	IA	2.16%	74.16%	76.05%	4.55%	0.57%	0.60%	-1.53%	6.28%
5	Community Bankers Trust Corporation	Glen Allen	VA	11.50%	50.77%	83.91%	0.94%	0.37%	0.79%	-0.35%	3.91%
6	Peoples Bancorp	Lynden	WA	3.25%	92.44%	89.83%	0.80%	0.10%	0.37%	0.66%	5.38%
7	Community First Bancshares Inc.	Union City	TN	1.81%	77.79%	83.27%	1.49%	0.78%	1.52%	-0.01%	5.82%
8	First Financial Service Corporation	Elizabethtown	KY	2.04%	90.03%	76.54%	1.71%	0.07%	0.65%	0.59%	5.09%
9	The ANB Corporation	Terrell	TX	6.75%	62.69%	81.64%	1.15%	0.39%	0.51%	0.55%	5.73%
10	Mercantile Bank Corporation	Grand Rapids	MI	0.76%	84.26%	72.60%	2.66%	1.07%	1.14%	-0.09%	5.05%

Continued

I. Introductory materials

Table 3.6 Top and Bottom 10 TARP Participants by Size and Age

The table below shows top 10 and bottom 10 TARP participants for bank size in terms of total assets (large, medium, and small) and bank maximum age for the banks in the institution structure (above and below the median for the group of 39) for the banks that received TARP capital injections along with a set of financial characteristics in 2008:Q4, when the TARP program started. The data is compiled by the authors based on the Call Reports and SNL Financial and National Information Center where data for the institutions is not available in the Call Reports.—cont'd

Panel E Small Banks - Top 10 in Terms of Bailout Amount

Rank	Name of Participating Institution	City	State	(1) Bailout ($thousands)	(2) Bailout/Equity	(3) Repaid Early	(4) Missed Pay	(5) Log (Total Assets)	(6) Equity/Assets	(7) RWA Ratio
1	Berkshire Hills Bancorp, Inc.	Pittsfield	MA	$40,000	60.78%	Yes	No	5.96	7.14%	70.35%
2	Washington Banking Company	Oak Harbor	WA	$26,380	25.31%	No	No	5.95	11.60%	97.67%
3	Patriot Bancshares, Inc.	Houston	TX	$26,038	23.19%	No	No	5.98	11.65%	93.47%
4	Peoples Bancorp of North Carolina, Inc.	Newton	NC	$25,054	28.22%	No	No	5.98	9.19%	87.24%
5	Crescent Financial Corporation	Cary	NC	$24,900	23.81%	No	No	5.99	10.80%	86.18%
6	Heritage Financial Corporation	Olympia	WA	$24,000	25.72%	Yes	No	5.98	9.87%	84.17%
7	Bridge Capital Holdings	San Jose	CA	$23,864	22.07%	No	No	5.98	11.40%	85.63%
8	Severn Bancorp, Inc.	Annapolis	MD	$23,393	17.60%	No	No	5.99	13.52%	79.78%
9	Park Bancorporation, Inc.	Madison	WI	$23,200	33.37%	No	No	5.91	8.53%	94.65%
10	Central Bancorp, Inc.	Somerville	MA	$22,500	51.84%	No	No	5.74	7.87%	67.97%

Rank	Name of Participating Institution	City	State	(8) Liquidity Ratio	(9) Loans/Assets	(10) Deposits/Assets	(11) NPL Ratio	(12) Charge-Offs Ratio	(13) Provisions/Loans	(14) ROA	(15) Overhead Costs/Assets
1	Berkshire Hills Bancorp, Inc.	Pittsfield	MA	6.94%	50.65%	79.09%	0.03%	-0.01%	0.85%	0.41%	1.12%
2	Washington Banking Company	Oak Harbor	WA	1.57%	91.97%	83.30%	0.23%	0.48%	0.61%	1.10%	5.10%
3	Patriot Bancshares, Inc.	Houston	TX	2.57%	93.26%	69.11%	0.30%	0.25%	0.69%	0.06%	5.41%
4	Peoples Bancorp of North Carolina, Inc.	Newton	NC	2.19%	80.88%	77.82%	1.58%	0.37%	0.61%	0.74%	5.33%
5	Crescent Financial Corporation	Cary	NC	1.05%	81.13%	73.92%	1.67%	0.28%	0.83%	0.25%	4.99%
6	Heritage Financial Corporation	Olympia	WA	6.44%	85.57%	89.57%	0.57%	0.29%	0.92%	0.79%	4.87%
7	Bridge Capital Holdings	San Jose	CA	2.71%	73.62%	84.23%	2.34%	3.09%	4.36%	-0.60%	5.25%
8	Severn Bancorp, Inc.	Annapolis	MD	1.46%	91.75%	70.71%	6.41%	0.00%	0.32%	0.00%	1.22%
9	Park Bancorporation, Inc.	Madison	WI	4.69%	88.65%	73.95%	0.62%	0.74%	1.03%	0.47%	5.01%
10	Central Bancorp, Inc.	Somerville	MA	5.07%	82.71%	64.08%	2.15%	0.02%	0.29%	-0.85%	5.37%

The table below shows top 10 and bottom 10 TARP participants for bank size in terms of total assets (large, medium, and small) and bank maximum age for the banks in the institution structure (above and below the median for the group of 39) for the banks that received TARP capital injections along with a set of financial characteristics in 2008:Q4, when the TARP program started. The data is compiled by the authors based on the Call Reports and SNL Financial and National Information Center where data for the institutions is not available on the Call Reports.—cont'd

Panel F Small Banks - Bottom 10 in Terms of Bailout Amount

Rank	Name of Participating Institution	City	State	(1) Bailout ($thousands)	(2) Bailout/Equity	(3) Repaid Early	(4) Missed Pay	(5) Log (Total Assets)	(6) Equity/Assets	(7) RWA Ratio
1	The Freeport State Bank	Harper	KS	$301	27.82%	No	No	4.28	5.63%	54.27%
2	Haviland Bancshares, Inc.	Haviland	KS	$425	12.93%	Yes	No	4.44	11.84%	70.92%
3	Farmers & Merchants Financial Corporation	Argonia	KS	$442	25.48%	No	No	4.35	7.67%	64.42%
4	Kirksville Bancorp Inc.	Kirksville	MO	$470	19.08%	No	No	4.34	11.31%	74.61%
5	Community Bancshares of Kansas, Inc.	Goff	KS	$500	16.20%	No	No	4.42	11.75%	72.44%
6	The Victory Bancorp, Inc. (The Victory Bank)	Limerick	PA	$541	7.21%	No	No	4.36	32.41%	89.14%
7	Colonial American Bank	West Conshohocken	PA	$574	20.49%	No	No	4.46	9.68%	66.09%
8	Butler Point, Inc.	Catlin	IL	$607	16.60%	No	No	4.61	8.98%	49.71%
9	Corning Savings and Loan Association	Corning	AR	$638	17.34%	No	No	4.51	11.42%	67.37%
10	Green City Bancshares, Inc.	Green City	MO	$651	21.01%	Yes	No	4.49	10.12%	71.81%

Rank	Name of Participating Institution	City	State	(8) Liquidity Ratio	(9) Loans/Assets	(10) Deposits/Assets	(11) NPL Ratio	(12) Charge-Offs Ratio	(13) Provisions/Loans	(14) ROA	(15) Overhead Costs/Assets
1	The Freeport State Bank	Harper	KS	2.43%	48.22%	93.68%	1.54%	0.00%	0.70%	0.29%	5.07%
2	Haviland Bancshares, Inc.	Haviland	KS	9.49%	63.48%	83.60%	0.17%	-0.01%	0.00%	1.43%	4.70%
3	Farmers & Merchants Financial Corporation	Argonia	KS	6.88%	72.72%	86.95%	0.01%	0.23%	0.68%	0.20%	7.62%
4	Kirksville Bancorp, Inc.	Kirksville	MO	5.38%	76.80%	85.19%	0.01%	0.01%	0.07%	-0.81%	7.12%
5	Community Bancshares of Kansas, Inc.	Goff	KS	16.65%	74.34%	78.69%	0.01%	0.01%	1.23%	-0.85%	3.76%
6	The Victory Bancorp, Inc. (The Victory Bank)	Limerick	PA	4.20%	77.99%	67.02%	0.00%	0.00%	1.10%	-12.38%	15.01%
7	Colonial American Bank	West Conshohocken	PA	0.96%	67.17%	86.32%	0.58%	0.26%	0.64%	-6.13%	12.93%
8	Butler Point, Inc.	Catlin	IL	4.22%	46.96%	85.54%	4.95%	0.00%	0.38%	0.09%	6.38%
9	Corning Savings and Loan Association	Corning	AR	19.22%	69.49%	83.99%	2.96%	-0.12%	-0.01%	4.84%	1.54%
10	Green City Bancshares, Inc.	Green City	MO	17.90%	40.41%	74.30%	2.96%	0.05%	0.24%	0.31%	5.21%

Continued

Table 3.6   Top and Bottom 10 TARP Participants by Size and Age

The table below shows top 10 and bottom 10 TARP participants for bank size in terms of total assets (large, medium, and small) and bank maximum age for the banks in the institution structure (above and below the median for the group of 39) for the banks that received TARP capital injections along with a set of financial characteristics in 2008:Q4, when the TARP program started. The data is compiled by the authors based on the Call Reports and SNL Financial and National Information Center where data for the institutions is not available in the Call Reports.—cont'd

Panel G Old Banks (Highest Bank Age in the Institution Structure) - Top 10 in Terms of Bailout Amount

Rank	Name of Participating Institution	City	State	(1) Bailout ($thousands)	(2) Bailout /Equity	(3) Repaid Early	(4) Missed Pay	(5) Log (Total Assets)	(6) Equity/ Assets	(7) RWA Ratio
1	Bank of America Corporation	Charlotte	NC	$25,000,000	13.01%	Yes	No	75	11.05%	69.72%
2	Citigroup Inc.	New York	NY	$25,000,000	16.84%	No	No	91	8.42%	44.75%
3	JPMorgan Chase & Co.	New York	NY	$25,000,000	9.45%	Yes	No	84	10.90%	52.29%
4	Wells Fargo & Company	San Francisco	CA	$25,000,000	23.42%	Yes	No	156	8.61%	81.60%
5	The PNC Financial Services Group Inc.	Pittsburgh	PA	$7,579,200	30.01%	Yes	No	163	8.71%	84.46%
6	U.S. Bancorp	Minneapolis	MN	$6,599,000	28.62%	Yes	No	145	8.59%	84.40%
7	SunTrust Banks, Inc.	Atlanta	GA	$4,850,000	24.87%	No	No	117	10.54%	86.14%
8	Capital One Financial Corporation	McLean	VA	$3,555,199	14.62%	Yes	No	75	15.59%	71.85%
9	Regions Financial Corporation	Birmingham	AL	$3,500,000	24.12%	No	No	80	10.19%	80.48%
10	Fifth Third Bancorp	Cincinnati	OH	$3,408,000	24.91%	No	No	155	10.47%	88.80%

Rank	Name of Participating Institution	City	State	(8) Liquidity Ratio	(9) Loans/ Assets	(10) Deposits/ Assets	(11) NPL Ratio	(12) Charge- Offs Ratio	(13) Provisions/ Loans	(14) ROA	(15) Overhead Costs/ Assets
1	Bank of America Corporation	Charlotte	NC	3.28%	52.10%	55.51%	3.19%	1.79%	2.89%	0.52%	3.98%
2	Citigroup Inc.	New York	NY	10.29%	43.06%	55.46%	3.41%	1.83%	4.07%	0.16%	5.90%
3	JPMorgan Chase & Co.	New York	NY	7.19%	30.74%	47.10%	3.33%	1.32%	2.84%	0.99%	3.74%
4	Wells Fargo & Company	San Francisco	CA	5.37%	64.04%	64.05%	2.93%	0.86%	1.72%	0.29%	2.22%
5	The PNC Financial Services Group Inc.	Pittsburgh	PA	6.54%	62.17%	69.38%	2.80%	0.30%	0.76%	0.17%	2.10%
6	U.S. Bancorp	Minneapolis	MN	3.28%	70.14%	64.10%	2.57%	0.97%	1.68%	1.28%	4.50%
7	SunTrust Banks, Inc.	Atlanta	GA	3.03%	70.80%	64.89%	3.79%	1.19%	1.89%	0.53%	4.70%
8	Capital One Financial Corporation	McLean	VA	5.63%	59.86%	75.21%	1.67%	3.08%	4.92%	0.10%	7.31%
9	Regions Financial Corporation	Birmingham	AL	7.17%	69.33%	67.36%	2.06%	1.57%	2.08%	-3.88%	8.40%
10	Fifth Third Bancorp	Cincinnati	OH	9.08%	65.79%	67.38%	4.03%	3.15%	5.30%	-1.47%	5.42%

The table below shows top 10 and bottom 10 TARP participants for bank size in terms of total assets (large, medium, and small) and bank maximum age for the banks in the institution structure (above and below the median for the group of 39) for the banks that received TARP capital injections along with a set of financial characteristics in 2008:Q4, when the TARP program started. The data is compiled by the authors based on the Call Reports and SNL Financial and National Information Center where data for the institutions is not available in the Call Reports.—cont'd

Panel H Old Banks (Highest Bank Age in the Institution Structure) - Bottom 10 in Terms of Bailout Amount

Rank	Name of Participating Institution	City	State	(1) Bailout ($thousands)	(2) Bailout /Equity	(3) Repaid Early	(4) Missed Pay	(5) Log (Total Assets)	(6) Equity/ Assets	(7) RWA Ratio
1	The Freeport State Bank	Harper	KS	$301	27.82%	No	No	49	5.63%	54.27%
2	Haviland Bancshares, Inc.	Haviland	KS	$425	12.93%	Yes	No	105	11.84%	70.92%
3	Farmers & Merchants Financial Corporation	Argonia	KS	$442	25.48%	No	No	107	7.67%	64.42%
4	Community Bancshares of Kansas, Inc.	Goff	KS	$500	16.20%	No	No	104	11.75%	72.44%
5	Butler Point, Inc	Catlin	IL	$607	16.60%	No	No	104	8.98%	49.71%
6	Green City Bancshares, Inc.	Green City	MO	$651	21.01%	Yes	No	65	10.12%	71.81%
7	Midwest Regional Bancorp, Inc.	Festus	MO	$700	9.33%	Yes	No	114	18.27%	71.27%
8	Farmers State Bankshares, Inc.	Holton	KS	$700	16.25%	No	No	108	9.46%	66.50%
9	First State Bank of Mobeetie	Mobeetie	TX	$731	15.67%	Yes	No	102	5.54%	32.50%
10	Banner County Ban Corporation	Harrisburg	NE	$795	21.71%	No	No	44	9.10%	73.41%

Rank	Name of Participating Institution	City	State	(8) Liquidity Ratio	(9) Loans/ Assets	(10) Deposits/ Assets	(11) NPL Ratio	(12) Charge-Offs Ratio	(13) Provisions/ Loans	(14) ROA	(15) Overhead Costs/Assets
1	The Freeport State Bank	Harper	KS	2.43%	48.22%	93.68%	1.54%	0.00%	0.70%	0.29%	5.07%
2	Haviland Bancshares, Inc.	Haviland	KS	9.49%	63.48%	83.60%	0.17%	-0.01%	0.00%	1.43%	4.70%
3	Farmers & Merchants Financial Corporation	Argonia	KS	6.88%	72.72%	86.95%	0.01%	0.23%	0.68%	0.20%	7.62%
4	Community Bancshares of Kansas, Inc.	Goff	KS	16.65%	74.34%	78.69%	0.01%	0.01%	1.23%	-0.85%	3.76%
5	Butler Point, Inc.	Catlin	IL	4.22%	46.96%	85.54%	4.95%	0.26%	0.38%	0.09%	6.38%
6	Green City Bancshares, Inc.	Green City	MO	17.90%	40.41%	74.30%	2.96%	0.05%	0.24%	0.31%	5.21%
7	Midwest Regional Bancorp, Inc.	Festus	MO	17.69%	61.60%	69.18%	1.85%	2.06%	2.06%	-2.05%	5.83%
8	Farmers State Bankshares, Inc.	Holton	KS	2.41%	58.57%	82.32%	2.63%	0.93%	0.38%	0.25%	6.20%
9	First State Bank of Mobeetie	Mobeetie	TX	22.05%	18.22%	94.39%	0.63%	0.05%	0.68%	1.00%	2.89%
10	Banner County Ban Corporation	Harrisburg	NE	6.70%	72.74%	89.90%	0.35%	0.02%	0.22%	0.98%	4.66%

Continued

I. Introductory materials

Table 3.6 Top and Bottom 10 TARP Participants by Size and Age

The table below shows top 10 and bottom 10 TARP participants (for bank size in terms of total assets (large, medium, and small) and bank maximum age for the banks in the institution structure (above and below the median for the group of 39) for the banks that received TARP capital injections along with a set of financial characteristics in 2008:Q4, when the TARP program started. The data is compiled by the authors based on the Call Reports and SNL Financial and National Information Center where data for the institutions is not available in the Call Reports.—cont'd

Panel I Young Banks (Lowest Bank Age in the Institution Structure) - Top 10 in Terms of Bailout Amount

Rank	Name of Participating Institution	City	State	(1) Bailout ($thousands)	(2) Bailout /Equity	(3) Repaid Early	(4) Missed Pay	(5) Log (Total Assets)	(6) Equity/ Assets	(7) RWA Ratio
1	Morgan Stanley	New York	NY	$10,000,000	172.11%	Yes	No	19	10.00%	77.31%
2	The Goldman Sachs Group, Inc.	New York	NY	$10,000,000	73.21%	Yes	No	18	8.37%	92.94%
3	American Express Company	New York	NY	$3,388,890	111.57%	Yes	No	19	12.36%	100.49%
4	CIT Group Inc.	New York	NY	$2,330,000	436.70%	Yes	No	8	15.25%	68.63%
5	South Financial Group, Inc.	Greenville	SC	$347,000	21.73%	Yes	No	22	11.77%	86.49%
6	East West Bancorp	Pasadena	CA	$306,546	18.18%	Yes	No	36	13.58%	83.40%
7	Sterling Financial Corporation	Spokane	WA	$303,000	23.43%	No	No	25	10.11%	77.22%
8	UCBH Holdings, Inc.	San Francisco	CA	$298,737	18.74%	No	No	34	11.83%	73.85%
9	Flagstar Bancorp, Inc.	Troy	MI	$266,657	39.76%	No	Yes	21	4.74%	61.34%
10	PrivateBancorp, Inc.	Chicago	IL	$243,815	27.98%	No	No	19	8.99%	90.35%

Rank	Name of Participating Institution	City	State	(8) Liquidity Ratio	(9) Loans/ Assets	(10) Deposits/ Assets	(11) NPL Ratio	(12) Charge-Offs Ratio	(13) Provisions/ Loans	(14) ROA	(15) Overhead Costs/ Assets
1	Morgan Stanley	New York	NY	51.81%	25.57%	79.98%	2.32%	0.25%	0.35%	-0.92%	1.62%
2	The Goldman Sachs Group, Inc.	New York	NY	7.53%	2.62%	27.62%	0.00%	0.00%	0.05%	-0.15%	0.68%
3	American Express Company	New York	NY	16.18%	76.57%	29.92%	2.48%	6.54%	7.96%	3.90%	14.74%
4	CIT Group Inc.	New York	NY	23.36%	57.67%	75.05%	0.31%	2.83%	1.84%	0.45%	3.74%
5	South Financial Group, Inc.	Greenville	SC	2.15%	75.43%	71.20%	4.04%	2.18%	3.36%	-3.99%	8.28%
6	East West Bancorp	Pasadena	CA	3.01%	66.46%	65.79%	2.60%	1.71%	2.80%	-0.32%	3.91%
7	Sterling Financial Corporation	Spokane	WA	1.11%	71.40%	65.48%	5.48%	2.42%	3.49%	-2.54%	6.81%
8	UCBH Holdings, Inc.	San Francisco	CA	4.29%	64.34%	67.21%	6.11%	1.31%	3.03%	-0.40%	4.10%
9	Flagstar Bancorp, Inc.	Troy	MI	3.61%	73.75%	55.86%	8.95%	0.11%	1.69%	-1.48%	1.86%
10	PrivateBancorp, Inc.	Chicago	IL	2.27%	78.65%	79.30%	1.48%	1.42%	2.23%	-0.49%	3.40%

The table below shows top 10 and bottom 10 TARP participants for bank size in terms of total assets (large, medium, and small) and bank maximum age for the banks in the institution structure (above and below the median for the group of 39) for the banks that received TARP capital injections along with a set of financial characteristics in 2008:Q4, when the TARP program started. The data is compiled by the authors based on the Call Reports and SNL Financial and National Information Center where data for the institutions is not available in the Call Reports.—cont'd

Panel J Young Banks (Lowest Bank Age in the Institution Structure) - Bottom 10 in Terms of Bailout Amount

Rank	Name of Participating Institution	City	State	(1) Bailout ($thousands)	(2) Bailout /Equity	(3) Repaid Early	(4) Missed Pay	(5) Log (Total Assets)	(6) Equity/ Assets	(7) RWA Ratio
1	Kirksville Bancorp, Inc.	Kirksville	MO	$470	19.08%	No	No	3	11.31%	74.61%
2	The Victory Bancorp, Inc. (The Victory Bank)	Limerick	PA	$541	7.21%	No	No	0	32.41%	89.14%
3	Colonial American Bank	West Conshohocken	PA	$574	20.49%	No	No	1	9.68%	66.09%
4	Corning Savings and Loan Association	Corning	AR	$638	17.34%	No	No	34	11.42%	67.37%
5	BankGreenville	Greenville	SC	$1,000	10.47%	No	No	2	11.56%	77.86%
6	Bank Financial Services, Inc.	Eden Prarie	MN	$1,004	25.21%	No	No	4	5.73%	51.04%
7	Community Holding Company of Florida, Inc.	Miramar Beach	FL	$1,050	10.99%	No	No	1	20.72%	74.66%
8	Independence Bank	East Greenwich	RI	$1,065	20.07%	No	No	5	8.72%	58.36%
9	First Advantage Bancshares Inc.	Coon Rapids	MN	$1,177	24.83%	No	No	5	10.54%	89.67%
10	Fort Lee Federal Savings Bank	Fort Lee	NJ	$1,300	32.35%	No	No	8	6.57%	62.71%

Rank	Name of Participating Institution	City	State	(8) Liquidity Ratio	(9) Loans/ Assets	(10) Deposits/ Assets	(11) NPL Ratio	(12) Charge-Offs Ratio	(13) Provisions/ Loans	(14) ROA	(15) Overhead Costs/ Assets
1	Kirksville Bancorp, Inc.	Kirksville	MO	5.38%	76.80%	85.19%	0.01%	0.01%	0.07%	-0.81%	7.12%
2	The Victory Bancorp, Inc. (The Victory Bank)	Limerick	PA	4.20%	77.99%	67.02%	0.00%	0.00%	1.10%	-12.38%	15.01%
3	Colonial American Bank	West Conshohocken	PA	0.96%	67.17%	86.32%	0.58%	0.00%	0.64%	-6.13%	12.93%
4	Corning Savings and Loan Association	Corning	AR	19.22%	69.49%	83.99%	2.96%	-0.12%	-0.01%	4.84%	1.54%
5	BankGreenville	Greenville	SC	1.42%	66.16%	70.48%	2.24%	0.00%	0.40%	-0.07%	4.86%
6	Bank Financial Services, Inc.	Eden Prarie	MN	0.62%	70.11%	65.22%	2.36%	0.25%	0.31%	-0.59%	1.77%
7	Community Holding Company of Florida, Inc.	Miramar Beach	FL	18.96%	51.58%	78.87%	1.51%	1.12%	2.06%	-2.87%	7.08%
8	Independence Bank	East Greenwich	RI	23.85%	71.55%	65.29%	2.08%	0.52%	-0.59%	-0.51%	8.35%
9	First Advantage Bancshares Inc.	Coon Rapids	MN	4.25%	88.37%	82.82%	6.51%	0.23%	1.89%	-0.89%	6.08%
10	Fort Lee Federal Savings Bank	Fort Lee	NJ	17.02%	76.13%	93.19%	0.41%	0.14%	0.00%	0.05%	1.43%

TABLE 3.7 All banks that received TARP funds.

TARP Purchase Date	Name of Participating Institution	Institution City	Institution State	TARP Investment Description	TARP Investment Amount
			Involuntary Participants		
10/28/2008	Bank of America Corporation	Charlotte	NC	Preferred Stock w/ Warrants	$15,000,000,000
1/9/2009	Bank of America Corporation	Charlotte	NC	Preferred Stock w/ Warrants	$10,000,000,000
10/28/2008	The Bank of New York Mellon Corporation	New York	NY	Preferred Stock w/ Warrants	$3,000,000,000
10/28/2008	Citigroup Inc.	New York	NY	Common Stock w/ Warrants	$25,000,000,000
10/28/2008	The Goldman Sachs Group, Inc.	New York	NY	Preferred Stock w/ Warrants	$10,000,000,000
10/28/2008	JPMorgan Chase & Co.	New York	NY	Preferred Stock w/ Warrants	$25,000,000,000
10/28/2008	Morgan Stanley	New York	NY	Preferred Stock w/ Warrants	$10,000,000,000
10/28/2008	State Street Corporation	Boston	MA	Preferred Stock w/ Warrants	$2,000,000,000
10/28/2008	Wells Fargo & Company	San Francisco	CA	Preferred Stock w/ Warrants	$25,000,000,000
			All Other Participants		
11/14/2008	Bank of Commerce Holdings	Redding	CA	Preferred Stock w/ Warrants	$17,000,000
11/14/2008	1st FS Corporation	Hendersonville	NC	Preferred Stock w/ Warrants	$16,369,000
11/14/2008	UCBH Holdings, Inc.	San Francisco	CA	Preferred Stock w/ Warrants	$298,737,000
11/14/2008	Northern Trust Corporation	Chicago	IL	Preferred Stock w/ Warrants	$1,576,000,000
11/14/2008	SunTrust Banks, Inc.	Atlanta	GA	Preferred Stock w/ Warrants	$3,500,000,000
11/14/2008	Broadway Financial Corporation	Los Angeles	CA	Preferred Stock	$9,000,000
11/14/2008	Washington Federal, Inc.	Seattle	WA	Preferred Stock w/ Warrants	$200,000,000
11/14/2008	BB&T Corp.	Winston-Salem	NC	Preferred Stock w/ Warrants	$3,133,640,000
11/14/2008	M&T Bank Corporation (Provident Bancshares Corp.)	Baltimore	MD	Preferred Stock w/ Warrants	$151,500,000
11/14/2008	Umpqua Holdings Corp.	Portland	OR	Preferred Stock w/ Warrants	$214,181,000
11/14/2008	Comerica Inc.	Dallas	TX	Preferred Stock w/ Warrants	$2,250,000,000
11/14/2008	Regions Financial Corporation	Birmingham	AL	Preferred Stock w/ Warrants	$3,500,000,000
11/14/2008	Capital One Financial Corporation	McLean	VA	Preferred Stock w/ Warrants	$3,555,199,000
11/14/2008	First Horizon National Corporation	Memphis	TN	Preferred Stock w/ Warrants	$866,540,000
11/14/2008	Huntington Bancshares	Columbus	OH	Preferred Stock w/ Warrants	$1,398,071,000
11/14/2008	KeyCorp	Cleveland	OH	Preferred Stock w/ Warrants	$2,500,000,000
11/14/2008	Valley National Bancorp	Wayne	NJ	Preferred Stock w/ Warrants	$300,000,000
11/14/2008	Zions Bancorporation	Salt Lake City	UT	Preferred Stock w/ Warrants	$1,400,000,000
11/14/2008	Marshall & Ilsley Corporation	Milwaukee	WI	Preferred Stock w/ Warrants	$1,715,000,000
11/14/2008	U.S. Bancorp	Minneapolis	MN	Preferred Stock w/ Warrants	$6,599,000,000
11/14/2008	TCF Financial Corporation	Wayzata	MN	Preferred Stock w/ Warrants	$361,172,000
11/21/2008	First Niagara Financial Group	Lockport	NY	Preferred Stock w/ Warrants	$184,011,000
11/21/2008	HF Financial Corp.	Sioux Falls	SD	Preferred Stock w/ Warrants	$25,000,000

Table 3.7 All banks that received TARP funds.—cont'd

TARP Purchase Date	Name of Participating Institution	Institution City	Institution State	TARP Investment Description	TARP Investment Amount
				All Other Participants (cont.)	
11/21/2008	Centerstate Banks of Florida Inc.	Davenport	FL	Preferred Stock w/ Warrants	$27,875,000
11/21/2008	City National Corporation	Beverly Hills	CA	Preferred Stock w/ Warrants	$400,000,000
11/21/2008	First Community Bankshares Inc.	Bluefield	VA	Preferred Stock w/ Warrants	$41,500,000
11/21/2008	Western Alliance Bancorporation	Las Vegas	NV	Preferred Stock w/ Warrants	$140,000,000
11/21/2008	Webster Financial Corporation	Waterbury	CT	Preferred Stock w/ Warrants	$400,000,000
11/21/2008	Pacific Capital Bancorp	Santa Barbara	CA	Common Stock w/ Warrants	$195,045,000
11/21/2008	Heritage Commerce Corp.	San Jose	CA	Preferred Stock w/ Warrants	$40,000,000
11/21/2008	Ameris Bancorp	Moultrie	GA	Preferred Stock w/ Warrants	$52,000,000
11/21/2008	Porter Bancorp Inc.	Louisville	KY	Preferred Stock w/ Warrants	$35,000,000
11/21/2008	Banner Corporation	Walla Walla	WA	Preferred Stock w/ Warrants	$124,000,000
11/21/2008	Cascade Financial Corporation	Everett	WA	Preferred Stock w/ Warrants	$38,970,000
11/21/2008	Columbia Banking System, Inc.	Tacoma	WA	Preferred Stock w/ Warrants	$76,898,000
11/21/2008	Heritage Financial Corporation	Olympia	WA	Preferred Stock w/ Warrants	$24,000,000
11/21/2008	First PacTrust Bancorp, Inc.	Chula Vista	CA	Preferred Stock w/ Warrants	$19,300,000
11/21/2008	Severn Bancorp, Inc.	Annapolis	MD	Preferred Stock w/ Warrants	$23,393,000
11/21/2008	Boston Private Financial Holdings, Inc.	Boston	MA	Preferred Stock w/ Warrants	$154,000,000
11/21/2008	Associated Banc-Corp	Green Bay	WI	Preferred Stock w/ Warrants	$525,000,000
11/21/2008	Trustmark Corporation	Jackson	MS	Preferred Stock w/ Warrants	$215,000,000
11/21/2008	First Community Corporation	Lexington	SC	Preferred Stock w/ Warrants	$11,350,000
11/21/2008	Taylor Capital Group	Rosemont	IL	Preferred Stock w/ Warrants	$104,823,000
11/21/2008	Nara Bancorp, Inc.	Los Angeles	CA	Preferred Stock w/ Warrants	$67,000,000
12/5/2008	Midwest Banc Holdings, Inc.	Melrose Park	IL	Mandatorily Convertible Preferred Stock w/ Warrants	$89,388,000
12/5/2008	MB Financial Inc.	Chicago	IL	Preferred Stock w/ Warrants	$196,000,000
12/5/2008	First Midwest Bancorp, Inc.	Itasca	IL	Preferred Stock w/ Warrants	$193,000,000
12/5/2008	United Community Banks, Inc.	Blairsville	GA	Preferred Stock w/ Warrants	$180,000,000
12/5/2008	WesBanco, Inc.	Wheeling	WV	Preferred Stock w/ Warrants	$75,000,000
12/5/2008	Encore Bancshares Inc.	Houston	TX	Preferred Stock w/ Warrants	$34,000,000
12/5/2008	Manhattan Bancorp	El Segundo	CA	Preferred Stock w/ Warrants	$1,700,000
12/5/2008	Iberiabank Corporation	Lafayette	LA	Preferred Stock w/ Warrants	$90,000,000
12/5/2008	Eagle Bancorp, Inc.	Bethesda	MD	Preferred Stock w/ Warrants	$38,235,000
12/5/2008	Sandy Spring Bancorp, Inc.	Olney	MD	Preferred Stock w/ Warrants	$83,094,000
12/5/2008	Coastal Banking Company, Inc.	Fernandina Beach	FL	Preferred Stock w/ Warrants	$9,950,000
12/5/2008	East West Bancorp	Pasadena	CA	Preferred Stock w/ Warrants	$306,546,000
12/5/2008	South Financial Group, Inc.	Greenville	SC	Preferred Stock w/ Warrants	$347,000,000
12/5/2008	Great Southern Bancorp	Springfield	MO	Preferred Stock w/ Warrants	$58,000,000
12/5/2008	Cathay General Bancorp	Los Angeles	CA	Preferred Stock w/ Warrants	$258,000,000
12/5/2008	Southern Community Financial Corp.	Winston-Salem	NC	Preferred Stock w/ Warrants	$42,750,000
12/5/2008	CVB Financial Corp	Ontario	CA	Preferred Stock w/ Warrants	$130,000,000
12/5/2008	First Defiance Financial Corp.	Defiance	OH	Preferred Stock w/ Warrants	$37,000,000
12/5/2008	First Financial Holdings Inc.	Charleston	SC	Preferred Stock w/ Warrants	$65,000,000
12/5/2008	Superior Bancorp Inc.	Birmingham	AL	Trust Preferred Securities w/ Warrants	$69,000,000
12/5/2008	Southwest Bancorp, Inc.	Stillwater	OK	Preferred Stock w/ Warrants	$70,000,000
12/5/2008	Popular, Inc.	San Juan	PR	Trust Preferred Securities w/ Warrants	$935,000,000
12/5/2008	Blue Valley Ban Corp	Overland Park	KS	Preferred Stock w/ Warrants	$21,750,000

Continued

Table 3.7 All banks that received TARP funds.—cont'd

TARP Purchase Date	Name of Participating Institution	Institution City	Institution State	TARP Investment Description	TARP Investment Amount
		All Other Participants (cont.)			
12/5/2008	Central Federal Corporation	Fairlawn	OH	Preferred Stock w/ Warrants	$7,225,000
12/5/2008	Bank of Marin Bancorp	Novato	CA	Preferred Stock w/ Warrants	$28,000,000
12/5/2008	BNC Bancorp	Thomasville	NC	Preferred Stock w/ Warrants	$31,260,000
12/5/2008	Central Bancorp, Inc.	Somerville	MA	Preferred Stock w/ Warrants	$10,000,000
12/5/2008	Southern Missouri Bancorp, Inc.	Poplar Bluff	MO	Preferred Stock w/ Warrants	$9,550,000
12/5/2008	State Bancorp, Inc.	Jericho	NY	Preferred Stock w/ Warrants	$36,842,000
12/5/2008	TIB Financial Corp	Naples	FL	Preferred Stock w/ Warrants	$37,000,000
12/5/2008	Unity Bancorp, Inc.	Clinton	NJ	Preferred Stock w/ Warrants	$20,649,000
12/5/2008	Old Line Bancshares, Inc.	Bowie	MD	Preferred Stock w/ Warrants	$7,000,000
12/5/2008	FPB Bancorp, Inc.	Port S. Lucie	FL	Preferred Stock w/ Warrants	$5,800,000
12/5/2008	Sterling Financial Corporation	Spokane	WA	Common Stock w/ Warrants	$303,000,000
12/5/2008	Oak Valley Bancorp	Oakdale	CA	Preferred Stock w/ Warrants	$13,500,000
12/12/2008	Old National Bancorp	Evansville	IN	Preferred Stock w/ Warrants	$100,000,000
12/12/2008	Capital Bank Corporation	Raleigh	NC	Preferred Stock w/ Warrants	$41,279,000
12/12/2008	Pacific International Bancorp	Seattle	WA	Preferred Stock w/ Warrants	$6,500,000
12/12/2008	SVB Financial Group	Santa Clara	CA	Preferred Stock w/ Warrants	$235,000,000
12/12/2008	LNB Bancorp Inc.	Lorain	OH	Preferred Stock w/ Warrants	$25,223,000
12/12/2008	Wilmington Trust Corporation	Wilmington	DE	Preferred Stock w/ Warrants	$330,000,000
12/12/2008	Susquehanna Bancshares, Inc	Lititz	PA	Preferred Stock w/ Warrants	$300,000,000
12/12/2008	Signature Bank	New York	NY	Preferred Stock w/ Warrants	$120,000,000
12/12/2008	HopFed Bancorp	Hopkinsville	KY	Preferred Stock w/ Warrants	$18,400,000
12/12/2008	Citizens Republic Bancorp, Inc.	Flint	MI	Preferred Stock w/ Warrants	$300,000,000
12/12/2008	Indiana Community Bancorp	Columbus	IN	Preferred Stock w/ Warrants	$21,500,000
12/12/2008	Bank of the Ozarks, Inc.	Little Rock	AR	Preferred Stock w/ Warrants	$75,000,000
12/12/2008	Center Financial Corporation	Los Angeles	CA	Preferred Stock w/ Warrants	$55,000,000
12/12/2008	NewBridge Bancorp	Greensboro	NC	Preferred Stock w/ Warrants	$52,372,000
12/12/2008	Sterling Bancshares, Inc.	Houston	TX	Preferred Stock w/ Warrants	$125,198,000
12/12/2008	The Bancorp, Inc.	Wilmington	DE	Preferred Stock w/ Warrants	$45,220,000
12/12/2008	TowneBank	Portsmouth	VA	Preferred Stock w/ Warrants	$76,458,000
12/12/2008	Wilshire Bancorp, Inc.	Los Angeles	CA	Preferred Stock w/ Warrants	$62,158,000
12/12/2008	Valley Financial Corporation	Roanoke	VA	Preferred Stock w/ Warrants	$16,019,000
12/12/2008	Independent Bank Corporation	Ionia	MI	Mandatorily Convertible Preferred Stock w/ Warrants	$74,426,000
12/12/2008	Pinnacle Financial Partners, Inc.	Nashville	TN	Preferred Stock w/ Warrants	$95,000,000
12/12/2008	First Litchfield Financial Corporation	Litchfield	CT	Preferred Stock w/ Warrants	$10,000,000
12/12/2008	National Penn Bancshares, Inc.	Boyertown	PA	Preferred Stock w/ Warrants	$150,000,000
12/12/2008	Northeast Bancorp	Lewiston	ME	Preferred Stock w/ Warrants	$4,227,000
12/12/2008	Citizens South Banking Corporation	Gastonia	NC	Preferred Stock w/ Warrants	$20,500,000
12/12/2008	Virginia Commerce Bancorp	Arlington	VA	Preferred Stock w/ Warrants	$71,000,000
12/12/2008	Fidelity Bancorp, Inc.	Pittsburgh	PA	Preferred Stock w/ Warrants	$7,000,000
12/12/2008	LSB Corporation	North Andover	MA	Preferred Stock w/ Warrants	$15,000,000
12/19/2008	Intermountain Community Bancorp	Sandpoint	ID	Preferred Stock w/ Warrants	$27,000,000
12/19/2008	Community West Bancshares	Goleta	CA	Preferred Stock w/ Warrants	$15,600,000
12/19/2008	Synovus Financial Corp.	Columbus	GA	Preferred Stock w/ Warrants	$967,870,000
12/19/2008	Tennessee Commerce Bancorp, Inc.	Franklin	TN	Preferred Stock w/ Warrants	$30,000,000

Table 3.7   All banks that received TARP funds.—cont'd

TARP Purchase Date	Name of Participating Institution	Institution City	Institution State	TARP Investment Description	TARP Investment Amount
		All Other Participants (cont.)			
12/19/2008	Community Bankers Trust Corporation	Glen Allen	VA	Preferred Stock w/ Warrants	$17,680,000
12/19/2008	BancTrust Financial Group, Inc.	Mobile	AL	Preferred Stock w/ Warrants	$50,000,000
12/19/2008	Enterprise Financial Services Corp.	St. Louis	MO	Preferred Stock w/ Warrants	$35,000,000
12/19/2008	Mid Penn Bancorp, Inc.	Millersburg	PA	Preferred Stock w/ Warrants	$10,000,000
12/19/2008	Summit State Bank	Santa Rosa	CA	Preferred Stock w/ Warrants	$8,500,000
12/19/2008	VIST Financial Corp.	Wyomissing	PA	Preferred Stock w/ Warrants	$25,000,000
12/19/2008	Wainwright Bank & Trust Company	Boston	MA	Preferred Stock w/ Warrants	$22,000,000
12/19/2008	Whitney Holding Corporation	New Orleans	LA	Preferred Stock w/ Warrants	$300,000,000
12/19/2008	The Connecticut Bank and Trust Company	Hartford	CT	Preferred Stock w/ Warrants	$5,448,000
12/19/2008	CoBiz Financial Inc.	Denver	CO	Preferred Stock w/ Warrants	$64,450,000
12/19/2008	Santa Lucia Bancorp	Atascadero	CA	Preferred Stock w/ Warrants	$4,000,000
12/19/2008	Seacoast Banking Corporation of Florida	Stuart	FL	Preferred Stock w/ Warrants	$50,000,000
12/19/2008	Horizon Bancorp	Michigan City	IN	Preferred Stock w/ Warrants	$25,000,000
12/19/2008	Fidelity Southern Corporation	Atlanta	GA	Preferred Stock w/ Warrants	$48,200,000
12/19/2008	Community Financial Corporation	Staunton	VA	Preferred Stock w/ Warrants	$12,643,000
12/19/2008	Berkshire Hills Bancorp, Inc.	Pittsfield	MA	Preferred Stock w/ Warrants	$40,000,000
12/19/2008	First California Financial Group, Inc	Westlake Village	CA	Preferred Stock w/ Warrants	$25,000,000
12/19/2008	AmeriServ Financial, Inc	Johnstown	PA	Preferred Stock w/ Warrants	$21,000,000
12/19/2008	Security Federal Corporation	Aiken	SC	Preferred Stock w/ Warrants	$18,000,000
12/19/2008	Wintrust Financial Corporation	Lake Forest	IL	Preferred Stock w/ Warrants	$250,000,000
12/19/2008	Flushing Financial Corporation	Lake Success	NY	Preferred Stock w/ Warrants	$70,000,000
12/19/2008	Monarch Financial Holdings, Inc.	Chesapeake	VA	Preferred Stock w/ Warrants	$14,700,000
12/19/2008	StellarOne Corporation	Charlottesville	VA	Preferred Stock w/ Warrants	$30,000,000
12/19/2008	Union First Market Bankshares Corporation	Bowling Green	VA	Preferred Stock w/ Warrants	$59,000,000
12/19/2008	Tidelands Bancshares, Inc	Mt. Pleasant	SC	Preferred Stock w/ Warrants	$14,448,000
12/19/2008	Bancorp Rhode Island, Inc.	Providence	RI	Preferred Stock w/ Warrants	$30,000,000
12/19/2008	Hewborn Bancshares, Inc.	Lee's Summit	MO	Preferred Stock w/ Warrants	$30,255,000
12/19/2008	The Elmira Savings Bank, FSB	Elmira	NY	Preferred Stock w/ Warrants	$9,090,000
12/19/2008	Alliance Financial Corporation	Syracuse	NY	Preferred Stock w/ Warrants	$26,918,000
12/19/2008	Heartland Financial USA, Inc.	Dubuque	IA	Preferred Stock w/ Warrants	$81,698,000
12/19/2008	Citizens First Corporation	Bowling Green	KY	Preferred Stock w/ Warrants	$8,779,000
12/19/2008	FFW Corporation	Wabash	IN	Preferred Stock w/ Exercised Warrants	$7,289,000
12/19/2008	Plains Capital Corporation	Dallas	TX	Preferred Stock w/ Exercised Warrants	$87,631,000
12/19/2008	Tri-County Financial Corporation	Waldorf	MD	Preferred Stock w/ Exercised Warrants	$15,540,000
12/19/2008	OneUnited Bank	Boston	MA	Preferred Stock	$12,063,000
12/19/2008	Patriot Bancshares, Inc.	Houston	TX	Preferred Stock w/ Exercised Warrants	$26,038,000
12/19/2008	Pacific City Financial Corporation	Los Angeles	CA	Preferred Stock w/ Exercised Warrants	$16,200,000
12/19/2008	Marquette National Corporation	Chicago	IL	Preferred Stock w/ Exercised Warrants	$35,500,000
12/19/2008	Exchange Bank	Santa Rosa	CA	Preferred Stock w/ Exercised Warrants	$43,000,000
12/19/2008	Monadnock Bancorp, Inc.	Peterborough	NH	Preferred Stock w/ Exercised Warrants	$1,834,000
12/19/2008	Bridgeview Bancorp, Inc.	Bridgeview	IL	Preferred Stock w/ Exercised Warrants	$38,000,000
12/19/2008	Fidelity Financial Corporation	Wichita	KS	Preferred Stock w/ Exercised Warrants	$36,282,000
12/19/2008	Patapsco Bancorp, Inc.	Dundalk	MD	Preferred Stock w/ Exercised Warrants	$6,000,000
12/19/2008	NCAL Bancorp	Los Angeles	CA	Preferred Stock w/ Exercised Warrants	$10,000,000

Continued

Table 3.7 All banks that received TARP funds.—cont'd

TARP Purchase Date	Name of Participating Institution	Institution City	Institution State	TARP Investment Description	TARP Investment Amount
			All Other Participants (cont.)		
12/19/2008	FCB Bancorp, Inc.	Louisville	KY	Preferred Stock w/ Exercised Warrants	$9,294,000
12/23/2008	First Financial Bancorp	Cincinnati	OH	Preferred Stock w/ Warrants	$80,000,000
12/23/2008	Bridge Capital Holdings	San Jose	CA	Preferred Stock w/ Warrants	$23,864,000
12/23/2008	International Bancshares Corporation	Laredo	TX	Preferred Stock w/ Warrants	$216,000,000
12/23/2008	First Sound Bank	Seattle	WA	Preferred Stock w/ Warrants	$7,400,000
12/23/2008	M&T Bank Corporation	Buffalo	NY	Preferred Stock w/ Warrants	$600,000,000
12/23/2008	Emclaire Financial Corp.	Emlenton	PA	Preferred Stock w/ Warrants	$7,500,000
12/23/2008	Park National Corporation	Newark	OH	Preferred Stock w/ Warrants	$100,000,000
12/23/2008	Green Bankshares, Inc.	Greeneville	TN	Preferred Stock w/ Warrants	$72,278,000
12/23/2008	Cecil Bancorp, Inc.	Elkton	MD	Preferred Stock w/ Warrants	$11,560,000
12/23/2008	Financial Institutions, Inc.	Warsaw	NY	Preferred Stock w/ Warrants	$37,515,000
12/23/2008	Fulton Financial Corporation	Lancaster	PA	Preferred Stock w/ Warrants	$376,500,000
12/23/2008	United Bancorporation of Alabama, Inc.	Atmore	AL	Preferred Stock w/ Warrants	$10,300,000
12/23/2008	MutualFirst Financial, Inc.	Muncie	IN	Preferred Stock w/ Warrants	$32,382,000
12/23/2008	BCSB Bancorp, Inc.	Baltimore	MD	Preferred Stock w/ Warrants	$10,800,000
12/23/2008	HMN Financial, Inc.	Rochester	MN	Preferred Stock w/ Warrants	$26,000,000
12/23/2008	First Community Bank Corporation of America	Pinellas Park	FL	Preferred Stock w/ Warrants	$10,685,000
12/23/2008	Sterling Bancorp	New York	NY	Preferred Stock w/ Warrants	$42,000,000
12/23/2008	Intervest Bancshares Corporation	New York	NY	Preferred Stock w/ Warrants	$25,000,000
12/23/2008	Peoples Bancorp of North Carolina, Inc.	Newton	NC	Preferred Stock w/ Warrants	$25,054,000
12/23/2008	Parkvale Financial Corporation	Monroeville	PA	Preferred Stock w/ Warrants	$31,762,000
12/23/2008	Timberland Bancorp, Inc.	Hoquiam	WA	Preferred Stock w/ Warrants	$16,641,000
12/23/2008	1st Constitution Bancorp	Cranbury	NJ	Preferred Stock w/ Warrants	$12,000,000
12/23/2008	Central Jersey Bancorp	Oakhurst	NJ	Preferred Stock w/ Warrants	$11,300,000
12/23/2008	Western Illinois Bancshares Inc.	Monmouth	IL	Preferred Stock w/ Exercised Warrants	$6,855,000
12/23/2008	Saigon National Bank	Westminster	CA	Preferred Stock w/ Exercised Warrants	$1,549,000
12/23/2008	Capital Pacific Bancorp	Portland	OR	Preferred Stock w/ Exercised Warrants	$4,000,000
12/23/2008	Uwharrie Capital Corp	Albemarle	NC	Preferred Stock w/ Exercised Warrants	$10,000,000
12/23/2008	Mission Valley Bancorp	Sun Valley	CA	Preferred Stock	$5,500,000
12/23/2008	The Little Bank, Incorporated	Kinston	NC	Preferred Stock w/ Exercised Warrants	$7,500,000
12/23/2008	Pacific Commerce Bank	Los Angeles	CA	Preferred Stock w/ Exercised Warrants	$4,060,000
12/23/2008	Citizens Community Bank	South Hill	VA	Preferred Stock w/ Exercised Warrants	$3,000,000
12/23/2008	Seacoast Commerce Bank	Chula Vista	CA	Preferred Stock w/ Exercised Warrants	$1,800,000
12/23/2008	TCNB Financial Corp.	Dayton	OH	Preferred Stock w/ Exercised Warrants	$2,000,000
12/23/2008	Leader Bancorp, Inc.	Arlington	MA	Preferred Stock w/ Exercised Warrants	$5,830,000
12/23/2008	Nicolet Bankshares, Inc.	Green Bay	WI	Preferred Stock w/ Exercised Warrants	$14,964,000
12/23/2008	Magna Bank	Memphis	TN	Preferred Stock w/ Exercised Warrants	$13,795,000
12/23/2008	Western Community Bancshares, Inc.	Palm Desert	CA	Preferred Stock w/ Exercised Warrants	$7,290,000
12/23/2008	Community Investors Bancorp, Inc.	Bucyrus	OH	Preferred Stock w/ Exercised Warrants	$2,600,000
12/23/2008	Capital Bancorp, Inc.	Rockville	MD	Preferred Stock w/ Exercised Warrants	$4,700,000
12/23/2008	Cache Valley Banking Company	Logan	UT	Preferred Stock w/ Exercised Warrants	$4,767,000
12/23/2008	Citizens Bancorp	Nevada City	CA	Preferred Stock w/ Exercised Warrants	$10,400,000
12/23/2008	Tennessee Valley Financial Holdings, Inc.	Oak Ridge	TN	Preferred Stock w/ Exercised Warrants	$3,000,000
12/23/2008	Pacific Coast Bankers' Bancshares	San Francisco	CA	Preferred Stock w/ Exercised Warrants	$11,600,000

Table 3.7 All banks that received TARP funds.—cont'd

TARP Purchase Date	Name of Participating Institution	Institution City	Institution State	TARP Investment Description	TARP Investment Amount
		All Other Participants (cont.)			
12/31/2008	SunTrust Banks, Inc.	Atlanta	GA	Preferred Stock w/ Warrants	$1,350,000,000
12/31/2008	The PNC Financial Services Group Inc.	Pittsburgh	PA	Preferred Stock w/ Warrants	$7,579,200,000
12/31/2008	Fifth Third Bancorp	Cincinnati	OH	Preferred Stock w/ Warrants	$3,408,000,000
12/31/2008	Hampton Roads Bankshares, Inc.	Norfolk	VA	Common Stock w/ Warrants	$80,347,000
12/31/2008	CIT Group Inc.	New York	NY	Contingent Value Rights	$2,330,000,000
12/31/2008	West Bancorporation, Inc.	West Des Moines	IA	Preferred Stock w/ Warrants	$36,000,000
12/31/2008	First Banks, Inc.	Clayton	MO	Preferred Stock w/ Exercised Warrants	$295,400,000
1/9/2009	FirstMerit Corporation	Akron	OH	Preferred Stock w/ Warrants	$125,000,000
1/9/2009	Farmers Capital Bank Corporation	Frankfort	KY	Preferred Stock w/ Warrants	$30,000,000
1/9/2009	Peapack–Gladstone Financial Corporation	Gladstone	NJ	Preferred Stock w/ Warrants	$28,685,000
1/9/2009	Commerce National Bank	Newport Beach	CA	Preferred Stock w/ Warrants	$5,000,000
1/9/2009	The First Bancorp, Inc.	Damariscotta	ME	Preferred Stock w/ Warrants	$25,000,000
1/9/2009	Sun Bancorp, Inc.	Vineland	NJ	Preferred Stock w/ Warrants	$89,310,000
1/9/2009	Crescent Financial Corporation	Cary	NC	Preferred Stock w/ Warrants	$24,900,000
1/9/2009	American Express Company	New York	NY	Preferred Stock w/ Warrants	$3,388,890,000
1/9/2009	Central Pacific Financial Corp.	Honolulu	HI	Common Stock w/ Warrants	$135,000,000
1/9/2009	Centrue Financial Corporation	St. Louis	MO	Preferred Stock w/ Warrants	$32,668,000
1/9/2009	Eastern Virginia Bankshares, Inc.	Tappahannock	VA	Preferred Stock w/ Warrants	$24,000,000
1/9/2009	Colony Bankcorp, Inc.	Fitzgerald	GA	Preferred Stock w/ Warrants	$28,000,000
1/9/2009	Independent Bank Corp.	Rockland	MA	Preferred Stock w/ Warrants	$78,158,000
1/9/2009	Cadence Financial Corporation	Starkville	MS	Preferred Stock w/ Warrants	$44,000,000
1/9/2009	LCNB Corp.	Lebanon	OH	Preferred Stock w/ Warrants	$13,400,000
1/9/2009	Center Bancorp, Inc.	Union	NJ	Preferred Stock w/ Warrants	$10,000,000
1/9/2009	F.N.B. Corporation	Hermitage	PA	Preferred Stock w/ Warrants	$100,000,000
1/9/2009	C&F Financial Corporation	West Point	VA	Preferred Stock w/ Warrants	$20,000,000
1/9/2009	North Central Bancshares, Inc.	Fort Dodge	IA	Preferred Stock w/ Warrants	$10,200,000
1/9/2009	Carolina Bank Holdings, Inc.	Greensboro	NC	Preferred Stock w/ Warrants	$16,000,000
1/9/2009	First Bancorp	Troy	NC	Preferred Stock w/ Warrants	$65,000,000
1/9/2009	First Financial Service Corporation	Elizabethtown	KY	Preferred Stock w/ Warrants	$20,000,000
1/9/2009	Codorus Valley Bancorp, Inc.	York	PA	Preferred Stock w/ Warrants	$16,500,000
1/9/2009	MidSouth Bancorp, Inc.	Lafayette	LA	Preferred Stock w/ Warrants	$20,000,000
1/9/2009	First Security Group, Inc.	Chattanooga	TN	Preferred Stock w/ Warrants	$33,000,000
1/9/2009	Shore Bancshares, Inc.	Easton	MD	Preferred Stock w/ Warrants	$25,000,000
1/9/2009	The Queensborough Company	Louisville	GA	Preferred Stock w/ Exercised Warrants	$12,000,000
1/9/2009	American State Bancshares, Inc.	Great Bend	KS	Preferred Stock w/ Exercised Warrants	$6,000,000
1/9/2009	Security California Bancorp	Riverside	CA	Preferred Stock w/ Exercised Warrants	$6,815,000
1/9/2009	Security Business Bancorp	San Diego	CA	Preferred Stock w/ Exercised Warrants	$5,803,000
1/9/2009	Sound Banking Company	Morehead City	NC	Preferred Stock w/ Exercised Warrants	$3,070,000
1/9/2009	Mission Community Bancorp	San Luis Obispo	CA	Preferred Stock	$5,116,000
1/9/2009	Redwood Financial Inc.	Redwood Falls	MN	Preferred Stock w/ Exercised Warrants	$2,995,000
1/9/2009	Surrey Bancorp	Mount Airy	NC	Preferred Stock w/ Exercised Warrants	$2,000,000
1/9/2009	Independence Bank	East Greenwich	RI	Preferred Stock w/ Exercised Warrants	$1,065,000
1/9/2009	Valley Community Bank	Pleasanton	CA	Preferred Stock w/ Exercised Warrants	$5,500,000
1/9/2009	Rising Sun Bancorp	Rising Sun	MD	Preferred Stock w/ Exercised Warrants	$5,983,000

Continued

I. Introductory materials

Table 3.7 All banks that received TARP funds.—cont'd

TARP Purchase Date	Name of Participating Institution	Institution City	Institution State	TARP Investment Description	TARP Investment Amount
		All Other Participants (cont.)			
1/9/2009	Community Trust Financial Corporation	Ruston	LA	Preferred Stock w/ Exercised Warrants	$24,000,000
1/9/2009	GrandSouth Bancorporation	Greenville	SC	Preferred Stock w/ Exercised Warrants	$9,000,000
1/9/2009	Texas National Bancorporation	Jacksonville	TX	Preferred Stock w/ Exercised Warrants	$3,981,000
1/9/2009	Congaree Bancshares, Inc.	Cayce	SC	Preferred Stock w/ Exercised Warrants	$3,285,000
1/9/2009	New York Private Bank & Trust Corporation	New York	NY	Preferred Stock w/ Exercised Warrants	$267,274,000
1/16/2009	Home Bancshares, Inc.	Conway	AR	Preferred Stock w/ Warrants	$50,000,000
1/16/2009	Washington Banking Company	Oak Harbor	WA	Preferred Stock w/ Warrants	$26,380,000
1/16/2009	New Hampshire Thrift Bancshares, Inc.	Newport	NH	Preferred Stock w/ Warrants	$10,000,000
1/16/2009	Bar Harbor Bankshares	Bar Harbor	ME	Preferred Stock w/ Warrants	$18,751,000
1/16/2009	Somerset Hills Bancorp	Bernardsville	NJ	Preferred Stock w/ Warrants	$7,414,000
1/16/2009	SCBT Financial Corporation	Columbia	SC	Preferred Stock w/ Warrants	$64,779,000
1/16/2009	S&T Bancorp	Indiana	PA	Preferred Stock w/ Warrants	$108,676,000
1/16/2009	ECB Bancorp, Inc.	Engelhard	NC	Preferred Stock w/ Warrants	$17,949,000
1/16/2009	First BanCorp	San Juan	PR	Mandatorily Convertible Preferred Stock w/ Warrants	$424,174,000
1/16/2009	Texas Capital Bancshares, Inc.	Dallas	TX	Preferred Stock w/ Warrants	$75,000,000
1/16/2009	Yadkin Valley Financial Corporation	Elkin	NC	Preferred Stock w/ Warrants	$36,000,000
1/16/2009	Carver Bancorp, Inc	New York	NY	Preferred Stock	$18,980,000
1/16/2009	Citizens & Northern Corporation	Wellsboro	PA	Preferred Stock w/ Warrants	$26,440,000
1/16/2009	MainSource Financial Group, Inc.	Greensburg	IN	Preferred Stock w/ Warrants	$57,000,000
1/16/2009	MetroCorp Bancshares, Inc.	Houston	TX	Preferred Stock w/ Warrants	$45,000,000
1/16/2009	United Bancorp, Inc.	Tecumseh	MI	Preferred Stock w/ Warrants	$20,600,000
1/16/2009	Old Second Bancorp, Inc.	Aurora	IL	Preferred Stock w/ Warrants	$73,000,000
1/16/2009	Pulaski Financial Corp	Creve Coeur	MO	Preferred Stock w/ Warrants	$32,538,000
1/16/2009	OceanFirst Financial Corp.	Toms River	NJ	Preferred Stock w/ Warrants	$38,263,000
1/16/2009	Community 1st Bank	Roseville	CA	Preferred Stock w/ Exercised Warrants	$2,550,000
1/16/2009	TCB Holding Company	The Woodlands	TX	Preferred Stock w/ Exercised Warrants	$11,730,000
1/16/2009	Centra Financial Holdings, Inc.	Morgantown	WV	Preferred Stock w/ Exercised Warrants	$15,000,000
1/16/2009	First Bankers Trustshares, Inc.	Quincy	IL	Preferred Stock w/ Exercised Warrants	$10,000,000
1/16/2009	Pacific Coast National Bancorp	San Clemente	CA	Preferred Stock w/ Exercised Warrants	$4,120,000
1/16/2009	Community Bank of the Bay	Oakland	CA	Preferred Stock	$1,747,000
1/16/2009	Redwood Capital Bancorp	Eureka	CA	Preferred Stock w/ Exercised Warrants	$3,800,000
1/16/2009	Syringa Bancorp	Boise	ID	Preferred Stock w/ Exercised Warrants	$8,000,000
1/16/2009	Idaho Bancorp	Boise	ID	Preferred Stock w/ Exercised Warrants	$6,900,000
1/16/2009	Puget Sound Bank	Bellevue	WA	Preferred Stock w/ Exercised Warrants	$4,500,000
1/16/2009	United Financial Banking Companies, Inc.	Vienna	VA	Preferred Stock w/ Exercised Warrants	$5,658,000
1/16/2009	Dickinson Financial Corporation II	Kansas City	MO	Preferred Stock w/ Exercised Warrants	$146,053,000
1/16/2009	The Baraboo Bancorporation	Baraboo	WI	Preferred Stock w/ Exercised Warrants	$20,749,000
1/16/2009	Bank of Commerce	Charlotte	NC	Preferred Stock w/ Exercised Warrants	$3,000,000
1/16/2009	State Bankshares, Inc.	Fargo	ND	Preferred Stock w/ Exercised Warrants	$50,000,000
1/16/2009	BNCCORP, Inc.	Bismarck	ND	Preferred Stock w/ Exercised Warrants	$20,093,000
1/16/2009	First Manitowoc Bancorp, Inc.	Manitowoc	WI	Preferred Stock w/ Exercised Warrants	$12,000,000
1/16/2009	Southern Bancorp, Inc.	Arkadelphia	AR	Preferred Stock	$11,000,000
1/16/2009	Morrill Bancshares, Inc.	Merriam	KS	Preferred Stock w/ Exercised Warrants	$13,000,000
1/16/2009	Treaty Oak Bancorp, Inc.	Austin	TX	Warrants	$3,268,000

Table 3.7 All banks that received TARP funds.—cont'd

TARP Purchase Date	Name of Participating Institution	Institution City	Institution State	TARP Investment Description	TARP Investment Amount
			All Other Participants (cont.)		
1/23/2009	1st Source Corporation	South Bend	IN	Preferred Stock w/ Warrants	$111,000,000
1/23/2009	Princeton National Bancorp, Inc.	Princeton	IL	Preferred Stock w/ Warrants	$25,083,000
1/23/2009	AB&T Financial Corporation	Gastonia	NC	Preferred Stock w/ Warrants	$3,500,000
1/23/2009	First Citizens Banc Corp	Sandusky	OH	Preferred Stock w/ Warrants	$23,184,000
1/23/2009	WSFS Financial Corporation	Wilmington	DE	Preferred Stock w/ Warrants	$52,625,000
1/23/2009	Commonwealth Business Bank	Los Angeles	CA	Preferred Stock w/ Exercised Warrants	$7,701,000
1/23/2009	Three Shores Bancorporation, Inc.	Orlando	FL	Preferred Stock w/ Exercised Warrants	$5,677,000
1/23/2009	CalWest Bancorp	Rancho Santa Margarita	CA	Preferred Stock w/ Exercised Warrants	$4,656,000
1/23/2009	Fresno First Bank	Fresno	CA	Preferred Stock w/ Exercised Warrants	$1,968,000
1/23/2009	First ULB Corp.	Oakland	CA	Preferred Stock w/ Exercised Warrants	$4,900,000
1/23/2009	Alarion Financial Services, Inc.	Ocala	FL	Preferred Stock w/ Exercised Warrants	$6,514,000
1/23/2009	Midland States Bancorp, Inc.	Effingham	IL	Preferred Stock w/ Exercised Warrants	$10,189,000
1/23/2009	Moscow Bancshares, Inc.	Moscow	TN	Preferred Stock w/ Exercised Warrants	$6,216,000
1/23/2009	Farmers Bank	Windsor	VA	Preferred Stock w/ Exercised Warrants	$8,752,000
1/23/2009	California Oaks State Bank	Thousand Oaks	CA	Preferred Stock w/ Exercised Warrants	$3,300,000
1/23/2009	Pierce County Bancorp	Tacoma	WA	Preferred Stock w/ Exercised Warrants	$6,800,000
1/23/2009	Calvert Financial Corporation	Ashland	MO	Preferred Stock w/ Exercised Warrants	$1,037,000
1/23/2009	Liberty Bancshares, Inc.	Jonesboro	AR	Preferred Stock w/ Exercised Warrants	$57,500,000
1/23/2009	Crosstown Holding Company	Blaine	MN	Preferred Stock w/ Exercised Warrants	$10,650,000
1/23/2009	BancFirst Capital Corporation	Macon	MS	Preferred Stock w/ Exercised Warrants	$15,500,000
1/23/2009	Southern Illinois Bancorp, Inc.	Carmi	IL	Preferred Stock w/ Exercised Warrants	$5,000,000
1/23/2009	FPB Financial Corp.	Hammond	LA	Preferred Stock w/ Exercised Warrants	$3,240,000
1/23/2009	Stonebridge Financial Corp.	West Chester	PA	Preferred Stock w/ Exercised Warrants	$10,973,000
1/30/2009	Peoples Bancorp Inc.	Marietta	OH	Preferred Stock w/ Warrants	$39,000,000
1/30/2009	Anchor BanCorp Wisconsin Inc.	Madison	WI	Preferred Stock w/ Warrants	$110,000,000
1/30/2009	Parke Bancorp, Inc.	Sewell	NJ	Preferred Stock w/ Warrants	$16,288,000
1/30/2009	Central Virginia Bankshares, Inc.	Powhatan	VA	Preferred Stock w/ Warrants	$11,385,000
1/30/2009	Flagstar Bancorp, Inc.	Troy	MI	Preferred Stock w/ Warrants	$266,657,000
1/30/2009	Middleburg Financial Corporation	Middleburg	VA	Preferred Stock w/ Warrants	$22,000,000
1/30/2009	Peninsula Bank Holding Co.	Palo Alto	CA	Preferred Stock w/ Warrants	$6,000,000
1/30/2009	PrivateBancorp, Inc.	Chicago	IL	Preferred Stock w/ Warrants	$243,815,000
1/30/2009	Central Valley Community Bancorp	Fresno	CA	Preferred Stock w/ Warrants	$7,000,000
1/30/2009	Plumas Bancorp	Quincy	CA	Preferred Stock w/ Warrants	$11,949,000
1/30/2009	Stewardship Financial Corporation	Midland Park	NJ	Preferred Stock w/ Warrants	$10,000,000
1/30/2009	Oak Ridge Financial Services, Inc.	Oak Ridge	NC	Preferred Stock w/ Warrants	$7,700,000
1/30/2009	First United Corporation	Oakland	MD	Preferred Stock w/ Warrants	$30,000,000
1/30/2009	Community Partners Bancorp	Middletown	NJ	Preferred Stock w/ Warrants	$9,000,000
1/30/2009	Guaranty Federal Bancshares, Inc.	Springfield	MO	Preferred Stock w/ Warrants	$17,000,000
1/30/2009	Annapolis Bancorp, Inc.	Annapolis	MD	Preferred Stock w/ Warrants	$8,152,000
1/30/2009	DNB Financial Corporation	Downingtown	PA	Preferred Stock w/ Warrants	$11,750,000
1/30/2009	Firstbank Corporation	Alma	MI	Preferred Stock w/ Warrants	$33,000,000
1/30/2009	Valley Commerce Bancorp	Visalia	CA	Preferred Stock w/ Exercised Warrants	$7,700,000
1/30/2009	Greer Bancshares Incorporated	Greer	SC	Preferred Stock w/ Exercised Warrants	$9,993,000
1/30/2009	Ojai Community Bank	Ojai	CA	Preferred Stock w/ Exercised Warrants	$2,080,000

Continued

I. Introductory materials

Table 3.7 All banks that received TARP funds.—cont'd

TARP Purchase Date	Name of Participating Institution	Institution City	Institution State	TARP Investment Description	TARP Investment Amount
		All Other Participants (cont.)			
1/30/2009	Adbanc, Inc	Ogallala	NE	Preferred Stock w/ Exercised Warrants	$12,720,000
1/30/2009	Beach Business Bank	Manhattan Beach	CA	Preferred Stock w/ Exercised Warrants	$6,000,000
1/30/2009	Legacy Bancorp, Inc.	Milwaukee	WI	Preferred Stock	$5,498,000
1/30/2009	First Southern Bancorp, Inc.	Boca Raton	FL	Preferred Stock w/ Exercised Warrants	$10,900,000
1/30/2009	Country Bank Shares, Inc.	Milford	NE	Preferred Stock w/ Exercised Warrants	$7,525,000
1/30/2009	Katahdin Bankshares Corp.	Houlton	ME	Preferred Stock w/ Exercised Warrants	$10,449,000
1/30/2009	Rogers Bancshares, Inc.	Little Rock	AR	Preferred Stock w/ Exercised Warrants	$25,000,000
1/30/2009	UBT Bancshares, Inc.	Marysville	KS	Preferred Stock w/ Exercised Warrants	$8,950,000
1/30/2009	Bankers' Bank of the West Bancorp, Inc.	Denver	CO	Preferred Stock w/ Exercised Warrants	$12,639,000
1/30/2009	W.T.B. Financial Corporation	Spokane	WA	Preferred Stock w/ Exercised Warrants	$110,000,000
1/30/2009	AMB Financial Corp.	Munster	IN	Preferred Stock w/ Exercised Warrants	$3,674,000
1/30/2009	Goldwater Bank, N.A.	Scottsdale	AZ	Preferred Stock w/ Exercised Warrants	$2,568,000
1/30/2009	Equity Bancshares, Inc.	Wichita	KS	Preferred Stock w/ Exercised Warrants	$8,750,000
1/30/2009	WashingtonFirst Bankshares, Inc.	Reston	VA	Preferred Stock w/ Exercised Warrants	$6,633,000
1/30/2009	Central Bancshares, Inc.	Houston	TX	Preferred Stock w/ Exercised Warrants	$5,800,000
1/30/2009	Hilltop Community Bancorp, Inc.	Summit	NJ	Preferred Stock w/ Exercised Warrants	$4,000,000
1/30/2009	Northway Financial, Inc.	Berlin	NH	Preferred Stock w/ Exercised Warrants	$10,000,000
1/30/2009	Monument Bank	Bethesda	MD	Preferred Stock w/ Exercised Warrants	$4,734,000
1/30/2009	Metro City Bank	Doraville	GA	Preferred Stock w/ Exercised Warrants	$7,700,000
1/30/2009	F & M Bancshares, Inc.	Trezevant	TN	Preferred Stock w/ Exercised Warrants	$4,609,000
1/30/2009	First Resource Bank	Exton	PA	Preferred Stock w/ Exercised Warrants	$2,600,000
2/6/2009	MidWestOne Financial Group, Inc.	Iowa City	IA	Preferred Stock w/ Warrants	$16,000,000
2/6/2009	Lakeland Bancorp, Inc.	Oak Ridge	NJ	Preferred Stock w/ Warrants	$59,000,000
2/6/2009	Monarch Community Bancorp, Inc.	Coldwater	MI	Preferred Stock w/ Warrants	$6,785,000
2/6/2009	The First Bancshares, Inc.	Hattiesburg	MS	Preferred Stock w/ Warrants	$5,000,000
2/6/2009	Carolina Trust Bank	Lincolnton	NC	Preferred Stock w/ Warrants	$4,000,000
2/6/2009	Alaska Pacific Bancshares, Inc.	Juneau	AK	Preferred Stock w/ Warrants	$4,781,000
2/6/2009	PGB Holdings, Inc.	Chicago	IL	Preferred Stock	$3,000,000
2/6/2009	The Freeport State Bank	Harper	KS	Preferred Stock w/ Exercised Warrants	$301,000
2/6/2009	Stockmens Financial Corporation	Rapid City	SD	Preferred Stock w/ Exercised Warrants	$15,568,000
2/6/2009	US Metro Bank	Garden Grove	CA	Preferred Stock w/ Exercised Warrants	$2,861,000
2/6/2009	First Express of Nebraska, Inc.	Gering	NE	Preferred Stock w/ Exercised Warrants	$5,000,000
2/6/2009	Mercantile Capital Corp.	Boston	MA	Preferred Stock w/ Exercised Warrants	$3,500,000
2/6/2009	Citizens Commerce Bancshares, Inc.	Versailles	KY	Preferred Stock w/ Exercised Warrants	$6,300,000
2/6/2009	Liberty Financial Services, Inc.	New Orleans	LA	Preferred Stock	$5,645,000
2/6/2009	Lone Star Bank	Houston	TX	Preferred Stock w/ Exercised Warrants	$3,072,000
2/6/2009	Union First Market Bankshares Corporation	Bowling Green	VA	Preferred Stock	$33,900,000
2/6/2009	Banner County Ban Corporation	Harrisburg	NE	Preferred Stock w/ Exercised Warrants	$795,000
2/6/2009	Centrix Bank & Trust	Bedford	NH	Preferred Stock w/ Exercised Warrants	$7,500,000
2/6/2009	Todd Bancshares, Inc.	Hopkinsville	KY	Preferred Stock w/ Exercised Warrants	$4,000,000
2/6/2009	Georgia Commerce Bancshares, Inc.	Atlanta	GA	Preferred Stock w/ Exercised Warrants	$8,700,000
2/6/2009	First Bank of Charleston, Inc.	Charleston	WV	Preferred Stock w/ Exercised Warrants	$3,345,000
2/6/2009	F & M Financial Corporation	Salisbury	NC	Preferred Stock w/ Exercised Warrants	$17,000,000
2/6/2009	The Bank of Currituck	Moyock	NC	Preferred Stock w/ Exercised Warrants	$4,021,000

Continued

Table 3.7 All banks that received TARP funds.—cont'd

TARP Purchase Date	Name of Participating Institution	Institution City	Institution State	TARP Investment Description	TARP Investment Amount
		All Other Participants (cont.)			
2/6/2009	CedarStone Bank	Lebanon	TN	Preferred Stock w/ Exercised Warrants	$3,564,000
2/6/2009	Community Holding Company of Florida, Inc.	Miramar Beach	FL	Preferred Stock w/ Exercised Warrants	$1,050,000
2/6/2009	Hyperion Bank	Philadelphia	PA	Preferred Stock w/ Exercised Warrants	$1,552,000
2/6/2009	Pascack Bancorp, Inc.	Westwood	NJ	Preferred Stock w/ Exercised Warrants	$3,756,000
2/6/2009	First Western Financial, Inc.	Denver	CO	Preferred Stock w/ Exercised Warrants	$8,559,000
2/13/2009	2CR Holdings, Inc.	Moline	IL	Preferred Stock w/ Warrants	$38,237,000
2/13/2009	Wesamerica Bancorporation	San Rafael	CA	Preferred Stock w/ Warrants	$83,726,000
2/13/2009	The Bank of Kentucky Financial Corporation	Crestview Hills	KY	Preferred Stock w/ Warrants	$34,000,000
2/13/2009	PremierWest Bancorp	Medford	OR	Preferred Stock w/ Warrants	$41,400,000
2/13/2009	Carrollton Bancorp	Baltimore	MD	Preferred Stock w/ Warrants	$9,201,000
2/13/2009	FNB United Corp.	Asheboro	NC	Preferred Stock w/ Warrants	$51,500,000
2/13/2009	First Menasha Bancshares, Inc.	Neenah	WI	Preferred Stock w/ Exercised Warrants	$4,797,000
2/13/2009	1st Enterprise Bank	Los Angeles	CA	Preferred Stock w/ Exercised Warrants	$4,400,000
2/13/2009	DeSoto County Bank	Horn Lake	MS	Preferred Stock w/ Exercised Warrants	$1,173,000
2/13/2009	Security Bancshares of Pulaski County, Inc.	Waynesville	MO	Preferred Stock w/ Exercised Warrants	$2,152,000
2/13/2009	State Capital Corporation	Greenwood	MS	Preferred Stock w/ Exercised Warrants	$15,000,000
2/13/2009	BankGreenville	Greenville	SC	Preferred Stock w/ Exercised Warrants	$1,000,000
2/13/2009	Corning Savings and Loan Association	Corning	AR	Preferred Stock w/ Exercised Warrants	$638,000
2/13/2009	Financial Security Corporation	Basin	WY	Preferred Stock w/ Exercised Warrants	$5,000,000
2/13/2009	CoreEast Bankshares, Inc.	Lamar	CO	Preferred Stock w/ Exercised Warrants	$10,000,000
2/13/2009	Santa Clara Valley Bank, N.A.	Santa Paula	CA	Preferred Stock w/ Exercised Warrants	$2,900,000
2/13/2009	Reliance Bancshares, Inc.	Frontenac	MO	Preferred Stock w/ Exercised Warrants	$40,000,000
2/13/2009	Regional Bankshares, Inc.	Hartsville	SC	Preferred Stock w/ Exercised Warrants	$1,500,000
2/13/2009	Peoples Bancorp	Lynden	WA	Preferred Stock w/ Exercised Warrants	$18,000,000
2/13/2009	First Choice Bank	Cerritos	CA	Preferred Stock w/ Exercised Warrants	$2,200,000
2/13/2009	Cregg Bancshares, Inc	Ozark	MO	Preferred Stock w/ Exercised Warrants	$825,000
2/13/2009	Hometown Bancshares, Inc.	Corbin	KY	Preferred Stock w/ Exercised Warrants	$1,900,000
2/13/2009	Midwest Regional Bancorp, Inc.	Festus	MO	Preferred Stock w/ Exercised Warrants	$700,000
2/13/2009	Bern Bancshares, Inc.	Bern	KS	Preferred Stock w/ Exercised Warrants	$985,000
2/13/2009	North-west Bancorporation, Inc.	Spokane	WA	Preferred Stock w/ Exercised Warrants	$10,500,000
2/13/2009	Liberty Bancshares, Inc.	Springfield	MO	Preferred Stock w/ Exercised Warrants	$21,900,000
2/13/2009	F&M Financial Corporation	Clarksville	TN	Preferred Stock w/ Exercised Warrants	$17,243,000
2/13/2009	Meridian Bank	Devon	PA	Preferred Stock w/ Exercised Warrants	$6,200,000
2/13/2009	Nor-hwest Commercial Bank	Lakewood	WA	Preferred Stock w/ Exercised Warrants	$1,992,000
2/20/2009	Royal Bancshares of Pennsylvania, Inc.	Narberth	PA	Preferred Stock w/ Warrants	$30,407,000
2/20/2009	First Merchants Corporation	Muncie	IN	Preferred Stock w/ Warrants	$69,600,000
2/20/2009	Northern States Financial Corporation	Waukegan	IL	Preferred Stock w/ Warrants	$17,211,000
2/20/2009	Sonoma Valley Bancorp	Sonoma	CA	Preferred Stock w/ Exercised Warrants	$8,653,000
2/20/2009	Guaranty Bancorp, Inc.	Woodsville	NH	Preferred Stock w/ Exercised Warrants	$6,920,000
2/20/2009	The Private Bank of California	Los Angeles	CA	Preferred Stock w/ Exercised Warrants	$5,450,000
2/20/2009	Lafayette Bancorp, Inc.	Oxford	MS	Preferred Stock w/ Exercised Warrants	$1,998,000
2/20/2009	Liberty Shares, Inc.	Hinesville	GA	Preferred Stock w/ Exercised Warrants	$17,280,000
2/20/2009	White River Bancshares Company	Fayetteville	AR	Preferred Stock w/ Exercised Warrants	$16,800,000
2/20/2009	United American Bank	San Mateo	CA	Preferred Stock w/ Exercised Warrants	$8,700,000

Table 3.7 All banks that received TARP funds.—cont'd

TARP Purchase Date	Name of Participating Institution	Institution City	Institution State	TARP Investment Description	TARP Investment Amount
		All Other Participants (cont.)			
2/20/2009	Crazy Woman Creek Bancorp, Inc.	Buffalo	WY	Preferred Stock w/ Exercised Warrants	$3,100,000
2/20/2009	First Priority Financial Corp.	Malvern	PA	Preferred Stock w/ Exercised Warrants	$4,579,000
2/20/2009	Mid-Wisconsin Financial Services, Inc.	Medford	WI	Preferred Stock w/ Exercised Warrants	$10,000,000
2/20/2009	Market Bancorporation, Inc.	New Market	MN	Preferred Stock w/ Exercised Warrants	$2,060,000
2/20/2009	Hometown Bancorp of Alabama, Inc.	Oneonta	AL	Preferred Stock w/ Exercised Warrants	$3,250,000
2/20/2009	Security State Bancshares, Inc.	Charleston	MO	Preferred Stock w/ Exercised Warrants	$12,500,000
2/20/2009	CBB Bancorp	Cartersville	GA	Preferred Stock w/ Exercised Warrants	$2,644,000
2/20/2009	BancPlus Corporation	Ridgeland	MS	Preferred Stock w/ Exercised Warrants	$48,000,000
2/20/2009	Central Community Corporation	Temple	TX	Preferred Stock w/ Exercised Warrants	$22,000,000
2/20/2009	First Banc Trust Corporation	Paris	IL	Preferred Stock w/ Exercised Warrants	$7,350,000
2/20/2009	Premier Service Bank	Riverside	CA	Preferred Stock w/ Exercised Warrants	$4,000,000
2/20/2009	Florida Business BancGroup, Inc.	Tampa	FL	Preferred Stock w/ Exercised Warrants	$9,495,000
2/20/2009	Hamilton State Bancshares	Hoschton	GA	Preferred Stock w/ Exercised Warrants	$7,000,000
2/27/2009	Lakeland Financial Corporation	Warsaw	IN	Preferred Stock w/ Warrants	$56,044,000
2/27/2009	First M&F Corporation	Kosciusko	MS	Preferred Stock w/ Warrants	$30,000,000
2/27/2009	Southern First Bancshares, Inc.	Greenville	SC	Preferred Stock w/ Warrants	$17,299,000
2/27/2009	Integra Bank Corporation	Evansville	IN	Preferred Stock w/ Warrants	$83,586,000
2/27/2009	Community First Inc.	Columbia	TN	Preferred Stock w/ Exercised Warrants	$17,806,000
2/27/2009	BNC Financial Group, Inc.	New Canaan	CT	Preferred Stock w/ Exercised Warrants	$4,797,000
2/27/2009	California Bank of Commerce	Lafayette	CA	Preferred Stock w/ Exercised Warrants	$4,000,000
2/27/2009	Columbine Capital Corp.	Buena Vista	CO	Preferred Stock w/ Exercised Warrants	$2,260,000
2/27/2009	National Bancshares, Inc.	Bettendorf	IA	Preferred Stock w/ Exercised Warrants	$24,664,000
2/27/2009	First State Bank of Mobeetie	Mobeetie	TX	Preferred Stock w/ Exercised Warrants	$731,000
2/27/2009	Ridgestone Financial Services, Inc.	Brookfield	WI	Preferred Stock w/ Exercised Warrants	$10,900,000
2/27/2009	Community Business Bank	West Sacramento	CA	Preferred Stock w/ Exercised Warrants	$3,976,000
2/27/2009	D.L. Evans Bancorp	Burley	ID	Preferred Stock w/ Exercised Warrants	$19,891,000
2/27/2009	TriState Capital Holdings, Inc.	Pittsburgh	PA	Preferred Stock w/ Exercised Warrants	$23,000,000
2/27/2009	Green City Bancshares, Inc.	Green City	MO	Preferred Stock w/ Exercised Warrants	$651,000
2/27/2009	First Gothenburg Bancshares, Inc.	Gothenburg	NE	Preferred Stock w/ Exercised Warrants	$7,570,000
2/27/2009	Green Circle Investments, Inc.	Clive	IA	Preferred Stock w/ Exercised Warrants	$2,400,000
2/27/2009	Private Bancorporation, Inc.	Minneapolis	MN	Preferred Stock w/ Exercised Warrants	$4,960,000
2/27/2009	Regent Capital Corporation	Nowata	OK	Preferred Stock w/ Exercised Warrants	$2,655,000
2/27/2009	Central Bancorp, Inc.	Garland	TX	Preferred Stock w/ Exercised Warrants	$22,500,000
2/27/2009	Medallion Bank	Salt Lake City	UT	Preferred Stock w/ Exercised Warrants	$11,800,000
2/27/2009	PSB Financial Corporation	Many	LA	Preferred Stock w/ Exercised Warrants	$9,270,000
2/27/2009	Avenue Financial Holdings, Inc.	Nashville	TN	Preferred Stock w/ Exercised Warrants	$7,400,000
2/27/2009	Howard Bancorp, Inc.	Ellicott City	MD	Preferred Stock w/ Exercised Warrants	$5,983,000
2/27/2009	FNB Bancorp	South San Francisco	CA	Preferred Stock w/ Exercised Warrants	$12,000,000
2/27/2009	The Victory Bancorp, Inc.	Limerick	PA	Preferred Stock w/ Exercised Warrants	$541,000
2/27/2009	Catskill Hudson Bancorp, Inc	Rock Hill	NY	Preferred Stock w/ Exercised Warrants	$3,000,000
2/27/2009	Midtown Bank & Trust Company	Atlanta	GA	Preferred Stock w/ Exercised Warrants	$5,222,000
3/6/2009	HCSB Financial Corporation	Loris	SC	Preferred Stock w/ Warrants	$12,895,000
3/6/2009	First Busey Corporation	Urbana	IL	Preferred Stock w/ Warrants	$100,000,000
3/6/2009	First Federal Bancshares of Arkansas, Inc.	Harrison	AR	Preferred Stock w/ Warrants	$16,500,000

Table 3.7 All banks that received TARP funds.—cont'd

TARP Purchase Date	Name of Participating Institution	Institution City	Institution State	TARP Investment Description	TARP Investment Amount
		All Other Participants (cont.)			
3/6/2009	Citzens Bancshares Corporation	Atlanta	GA	Preferred Stock	$7,462,000
3/6/2009	ICB Financial	Ontario	CA	Preferred Stock w/ Exercised Warrants	$6,000,000
3/6/2009	First Texas BHC, Inc.	Fort Worth	TX	Preferred Stock w/ Exercised Warrants	$13,533,000
3/6/2009	Farmer's & Merchants Bancshares, Inc.	Houston	TX	Preferred Stock w/ Exercised Warrants	$11,000,000
3/6/2009	Blue Ridge Bancshares, Inc.	Independence	MO	Preferred Stock w/ Exercised Warrants	$12,000,000
3/6/2009	First Reliance Bancshares, Inc.	Florence	SC	Preferred Stock w/ Exercised Warrants	$15,349,000
3/6/2009	Merchants and Planters Bancshares, Inc.	Toone	TN	Preferred Stock w/ Exercised Warrants	$1,881,000
3/6/2009	First Southwest Bancorporation, Inc.	Alamosa	CO	Preferred Stock w/ Exercised Warrants	$5,500,000
3/6/2009	Germantown Capital Corporation, Inc.	Germantown	TN	Preferred Stock w/ Exercised Warrants	$4,967,000
3/6/2009	BOH Holdings, Inc.	Houston	TX	Preferred Stock w/ Exercised Warrants	$10,000,000
3/6/2009	AmeriBank Holding Company	Collinsville	OK	Preferred Stock w/ Exercised Warrants	$2,492,000
3/6/2009	Highlands Independent Bancshares, Inc.	Sebring	FL	Preferred Stock w/ Exercised Warrants	$6,700,000
3/6/2009	Pinnacle Bank Holding Company, Inc.	Orange City	FL	Preferred Stock w/ Exercised Warrants	$4,389,000
3/6/2009	Blue River Bancshares, Inc.	Shelbyville	IN	Preferred Stock w/ Exercised Warrants	$5,000,000
3/6/2009	Marine Bank & Trust Company	Vero Beach	FL	Preferred Stock w/ Exercised Warrants	$3,000,000
3/6/2009	Community Bancshares of Kansas, Inc.	Goff	KS	Preferred Stock w/ Exercised Warrants	$500,000
3/6/2009	Regent Bancorp, Inc.	Davie	FL	Preferred Stock w/ Exercised Warrants	$9,982,000
3/6/2009	Bark Bancorporation, Inc.	Madison	WI	Preferred Stock w/ Exercised Warrants	$23,200,000
3/6/2009	PeoplesSouth Bancshares, Inc.	Colquitt	GA	Preferred Stock w/ Exercised Warrants	$12,325,000
3/13/2009	First Place Financial Corp.	Warren	OH	Preferred Stock w/ Warrants	$72,927,000
3/13/2009	Salisbury Bancorp, Inc.	Lakeville	CT	Preferred Stock w/ Warrants	$8,816,000
3/13/2009	First Northern Community Bancorp	Dixon	CA	Preferred Stock w/ Warrants	$17,390,000
3/13/2009	Discover Financial Services	Riverwoods	IL	Preferred Stock w/ Warrants	$1,224,558,000
3/13/2009	Provident Community Bancshares, Inc.	Rock Hill	SC	Preferred Stock w/ Warrants	$9,266,000
3/13/2009	First American International Corp.	Brooklyn	NY	Preferred Stock	$17,000,000
3/13/2009	BancIndependent, Inc.	Sheffield	AL	Preferred Stock w/ Exercised Warrants	$21,100,000
3/13/2009	Haviland Bancshares, Inc.	Haviland	KS	Preferred Stock w/ Exercised Warrants	$425,000
3/13/2009	First United Bancorp, Inc.	Boca Raton	FL	Preferred Stock w/ Exercised Warrants	$10,000,000
3/13/2009	Madison Financial Corporation	Richmond	KY	Preferred Stock w/ Exercised Warrants	$3,370,000
3/13/2009	First National Corporation	Strasburg	VA	Preferred Stock w/ Exercised Warrants	$13,900,000
3/13/2009	St. Johns Bancshares, Inc.	St. Louis	MO	Preferred Stock w/ Exercised Warrants	$3,000,000
3/13/2009	Backhawk Bancorp, Inc.	Beloit	WI	Preferred Stock w/ Exercised Warrants	$10,000,000
3/13/2009	IBW Financial Corporation	Washington	DC	Preferred Stock	$6,000,000
3/13/2009	Butler Point, Inc.	Catlin	IL	Preferred Stock	$607,000
3/13/2009	Bank of George	Las Vegas	NV	Preferred Stock w/ Exercised Warrants	$2,672,000
3/13/2009	Moneytree Corporation	Lenoir City	TN	Preferred Stock w/ Exercised Warrants	$9,516,000
3/13/2009	Sovereign Bancshares, Inc.	Dallas	TX	Preferred Stock w/ Exercised Warrants	$18,215,000
3/13/2009	First Intercontinental Bank	Doraville	GA	Preferred Stock w/ Exercised Warrants	$6,398,000
3/20/2009	Heritage Oaks Bancorp	Paso Robles	CA	Preferred Stock w/ Warrants	$21,000,000
3/20/2009	Community First Bancshares Inc.	Union City	TN	Preferred Stock w/ Exercised Warrants	$20,000,000
3/20/2009	First N3C Bank Holding Company	New Orleans	LA	Preferred Stock w/ Exercised Warrants	$17,836,000
3/20/2009	First Colebrook Bancorp, Inc.	Colebrook	NH	Preferred Stock w/ Exercised Warrants	$4,500,000
3/20/2009	Kirksville Bancorp, Inc.	Kirksville	MO	Preferred Stock w/ Exercised Warrants	$470,000
3/20/2009	Peoples Bancshares of TN, Inc.	Madisonville	TN	Preferred Stock w/ Exercised Warrants	$3,900,000

Continued

I. Introductory materials

3. Descriptions of TARP

Table 3.7 All banks that received TARP funds.—cont'd

TARP Purchase Date	Name of Participating Institution	Institution City	Institution State	TARP Investment Description	TARP Investment Amount
		All Other Participants (cont.)			
3/20/2009	Premier Bank Holding Company	Tallahassee	FL	Preferred Stock w/ Exercised Warrants	$9,500,000
3/20/2009	Citizens Bank & Trust Company	Covington	LA	Preferred Stock w/ Exercised Warrants	$2,400,000
3/20/2009	Farmers & Merchants Financial Corporation	Argonia	KS	Preferred Stock w/ Exercised Warrants	$442,000
3/20/2009	Farmers State Bankshares, Inc.	Holton	KS	Preferred Stock w/ Exercised Warrants	$700,000
3/27/2009	SBT Bancorp, Inc.	Simsbury	CT	Preferred Stock w/ Exercised Warrants	$4,000,000
3/27/2009	CSRA Bank Corp.	Wrens	GA	Preferred Stock w/ Exercised Warrants	$2,400,000
3/27/2009	Trinity Capital Corporation	Los Alamos	NM	Preferred Stock w/ Exercised Warrants	$35,539,000
3/27/2009	Clover Community Bankshares, Inc.	Clover	SC	Preferred Stock w/ Exercised Warrants	$3,000,000
3/27/2009	Pathway Bancorp	Cairo	NE	Preferred Stock w/ Exercised Warrants	$3,727,000
3/27/2009	Colonial American Bank	West Conshohocken	PA	Preferred Stock w/ Exercised Warrants	$574,000
3/27/2009	MS Financial, Inc.	Kingwood	TX	Preferred Stock w/ Exercised Warrants	$7,723,000
3/27/2009	Triad Bancorp, Inc.	Frontenac	MO	Preferred Stock w/ Exercised Warrants	$3,700,000
3/27/2009	Alpine Banks of Colorado	Glenwood Springs	CO	Preferred Stock w/ Exercised Warrants	$70,000,000
3/27/2009	Naples Bancorp, Inc.	Naples	FL	Preferred Stock w/ Exercised Warrants	$4,000,000
3/27/2009	CBS Banc-Corp.	Russellville	AL	Preferred Stock w/ Exercised Warrants	$24,300,000
3/27/2009	IBT Bancorp, Inc.	Irving	TX	Preferred Stock w/ Exercised Warrants	$2,295,000
3/27/2009	Spirit BankCorp, Inc.	Bristow	OK	Preferred Stock w/ Exercised Warrants	$30,000,000
3/27/2009	Maryland Financial Bank	Towson	MD	Preferred Stock w/ Exercised Warrants	$1,700,000
3/27/2009	First Capital Bancorp, Inc.	Glen Allen	VA	Preferred Stock w/ Warrants	$10,958,000
4/3/2009	Tri-State Bank of Memphis	Memphis	TN	Preferred Stock	$2,795,000
4/3/2009	Fortune Financial Corporation	Arnold	MO	Preferred Stock w/ Exercised Warrants	$3,100,000
4/3/2009	BancStar, Inc.	Festus	MO	Preferred Stock w/ Exercised Warrants	$8,600,000
4/3/2009	Titonka Bancshares, Inc	Titonka	IA	Preferred Stock w/ Exercised Warrants	$2,117,000
4/3/2009	Millennium Bancorp, Inc.	Edwards	CO	Preferred Stock w/ Exercised Warrants	$7,260,000
4/3/2009	TriSummit Bank	Kingsport	TN	Preferred Stock w/ Exercised Warrants	$2,765,000
4/3/2009	Prairie Star Bancshares, Inc.	Olathe	KS	Preferred Stock w/ Exercised Warrants	$2,800,000
4/3/2009	Community First Bancshares, Inc.	Harrison	AR	Preferred Stock w/ Exercised Warrants	$12,725,000
4/3/2009	BCB Holding Company, Inc.	Theodore	AL	Preferred Stock w/ Exercised Warrants	$1,706,000
4/10/2009	City National Bancshares Corporation	Newark	NJ	Preferred Stock	$9,439,000
4/10/2009	First Business Bank, N.A.	San Diego	CA	Preferred Stock w/ Exercised Warrants	$2,211,000
4/10/2009	SV Financial, Inc.	Sterling	IL	Preferred Stock w/ Exercised Warrants	$4,000,000
4/10/2009	Capital Commerce Bancorp, Inc.	Milwaukee	WI	Preferred Stock w/ Exercised Warrants	$5,100,000
4/10/2009	Metropolitan Capital Bancorp, Inc.	Chicago	IL	Preferred Stock w/ Exercised Warrants	$2,040,000
4/17/2009	Bank of the Carolinas Corporation	Mocksville	NC	Preferred Stock w/ Warrants	$13,179,000
4/17/2009	Penn Liberty Financial Corp.	Wayne	PA	Preferred Stock w/ Exercised Warrants	$9,960,000
4/17/2009	Tifton Banking Company	Tifton	GA	Preferred Stock w/ Exercised Warrants	$3,800,000
4/17/2009	Patterson Bancshares, Inc	Patterson	LA	Preferred Stock w/ Exercised Warrants	$3,690,000
4/17/2009	BNB Financial Services Corporation	New York	NY	Preferred Stock w/ Exercised Warrants	$7,500,000
4/17/2009	Omega Capital Corp.	Lakewood	CO	Preferred Stock w/ Exercised Warrants	$2,816,000
4/24/2009	Mackinac Financial Corporation	Manistique	MI	Preferred Stock w/ Warrants	$11,000,000
4/24/2009	Birmingham Bloomfield Bancshares, Inc	Birmingham	MI	Preferred Stock w/ Exercised Warrants	$1,635,000
4/24/2009	Vision Bank - Texas	Richardson	TX	Preferred Stock w/ Exercised Warrants	$1,500,000
4/24/2009	Oregon Bancorp, Inc.	Salem	OR	Preferred Stock w/ Exercised Warrants	$3,216,000
4/24/2009	Peoples Bancorporation, Inc.	Easley	SC	Preferred Stock w/ Exercised Warrants	$12,660,000

Continued

Table 3.7 All banks that received TARP funds.—cont'd

TARP Purchase Date	Name of Participating Institution	Institution City	Institution State	TARP Investment Description	TARP Investment Amount
			All Other Participants (cont.)		
4/24/2009	Indiana Bank Corp.	Dana	IN	Preferred Stock w/ Exercised Warrants	$1,312,000
4/24/2009	Business Bancshares, Inc.	Clayton	MO	Preferred Stock w/ Exercised Warrants	$15,000,000
4/24/2009	Standard Bancshares, Inc.	Hickory Hills	IL	Preferred Stock w/ Exercised Warrants	$60,000,000
4/24/2009	York Traditions Bank	York	PA	Preferred Stock w/ Exercised Warrants	$4,871,000
4/24/2009	Grand Capital Corporation	Tulsa	OK	Preferred Stock w/ Exercised Warrants	$4,000,000
4/24/2009	Allied First Bancorp, Inc.	Oswego	IL	Preferred Stock w/ Exercised Warrants	$3,652,000
4/24/2009	Frontier Bancshares, Inc.	Austin	TX	Subordinated Debentures w/ Exercised Warrants	$3,000,000
5/1/2009	Village Bank and Trust Financial Corp.	Midlothian	VA	Preferred Stock w/ Warrants	$14,738,000
5/1/2009	CenterBank	Milford	OH	Preferred Stock w/ Exercised Warrants	$2,250,000
5/1/2009	Georgia Primary Bank	Atlanta	GA	Preferred Stock w/ Exercised Warrants	$4,500,000
5/1/2009	Union Bank & Trust Company	Oxford	NC	Preferred Stock w/ Exercised Warrants	$3,194,000
5/1/2009	FPK Financial Corporation	Chicago	IL	Preferred Stock w/ Exercised Warrants	$4,000,000
5/1/2009	OSB Financial Services, Inc.	Orange	TX	Subordinated Debentures w/ Exercised Warrants	$6,100,000
5/1/2009	Security State Bank Holding-Company	Jamestown	ND	Subordinated Debentures w/ Exercised Warrants	$10,750,000
5/8/2009	Highlands Bancorp, Inc.	Vernon	NJ	Preferred Stock w/ Exercised Warrants	$3,091,000
5/8/2009	One Georgia Bank	Atlanta	GA	Preferred Stock w/ Exercised Warrants	$5,500,000
5/8/2009	Gateway Bancshares, Inc.	Ringgold	GA	Preferred Stock w/ Exercised Warrants	$6,000,000
5/8/2009	Freeport Bancshares, Inc.	Freeport	IL	Subordinated Debentures w/ Exercised Warrants	$3,000,000
5/8/2009	Investors Financial Corp of Pettis County, Inc.	Sedalia	MO	Subordinated Debentures w/ Exercised Warrants	$4,000,000
5/8/2009	Sword Financial Corporation	Horicon	WI	Subordinated Debentures w/ Exercised Warrants	$13,644,000
5/8/2009	Premier Bancorp, Inc.	Wilmette	IL	Subordinated Debentures	$6,784,000
5/15/2009	Mercantile Bank Corporation	Grand Rapids	MI	Preferred Stock w/ Warrants	$21,000,000
5/15/2009	Northern State Bank	Closter	NJ	Preferred Stock w/ Exercised Warrants	$1,341,000
5/15/2009	Western Reserve Bancorp, Inc	Medina	OH	Preferred Stock w/ Exercised Warrants	$4,700,000
5/15/2009	Community Financial Shares, Inc.	Glen Ellyn	IL	Preferred Stock w/ Exercised Warrants	$6,970,000
5/15/2009	Worthington Financial Holdings, Inc.	Huntsville	AL	Preferred Stock w/ Exercised Warrants	$2,720,000
5/15/2009	First Community Bancshares, Inc	Overland Park	KS	Preferred Stock w/ Exercised Warrants	$14,800,000
5/15/2009	Southern Heritage Bancshares, Inc.	Cleveland	TN	Preferred Stock w/ Exercised Warrants	$4,862,000
5/15/2009	Foresight Financial Group, Inc.	Rockford	IL	Preferred Stock w/ Exercised Warrants	$15,000,000
5/15/2009	IBC Bancorp, Inc.	Chicago	IL	Subordinated Debentures	$4,205,000
5/15/2009	Bosobel Bancorp, Inc	Boscobel	WI	Subordinated Debentures w/ Exercised Warrants	$5,586,000
5/15/2009	Erogan Bankshares, Inc.	Kaukauna	WI	Subordinated Debentures w/ Exercised Warrants	$2,400,000
5/15/2009	Riverside Bancshares, Inc.	Little Rock	AR	Subordinated Debentures w/ Exercised Warrants	$1,100,000
5/15/2009	Deerfield Financial Corporation	Deerfield	WI	Subordinated Debentures w/ Exercised Warrants	$2,639,000
5/15/2009	Market Street Bancshares, Inc.	Mt. Vernon	IL	Subordinated Debentures w/ Exercised Warrants	$20,300,000
5/22/2009	The Landrum Company	Columbia	MO	Preferred Stock w/ Exercised Warrants	$15,000,000
5/22/2009	First Advantage Bancshares Inc.	Coon Rapids	MN	Preferred Stock w/ Exercised Warrants	$1,177,000
5/22/2009	Fort Lee Federal Savings Bank	Fort Lee	NJ	Preferred Stock w/ Exercised Warrants	$1,300,000
5/22/2009	Blackridge Financial, Inc.	Fargo	ND	Preferred Stock w/ Exercised Warrants	$5,000,000
5/22/2009	Illinois State Bancorp, Inc.	Chicago	IL	Preferred Stock w/ Exercised Warrants	$6,272,000
5/22/2009	Universal Bancorp	Bloomfield	IN	Preferred Stock w/ Exercised Warrants	$9,900,000
5/22/2009	Franklin Bancorp, Inc.	Washington	MO	Preferred Stock w/ Exercised Warrants	$5,097,000
5/22/2009	Commonwealth Bancshares, Inc.	Louisville	KY	Subordinated Debentures w/ Exercised Warrants	$20,400,000
5/22/2009	Premier Financial Corp	Dubuque	IA	Subordinated Debentures w/ Exercised Warrants	$6,349,000

I. Introductory materials

Table 3.7   All banks that received TARP funds.—cont'd

TARP Purchase Date	Name of Participating Institution	Institution City	Institution State	TARP Investment Description	TARP Investment Amount
		All Other Participants (cont.)			
5/22/2009	F & C Bancorp, Inc.	Holden	MO	Subordinated Debentures w/ Exercised Warrants	$2,993,000
5/22/2009	Diamond Bancorp, Inc.	Washington	MO	Subordinated Debentures w/ Exercised Warrants	$20,445,000
5/22/2009	United Bank Corporation	Barnesville	GA	Subordinated Debentures w/ Exercised Warrants	$14,400,000
5/29/2009	Community Bank Shares of Indiana, Inc.	New Albany	IN	Preferred Stock w/ Warrants	$19,468,000
5/29/2009	American Premier Bancorp	Arcadia	CA	Preferred Stock w/ Exercised Warrants	$1,800,000
5/29/2009	CB Holding Corp.	Aledo	IL	Preferred Stock w/ Exercised Warrants	$4,114,000
5/29/2009	Citizens Bancshares Co.	Chillicothe	MO	Preferred Stock w/ Exercised Warrants	$24,990,000
5/29/2009	Grand Mountain Bancshares, Inc.	Granby	CO	Preferred Stock w/ Exercised Warrants	$3,076,000
5/29/2009	Two Rivers Financial Group	Burlington	IA	Preferred Stock w/ Exercised Warrants	$12,000,000
5/29/2009	Fidelity Bancorp, Inc	Baton Rouge	LA	Subordinated Debentures w/ Exercised Warrants	$3,942,000
6/5/2009	Chambers Bancshares, Inc.	Danville	AR	Subordinated Debentures w/ Exercised Warrants	$19,817,000
6/5/2009	Covenant Financial Corporation	Clarksdale	MS	Preferred Stock w/ Exercised Warrants	$5,000,000
6/5/2009	First Trust Corporation	New Orleans	LA	Subordinated Debentures w/ Exercised Warrants	$17,969,000
6/5/2009	OneFinancial Corporation	Little Rock	AR	Subordinated Debentures w/ Exercised Warrants	$17,300,000
6/12/2009	Berkshire Bancorp, Inc.	Wyomissing	PA	Preferred Stock w/ Exercised Warrants	$2,892,000
6/12/2009	First Vernon Bancshares, Inc.	Vernon	AL	Preferred Stock w/ Exercised Warrants	$6,000,000
6/12/2009	SouthFirst Bancshares, Inc.	Sylacauga	AL	Preferred Stock w/ Exercised Warrants	$2,760,000
6/12/2009	Virginia Company Bank	Newport News	VA	Preferred Stock w/ Exercised Warrants	$4,700,000
6/12/2009	Enterprise Financial Services Group, Inc.	Allison Park	PA	Preferred Stock w/ Exercised Warrants	$4,000,000
6/12/2009	First Financial Bancshares, Inc.	Lawrence	KS	Subordinated Debentures w/ Exercised Warrants	$3,756,000
6/12/2009	River Valley Bancorporation, Inc.	Wausau	WI	Subordinated Debentures w/ Exercised Warrants	$15,000,000
6/19/2009	Merchants and Manufacturers Bank Corporation	Joliet	IL	Subordinated Debentures w/ Exercised Warrants	$3,510,000
6/19/2009	RCB Financial Corporation	Rome	GA	Preferred Stock w/ Exercised Warrants	$8,900,000
6/19/2009	Manhattan Bancshares, Inc.	Manhattan	IL	Subordinated Debentures w/ Exercised Warrants	$2,639,000
6/19/2009	Biscayne Bancshares, Inc.	Coconut Grove	FL	Subordinated Debentures w/ Exercised Warrants	$6,400,000
6/19/2009	Duke Financial Group, Inc.	Minneapolis	MN	Subordinated Debentures w/ Exercised Warrants	$12,000,000
6/19/2009	Farmers Enterprises, Inc.	Great Bend	KS	Subordinated Debentures w/ Exercised Warrants	$12,000,000
6/19/2009	Century Financial Services Corporation	Santa Fe	NM	Subordinated Debentures w/ Exercised Warrants	$10,000,000
6/19/2009	NEMO Bancshares Inc.	Madison	MO	Subordinated Debentures w/ Exercised Warrants	$2,330,000
6/19/2009	University Financial Corp, Inc.	St. Paul	MN	Subordinated Debentures	$11,926,000
6/19/2009	Suburban Illinois Bancorp, Inc.	Elmhurst	IL	Subordinated Debentures w/ Exercised Warrants	$15,000,000
6/26/2009	Hartford Financial Services Group, Inc.	Hartford	CT	Preferred Stock w/ Warrants	$3,400,000,000
6/26/2009	Vertex Holdings, Inc.	Dallas	TX	Preferred Stock w/ Exercised Warrants	$3,000,000
6/26/2009	Waukesha Bankshares, Inc.	Waukesha	WI	Preferred Stock w/ Exercised Warrants	$5,625,000
6/26/2009	FC Holdings, Inc.	Houston	TX	Preferred Stock w/ Exercised Warrants	$21,042,000
6/26/2009	Security Capital Corporation	Batesville	MS	Preferred Stock w/ Exercised Warrants	$17,388,000
6/26/2009	First Alliance Bancshares, Inc.	Cordova	TN	Preferred Stock w/ Exercised Warrants	$3,422,000
6/26/2009	Gulfstream Bancshares, Inc.	Stuart	FL	Preferred Stock w/ Exercised Warrants	$7,500,000
6/26/2009	Gold Canyon Bank	Gold Canyon	AZ	Preferred Stock w/ Exercised Warrants	$1,607,000
6/26/2009	M&F Bancorp, Inc.	Durham	NC	Preferred Stock	$11,735,000
6/26/2009	Metropolitan Bank Group, Inc.	Chicago	IL	Preferred Stock w/ Exercised Warrants	$71,526,000
6/26/2009	NC Bancorp, Inc.	Chicago	IL	Preferred Stock w/ Exercised Warrants	$6,880,000
6/26/2009	Alliance Bancshares, Inc.	Dalton	GA	Preferred Stock w/ Exercised Warrants	$2,986,000
6/26/2009	Stearns Financial Services, Inc.	St. Cloud	MN	Subordinated Debentures w/ Exercised Warrants	$24,900,000

Continued

Table 3.7 All banks that received TARP funds.—cont'd

TARP Purchase Date	Name of Participating Institution	Institution City	Institution State	TARP Investment Description	TARP Investment Amount
		All Other Participants (cont.)			
6/26/2009	Signature Bancshares, Inc.	Dallas	TX	Subordinated Debentures w/ Exercised Warrants	$1,700,000
6/26/2009	Fremont Bancorporation	Fremont	CA	Subordinated Debentures w/ Exercised Warrants	$35,000,000
6/26/2009	Alliance Financial Services Inc.	Saint Paul	MN	Subordinated Debentures w/ Exercised Warrants	$12,000,000
7/10/2009	Lincoln National Corporation	Radnor	PA	Preferred Stock w/ Warrants	$950,000,000
7/10/2009	Bancorp Financial, Inc.	Oak Brook	IL	Preferred Stock w/ Exercised Warrants	$13,669,000
7/17/2009	Brotherhood Bancshares, Inc.	Kansas City	KS	Preferred Stock w/ Exercised Warrants	$11,000,000
7/17/2009	SouthCrest Financial Group, Inc.	Fayetteville	GA	Preferred Stock w/ Exercised Warrants	$12,900,000
7/17/2009	Harbor Bankshares Corporation	Baltimore	MD	Preferred Stock	$6,800,000
7/17/2009	First South Bancorp, Inc.	Lexington	TN	Subordinated Debentures w/ Exercised Warrants	$50,000,000
7/17/2009	Great River Holding Company	Baxter	MN	Subordinated Debentures w/ Exercised Warrants	$8,400,000
7/17/2009	Plato Holdings Inc.	Saint Paul	MN	Subordinated Debentures w/ Exercised Warrants	$2,500,000
7/24/2009	Yadkin Valley Financial Corporation	Elkin	NC	Preferred Stock w/ Warrants	$13,312,000
7/24/2009	Community Bancshares, Inc.	Kingman	AZ	Preferred Stock w/ Exercised Warrants	$3,872,000
7/24/2009	Florida Bank Group, Inc.	Tampa	FL	Preferred Stock w/ Exercised Warrants	$20,471,000
7/24/2009	First American Bank Corporation	Elk Grove Village	IL	Subordinated Debentures w/ Exercised Warrants	$50,000,000
7/31/2009	Chicago Shore Corporation	Chicago	IL	Preferred Stock w/ Exercised Warrants	$7,000,000
7/31/2009	Financial Services of Winger, Inc.	Winger	MN	Subordinated Debentures w/ Exercised Warrants	$3,742,000
8/7/2009	The ANB Corporation	Terrell	TX	Preferred Stock w/ Exercised Warrants	$20,000,000
8/7/2009	U.S. Century Bank	Miami	FL	Preferred Stock w/ Exercised Warrants	$50,236,000
8/14/2009	Bank Financial Services, Inc.	Eden Prairie	MN	Preferred Stock w/ Exercised Warrants	$1,004,000
8/21/2009	KS Bancorp, Inc.	Smithfield	NC	Preferred Stock w/ Exercised Warrants	$4,000,000
8/21/2009	AmFirst Financial Services, Inc.	McCook	NE	Subordinated Debentures w/ Exercised Warrants	$5,000,000
8/28/2009	First Independence Corporation	Detroit	MI	Preferred Stock	$3,223,000
8/28/2009	First Guaranty Bancshares, Inc.	Hammond	LA	Preferred Stock w/ Exercised Warrants	$20,699,000
8/28/2009	CoastalSouth Bancshares, Inc.	Hilton Head Island	SC	Preferred Stock w/ Exercised Warrants	$16,015,000
8/28/2009	TCB Corporation	Greenwood	SC	Subordinated Debentures w/ Exercised Warrants	$9,720,000
9/4/2009	The State Bank of Bartley	Bartley	NE	Subordinated Debentures w/ Exercised Warrants	$1,697,000
9/11/2009	Pathfinder Bancorp, Inc.	Oswego	NY	Preferred Stock w/ Warrants	$6,771,000
9/11/2009	Community Bancshares of Mississippi, Inc.	Brandon	MS	Preferred Stock w/ Exercised Warrants	$52,000,000
9/11/2009	Heartland Bancshares, Inc.	Franklin	IN	Preferred Stock w/ Exercised Warrants	$7,000,000
9/11/2009	PFSB Bancorporation, Inc.	Pigeon Falls	WI	Preferred Stock w/ Exercised Warrants	$1,500,000
9/11/2009	First Eagle Bancshares, Inc.	Hanover Park	IL	Subordinated Debentures w/ Exercised Warrants	$7,500,000
9/18/2009	IA Bancorp, Inc.	Iselin	NJ	Preferred Stock w/ Exercised Warrants	$5,976,000
9/18/2009	HomeTown Bankshares Corporation	Roanoke	VA	Preferred Stock w/ Exercised Warrants	$10,000,000
9/25/2009	Heritage Bankshares, Inc.	Norfolk	VA	Preferred Stock w/ Exercised Warrants	$10,103,000
9/25/2009	Mountain Valley Bancshares, Inc.	Cleveland	GA	Preferred Stock w/ Exercised Warrants	$3,300,000
9/25/2009	Grand Financial Corporation	Hattiesburg	MS	Subordinated Debentures w/ Exercised Warrants	$2,443,320
9/25/2009	Guaranty Capital Corporation	Belzoni	MS	Subordinated Debentures	$14,000,000
9/25/2009	GulfSouth Private Bank	Destin	FL	Preferred Stock w/ Exercised Warrants	$7,500,000
9/25/2009	Steele Street Bank Corporation	Denver	CO	Subordinated Debentures w/ Exercised Warrants	$11,019,000
10/2/2009	Premier Financial Bancorp, Inc.	Huntington	WV	Preferred Stock w/ Warrants	$22,252,000
10/2/2009	Providence Bank	Rocky Mount	NC	Preferred Stock w/ Exercised Warrants	$4,000,000
10/23/2009	Regents Bancshares, Inc.	Vancouver	WA	Preferred Stock w/ Exercised Warrants	$12,700,000
10/23/2009	Cardinal Bancorp II, Inc.	Washington	MO	Subordinated Debentures w/ Exercised Warrants	$6,251,000

I. Introductory materials

Table 3.7 All banks that received TARP funds.—cont'd

TARP Purchase Date	Name of Participating Institution	Institution City	Institution State	TARP Investment Description	TARP Investment Amount
		All Other Participants (cont.)			
10/30/2009	Randolph Bank & Trust Company	Asheboro	NC	Preferred Stock w/ Exercised Warrants	$6,229,000
10/30/2009	WashingtonFirst Bankshares, Inc.	Reston	VA	Preferred Stock	$6,842,000
11/6/2009	F & M Bancshares, Inc.	Trecevant	TN	Preferred Stock	$3,535,000
11/13/2009	Fidelity Federal Bancorp	Evansville	IN	Preferred Stock w/ Exercised Warrants	$6,657,000
11/13/2009	Community Pride Bank Corporation	Ham Lake	MN	Subordinated Debentures w/ Exercised Warrants	$4,400,000
11/13/2009	HPK Financial Corporation	Chicago	IL	Preferred Stock w/ Exercised Warrants	$5,000,000
11/20/2009	Presidio Bank	San Francisco	CA	Preferred Stock w/ Exercised Warrants	$10,800,000
11/20/2009	McLeod Bancshares, Inc.	Shorewood	MN	Preferred Stock w/ Exercised Warrants	$6,000,000
11/20/2009	Metropolitan Capital Bancorp, Inc.	Chicago	IL	Preferred Stock	$2,348,000
12/4/2009	Broadway Financial Corporation	Los Angeles	CA	Preferred Stock	$6,000,000
12/4/2009	Delmar Bancorp	Delmar	MD	Preferred Stock w/ Exercised Warrants	$9,000,000
12/4/2009	Liberty Bancshares, Inc.	For. Worth	TX	Preferred Stock w/ Exercised Warrants	$6,500,000
12/11/2009	First Community Financial Partners, Inc.	Joliet	IL	Preferred Stock w/ Exercised Warrants	$22,000,000
12/11/2009	Wachusett Financial Services, Inc.	Clinton	MA	Preferred Stock w/ Exercised Warrants	$12,000,000
12/11/2009	Nationwide Bankshares, Inc.	West Point	NE	Subordinated Debentures w/ Exercised Warrants	$2,000,000
12/11/2009	GrandSouth Bancorporation	Greenville	SC	Preferred Stock	$6,319,000
12/11/2009	1st Enterprise Bank	Los Angeles	CA	Preferred Stock	$6,000,000
12/11/2009	First Resource Bank	Exton	PA	Preferred Stock	$2,417,000
12/11/2009	First Western Financial, Inc.	Denver	CO	Preferred Stock	$11,881,000
12/11/2009	Meridian Bank	Devon	PA	Preferred Stock	$6,335,000
12/11/2009	The Victory Bancorp, Inc.	Limerick	PA	Preferred Stock w/ Exercised Warrants	$1,505,000
12/11/2009	First Business Bank, N.A.	San Diego	CA	Preferred Stock	$2,032,000
12/18/2009	Layton Park Financial Group	Milwaukee	WI	Preferred Stock w/ Exercised Warrants	$3,000,000
12/18/2009	Centric Financial Corporation	Harrisburg	PA	Preferred Stock w/ Exercised Warrants	$6,056,000
12/18/2009	Valley Financial Group, Ltd., 1st State Bank	Saginaw	MI	Preferred Stock w/ Exercised Warrants	$1,300,000
12/18/2009	Cache Valley Banking Company	Logan	UT	Preferred Stock	$4,640,000
12/18/2009	Birmingham Bloomfield Bancshares, Inc	Birmingham	MI	Preferred Stock	$1,744,000
12/18/2009	First Priority Financial Corp.	Malvern	PA	Preferred Stock	$4,596,000
12/18/2009	Northern State Bank	Closter	NJ	Preferred Stock	$1,230,000
12/18/2009	Union Bank & Trust Company	Oxford	NC	Preferred Stock	$2,997,000
12/22/2009	First Freedom Bancshares, Inc.	Lebanon	TN	Preferred Stock w/ Exercised Warrants	$8,700,000
12/22/2009	First Choice Bank	Cerritos	CA	Preferred Stock	$2,836,000
12/22/2009	Highlands Bancorp, Inc.	Vernon	NJ	Preferred Stock	$2,359,000
12/22/2009	Medallion Bank	Salt Lake City	UT	Preferred Stock w/ Exercised Warrants	$9,698,000
12/22/2009	Catskill Hudson Bancorp, Inc	Rock Hill	NY	Preferred Stock w/ Exercised Warrants	$3,500,000
12/22/2009	TriSummit Bank	Kingsport	TN	Preferred Stock	$4,237,000
12/29/2009	Atlantic Bancshares, Inc.	Bluffton	SC	Preferred Stock w/ Exercised Warrants	$2,000,000
12/29/2009	Union Financial Corporation	Albuquerque	NM	Preferred Stock w/ Exercised Warrants	$2,179,000
12/29/2009	Mainline Bancorp, Inc.	Ebensburg	PA	Preferred Stock w/ Exercised Warrants	$4,500,000
12/29/2009	FBHC Holding Company	Boulder	CO	Subordinated Debentures w/ Exercised Warrants	$3,035,000
12/29/2009	Western Illinois Bancshares Inc.	Monmouth	IL	Preferred Stock	$4,567,000
12/29/2009	DeSoto County Bank	Horn Lake	MS	Preferred Stock	$1,508,000
12/29/2009	Lafayette Bancorp, Inc.	Oxford	MS	Preferred Stock	$2,453,000
12/29/2009	Private Bancorporation, Inc.	Minneapolis	MN	Preferred Stock	$3,262,000

Table 3.7 All banks that received TARP funds.—cont'd

TARP Purchase Date	Name of Participating Institution	Institution City	Institution State	TARP Investment Description	TARP Investment Amount
		All Other Participants (cont.)			
12/29/2009	CBB Bancorp	Cartersville	GA	Preferred Stock	$1,753,000
12/29/2009	Illinois State Bancorp, Inc.	Chicago	IL	Preferred Stock w/ Exercised Warrants	$4,000,000
Total				**Total Purchase Amount**	**$204,893,941,320**

The table above sourced from the US Treasury website shows all the banks that received TARP capital injections.

TABLE 3.8 All banks that paid back TARP funds early (no later than 2010:Q4).

Name of Participating Institution	Institution City	Institution State	Investment Fully Repaid Early 2009-2010 (less Warrants)	Capital Repayment Date*
Involuntary Participants (Fully Repaid)				
Bank of America Corporation	Charlotte	NC	Full Repayment	12/9/2009
Bank of America Corporation	Charlotte	NC	Full Repayment	12/9/2009
The Bank of New York Mellon Corporation	New York	NY	Full Repayment	6/17/2009
Citigroup Inc.	New York	NY	Full Repayment	12/6/2010
The Goldman Sachs Group, Inc.	New York	NY	Full Repayment	6/17/2009
JPMorgan Chase & Co.	New York	NY	Full Repayment	6/17/2009
Morgan Stanley	New York	NY	Full Repayment	6/17/2009
State Street Corporation	Boston	MA	Full Repayment	6/17/2009
Wells Fargo & Company	San Francisco	CA	Full Repayment	12/23/2009
All Other Participants (Fully Repaid)				
Northern Trust Corporation	Chicago	IL	Full Repayment	6/17/2009
Washington Federal, Inc.	Seattle	WA	Full Repayment	5/27/2009
BB&T Corp.	Winston-Salem	NC	Full Repayment	6/17/2009
Umpqua Holdings Corp.	Portland	OR	Full Repayment	2/17/2010
Comerica Inc.	Dallas	TX	Full Repayment	3/17/2010
Capital One Financial Corporation	McLean	VA	Full Repayment	6/17/2009
First Horizon National Corporation	Memphis	TN	Full Repayment	12/22/2010
Huntington Bancshares	Columbus	OH	Full Repayment	12/22/2010
U.S. Bancorp	Minneapolis	MN	Full Repayment	6/17/2009
TCF Financial Corporation	Wayzata	MN	Full Repayment	4/22/2009
First Niagara Financial Group	Lockport	NY	Full Repayment	5/27/2009
HF Financial Corp.	Sioux Falls	SD	Full Repayment	6/3/2009
Centerstate Banks of Florida Inc.	Davenport	FL	Full Repayment	9/30/2009
First Community Bankshares Inc.	Bluefield	VA	Full Repayment	7/8/2009
Columbia Banking System, Inc.	Tacoma	WA	Full Repayment	8/11/2010
Heritage Financial Corporation	Olympia	WA	Full Repayment	12/22/2010
First PacTrust Bancorp, Inc.	Chula Vista	CA	Full Repayment	12/15/2010
Trustmark Corporation	Jackson	MS	Full Repayment	12/9/2009
WesBanco, Inc.	Wheeling	WV	Full Repayment	9/9/2009
Manhattan Bancorp	El Segundo	CA	Full Repayment	9/16/2009
Iberiabank Corporation	Lafayette	LA	Full Repayment	3/31/2009
East West Bancorp	Pasadena	CA	Full Repayment	12/29/2010
Bank of Marin Bancorp	Novato	CA	Full Repayment	3/31/2009
Old Line Bancshares, Inc.	Bowie	MD	Full Repayment	7/15/2009
Old National Bancorp	Evansville	IN	Full Repayment	3/31/2009
SVB Financial Group	Santa Clara	CA	Full Repayment	12/23/2009
Signature Bank	New York	NY	Full Repayment	3/31/2009
Bank of the Ozarks, Inc.	Little Rock	AR	Full Repayment	11/4/2009
Sterling Bancshares, Inc.	Houston	TX	Full Repayment	5/5/2009
The Bancorp, Inc.	Wilmington	DE	Full Repayment	3/10/2010
First Litchfield Financial Corporation	Litchfield	CT	Full Repayment	4/7/2010
LSB Corporation	North Andover	MA	Full Repayment	11/18/2009
Wainwright Bank & Trust Company	Boston	MA	Full Repayment	11/24/2009
Berkshire Hills Bancorp, Inc.	Pittsfield	MA	Full Repayment	5/27/2009
Security Federal Corporation	Aiken	SC	Full Repayment	9/29/2010
Wintrust Financial Corporation	Lake Forest	IL	Full Repayment	12/22/2010
Flushing Financial Corporation	Lake Success	NY	Full Repayment	10/28/2009
Monarch Financial Holdings, Inc.	Chesapeake	VA	Full Repayment	12/23/2009
Union First Market Bankshares Corporation	Bowling Green	VA	Full Repayment	11/18/2009
Bancorp Rhode Island, Inc.	Providence	RI	Full Repayment	8/5/2009
Alliance Financial Corporation	Syracuse	NY	Full Repayment	5/13/2009
First Financial Bancorp	Cincinnati	OH	Full Repayment	2/24/2010
Fulton Financial Corporation	Lancaster	PA	Full Repayment	7/14/2010
United Bancorporation of Alabama, Inc.	Atmore	AL	Full Repayment	9/3/2010
1st Constitution Bancorp	Cranbury	NJ	Full Repayment	10/27/2010
Central Jersey Bancorp	Oakhurst	NJ	Full Repayment	11/24/2010
Mission Valley Bancorp	Sun Valley	CA	Full Repayment	8/20/2010
Leader Bancorp, Inc.	Arlington	MA	Full Repayment	11/24/2010
Capital Bancorp, Inc.	Rockville	MD	Full Repayment	12/30/2010

TABLE 3.8 All banks that paid back TARP funds early (no later than 2010: Q4).—cont'd

Name of Participating Institution	Institution City	Institution State	Investment Fully Repaid Early 2009-2010 (less Warrants)	Capital Repayment Date*
All Other Participants (Fully Repaid) cont.				
The PNC Financial Services Group Inc.	Pittsburgh	PA	Full Repayment	2/10/2010
FirstMerit Corporation	Akron	OH	Full Repayment	4/22/2009
Commerce National Bank	Newport Beach	CA	Full Repayment	10/7/2009
Sun Bancorp, Inc.	Vineland	NJ	Full Repayment	4/8/2009
American Express Company	New York	NY	Full Repayment	6/17/2009
Independent Bank Corp.	Rockland	MA	Full Repayment	4/22/2009
LCNB Corp.	Lebanon	OH	Full Repayment	10/21/2009
F.N.B. Corporation	Hermitage	PA	Full Repayment	9/9/2009
Shore Bancshares, Inc.	Easton	MD	Full Repayment	4/15/2009
Surrey Bancorp	Mount Airy	NC	Full Repayment	12/29/2010
Texas National Bancorporation	Jacksonville	TX	Full Repayment	5/19/2010
Bar Harbor Bankshares	Bar Harbor	ME	Full Repayment	2/24/2010
Somerset Hills Bancorp	Bernardsville	NJ	Full Repayment	5/20/2009
SCBT Financial Corporation	Columbia	SC	Full Repayment	5/20/2009
Texas Capital Bancshares, Inc.	Dallas	TX	Full Repayment	5/13/2009
Carver Bancorp, Inc	New York	NY	Full Repayment	8/27/2010
Citizens & Northern Corporation	Wellsboro	PA	Full Repayment	8/4/2010
OceanFirst Financial Corp.	Toms River	NJ	Full Repayment	12/30/2009
Centra Financial Holdings, Inc.	Morgantown	WV	Full Repayment	3/31/2009
Community Bank of the Bay	Oakland	CA	Full Repayment	9/29/2010
First Manitowoc Bancorp, Inc.	Manitowoc	WI	Full Repayment	5/27/2009
Southern Bancorp, Inc.	Arkadelphia	AR	Full Repayment	8/6/2010
1st Source Corporation	South Bend	IN	Full Repayment	12/29/2010
First ULB Corp.	Oakland	CA	Full Repayment	4/22/2009
Midland States Bancorp, Inc.	Effingham	IL	Full Repayment	12/23/2009
California Oaks State Bank	Thousand Oaks	CA	Full Repayment	12/8/2010
Middleburg Financial Corporation	Middleburg	VA	Full Repayment	12/23/2009
First Southern Bancorp, Inc.	Boca Raton	FL	Full Repayment	6/16/2010
Hilltop Community Bancorp, Inc.	Summit	NJ	Full Repayment	4/21/2010
The First Bancshares, Inc.	Hattiesburg	MS	Full Repayment	9/29/2010
PGB Holdings, Inc.	Chicago	IL	Full Repayment	8/13/2010
Liberty Financial Services, Inc.	New Orleans	LA	Full Repayment	9/24/2010
State Capital Corporation	Greenwood	MS	Full Repayment	9/29/2010
First Choice Bank	Cerritos	CA	Full Repayment	9/24/2010
Midwest Regional Bancorp, Inc.	Festus	MO	Full Repayment	11/10/2009
Lafayette Bancorp, Inc.	Oxford	MS	Full Repayment	9/29/2010
BancPlus Corporation	Ridgeland	MS	Full Repayment	9/29/2010
Lakeland Financial Corporation	Warsaw	IN	Full Repayment	6/9/2010
First M&F Corporation	Kosciusko	MS	Full Repayment	9/29/2010
First State Bank of Mobeetie	Mobeetie	TX	Full Repayment	4/14/2010
Green City Bancshares, Inc.	Green City	MO	Full Repayment	7/14/2010
PSB Financial Corporation	Many	LA	Full Repayment	9/29/2010
Citizens Bancshares Corporation	Atlanta	GA	Full Repayment	8/13/2010
Discover Financial Services	Riverwoods	IL	Full Repayment	4/21/2010
First American International Corp.	Brooklyn	NY	Full Repayment	8/13/2010
Haviland Bancshares, Inc.	Haviland	KS	Full Repayment	12/29/2010
1st United Bancorp, Inc.	Boca Raton	FL	Full Repayment	11/18/2009
IBW Financial Corporation	Washington	DC	Full Repayment	9/3/2010
Tri-State Bank of Memphis	Memphis	TN	Full Repayment	8/13/2010
Premier Bancorp, Inc.	Wilmette	IL	Full Repayment	8/13/2010
IBC Bancorp, Inc.	Chicago	IL	Full Repayment	9/10/2010
First Vernon Bancshares, Inc.	Vernon	AL	Full Repayment	9/29/2010
University Financial Corp, Inc.	St. Paul	MN	Full Repayment	7/30/2010
Hartford Financial Services Group, Inc.	Hartford	CT	Full Repayment	3/31/2010
Security Capital Corporation	Batesville	MS	Full Repayment	9/29/2010
M&F Bancorp, Inc.	Durham	NC	Full Repayment	8/20/2010
Signature Bancshares, Inc.	Dallas	TX	Full Repayment	12/15/2010
Lincoln National Corporation	Radnor	PA	Full Repayment	6/30/2010

Continued

TABLE 3.8   All banks that paid back TARP funds early (no later than 2010: Q4).—cont'd

Name of Participating Institution	Institution City	Institution State	Investment Fully Repaid Early 2009-2010 (less Warrants)	Capital Repayment Date*
All Other Participants (Fully Repaid) cont.				
Community Bancshares of Mississippi, Inc.	Brandon	MS	Full Repayment	9/29/2010
First Eagle Bancshares, Inc.	Hanover Park	IL	Full Repayment	9/17/2010
Guaranty Capital Corporation	Belzoni	MS	Full Repayment	7/30/2010
Nationwide Bankshares, Inc.	West Point	NE	Full Repayment	12/29/2010
First Choice Bank	Cerritos	CA	Full Repayment	9/24/2010
Lafayette Bancorp, Inc.	Oxford	MS	Full Repayment	9/29/2010
All Other Participants (Partially Repaid)				
Valley National Bancorp	Wayne	NJ	Partial Repayment	6/3/2009
City National Corporation	Beverly Hills	CA	Partial Repayment	12/30/2009
Webster Financial Corporation	Waterbury	CT	Partial Repayment	3/3/2010
Boston Private Financial Holdings, Inc.	Boston	MA	Partial Repayment	1/13/2010
Eagle Bancorp, Inc.	Bethesda	MD	Partial Repayment	12/23/2009
Sandy Spring Bancorp, Inc.	Olney	MD	Partial Repayment	7/21/2010
CVB Financial Corp	Ontario	CA	Partial Repayment	8/26/2009
Susquehanna Bancshares, Inc	Lititz	PA	Partial Repayment	4/21/2010
Horizon Bancorp	Michigan City	IN	Partial Repayment	11/10/2010
Magna Bank	Memphis	TN	Partial Repayment	11/24/2009
Peapack-Gladstone Financial Corporation	Gladstone	NJ	Partial Repayment	1/6/2010
United Financial Banking Companies, Inc.	Vienna	VA	Partial Repayment	12/15/2010
State Bankshares, Inc.	Fargo	ND	Partial Repayment	8/12/2009
FPB Financial Corp.	Hammond	LA	Partial Repayment	12/16/2009
Lakeland Bancorp, Inc.	Oak Ridge	NJ	Partial Repayment	8/4/2010
Westamerica Bancorporation	San Rafael	CA	Partial Repayment	9/2/2009
The Bank of Kentucky Financial Corporation	Crestview Hills	KY	Partial Repayment	12/22/2010
Frontier Bancshares, Inc.	Austin	TX	Partial Repayment	11/24/2009
All Other Participants (Other Chnages in Payment Status)				
South Financial Group, Inc.	Greenville	SC	Shares Sold to Another Institution	9/30/2010
The Bank of Currituck	Moyock	NC	Shares Sold to Another Institution	12/3/2010
TIB Financial Corp	Naples	FL	Shares Sold to Another Institution	9/30/2010
CIT Group Inc.	New York	NY	Bankruptcy, Amount Not Recovered	2/8/2010
Pacific Coast National Bancorp	San Clemente	CA	Bankruptcy, Amount Not Recovered	2/11/2010

3.1.7.1 Top and bottom 10 institutions by size and age

Table 3.6 Panels A-J show the bank names, city and state, as they appear in the US Treasury Report, ranked in terms of dollar bailout amount, and a number of bailout and financial ratios as of 2008:Q4, when the TARP program commenced. As above, financial information is sourced from the Call Reports aggregated to the holding company level, and using SNL Financial for institutions not covered in the Call Reports.

Specifically, we present the top 10 and bottom 10 participants, respectively, in terms of dollar bailout amount (expressed in $ thousands), for the following size and age groups: 1) *large banks* (GTA exceeding $3 billion) in Panels A and B; 2) *medium-size banks* (GTA exceeding $1 billion and up to $3 billion) in Panels C and D; 3) *small banks* (GTA up to $1 billion) in Panels E and F; 4) *older banks* (with maximum bank age in the institution structure greater than or equal to the median age of 39 years old) in Panels G and H; and 5) *younger banks* (with maximum bank age in the institution structure less than the median age of 39 years old) in Panels I and J.

Panels A-J reveal a large variety of bailout amounts that went to the various participants and post-bailout behavior in terms of repaying early or not by no later than 2010:Q4 or missing or not dividend payments. While large and older institutions tended to get higher dollar bailout amounts, the amounts injected were often relatively meaningful relative to the banks' total equity in almost all cases, including for smaller institutions. The financial strength indicators for the participants reveal varied profiles as measured by capital, risk-weighted assets, liquidity, loans/assets, deposits/assets, nonperforming loans, charge-offs, provisions/loans, profitability and overhead costs ratios, with very few consistent patterns across them.

For brevity, we only discuss next in detail Panels A and B for top 10 and bottom 10 large bank participants, and invite readers to review details for other tables for which they may have special interests.

Looking at Panel A, showing top 10 large bailout recipients, as expected, we observe that six of them are involuntary participants in the program. The amounts injected range from $25 billion the highest amount going to four different institutions, Bank of America, Citigroup, JP Morgan Chase, and Wells Fargo, to $3.6 billion the lowest amount going to Capital One. These also represent large amounts relative to the institution's total equity capital.[5] We also see that eight out of 10 banks repaid early by 2010:Q4, and none of them missed dividend payments. In terms of financial condition in 2008:Q4, these institutions appear to be generally well capitalized with equity ratios ranging between 8.42% to 15.59%. Their loans relative to assets range between 2.62% to 70.80% and their deposits to assets between 27.62% and 79.98%. They have varied risk, liquidity, and profitability profiles. Thus, their risk-weighted assets ratios are between 44.75% and 92.94%, their nonperforming loans ratios are between 0% and 3.79%, charge-off ratios between 0% and 3.08%, and provisions to loans ratios between 0.05% and 4.92%. Their liquidity ratios range between 3.03% and 51.81%. Some are more profitable than others, and two register negative ROAs, but most have positive profitability. Finally, overhead costs ratios, often regarded as measures of management quality, where lower ratios suggest higher cost efficiency and better management quality, range between 0.68% to 7.31%.

Looking at Panel B, showing the bottom 10 large bailout recipients, the amounts injected range from $52 million, the lowest amount going to WSFS Financial Corporation, to $78 million, the highest amount going to Independent Bank Corporation. The bailout amounts, despite being much smaller than those of the top 10 group for large institutions, are relatively

---

[5] Note that some ratios may appear large also because equity is based on the Call Report aggregated equity value of all commercial banks under the holding company structure.

meaningful relative to these banks' total equity capital, and range between 4.13% and 28.06%. Only five out of 10 banks repaid early by 2010: Q4, and no institution missed its dividend payments. The banks' equity capital ratios range between 5.90% to 13.80%, so that some are much more capitalized than others. As is the case for the top 10 group above for large institutions, these banks also have a mix of risk, liquidity, and profitability profiles, with some having very high nonperforming loans ratios reaching as high as 7.75% and 3 out of 10 institutions having negative ROAs, but others having very low risks, high liquidity ratios, and relatively high profitability. Finally, their overhead costs ratios range between 1.14% and 5.42%.[34]

3.1.7.2 Use of Capital Surveys (Capital Purchase Program)

In order to determine how effective the TARP program was, the US Treasury surveyed the participating institutions, asking them how they employed the capital infusions each year. The surveys include participants in the CPP as well as participants in the CDCI, another program of the Office of Financial Stability (OFS). The purpose of the surveys was to obtain insights into lending, financial intermediation, and capital building activities of all recipients. More precisely, the participants could report on multiple uses of capital from the following eight categories: (1) increase lending or reduce lending less than otherwise would have occurred; (2) increase securities purchased (ABS, MBS, etc.); (3) make other investments; (4) increase reserves for nonperforming assets; (5) reduce borrowings; (6) increase charge-offs; (7) purchase another financial institution or purchase assets from another financial institution; and (8) hold as nonleveraged increase to total capital. Table 3.9 shows summaries of the surveys conducted over 2009–2017. These summaries list the percentage of respondents that cited each of the eight uses listed in the survey (in order of the most frequently cited).

A total of 664 institutions surveyed submitted responses out of 738 total recipients (90%) with funds (CCP and CDCI programs) in 2009. This number declined over time to as low as 40% in 2012 and reached 63% in 2017 (the last survey year). Across all years, a majority of respondents (85% in 2009, 82% in 2010, 81% in 2011, 77% in 2012, 76% in 2013, 80% in 2014 and 2015, 78% in 2016, and 73% in 2017) cited that their institutions increased lending or reduced lending less than otherwise would have occurred after the receipt of the capital injections. Other highly cited uses of the capital are holding the capital as a nonleveraged increase to total capital and increasing reserves for nonperforming assets.

TABLE 3.9 US. Treasury annual use of capital survey for the TARP[a].

Panel A: Annual Use of Capital Survey for Years 2009, 2010, 2011, and 2012.

Rank	Cited Use of Capital	2009 Survey Number of Respondents	2009 Survey Percentage of Respondents	2010 Survey Number of Respondents	2010 Survey Percentage of Respondents	2011 Survey Number of Respondents	2011 Survey Percentage of Respondents	2012 Survey Number of Respondents	2012 Survey Percentage of Respondents
1	Increase lending or reduce lending less than otherwise would have occurred	565	85.2%	465	81.5%	304	80.6%	141	76.6%
2	Held as non-leveraged increase to total capital	352	53.1%	273	48.9%	179	47.5%	73	39.7%
3	Increase reserves for non-performing assets	306	46.2%	252	45.2%	153	40.6%	65	35.3%
4	Increase securities purchased (ABS, MBS, etc.)	241	36.3%	211	37.8%	146	38.7%	56	30.4%
5	Reduce borrowings	279	42.1%	211	37.8%	137	36.3%	55	29.9%
6	Make other investments	251	37.9%	184	33.0%	125	33.2%	50	27.2%
7	Increase charge-offs	83	12.5%	56	10.0%	41	10.9%	15	8.2%
8	Purchase another financial institution or purchase assets from another financial institution	82	12.4%	57	10.2%	30	8.0%	9	4.9%
	Total number of respondents	664		558		398		188	

	2009	2010	2011	2012
Number of participants with funds	738	679	640	473
Total Respondents	664	558	398	188
CPP respondents	635	485	336	151
CDCI respondents	29	73	62	37
Total Respondent rate by count	90%	82%	67%	40%

Note: 29 institutions converted from CPP in 2009. Terms for the CDCI program were announced in February 2010.

Continued

I. Introductory materials

Table 3.9   US. Treasury annual use of capital survey for the TARP[a].—cont'd

Panel B: Annual Use of Capital Survey for Year 2013

Rank	Cited Use of Capital	2013 Survey	
		Number of Respondents	Percentage of Respondents
1	Increase lending or reduce lending less than otherwise would have occurred	114	75.5%
2	Held as non-leveraged increase to total capital	60	39.7%
3	Increase reserves for non-performing assets	55	36.4%
4	Increase securities purchased (ABS, MBS, etc.)	30	19.9%
5	Reduce borrowings	35	23.2%
6	Make other investments	14	9.3%
7	Increase charge-offs	37	24.5%
8	Purchase another financial institution or purchase assets from another financial institution	8	10.1%
	Total number of respondents	151	

Number of participants with funds	2013
	322
Total Respondents	151
CPP respondents	101
CDCI respondents	50
Total Respondent rate by count	47%

Panel C: Annual Use of Capital Survey for Year 2014

Rank	Cited Use of Capital	2014 Survey	
		Number of Respondents	Percentage of Respondents
1	Increase lending or reduce lending less than otherwise would have occurred	63	79.7%
2	Held as non-leveraged increase to total capital	27	34.2%
3	Increase reserves for non-performing assets	28	35.4%
4	Increase securities purchased (ABS, MBS, etc.)	13	16.5%
5	Reduce borrowings	9	11.4%
6	Make other investments	11	23.9%
7	Increase charge-offs	16	20.3%
8	Purchase another financial institution or purchase assets from another financial institution	9	11.4%
	Total number of respondents	79	

Number of participants with funds	2014
	148
Total Respondents	79
CPP respondents	34
CDCI respondents	45
Total Respondent rate by count	53%

Table 3.9 US. Treasury annual use of capital survey for the TARP[a].—cont'd

Panel D: Annual Use of Capital Survey for Year 2015

Rank	Cited Use of Capital	2015 Survey	
		Number of Respondents	Percentage of Respondents
1	Increase lending or reduce lending less than otherwise would have occurred	53	77.9%
2	Held as non-leveraged increase to total capital	24	35.3%
3	Increase reserves for non-performing assets	19	27.9%
4	Increase securities purchased (ABS, MBS, etc.)	11	16.2%
5	Reduce borrowings	11	16.2%
6	Make other investments	11	16.2%
7	Increase charge-offs	10	14.7%
8	Purchase another financial institution or purchase assets from another financial institution	3	4.4%
	Total number of respondents	**68**	

	2015
Number of participants with funds	100
Total Respondents	68
CPP respondents	18
CDCI respondents	50
Total Respondent rate by count	**68%**

Panel E: Annual Use of Capital Survey for Year 2016

Rank	Cited Use of Capital	2016 Survey	
		Number of Respondents	Percentage of Respondents
1	Increase lending or reduce lending less than otherwise would have occurred	38	77.6%
2	Held as non-leveraged increase to total capital	16	32.7%
3	Increase reserves for non-performing assets	13	26.5%
4	Increase securities purchased (ABS, MBS, etc.)	9	18.4%
5	Reduce borrowings	9	18.4%
6	Make other investments	9	18.4%
7	Increase charge-offs	11	22.4%
8	Purchase another financial institution or purchase assets from another financial institution	3	6.1%
	Total number of respondents	**49**	

Continued

I. Introductory materials

Table 3.9 US. Treasury annual use of capital survey for the TARP[a].—cont'd

	2016
Number of participants with funds	76
Total Respondents	49
CPP respondents	8
CDCI respondents	41
Total Respondent rate by count	64%

Panel F: Annual Use of Capital Survey for Year 2017

		2017 Survey	
Rank	**Cited Use of Capital**	**Number of Respondents**	**Percentage of Respondents**
1	Increase lending or reduce lending less than otherwise would have occurred	19	73.1%
2	Held as non-leveraged increase to total capital	3	11.5%
3	Increase reserves for non-performing assets	8	30.8%
4	Increase securities purchased (ABS, MBS, etc.)	1	3.8%
5	Reduce borrowings	3	11.5%
6	Make other investments	4	15.4%
7	Increase charge-offs	5	19.2%
8	Purchase another financial institution or purchase assets from another financial institution	1	3.8%
	Total number of respondents	**26**	

	2017
Number of participants with funds	41
Total Respondents	26
CPP respondents	7
CDCI respondents	19
Total Respondent rate by count	63%

Note: 29 institutions converted from CPP in 2009. Terms for the CDCI program were announced in February 2010. Survey summaries for 2009-14 and 2017 were taken from the US Treasury website, while survey summaries for 2015-16 were compiled by the authors based on the granular data by institution provided on the US Treasury at https://www.treasury.gov/initiatives/financial-stability/TARP-Programs/bank-investment-programs/cap/use-of-capital/Pages/default.aspx.
[a]https://www.treasury.gov/initiatives/financial-stability/TARP-Programs/bank-investment-programs/cap/use-of-capital/Pages/default.aspx and https://www.treasury.gov/initiatives/financial-stability/TARP-Programs/bank-investment-programs/cap/use-of-capital/PublishingImages and https://www.treasury.gov/initiatives/financial-stability/TARP-Programs/bank-investment-programs/cap/Pages/payments.aspx.

3.2 Other bank bailouts in the US during the Global Financial Crisis

While TARP appears to be the most prominent program in response to the financial crisis, the US government took many other actions around the same time.

For example, the Federal Reserve also injected liquidity into banks during the crisis using other programs. On August 17, 2007, it instituted the Term Discount Window (TDW) Program, a temporary program that provided discount window funds with maturities beyond overnight, funds being initially made available for up to 30 days and later extended to 90 days.

On December 12, 2007, the Term Auction Facility (TAF) was created to address the potential stigma associated with using the discount window, and it included a series of auctions for funds at maturities of either 28 or 84 days available to qualify depository institutions in generally healthy condition. See Berger, Black, Bouwman, and Dlugosz (2017) for more details.

On October 14, 2008, the FDIC instituted the Temporary Liquidity Guarantee Program (TLGP) which consisted of two guarantee programs meant to calm market fears and encourage liquidity in the interbank lending market. One program was the Federal Deposit Transaction Account Guarantee Program (TAGP), which provided temporary full FDIC guarantees for domestic noninterest-bearing transaction accounts, low-interest checking accounts (Negotiable Orders of Withdrawal or NOW accounts), and Interest on Lawyers Trust Accounts (IOLTAs) held at participating banks and thrifts through December 31, 2009. The deadline of the program was extended twice and expired on December 31, 2010. The other program was the Transaction Debt Guarantee Program (TDGP) which provided guarantees on new issues of senior unsecured debt.

In terms of costs, the FDIC reported that 122 entities issued TLGP debt and at its peak, the TDGP guaranteed $345.8 billion of outstanding debt. The FDIC collected $10.4 billion in fees and surcharges under the TDGP and paid $153 million in losses resulting from six participating entities defaulting on debt issued under the TDGP. For the TAGP, the FDIC collected $1.2 billion in fees and total estimated TAGP losses were $2.1 billion on failures as of December 31, 2012.

The SBLF (Small Business Lending Fund) was a $30 billion dedicated fund created as part of the 2010 Small Business Jobs Act to encourage lending to small business customers by providing low-cost Tier 1 capital to qualified community banks with assets of less than $10 billion and community development financial institutions (CDFIs). It had the goal to help Main Street banks and small businesses work together to help create jobs and promote economic growth in local communities across the nation.

Treasury invested over $4.0 billion in 332 institutions through the SBLF program. These amounts include investments of $3.9 billion in 281 community banks and $104 million in 51 CDLFs. Collectively, these institutions operate in over 3000 locations across 47 states and the District of Columbia. Banks paid for SBLF funds via dividends on the stock purchased by the Treasury. The dividend rate was reduced as their level of small business lending increased. Thus, the program incentivized institutions to increase their lending using SBLF funds immediately to ensure they are paying the lowest rate for them (Cortés and Millington, 2014).[7]

The Federal Home Loan Bank (FHLB) system also served as reliable and low-cost source of funding for local banks during the crisis to support mortgage lending. There are 12 Federal Home Loan Banks in the US, and they operate throughout the US. To use the Home Loan Bank credit, community development and mortgage finance products, a financial institution must first become a member of a Home Loan Bank. The Federal Loan Banks operate as a cooperative in that the members own them.

The Federal Reserve also engaged in unconventional monetary policy throughout and after the crisis under which it massively purchased mortgage-backed securities (MBSs) and US Treasuries. Quantitative Easing (QE) was implemented in four phases, QE1, QE2, QE3, and QE4, with pauses in between them. Readers can see Box 1.1 in Chapter 1 for exact amounts in each of the QE programs.

Finally, as discussed in Chapter 1, another related bank bailout is that of a very large insurance company, American International Group (AIG). AIG owed significant amount of funds to a number of large banks. The government used loans and capital injections for the bailout and insisted on dollar-for-dollar full payments to their counterparty banks, avoiding large losses for these banks, effectively making this a bank bailout.

3.3 Bailouts in other nations during the Global Financial Crisis, European Sovereign Debt Crisis, and other times

The Global Financial Crisis emerged in Europe shortly after it started in the US. The problems continued with several European country-level sovereign debt crises. Similar to the US, in 2008, European markets experienced a general loss of confidence, while several large European cross-border banking organizations suffered serious capital and liquidity problems. Unlike the US, the EU macroprudential supervision was conducted at both the European and the member country level, although in principle,

[7] https://www.clevelandfed.org/newsroom-and-events/publications/economic-trends/2014-economic-trends/et-20141125-gauging-the-impact-of-small-business-lending-funds.aspx.

national regulators were responsible for their own macroprudential policies.[8] Thus, implementing effective remedies for the crisis was slower and different in the EU than the US (e.g., Pisani-Ferry and Sapir, 2010).

On September 27 and September 30, 2008, Fortis and Dexia were the first large institutions to be bailed out by the Benelux nations of Belgium, Luxembourg, and Netherlands. On September 30, 2008, the government of Ireland also announced its decision to guarantee all deposits and debts of six Irish banks and all their subsidiaries abroad. This was the beginning of other similar national initiatives, and upon meetings at the EU level, it was agreed that the economic situation needed a coordinated response at the EU level as well.

The European Commission played a very active role in dealing with the financial crisis and revised the State Aid framework to allow member states to put in place an effective response. It authorized national governments to provide state aid and guarantees to financial institutions.

To address financial market distress, several bank aid approaches were taken from consolidating banks in Spain to establish "a bad bank" in Germany, and nationalizing banks in the UK and the Netherlands. In all cases, the financial institutions were rescued using taxpayers' money. The various types of liquidity and capital support helped prevent the failure of systemically important institutions and restore confidence, but transferred significant risks to the sovereigns. At the end of 2009, this evolved into the European Sovereign Debt Crisis encompassing the EU member states of Greece, Ireland, Portugal, Spain, and Cyprus, which could not repay or refinance their government debt or bail out stressed banks without aid from third-party organizations such as the European Central Bank (ECB), the International Monetary Fund (IMF), and the European Financial Stability Facility (EFSF). In 2010, 17 countries in the EU voted to create the EFSF to address the European Sovereign Debt Crisis. The EFSF lasted until 2012.[9]

To reduce negative spillovers in the banking system and enhance financial stability in the EU countries, from 2008 to 2016, the European Commission approved a total of about €5.0 trillion of state aid that may be

---

[8] Since the establishment of the Banking Union in 2014, the largest banks in the Euro area are under the direct supervision of the ECB.

[9] At the heart of the European Sovereign Debt Crisis, policymakers decided to form a Banking Union in order to break the link between distressed sovereigns and distressed banks. This implied three important decisions: (1) largest banks would become subject to the Single Supervisory Mechanism (SSM), which transferred regulatory oversight from national regulators to the ECB; (2) European Stability Mechanism (ESM) was formed as a central source of financing for bank bailouts; and (3) the BRRD and the SRM were established to resolve large failed banking organizations.

granted for 28 EU countries, out of which about €1.9 trillion was effectively implemented (see Table 3.10).[10] The implemented measures account for about 13.1% of 2016 EU GDP, but there was significant variety across countries. Four different types of bailout support were used: guarantees on bank liabilities, 61.0% of the total; capital injections (recapitalizations), 23.9% of the total; asset relief interventions, 9.7% of the total; and bank liquidity support, 5.4% of the total. Guarantees on bank liabilities is the most commonly used instrument during the crisis in the EU, providing bank debtors with an implicit guarantee if the bank fails to repay its debts. It accounts for 8% of the 2016 EU GDP over 2008–2016 but registers the highest volumes at the peak of the crisis in 2009 and 2010, and then steadily declines over the rest of the period. Recapitalizations are the second most used instrument under which the government relieves banks of "toxic" assets, representing 3.1% of the 2016 EU GDP. Greece, Italy, Ireland, Portugal, and Spain (GIIPS countries), which suffered great instabilities during the crisis, were the main users of all support measures over 2008–16, using 44% of all guarantee support, 42% of the capital injections, 21% of all asset relief support, and 29% of the liquidity measures.

The types of aid measures used varied across individual EU countries as well. The highest amounts of outstanding guarantees were used by Ireland accounting for 24% of the total EU used, while capital injections were used in close amounts 13%–14% of the EU total by Germany, Ireland, and Spain. Asset relief support was highest in Germany with 42% of the total EU. Finally, liquidity support was highest in the UK and the Netherlands, with 32% and 29%, respectively, of the total EU used. Eastern European countries used the least amount of support, likely due to having many foreign-owned banks, which were already bailed out by their home country.

There is no centralized location listing all banks in the EU that received bailouts as for the US TARP program. The closest are some recent research papers that compile themselves lists of such institutions by manually collecting the information from various sources and annual reports. We show in Table 3.11 a short list of 30 large institutions (€20 billion or more in assets) from 15 EU countries that underwent bailouts of three types (guarantees, capital injections, and liquidity injections), the list being adapted after Ongena and Nistor-Mutu (2019). Importantly, Ongena and Nistor-Mutu (2019) note that these banks were subject to 106 different aid events so that some banks received multiple aids leading to 36 state guarantees events, 35 capital injections, and 35 liquidity injection events. Out of 30 banks, six banks received all three types of aid, 14 banks received two types, and 10 banks received only one type.

---

[10] See European Commission website at http://ec.europa.eu/competition/state_aid/scoreboard/index_en.html.

TABLE 3.10 European Bailout Programs 2008-2016

No.	EU Member State	EU Approved Aid Instrument over 2008-16 (€ Billion)					EU Used Aid Instrument over 2008-16 (€ Billion)				
		Approved Recapitalizations	Approved Impaired Asset Measures	Approved Guarantees	Approved Other Liquidity Measures	Total or Max Aid Approved	Used Recapitalizations	Used Impaired Asset Measures	Used Guarantees	Used Other Liquidity Measures	Total or Max Aid Used
1	Belgium	23.3	28.2	275.8	20.5	347.8	20.8	21.8	46.8	0.0	89.4
2	Bulgaria	0.0	0.0	0.0	1.7	1.7	0.0	0.0	0.0	0.0	0.0
3	Czech Republic	0.0	0.0	0.0	0.0	0.0	0.0	0.0	0.0	0.0	0.0
4	Denmark	14.6	2.3	580.0	4.9	601.8	10.8	0.3	145.0	2.0	158.1
5	Germany	114.6	82.8	447.8	9.5	654.6	64.2	80.0	135.0	4.7	283.9
6	Estonia	0.0	0.0	0.0	0.0	0.0	0.0	0.0	0.0	0.0	0.0
7	Ireland	92.4	57.2	376.0	40.7	566.4	62.8	2.6	284.3	0.9	350.5
8	Greece	59.6	0.0	93.4	8.0	161.0	46.7	0.0	62.3	6.9	115.9
9	Spain	174.3	139.9	200.0	30.0	544.2	61.9	32.9	72.0	19.3	186.0
10	France	29.2	4.7	319.8	8.7	362.3	25.0	1.2	92.7	0.0	119.0
11	Croatia	0.0	0.0	0.0	0.0	0.0	0.0	0.0	0.0	0.0	0.0
12	Italy	25.8	0.4	150.0	0.0	176.2	11.5	0.3	85.7	0.0	97.5
13	Cyprus	3.5	0.0	6.0	0.0	9.5	3.5	0.0	2.8	1.0	6.3
14	Latvia	0.8	0.5	5.1	2.1	8.5	0.5	0.4	0.5	0.0	2.5
15	Lithuania	0.8	0.6	0.3	0.0	1.8	0.3	0.0	0.0	0.0	0.3
16	Luxembourg	2.5	0.0	4.5	0.3	7.3	2.6	0.0	3.8	0.1	6.5
17	Hungary	1.1	0.1	5.4	3.9	10.4	0.2	0.0	0.0	2.5	2.8
18	Malta	0.0	0.0	0.0	0.0	0.0	0.0	0.0	0.0	0.0	0.0
19	Netherlands	39.8	30.6	200.0	52.9	323.4	23.0	5.0	40.9	30.4	99.3
20	Austria	40.1	0.6	75.0	0.0	115.7	11.8	0.5	19.3	0.0	31.7
21	Poland	43.2	0.0	29.3	0.0	72.5	0.0	0.1	0.0	0.0	0.1
22	Portugal	34.8	4.4	28.2	6.1	73.5	14.5	3.2	16.6	3.8	38.2
23	Romania	0.0	0.0	0.0	0.0	0.0	0.0	0.0	0.0	0.0	0.0
24	Slovenia	4.5	3.8	12.0	0.0	20.3	3.6	0.3	2.2	0.0	6.1
25	Slovakia	0.7	0.0	2.8	0.0	3.5	0.0	0.0	0.0	0.0	0.0
26	Finland	4.0	0.0	50.0	0.0	54.0	0.0	0.0	0.1	0.0	0.1
27	Sweden	5.0	0.0	156.0	0.5	161.6	0.8	0.0	19.9	0.0	20.7
28	UK	114.6	248.1	364.5	39.9	767.1	100.1	40.4	158.2	33.3	332.1
	Total	929.4	604.3	3,381.6	229.7	5,045.0	464.6	189.2	1,188.1	105.0	1,946.9
	% of Total	16.4%	12.0%	67.0%	4.6%	100.0%	23.9%	9.7%	61.0%	5.4%	100.0%
	% of 2016 EU GDP	5.6%	4.1%	22.7%	1.5%	33.8%	3.1%	1.3%	8.0%	0.7%	13.1%

(Source: European Commission)

I. Introductory materials

TABLE 3.11 Individual European bank bailouts 2008–14.

No.	Bank	Country	Guarantees	Recapitalizations	Liquidity Injections
1	Allied Irish Banks plc	Ireland	x	x	x
2	Banca Piccolo Credito Valtelline	Italy		x	
3	Banca Popolare di Milano SCaRL	Italy	x	x	
4	Banco BPI SA	Portugal		x	
5	Banco Comercial Português, SAMi	Portugal	x	x	
6	Banco de Sabadell SA	Spain	x	x	x
7	Banco Espirito Santo SA	Portugal	x		
8	Bank of Cyprus Public Company	Cyprus	x		x
9	Bank of Ireland	Ireland	x	x	x
10	BNP Paribas	France		x	x
11	Caixabank, S.A.	Spain		x	x
12	Commerzbank AG	Germany	x	x	
13	Crédit Agricole S.A.	France		x	x
14	Danske Bank A/S	Denmark	x	x	
15	Erste Group Bank AG	Austria	x	x	
16	First Investment Bank AD	Bulgaria			x
17	ING Groep NV	Netherlands	x	x	x
18	Intesa Sanpaolo	Italy	x		
19	KBC Groep NV	Belgium		x	x
20	Lloyds Banking Group Plc	United Kingdom	x	x	x
21	Mediobanca SpA	Italy	x		
22	Natixis SA	France		x	x
23	OTP Bank Plc	Hungary			x
24	Raiffeisen Bank International AG	Austria	x	x	x
25	Royal Bank of Scotland Group Plc	United Kingdom	x	x	x
26	Société Générale SA	France		x	
27	Spar Nord Bank	Denmark		x	
28	Swedbank AB	Sweden	x		
29	Unione di Banche Italiane Scpa-U	Italy	x		
30	Volksbank Vorarlberg e.Gen.	Austria	x	x	

Source: Ongena and Nistor-Muttu (2019).

Similar to the US, EU member states made extensive use of various forms of government support to stabilize their banking sectors. In contrast, however, the EU approved support amounts much higher than used and guarantees rather than capital injections were the most important type of aid used, suggesting differences in the aid type choice and implementation (Gropp and Tonzer, 2016).

3.4 Bail-ins in the US and other nations

3.4.1 Orderly Liquidation Authority (OLA) and Total Loss-Absorbing Capacity (TLAC) requirements in the US

In the US, Title II of the Dodd–Frank Act of 2010 (Section 202) introduced the OLA bail-in regime. The resolution process applies to "covered financial corporations," broadly referred as BHCs and other holding companies engaged in financial activities that are "in default or danger of default," and whose failure would have serious adverse effects on US financial stability.

The FDIC is charged as receiver of such an entity and would assume broad statutory authority to wind down and sell off the financial company. The FDIC uses a single point of entry (SPOE) strategy in which only the US top-tier parent holding company is placed into receivership (including claims of shareholders and most unsecured creditors who absorb losses), management is dismissed and the institution is orderly liquidated, while solvent subsidiaries are transferred to a newly established bridge financial company and continue operations as usual to avoid further disruptions to the financial system. Title II of the Act also establishes in the Treasury the Orderly Liquidation Fund (OLF), a fund managed by the FDIC to: (1) enable the FDIC to implement its authorities in the Act; and (2) cover the cost of authorized actions, including the orderly liquidation of covered financial companies. The fund is capitalized by collecting risk-based assessment fees on any BHC with total consolidated assets equal to or greater than $50 billion and any nonbank financial company supervised by the Board of Governors. Thus, OLA relies on the OLF to provide financing to the financial company in receivership when private funding is not available.

OLA has been implemented, but it has not been triggered yet. However, as discussed in Chapter 17, research suggests that OLA has significantly changed bank capital behavior.

In December 2016, the Federal Reserve Board of Governors finalized total loss absorbing capacity (TLAC) rules that require banks to have sufficient loss absorbing capacity on both going- and gone-concern bases for cases of severe distress. Because a bank's regulatory capital is likely to be significantly exhausted in the run up to a resolution, banks are required to have sufficient bail-inable instruments (common equity and eligible subordinated long-term debt) that can be written down to recapitalize operating subsidiaries. Eligible TLAC debt securities must be subordinate to all other creditors and claims (except equity) and are subject to a 100% haircut for amounts due to be paid within one year. TLAC must also have a remaining maturity of at least one year and include no provision by which holders could circumvent the loss-bearing purposes of TLAC debt. In case of distress, supervisors will convert TLAC debt (also called "bail-in" debt) into equity at either the parent or subsidiary level (e.g., Flannery and Bliss, 2019).[11] The eight US Globally Systemically Important Banks (G-SIBs) are subject to a minimum TLAC requirement of 21.5%–23% and a minimum long-term debt requirement of 7%–10%. Subject institutions had to comply with these requirements by January 1, 2019.

3.4.2 Other historical bail-ins: double liability during the Great Depression in the US

Another form of bail-in used in the US in the past is "double liability." Today, bank shareholders are liable only for the amount of their investment if the bank becomes insolvent and have no personal responsibility for the bank debts. However, between the Civil War and the Great Depression (nearly three quarters of a century), shareholders had double liability. When a bank became insolvent, shareholders would lose both their investments (as under limited liability) and also had to pay an amount that could be as high as the current value of their shares in compensation to depositors and creditors. The goals were to both mitigate excessive bank risk and provide a safety net for depositors.

This system of "double liability" was actively and vigorously enforced throughout the period of its existence, generating an enormous volume of litigation, including about 50 decisions by the US Supreme Court and hundreds more in the state courts and lower federal courts (e.g., Macey and Miller, 1992). The regime of bank double liability was abandoned due to three reasons: (1) it had failed to protect bank creditors; (2) it did not maintain public confidence in the banking system; and (3) deposit insurance was a far preferable means for accomplishing the regulatory objectives. However, double liability helped enforce shareholder

---

[11] There are two main implementations discussed in the context of TLAC requirements: "single point of entry" (SPOE) and "multiple points of entry" (MPOE). The SPOE approach recapitalizes the firm's ultimate parent under the "home" supervisory authority, which expects the parent to downstream new equity to its subsidiaries. Under an MPOE approach, multiple subsidiaries will issue TLAC obligations in the market, and their solvency problems can be addressed by various host supervisors.

incentives to assess the risk of investments accurately and to better monitor bank managers.[12]

The Global Financial Crisis brought attention back to this mechanism, and one such proposal was to reintroduce double liability into the banking system to directly increase financial intermediaries' skin in the game (Leijonhufvud, 2010; Hendrickson, 2014; Salter, Veetil, and White, 2017; Anderson, Barth, Choi, 2018).

3.4.3 Other historical bail-ins: Long-Term Capital Management (LTCM)

A combination bailout—bail-in is the resolution of the world's largest hedge fund Long-Term Capital Management (LTCM) in 1998. As Berger and Bouwman (2016) point out, LTCM was following an arbitrage strategy meant to make money irrespective whether prices were rising or falling. When Russia defaulted on its sovereign debt on August 17, 1998, investors shifted from other government paper to the safe US Treasuries and this led to unexpected widening of spreads on supposedly low-risk portfolios. By end of August 1998, LTCM's capital had dropped dramatically to $2.3 billion, less than 50% of its December 1997 value, with assets standing at $126 billion. In the first 3 weeks of September, LTCM's capital fell even more to $600 million without diminishing the portfolio, and banks commenced to distrust its ability to meet margin calls.

In order to avert a probable catastrophic breakdown due to the collapse of the largest hedge fund, the Federal Reserve Bank of New York organized a $3.5 billion rescue plan by LTCM's major private creditors on September 23, 1998. In the last quarter of 1998, several large banks had to assume considerable write-offs due to losses on their investments. Thus, the rescue of LTCM was essentially a bail-in mandated by the government in which financing was provided by a group of private-sector financial institutions.

3.4.4 Bank Recovery and Resolution Directive (BRRD) in Europe

Similar to OLA in the US, in Europe, the BRRD and the Single Resolution Mechanism (SRM) were finalized on June 1, 2014 and became effective in January 2016. BRRD creates a common framework for bank resolution across all the EU member states to deal with complex

---

[12] The policy of double or higher liability was around same period also internationally in other countries like the UK, Scotland, Sweden, and Canada (see Salter, Veetil, and White, 2017).

systemically important institutions. SRM is charged to implement BRRD within the euro area in conjunction with the ECB and national resolution authorities and has access to funds to funds to assist with resolutions via the Single Resolution Fund (SRF). Once an institution reaches the point of nonviability being declared as "failing or likely to fail," a bail-in tool empowers regulators to conduct a fast recapitalization of a troubled institution prior to default by writing-off or converting liabilities to equity and requiring creditors take losses on holdings according to hierarchy. In particular, BRRD establishes that the bail-in procedure will affect equity holders (whose equity will be written off), followed by subordinated debtholders, and then senior unsecured debtholders, and uninsured depositors (all of which may take losses by conversions of debt to equity and/or write-offs). This is intended to minimize costs for taxpayers and real economy.

The bail-in resolution also includes other tools, such as a sale of business tool which allows the resolution authority to sell all or part of a failing bank to another institution that provides capital, a bridge institution under which good assets are transferred into a new temporary institution for sale, and an asset separation tool under which bad assets are isolated or transferred to an asset vehicle for orderly winding down, or capital provision by other banking or nongovernment organizations.[13] If private sector funding is insufficient, the EU framework allows the government to provide further capital injections with the benefit of private sector investors having already absorbed the first losses. This last type of aid to failing banks is only granted if the bank is put into resolution and after bail-in of at least 8% of the bank's total liabilities. Throughout the process, the bank continues franchise operations, and it is expected to emerge with a stronger capital position.

While bank resolution did not require bail-in of uninsured creditors before 2016 in the EU, several idiosyncratic and systemic resolutions suggest that this regime was, at least partially, already in place before its full implementation. We next discuss some bail-in examples for the EU banks before and after the BRRD full implementation, particularly for Cyprus, Greece, Italy, Portugal, and Spain.

3.4.5 Examples of EU bail-ins

3.4.5.1 *Cyprus' experience*

Bail-ins were first brought into attention in 2013 after government officials resorted to them in Cyprus.[14] To approve a €10 billion bailout

---

[13] https://srb.europa.eu/en/content/tasks-tools.

[14] https://www.economist.com/the-economist-explains/2013/04/07/what-is-a-bail-in.

package to Cyprus banks in 2013, the EU and international authorities demanded the bail-in of the creditors of the biggest two banks in Cyprus, while sparing insured depositors. However, in the case of Cyprus banks, the absence of any significant intermediate liability between equity and deposits made uninsured depositor haircut very deep. Uninsured depositors of the Cyprus Popular Bank (also known as Laiki Bank, second largest bank) lost everything as the bank failed, while about 48% of uninsured deposits in the Bank of Cyprus (largest commercial bank) also incurred losses. In response, these latter depositors were given stock in the bank, but the stock's value was way below most depositor's losses.

3.4.5.2 Greece's experience

Greece also experienced bail-ins, but in a more limited way. Greece is another EU country which sent great shock waves across the EU due to its severe and long crisis over 2009−2016, which was often in the media forefront. The recapitalization of the banking system was finished in 2015 to circumvent difficulties with the BRRD rules which would have harmed uninsured depositors, many of which were small and medium enterprises (SMEs).

Nevertheless, some partial bail-ins did take place. In April 2015, Panellinia Bank was resolved by relocating selected assets and liabilities to Piraeus Bank using a tender process. The common and preferred shares stayed in the entity in liquidation and were wiped out, while the bank had no outstanding subordinated debt to be converted to equity. In December 2015, Cooperative Bank of Peloponnese was also put in resolution, as it was not able to repair its capital shortfall and its deposits were relocated to the National Bank of Greece using a tender process and financed by the Greek Resolution Fund. In this case as well, the equity was wiped out while liabilities were bailed-in. Moreover, two of the four main Greek banks (National Bank of Greece and Piraeus Bank) underwent "precautionary" recapitalizations which used public funds at the end of 2015, rather than being resolved via a *de facto* bail-in, in the aftermath of the capital shortfalls from the ECB stress test. However, to comply with state aid rules, most bondholders were bailed-in using conversion of debt to equity, and some senior subordinated debtholders and preferred shareholders also suffered losses.

3.4.5.3 Italy's experience

Italy also had some tough bail-in decisions to deal with due to precarious economic conditions and a stressed banking sector owning high volumes of bad loans. In late 2015 before the BRRD was in full effect, Italy approved the bail-in resolution plans for four small Italian banks having overall total assets of €47 billion (Banca Marche, Banca Popolare dell'Etruria, Cassa di Risparmio di Ferrara, and Cassa di Risparmio della

Provincia di Chieti). In these bail-in cases, all assets and liabilities were moved to bridge banks, and senior bondholders were spared, but equity holders and subordinated debtholders did incur losses. These bail-in resolutions met with public uproar as many bank subordinated debtholders were retail customers who were missold the investments and falsely made to believe they were buying safe assets. After these events, authorities began to forbid sales of subordinated debt to retail clients and evaluated such resolution decisions more cautiously.

The new EU BRRD bail-in rules were the default option from 2016 on, and disallowed the use of taxpayer money to save banks. However, in certain situations, EU authorities could decide that a bail-in resolution was not in the public interest, i.e. jeopardized financial stability, interposed in the provision of critical functions, or imperiled depositors. This was the case of two large troubled banks—Banca Popolare di Vicenza and Veneto Banca—in the region of Veneto in May 2017 described below. In contrast to the earlier four bail-ins, in these cases, the Italian government ruled out a bail-in of depositors and instead requested approval for a government bailout of these banks and the EU authorities found that it was "not warranted in the public interest" to put them into bail-in as they were perceived by the EU as posing no significant adverse impact on financial stability and were better dealt with under the Italian insolvency law.[15] Another important argument was that avoiding losses for senior creditors and retail subordinated debtholders were important in Italy, as uninsured bank liabilities accounted for more than 10% of all household wealth and losses to retail holders could have undermined depositor confidence and created political chaos. However, critics suggest that the BRRD bail-in rules failed when dealing with legacy situations like those inherent in the Italian banks.

Banca Popolare di Vicenza (10th largest) and Veneto Banca (11th largest) are two banks that were declared by the ECB as "failing or likely to fail" due to lack of capital in June 2017 and were stressed due to high levels of bad loans (about €10 and €9 billion, respectively) and underlying challenges in their business models. The Italian government pronounced them dead. Upon the EU Commission approval, their "good" assets were sold to Intesa Sanpaolo, Italy's second largest bank by assets for €1, and their "bad" ones were put into a "bad bank." Intesa Sanpaolo was paid €3.5 billion by the government to counterbalance the effect of the additional assets on its capital ratios and another €1.3 billion to offset integration costs, including any closures of branches. The government also provided another €12 billion in guarantees to cover other potential losses.

---

[15] https://www.economist.com/finance-and-economics/2017/07/01/the-complicated-failure-of-two-italian-lenders; https://www.ft.com/content/c813eb7e-5fdf-11e7-91a7-502f7ee26895.

In June 2017, Italy's fourth largest bank, Banca Monte dei Paschi di Siena S.p.A (BMPS) also underwent a precautionary recapitalization with a bail-in. The bank battled for years to recuperate from poor management problems and a large pile of bad loans (worth about €28.6 billion). The bank had two capital increases since 2014, but its situation became hazardous and uncertain after a private recapitalization plan failed in December 2016. At the end of June, the Italian government received approval from the EU to bail out the bank, injecting €5.4 billion (giving it a 70% stake) into the bank, as part of a total boost of €8.1 billion.[16]

In exchange, the bank had to commit to a major bank restructuring overhaul over a five-year period to recover and restore confidence (including securitizing and selling bad loans, strict cost controls,cap on top executive pay, reducing the number of employees, and shutting down a significant number of branches, increase profitability, improving Tier 1 common capital (CET1) ratio. In addition, the BMPS bailout required that bank's shareholders and junior creditors take losses first, for an appraised €4.3 billion to minimize the bill of the government. Retail investors, owning about €200 million in junior bonds, were to be remunerated for having been missold the products.

3.4.5.4 Portugal's experience

Portugal used a bail-in in the resolution of Banco Espirito Santo (BES) in the summer of 2014 (before BRRD full implementation). The Portuguese authorities employed a bridge bank strategy and established Novo Banco to house the bank's "good" assets and liabilities, together with an equity injection from the Portugal Resolution Fund. In addition, senior bondholders and depositors were transferred to Novo Banco and did not incur losses. However equity holders and subordinated debtholders were left behind in the legacy bank and suffered severe losses. Later in November 2015, the ECB stress test found a €1.4 billion capital gap in the bank. In late December, authorities took the decision after 18 months of resolution to retransfer five tranches out of 52 fixed rate senior unsecured bonds directed toward institutional investors and issued under the Portuguese law, and having a face value of €1.985 billion, back to BES to be wiped out. The arbitrary choice of the five bonds and late timing was not well received by market participants and instigated great ambiguity as the "*pari-passu*" of equality among senior bondholders was violated. Some of the investors took legal action against this decision, while Bank of Portugal later offered some reimbursement for the bondholders.[17]

[16] https://www.cnbc.com/2017/07/05/italy-swoops-in-to-save-another-bank-leaving-taxpayers-on-the-hook-for-over-25-billion.html.

[17] https://www.euromoney.com/article/b12kp0jkw480cg/novo-banco-bail-in-may-breach-brrd-transfer-rules.

In December 2015, another Portuguese bank, Banco Internacional do Funchal (also known as BANIF, seventh largest bank) was resolved employing the same "good bank–bad bank" split, where the "good" assets were sold to Santander using state support (€2.26 billion), and another entity was established to keep some of the "bad" assets. As part of the resolution, depositors and senior bondholders were moved to Santander, evading any bail-in, but equity holders and subordinated bondholders remained in the original BANIF institution and incurred losses. A major part of the subordinated debt was owned by retail investors fronting losses as BANIF was liquidated, which led to public turmoil.[18]

3.4.5.5 *Spain's experience*

Spain also underwent a bank bail-in. Banco Popular (sixth largest bank) had been in difficulty since the collapse of Spain's national property bubble in 2008 for a long time and was battling with €7.9 billion worth of nonperforming loans. It raised equity from shareholders three times over 2012–16, a strategy that did not work out well, and eventually looked for a buyer. Nevertheless, an unexpected run on deposits amplified the bank's funding problems. On June 6, 2017, ECB deemed it as "failing or likely to fail," as its significant liquidity deterioration made the institution "unable to pay its debts or other liabilities as they fell due," and informed the EU Single Resolution Board to adopt a resolution scheme. One day later, Banco Santander (Spain's largest bank) announced its purchase of Banco Popular for a nominal €1 and conducted a capital increase of €7 billion to cover the capital and provisions needed to bolster Banco Popular's finances.[19] This deal led to shareholders being wiped out as well as some bondholders (including owners of contingent convertible (CoCos) debt which turned into equity), but the institution continued to operate under "normal business conditions" as a new solvent and liquid member of Santander Group. Distinct from resolutions in other countries, the Spanish and the EU authorities announced that this bail-in was a success and showed that the system passed its first BRRD test, given that the EU bail-in rules were respected, and no taxpayer money was needed for this resolution.

---

[18] https://www.euromoney.com/article/b12kp0zxch2kvg/portugal-banking-the-long-shadow-of-banif-and-bes.

[19] For more details see: https://www.independent.co.uk/news/business/news/santander-banco-popular-bankd-takeover-rescue-1-collapse-eu-spain-a7776561.html; and https://www.economist.com/the-economist-explains/2017/06/23/how-the-euro-zone-deals-with-failing-banks.

3.4.6 Bail-in/bailout hybrid—German bankers associations and the government in Germany over normal times and financial crises

The German banking sector is unique in the EU in that it has three pillars: private-sector (nationwide and foreign banks), public sector (savings banks and Landesbanken), and cooperative banks, which differ in ownership structure and geographical reach (see Brunner, Decressin, Hardy, and Kudela, 2004; Dam and Koetter, 2012; Berger, Bouwman, Kick, and Schaeck, 2016; Gropp and Tonzer, 2016). In addition, there are also differences in the design of safety net arrangements and the implementation of rescue packages for the banks.

In contrast to bailouts in the US and other countries where capital injections typically come from the public sector or taxpayers, Germany has a unique banking system in which it is predominantly the German bankers associations' insurance schemes which are providing the capital to banks in financial distress. Each of the three banking pillars in Germany has one umbrella bankers association and member institutions receive mandatory insurance from their umbrella organization. All insurance schemes are risk-based and funded by banks rather than the taxpayers. Capital support by the insurance scheme requires approval by its board or a committee of the insurance scheme and targets the weakest institutions. Once a bankers association insurance scheme deems a bank to be insolvent and there is no other bank available to acquire the distressed institution, the bank receives capital support from the association to meet regulatory requirements. Therefore, capital injections from the German bankers associations' insurance schemes could be regarded as either bail-ins because they are not extended by a government entity or organization buttressed by government, or bailouts because the injections are from a mutual organization rather than individual private counterparties. Later on, in Chapter 16, we simply refer to them as bailouts as they are more commonly referred to in the research literature.

An exception is the Global Financial Crisis, during which both the German government and bankers association insurance schemes provided capital support to the banks. Particularly, Berger, Bouwman, Kick, and Schaeck (2016) note that during the crisis, the government support in Germany came directly from the Financial Market Stabilization Fund. They find that during their sample period of 1999–2009, six German banks received such government support, while many more were supported by the bankers associations.

3.4.7 Other bail-in instruments: Contingent convertible bonds (CoCos)

Closely related to bail-in instruments are contingent convertible bonds (CoCos). CoCos have been proposed as a mechanism for promptly recapitalizing financial institutions and enhancing financial stability due to their conversion feature, as they can absorb losses when the capital of the issuing bank falls below a certain level (e.g., Calomiris and Herring, 2011, 2013; Flannery, 2014, 2016). CoCos have been proposed as instruments for facilitation of bail-ins and for helping bank regulators to address the TBTF problem,[20] due to similarities with the bail-in mechanisms. Similar to bail-ins (often known as gone-concern contingent capital because they absorb losses usually when a bank fails), CoCos (often known as going-concern contingent capital because they recapitalize the bank while it is still a going concern) are debt instruments that convert to equity as a firm's assets lose value.

CoCos differ from bail-ins in two ways. One is the trigger for conversion from debt to equity, which can be bank specific, systemic, or dual. In general, CoCos convert debt to equity as a firm nears but has not yet reached financial distress, while bail-in converts debt to equity once a firm reaches the point of nonviability. The second differentiating feature is the conversion ratio (rate at which debt is swapped for equity) and impact on the original shareholders. The conversion of CoCos dilutes the original shareholders, while a bail-in is attended by a reorganization that wipes out original shareholders. CoCos' effectiveness depends on the design of the trigger and the conversion rate, and the instrument can take a variety of forms such as a standby loan, a catastrophe bond, a surplus note, or a call option-enhanced reverse convertible.

3.5 Bankruptcy/failure

Policymakers in the US also consider other bailout and bail-in alternatives which include policies of avoiding intervention, such as expanding the role of bankruptcy for large banking organizations and failure of the banks.

The Financial CHOICE Act, H.R.10 of the 115th Congress, was introduced in the US House of Representatives on April 26, 2017, by Representative Jeb Hensarling and passed the House on June 8, 2017. It would have repealed certain provisions of the Dodd—Frank Act of 2010 and other laws. In particular, the CHOICE Act would repeal OLA and establish a new section of the US bankruptcy code (Chapter 14), which could more readily

---

[20] Other uses are to signal bank risk and encourage timely voluntary offerings of equity into the market by banks that have suffered significant losses.

resolve failed large complex financial institutions, especially those that submitted resolution plans (living wills) reviewed by the Federal Reserve and the FDIC under Title I of the Dodd–Frank Act.[21] Importantly, Chapter 14 would mirror many features of the FDIC's single point of entry (SPOE) model. However, resolutions would be conducted under the auspices of a bankruptcy court and would not include regulatory intervention or access to the OLF. As of now, the US Treasury acknowledges that Chapter 14 may not be feasible in some cases for large complex cross-border financial institutions if there is insufficient private financing, in which case the bail-in tool OLA may remain as an emergency tool for them.[22,23]

3.6 Reorganization using living wills

Living wills or resolution plans are regarded as a potential alternative way to resolve the distress and impending failure of TBTF banking organizations without government or private sector aid. Section 165(d) of the Dodd–Frank Act requires banks with $50 billion or more in assets to submit resolution plans annually to the Federal Reserve and the FDIC and substantial parts of plans are also disclosed to the public. The plans must describe substantive, detailed strategies for the bank's rapid and orderly resolution in case of financial difficulties or failure using the US bankruptcy process. From a theoretical viewpoint, living wills are much like the bankruptcy option discussed above except that they are designed to be more orderly and likely preserve more of the financially viable parts of the organization. Figs. 3.2 and 3.3 provide excerpts from actual living wills posted by two large US BHCs in 2017, JPMorgan Chase & Co, and Wells Fargo & Company, respectively.

The first set of plans were produced in July 2012 by banks with $250 billion or more in assets, followed by banks at or above $100 billion in July 2013, while the rest of the eligible institutions were filed in December 2013. These plans were submitted annually by the banks thereafter. The regulators can approve the living wills or reject them if they are not credible in order for the bank to improve the plan and develop a robust resolution strategy. Institutions that have their living will plans rejected can have harsher penalties imposed in terms of higher capital and

[21] https://www.congress.gov/bill/115th-congress/house-bill/10.

[22] https://www.davispolk.com/files/2018-09-17_financial_services_regulatory_reform_tool.pdf; https://www.hoover.org/research/making-failure-feasible; https://www.finregreform.com/single-post/2018/02/22/treasury-retain-but-reform-ola-add-new-chapter-14-to-bankruptcy-code/.

[23] Other similar bankruptcy plan proposals for TBTF banking organizations have been described in Hoenig, Morris, and Spong (2009) and Jackson (2009, 2015).

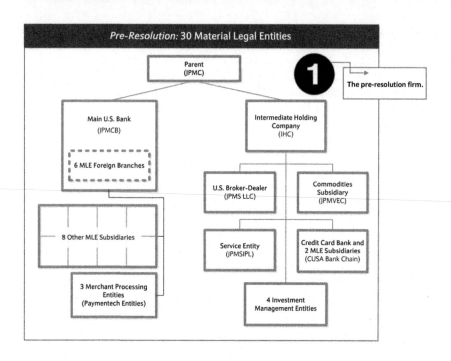

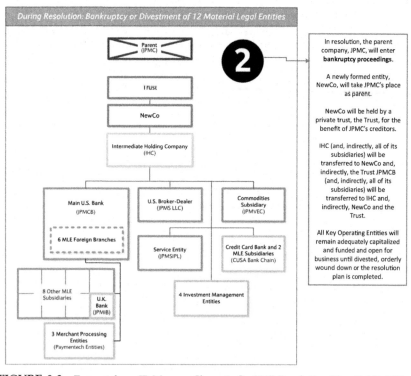

FIGURE 3.2 Excerpt from JP Morgan Chase & Co 2017 Resolution Plan Public Filing Corporate Structure Before, During, and After Resolution. https://www.federalreserve.gov/supervisionreg/resolution-plans/jpmorgan-chase-1g-20170701.pdf. (continued)

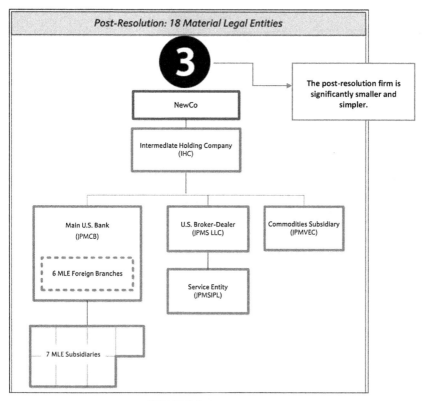

FIGURE 3.2 (continued)

liquidity requirements or make changes to their organizational structure. For example, Wells Fargo & Co. had its living will plan rejected in December 2016 and this led to prohibition of the bank from establishing international bank entities or acquiring nonbank subsidiaries.

In April 2019, the Federal Reserve and the FDIC signed off on an interagency proposal to streamline current requirements and let agency officials concentrate their efforts on the riskier firms.[24] Essentially, the proposal exempts several U.S. regional bank holding companies from having to file resolution plans and reduces "living wills" submission requirements for all other banks.[25] It creates risk-based bank categories to determine the requirements for submitting living wills, while extending

[24] Rocha, Polo, April 17, 2019, "FDIC approves proposal reducing bank 'living wills' requirements", SNL Bank and Thrift Daily.

[25] The Financial Institution Living Will Improvement Act of 2018 (HR. 4292) which passed the House in January 2018 also proposed that institutions file plans every 2 years instead of annually.

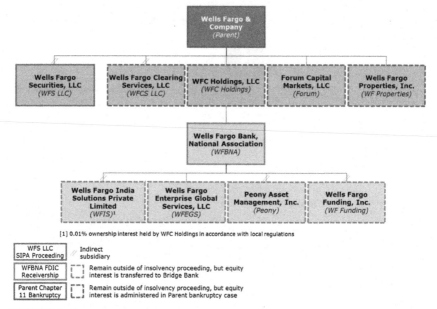

FIGURE 3.3   Excerpt from Wells Fargo & Co 2017 resolution plan public filing: Resolution regimes of material entities. https://www.federalreserve.gov/supervisionreg/resolution-plans/wells-fargo-2g-20170701.pdf.

the cycle of submission for banks. It also introduced alternating full plans (the same comprehensive plans that banks submit today) and targeted plans (which include only the core elements of the full plan such as capital, liquidity, changes from new regulatory policies, and information requests from agencies) to ease the regulatory burden.

Under the proposal, Category I filers—the eight US G-SIBs—are required to submit their plan every 2 years and alternate full and targeted plan review cycles. Category II (banks with assets of greater or equal to $700 billion or greater or equal to $75 billion in cross-jurisdictional activity) and Category III filers (banks with assets greater or equal to $250 billion or greater or equal to $75 billion in nonbank assets, weighted short-term wholesale funding, or off-balance sheet exposure) include 13 institutions and are both triennial being a 3-year cycle, also alternating full and targeted plans.[26] Finally, another 53 foreign banking organizations (FBOs) are on reduced plans on a 3-year cycle. All other institutions are no longer required to submit resolution plans.

---

[26] These 13 institutions are: Barclays, Capital One, Credit Suisse, Deutsche Bank, HSBC, Mizuho Bank, MUFG, Northern Trust, PNC Financial Services, Royal Bank of Canada, Toronto-Dominion Bank, UBS, and U.S. Bancorp.

In October 2019, the Federal Reserve completed the measure on living wills formally floated in the April proposal. The rules will go into effect after publication in the Federal Register.[27]

Resolution plans may be useful as they provide regulators with critical information about a large bank's organizational structure and may motivate banks to simplify their structures, both of which could help in a bankruptcy-like situation. However, it may also be possible that living wills may be only helpful for bankruptcy during normal times and may not work during financial crises and panics, when resolution solutions are needed the most. During a Brookings Institution discussion in late 2018, Timothy Geithner and Ben Bernanke mentioned that the "so-called living wills that the largest banks have to submit every year would not work in a financial panic."[28]

Based on the Federal Reserve regulatory-issued guidance for the large financial institutions post-crisis framework,[29] a living will is a tool for "enhancing resiliency of a firm to lower the probability of its failure" and for "reducing the impact on the financial system and the broader economy in the event of a firm's failure or material weakness." The resolution strategies address the complexity must not pose systemic risk and address the complexity and interconnectivity of the firm's operations, while excluding reliance on extraordinary support measures to prevent failure of the firm. In Chapter 4, we review some theoretical arguments from Cetorelli and Traina (2018) about the living will regulation and effects on banks' cost of capital.

3.7 Regulatory forbearance

Another policy to deal with distress of large institutions is to use "regulatory forbearance." This involves allowing financial institutions to continue operating when their capital is below the regulatory requirements or even fully depleted, deferring significant regulatory intervention or failure. Some might think of this as more of a lack of policy than a policy. The rationales for this are to save on closure costs, defer dealing with problems, or simply hope that problems will get resolved by themselves. However, such lack of regulatory action can lead to long-term problems.

---

[27] https://www.nytimes.com/2019/10/10/business/economy/federal-reserve-bank-regulations.html.

[28] https://wallstreetreview.com/2018/09/12/bank-living-wills-wont-save-financial-system-from-a-panic-bernanke-and-geithner-agree/.

[29] https://www.federalreserve.gov/supervisionreg/srletters/sr1217.htm.

Forbearance was applied widely in the 1980s in the savings and loans (S&Ls) crisis. S&Ls, also called thrifts, are generally smaller than banks in assets, but they are important for the US mortgage market. In 1980, the US had 4000 thrifts with $600 billion in assets, with $480 billion in mortgage loans. This was half of the approximately $960 billion in home mortgages outstanding at that time (Federal Reserve Board of Governors, 2013).[30] S&Ls were heavily concentrated in mortgages by regulation, and relied on deposits with short maturities for their funding, making them especially vulnerable to increases in interest rates.

In late 1970s and early 1980s, both inflation and interest rates rose dramatically, creating major problems for S&Ls. Because variable-rate mortgages were illegal, S&Ls primarily made long-term fixed-rate mortgages. When interest rates rose, S&Ls had to borrow at high rates in the short-term while being locked in low rates on their mortgage loans in the long-term, wiping out the S&Ls' net worth and depleting their book capital as well. Regulators lacked sufficient resources to deal with losses that S&Ls were suffering, so they largely let the institutions with low or negative capital stay open, delaying their closings and pushing the problems off into the future, and thus exhibiting regulatory forbearance. In place, they took steps to deregulate the industry in the hope that it could grow out of its problems. In 1980, the Congress passed and the President signed the Depository Institutions Deregulation and Monetary Control Act (DIDMCA), while in 1982, they passed the Garn–St. Germain Act which reduced some of the restrictions for thrift activities and expanded investment opportunities for them. The S&Ls problems, however, grew even more severe as moral hazard incentives to gamble for resurrection from the lack of capital led to additional credit risk and other problems. Ultimately, taxpayers suffered massive losses in the long run.

The problems were resolved somewhat by late 1980s, when Congress decided to address the S&Ls' problems. In 1989, it passed the Financial Institutions Reform, Recovery and Enforcement Act that instituted a number of reforms for the S&Ls. Both the main S&L regulator (the Federal Home Loan Bank Board) and the thrifts' insurance fund, known as the FSLIC, were dissolved. As a replacement, Congress created the Office of Thrift Supervision (OTS) and placed thrifts' insurance under the FDIC. In addition, it created the Resolution Trust Corporation (RTC) to resolve the remaining troubled S&Ls. The RTC closed 747 S&Ls with assets of over $407 billion. The RTC was ultimately closed in 1995. The ultimate cost to taxpayers was estimated to be as high as $124 billion.[31]

---

[30] https://www.federalreservehistory.org/essays/savings_and_loan_crisis.

[31] https://www.federalreservehistory.org/essays/savings_and_loan_crisis.

3.8 Breaking up large banking organizations

A final way to deal with large systemically important institutions distress is to break up the institutions. There are two sets of proposals for this. One set calls for breaking large institutions into smaller nonsystemically important ones that can be easier to manage when they pose "grave" systemic threats. Another set calls for breaking up different types of activities of banks or repealing the Gramm—Leach—Bliley Act of 1999 and going back to Glass—Steagall Act restrictions on combining commercial and investment banks. These have often been voiced as a solution by presidential candidates, including Donald Trump, Bernie Sanders, Elizabeth Warren, and many others, and it is sometimes referred to as the "21st Century Glass—Steagall Act."[32]

The Financial Stability Oversight Council (FSOC) established by the Dodd—Frank Act of 2010 has key responsibilities to identify and monitor buildups of risk in the financial system, designate certain institutions as systemically important financial institutions (SIFIs), and respond to emerging threats to financial system stability. Other detailed responsibilities include recommending and requiring by 2/3 vote tougher capital, liquidity, and risk management when financial institutions get "too big." Finally, FSOC can also approve by 2/3 vote the breakup of complex financial institutions that impose severe systemic threat to the financial system. No such breakups have yet been made.

Closely related, the Federal Reserve Bank of Minneapolis issued in January 2017, the so-called "Minneapolis Plan".[33] This is a proposal to end too-big-to-fail and reduce substantially the risk of financial crises and bank bailouts. The plan suggests several significant policy changes, including increasing minimum capital requirements for G-SIBs to 23.5% of risk-weighted assets and forcing these banks to no longer be systemically important as judged by the US Treasury (break themselves up) or else face gradual 5% per year increases in their capital requirements up to a maximum of 38% of risk-weighted assets. This plan has not been enacted and is subject to public comments.

[32] https://www.politico.com/2020-election/candidates-views on the issues/economy/big-banks/; https://fortune.com/2017/05/03/donald-trump-break-breaking-up-big-banks-glass-steagall/; https://www.americanbanker.com/opinion/another-political-storm-is-brewing-for-big-banks; https://money.cnn.com/2017/05/09/investing/donald-trump-glass-steagall/index.html.

[33] See Federal Reserve bank of Minneapolis (2017) available at: https://www.minneapolisfed.org/news-and-events/news-releases/minneapolis-fed-releases-final-plan-to-end-too-big-to-fail.

[34] Note that some ratios may appear large also because equity capital, the denominator of the ratio, is based on the Call Report aggregated equity value of all commercial banks under the holding company structure.

References

Anderson, H., Barth, D., & Choi, D. B. (2018). *Reducing moral hazard at the expense of market discipline: The effectiveness of double liability before and during the Great Depression.* Office of Financial Research Research Paper. no. 18–06.

Barofsky, N. (2013). *Bailout: How Washington abandoned Main Street while rescuing wall street.* Simon and Schuster.

Bayazitova, D., & Shivdasani, A. (2012). Assessing TARP. *The Review of Financial Studies, 25*(2), 377–407.

Berger, A. N., Black, L. K., Bouwman, C. H. S., & Dlugosz, J. (2017). Bank loan supply responses to Federal Reserve emergency liquidity facilities. *Journal of Financial Intermediation, 32*, 1–15.

Berger, A. N., & Bouwman, C. H. S. (2016). *Bank liquidity creation and financial crises.* Elsevier – North Holland.

Berger, A. N., Bouwman, C. H. S., Kick, T., & Schaeck, K. (2016). Bank liquidity creation following regulatory interventions and capital support. *Journal of Financial Intermediation, 26*, 115–141.

Bernanke, B. S. (2015). *The courage to act: A memoir of a crisis and its aftermath.* WW Norton & Company.

Brunner, A. D., Decressin, J., Hardy, D. C. L., & Kudela, B. (2004). *Germany's three-pillar banking system: Cross-country perspectives in Europe* (Vol. 233). International Monetary Fund.

Bush, G. W. (2008). *President Bush discusses Emergency Economic Stabilization Act of 2008.* White House Press Release. Available at https://georgewbush-whitehouse.archives.gov/news/releases/2008/10/20081003-11.html.

Calomiris, C. W., & Herring, R. J. (2011). *Why and how to design a contingent convertible debt requirement* (Working Paper).

Calomiris, C. W., & Herring, R. J. (2013). How to design a contingent convertible debt requirement that helps solve our too-big-to-fail problem. *The Journal of Applied Corporate Finance, 25*, 39–62.

Cetorelli, N., & Traina, J. (2018). *Resolving 'too big to fail'* (Working Paper).

Congressional Oversight Panel. (2009). Taking stock: What has the Troubled Asset Relief Program achieved. Congressional Oversight Panel. Available at: https://fraser.stlouisfed.org/files/docs/historical/fct/cop_report_20091209.pdf.

Congressional Oversight Panel. (2010). Assessing the TARP on the eve of its expiration. Congressional Oversight Panel. Available at: https://fraser.stlouisfed.org/files/docs/historical/fct/cop_report_20100916.pdf.

Cortés, K., & Millington, S. (2014). *Gauging the impact of the small business lending fund.* Federal Reserve Bank of Cleveland. Economic Trends.

Dam, L., & Koetter, M. (2012). Bank bailouts and moral hazard: Evidence from Germany. *The Review of Financial Studies, 25*(8), 2343–2380.

Duchin, R., & Sosyura, D. (2012). The politics of government investment. *Journal of Financial Economics, 106*(1), 24–48.

Federal Reserve Bank of Minneapolis. (2017). *The Federal Reserve Bank of Minneapolis plan to end too big to fail.* Available at https://www.minneapolisfed.org/~/media/files/publications/studies/endingtbtf/the-minneapolis-plan/the-minneapolis-plan-to-end-too-big-to-fail-final.pdf?la=en.

Federal Reserve Board of Governors. (2013). *Savings and loan crisis.* Available at https://www.federalreservehistory.org/essays/savings_and_loan_crisis.

Flannery, M. J. (2014). Contingent capital instruments for large financial institutions: A review of the literature. *Annual Review of Financial Economics, 6*(1), 225–240.

Flannery, M. J. (2016). Stabilizing large financial institutions with contingent capital certificates. Quarterly Journal of Finance, 6(2), 1650006.

Flannery, M. J., & Bliss, R. R. (2019). Market discipline in regulation: Pre-and post-crisis. In *Oxford Handbook of Banking* (3rd Edition).

Gropp, R., & Tonzer, L. (2016). State aid and guarantees in Europe. In *The Palgrave Handbook of European Banking*. Springer, 349–81.

Hendrickson, J. R. (2014). Contingent liability, capital requirements, and financial reform. *Cato J, 34*, 129.

Hilsenrath, J., Solomon, D., & Paletta, D. (2008). Paulson, Bernanke strained for consensus in bailout. *Wall Street Journal*.

Hoenig, T. M., Morris, C. S., & Spong, K. (2009). *The Kansas City Plan. Chapter 10 In Ending government bailouts as we know them*. Hoover Institution Press.

Isaac, W. M. (2010). *Senseless panic: How Washington failed America*. John Wiley and Sons.

Jackson, T. H. (2009). *Chapter 11F: A proposal for the use of bankruptcy to resolve financial institutions. Chapter 11 in Ending government bailouts as we know them*. Hoover Institution Press.

Jackson, T. H. (2015). *Building on bankruptcy: A revised Chapter 14 proposal for the recapitalization, reorganization, or liquidation of large financial institutions. Chapter 2 in Making failure feasible*. Hoover Institution Press.

Leijonhufvud, A. (2010). *A modest proposal*. (Accessed 20 September 2010).

Macey, J. R., & Miller, G. P. (1992). *Double liability of bank shareholders: History and implications* (Working Paper).

Massad, T. G. (2011). *Written testimony before the* Senate Committee on Banking, Housing, and Urban Affairs. Available at https://www.treasury.gov/press-center/press-releases/Pages/tg1108.aspx.

Mukherjee, T., & Pana, E. (2018). The distribution of the capital purchase program funds: Evidence from bank internal capital markets. *Financial Markets, Institutions & Instruments, 27*(4), 125–143.

Nistor-Mutu, S., Ongena, S., The impact of policy interventions on systemic risk across banks. 2019. (Working Paper).

Paulson, H. M. (2013). *On the brink: Inside the race to stop the collapse of the global financial system—with original new material on the five year anniversary of the financial crisis* (Business Plus).

Pisani-Ferry, J., & Sapir, A. (2010). Banking crisis management in the EU: An early assessment. *Economic Policy, 25*(62), 341–373.

Salter, A. W., Veetil, V., & White, L. H. (2017). Extended shareholder liability as a means to constrain moral hazard in insured banks. *The Quarterly Review of Economics and Finance, 63*, 153–160.

Solomon, D., & Enrich, D. (2008). Devil is in bailout's details. *The Wall Street Journal*.

Zingales, L. (2011). *Oral Testimony of Luigi Zingales on overall impact of TARP on financial stability*. Congressional Oversight Panel.

Theoretical background on bank bailouts, bail-ins, and other resolution approaches

Chapter 4 reviews the theories behind the different resolution approaches for financially distressed banks: 1) bailouts; 2) bail-ins; 3) bankruptcy/failure (bankruptcy of the BHC and failure of the bank); 4) reorganization using living wills; and 5) forbearance. In line with the major focuses of the book, most of the discussion is on bailouts and bail-ins.

Sections 4.1—4.4 trace the theoretical pathways through which bailouts and bail-ins may or may not achieve their ultimate goals or outcomes of reducing systemic risk and improving the real economy. Of course, there are no direct routes from bailouts and bail-ins to systemic risk or the real economy. Instead, these resolution approaches must first affect the bailed-out or bailed-in banks' behavior, the functioning of their markets, and their stakeholders, which we refer to as intermediate outcomes. These intermediate financial and economic outcomes may then affect the ultimate outcomes for systemic risk and the real economy.

Section 4.1 discusses the channels through which bailouts may directly affect a large number of intermediate financial and economic outcomes for banks, their markets, and their stakeholders. These outcomes essentially cover all of the intermediate outcomes of TARP studied in the literature and reviewed in Part II below. These intermediate outcomes are the valuation; market discipline by shareholders, uninsured creditors, and insured depositors; market leverage risk of the bailed-out banks; competition as measured by bailed-out bank market share and market power; credit supply, portfolio risk, and systemic importance of these banks; and the valuation and spending behavior of the banks' credit customers. The directions of these effects—positive, negative, or ambiguous—are displayed in Table 4.1. Section 4.2 and Table 4.2 provide similar corresponding

TABLE 4.1 Primary channels from bailouts to intermediate financial and economic outcomes.

No.	Primary channels for bailouts	Bank stock valuation	Bank market discipline (shareholders)	Bank market discipline (uninsured creditors)	Bank market discipline (insured depositors)	Bank market leverage risk	Bank competition (market share)	Bank competition (market power)	Bank credit supply	Bank portfolio risk	Bank systemic importance	Credit customers (valuation)	Credit customers (investments, employment, & other spending effects)
1	Stigma	−	+	+	+	+	−	−	−	?	?	−	−
2	Safety	+	−	−	−	−	+	+	+	?	?	+	+
3	Predation	?	?	+	+	?	+	−	+	+	?	+	+
4	Charter value / quiet life	+	−	−	−	+	−	+	−	−	?	−	−
5	Cost disadvantage	−	+	+	+	−	−	−	−	−	?	−	−
6	Cost advantage	+	−	−	−	+	+	+	+	+	?	+	+
7	Increased moral hazard	?	?	+	+	?	?	+	?	+	?	?	?
8	Decreased moral hazard	?	?	−	−	?	?	−	?	−	?	?	?
9	Capital priority	−	+	+	+	+	−	−	−	?	?	−	−
10	Capital cushion	+	−	−	−	−	+	+	+	?	?	+	+
11	TBTF (size)	+	−	−	−	−	+	?	?	?	+	?	?
12	TITF (interconnectedness)	+	−	−	−	−	?	?	?	?	+	?	?
13	TMTF (herding)	+	−	−	−	−	?	?	?	?	+	?	?

This table shows the signs of the effects of 13 channels of bailouts on 12 intermediate financial and economic outcomes for banks and their stakeholders. "+" indicates a positive direct effect, "−" signifies a negative direct outcome, and "?" signals an ambiguous direct effect or no effect.

TABLE 4.2 Primary channels from bail-ins to intermediate financial and economic outcomes.

No.	Primary channels for bail-ins	Bank stock valuation	Bank market discipline (shareholders)	Bank market discipline (uninsured creditors)	Bank market discipline (insured depositors)	Bank market leverage risk	Bank competition (market share)	Bank competition (market power)	Bank credit supply	Bank portfolio risk	Bank systemic importance	Credit customers (valuation)	Credit customers (investments, employment, & other spending effects)
1	Stigma	−	+	+	+	+	−	−	−	?	?	−	−
2	Safety	N/A	N/A	N/A	N/A	N/A	N/A	N/A	N/A	N/A	N/A	N/A	N/A
3	Predation	?	?	+	+	?	+	−	+	+	?	+	+
4	Charter value / quiet life	N/A	N/A	N/A	N/A	N/A	N/A	N/A	N/A	N/A	N/A	N/A	N/A
5	Cost disadvantage	−	+	+	+	+	−	−	−	−	?	−	−
6	Cost advantage	N/A	N/A	N/A	N/A	N/A	N/A	N/A	N/A	N/A	N/A	N/A	N/A
7	Increased moral hazard	N/A	N/A	N/A	N/A	N/A	N/A	N/A	N/A	N/A	N/A	N/A	N/A
8	Decreased moral hazard	?	?	?	?	?	?	−	?	−	?	?	?
9	Capital priority	N/A	N/A	N/A	N/A	N/A	N/A	N/A	N/A	N/A	N/A	N/A	N/A
10	Capital conversion	−	+	+	+	?	−	−	−	?	?	−	−
11	Capital cushion	+	−	−	−	−	+	+	+	?	?	+	+
12	TBTF (size)	N/A	N/A	N/A	N/A	N/A	N/A	N/A	N/A	N/A	N/A	N/A	N/A
13	TITF (interconnectedness)	N/A	N/A	N/A	N/A	N/A	N/A	N/A	N/A	N/A	N/A	N/A	N/A
14	TMTF (herding)	N/A	N/A	N/A	N/A	N/A	N/A	N/A	N/A	N/A	N/A	N/A	N/A

This table shows the signs of the effects of 14 channels of bail-ins on 12 intermediate financial and economic outcomes. "+" indicates a positive direct effect on the intermediate outcome, "−" signifies a negative direct effect, "?" signals an ambiguous direct effect or no effect, while "N/A" signals that some of the channels do not apply to bail-ins.

TABLE 4.3   Relations between the intermediate financial and economic outcomes of bailouts and bail-ins and the ultimate outcomes of systemic risk and the real economy.

No.	Relations between intermediate outcomes of bailouts and bail-ins and the ultimate outcomes	Systemic risk	Real economy
1	Bank stock valuation	−	?
2	Bank market discipline (stockholders)	?	?
3	Bank market discipline (uninsured creditors)	?	?
4	Bank market discipline (insured depositors)	?	?
5	Bank leverage risk	+	?
6	Bank competition (market share)	?	?
7	Bank competition (market power)	?	?
8	Bank credit supply	+	?
9	Bank portfolio risk	+	?
10	Bank systemic importance	+	?
11	Credit customers (valuation)	?	?
12	Credit customers (investments, employment and other spending effects)	?	+

This table shows the signs of the relation between the 12 intermediate financial and economic outcomes for banks, their markets, and their stakeholders for bailouts and bail-ins and the two ultimate outcomes of systemic risk and the real economy. "+" indicates a positive relation between the intermediate outcome and the ultimate outcome, "−" signifies a negative relation, and "?" signals an ambiguous or no relation.

information for bail-ins. Section 4.3 and Table 4.3 show the relations between these intermediate outcomes and the ultimate outcomes for systemic risk and real economy that determine whether bailouts and bail-ins achieve their main goals. Section 4.4 and Table 4.4 complete the circles by showing the interactions between systemic risk and the real economy. Thus, the

TABLE 4.4   Relations between systemic risk and the real economy.

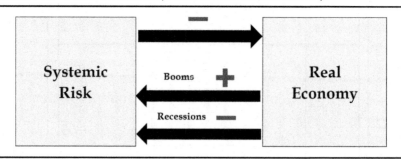

This table shows the relations of the two ultimate outcomes of systemic risk and the real economy with each other. "+" indicates a positive relation, "−" signifies a negative relation, and "?" signals an ambiguous or no relation.

effects of bailouts and bail-ins on these ultimate outcomes can be traced (1) through the direct channels that affect the intermediate financial and economic outcomes, (2) to the effects on systemic risk and the real economy, and (3) finally to the interactions of these two ultimate outcomes.

The discussion of the channels in Sections 4.1–4.4 includes only some of the theoretical literature. Section 4.5 reviews additional theoretical research on bailouts, bail-ins, and comparisons among them and one other resolution approach, bankruptcy/failure. Section 4.6 discusses research on the final two resolution approaches, reorganization using living wills and forbearance.

4.1 Direct channels from bailouts to intermediate financial and economic outcomes for banks, their markets, and their stakeholders

In this section, we closely follow Table 4.1, which shows the signs of the effects of 13 channels of bailouts on 12 intermediate financial and economic outcomes for banks and their stakeholders. We go row by row in the table, where "+" indicates a positive direct effect on the intermediate outcome, "−" signifies a negative direct effect, and "?" signals an ambiguous direct effect or no effect. Of course, there are many types of bank bailouts that may work in different fashions. For simplicity, the bailout results in the table are for preferred equity injections, such as the TARP bailout discussed in Chapter 3. While there may be some different effects of other bailout types—such as liquidity injections and blanket guarantees of liabilities—most of the effects of other bailout types are likely to be similar. The 13 channels are adapted from research contributions of Berger and Roman (2015, 2017), Berger (2018), Berger, Makaew, and Roman (2019), Roman (2020), and Berger, Roman, and Sedunov (2020), who develop and base their channels on extant theory. We extrapolate considerably from these papers, which each typically only focuses on a small number of outcomes, while we try here to determine to the extent possible the direct effects of every channel on every intermediate outcome.

While there are 156 combinations shown in Table 4.1—13 channels times 12 intermediate financial and economic outcomes—we are able to simplify the discussion of the table in several ways. First, we note that many of the channels are related to each other and most come in pairs that are opposites of each other. To facilitate the exposition, we group related channels in the following discussion. Second, we do not discuss the bank systemic importance outcome when determining the effects of the first 10 channels. This is because only the final three channels which are explicitly designed to increase such importance have such effects. Third, we point out in advance that some of the outcomes always go in the same directions. For all 13 channels, the market discipline from insured depositors has the same sign as the market discipline from unsecured creditors. All debtholders react in the same direction to bank risk, although the reactions of insured depositors are more muted because of deposit insurance protection. For all channels, the effects on bank credit supply and on credit customers' valuations and spending all also have the same signs. It is through increased or decreased credit that credit customers are helped or harmed by the bailouts, and, as a result, their spending increases or decreases.

Stigma versus safety channels—Rows 1 and 2 of Table 4.1 show the *stigma* and *safety channels* for bailouts, which are opposites of each other and only one can hold for a given bank at a given time. Under the *stigma channel*, bailouts come with a stigma of being more likely to fail or become more financially distressed (e.g., Hoshi and Kashyap, 2010). As shown in Row 1, such stigma may decrease banks' stock valuations, as shown with "−," and increase market discipline from shareholders, uninsured creditors, and insured depositors, as indicated by "+s." The depressed equity values increase banks' market leverage risk. Bailed-out banks may also lose market share and market power and reduce their supplies of credit as they face higher costs and/or reduced availability of funds. The effects on portfolio risk are ambiguous, as indicated by "?," as the banks may issue less total credit, reducing portfolio risk, but more of it may go to riskier borrowers, increasing such risk. Finally, the reduced credit supply can have negative effects on credit customers' valuations and spending, including reduced investments, employment, and other spending.

Under the opposing *safety channel*, bailed-out banks may be perceived as safer due to the recapitalization itself, the selection criteria of the intervention (e.g., TARP targeted "healthy, viable institutions"), and/or a perception that these banks are more likely to be bailed out in the future. In all cases, the intermediate effects of the perception of safety are exactly opposed to those of stigma and follow the same logic.

Predation versus charter value/quiet life channels—Rows 3 and 4 of Table 4.1 show the *predation* and *charter value/quiet life channels* for bailouts, which in most but not all cases, are opposites of each other and only one can hold for a given bank at a given time. Under the *predation channel*, banks may use the capital from the intervention to act more aggressively in the market. As shown in Row 3, predation behavior can lead to ambiguous effects as indicated by "?s" on banks' market valuation, market discipline by shareholders, and market leverage risk. Predation can increase perceived bank risk, depressing stock prices, increasing discipline from all stakeholders, and raising market leverage risk.

However, predation can alternatively increase stock prices, decrease discipline from shareholders, and reduce market leverage risk due to shareholders' agency problems as they may seek higher rather than lower bank risk, yielding "?s." In both cases, predation is expected to increase market discipline from uninsured creditors and insured depositors, as indicated by "+s." Aggressiveness from predation by bailed-out banks may be manifested by taking market share away from financially constrained peers,[1] resulting in higher market shares, or by offering customers lower rates and fees on loans and higher rates on deposits and other funds, resulting in lower market power. Bailed-out banks under predation may also increase their supplies of credit, particularly risky credit, which may also raise portfolio risks, both indicated by "+s" (e.g., Telser, 1966; Fudenberg and Tirole, 1986). Ultimately, the increased credit supply can have positive effects on credit customers' valuation and their investments, employment, and other spending.

Under the almost opposing *charter value/quiet life channel*, the additional safety from the bailout may increase bank charter value and/or allow for a "quiet life," decreasing incentives for aggressive behavior in the market (e.g., Hicks, 1935; Keeley, 1990; Cordella and Yeyati, 2003; Gropp, Hakenes, and Schnabel, 2011). The intermediate outcomes of the perception of higher charter value are exactly opposed to those of predation and follow the same logic for all but market valuation, shareholder discipline, and bank market leverage risk, which were ambiguous above under predation. In contrast, increased charter value from the bailouts can increase perception of improved bank fundamentals which can increase stock market prices, decrease discipline from shareholders, and decrease market leverage risk.

Cost disadvantage versus advantage channels—Rows 5 and 6 of Table 4.1 show the *cost disadvantage* and *cost advantage channels* for bailouts, which are opposites, and only one can hold for a given bank at a given time. Under the *cost disadvantage channel*, bailout funds can be more expensive than other sources of funding provided by the market. As shown in Row 5, such cost disadvantage may decrease banks' stock valuations, as shown with "−," and increase market discipline from shareholders, uninsured creditors, and insured depositors, as indicated by "+s." The depressed equity values also increase the banks' market leverage risk. Due to the cost disadvantage, bailed-out banks may

---

[1] Some anecdotal evidence suggests that some TARP bailout recipients used the funds to acquire peers with poorer capital ratios. For example, MB Financial acquired in 2009 several failing institutions: Benchmark Bank, Corus Bank NA, InBank, and Heritage Community Bank. M&T Bank Corp, New York, also acquired all the outstanding common stock of Provident Bankshares Corp in 2009 and Wilmington Trust Corporation in 2010.

decrease their portfolio sizes, resulting in lower market shares and may have increased marginal costs, so they may increase price (by a lesser amount), leading to lower market power. Thus, both market share and market power are indicated by "−s." The relatively expensive funds from bailouts induce banks to decrease their supplies of bank credit and reduce portfolio risk. The reduced credit supplies can have negative effects on credit customers' valuations and spending.

Under the opposing *cost advantage channel*, bailout funds may be relatively cheap compared to other sources of funding provided by the market, sending a positive signal to the market. In all cases, the intermediate outcomes of the bailed-out banks' cost advantage are exactly opposed to those of cost disadvantage and follow the same logic.

Increased versus decreased moral hazard channels—Rows 7 and 8 of Table 4.1 show the *increased moral hazard* and *decreased moral hazard channels* for bailouts, which are opposites of each other, and only one can hold for a given bank at a given time. Under the *increased moral hazard channel*, bank moral hazard incentives of bailed-out banks may increase because of a perceived increased probability of future bailouts which may protect the bank or some stakeholders (e.g., Acharya and Yorulmazer, 2007; Kashyap, Rajan, and Stein, 2008; Black and Hazelwood, 2013; Li, 2013; Duchin and Sosyura, 2014). As shown in Row 7, such increased moral hazard can have ambiguous effects on bank stock valuation, shareholder discipline, and market leverage risk. Increased moral hazard can increase perception of intensified bank risk which can decrease stock prices, increase discipline from all stakeholders, and increase market leverage risk. However, it can also have the opposite effects due to shareholders' agency problems as they may seek higher rather than lower risk-taking. In both cases, increased moral hazard is expected to increase market discipline from uninsured creditors and insured depositors. Under the *increased moral hazard channel*, banks may have incentives to shift into riskier portfolios to offset potential reductions in market leverage risk from the bailout (e.g., Koehn and Santomero, 1980; Kim and Santomero, 1988; Besanko and Kanatas, 1996; Calem and Rob, 1999). This has ambiguous effects on market share, but leads to higher measured market power because the riskier pool of customers pays higher interest rates. Creditors may also charge more if they perceive the bailed-out banks as riskier, but this increase will be less than enough to compensate for the riskier asset portfolio. While portfolio risk increases, the effects on credit supply are ambiguous, as the banks may increase, decrease, or not change their overall credit supply. This further suggests that effects on credit customers' valuations and spending are ambiguous as well.

Under the opposing *decreased moral hazard channel*, bailouts can reduce bank moral hazard incentives to take excessive risks induced by various aspects of the government safety net for banks due to increased restrictions imposed by supervisors (e.g., Kashyap, Rajan, and Stein, 2008; Hart and Zingales, 2011; Admati, DeMarzo, Hellwig, and Pfleiderer, 2013; Berger and Bouwman, 2013; Acharya, Mehran, and Thakor, 2016). In all cases, the intermediate outcomes of the perception of such decreased moral hazard are exactly opposed to those of the increased moral hazard and follow the same logic.

Capital priority versus capital cushion channels—Rows 9 and 10 of Table 4.1 show the *capital priority* and *capital cushion channels* for bailouts, which are opposites of each other. Under the *capital priority channel*, injections of capital such as preferred equity of TARP may have priority over other stakeholders, including common shareholders. Injecting preferred equity can reduce the market value of common equity through lower market equity prices and/or less common equity issuance by making such equity more expensive to raise. This can occur via: (1) higher costs such as interest payments to be paid to the preferred shareholders before any profits reach common shareholders; (2) the rate paid on the equity injection may be a penalty rather than a subsidized rate; and/or (3) the capital injection may come with a stigma of being more likely to fail or become financially distressed, hurting confidence in the bank. As shown in Row 9, such capital priority effects and induced reduced confidence may decrease banks' stock valuations and increase market discipline from shareholders, uninsured creditors, and insured depositors. The depressed equity values increase banks' leverage risk. Bailed-out banks may also lose market share and market power and reduce their supply of credit as they face higher costs and/or reduced availability of funds. The effects on portfolio risk are ambiguous, as the banks may issue less total credit, reducing portfolio risk, but more of it may go to riskier borrowers, increasing such risk. Ultimately, the reduced credit supply can have negative effects on credit customers' valuations and spending.

Under the opposing *capital cushion channel*, bailouts may boost the bank market value through higher market common equity prices and/or more equity issuance. There are three mechanisms through which this may happen: (1) reducing risk and making the institutions less likely to fail by providing an extra layer of funds to absorb losses; (2) providing the funding at a subsidized rate; and (3) boosting public confidence in the bank due to government backing or signaling of safety. In all cases, the intermediate outcomes of the capital cushion are exactly opposed to those of capital priority and follow the same logic.

Too-big-to-fail (size), too-interconnected-to-fail (interconnectedness), and too-many-to-fail (herding) channels—Rows 11, 12, and 13 of Table 4.1 show the *too-big-to-fail (size)*, *too-interconnected-to-fail (interconnectedness)*, and *too-many-to-fail (herding) channels* for bailouts. Regulatory interventions via bailouts may increase the probabilities of such future bailouts, encouraging banks to grow to gain too-big-to-fail (TBTF) protections, to become more interconnected—i.e., enter into more contracts (e.g., loans, derivatives) with other banks—to gain too-interconnected-to-fail (TITF) protections, and to engage in herding behavior—such as engaging in similar investments—to gain too-many-to-fail (TMTF) protections (e.g., Acharya and Yorulmazer, 2007, 2008; Brown and Dinc, 2011). The bailed-out banks' increased TBTF, TITF, and TMTF protections induce increased stock market valuations and reduced market discipline from all stakeholders (shareholders, uninsured creditors, and insured creditors), as well as reduced market leverage risk. To enhance their TBTF protections, banks have incentives to expand either organically or via mergers and acquisitions (M&As), although for the purposes of our discussion, we assume that TBTF status can only be realistically achieved through M&As. This may increase their market shares and systemic importance, but have no clear effects on market power, credit supply, portfolio risk, or credit customers. TITF and TMTF increase systemic importance, but have no clear effects on market share or these other intermediate outcomes.

4.2 Direct channels from bail-ins to intermediate financial and economic outcomes for banks, their markets, and their stakeholders

We next follow Table 4.2, which shows the signs of the effects of the channels for bail-ins. We include the same 13 channels on the same 12 intermediate financial and economic outcomes as above for bailouts, but here we also include a 14th additional channel specific to bail-ins. In addition to "+," "−," and "?," we include "N/A" to signal that some of the bailout channels do not apply to bail-ins. For simplicity, the bail-in results in the table are for bail-in interventions such as in the Orderly Liquidation Authority (OLA) program in the US discussed in Chapter 3, but most of the findings likely generalize to other bail-ins.

We again group related channels and again some of the outcomes always go in the same directions. We do not discuss bank systemic importance at all here, as the final three channels to increase systemic importance do not apply to bail-ins.

Stigma versus safety channels—Rows 1 and 2 of Table 4.2 show the *stigma* and *safety channels* for bail-ins. As above for bailouts, stigma from bail-ins may decrease stock valuations and increase market discipline from shareholders, uninsured creditors, and insured depositors. Depressed equity prices can increase banks' market leverage risk. Bailed-in banks may also lose market share and market power and reduce their supply of credit as they face higher costs and/or reduced availability of funds, as above for bailouts. The effects on portfolio risk are ambiguous, as the bailed-in banks may issue less total credit, reducing portfolio risk, but more of it may go to riskier borrowers, increasing such risk. Finally, the reduced credit supply can have negative effects on credit customers' valuations and spending.

There is no *safety channel* under bail-ins, as indicated by the row of "N/As." Even if bail-ins were to signal more future bail-ins, this would not be an assurance of safety.

Predation versus charter value/quiet life channels—Under the *predation channel* in Row 3 of Table 4.2, predation behavior under bail-in in an effort "to gamble for resurrection" can increase the perception of increased bank risk, which can depress banks' market valuation and increase market discipline from all stakeholders (shareholders, uninsured creditors, and insured creditors), as well as increase market leverage. However, because shareholders may prefer the higher risk from predation behavior, stock prices may alternatively increase, raising valuation and decreasing leverage risk, yielding "?s" for these effects. Aggressiveness from predation by bailed-in banks may manifest by taking market share away from peers, resulting in higher market share, or offering customers lower rates and fees on loans and higher rates on deposits and other funds, resulting in lower market power. Bailed-in banks under predation may also increase their supplies of risky credit, which may raise portfolio risks. Ultimately, the increased credit supplies can have positive effects on credit customers' valuation and spending, including increased investments and employment.

There is no *charter value/quiet life channel* under bail-ins as bail-ins clearly destroy charter value as shown by the row of "N/As."

Cost disadvantage versus advantage channels—Under the *cost disadvantage channel* in Row 5, bail-in funds can be more expensive relative to other sources of funding provided by the market. This sends a negative signal to the market. Such cost disadvantages may decrease banks' stock valuations and increase market discipline from shareholders, uninsured creditors, and insured depositors. Depressed stock prices increase market leverage risk. Due to the cost disadvantages, bailed-in banks may decrease their portfolio sizes, resulting in lower market shares and may have increases in marginal cost so they may increase price (by a lesser amount), leading to lower market power. The relatively expensive funds from bail-ins induce banks to decrease their supplies of bank credit and reduce portfolio risk. The reduced credit supplies can have negative effects on credit customers' valuations and spending.

There is no *cost advantage channel* under bail-ins as bail-ins do not provide subsidized funds, indicated by the row of "N/As."

Increased versus decreased moral hazard channels—There is no *increased moral hazard channel* under bail-ins as there is no subsidy to risk-taking under bail-ins, shown by the Row 7 of "N/As."

Under the *decreased moral hazard channel* in Row 8, bail-ins can reduce bank moral hazard incentives to take excessive risks because under bail-ins, the costs of bank distress and failure are all borne by private stakeholders, which may become more sensitive to risk. It is unclear whether the decreased moral hazard from bail-ins is enough to offset other negative effects of bail-ins for stakeholders and be regarded as a positive signal by the market. Thus, effects from decreased moral hazard are uncertain on banks' stock valuation, market discipline from all stakeholders (shareholders, uninsured creditors, and insured depositors) and bank market leverage risk, shown with "?s." Under the *decreased moral hazard channel*, the increase in private capital from bail-ins may result in shifts into safer portfolios. This has ambiguous effects on market share shown with "?," but can lead to lower measured market power shown with "−." This is because the safer pool of customers pays lower interest rates for loan products, which is partially offset by lower interest rates from creditors. While banks may decrease portfolio risk, the effects on their total supply of credit are ambiguous, as banks may decrease the supplies of credit to riskier borrowers, increase supplies to safer borrowers, or shift from riskier to safer borrowers without changing overall credit supply. As before, this further suggests that effects on credit customers' valuations and spending, including investments and employment, are uncertain.

Capital priority, capital cushion, and capital conversion channels—As shown in Rows 9 and 10 of Table 4.2, there are no *capital priority* and *capital cushion channels* for bail-ins, as there are no injections of preferred equity as there were in the TARP version of bailouts above.

However, we add a new channel, the *capital conversion channel*, that is relevant for bail-ins, but not for bailouts. Under this new channel, shown in Row 11 of Table 4.2, bail-ins via equity wipeouts and conversions of debt to equity can harm certain stakeholders and bank market confidence. This may occur because the equity wipeouts of original shareholders and conversions of debtholders into shareholders are undesired outcomes for these stakeholders imposing significant losses on them and creating potential panic among all stakeholders. This could also occur because the capital conversion likely comes with a stigma that the bank may be more likely to fail or become financially distressed, hurting market confidence in the bank and increasing market discipline from all stakeholders. However, the effects on market leverage risk are ambiguous because the wipeout of the original shareholders and conversion of debt to equity inherent in this channel may actually decrease leverage risk. Due to the reduced confidence, market share and market power are likely to be decreased, as is credit supply, while the effect on portfolio risk is ambiguous. The reduced credit supply can have negative effects on credit customers.

Too-big-to-fail (size), too-interconnected-to-fail (interconnectedness), and too-many-to-fail (herding) channels—Rows 12, 13, and 14 of

Table 4.2 show "N/A" for these channels for bail-ins. Bail-ins are undesirable outcomes, so it would not be sensible to try to increase the probabilities of bail-ins.[2]

4.3 Relations between the intermediate outcomes of bailouts and bail-ins and the ultimate outcomes of systemic risk and the real economy

Here, we closely follow Table 4.3, which shows the signs of the relation between the 12 intermediate financial and economic outcomes for banks, their markets, and their stakeholders for bailouts and bail-ins and the two ultimate outcomes of systemic risk and the real economy. Analogously to prior sections and tables, "+" indicates a positive relation between the intermediate outcome and the ultimate outcome, "−" signifies a negative relation, and "?" signals an ambiguous or no relation.

To be clear, independent of whether bailouts or bail-ins positively or negatively affect each intermediate outcome, we assess the relations between positive intermediate outcomes and the ultimate outcomes. Thus, the table entries evaluate how increases in bank stock valuations, increases in market discipline by various stakeholders, etc. are related to systemic risk and the real economy.

Starting with the systemic risk column, banks' stock valuation in Row 1 is negatively associated with bank systemic risk. Increased stock valuations reduce bank leverage risk, which decreases the bank's contribution to systemic risk. Consistent with this, increased bank leverage risk in column 5 is positively related to systemic risk. In rows 2−4, market discipline by shareholders, uninsured creditors, and insured depositors have ambiguous associations with bank systemic risk. On the one hand, more market discipline reduces systemic risk by keeping the bank from taking excessive risks, while on the other hand, more discipline is costly to the bank, depressing market valuation, which increases the bank's contribution to systemic risk. In rows 6, 7, 11, and 12, the nonfinancial outcomes of bank market share and market power and credit customers' valuation and spending do not have any obvious significant relations with systemic risk. In rows 8-10, we see that bank credit supply, portfolio risk, and systemic importance, all have positive associations with bank systemic risk because anything that makes the bank riskier or more systemically important increases its contribution to systemic risk.

Turning to the findings for the real economy, the only intermediate outcome of bailouts and bail-ins which has unambiguous relations with the real economy is the positive associations for bank credit customers' spending. Thus, credit customers must alter their investments, employment, and/or other spending on goods and services in order to affect the real economy.

4.4 Relations between the ultimate outcomes of systemic risk and the real economy

A final set of links is the relations of the two ultimate outcomes of systemic risk and the real economy with each other. These relations are described here and shown in Table 4.4. Again, we use "+," "−,"and "?" indicators. Analogously to the prior section and table, we assess the effects of an increase in systemic risk on the real economy and the effects of an improvement in the real economy on systemic risk.

Starting with the effects of systemic risk on the real economy, systemic risk has a strong negative effect on the real economy. High systemic risk can cause a financial system collapse that reduces credit and equity supplied to firms and imperils the real economy as witnessed by the Great Recession that followed the Global Financial Crisis, and the Great Depression that followed the financial panic that started in 1929.

Looking next at the effects of the real economy on systemic risk, the relations depend in large part on the segment of the economic cycle. During a boom in the real economy, further real economic improvements can increase systemic risk. They may exacerbate lending booms, lead to lax enforcement of material adverse change clauses on loan commitments, excessive bank liquidity creation, etc., that result in excessive bank risk and asset pricing bubbles that burst and cause financial crises. These processes and the research on them are described above in Chapter 2. However, improvements in the real economy can also reduce systemic risk during recessions. Increases in employment and GDP during problematic economic times may improve banks' portfolio quality and create profitable lending opportunities, reducing banks' risks and decreasing the risk of the financial system.

---

[2] If anything, banks might try to avoid systemic importance under bail-ins, similar to the way that some banks try to stay under the Dodd−Frank asset thresholds due to harsher regulatory treatment (e.g., Bouwman, Hu, and Johnson, 2018; Bindal, Bouwman, Hu, and Johnson, 2020)

4.5 Additional theoretical research on bailouts, bail-ins, and comparisons among them and bankruptcy/failure

4.5.1 Additional theoretical research on bailouts

Most of the theoretical arguments on bailouts are mentioned above in the channels discussions, but others are also important.

Allen, Carletti, Goldstein, and Leonello (2018) find that bailouts can be welfare improving because they induce banks to improve their liquidity provision. Merton and Thakor (2019) provide a new perspective on why bailing out banks may be socially efficient — because depositors are "customers" who provide financing to the bank but never want to be exposed to its credit risk (unlike investors who provide financing).[3] However, Allen, Carletti, Goldstein, and Leonello (2018) find that bailouts may also increase the likelihood of runs or create distortions in banks' behavior. Acharya and Thakor (2016) look at bailouts as part of the optimal central bank regulatory policy in the presence of the "liquidation externalities" of excessive bank leverage. They discuss trade-offs between greater use of equity which can lead to lower *ex ante* bank liquidity and greater use of debt which can lead to a higher probability of inefficient bank liquidation. Other theoretical papers on bailouts also suggest that bailouts or anticipation of bailouts may adversely affect banks' risk-taking incentives, and ultimately the appeal of the public intervention (e.g., Farhi and Tirole, 2012; Nosal and Ordoñez, 2016; Keister and Narasiman, 2016).

Philippon and Schnabl (2013) solve for the optimal bailout intervention to recapitalize a banking sector that restricts lending to firms because of debt overhang. They find that the efficient recapitalization program injects capital against preferred stock plus warrants. They argue that preferred stock plus warrants reduce opportunistic participation by banks that do not require recapitalization, although conditional implementation limits free-riding by banks that benefit from lower credit risk because of other banks' participation.

Focusing on systemic risk, Choi (2014) finds that despite the fact that financial contagion originates in weaker institutions, systemic risk can critically depend on the financial health of stronger banks in the contagion

---

[3] Acharya and Thakor (2016) look at bailouts as part of the optimal central bank regulatory policy in the presence of the "liquidation externalities" of excessive bank leverage. They discuss trade-offs between greater use of equity which can lead to lower *ex ante* bank liquidity and greater use of debt which can lead to a higher probability of inefficient bank liquidation.

chain. He argues that supporting the strong, rather than the weak, can more effectively enhance systemic stability.[4]

4.5.2 Additional theoretical research on bail-ins

The theoretical work on bail-ins focuses on the effects of bail-ins on bank incentives, systemic risk, and other benefits and costs of bail-ins. Starting with bank incentives, Avgouleas and Goodhart (2016) argue that replacing the implicit public guarantee with a system of private penalties under bail-ins is expected to reduce moral hazard, increase market discipline, and improve bank management *ex ante* behavior. Dewatripont and Tirole (2018) argue that bail-ins can complement liquidity regulation.

A number of other papers find limited benefits of bail-ins on bank systemic risk. Huser, Halaj, Kok, Perales, and van der Kraaij (2018) assess the possible contagion effects and systemic implications of bail-ins using a multi-layered network model. In the model, each layer represents the securities' cross-holdings of a specific seniority among the largest banking groups in the euro area, and the bail-in of a bank is simulated to identify the direct contagion risk to the other banks in the network. They find that shareholders and subordinated creditors are always affected by the bail-in, while senior unsecured creditors are affected in 75% of the cases. The bail-in significantly reshapes interbank linkages within specific seniority layers. The authors recommend careful monitoring of the impact of bail-ins on the systemic risk of the banks under resolution. Walther and White (2017) show that precautionary regimes of long-term debt can signal adverse information about a bank's balance sheet and cause a bank run, leading to an overly weak bail-in regime. In the context of Greece, Zenios (2016) discusses that bail-ins can create systemic problems through widespread credit crunch on the demand side (bailed-in depositors) as a result of write-downs. He recommends that in order for bail-ins to play their role as a deterrent to excessive risk-taking, bail-in policies and the bail-in percent should be well communicated to the public and should allow fair treatment of creditors within their seniority class and among each other and not just be compared with the disastrous alternative of bank failures.

Several papers argue that bail-ins cannot handle the simultaneous balance sheet insolvency of several banks. Persaud (2014) and Hadjiemmanuil (2016) argue that bail-ins work well in idiosyncratic bank failures (the institution failed due to its own actions), but in the presence of systemic crises, bail-ins might make matters even worse. They suggest that in a context of widespread distress, the application of bail-in in a

---

[4] For a review of the theory about government guarantees and moral hazard, see Allen, Carletti, Goldstein, and Leonello (2018).

single (failing) bank may push creditors of other banks to reconsider their positions, thus precipitating an across-the-board flight to quality.

Avgouleas and Goodhart (2016) also argue that the bail-in tool may be particularly superior to bailout in cases of idiosyncratic failure. However, bail-in regimes may not eradicate the need for bailouts where there is a threat of systemic collapse, i.e., when a number of banks have entered concurrently into difficulties, or in the event of the failure of a large complex cross-border bank. In contrast, Grauwe (2013) suggests that bail-in does not lead to runs in other banks as per the FDIC experience of purchase and assumptions of small banks.

Mitts (2015) discusses deficiencies of OLA approach and argues that a major omission by policymakers and academics is understanding the microlevel managerial incentives resulting from the OLA's incapacity to respond to banks' simultaneous balance sheet insolvencies. By holding correlated asset portfolios and serving as counterparties to similarly situated financial institutions, managers can strategically increase the likelihood of government bailouts rather than bail-ins.

Several researchers point out that current bail-in regimes may not distinguish well between cases of bank illiquidity- versus insolvency-driven systemic risk. Systemic risk effects could be better contained if attempting to prevent cases of short-term illiquidity from deteriorating into long-term insolvency by intervening sufficiently early while a distressed firm is still balance-sheet solvent (e.g., Persaud, 2014; Mitts, 2015; Avgouleas and Goodhart, 2016; Hadjiemmanuil, 2016).[5]

Many other costs and benefits of bail-ins have been voiced in the literature, with implications for regulation and policy. Avgouleas and Goodhart (2016) balance a long list of actual or hypothetical benefits and drawbacks of bail-ins relative to bailouts. Aside from the benefits and costs already discussed above, they mention that bail-ins better protect taxpayers and mitigate sovereign-bank debt "doom-loop in which banks and sovereigns drag each other down," while placing the recapitalization burden more fairly and removing unfair competitive advantages of TBTF banks. Avgouleas and Goodhart (2016) also mention that an important weakness of bail-ins is potentially severe reputational contagion. OLA bail-in resolution in the US uses a top–down approach in which the parent BHC is put under resolution while allowing the subsidiaries to continue operations. However, subsidiaries may have trouble continuing on their own without the parent BHC due to lack of market confidence. The authors argue that the parent liquidation can likely trigger panic and flight from the entire group, including the apparently unaffected subsidiaries.

---

[5] The current statutory limitations on resolution of failed banks may prevent OLA from intervening unless the firm is already in default or danger of default.

Furthermore, the liquidation of one entity can also put into question the health of other banks, triggering contagious events.

Finally, several researchers predict international cooperation challenges for bailed-in institutions with operations in multiple nations. Even where regulatory agreements are in place, it may be doubtful that bilateral arrangements will hold in the event of cross-border banking crises and bail-in events, involving a transfer of funds from one jurisdiction to another. For example, host regulators may force foreign subsidiaries to operate as ring-fenced entities, leading to inefficient internal capital markets and inability to shift resources from healthy to troubled subsidiaries (e.g., Carmassi and Herring, 2015; Lupo-Pasini and Buckley, 2015; Avgouleas and Goodhart, 2016; Hadjiemmanuil, 2016).

4.5.3 Additional theoretical research on contingent convertibles (CoCos)

As mentioned above, contingent convertibles are another bail-in tool. Theoretical research shows that CoCos may be able to signal risk, improve bank incentives, and encourage timely voluntary offerings of equity into the market by banks in distress (Calomiris and Herring, 2011, 2013; Flannery, 2017; Himmelberg and Tsyplakov, 2017). For example, Calomiris and Herring (2011) develop a proposal for a contingent capital (CoCo) requirement to be used as a prudential tool. The authors explain that CoCos can create strong incentives for the prompt recapitalization of banks after significant losses of equity, but before the bank has run out of options to access the equity market. The incentive feature of a properly designed CoCo would encourage effective risk management by banks, provide a more effective solution to the TBTF problem, and address ambiguity about the adequate amount of capital banks need to hold. They maintain that if a CoCo requirement had been in place in 2007, the disruptive failures of large financial institutions and the systemic meltdown after September 2008 could have been avoided. Calomiris and Herring (2013) show that CoCos can play a key role along with the minimum capital requirements, and if adequately designed, they can provide adequate capital relative to risk taken, and can do it at a lower cost than the simple capital requirements. The authors also maintain that encouraging timely voluntary offerings of equity into the market by banks that suffered significant losses is the most important goal to pursue when dealing with banks' TBTF problem. Himmelberg and Tsyplakov (2017) study the optimal design and *ex ante* incentive effects of CoCos and find that CoCos can induce powerful incentive effects for the banks with first-order implications for the dynamics of capital structure management. They show that if conversion terms are dilutive for existing shareholders, banks would have incentives to reduce likelihood of triggering the CoCos by pursuing lower leverage, leading to less defaults and lower borrowing costs. However, if at conversion, bond principal is written down without diluting shareholders, then banks would have perverse incentives to pursue higher leverage and destroy capital.

A number of papers investigate systemic risk and risk implications of CoCos and find ambiguous results. Some researchers find that CoCos can intensify bank contagion and systemic risk that could ultimately endanger the financial system and the real economy (Chan and Wijnbergen, 2014, 2017; Zombirt, 2015). For example, Chan and Wijnbergen (2014) document that CoCos increase systemic risk. They show that while the CoCo conversion of the issuing bank may bring the bank back into compliance with the prevailing capital requirements, it will also raise the probability of the bank being run because conversion is a negative signal to depositors about bank asset quality. Furthermore, conversion also imposes a negative externality on other banks in the system in the case of correlated asset returns, so that bank runs become more likely in the banking system, and systemic risk goes up after conversion.

Chan and Wijnbergen (2017) also investigate effects of the CoCo design on bank risk shifting incentives and financial fragility. They document that the CoCo conversion enhances the issuer's loss absorption capacity, but leads to wealth transfers between CoCo holders and shareholders, thus giving rise to risk-shifting incentives to shareholders. For written-down CoCos, the risk-shifting incentive is always present, while for equity-converting CoCos, it depends on the dilutive power of the CoCo. They maintain that some types of CoCos are possibly riskier than issuing subordinated debt instead. In order to avoid these effects, banks' use of CoCos should be complemented with increasing bank capital and should not be treated as true substitutes for equity. Zombirt (2015) also warns that there are still unknown threats connected with CoCos that could endanger future adequate functioning of the financial system and real economy. Another paper, Bleich (2014), analyzes how the design of CoCos affects the stability of bank funding and distinguishes among three different types of CoCos: Conversion-to-Equity CoCos, Principal Write-down CoCos with a full write-down feature, and Principal Write-down CoCos with a partial write-down feature. While the author finds that the first two unambiguously enhance the bank funding stability, the latter can raise solvency risk and can be a source of ambiguity for the bank's *ex post* solvency. This suggests caution for the regulatory treatment of CoCos with a partial write-down feature.

Conversely, some other papers find increased stability effects and better taxpayers protection (De Spiegeleer, Hocht, and Schoutens, 2015; Allen and Tang, 2016; Avdjiev, Bolton, Jiang, Kartasheva, and Bogdanova, 2017; Ammann, Blickle, and Ehmann, 2017; Himmelberg and Tsyplakov,

2017; Hwang, 2017). For example, Allen and Tang (2016) document that CoCos can reduce systemic risk by automatically recapitalizing banks during financial crises if the trigger mechanism is adequately designed. They propose a dual trigger mechanism based on the aggregate systemic risk in the banking system (ΔCoVaR) and the individual bank's contribution to overall systemic risk (ΔCoVaR). The dual trigger is highly correlated with system-wide insolvency risk and prices systemic risk. Using a 99% trigger cut-off, systemic CoCos issued by Lehman Brothers and Bear Stearns would have been triggered in November 2007, months prior to their actual resolutions. Consistently, Avdjiev, Bolton, Jiang, Kartasheva, and Bogdanova (2017) find that CoCo issuance reduces bank credit risk, leading to a decline in the issuers' CDS spreads.

Finally, Hwang (2017) directly considers the case of CoCos as tools of bail-ins and finds that CoCos may be more or less effective to recapitalize the institutions, depending on the conversion trigger chosen. If the issuing institution is nonviable and therefore a trigger condition is met, the CoCo bond is written down or converted to equity and hence, the bank can be recapitalized at the expense of creditors, rather than taxpayers. However, the trigger condition could be either rule-based or discretion-based. The paper shows that bailout is more likely and creditor bail-in is less likely when a discretionary trigger is used.

4.5.4 Research on bankruptcy/failure

While there is theoretical research on bank failure, there is no theoretical research to our knowledge that focuses on BHC bankruptcy alone or the combination of bankruptcy of the BHC and failure of the bank as under the proposed CHOICE Act or other similar bank bankruptcy proposals. Berger, Himmelberg, Roman, and Tsyplakov (2020), which is discussed in the next subsection, does essentially cover the bankruptcy/failure option, but only in the context of comparing it to bailouts and bail-ins.

4.5.5 Research comparing bailouts, bail-ins, and bankruptcy/failure

Berger, Himmelberg, Roman, and Tsyplakov (2020) develop a dynamic model of the socially optimal designs of three regulatory regimes for handling potential failure of a large bank and the bankruptcy of its bank holding company (BHC): bailout, bail-in, and no regulatory intervention in which the bank is allowed to fail and the BHC becomes bankrupt. We hereafter refer to the last approach of these authors as bankruptcy/failure to distinguish it from forbearance discussed below, which involves even less regulatory intervention and no bankruptcy or failure at least in the short-run.

The authors find that among the three regimes, only optimal bail-ins result in banks preemptively rebuilding capital during distress. This result occurs because the market rewards the BHC for precommitting to recapitalize in the event of financial distress with lower cost of debt and higher debt capacity *ex ante*. This key finding occurs because of the dynamic nature of the model—the *ex ante* market rewards for precommitment cannot be developed using a static model.

Additionally, under the bankruptcy/failure regime, both the BHC and the rest of society are worst off. The BHC is worst off because there are no recapitalizations either by the regulator in the case of bailout or by the BHC. In the event of distress, the BHC is more likely to become bankrupt and the bank is more likely to fail. The rest of society is also worst off under bankruptcy/failure because of the higher likelihood of bank default.

Finally, the optimally designed bailout and bail-in regimes have similar social welfare values in the base case of the model. However, when the social welfare costs of using and risking public taxpayer funds to bail out private-sector BHCs and/or the transactions costs of raising and distributing bailout funds are included in the model, bail-ins have higher social values than bailouts.

Leanza, Sbuelz, and Tarelli (2019) use a static structural model to study the optimal liability structure of a bank under different resolution regimes and capital requirements. Similar to one of the results in Berger, Himmelberg, Roman, and Tsyplakov (2020), they show that compared to a bailout regime, banks choose higher capital ratios under bail-in so that a credible bail-in regime endogenously reduces leverage and mitigates default risk. The costs of bank failures are shifted to equity holders and debt holders, so equity and bond prices become more sensitive to bank risk. However, the theoretical mechanism in this paper is quite different from the first because their model is static and cannot capture the value to shareholders from the pre-commitment to recapitalize. These authors also consider a mixed regime, in which the government can still bail out the bank even in the presence of bail-inable debt, and show that the credibility of the bail-in tool is essential. Even for a relatively small risk-adjusted probability of bailout, the incentives for shareholders to raise leverage and to take advantage of the implicit government guarantee significantly affect the optimal debt structure. Clayton and Schaab (2019) model bank capital structure as a mix of standard debt, which liquidates the bank, and bail-in debt which is written down to restore solvency of the institution. They find that in the presence of fire sale externalities induced by bank failure and moral hazard from bailouts, banks' incentives are to choose too much standard debt relative to bail-in debt, hence a bail-in regime is the optimal policy and can fully replace bailouts. To prevent self-fulfilling crises in the debt markets that bail-ins can induce, debt guarantees should be accompanied by lender of last resort policies. Pandolfi (2018) studies a related incentive problem to Clayton and Scaab (2019), and finds that bailouts may be desirable in conjunction with bail-ins when bail-ins limit investment scale by weakening bank incentives. Also focusing on incentives, Keister and Mitkov (2017) show that banks will not bail in their creditors if they anticipate that bailouts could occur.

Also analyzing three crisis resolution mechanisms for banks, Klimek, Poledna, Farmer, and Thurner (2015) employ an agent-based model to study the economic and financial ramifications of bank closure via a purchase and assumption transaction, a bailout, or bail-in. Authors find that the best bank resolution mechanism with respect to financial system stability and productivity depends on the state of the economy. For economies in recession with high unemployment, the bail-in tool provides the most efficient resolution mechanism, while for economies with low unemployment and high productivity, the optimal resolution is to close the distressed institution via a purchase and assumption transaction. Their findings suggest that taxpayer-funded bailout schemes underperform bail-ins with private sector involvement.

Finally, looking at various international cases of banking crises, Dewatripont (2014) discuss the pros and cons of bailouts and bail-ins. He stresses that financial instability can be costlier than bailouts, and that speedy recapitalization through a bailout can be crucial to minimize the effect on the economy. He shows that in many cases, the public money is eventually repaid in full and argues that the negative impact of bailouts in terms of moral hazard and of taxpayer risk can be contained by punishing managers and shareholders that receive bailouts. He argues that pre-funded bailouts should not be ruled out as an alternative/complement to bail-in, especially to deal with negative macroeconomic shocks. However, he also suggests that policymakers should ensure that markets understand that the risk of bail-in is concentrated in long-term bank liabilities.

4.6 Theoretical research on reorganization using living wills

As discussed in Chapter 3, living wills or resolution plans are mandated by the Dodd-Frank Act, and are a potential alternative way to resolve the distress and impending failure of banking organizations without government or private sector aid. The plans describe substantive, detailed strategies for the bank's rapid and orderly resolution in case of financial difficulties or failure using the bankruptcy process. From a theoretical viewpoint, living wills are much like the bankruptcy/failure option discussed above, except that they are designed to be more orderly and likely to preserve more of the financially viable parts of the organization.

There is only one paper to our knowledge addressing living wills in the US. Cetorelli and Traina (2018) discuss the living will regulation and its effects on banks' cost of capital. They also provide some theoretical intuition on the channels through which living wills may work and reduce the need for bailouts. They suggest that if living wills are credible, they should reduce agency costs of letting the institution fail due to two mechanisms: (1) living wills can increase the regulator's bargaining power due to less uncertainty about hidden costs of failure; and (2) they can also increase the political costs to bailing out the institution, given that regulators publicly signaled they would not do so.

4.7 Theoretical research on forbearance

As mentioned in Chapter 3, "regulatory forbearance" or "capital forbearance" is another alternative response to bank financial distress. This involves allowing banks with very low or negative capital ratios to continue operating without significant regulatory intervention or failure. This approach is sometimes used to save on closure costs, postpone dealing with problems until another regulator is in charge, or in the hope that the problems will be reversed on their own. However, it may create elevated credit risk problems and result in large losses to taxpayers in the long-run.

One widespread illustrative episode in the US banking crisis history was the savings and loan (S&L) crisis in the 1980s. The crisis began when monetary policy tightened in 1979, raising short-term interest rates to very high levels. S&Ls held large quantities of 30-year fixed-rate mortgages because of regulation requiring such investments and forbidding the use of adjustable rate mortgages. Thus, they were financing long-term mortgages at much lower rates than they were paying for their short-term deposits, essentially destroying their capital. Regulatory forbearance at the state and federal level was used widely and led to flawed examination and supervision measures allowing a large number of troubled S&Ls to continue to operate with low or negative equity capital. The Federal Savings and Loan Insurance Corporation (FSLIC) did not close the S&Ls, which would have forced them to realize the losses, and the supervisors generally did not act either. In some cases, the low capital exacerbated the moral hazard incentives to take on excessive portfolio risk, including some criminal activity and political involvement (e.g., Charles Keating, Lincoln Savings and Loan Association, and the "Keating Five" Senators).

Kormendi, Bernard, Pirrong, and Snyder (1989) argue that FSLIC actions during the 1980s increased resolution costs of problematic S&Ls because in organizing the sale of S&Ls, a $1 increase in tax benefits to acquirers was offset by only a 40 cents reduction in FSLIC costs. Thus, from a consolidated government estimation of costs, FSLIC actions had negative rather than positive effects.

Many of these problems were finally addressed by the Financial Institutions Reform, Recovery, and Enforcement Act of 1989 (FIRREA). It closed the FSLIC, transferring deposit insurance of the S&Ls to the FDIC. Among other actions, it also created the Resolution Trust Corporation (RTC). The RTC took on the assets of the failed S&Ls and eventually successfully sold them off slowly over time by coupling the undesirable bad assets with the desirable good assets.

Kane (2003) discusses lessons from the S&L financial crisis in the US and mentions that the major lesson to learn is how dangerous regulatory and bank risk-taking can reinforce each other. He mentions that, individual insolvencies persisting for years implies that regulators may have sold insolvent institutions' protection against failure and conspired at least implicitly with internal and external auditors to hide huge financial holes in the individual institutions' balance sheets. This helped the lending policies of troubled institutions escape the ordinary market and depositor discipline.

References

Acharya, V. V., Mehran, H., & Thakor, A. V. (2016). Caught between Scylla and charybdis? Regulating bank leverage when there is rent seeking and risk shifting. *The Review of Corporate Finance Studies, 5*(1), 36–75.

Acharya, V. V., & Thakor, A. V. (2016). The dark side of liquidity creation: Leverage and systemic risk. *Journal of Financial Intermediation, 28*, 4–21.

Acharya, V. V., & Yorulmazer, T. (2007). Too many to fail—An analysis of time-inconsistency in bank closure policies. *Journal of Financial Intermediation, 16*(1), 1–31.

Acharya, V. V., & Yorulmazer, T. (2008). Cash-in-the-market pricing and optimal resolution of bank failures. *The Review of Financial Studies, 21*(6), 2705–2742.

Admati, A. R., DeMarzo, P. M., Hellwig, M. F., & Pfleiderer, P. C. (2013). *Fallacies, irrelevant facts, and myths in the discussion of capital regulation: Why bank equity is not socially expensive* (Working Paper).

Allen, F., Carletti, E., Goldstein, I., & Leonello, A. (2018). Government guarantees and financial stability. *Journal of Economic Theory, 177*, 518–557.

Allen, L., & Tang, Y. (2016). What's the contingency? A proposal for bank contingent capital triggered by systemic risk. *Journal of Financial Stability, 26*, 1–14.

Ammann, M., Blickle, K., & Ehmann, C. (2017). Announcement effects of contingent convertible securities: Evidence from the global banking industry. *European Financial Management, 23*(1), 127–152.

Avdjiev, S., Bogdanova, B., Bolton, P., Jiang, W., & Kartasheva, A. (2017). *CoCo issuance and bank fragility* (Working Paper).

Avgouleas, E., & Goodhart, C. (2016). An anatomy of bank bail-ins—Why the eurozone needs a fiscal backstop for the banking sector. *European Economy, 2*, 75–90.

Berger, A. N. (2018). The benefits and costs of the TARP bailouts: A critical assessment. *Quarterly Journal of Finance, 8*(02), 1–29.

Berger, A. N., & Bouwman, C. H. S. (2013). How does capital affect bank performance during financial crises? *Journal of Financial Economics, 109*(1), 146–176.

Berger, A. N., Himmelberg, C. P., Roman, R. A., & Tsyplakov, S. (2020). *Bank bailouts, bail-ins, or no regulatory intervention?. A dynamic model and empirical tests of optimal regulation* (Working Paper).

Berger, A. N., Makaew, T., & Roman, R. A. (2019). Do business borrowers benefit from bank bailouts? The effects of TARP on loan contract terms. *Financial Management, 48*(2), 575–639.

Berger, A. N., & Roman, R. A. (2015). Did TARP banks get competitive advantages? *Journal of Financial and Quantitative Analysis, 50*(6), 1199–1236.

Berger, A. N., & Roman, R. A. (2017). Did saving Wall Street really save Main Street? The real effects of TARP on local economic conditions. *Journal of Financial and Quantitative Analysis, 52*(5), 1827–1867.

Berger, A. N., Roman, R. A., & Sedunov, J. (2020). Did TARP reduce or increase systemic risk? The effects of government aid on financial system stability. *Journal of Financial Intermediation*. forthcoming.

Besanko, D., & Kanatas, G. (1996). The regulation of bank capital: Do capital standards promote bank safety? *Journal of Financial Intermediation, 5*(2), 160–183.

Bindal, S., Bouwman, C. H., Hu, S., & Johnson, S. A. (2020). Bank regulatory size thresholds, merger and acquisition behavior, and small business lending. *Journal of Corporate Finance, 62*, 101519.

Black, L. K., & Hazelwood, L. N. (2013). The effect of TARP on bank risk-taking. *Journal of Financial Stability, 9*(4), 790–803.

Bleich, D. (2014). *Contingent convertible bonds and the stability of bank funding: The case of partial writedown* (Working Paper).

Bouwman, C. H. S., Hu, S., & Johnson, S. A. (2018). Differential bank behaviors around the Dodd–Frank Act size thresholds. *Journal of Financial Intermediation, 34*, 47–57.

Brown, C. O., & Dinç, I. S. (2011). Too many to fail? Evidence of regulatory forbearance when the banking sector is weak. *The Review of Financial Studies, 24*(4), 1378–1405.

Calem, P., & Rob, R. (1999). The impact of capital-based regulation on bank risk-taking. *Journal of Financial Intermediation, 8*(4), 317–352.

Calomiris, C. W., & Herring, R. J. (2011). *Why and how to design a contingent convertible debt requirement* (Working Paper).

Calomiris, C. W., & Herring, R. J. (2013). How to design a contingent convertible debt requirement that helps solve our too-big-to-fail problem. *Journal of Applied Corporate Finance, 25*(2), 39–62.

Carmassi, J., & Herring, R. J. (2015). *Corporate structures, transparency and resolvability of global systemically important banks* (Working Paper).

Cetorelli, N., & Traina, J. (2018). *Resolving 'too big to fail'* (Working Paper).

Chan, S., & Van Wijnbergen, S. (2014). CoCos, contagion and systemic risk. Working Paper.

Chan, S., & Van Wijnbergen, S. (2017). CoCo design, risk shifting incentives and capital regulation. Working Paper.

Choi, D. B. (2014). Heterogeneity and stability: Bolster the strong, not the weak. *The Review of Financial Studies, 27*(6), 1830–1867.

Clayton, C., & Schaab, A. (2019). *Bail-ins, optimal regulation, and crisis resolution* (Working Paper).

Cordella, T., & Yeyati, E. L. (2003). Bank bailouts: Moral hazard vs. value effect. *Journal of Financial Intermediation, 12*(4), 300–330.

De Spiegeleer, J., Höcht, S., & Schoutens, W. (2015). *Are banks now safer? What can we learn from the CoCo markets?* (Working Paper).

Dewatripont, M. (2014). European banking, bailout, bail-in and state aid control. *International Journal of Industrial Organization, 34*, 37–43.

Dewatripont, M., & Tirole, J. (2018). *Liquidity regulation, bail-ins and bailouts* (Working paper).

Duchin, R., & Sosyura, D. (2014). Safer ratios, riskier portfolios: Banks' response to government aid. *Journal of Financial Economics, 113*(1), 1–28.

Farhi, E., & Tirole, J. (2012). Collective moral hazard, maturity mismatch, and systemic bailouts. *The American Economic Review, 102*(1), 60–93.

Flannery, M. J. (2017). Stabilizing large financial institutions with contingent capital certificates. In *The Most Important Concepts in Finance*. Edward Elgar Publishing.

Fudenberg, D., & Tirole, J. (1986). A "signal-jamming" theory of predation. *The RAND Journal of Economics*, 366–376.

Grauwe, P. D. (2013). *The new bail-in doctrine: A recipe for banking crises and depression in the Eurozone*. Centre for European Policy Studies.

Gropp, R., Hakenes, H., & Schnabel, I. (2011). Competition, risk-shifting, and public bail-out policies. *The Review of Financial Studies*, 24(6), 2084–2120.

Hadjiemmanuil, C. (2016). *Bank resolution financing in the banking union* (Working Papers).

Hart, O., & Zingales, L. (2011). A new capital regulation for large financial institutions. *American Law and Economics Review*, 13(2), 453–490.

Hicks, J. R. (1935). Annual survey of economic theory: The theory of monopoly. *Econometrica. Journal of the Econometric Society*, 1–20.

Kane, E. J. (2003). What lessons might crisis countries in Asia and Latin America have learned from the S&L mess. *Business Economics*, 38(1), 21–30.

Himmelberg, C. P., & Tsyplakov, S. (2017). *Optimal terms of contingent capital, incentive effects, and capital structure dynamics* (Working Paper).

Hoshi, T., & Kashyap, A. K. (2010). Will the U.S. bank recapitalization succeed?: Eight lessons from Japan. *Journal of Financial Economics*, 97, 398–417.

Huser, A. C., Hałaj, G., Kok, C., Perales, C., & van der Kraaij, A. (2018). The systemic implications of bail-in: A multi-layered network approach. *Journal of Financial Stability*, 38, 81–97.

Hwang, S. (2017). *Does the CoCo bond effectively work as a bail-in tool?* (Working Paper).

Kashyap, A., Rajan, R., & Stein, J. (2008). *Rethinking capital regulation. Maintaining stability in a changing financial system* 43171.

Keeley, M. C. (1990). Deposit insurance, risk, and market power in banking. *The American Economic Review*, 80(5), 1183–1200.

Keister, T., & Mitkov, Y. (2017). *Bailouts, bail-ins and banking crises* (Working Paper).

Keister, T., & Narasiman, V. (2016). Expectations vs. fundamentals-driven bank runs: When should bailouts be permitted? *Review of Economic Dynamics*, 21, 89–104.

Kim, D., & Santomero, A. M. (1988). Risk in banking and capital regulation. *The Journal of Finance*, 43(5), 1219–1233.

Klimek, P., Poledna, S., Farmer, J. D., & Thurner, S. (2015). To bail-out or to bail-in? Answers from an agent-based model. *Journal of Economic Dynamics and Control*, 50, 144–154.

Koehn, M., & Santomero, A. M. (1980). Regulation of bank capital and portfolio risk. *The Journal of Finance*, 35(5), 1235–1244.

Kormendi, R. C., Bernard, V. L., Pirrong, S. C., & Snyder, S. A. (1989). Crisis resolution in the thrift industry: Beyond the December deals. In *Report of the Mid-America Institute Task Force on the Thrift Crisis*. University of Michigan.

Leanza, L., Sbuelz, A., & Tarelli, A. (2019). *Bail-in vs bail-out: Bank resolution and liability structure* (Working Paper).

Li, L. (2013). TARP funds distribution and bank loan supply. *Journal of Banking and Finance*, 37(12), 4777–4792.

Lupo-Pasini, F., & Buckley, R. P. (2015). International coordination in cross-border bank bail-ins: Problems and prospects. *European Business Organization Law Review*, 16(2), 203–226.

Merton, R. C., & Thakor, R. T. (2019). Customers and investors: a framework for understanding the evolution of financial institutions. *Journal of Financial Intermediation*, 39, 4–18.

Mitts, J. (2015). Systemic risk and managerial incentives in the Dodd-Frank Orderly Liquidation Authority. *Journal of Financial Regulation*, 1(1), 51–94.

Nosal, J. B., & Ordoñez, G. (2016). Uncertainty as commitment. *Journal of Monetary Economics*, 80, 124–140.

Pandolfi, L. (2018). *Bail-in vs. Bailout: A false dilemma?* (Working Paper).

Persaud, A. (2014). *Why bail-in securities are fool's gold* (Working Paper).

Philippon, T., & Schnabl, P. (2013). Efficient recapitalization. *The Journal of Finance*, 68(1), 1–42.

Roman, R. A. (2020). Winners and losers from supervisory enforcement actions against banks. *Journal of Corporate Finance, 62.*

Telser, L. G. (1966). Cutthroat competition and the long purse. *The Journal of Law and Economics, 9,* 259–277.

Walther, A., & White, L. (2017). *Bail-ins and bailouts in bank resolution* (Working Paper).

Zenios, S. A. (2016). Fairness and reflexivity in the Cyprus bail-in. *Empirica, 43,* 579–606.

Zombirt, J. (2015). Contingent convertible bonds as an alternative to strengthen banks' ability in financing a real economy. *Entrepreneurial Business and Economics Review, 3,* 135–149.

Empirical research on TARP

Introduction to Part II

Part II discusses empirical research on Troubled Asset Relief Program (TARP) and includes 11 chapters. The material here covers research results and excludes institutional details of TARP, which are provided earlier in Chapter 3. The research reviewed here covers only the main component of the TARP program—the CPP (Capital Purchase Program) capital injections into bank holding companies (BHCs) and banks—and we continue to use the term "TARP" to mean only these. This part of the book may be studied as a stand-alone primer on TARP research by readers that are less interested in other bailouts and bail-ins.

The tree of knowledge for Part II shows leaves with the fruits of all the references for the 11 chapters in this part of the book. The leaves proceed in a counter-clockwise fashion until we reach the top of the tree with the two chapters on the effects of TARP on the ultimate goals of the program—boosting the real economy and reducing the risks of the financial system. Each leaf shows the topic of the corresponding chapter with the references for that chapter, which bear the fruits of knowledge about the topic.

As a guide to Part II, Chapter 5 details the main methodologies used in the empirical TARP literature. It summarizes the difference-in-difference (DID) procedure, which is used in most of the studies, and also covers instrumental variables (IV), propensity score matching (PSM), Heckman sample selection correction, and placebo approaches used in some of the empirical studies of the various aspects of TARP. Chapter 6 reviews the research on the determinants of applying for and receiving TARP funds and exiting early from the program. Chapter 7 summarizes findings on the effects of the program on the recipient banks' valuations. Chapter 8 gives the research on the effects of TARP on market discipline. Chapter 9 covers the findings on banks' leverage risk. Chapter 10 goes over the results on the effects of TARP on bank competition. Chapters 11 and 12 discuss the closely related effects of TARP on banks' credit supply and portfolio risks, respectively. Chapter 13 covers the effects of the program on recipient banks' credit customers, including changes in their market values, investments, and other spending effects. Finally, Chapters 14 and 15 summarize the papers on the extent to which TARP accomplished its two main goals of improving the real economy and reducing systemic risk, respectively. Each chapter contains a short conclusions-and-caveats section at the end that summarizes the implications of the research reviewed in the chapter.

Importantly, the topics of the chapters are not entirely independent of one another. The direct effects of TARP in one area have indirect effects on other areas. For example, to the extent that TARP increased bank credit supply, bank portfolio risks and systemic risk may have also increased, loan customers may have been made better off, and the real economy might have been stimulated. In what follows, we focus on each direct research result once and simply acknowledge the indirect effects later. Thus, when we cover the changes in bank credit supply in Chapter 11, we do not discuss the indirect impacts of these changes on bank portfolio risks, loan customers, the real economy, and systemic risk. We mention these indirect effects later in Chapters 12, 13, 14, and 15, respectively. Notably, some of the indirect effects in later chapters also go in the other direction from the direct effects studied in earlier chapters. For example, to the extent that TARP may have reduced systemic risk, bank credit supply quantities may have increased as financially healthier banks were in better positions to lend. Again, we simply acknowledge these indirect effects in the later chapters.

Part II: Empirical research on TARP

5. Methodologies

Bayaziteva and Shivdasani, 2012; Beck, Levine, and Levkov, 2010; Berger and Roman, 2015; Berger, Roman and Sedunov, 2020; Duchin and Sosyura, 2012, 2014; Heckman, 1979; Li, 2013; Wooldridge, 2002.

6. Determinants

Bayaziteva and Shivdasani, 2012; Berger, 2018; Berger and Roman, 2015, 2017; Berger, Makaew, and Roman, 2019; Berger, Roman, and Sedunov, 2020; Blau, Brough, and Thomas, 2013; Cadman, Carter, and Lynch, 2012; Calomiris and Khan, 2015; Chavaz and Rose, 2019; Cornett, Li, and Tehranian, 2013; Duchin and Sosyura, 2012, 2014; Jordan, Rice, Sanchez, and Wort, 2009; Li, 2013; Liu, Kolari, Tippens, and Fraser, 2013; Ng, Vasvari, and Wittenberg-Moerman, 2016; Paletta and Enrich, 2009; Pana and Wilson, 2012; Roman, 2019; Taliaferro, 2009; Wilson and Wu, 2012.

7. Banks' valuations

Bayaziteva and Shivdasani, 2012; Carow and Salotti, 2014; Croce, Hertig, and Nowak, 2016; Duffie, Saita, and Wang, 2007; Farruggio, Michalak, and Uhde, 2013; Kim and Stock, 2012; King, 2009; Liu, Kolari, Tippens, and Fraser, 2013; Ng, Vasvari, and Wittenberg-Moerman, 2016; Veronesi and Zingales, 2010; Zanzalari, 2016.

8. Market discipline

Bank for International Settlements, 2006; Berger, 1991; Berger, El Ghoul, Guedhami, and Roman, 2020; Berger, Lamers, Roman, and Schoors, 2019; Duchin and Sosyura, 2014; Flannery, 1998; Flannery and Bliss, 2019 Flannery and Nikolova, 2004; Flannery and Sorescu, 1996; Forssbæck and Nielsen, 2015; Gropp, Vesala, and Vulpes, 2006; Marsh and Roman, 2018.

9. Leverage risk

Acharya, Pedersen, Philippon, and Richardson, 2017; Berger, Roman, and Sedunov, 2020; Calabrese, Degl'Innocenti, and Osmetti, 2017; Duchin and Sosyura, 2014; Li, 2013.

10. Bank competition

Beck, Levine, and Levkov, 2010; Berger and Roman, 2015; Calderon and Schaeck, 2012; Carow, Alvira and Nuñez-Torres, 2019; Congressional Oversight Panel, 2011; French, Baily, Campbell, Cochrane, Diamond, Duffie, Kashyap, Mishkin, Rajan, Scharfstein, Shiller, Shin, Slaughter, Stein, and Stulz, 2010; Gropp, Hakenes, and Schnabel, 2011; Hakenes and Schnabel, 2010; Koetter and North, 2016; Lerner, 1933.

11. Credit supply

Bain, 1959; Bassett, Demiralp, and Lloyd, 2017; Berger and Black, 2019; Berger and Bouwman, 2016; Berger, Black, Bouwman, and Dlugosz, 2017; Berger, Cerqueiro, and Penas, 2015; Berger, Makaew, and Roman, 2019; Berger and Roman, 2017; Berger, Saunders, Scalise, and Udell, 1998; Berrospide and Edge, 2010; Black and Hazelwood, 2013; Boot and Thakor, 2000; Cao-Alvira and Nuñez-Torres, 2019; Carbo-Valverde, Rodriguez-Fernandez, and Udell, 2009; Carpenter, Demiralp, and Eisenschmidt, 2014; Cetorelli and Strahan, 2006; Chang, Contessi and Francis, 2014; Chavaz and Rose, 2019; Chu, Zhang and Zhao, 2019; Contessi and Francis, 2011; Cornett, McNutt, Strahan, and Tehranian, 2011; Cortés, Demyanyk, Li, Loutskina, Strahan, 2020; Degryse, Morales-Acevedo, and Ongena, 2019; Duchin and Sosyura, 2014; Ivashina and Scharfstein, 2010; Jang, 2017; Koetter and Noth, 2016; Li, 2013; Liu, Liu, and Srinivasan, 2017; Montgomery and Takahashi, 2014; Peterson and Rajan, 1995; Puddu and Waelchli, 2015; Sheng, 2017; Taliaferro, 2009; Wu, 2015; Zheng, 2017.

12. Portfolio risk

Acharya and Ryan, 2016; Agarwal and Zhang, 2018; Berger, Imbierowicz, and Rauch, 2016; Berger, Makaew, and Roman, 2019; Berger and Roman, 2017; Black and Hazelwood, 2013; Bunkanwanicha, Di Giuli, and Salvadè, 2019; Cao-Alvira and Nuñez-Torres, 2019; Chavaz and Rose, 2019; Cole and White, 2012; Cordella and Yeyati, 1998; Duchin and Sosyura, 2014; Jungherr, 2018; Kim, Kim, and Lee, 2019.

13. Banks' credit customers

Berger, Molyneux, and Wilson, 2020; Lin, Liu, and Srinivasan, 2017; Norden, Roosenboom, and Wang, 2013; Norden, Udell, and Wang, 2020; Sheng, 2017; Song and Uzmanoglu, 2016.

14. Real economy

Berger and Roman, 2017; Contreras, Delis, Ghosh, and Hasan, 2019; Contreras, Ghosh, and Kong, 2019.

15. Systemic risk

Acharya, Engle, and Richardson, 2012; Acharya, Pedersen, Philippon, and Richardson, 2017; Adrian and Brunnermeier, 2016; Berger and Roman, 2017; Berger, Roman, and Sedunov, 2020; Brownlees and Engle, 2017; Choi, 2014; Coffey, Hrung, and Sarkar, 2009; Del Viva, Kasanen, Saunders, and Trigeorgis, 2017; Duchin and Sosyura, 2014; Farruggio, Michalak, and Uhde, 2013; Huerta, Perez-Liston, and Jackson, 2011; Nguyen and Enomoto, 2009; Semian and Drake, 2016.

5

Methodologies used in most of the TARP empirical studies

This chapter covers the empirical methodologies used in most of the TARP empirical research. As indicated above, TARP studies generally use difference-in-difference (DID) methods as the main specification, which we cover in Section 5.1 below. To test the robustness of the DID results and account for endogeneity and/or sample selection concerns, researchers also use other robustness techniques and tests. The most important ones are instrumental variables (IV) described in Section 5.2, propensity score matching (PSM) described in Section 5.3, Heckman sample selection models covered in Section 5.4, and/or placebo tests discussed in Section 5.5. Additional methods and robustness checks are not covered in detail here in the interest of brevity. Section 5.6 provides some brief conclusions and caveats.

5.1 The difference-in-difference (DID) methodology

The DID methodology is often used in the banking literature and elsewhere to compare a treatment group to a control group before and after treatment. For the TARP research, the treatment group usually consists of banks that received TARP funds, and the control group consists of other banks that did not receive the funds.[1] In some of the research, the treatment is at the state level—the proportion of banks in the state that received TARP bailouts. In some cases, treatment is at the individual loan level, comparing the terms of credit on loans from TARP banks with those from non-TARP banks before and after the TARP treatment. For expositional purposes, we begin with the DID model at the bank level, which typically takes the form:

$$Y_{it} = \beta_0 + \beta_1 \cdot TARP\ RECIPIENT_i + \beta_2 \cdot POST\ TARP_t \\ \times TARP\ RECIPIENT_i + \beta_3 \cdot X_{it-1} + \beta_4 \cdot TIME_t + \varepsilon_{it}. \tag{5.1}$$

where i indexes the banks, t indicates the year-quarter in time, and Y_{it} is the outcome variable under consideration—such as a measure of competitive advantage, lending amount, systemic risk contribution, real economic indicator, etc.

$TARP\ RECIPIENT_i$ is usually a dummy variable equal to one if the bank was provided with TARP capital support. It is included in the regression uninteracted to control for any constant or long-term differences in Y_{it} between TARP and non-TARP banks that are unrelated to the receipt of the TARP funds. In some robustness checks, the $TARP\ RECIPIENT_i$ dummy is replaced by a continuous measure of the amount of funds injected. In some of the papers' main specifications and/or robustness checks, Eq. (5.1) above is modified to include bank fixed effects. In these cases, the $TARP\ RECIPIENT_i$ dummy is omitted, as it would be perfectly collinear with the bank fixed effects, but the interaction term remains intact.

$POST\ TARP_t$ is a dummy equal to one in the period after the TARP program initiation and equal to 0 in the pre-TARP period. In most cases, the TARP period is specified as starting in 2009:Q1. Most of the studies end the post-TARP period in 2012:Q4. The datasets usually start in 2005: Q1 or 2005:Q2, so there are approximately equal numbers of observations before and after TARP initiation. Some studies try using 2008:Q4 as an

---

[1] Most TARP studies use the full universe of private and public US banks and compare TARP banks with non-TARP banks. Some studies focus on publicly listed banks and bank holding companies (BHCs) only, and compare publicly listed TARP recipients with institutions for which the TARP application was not approved (e.g., Duchin and Sosyura, 2012, 2014; Berger, Roman, and Sedunov, 2020). They exclude from the analysis any entities that did not apply for TARP as it is not known whether they did not apply because it was discouraged or did not need assistance. This approach helps account for the selection of TARP banks, but can only be accomplished for the publicly listed institutions. The authors of these studies determine the status of each application for all TARP-eligible public banks and BHCs from 2008:Q4 to 2009:Q4 by reading quarterly filings, annual reports, and proxy statements of all TARP-eligible public banks and BHCs from 2008:Q4 to 2009:Q4.

alternative starting date for TARP, which is when the very first banks received the TARP capital injections. Some of the early studies also use an earlier ending date for the post-TARP period because of data availability, and the results are generally materially unchanged. $POST\ TARP_t$ does not appear in uninteracted form on the right-hand side of Eq. (5.1) because it is subsumed by the time fixed effects ($TIME_t$) described below.

$POST\ TARP_t \times TARP\ RECIPIENT_i$ is the DID term and captures the effect of the treatment (TARP capital injections) on the treated (TARP recipients) compared to the untreated (non-TARP banks) after treatment. This is the key exogenous variable under consideration, and most of the hypotheses tested are about its coefficient, β_2.

A few of the TARP studies also examine the dynamic effects of TARP in a similar fashion to Beck, Levine, and Levkov (2010). In these studies, the DID term $POST\ TARP_t \times TARP\ RECIPIENT_i$ is replaced by a series of dummy variables, such as $POST\ TARP\ 2009_t \times TARP\ RECIPIENT_i$, $POST\ TARP\ 2010_t \times TARP\ RECIPIENT_i$, etc., so that the effects can be measured separately for each year over the post-TARP period. In some cases, the results are measured for quarters, as opposed to years. In some studies, the dynamics of the pre-TARP periods are also estimated to help rule out that the effects of the program started beforehand.

The X_{it-1} is a vector of control variables to take into account other factors affecting the outcome variable Y_{it} and mitigate potential omitted variable problems that could bias the coefficient estimates. While these controls differ somewhat across studies, we briefly describe the controls used in one fairly representative study, Berger and Roman (2015). Justifications for these individual variables may be found in that paper. These authors control for proxies for CAMELS, the declared set of financial criteria used by regulators for evaluating banks, as indicators of a bank's financial health. The CAMELS proxies include capital adequacy measured by equity capital divided by gross total assets (GTA),[2] asset quality using the fraction of nonperforming loans to total loans, management quality based on a dummy for whether the bank received a corrective action by its regulator in quarter t-1, earnings proxied by return on assets (ROA), liquidity measured by the ratio of cash to deposits, and sensitivity to market risk using the ratio of the absolute difference (gap) between short-term assets and short-term liabilities to GTA. Other bank characteristics controls include bank size measured by thenatural logarithm of GTA, bank age given by the age in years of the commercial bank or the oldest bank owned by the BHC (when there are multiple banks

---

[2] GTA equals total assets plus the allowance for loan and lease losses and the allocated transfer risk reserve (a reserve for certain foreign loans). Total assets on Call Reports deduct these two reserves, which are held to cover potential credit losses. These reserves are added back to measure the full value of the assets financed.

owned by a BHC), a dummy for whether a bank received discount window loans and/or Term Auction Facility (TAF) funding during the crisis, a dummy for whether the bank acquired another institution, a dummy for whether the entity is a BHC, an indicator for whether the bank or its BHC is publicly listed, a metropolitan dummy for whether the majority of the bank's deposits are in metropolitan markets (Metropolitan Statistical Areas (MSAs) or New England County Metropolitan Areas (NECMAs)), the weighted average across the bank's local deposit markets of the Herfindahl—Hirschman Index (HHI) of deposit market concentration data from the Federal Deposit Insurance Corporation (FDIC) Summary of Deposits, and the ratio of the number of branches over GTA multiplied by 1000.

$TIME_t$ is a series of time fixed effects for all the year-quarters but one to take into account the many policy and economic changes that took place over time and affected all banks. ε_{it} represents an error term.

A second DID regression model used in some of the TARP studies allows for the possibility that banks that repaid TARP funds early may behave differently from other TARP recipients. This model typically takes the form:

$$
\begin{aligned}
Y_{it} = {} & \delta_0 + \delta_1 \cdot TARP\ RECIPIENT\ NOT\ REPAID_i \\
& + \delta_2 \cdot TARP\ RECIPIENT\ REPAID_i \\
& + \delta_3 \cdot POST\ TARP_t \times TARP\ RECIPIENT\ NOT\ REPAID_i \quad (5.2) \\
& + \delta_4 \cdot POST\ TARP_t \times TARP\ RECIPIENT\ REPAID_i \\
& + \delta_5 \cdot X_{it-1} + \delta_6 \cdot TIME_t + \eta_{it}.
\end{aligned}
$$

All variables in Eq. (5.2) are the same as in Eq. (5.1), except that $TARP\ RECIPIENT\ NOT\ REPAID_i$, which equals one if the bank did not repay in 2009—10 and $TARP\ RECIPIENT\ REPAID_i$, which equals one if the bank repaid early in 2009—10, replace $TARP\ RECIPIENT_i$, and η_{it} replaces ε_{it} as the error term. $POST\ TARP_t \times TARP\ RECIPIENT\ NOT\ REPAID_i$ and $POST\ TARP_t \times TARP\ RECIPIENT\ REPAID_i$ are the DID terms and capture the effects of the TARP treatment on the TARP recipients that did not and did repay early, respectively. δ_3 and δ_4 can be compared and tested for equality to each other to see if the effects on TARP on the two groups differ.

5.2 The instrumental variables (IV) methodology

The instrumental variables (IV) methodology is often used in conjunction with the DID methodology in Eqs. (5.1) and (5.2) because the $TARP\ RECIPIENT_i$, $TARP\ RECIPIENT\ NOT\ REPAID_i$, and $TARP\ RECIP$-$IENT\ REPAID_i$ variables are not assigned randomly and may be endogenous. TARP funds might have been more often provided to the strongest and largest banks because of the US Treasury's TARP selection criterion of "healthy, viable institutions" and the initial TARP funds disbursement to the largest banks discussed above. This may yield spurious relations between *TARP RECIPIENT$_i$* and the dependent variables Y_{it} in these equations because stronger banks and/or larger banks may have been more likely to gain a competitive advantage, lend more, etc. *TARP RECIPIENT NOT REPAID$_i$*, and *TARP RECIPIENT REPAID$_i$* may similarly have endogeneity problems because the banks had to be in relatively good financial health to repay the funds early, and this good health may also be correlated with the Y_{it} outcomes.

We briefly describe three instruments used in the literature multiple times for *TARP RECIPIENT$_i$*. These are:

(1) *SUBCOMMITTEES ON FINANCIAL INSTITUTIONS OR CAPITAL MARKETS$_i$*, a dummy that takes a value of one if a firm is headquartered in a district of a House member who served on the Financial Institutions Subcommittee or the Capital Markets Subcommittee of the House Committee on Financial Services in 2008 or 2009;

(2) *DEMOCRAT$_i$*, a dummy that takes a value of one if the local representative from the bank's headquarters location was a Democrat in the 2007–08 campaign election cycle; and

(3) *FED DIRECTOR$_i$*, a dummy that takes a value of one if one of the bank's directors was on the board of directors of one of the 12 Federal Reserve Banks (FRBs) or a branch in 2008 or 2009.

Without going into excessive detail, the subcommittees in (1) played a direct role in the development of Emergency Economic Stabilization Act (EESA), prepared voting recommendations for Congress on authorizing and expanding TARP, arranged meetings between banks and the US Treasury, and wrote letters to regulators and EESA provisions to help individual firms (Duchin and Sosyura, 2012). The Democrats in (2) were generally more in favor of government bailouts of private firms, and the directors in (3) may have had more influence over Federal Reserve-regulated banks (state-chartered member banks and all bank holding companies), and this influence may have resulted in a more favorable application evaluation process. Detailed arguments for these instruments may be found in the papers that employed them (e.g., Bayazitova and Shivdasani, 2012; Li, 2013; Duchin and Sosyura, 2014; Berger and Roman, 2015). While these arguments suggest that the proposed instruments should be positively related to TARP decisions, these political and regulatory instruments are unlikely to be directly related to banks' behavior after TARP implementation, satisfying the exclusion restriction.

We next discuss briefly two instruments used for *TARP RECIPIENT NOT REPAID$_i$* and *TARP RECIPIENT REPAID$_i$*. These are:

(1) *CEO COMPENSATION$_i$*, a dummy that takes a value of one if a bank's CEO had total compensation greater than $500,000 in 2008; and

(2) *COINCIDENT INDEX$_i$*, which combines four state-level indicators (nonfarm payroll employment, average hours worked in manufacturing, the unemployment rate, and wage and salary disbursements deflated by the Consumer Price Index) to summarize economic conditions in a single statistic for the state, and then allocates this to the banks based on their deposit presence in the states.

Briefly, banks with *CEO COMPENSATION$_i$* equals; 1 may be more likely to exit TARP early due to TARP's restrictions on executive pay, and banks in states with higher *COINCIDENT INDEX$_i$* may be more likely to repay TARP early because they can raise capital more easily through retained earnings.

The IV procedures used to estimate Eqs. (5.1) and (5.2) take into account that the potentially endogenous explanatory variables *TARP RECIPIENT$_i$*, *TARP RECIPIENT NOT REPAID$_i$*, and *TARP RECIPIENT REPAID$_i$* are binary dummies. The studies employ the dummy endogenous variable model as suggested in Wooldridge (2002, sec. 18.4.1). The first stage for Eq. (5.1) uses a probit model in which the *TARP RECIPIENT$_i$* dummy is regressed on whichever of the political and regulatory instruments *SUBCOMMITTEES ON FINANCIAL INSTITUTIONS OR CAPITAL MARKETS$_i$*, *DEMOCRAT$_i$*, and/or *FED DIRECTOR$_i$* is used in the particular study and all control variables from the main regression model in the study. The predicted probability obtained from the first stage is employed as an instrument for the final stage. Similarly, for Eq. (5.2), first-stage probit regressions for *TARP RECIPIENT NOT REPAID$_i$* and *TARP RECIPIENT REPAID$_i$* are run on the political and regulatory instruments plus whichever of the two extra instruments for early program exit decisions, *CEO COMPENSATION$_i$*, and/or *COINCIDENT INDEX$_i$* are employed in the study as well as the relevant control variables, and the predicted probabilities obtained are again used as instruments for the final stage.

5.3 The propensity score matching (PSM) methodology

As discussed above regarding the IV methodology, the selection of TARP banks may be systemically related to other variables that are related to the dependent variables in Eqs. (5.1) and (5.2). Another way to address the potential concern of selection bias that is used in many studies is propensity score matching (PSM) analysis. PSM narrows the set of non-TARP banks in the regression sample to those with similar likelihoods to obtain TARP funding as the TARP banks. The purpose is to help dispel the competing explanation that the results of estimating Eqs. (5.1) and (5.2) spuriously reflect differences in the characteristics of recipients and nonrecipients, rather than the effects of TARP on the dependent variables.

Using a probit regression, the propensity scores of all banks are estimated based on some or all of the characteristics of the banks in the pre-treatment period specified in the control variables of the main regressions. A propensity score is the probability of a bank receiving TARP funds, based on the bank's pre-treatment characteristics. Each TARP bank is assigned to its corresponding non-TARP bank matches based on the absolute differences in propensity scores. Banks with the smallest differences are considered matches and are included in the analyses. Researchers use matching techniques without and with replacement. Thus, in the matching without replacement, each treated TARP bank is matched with the nearest untreated non-TARP control bank(s). In contrast, in the matching with replacement, each treated bank is matched to the nearest control bank(s), even if the latter is used more than once. In most cases, each TARP bank is matched with one, two, or three other nearest neighbors.

5.4 Heckman's (1979) sample selection methodology

To address potential sample selection bias, some researchers also use Heckman's (1979) two-step procedure in conjunction with the DID main methodology. This approach controls for selection bias introduced by bank and government choices about TARP by incorporating TARP decisions into the econometric estimation. In the first step, they use the same or similar probit model from the IV estimation. In the second stage, the outcome variable is the dependent variable, and the self-selection parameter (inverse Mills ratio) estimated from the first stage is included. The coefficients on the DID variables indicate if the main results are robust and the statistical significance or insignificance of the coefficient on the inverse Mills ratio suggests whether sample selection bias is or is not a major issue.

5.5 The placebo test methodology

It is also possible that alternative confounding forces that affect TARP and non-TARP banks differently drive the results. Some researchers, therefore, also conduct placebo experiments in conjunction with the DID framework. In one type of experiment, researchers fictionally assume that TARP participation took place earlier, while still distinguishing between banks that received and did not receive TARP funds according to the "true" TARP program. For example, Berger, Roman, and Sedunov (2020) use an eight-year period immediately preceding TARP from 2000 to 2007 and assume that the fictional post-TARP period begins 5 years before the actual program. Thus, they rerun the regressions using the placebo sample (2000–07) and define placebo post-TARP as a dummy equal to one in 2004–07, the period after the fictional TARP initiation. If their main results reflect the true program and are not driven by alternative forces, researchers should not find significant results in the same direction for the DID terms in the placebo experiment.

In another type of placebo experiment, researchers allocate the TARP treatment randomly to banks and then reestimate the regressions with bootstrapped confidence intervals (e.g., Berger and Roman, 2015). Again, if the main results are representative of the effects of TARP rather than the impacts of other factors, there should not be significant results in the same direction in the placebo experiment.

5.6 Conclusions and caveats regarding methodology

As mentioned in Part I above, there are significant challenges in finding a convincing empirical strategy to identify the effects of bailouts. This is because we cannot observe the counterfactual of how the economy and financial system would have functioned without the bailouts. Thus, the best that researchers can generally do is to use the DID methodology to measure the effects of these bailouts by comparing the TARP banks, locations, or loans relative to those that were not bailed out.

A positive aspect of the researchis that TARP bailouts may be considered reasonable quasi-natural experiments, given that the prior circumstances reflected uncertainty whether the legislation would be passed, and the form in which the bailout was implemented was as a surprise to many. Therefore, results are most likely due to the TARP program itself, rather than other earlier events or anticipation of bailouts, although endogeneity and sample selection concerns may remain and are dealt with using the other methods.

The negative aspect, which we emphasize many times in the book, is that TARP and other bailouts and bail-ins also may affect other banks, locations, and loans, so that DID methodology which focuses on differences does not necessarily capture the total effects. For example, as discussed in Chapter 11 below on credit supply, DID calculates the change in difference in the supplies of TARP and non-TARP banks, rather than the sum of the credit changes by TARP and non-TARP banks. Non-TARP banks may have either decreased their credit due to stigma from not receiving funds or other factors. Alternatively, these other banks may have benefited from the rescue of the real economy and/or financial system provided by TARP and increased their credit.

In the remainder of Part II as well as the rest of the book, we endeavor to navigate through the difficulties and draw the best conclusions possible, emphasizing the relevant caveats.

References

Bayazitova, D., & Shivdasani, A. (2012). Assessing TARP. *The Review of Financial Studies, 25*(2), 377–407.

Beck, T., Levine, R., & Levkov, A. (2010). Big bad banks? The winners and losers from bank deregulation in the United States. *The Journal of Finance, 65*(5), 1637–1667.

Berger, A. N., & Roman, R. A. (2015). Did TARP banks get competitive advantages? *Journal of Financial and Quantitative Analysis, 50*(6), 1199–1236.

Berger, A. N., Roman, R. A., & Sedunov, J. (2020). Did TARP reduce or increase systemic risk? The effects of government aid on financial system stability. *Journal of Financial Intermediation.* forthcoming.

Duchin, R., & Sosyura, D. (2012). The politics of government investment. *Journal of Financial Economics, 106*(1), 24–48.

Duchin, R., & Sosyura, D. (2014). Safer ratios, riskier portfolios: Banks' response to government aid. *Journal of Financial Economics, 113*(1), 1–28.

Heckman, J. J. (1979). Sample selection bias as a specification error. *Econometrica, 47*(1), 153–161.

Li, L. (2013). TARP funds distribution and bank loan supply. *Journal of Banking and Finance, 37*(12), 4777–4792.

Wooldridge, J. M. (2002). *Econometric analysis of cross section and panel data.* MIT Press.

6

Determinants of applying for and receiving TARP funds and exiting early from the program

6.1 Determinants of applying for and receiving TARP funds

A number of papers investigate factors that affected the decisions of banks to apply for TARP funds and/or the US Treasury's decisions to approve these banks. The stated selection criteria in the press for TARP approval was that the program targeted "healthy, viable institutions," where such health was evaluated by the US Treasury upon consultation with the primary banking regulators to ensure that the institution was satisfactory from a safety and soundness standpoint. Specifically, the evaluation was based on the banks' CAMELS examination ratings and other financial performance ratios. Institutions deemed as the strongest in their health and viability by their primary regulators had their applications submitted to the US Treasury for final approval.

The US Government Accountability Office (2010) evaluation of the approval process for TARP applications finds that most of the institutions analyzed had satisfactory or better health. The evaluation also reveals that ¼ of the examination ratings used for approval were more than a year old, 5% were more than 16 months old, and about 18% of the 567 revised applications by them did not have a date for the most recent regulatory examination.

187

However, of the institutions evaluated, 66 or 12% of the institutions had financial weaknesses, including unsatisfactory examination ratings, unsatisfactory financial ratios, and/or formal enforcement actions around safety and soundness issues. Thus, it was widely speculated that discretionary factors other than bank health and merit, particularly regulatory and political influence, may have also helped some banks obtain TARP funds.

Some examples are illuminating. Duchin and Sosyura (2012) mention financial press reported cases in which politicians went as far as modifying the legislation to save firms in their home states in response to petitions by firms that were not strong enough financially to qualify for TARP capital (Paletta and Enrich, 2009). For example, in late September 2008, the OneUnited Bank from Boston had capital problems and received a cease-and-desist order from the FDIC for deficient lending practices and compensation abuse. Despite these, in December 2008, the bank received $12,063,000 capital from the TARP program. Over 2009–10, the bank missed its dividend payments to the US Treasury. The local representative was Barney Frank, the head of the Financial Services Committee, who acknowledges that he had included in an early version of the Emergency Economic Stabilization Act (ESSA) authorizing the TARP a provision aimed at helping this particular bank, although this was not in the final bill.[1] He also recommended to regulators that the bank be considered for capital under TARP. The bank's lawyer acknowledged having discussed the bank's financial situation over the phone not only with Frank but also with representative Maxine Waters (a member of the Financial Services Committee and Financial Institutions Subcommittee), who subsequently helped set up meetings between the US Treasury and the bank's management. Waters' husband was a OneUnited director in 2004–07 and held over $500,000 in OneUnited stock at the time of TARP. In 2010, the House Ethics Committee initiated an investigation of representative Waters' influence in the allocation of capital to OneUnited under TARP, and later that year recommended

---

[1] OneUnited owned a large amount of Fannie Mae preferred shares that suffered large losses after the government took over Fannie Mae. The language in the TARP bill (passed only weeks after that meeting) set out three criteria suitable for OneUnited's condition. The "Secretary [of the Treasury] shall take into consideration … providing financial assistance to financial institutions," the bill reads, that (1) have assets under $1 billion, (2) were at least adequately capitalized under regulatory guidelines as of June 30, 2008, and (3) owned preferred shares in Fannie Mae or Freddie Mac and were significantly hurt by the takeover. The bill stated that institutions "serving low- and moderate-income populations and other underserved communities" should be given consideration. More details at: https://www.propublica.org/article/bank-that-rep.-frank-helped-in-healthy-bank-bailout-now-struggling-730;   https://thehill.com/homenews/house/119099-bank-at-center-of-waters-controversy-got-12m-bailout

three charges against her for violating House ethics rules. The charges were cleared later in 2012.[2]

Audits of TARP capital investments in 2008–09 disclose documented outside inquiries on applications from 56 undisclosed banks.[3] The assumed attempts of external influence on regulators were so significant that on January 27, 2009, the US Treasury imposed a formal restriction on contacts with lobbyists regarding TARP applications to "limit lobbyist influence in federal investment decisions."[4]

A number of research papers investigate the possibilities of political and regulatory connections in TARP application and approval decisions. Duchin and Sosyura (2012) use hand-collected data on TARP applications for the capital of the public banks to study empirically which institutions participated in the program and whether political determinants may have played an important role in the decision to apply as well as the approval of the applications. A key part of their analysis is measuring political connections between banks and politicians and/or regulators. They measure political and regulatory influence in four different ways. First, they consider a bank to be connected if it employed a director in 2008–09 with simultaneous or former work experience at either a banking regulator or the US Treasury. A bank with some regulatory connection may have been treated more favorably in the application evaluation process. Second, they consider a bank's connection to members of the House Financial Services Committee and its two subcommittees—the Subcommittee on Financial institutions and the Subcommittee on Capital Markets—both of which played direct key roles in the development of the EESA in 2008, its modifications in 2009, and were charged with preparing voting recommendations for Congress on authorizing and expanding TARP. In a later paper, Duchin and Sosyura (2014) discuss how members of these subcommittees were shown to arrange meetings between banks and the Treasury, write letters to regulators, and write provisions into

---

[2] See WSJ, January 22, 2009, "Political Interference Seen in Bank Bailout Decisions," available at: https://www.wsj.com/articles/SB123258284337504295. Another example is in the ProPublica, June 30, 2009, "After Call From Senator Inouye's Office, Small Hawaii Bank Got U.S. Aid," available at: https://www.propublica.org/article/senator-inouye-small-hawaii-bank-aid-630 and Business Insider, July 1, 2009, "Hawaii Bank Got TARP Cash After Senator's Phone Call," available at: https://www.businessinsider.com/hawaii-bank-got-tarp-cash-after-senators-phone-call-2009-7

[3] See Quarterly Report to Congress of the TARP Special Inspector General, October 21, 2009, available at: https://www.sigtarp.gov/reports/congress/2009/October2009_Quarterly_Report_to_Congress.pdf

[4] See US Department of Treasury, 2009. Treasury secretary opens term with new rules to bolster transparency, limit lobbyist influence in federal investment decisions. Press release, January 27, available at: https://www.treasury.gov/press-center/press-releases/Pages/tg02.aspx

EESA to help particular firms. In their paper, a particular bank is considered to be connected to a Congress representative if it is headquartered in his or her district, given that banks may be able to ask their elected local representatives for help if they wanted government aid. The third Duchin and Sosyura (2012) measure is the bank's size-adjusted dollar amount of expenditures on lobbying Congress and banking regulators on the issues of banking, finance, or bankruptcy in 2008–09. Finally, they use the bank's size-adjusted dollar amount of campaign contributions to the House Financial Services Committee in the 2008 election cycle. These variables proxy for various mechanisms of a bank's influence on government officials involved in developing and implementing TARP. The authors also construct an index of political connections which incorporates all four of the proxies.

Duchin and Sosyura (2012) find several important results. First, they find that an overwhelming 80.2% of public banks submitted TARP applications. They argue this is consistent with the wide awareness of the TARP program and low cost of applying —applying was a simple procedure and banks were allowed to refuse the funds upon approval. The remaining 19.8% that did not apply for TARP in their sample were the best capitalized institutions, and thus had less need for additional capital.

The authors also look at the determinants of application approvals by the regulators. They find a strong positive association between bank regulatory and political connections and the likelihood that a TARP applicant is approved for funds, controlling for other bank fundamentals such as proxies of CAMELS ratings. The strong positive association is applicable for both connections to legislators—congressional committees charged with developing TARP—and connections to regulators and US Treasury in charge of the program implementation. They look at the importance of the various forms of political influence. Banks with directors connected to regulators were 9.1 percentage points more likely to be approved for TARP funds, controlling for other factors. Banks headquartered in the election districts of House members that were part of important finance committees were 6.3 percentage points more likely to be approved.[5] They also find that a one standard deviation increase in size-adjusted dollar lobbying expenditures leads to an increase of 7.6 percentage points in the likelihood of being approved. The figure for campaign contributions is 5.0% points. Using the aggregate index of political connections, the authors find that a one standard deviation

[5] Pana and Wilson (2012) also confirm results for credit unions. They find that the probability of receiving bailout funds jumps from 29% to 81% for the average credit union, if the institution's headquarters was in the district of a member of the US House Financial Services Committee.

increase in the bank index of political connections is associated with a 7.1 percentage points increase in the likelihood of approval for government investment.

Blau, Brough, and Thomas (2013) also find that politically connected banks were not only more likely to receive TARP funds, but they also received a greater amount of TARP support and received the support earlier than firms that were not politically involved. Overall, these results are consistent with more favorable application treatment for banks with political and regulatory ties.

Duchin and Sosyura (2012) also investigate the extent to which the allocation of TARP funds based on political and regulatory connections may have led to inefficient government investment. They distinguish between two opposing views of political influence: (1) political connections may reduce efficiency of the government investment by benefiting connected banks at the expense of the taxpayers; (2) political connections may improve the efficiency of government investment by resolving information asymmetry between banks and outside investors in the investment process. Using several measures of *ex post* performance of government investment—bank ROA, Tobin's Q, raw returns, market-adjusted returns, and industry-adjusted returns—the authors show evidence that politically connected banks underperform unconnected banks, consistent with the first view, and thus evidence of distortions in investment efficiency.

A number of other research papers also find political connections are important determinants for receiving TARP capital and use them as instrumental variables for the likelihood of obtaining TARP funds in their analyses (e.g., Li, 2013; Duchin and Sosyura, 2014; Berger and Roman, 2016, 2017; Berger, Makaew, and Roman, 2019; Chavaz and Rose, 2019; Berger, Roman, and Sedunov, 2020). All of these papers confirm that having a local representative on the Subcommittees for Financial Institutions and Capital Markets significantly increased the chance of getting TARP funds, and some of the studies (e.g., Li, 2013; Berger and Roman, 2015; Chavaz and Rose, 2019) also confirm that having a director with current or former experience at one the 12 Federal Reserve Banks (FRBs) or their 24 associated branches also significantly increased the likelihood of getting funds. For example, Li (2013) uses the full universe of private and public commercial banks and shows that political and regulatory connections played a significant role in the allocation of TARP funds. Among the various instruments employed, he shows that a bank had a 14.45% higher probability of receiving TARP funds if its local representative sat on the House subcommittee that oversaw federal banking regulators. If a local representative received a greater portion of their campaign contributions in the 2007–08 election cycle from local FIRE (finance, insurance, and real estate) industries, banks in their district would be 1.20% more likely to get TARP funds as well. Finally, a bank had a 27.05% significantly higher chance of receiving TARP funds if its executive was a director of one of the FRBs or one of the branches of the FRBs. Two papers (Berger and Roman, 2015; Ng, Vasvari, and Wittenberg-Moerman, 2016) also find some significant results for the political ideology of the local representative because Republicans were generally regarded as being more opposed to bank bailouts. For example, Berger and Roman (2016) find that having a bank local representative that is a Democrat in the 2007−08 campaign cycle increased the likelihood of getting TARP funds by 3.9%.

Another paper that analyzes which banks applied for and received TARP capital injections is Bayazitova and Shivdasani (2012). These authors find evidence of self-selection in the program participation, but consistent with Duchin and Sosyura (2012), they find that strong banks rather than weak ones opted out of participating in TARP. Thus, banks that did not participate had better capital ratios, more stable funding profiles, higher asset quality, and operated in local markets with better economic conditions. With regard to TARP application approvals, Bayazitova and Shivdasani (2012) find that capital injections seemed to have been motivated by the desire to lower financial distress costs. Approved banks were larger, posed greater risks on the financial system, but also had stronger asset quality than unapproved banks. Banks that were approved but later declined the funds had higher asset quality and operated in better local economic markets than those that accepted the funds, providing some evidence that perhaps better performing banks may have regarded the TARP capital injections as being too costly for them. To further support this point, Bayazitova and Shivdasani (2012) show that limits on CEO compensation (restrictions for compensation over $500,000) and the associated CEO personal costs from these government restrictions were particularly regarded as costly. Banks with CEO compensation in excess of $500,000 were 8% less likely to be approved and also were 11% more likely to reject funds after approval of the application. The rationale was that compensation restrictions may have given an advantage to non-TARP banks that could hire better executives with unrestricted compensation packages. The last finding is also confirmed by Cadman, Carter, and Lynch (2012), who find that increasing CEO compensation from the 25th to the 75th percentile of banks is associated with a doubling of the bank's averseness to accept TARP capital.

Jordan, Rice, Sanchez, and Wort (2009) find that banks that took funds under the TARP program had lower market-to-book ratios than banks that refrained from taking such funds. These authors find that both receipt of TARP funds and higher ratios of nonaccrual assets plus other real estate owned to total assets are associated with these lower market-to-book ratios for banks as of March 31, 2009.

Taliaferro (2009) also looks at characteristics of TARP participating banks and finds that banks that had high leverage and high expected costs of regulatory downgrades due, for example, to a high fraction of brokered deposits, tended to participate in the program. Banks that were likely to increase lending, either because of prior commitments or because of promising investment opportunities, and banks that soon faced a deteriorating balance sheet due to exposure to real estate loans were also more likely to receive TARP funds. However, he finds that exposure to past-due loans, also indicative of a deteriorating balance sheet, is negatively related to TARP participation, consistent with Treasury imposing a viability screen on this dimension.

Cadman, Carter, and Lynch (2012) also find greater subsequent executive turnover and lower pay increases in banks accepting funds, consistent with concerns about the potential TARP acceptance talent drain. Additionally, they find that proxies for self-serving behavior are related to declining funds, suggesting pay preservation as a potential motive. Despite the motives behind declining funding, it is not found that restrictions limited the objectives of the program based on banks' financial health or lending or may have allowed the government to allocate funds more effectively.

Cornett, Li, and Tehranian (2013) investigate how the pre-crisis health of banks is related to the probability of receiving TARP funds. They find that financial characteristics related to the probability of receiving TARP differ for relatively healthy ("overachiever") versus relatively unhealthy ("underachiever") banks. Consistent with TARP's goal of helping temporarily unhealthy banks get through a period of financial distress, they find that TARP "underachievers" had weaknesses in income production and experienced liquidity issues. In contrast, TARP "overachievers" performed well, seeing increases in their returns on loans, but had liquidity issues (from low levels of liquid assets and core deposits and drawdowns of loan commitments) which hurt the abilities of these banks to continue lending.[6]

6.2 Determinants of exiting TARP early

Exiting TARP early is a joint decision of the banks and the Treasury in consultation with the regulatory agencies. Banks wishing to return the

---

[6] In a similar line, Liu, Kolari, Tippens, and Fraser (2013) use a dynamic model of financial recovery of banks receiving TARP and compare recovering and nonrecovering banks. They find that recovering banks over time had stronger overall financial condition than nonrecovering banks, as evidenced by higher capital, loan quality, profits, dividends, liquidity (i.e., more short-term, more interest-sensitive assets than liabilities), and asset size.

TARP money to the Treasury early could apply to their primary regulators for permission. They had to demonstrate they were in a state of safety and soundness and sometimes had to raise private capital before being allowed to repay the funds and exit the program early. Industry groups, like the American Bankers Association, lobbied aggressively to allow banks to repay the funds quickly, saying it would send a positive signal to depositors and investors that the nation's banks were sound.[7]

Turning to the research on this issue, Bayazitova and Shivdasani (2012) analyze determinants for public banks repaying the TARP funds and exiting the program by November 30, 2009. The authors find that banks that repaid TARP capital early were larger, financially healthier with stronger capital ratios, and had better asset quality than banks that decided to remain in the program. Another important finding is that CEO compensation in excess of $500,000 in years prior to the program was a key determinant for these early exits, as it increased by 15%–17% the likelihood that the banks repay early. This is consistent with the idea that program CEO compensation restrictions have constituted significant concerns for these banks, motivating them to exit early. Bayazitova and Shivdasani (2012) also find weak evidence that banks in states with more economic growth as measured by the Federal Reserve Bank of Philadelphia's coincident index may also exit TARP earlier as they can raise cheaper financing in the local markets.

Results about high CEO compensation and local economic conditions are confirmed in Berger and Roman (2015), who use the broader universe of commercial banks in the United States. These authors also use an indicator for banks with excess compensation beyond $500,000 as an instrument for early TARP repayment until 2010:Q4, and find a strong positive effect.

Wilson and Wu (2012) look at the characteristics of the banks that fully or partially repaid the US Treasury's investments in TARP programs (CPP and TIP) before the end of 2009. Consistent with Bayzitova and Shivdasani (2012) and Berger and Roman (2015), Wilson and Wu (2012) find strong evidence that high levels of CEO pay in 2008 were associated with banks being significantly more likely to exit TARP. In addition, they find that larger publicly traded banks with better accounting performance as measured by ROA, better capital ratios, and stronger asset quality also exited early. Banks that raised private capital in 2009 were also significantly more likely to return the capital early. The original eight involuntary TARP recipients had weak tangible common equity ratios at the end of 2008 relative to other TARP recipients and raised common equity capital in 2009, and all at least partially exited the program early in 2009.

---

[7] https://www.cnbc.com/id/29991226/

Cadman, Carter, and Lynch (2012) additionally find that among banks accepting TARP funds, the likelihood of repaying before the end of 2009 is positively related to CEO incentive compensation. Finally, Cornett, Li, and Tehranian (2013) find that banks that repaid early are more likely to be large banks and have performance improvements during the time they held TARP funds. Overachiever banks, particularly large banks, which are more likely to repay TARP funds and to repay faster, are those that see larger improvements in loan portfolio quality and expense reduction. Underachiever banks that tend to repay also see improvements in loan portfolio quality and increases in deposit growth.

6.3 Conclusions and caveats from the TARP application, receipt, and exit research

The research reviewed here suggests that TARP decisions were made by both the banks and the US Treasury in consultation with the bank regulators, with a considerable amount of influence of political and regulatory connections over the latter's choices. The banks that voluntarily chose TARP funds appeared to be in many cases the ones that needed the capital injections, rather than those that were well capitalized. The banks that chose to exit early were those that no longer needed the funds and/or were constrained by the executive pay restrictions.

To some extent, the evidence suggests that the Treasury stuck to its mandate of improving the stability of the financial system by bailing out "healthy, viable institutions." However, there is also plenty of evidence that political and regulatory connections may have also played important roles in allocating these resources. These latter findings have numerous adverse consequences, including a likely economic misallocation of funds, increased incentives to spend real resources to influence government decisions, and potential loss of public confidence in the fairness of the government and the financial system. These findings are consistent with conclusions drawn by other surveys of TARP research (e.g., Calomiris and Khan, 2015; Berger, 2018; Roman, 2019).

A key caveat to this chapter is that most of the TARP application, receipt, and exit decisions were made in private, so the evidence presented here is largely circumstantial. For example, some of the research measures political connections using whether the bank is headquartered in a district of a House member who served on the Financial Institutions Subcommittee or the Capital Markets Subcommittee of the House Financial Services Committee. This is a circumstance that may have created the opportunity for the use of political connections to obtain TARP funds, but it is not ironclad proof that such connections were used.

References

Bayazitova, D., & Shivdasani, A. (2012). Assessing TARP. *The Review of Financial Studies, 25*(2), 377–407.

Berger, A. N. (2018). The benefits and costs of the TARP bailouts: A critical assessment. *Quarterly Journal of Finance, 8*(02), 1–29.

Berger, A. N., Makaew, T., & Roman, R. A. (2019). Do business borrowers benefit from bank bailouts?: The effects of TARP on loan contract terms. *Financial Management, 48*(2), 575–639.

Berger, A. N., & Roman, R. A. (2015). Did TARP banks get competitive advantages? *Journal of Financial and Quantitative Analysis, 50*(6), 1199–1236.

Berger, A. N., & Roman, R. A. (2017). Did saving Wall street really save Main Street?: The real effects of TARP on local economic conditions. *Journal of Financial and Quantitative Analysis, 52*(5), 1827–1867.

Berger, A. N., Roman, R. A., & Sedunov, J. (2020). Did TARP reduce or increase systemic risk? The effects of government aid on financial system stability. *Journal of Financial Intermediation.* forthcoming.

Blau, B. M., Brough, T. J., & Thomas, D. W. (2013). Corporate lobbying, political connections, and the bailout of banks. *Journal of Banking and Finance, 37*(8), 3007–3017.

Cadman, B., Carter, M. E., & Lynch, L. J. (2012). Executive compensation restrictions: Do they restrict firms' willingness to participate in TARP? *Journal of Business Finance and Accounting, 39*(7–8), 997–1027.

Calomiris, C. W., & Khan, U. (2015). An assessment of TARP assistance to financial institutions. *The Journal of Economic Perspectives, 29*(2), 53–80.

Chavaz, M., & Rose, A. K. (2019). Political borders and bank lending in post-crisis America. *Review of Finance, 23*(5), 935–959.

Cornett, M. M., Li, L., & Tehranian, H. (2013). The performance of banks around the receipt and repayment of TARP funds: Over-achievers versus under-achievers. *Journal of Banking and Finance, 37*(3), 730–746.

Duchin, R., & Sosyura, D. (2012). The politics of government investment. *Journal of Financial Economics, 106*(1), 24–48.

Duchin, R., & Sosyura, D. (2014). Safer ratios, riskier portfolios: Banks' response to government aid. *Journal of Financial Economics, 113*(1), 1–28.

Jordan, D. J., Rice, D., Sanchez, J., & Wort, D. H. (2009). *Taking TARP funds can be hazardous to your bank's wealth* (Working Paper).

Li, L. (2013). TARP funds distribution and bank loan supply. *Journal of Banking and Finance, 37*(12), 4777–4792.

Liu, W., Kolari, J. W., Tippens, T. K., & Fraser, D. R. (2013). Did capital infusions enhance bank recovery from the great recession? *Journal of Banking and Finance, 37*(12), 5048–5061.

Ng, J., Vasvari, F. P., & Wittenberg-Moerman, R. (2016). Media coverage and the stock market valuation of tarp participating banks. *European Accounting Review, 25*(2), 347–371.

Paletta, D., & Enrich, D. (2009). Political interference seen in bank bailout decisions. *Wall Street Journal January, 22.*

Pana, E., & Wilson, L. (2012). Political influence and TARP investments in credit unions. *The Quarterly Journal of Finance, 2*(04), 1250017.

Roman, R. A. (2019). Bank bailouts and bail-ins. *In Oxford Handbook of banking* (3rd Edition), 2019, 630–684

Taliaferro, R. (2009). How do banks use bailout money? Optimal capital structure, new equity, and the TARP (Working Paper).

Wilson, L., & Wu, Y. W. (2012). Escaping TARP. *Journal of Financial Stability, 8*(1), 32–42.

Effects of TARP on recipient banks' valuations

This chapter reviews the research about the effects of TARP on publicly listed recipient banks' market valuations. This research primarily employs event study methodology around key TARP event dates, and occasionally complements it with regression analyses of longer term stock returns. The vast majority of the studies focus on effects for common stock returns only, but a few studies also look at preferred stock, given that TARP injected mostly preferred equity into the banks, and/or overall bank wealth effects.

The effects of TARP on bank valuations around different TARP events—program announcement, individual injections of TARP capital, announcements of nonparticipation or rejection of approved funds, repayments of funds—may be the result of at least three sets of factors. First, one important set consists of the benefits and costs for the individual participant banks from the 13 primary bailout channels outlined in Chapter 4 Table 4.1. Seven of the channels—safety, charter value/ quiet life, cost advantage, capital cushion, TBTF (Size), TITF (Interconnectedness), and TMTF (Herding)—would predict increases in bank market valuations. Another three channels—stigma, cost disadvantage, capital priority—would predict decreases in bank market valuations, and three channels—predation, increased moral hazard, and decreased moral hazard—have ambiguous effects on market valuations. The second set consists of the benefits and costs for the banks not participating in TARP due to other banks possibly getting comparative advantages and gaining market shares and market power at their expense, as discussed later in Chapter 10. Finally, another third set consists of the benefits and costs for all banks from making the whole financial system safer or riskier as a result of the TARP bailouts. It is not always easy, but we try to distinguish where possible among these three sets of factors in this chapter.

Importantly, the expectations of benefits and costs from TARP and the importance of the three sets of factors outlined may vary with different TARP events, different groups of banks—voluntary participants, involuntary participants, and non-TARP banks—and different categories of stock—common stock and types of preferred stock. As examples of different TARP events, the program announcement, actual TARP capital injections, and repayments may have disparate effects. TARP repayments may result in shedding some of the cost advantages or disadvantages of the program participation by leaving it and/or may lead to perceived higher safety from demonstrating the ability to repay.

We cover stock market effects around the TARP program announcement dates in Section 7.1, effects around the TARP individual capital injections in Section 7.2, effects around decisions to not apply for TARP and rejections of previously approved funds in Section 7.3, and effects around TARP funds repayments in Section 7.4. Some studies distinguish between voluntary and involuntary participants, and we mention these different results where they exist. Section 7.5 provides concluding remarks.

7.1 Effects of TARP on banks' valuations of common stock, preferred stock, and overall bank valuation at TARP announcement dates

A number of papers look at traded TARP banks' valuations around the program announcement date of October 14, 2008, and with one exception, they find positive stock returns associated with this announcement.

Bayazitova and Shivdasani (2012) investigate raw and excess common stock returns for initial and later participants associated with the TARP program announcement on October 14, 2008, when the US Treasury announced it would buy preferred equity in the largest institutions.[1] They find strongly positive and significant average 2-day $(-1, 0)$ excess returns of 14.9% for the initial large, involuntary recipients, consistent with net benefits in the first set of factors outlined in the introduction of this chapter. The authors also report significantly positive excess returns for the later voluntary TARP recipients on the same date, despite the fact that it was unknown at that time whether these institutions would receive

[1] Official press release on the TARP announcement from US Treasury is at: https://www. treasury.gov/press-center/press-releases/Pages/hp1207.aspx. The release mentioned that: "Nine large financial institutions already have agreed to participate in this program, moving quickly and collectively to signal the importance of the program for the system. These healthy institutions have voluntarily agreed to participate on the same terms that will be available to small and medium-sized banks and thrifts across the nation."

TARP capital. This is consistent with the third set of factors and the explanation is that the TARP program improved equity valuations of all banks by lowering financial system risk.

Kim and Stock (2012) examine the impact of the TARP announcement on the market valuation of existing preferred stock for involuntary and voluntary TARP banks. They focus on two different types of outstanding preferred stock: (1) trust preferred stock, senior to the TARP preferred stock; and (2) nontrust preferred stock, with equal claims to the TARP preferred stock. For both involuntary and voluntary bank groups, they find that trust preferred stock increased in value more from TARP than did the nontrust preferred stock at the October 14 TARP program announcement date for different reasons. For the involuntary TARP banks, the authors argue this is due to TARP issuance providing an additional asset base for trust preferred stock (the capital priority theory), more than offsetting any potential greater reduction in default risk for the nontrust preferred (the default theory). For the voluntary banks, the positive trust preferred stock effects may be due to market expectations that some banks would apply for and receive TARP upon the October 14 announcement. The authors conclude that TARP may have transferred wealth from taxpayers to preferred shareholders, and that taxpayers seemed to especially subsidize preferred stockholders of selected weaker banks. In additional analyses, consistent with Bayazitova and Shivdasani (2012), Kim and Stock (2012) find that the common stock of both involuntary and voluntary banks was also significantly and positively affected by TARP October 14 program announcement. This is again consistent with the third set of factors, suggesting that TARP resulted in benefits for banks generally, causing the majority of US bank stock prices to rise.

Farruggio, Michalak, and Uhde (2013) also investigate bank common stock wealth effects around the TARP program announcement. They find that both the first announcement of TARP on September 19, 2008 and the announcement of the revised TARP on October 14, 2008 yielded significantly positive estimated abnormal returns of 8.55% and 3.95% respectively on the announcement day. Similar positive reactions are observed for an event window period of 4 days (-2; $+2$) around the announcement day, showing significant positive cumulated abnormal returns of 10.81% and 16.92%, respectively, consistent with the first and third sets of factors that aid the TARP banks.[2]

Zanzalari (2014) examines whether investors react differently to key TARP events depending on the bank size. The author finds that in the

---

[2] Results are also consistent with findings provided by King (2009) for the US market suggesting that TARP may be perceived by capital market investors as an effective instrument to provide single banks with necessary liquidity and prevent further financial market distortions.

5 days surrounding the TARP announcement, there is a positive market reaction for almost all banks, both participants and nonparticipants in the program. Overall, banks participating in the TARP program experience a 6.01% abnormal return compared to a 1.82% abnormal return for banks that did not participate in TARP. The magnitude of the investor reactions differs depending on bank size. Investors in the involuntary participants received an abnormal return of 10.67% in the 5-days surrounding the announcement compared to 10.17% return for other large banks, 5.60% abnormal return for midsize banks, and 1.59% abnormal return for small banks that would later receive TARP capital. Importantly, consistent with findings in Bayazitova and Shivdasani (2012) and Kim and Stock (2012), the author finds that non-TARP banks also saw positive abnormal returns. For example, large nonparticipating banks saw a 7.61% abnormal return, while midsize banks saw a 4.87% abnormal return, the exception being small nonparticipating banks which saw a small negative return. Investors in banks that did not enter into TARP and had positive stock returns at the October 14, 2008 announcement date may have seen the TARP announcement as a positive signal. This may be due to expectations that their banks will eventually enter TARP and derive benefits from the participation and/or because they believed that the overall banking industry would benefit from a safer financial system.

Veronesi and Zingales (2010) estimate the value of common stock and preferred stock in the 10 largest banks around the announcement of the TARP revised plan—a period from Friday, October 10th to Tuesday, October 14th. Adjusting the individual bank stock movement for the market movement by using actual market betas, they find that during the announcement period considered, banks' common shareholders did not benefit from the plan, suffering $2.8 billion losses. However, there is a wide variation across firms. While JP Morgan shareholders lost $34 billion, Morgan Stanley's gained $11 billion, and Citigroup's and Goldman's shareholders gained roughly $8 billion each. The authors also perform a similar event study analysis for the preferred equity and find that, in contrast, the preferred stock increased in price by 36%, well above the market return of 11%, while overall the preferred stock increased in value at the announcement of the plan by $6.7 billion. This indicates that preferred rather than common equity holders benefited most from the TARP announcement.

In addition, Veronesi and Zingales (2010) also compute the overall value increase due to the TARP plan announcement as the sum of the values of the three most variable components on the right-hand side of the balance sheet. They find that the market value of debt increased by $119 billion, the aggregate derivative liabilities increased by 5.5 billion, the market value of preferred equity increased by $6.7 billion, while the market value of common equity dropped by $2.8 billion. Thus, they estimate that the total value of financial claims in the top 10 banks increased by $128 billion as a result of the plan. Adjusting for the expected cost to taxpayers for TARP, they show that, systemic effects aside, TARP increased the value of the banks' financial claims by $132 billion at a taxpayers' cost of between $15 and $47 billion, thus providing a net financial benefit of between $84 billion and $107 billion, not including all the other effects on the financial system and the real economy. The net benefit is the mixture of two factors: (1) the government intervention reducing the enterprise value by 2.5%, possibly due to the inefficient restrictions imposed by the government; and (2) the bailout infusion increasing the perceived banks' safety by reducing the probability of bankruptcy, which could have otherwise caused a decline of 22% of the banks' enterprise value.

Also related to the potential value conferred by the TARP bailouts, Croci, Hertig, and Nowak (2016) find evidence that TARP managed to stave off further bank failures while avoiding funding nonviable banks. However, they also argue that more lenient standards for TARP assistance to voluntary participants could have prevented a significant number of additional banks from failing, reducing resolution costs for the FDIC.

7.2 Effects of TARP on recipient banks' valuations at TARP capital injections

Some researchers look at traded TARP banks' common stock wealth effects around the time of the individual capital injections. In contrast with valuation effects around TARP announcements, which in most cases yielded positive returns, common stock returns around individual injections are mostly either insignificantly or significantly negative. As noted above, the factors reflecting expectations of benefits and costs and affecting the valuation of bank stocks can change over time and with different events. Thus, individual capital injections effects may more often reflect costs rather than advantages from participation in the program.

Bayazitova and Shivdasani (2012) find that excess returns around the exact announcement dates of capital injections for the voluntary recipients are statistically insignificant. They argue that these announcement returns do not support either a positive certification or safety effect or an adverse signaling or stigma effect to discourage bank participation. Furthermore, using regression methodology which controls for other factors, the authors find that bank abnormal returns became positively correlated with the bank capital ratios following TARP infusions. This is consistent with the market having rewarded banks with more capital.

Farruggio, Michalak, and Uhde (2013) find significantly negative abnormal returns of −1.03% on the exact injection days, while cumulative abnormal returns for the main event window period of (2, +2) around injection event dates are significantly negative at −2.26%. These authors argue that these negative reactions are driven by investors' skepticism toward government capital assistance that may not necessarily help mitigate TARP banks' default risks.

Zanzalari (2014) examines whether investors react to the TARP capital infusions differently depending on the bank size. Overall, the author finds that all banks experience a negative cumulative abnormal return at injection times. Banks that received TARP capital had a significant cumulative abnormal return of approximately −2.45% compared to a −1.98% return for nonparticipating banks. More interestingly, when decomposing the overall effect into groups of banks, the involuntary banks had a negative cumulative abnormal return of −7.10%, while the other large TARP banks had a cumulative abnormal return of −7.62% compared to only −3.38% for small TARP banks. Large banks that did not receive TARP capital only saw a −4.27% abnormal return. Investors in banks that received TARP capital may have reacted negatively to the capital infusions due to one or more of the negative channels from the first set of factors outlined above or because the government preferred shares are ranked above common stock in bankruptcy.

Ng, Vasvari, and Wittenberg-Moerman (2016) use articles published in the Wall Street Journal to capture the extent of negative media coverage about the TARP program and its participant banks. They investigate whether this media sentiment affected the common stock valuation of the publicly traded BHCs over the period October 2008 to December 2009, when the capital injections took place. They find that over this time period, about 40% of the published articles had a negative tone about TARP. They also document that the negative media sentiment substantially decreased the stock returns over November 2008 to January 2010 for both TARP and non-TARP banks, but that it had a substantially stronger effect (48% larger negative effect) on the valuation of TARP banks. A one standard deviation increase in *media sentiment* resulted in TARP banks' monthly stock returns being lower by 1.59 percentage points relative to the non-TARP banks' returns. Thus, the adverse effect of media sentiment on the common stock performance of TARP banks was 48% stronger than the stock performance of the non-TARP banks, suggesting that media sentiment exerted downward pressure on the returns of TARP banks, adversely affecting their valuation.

The results on TARP media sentiment-induced negative stock returns may be explained by TARP banks facing significant valuation uncertainty, increasing difficulty of valuing them due to several competing costs from the first set of factors described above. Besides the overall downward pressure on stock prices for TARP banks, Ng, Vasvari, and Wittenberg-Moerman (2016) also show that the effect of the media coverage on the TARP banks' stock returns was significantly stronger for the larger banks, but that it did not vary with the banks' loan portfolio quality.

One study by Carow and Salotti (2014) finds that TARP capital injection announcements helped weaker banks, but not healthy banks. Consistent with TARP certifying weak banks as viable and TARP funds potentially being "low-cost" for them, their abnormal stock returns increased significantly by about 1.82% surrounding the announcement that these banks were accepted. In contrast, healthy banks experienced negative, but insignificant abnormal returns around their acceptance announcement.

Kim and Stock (2012) find evidence that the preferred stock of voluntary participants registered positive returns for the subsequent announcements of TARP preferred issuance. This suggests that the market may have perceived the issuance of TARP preferred as favorable information for the preferred stockholders due to one or more of the channels discussed above, although the government interference in bank ownership concerned many investors. Similar to Bayazitova and Shivdasani (2012) above, Kim and Stock (2012) also find that common stock returns on individual injections were not significantly affected.

Liu, Kolari, Tippens, and Fraser (2013) focus on a broader event window than other studies for assessing the effects of TARP capital injections. They find that, similar to the banks that did not repay their funds early, both voluntary and involuntary TARP banks that repaid early by end of 2010 as a group—labeled by the authors as "recovering" banks—registered significantly negative or insignificant returns in the quarter before receipt of TARP funds, as well as the quarter after receipt of TARP funds. However, the negative magnitudes are much larger for the non-repaying banks—a significant abnormal return of -6.27% relative to the insignificant -2.29% for "recovering" TARP banks. This is consistent with the idea that investors may have been able to identify weaker TARP banks to some extent before repayment.

7.3 Effects of TARP on recipient banks' valuations around announcements of non-participation in the program or rejecting approved TARP funds

One paper looks at traded banks' valuations around times of banks' announcing their non-participation in the program and/or declining preapproved TARP funds. Bayazitova and Shivdasani (2012) find that excess returns around announcements of banks' declining participation in TARP and those rejecting TARP funds after receiving initial approval are both statistically insignificant. Similar to the injection effects above and reflecting the first set of factors, these results do not support either a positive certification or safety effect or an adverse signaling or stigma effect to discourage bank participation.

7.4 Effects of TARP on recipient banks' valuations at TARP repayment

Finally, a number of researchers investigate traded TARP banks' wealth effects around banks' announcements of TARP funds repayments and unanimously document positive stock market reactions for common stockholders. Repayment of funds sheds some of the cost advantages or disadvantages of TARP as banks are exiting the program. Stock market effects around repayments may reflect both investors' reactions to healthy banks that demonstrate their ability to repay the funds as well as to the government's signaling of confidence in these banks by allowing them to repay. These effects may also reflect that any stigma and other disadvantages attached to the program, such as cost disadvantages or executive compensation restrictions, would be lifted.

Liu, Kolari, Tippens, and Fraser (2013) measure wealth effects over time from receipt of TARP funds to later payment using a combined sample of involuntary and voluntary participants. They find that participant banks' buy-and-hold returns were significantly positive at 1.7% in the period from the receipt to the repayment of funds, and buy-and-hold wealth gains were significantly and economically larger at 14.02%, equivalent to an increase of $329 billion in the quarter after TARP repayment. Results hold when the authors redo the analysis excluding the involuntary participants. They argue that this positive result in the post-repayment period reflects partially that banks are opaque because investors could only partially identify recovering banks before their repayments. Additional cross-sectional analyses reveal that documented positive returns after repayment were related to both removing compensation restrictions and recovering financial conditions, consistent with benefits in the first set of factors outlined.

Liu, Kolari, Tippens, and Fraser (2013) also find similar effects for banks that had not repaid their TARP funds by the end of 2010. One year after receiving funds, nonrepaying TARP banks continued to have negative and significant quarterly average abnormal returns of −3.69%, so that these banks did not experience wealth gains. They infer from these findings that investors were able to some extent to identify nonrecovering TARP banks. The authors develop a dynamic hazard recovery model in the fashion of Duffie, Saita, and Wang (2007) that exploits time-series movements in explanatory covariates and estimates the probabilities of TARP banks repaying the funds or quarterly "recovery intensities" relative to other TARP banks. Using these estimates, Liu, Kolari, Tippens, and Fraser (2013) also find a significantly positive relation between the estimated wealth gains of TARP banks and their average recovery intensities, suggesting that TARP may have fostered stock price recovery. In addition, they find that this relation is strongest for nonrepaying TARP banks, suggesting that investors may be forming expectations about these banks' potential recovery based on their financial condition.

Farruggio, Michalak, and Uhde (2013) find that bank stock abnormal returns are insignificantly positive at 0.04% on repayment days, while cumulative abnormal returns are significantly positive at 0.90% for the main event window period of (−2, +2) days around repayment. The slightly positive share price response to capital repayments suggests that capital market investors may perceive repayments by banks as general signals of financial recovery.

Zanzalari (2014) examines whether investors' reactions to TARP repayments depend on bank size. The author finds that overall reactions to TARP capital repayment were significantly positive for all participating banks. Investors reacted positively to the repayments of TARP capital, registering a 1.85% abnormal return for all TARP banks as a group. When decomposing into individual groups, the author finds a 1.75% abnormal return for the banks that were required to take TARP, a 0.73% abnormal return for other large banks that received TARP capital, and a 3.52% abnormal return for small banks that received TARP capital. Zanzalari (2014) argues that investors may have reacted positively to the capital repayments for the involuntary banks, as they were less likely to lose their management team due to compensation restrictions. Interestingly, the larger cumulative average abnormal returns during this event window are for small rather than large banks that paid back TARP capital. Investors in repaying banks may have seen TARP repayment as a positive signal that the banks are better capitalized. Furthermore, investors no longer had to come second to the government in bankruptcy proceedings, and the high dividend payments to the government and other restrictions would cease.

Bayazitova and Shivdasani (2012) investigate the first round of public announcements for banks repaying TARP funds (95 announcements, excluding banks whose stock did not trade on that day) and find that the excess returns average 0.5% over the (−1, 0) interval, but they are not statistically significant. However, when dividing the sample into announcements accompanied by equity issuance and those without such equity issuance news, they find very different results. Repayment announcements for banks uncontaminated with equity issuance news experience significantly positive excess returns, averaging 1.9%, while announcements for banks that contemporaneously disclose equity issuance have significant excess returns averaging −2.2%. The authors argue that these returns may underestimate the impact of repaying TARP due to substantial media and equity analysts' focus and speculation around the likelihood of repayment by the TARP banks. The positive market reaction around TARP repayment announcements for the former participants is consistent with shedding the increased costs of participation in TARP, while the approval to repay TARP may signal positive information about the repaying banks' financial health.

7.5 Conclusions and caveats from the TARP stock valuation research

The research summarized here suggests that TARP key events had some important valuation effects on the participant banks. In almost all cases, there are positive and significant common stock abnormal returns, and in all cases analyzed, positive and significant preferred stock abnormal returns around TARP program announcements for both TARP and non-TARP banks. This is consistent with the idea that TARP may have made the banking sector stronger by reducing the risk of financial collapse. This increased bank valuation may be regarded as a channel for reducing systemic risk, as discussed further in Chapter 15. However, common stock returns around individual capital injections are mostly either insignificantly or significantly negative, consistent with various concerns about program conditions or bank conditions. Thus, TARP may have helped the financial system more than the individual banks receiving the funds. The common stock returns around announcements of nonparticipation or decline of approved funds are insignificant, suggesting neither a positive certification effect nor an adverse signaling effect to discourage bank participation. Finally, bank capital repayments register unanimously positive common stock returns, consistent with repaying banks being viewed as better capitalized and signaling stronger health, as well as possibly reflecting good news from the removal of some of the investor concerns from compensation and other restrictions associated with the TARP program.

However, it is important to highlight some limitations related to event studies, the dominant methodology used in the studies in this chapter. In particular, the valuation changes around TARP events may also be partially driven by other confounding bank characteristics or macro conditions that are not specifically related to the TARP program, but may be correlated with TARP and that cannot be controlled for in the event studies. Only a few papers complemented the event studies with regression analyses that control for bank and market characteristics at the time of TARP key events; thus, some results may be interpreted with caution.

References

Bayazitova, D., & Shivdasani, A. (2012). Assessing TARP. *The Review of Financial Studies, 25*(2), 377–407.

Carow, K. A., & Salotti, V. (2014). The US Treasury's Capital Purchase Program: Treasury's selectivity and market returns across weak and healthy banks. *Journal of Financial Research, 37*(2), 211–241.

Croci, E., Hertig, G., & Nowak, E. (2016). Decision-making during the credit crisis, did the treasury let commercial banks fail? *Journal of Empirical Finance, 38*, 476–497.

Duffie, D., Saita, L., & Wang, K. (2007). Multi-period corporate default prediction with stochastic covariates. *Journal of Financial Economics, 83*, 635–665.

Farruggio, C., Michalak, T. C., & Uhde, A. (2013). The light and dark side of TARP. *Journal of Banking and Finance, 37*(7), 2586–2604.

Kim, D. H., & Stock, D. (2012). Impact of the TARP financing choice on existing preferred stock. *Journal of Corporate Finance, 18*(5), 1121–1142.

King, M. R. (2009). *The cost of equity for global banks: A CAPM perspective from 1990 to 2009.* September: *BIS Quarterly Review.*

Liu, W., Kolari, J. W., Tippens, T. K., & Fraser, D. R. (2013). Did capital infusions enhance bank recovery from the great recession? *Journal of Banking and Finance, 37*(12), 5048–5061.

Ng, J., Vasvari, F. P., & Wittenberg-Moerman, R. (2016). Media coverage and the stock market valuation of TARP participating banks. *European Accounting Review, 25*(2), 347–371.

Veronesi, P., & Zingales, L. (2010). Paulson's gift. *Journal of Financial Economics, 97*(3), 339–368.

Zanzalari, D. (2014). Does bank size matter? Investor reactions to TARP (Working Paper).

Effects of TARP on market discipline

Market discipline in banking is roughly defined as the extent to which private-sector agents both absorb costs that are increasing in the risks that banks undertake and act based on these costs. The actions may be in the form of explicit prices charged, such as higher interest rates required to provide funds to riskier banks or lower fees paid for financial guarantees or derivatives provided by these banks. The actions may alternatively be withdrawn business opportunities, such as refusals to buy securities issued by riskier banks. The discipline may be by depositors, other debt holders, off-balance sheet customers, or shareholders (Berger, 1991). Market discipline is very important in banking to help offset moral hazard incentives created by deposit insurance and other elements of the government safety net for banks (e.g., Flannery, 1998; Flannery and Nikolova, 2004; Flannery and Bliss, 2019).[1]

As discussed in Chapter 4, TARP can be regarded as either a positive or negative signal to the market through several channels. The positive channels generally suggest that TARP banks may be safer, which can reduce stakeholders' incentives to monitor banks and price their securities and investments adequately (e.g., Flannery and Sorescu, 1996; Gropp, Vesala, and Vulpes, 2006). Alternatively, the negative channels may suggest more bank risk and result in enhanced market discipline, so the effects of TARP on market discipline are a key empirical issue.

The existing empirical literature covers market discipline by shareholders, subordinated debt holders, and depositors (both insured and

---

[1] Market discipline is one of the three pillars of the Basel Accords, together with minimum capital requirements and supervisory reviews. The market discipline pillar establishes minimum transparency criteria to help enable market participants to assess bank risk and help determine capital adequacy (Bank for International Settlements (2006), p. 226; Marsh and Roman, 2018).

uninsured), which we review in Sections 8.1, 8.2, and 8.3, respectively. Section 8.4 provides some brief conclusions and caveats from this research.

8.1 Market discipline by shareholders

Berger, El Ghoul, Guedhami, and Roman (2020) use the universe of publicly listed banks as identified in Duchin and Sosyura (2014) over 2006–10 and focus on the disciplining effects of bank equity holders on TARP banks. They find that investors discipline TARP banks by demanding higher prices for equity capital from the banks, consistent with more market discipline from the bailouts. Their findings appear to be driven by higher bank risk, heightened bailout restrictions such as executive compensation, and poor bank governance measured in different ways.

The studies on bank market valuation changes as a result of TARP discussed in Chapter 7 can also imply changes in market discipline. The findings in Chapter 7 that the announcement of the program was positive, the announcement of receipt of TARP funds was mostly insignificant or negative, and the announcement of early exit was positive suggest that additional safety of the system reduced market discipline generally. However, in some cases, market discipline increased on recipients due to some of the costs or conditions of the program or these banks.

8.2 Market discipline by subordinated debt holders

Forssbæck and Nielsen (2015) analyze disciplinary effects of TARP from subordinated debt holders using a sample of 123 BHCs over the period 2004–13. Predicted distress risk has a consistently positive and significant effect on subordinated debt spreads, suggesting the presence of market discipline. A higher bailout probability significantly reduces the risk-sensitivity of spreads for the full sample, indicating a moral hazard effect of recapitalizations. However, the effects disappear when the largest banks are dropped from the sample. Their results also indicate that the effects are transitory.

8.3 Market discipline by depositors

Finally, focusing on depositors, Berger, Lamers, Roman, and Schoors (2020) analyze whether depositors exert more or less market discipline on TARP banks. They look at changes in supply and demand for deposits by examining changes in deposit quantities and prices, and uncover some unexpected effects. They show that the amount of total deposits declines significantly, driven entirely by the insured depositors, suggesting either a decline in demand or supply or both. They further find a reduction in the demand for deposits as evidenced by the lower prices on deposits using deposit rate premiums computed from the Call Report and the actual deposit rate from RateWatch. These results are consistent with a reduction in TARP recipients' demand for deposits that dominates any supply reductions due to market discipline. Thus, TARP banks appear to have purposely reduced deposits, rather than experience withdrawals or runs from market discipline.

8.4 Conclusions and caveats from the market discipline research

The research evidence on TARP market discipline appears to be mixed and depends on the type of stakeholder and the time period analyzed. For the most part, it indicates that equity holders and subordinated debt holders, who are likely more sensitive to risk, exercise market discipline on TARP recipients in the post-TARP period and/or around certain key events. In contrast, depositors do not display significant discipline likely because they are mostly protected by deposit insurance and other government safety net provisions.

A key caveat here is that there are way too few research studies on the market discipline topic to draw any strong conclusions. We return to this issue in Chapter 29.

References

Bank for International Settlements. (2006). Basel II: International Convergence of Capital Measurement and Capital Standards: A Revised Framework— Comprehensive Version. Bank for International Settlements, June. Available at: https://www.bis.org/publ/bcbs128.pdf.

Berger, A. N. (1991). Market discipline in banking. In *Proceedings of a Conference on Bank Structure and Competition* (pp. 419–437). Chicago, Illinois: Federal Reserve Bank of Chicago.

Berger, A. N., El Ghoul, S., Guedhami, O., & Roman, R. A. (2020). *Risk or financial costs of strings attached: An evaluation of TARP and banks' cost of equity capital.* Working paper.

Berger, A. N., Lamers, M., Roman, R. A., & Schoors, K. (2020). *Unexpected effects of bank bailouts: Depositors need not apply and need not run.* Working paper.

Duchin, R., & Sosyura, D. (2014). Safer ratios, riskier portfolios: Banks' response to government aid. *Journal of Financial Economics, 113*(1), 1–28.

Flannery, M. (1998). Using market information in prudential bank supervision: A review of the us empirical evidence. *Journal of Money, Credit and Banking, 30,* 273–305.

Flannery, M. J., & Bliss, R. R. (2019). Market discipline in regulation, pre-and post-crisis. In *The Oxford Handbook of Banking.* Oxford: OUP.

Flannery, M. J., & Nikolova, S. (2004). *Market discipline of U.S. financial firms: Recent evidence and research issues, Chapter 9 in Market discipline across countries and industries.* Cambridge: The MIT Press.

Flannery, M. J., & Sorescu, S. M. (1996). Evidence of bank market discipline in subordinated debenture yields: 1983–1991. *The Journal of Finance, 51,* 1347–1377.

Forssbæck, J., & Nielsen, C. Y. (2015). *TARP and market discipline, Evidence on the moral hazard effects of bank recapitalizations.* Working Paper.

Gropp, R., Vesala, J., & Vulpes, G. (2006). Equity and bond market signals as leading indicators of bank fragility. *Journal of Money, Credit, and Banking, 38,* 399–428.

Marsh, W. B., & Roman, R. A. (2018). Bank financial restatements and market discipline. *Economic Review,* 25–53. Quarter II.

Effects of TARP on bank leverage risk

As indicated above in Chapter 1 and elsewhere, one of the two ultimate main goals of TARP was to reduce systemic risk. One of the ways to do this is to reduce the leverage risk of the individual TARP banks. This chapter investigates the extent to which this may have occurred.

The preferred equity injected by the US Treasury under the TARP is part of Tier 1 capital, a regulatory measure. Therefore, the program mechanically increased the regulatory ratios that include Tier 1 capital in the numerator, the Tier 1 risk-based capital ratio, the Tier 1 leverage ratio, and the Total (Tier 1 plus Tier 2) risk-based capital ratio. Thus, unless the banks reduced common equity or another component of Tier 1 capital or significantly increased the denominators of the regulatory ratios, the banks would be better capitalized on a regulatory basis. One research paper of which we are aware confirms that the Tier 1 risk-based capital ratio increased for TARP banks relative to non-TARP banks (Li, 2013).

However, the leverage ratios generally used in the bank research and systemic risk research literatures are derived from market-based or accounting-based measures of common equity, and do not include preferred equity. For the purposes of this chapter, we focus on the leverage risks based on common equity. Section 9.1 explains that the injections of preferred equity have no direct or mechanical effect on common equity. Nonetheless, common equity may be either increased or decreased by the TARP program. Thus, TARP banks may be made either safer or riskier based on common equity leverage ratios. Sections 9.2 and 9.3 summarize the small numbers of studies that measure the effects of TARP on market-based and accounting-based common equity leverage ratios, respectively. Importantly, part of the discussion in Section 9.2 refers back to the studies of the effects of TARP on bank stock prices reviewed in

Chapter 7, which also affect market-based leverage ratios. Section 9.4 gives conclusions and caveats from the findings.

9.1 Why TARP may either decrease or increase leverage risk based on common equity ratios

Table 4.1 in Chapter 4 shows a number of channels through which market leverage risk could be decreased or increased by bailouts like TARP, and many of these also apply to accounting-based leverage risk. Just to list two examples, the market values of existing common equity may be increased and market leverage risks decreased because of boosted confidence in the banks from the *safety channel*. In addition, the boosted confidence may make it easier for banks to raise more common equity, which would decrease both the market and accounting leverage ratios and risks. The *stigma channel* would have the opposite effects and decrease market and accounting common equity ratios and increase both types of leverage risks.

9.2 The effects of TARP on market-based leverage ratios

As discussed more thoroughly in Chapter 15, the systemic risk contribution of a bank depends in a crucial way on its market-based leverage. We focus on one particular market-based leverage ratio known as *LVG*, which is frequently used in the systemic risk literature (e.g., (Acharya, Pedersen, Philippon, and Richardson, 2017). Since market values of liabilities are very difficult to measure, researchers generally use book values of liabilities in the following approximation for bank i at time t:

$$LVG_{i,t} = \frac{\left(Book\ assets_{i,t} - Book\ equity_{i,t}\right) + Market\ equity_{i,t}}{Market\ equity_{i,t}}.$$

Thus, *LVG* is the book value of liabilities plus the market value of equity divided by the market value of equity (e.g.,Acharya, Pedersen, Philippon, and Richardson, 2017). To be clear, *LVG* can only be measured for publicly traded banking organizations, most of which are BHCs, since market values of equity are unavailable for most banks. We continue to refer to these organizations as banks for expositional convenience. As shown in Chapter 15, one of the most widely employed measures of a bank's contribution to systemic risk, Systemic Expected Shortfall (*SES*), is a linear combination of *LVG* and Marginal Expected Shortfall (*MES*), where *MES* measures how the bank's stock returns vary with market returns during periods of distress.

Berger, Roman, and Sedunov (2020) use the difference-in-difference (DID) methodology and find that TARP resulted in significantly decreased leverage risk as measured by *LVG* relative to non-TARP banks. To be clear, the decrease in *LVG* is relative, not absolute. Both TARP and non-TARP banks suffered increases in leverage risk, but the increase is significantly less for the TARP banks. Put another way, the DID results suggest that TARP significantly decreased leverage risk from what it otherwise would have been in the absence of the program. This decrease dominates the effects of changes in *MES*, and so is primarily responsible for making the systemic risk measure *SES* lower than it otherwise would have been, as shown in Chapter 15. The authors further find that this occurred primarily through changes in the price of existing common equity, rather than new common equity issues or dividend cutbacks to retain more common equity. Again, to be clear, the common equity prices of TARP banks did not rise, but rather fell less than those of otherwise comparable non-TARP banks.

It is likely that the DID method used in that study may understate the leverage risk reductions due to TARP because the DID measures only the reduction in *LVG* of TARP banks relative to non-TARP banks. It is quite possible that TARP may have also kept the *LVG* of non-TARP banks from rising as much as they would have otherwise as well. To the extent that TARP reduced systemic risk and kept the financial system from further collapse—discussed in more detail in Chapter 15—the equity prices of non-TARP banks may have also been higher due to TARP than they otherwise would have been. Thus, the *LVG* of non-TARP banks may have also decreased relative to what they otherwise would have been, so that the reported DID results may understate the risk reductions due to TARP.

9.3 The effects of TARP on accounting-based leverage ratios

Three studies—Duchin and Sosyura (2014), Calabrese, Degl'Innocenti, and Osmetti (2017), and Berger, Roman, and Sedunov (2020)—measure the effects of TARP on accounting-based common equity-to-assets ratio. These are standard accounting-based capital ratios used in the banking literature that are inverse measures of leverage. All three studies find that these standard capital ratios increased significantly for TARP banks, consistent with reductions in accounting-based leverage risk. Berger, Roman, and Sedunov (2020) also find that the entire increase is driven by increased internal equity from retained earnings, rather than raising external capital through new common equity issues.[1]

9.4 Conclusions and caveats regarding the effects of TARP on bank leverage risk

The research reviewed in this chapter suggests that TARP decreased both market and accounting leverage risk of TARP banks relative to non-TARP banks. However, two key caveats apply. First, there are very few studies on this topic, requiring more research as discussed in Chapter 29. Second, some of the event studies reviewed in Chapter 7 suggest initial stock price declines for TARP banks, while the Berger, Roman, and Sedunov (2020) results reported here suggest stock price increases over longer periods of time that lower *LVG* for TARP banks. The differing results may be due to the different time periods or other factors, also requiring more future research.

References

Acharya, V. V., Pedersen, L. H., Philippon, T., & Richardson, M. (2017). Measuring systemic risk. *The Review of Financial Studies, 30*(1), 2−47.

Berger, A. N., Roman, R. A., & Sedunov, J. (2020). Did TARP reduce or increase systemic risk? The effects of government aid on financial system stability. *Journal of Financial Intermediation.* forthcoming.

Calabrese, R., Degl'Innocenti, M., & Osmetti, S. A. (2017). The effectiveness of TARP-CPP on the US banking industry: A new copula-based approach. *European Journal of Operational Research, 256*(3), 1029−1037.

Duchin, R., & Sosyura, D. (2014). Safer ratios, riskier portfolios: Banks' response to government aid. *Journal of Financial Economics, 113*(1), 1−28.

Li, L. (2013). TARP funds distribution and bank loan supply. *Journal of Banking and Finance, 37*(12), 4777−4792.

---

[1] The issue of understatement of the effects for TARP banks due to changes in capital of non-TARP banks is less relevant for the accounting-based measure, since TARP likely only had small effects on the retained earnings of non-TARP banks.

10

Effects of TARP on bank competition

As discussed above in Chapter 1 and elsewhere, TARP was primarily intended to reduce systemic risk and improve the real economy. However, as is often the case with government policies, there may be unintended consequences. In this chapter, we evaluate the empirical evidence on one such potential unintended consequence—the effects of TARP in terms of distorting bank competition.

The general literature on regulatory interventions in the banking sector argues that public guarantees often distort competition (e.g., French, Baily, Campbell, Cochrane, Diamond, Duffie, Kashyap, Mishkin, Rajan, Scharfstein, Shiller, Shin, Slaughter, Stein, and Stulz, 2010; Gropp, Hakenes, and Schnabel, 2011; Calderon and Schaeck, 2012). From a theoretical standpoint, bailouts like TARP may result in recipient banks and their rivals gaining competitive advantages or disadvantages.

We describe in this chapter the only three empirical research studies to our knowledge that estimate these effects, and to the extent possible, investigate which of the channels are behind the results. Section 10.1 reviews the findings of Berger and Roman (2015) and Cao-Alvira and Núñez-Torres (2019) on the extent to which TARP banks gained competitive advantages from the program. Section 10.2 discusses the findings of Koetter and Noth (2016) on competitive distortions for banks that did not receive bailout funds. Finally, Section 10.3 concludes and discusses some additional issues and caveats.

10.1 Competitive advantages for TARP banks

Berger and Roman (2015) measure competitive advantages of TARP from two ways. First, they use changes in market shares, measured by the weighted-average local market asset shares, where the weights are the proportions of deposits in different local markets (locations of assets are not available), and the markets are Metropolitan Statistical Areas (MSAs), New England County Metropolitan Areas (NECMAs), or rural counties. Second, they employ changes in market power measured by the Lerner Index for bank gross total assets $(GTA)^1$ (Lerner, 1933). This is calculated as the price−cost margin divided by price $((PRICE−MC)/PRICE)$, where $PRICE$ is the price of GTA proxied by the ratio of total revenues (interest and noninterest income) to GTA and MC represents the marginal cost of GTA. A bank in perfect competition has a Lerner Index value of 0 and no market power $(PRICE = MC)$, while a bank with market power has a positive index. Details of these measures are provided in Berger and Roman (2015).

These authors were also the first to create the channels approach to test hypotheses about the effects of TARP discussed in Chapter 4. Berger and Roman (2015) develop three potential channels through which TARP may lead to higher market shares for TARP recipients: the *predation channel* (TARP banks may compete more aggressively), the *safety channel* (TARP banks may be considered safer), and the *cost advantage channel* (TARP funds may be cheaper than non-TARP funds). In contrast, they offer three different channels that may lead to lower market shares for TARP banks: the *charter value/quiet life channel* (bailout may increase charter value and/or allow for a "quiet life"), the *stigma channel* (TARP banks may be perceived as riskier), and the *cost disadvantage channel* (TARP funds may be more expensive than non-TARP funds). Notably, some of these channels are opposites of each other (e.g., the *safety* and *stigma channels*), and only one of each pair can hold for a given bank at a given time.

The authors' next four channels may increase market power as measured by Lerner Index, three of which also affect market share (the *safety channel*, the *charter value/quiet life channel*, and the *cost advantage channel*). The fourth channel is the *increased moral hazard channel* (reduction in discipline results in shifts into riskier portfolios). TARP banks may alternatively decrease their market power relative to non-TARP banks due to four different channels, three of which also affect market share (the *predation channel*, the *stigma channel*, and the *cost disadvantage channel*) plus the *decreased moral hazard channel* (increase in capital results in shifts into safer portfolios). The *increased moral hazard* and *decreased moral hazard channels* are opposites, and only one can hold for a given bank at a given time.

---

[1] GTA equals total assets plus the allowance for loan and lease losses and the allocated transfer risk reserve (a reserve for certain foreign loans). Total assets on Call Reports deduct these two reserves, which are held to cover potential credit losses. The authors add these reserves back to measure the full value of the assets financed.

Their difference-in-difference (DID) results suggest that TARP banks did get competitive advantages and increased both their market shares and market power. Their findings are also economically significant, suggesting that TARP recipients increased their local market shares by 9.14% and their Lerner Index of market power by 74.85%, evaluated relative to the means of market share and Lerner Index. When splitting the TARP participants by whether or not they repaid early, they find that the competitive advantages are primarily or entirely due to recipients that repaid early.

The authors are also able to assess which of the channels above are the strongest and weakest, largely by parsing through different sets of results, because the channels have predictions that vary by different outcome variables and sets of banks. Specifically, the authors differentiate among the findings for market shares measured in terms of assets; market power measured by the Lerner Index; the price and marginal cost components of the Lerner Index; banks that repaid early and those that did not; and so forth. They find that: (1) the *moral hazard channels* seem to be unimportant because *PRICE* does not change nearly as much as MC, and goes in two different directions for those banks that did and did not repay early, (2) the *cost disadvantage channel* appears to dominate the *cost advantage channel*, at least for the banks that repaid early, because when the cost effects are reduced by early repayment, the competitive advantages are amplified, and (3) the *safety channel*, the only remaining channel with positive influences on both market share and market power, appears to dominate the *stigma* and *cost disadvantage channels*, which have negative influences on both.

Berger and Roman (2015) also examine the dynamics of the relations between TARP and competitive advantage indicators for the TARP banks in a similar fashion to Beck, Levine, and Levkov (2010), as discussed in Chapter 5. They include a series of quarterly DID effects to trace out the effects over time of TARP on the competitive indicators for the TARP recipients.

They find that the impact of TARP on market share takes time to materialize and only becomes significantly positive in 2010:Q1, and this effect remains at a high level until the end of the sample period 2012:Q4. This may suggest that taking share away from competitors is a medium- to long-term strategic process. As for the impact of TARP on market power, the increase in banks' market power after TARP materializes very quickly, from the first quarter after TARP (2009:Q1), possibly because it may immediately affect banks' costs of funds. The effect eventually disappears in 2011. Thus, market share and market power record different patterns of increase post-TARP.

Cao-Alvira and Núñez-Torres (2019) replicate some of the market power analysis using a subset of 14 TARP and 10 non-TARP banks.

Specifically, they focus on banks engaged in the swap and securitization program with Fannie Mae as part of their analysis of the effects of TARP on these banks and their mortgage loan supply and modification behavior described in Chapters 11 and 12. For expositional convenience, we simply describe how their findings are consistent with or different from those in the full sample analysis of Berger and Roman (2015).

Most of the results in Cao-Alvira and Núñez-Torres (2019) are consistent with the earlier-described outcomes. These authors find that TARP increased the TARP banks' market power as measured by the Lerner Index, mostly from decreased costs of funding. However, a key difference is that these authors find that banks that repaid the TARP funds had about the same increase in the Lerner Index as those that did not, contrary to Berger and Roman's (2015) finding that the competitive advantages are primarily or entirely due to recipients that repaid early.

10.2 Competitive distortions for non-TARP banks

Koetter and Noth (2016) also find competitive distortions as a result of TARP, but in their case, they focus on the indirect effects of bailout expectations for sound unsupported TARP peers, i.e., those that did not actually receive bailout funds. They also differ from the other studies in that they focus on prices as evidence of competitive distortions, rather than market share or the Lerner Index (although the Lerner Index is based in part on prices). Rather than using actual bailouts, Koetter and Noth (2016) extrapolate bailout expectations for sound banks based on parameter estimates that separate banks that received TARP support from those that exited the market due to failures. They regress these generated bailout expectations on derived loan and deposit rates from the Uniform Bank Performance Reports charged by banks and volume changes by the banks after the end of the TARP program. Their findings match the theoretical channels identified in Hakenes and Schnabel (2010) for bailout competitive distortions among unsupported banks from increased competition among supported banks. They find that banks with higher bailout expectations increase loan rates, particularly for total loans and commercial and industrial (C&I) loans, and reduce deposit rates in the post-TARP period (2010:Q1-2013:Q3).

In terms of economic significance, Koetter and Noth (2016) find that one standard deviation increase in bailout expectations by unsupported banks increases loan interest rates by only 2.65 basis points. These increased interest margin effects are most pronounced in the immediate aftermath of TARP and then turn statistically insignificant after the year 2010, suggesting that competitive distortions among unsupported banks appear to have been small and short-lived. They find little in the way of loan volume changes.

10.3 Conclusions and caveats regarding TARP and competition

Combining the findings of these studies, the results in Koetter and Noth (2016) suggest that the results in Berger and Roman (2015) and Cao-Alvira and Núñez-Torres (2019) may somewhat understate the competitive distortions for TARP banks. This is because these other results are based on the differential effects of TARP banks relative to non-TARP banks. Thus, to the extent that some non-TARP banks gained market power as suggested by Koetter and Noth (2016), the competitive effects of TARP on TARP banks may be greater than estimated by Berger and Roman (2015) and Cao-Alvira and Núñez-Torres (2019).

All of these findings—the competitive advantages induced by increased market shares and market power due to actual TARP capital injections and the price changes for nonrecipients due to unrealized expectations of bailouts—represent competitive distortions that led to misallocations of resources and social costs from TARP. From a social viewpoint, resources should ideally be determined by market forces that reward the most efficient banks, rather than being determined by government bailouts.

We finally mention an additional issue with regard to the effects of TARP on bank competition that has not yet been fully investigated. It is possible that TARP may have altered the relative market powers of large and small banks. As indicated earlier, large banks more often received TARP bailouts than small banks, with most of the funds being given to the initial nine very large involuntary TARP participants (eight BHCs and one standalone investment bank that was subsequently acquired by one of the BHCs). This raises the possibility that TARP may have helped large banks gain market power relative to small banks, a concern raised by the Congressional Oversight Panel (2011). We return to this issue under future research topics in Chapter 29.

References

Beck, T., Levine, R., & Levkov, A. (2010). Big bad banks? The winners and losers from bank deregulation in the United States. *The Journal of Finance, 65*(5), 1637–1667.

Berger, A. N., & Roman, R. A. (2015). Did TARP banks get competitive advantages? *Journal of Financial and Quantitative Analysis, 50*(6), 1199–1236.

Calderon, C., & Schaeck, K. (2012). Bank bailouts, competitive distortions, and consumer welfare. *World Bank Working paper.*

Cao-Alvira, J. J., & Núñez-Torres, A. (2019). On TARP and agency securitization. *International Finance, 22*(2), 186–200.

Congressional, Oversight Panel (2011). *March Oversight Report.* Available at: https://www.govinfo.gov/content/pkg/CHRG-112shrg64832/pdf/CHRG-112shrg64832.pdf.

French, K. R., Baily, M. N., Campbell, J. Y., Cochrane, J. H., Diamond, D. W., Duffie, D., Kashyap, A. K., Mishkin, F. S., Rajan, R. G., Scharfstein, D. S., Shiller, R. J., Shin, H. S., Slaughter, M. J., Stein, J. C., & Stulz, R. M. (2010). *The Squam Lake Report, Fixing the Financial System*. University Press: Princeton, NJ: Princeton.

Gropp, R., Hakenes, H.a, & Schnabel, I. (2011). Competition, risk-shifting, and public bail-out policies. *The Review of Financial Studies, 24*(6), 2084–2120.

Hakenes, H., & Schnabel, I. (2010). Banks without parachutes: Competitive effects of government bail-out policies. *Journal of Financial Stability, 6*(3), 156–168.

Koetter, M., & Noth, F. (2016). Did TARP distort competition among sound unsupported banks? *Economic Inquiry, 54*(2), 994–1020.

Lerner, A. P. (1933). The concept of monopoly and the measurement of monopoly power". *Review of Economic Studies, 1*, 157–175.

11

Effects of TARP on bank credit supply

The effects of TARP on bank credit supply is the single most studied topic in the TARP research literature. Most, but not all, of this research uses the difference-in-difference (DID) methodology discussed in Chapter 5, and some also use instrumental variables (IV), propensity score matching (PSM), Heckman sample selection models, and/or placebo tests to confirm the robustness of the findings.

Most of these studies are of credit supply at the *extensive margin*, i.e., through changes in quantities of credit supplied. This research varies widely as to whether the credit quantities are measured at the bank level or at the borrower level, and whether the credit supplied is on the banks' balance sheets through loans or off the balance sheet through loan commitments. In some cases, the results differ by small versus large banks, and by small versus large borrowers. There is also some research on credit supply at the *intensive margin*, i.e., through more or less favorable loan contract terms (spread, amount, maturity, collateral, and covenants) for large borrowers that obtain syndicated loans. We cover all of these topics in this chapter.

In the introduction to Part II above, we note that the direct effects of TARP on one particular economic or financial outcome in some cases have indirect effects on other outcomes, and that we would discuss these indirect effects in the later chapters on the other outcomes. Following this approach, Section 11.1 examines the consequences for credit supply from the changes in bank competition associated with TARP documented in Chapter 10. Sections 11.2 and 11.3 cover the research findings on the direct effects of TARP on credit supply at the *extensive* and *intensive margins*, respectively. Section 11.4 provides conclusions from this research and caveats about drawing strong conclusions from the research findings.

223

One topic not covered here is the extent to which the different theoretical channels discussed in Chapter 4 may be behind the credit supply findings. To date, none of the empirical research on credit supply to our knowledge has been able to identify the underlying channels, and we recommend more research on this topic in Chapter 29.

Notably, in addition to the findings on credit supply quantities at the *extensive margin* and credit terms at the *intensive margin*, there is also research on the extent to which the changes in credit supply are tilted toward riskier or safer borrowers, often in the same research papers as the credit supply results. We withhold coverage of this research until Chapter 12, which reports on the effects of TARP on recipient banks' portfolio risks. We also withhold until Chapter 13 a discussion of the effects on the bank's loan customers of the changes in credit supply. As discussed earlier, the changes in credit supply also have indirect impacts on whether TARP achieved its main goals of improving the real economy and reducing systemic risk, and we defer discussion of these indirect impacts until Chapters 14 and 15, respectively.

11.1 Consequences for credit supply from changes in bank competition induced by TARP

The findings of increased market power and market shares for TARP banks in Chapter 10 have ambiguous consequences for credit supply. The direction of these effects depends on both the lending technologies used to serve the credit customers—transactions versus relationship lending technologies—and which among several alternative credit supply theories are most consistent with the data.

Under the traditional structure—conduct—performance (SCP) hypothesis of Bain (1959), the competitive advantages for TARP banks likely result in reduced credit supply for customers that are primarily screened and monitored using transactions lending technologies. Similar to any other transactions good or service, increased market power implies unfavorable prices and reduced credit supply to transactions customers.

In contrast, the treatment may be favorable for relationship borrowers. Under Petersen and Rajan's (1995) model, the higher market power and market share may encourage TARP banks to invest in relationships that allow them to enforce implicit contracts in which the bank subsidizes borrowers in the short run and charges more later in the relationships. Thus, there may be an increase in credit supply to relationship borrowers from the increased market power.

In contrast to the Bain's (1959) SCP model that applies to banks doing only transactions lending and the Petersen and Rajan's (1995) model of banks making only relationship loans, it seems likely that the same banks often engage in both types of lending. This may bring about different results because of the possibility of substitution between the two types of lending. Boot and Thakor (2000) model the effects of competition from other banks as well as from capital markets for banks that provide both types of credit.

In the Boot and Thakor (2000) model, the increase in market power from an external source like TARP would primarily increase bank market power relative to transactional borrowers. This is because banks are already somewhat protected from competition in serving relationship borrowers. Thus, TARP banks may have incentives to capture more rents by shifting from relationship lending to transactions lending, yielding the opposite conclusions from the models that consider banks supplying only transactions credit or only relationship credit.[1]

The extant empirical literature on the effects of bank competition on credit supply is as mixed as the theories. Some studies find positive effects of bank competition on credit supply (e.g., Cetorelli and Strahan, 2006), other studies find negative effects (e.g., Petersen and Rajan, 1995), others find results that depend on the measure of competition employed (e.g., Carbo-Valverde, Rodríguez-Fernández, and Udell, 2009), and still other research finds effects that differ depending on loan types (e.g., Berger, Cerqueiro, and Penas, 2015).[2] In addition, while most of this empirical literature is aimed at addressing credit to relationship borrowers, these borrowers are not always easily differentiated from transactional borrowers.

In the sections to follow on the empirical research on TARP and credit supply, we differentiate when possible between large or corporate business lending and small business lending. This is a very rough and imperfect approximation to transactions versus relationship borrowers.

11.2 Empirical research findings for the effects of TARP on credit supply at the *extensive margin*

Most of the studies of the effects of TARP on credit supply at the *extensive margin* find positive effects on credit quantities issued by both large and small banks to large corporations, small businesses, and consumers, but there is a significant minority that finds either no effects or

---

[1] Changes in competition from capital markets in Boot and Thakor's (2000) model would have very different effects from the changes in interbank competition from TARP discussed here.

[2] See surveys by Berger and Black (2019) and Degryse, Morales-Acevedo, and Ongena (2019) for more information.

negative credit supply effects. The results sometimes differ by bank size and by corporate versus small business lending, as well as by methodology, sample periods, and datasets. In some cases, the credit data are from only bank Call Reports that lack information on the borrowers, while in other cases, additional data from DealScan on corporate credits, Community Reinvestment Act (CRA) data on small business loans, Survey of Terms of Bank Lending (STBL) data on both large and small business loans, and Home Mortgage Disclosure Act (HMDA) data on residential mortgages are included.

We first cover studies finding positive credit supply effects. To be clear, a positive credit supply in the DID framework that is used by most of the studies does not necessarily mean that TARP banks increased their lending in absolute terms. In some cases, it may imply that these banks cut back their lending less than non-TARP banks after the TARP funds were injected.

Li (2013) covers essentially all US banks using the Call Reports and finds that TARP banks expanded their credit supply and increased quantities of all major types of loans. On average, TARP banks employed about one-third of their TARP capital to support new loans. Taliaferro (2009) uses a matched sample covering banks of all sizes and also finds increased lending from TARP, on the order of 13 cents of additional loans per dollar of TARP capital injection. Berrospide and Edge (2010) focus on large bank holding companies (BHCs) and use models of the effects of bank capital on lending to predict the effects of TARP capital injections on lending and find injections likely boosted BHC loan growth by several percent. Puddu and Waelchli (2015) use CRA data, which mostly cover lending by banks with over $1 billion in assets to small businesses. They find that TARP banks originate more small business loans than non-TARP banks, all else equal. Chavaz and Rose (2019) use all US banks in the HMDA dataset on mortgage lending and in the CRA dataset. They find that TARP increased mortgage and small business lending, but that these lending increases were significantly directed by political considerations. Specifically, more lending was allocated inside their home-representative's district, particularly if the representative supported the TARP, was subsequently reelected, and received more political contributions from the financial industry. Jang (2017) also uses the CRA data and finds that TARP banks with presence in both distressed counties (high foreclosure rates) and nondistressed counties (low foreclosure rates) increased their small business loan originations in the nondistressed counties as a result of TARP. This suggests that TARP mitigated the transmission of problems in distressed areas to nondistressed areas. Black and Hazelwood (2013) use C&I lending from the STBL. They find that outstanding C&I loans increased for small TARP banks. Carpenter, Demiralp, and Eisenschmidt (2014) also use the STBL, but include TARP and the Term Auction Facilities (TAF) data and find both were successful in increasing the supply of C&I loans. Berger and Roman (2017) use all banks in the Call Reports aggregated at the US state level and find increases in bank lending from TARP for C&I loans, and an even larger effect on commercial real estate (CRE) loans. Using the DealScan data on large commercial loans by large banks, Chu, Zhang, and Zhao (2019) find that large banks increase their contributions to syndicated loans after receiving TARP funding. Also focusing on the DealScan dataset, Berger, Makaew, and Roman (2019) find that after TARP funds are injected, TARP banks have a much higher likelihood of continuing to lend to their pre-TARP relationship loan customers. As well, Sheng (2017) finds statistically and economically significant increases in DealScan lending to corporations, a finding that becomes stronger when using PSM to compare TARP banks with similar non-TARP banks. Contessi and Francis (2011) combine banks and thrifts and find that TARP institutions experienced less lending contraction than non-TARP institutions for all types of loans and bank asset levels, with the most pronounced effects for real estate lending. Zheng (2017) finds that more TARP support is associated with less bank liquidity holding and significantly higher liquidity creation.[3] In sum, these studies find that TARP recipient banks increased their credit supplies relative to non-TARP banks or decreased their credit supplies less, and the findings hold for large and small banks, for large and small businesses, and for residential mortgages.

In contrast to these studies, some studies find essentially no positive effects of TARP on lending. Duchin and Sosyura (2014) study large publicly traded banks and find no change in credit supply quantities for large corporate loans or residential mortgages. Bassett, Demiralp, and Lloyd (2017) use a somewhat different approach, combining TARP with several other types of government support into a total government support (TGS) variable. They regress loan growth on TGS, lagged loan growth, and other controls rather than using the DID methodology. They find no significant increase in loan growth as a result of the government support. Wu (2015) studies the different effects of TARP, the discount window, and the TAF on very large syndicated loans using the Shared National Credit (SNC) database and finds only small increases to no significant effects of any of these programs.

Finally, three studies find reductions in credit supply by TARP banks. Using Call Report data, Montgomery and Takahashi (2014) find that TARP is associated with significant reductions in bank lending. Like

---

[3] Consistent with this, Chang, Contessi, and Francis (2014) find that banks that received TARP funds maintained lower cash-to-assets ratios (and thus lower excess reserves ratios), consistent with the view that the TARP capital injection possibly resulted in more lending or less contraction in lending for the TARP beneficiaries.

Bassett, Demiralp, and Lloyd (2017), Montgomery and Takahashi (2014) examine changes in lending while controlling for lagged changes in lending. Lin, Liu, and Srinivasan (2017) use DealScan loans to large corporations, focusing on changes in lending to the same borrower from the pre-TARP to the post-TARP period. They find significant negative effects on loan quantities for TARP banks relative to non-TARP banks, effects which are more pronounced for banks that are subject to future regulatory fines. Lastly, the Black and Hazelwood (2013) study cited above finds that outstanding C&I loans decreased for large TARP banks relative to large non-TARP banks.

Three of the studies on credit supply at the *extensive margin* cited above also include off-balance sheet guarantees. Such guarantees are contracts in which banks are obligated to supply future funds needed or requested by counterparties under certain conditions. Loan commitments account for most of the dollars of off-balance sheet guarantees of US banks (Berger and Bouwman, 2016). Li (2013) uses *total credit*, the sum of loans and off-balance sheet unused loan commitments. This may be considered a superior measure of total credit supply because some lending may not be voluntary, but driven by customer demand through drawdowns of unused commitments (e.g., Ivashina and Scharfstein, 2010; Cornett, McNutt, Strahan, and Tehranian, 2011; Berger, Black, Bouwman, and Dlugosz, 2017). This measure is not affected by customer-driven movements from off-balance sheet to the balance sheet, since the loan increases are fully offset by the decreases in unused loan commitments. Li (2013) finds that the effects of TARP on *total credit* are even larger than its effects on loans, suggesting that TARP also increased credit supply off the balance sheet. Duchin and Sosyura (2014) find no effects of TARP on loan commitments by large banks to large corporate borrowers. Berger and Roman (2017) investigate the effects of TARP on off-balance sheet guarantees of various types, and find positive effects on some loan commitments, particularly those related to real estate. Thus, two of the three studies find more positive effects of TARP on credit supply through off-balance sheet loan commitments, while the third study finds no effects for large corporate borrowers.

11.3 Empirical research findings for the effects of TARP on credit supply at the *intensive margin*

We are only aware of two studies of the effects of TARP on credit supply at the *intensive margin*. The Berger, Makaew, and Roman (2019) paper cited above also finds that TARP generally led to more favorable terms of credit for large commercial borrowers from large TARP banks using the DealScan dataset, an increase in credit supply at the *intensive margin.* Conditional on other determinants of credit terms, TARP recipient banks are found to grant loans on more favorable terms to the borrowers in all five dimensions studied—lower interest rate spreads, larger amounts, longer maturities, less frequency of collateral, and less restrictive covenants. These results hold whether or not the banks had prior lending relationships with the borrowers, consistent with the notion that TARP banks used the bailout funds to reach out to both new and existing borrowers. Smaller and unlisted borrowers benefit less, suggesting fewer benefits for financially constrained firms. The authors also trace out the effects of TARP over the 4 years following the TARP bailouts and find most of the improvements in contract terms are relatively long-lived.

Cao-Alvira and Núñez-Torres (2019) find lower spreads by TARP banks on conforming residential mortgages securitized by Fannie Mae, also indicative of increased credit supply at the *intensive margin.* However, a key difference from the C&I loans discussed above is that the securitized mortgages are not held by the bank for very long—they end up on the balance sheets of Fannie Mae and other investors. In contrast, most of the DealScan commercial loans are syndicated, and the lead banks typically keep parts of these loans.

11.4 Conclusions and caveats from the research findings for the effects of TARP on credit supply

The vast majority of the studies reviewed here use the DID framework. Most, but not all, suggest increased credit supply by TARP banks relative to non-TARP banks at both the *extensive* and *intensive margins,* for both large and small banks, for both large and small loan customers, and for both loans and loan commitments. Smaller numbers of studies find essentially no credit supply effects or negative effects. To put the different studies in perspective, of the papers reviewed above, 12 find loan supply increases at the *extensive margin,* two also find off-balance sheet loan commitment credit supply increases at the *extensive margin,* and two additionally find loan supply increases at the *intensive margin.* In contrast, three *extensive margin* studies find no loan supply changes, three find negative loan supply changes, and one finds no change in loan commitment credit supply. In a few cases, studies with multiple results are included in these lists more than once (e.g., Black and Hazelwood, 2013, with different findings for large and small banks). The differences in results across studies may be due to the use of different methodologies, time periods, datasets, and bank and borrower samples, but tracking down the detailed reasons for the different findings is beyond the scope of our investigation.

Several important caveats also apply to these findings. First, the DID studies do not test for whether TARP increased *total* credit supply. The DID framework calculates the change in difference in the supplies of TARP and non-TARP banks, rather than the sum of the credit changes by TARP and non-TARP banks. If non-TARP banks decreased their lending by a comparable amount, then the total effect may not be positive. This could have occurred because TARP banks became more aggressive and took market share from non-TARP banks, with no overall increase in lending. The US Treasury approval criteria of "healthy and viable banks" for TARP applications may have also inadvertently branded some non-TARP banks as "unhealthy" or "nonviable," reducing lending by these banks. This issue may apply more to credit supply at the *extensive margin*—it seems less likely that non-TARP banks significantly worsened their loan contract terms at the *intensive margin*. Supporting this conclusion, the only study of which we are aware on the behavior of non-TARP banks by Koetter and Noth (2016) finds only very small and temporary loan interest rate increases by these banks. As discussed in Chapter 15, to the extent that systemic risk was decreased by TARP, non-TARP banks may have alternatively also been made better off by the program and may have increased their lending.

Importantly, no papers other than Koetter and Noth (2016) to our knowledge address the issue of the effects of TARP on credit supply by non-TARP banks. Other bank credit supply literatures have examined the credit supply reactions of other local banks to bank mergers and acquisitions (M&As) (e.g., Berger, Saunders, Scalise, and Udell, 1998) and stress tests (e.g., Cortés, Demyanyk, Li, Loutskina, and Strahan, 2020). In Chapter 29, we recommend that the profession addresses this question for the effects of TARP on other local banks' credit supplies.

Another set of caveats regarding this literature is that even if total bank lending increased from TARP, it does not necessarily imply that borrowers were made better off or that TARP boosted the real economy. These issues are discussed further in Chapters 13 and 14, respectively.

References

Bain, J. S. (1959). *Industrial Organization* (2nd ed.). New York: John Wiley.

Bassett, W., Demiralp, S., & Lloyd, N. (2017). Government support of banks and bank lending. *Journal of Banking and Finance*, 105177.

Berger, A. N., & Black, L. K. (2019). *Small business lending: the roles of technology and regulation from pre-crisis to crisis to recovery* (3rd ed., pp. 431–469) Book chapter in Oxford Handbook of Banking.

Berger, A. N., Black, L. K., Bouwman, C. H. S., & Dlugosz, J. (2017a). Bank loan supply responses to Federal Reserve emergency liquidity facilities. *Journal of Financial Intermediation*, 32, 1–15.

Berger, A. N., & Bouwman, C. H. S. (2016). *Bank liquidity creation and financial crises*. Elsevier – North Holland.

Berger, A. N., Cerqueiro, G., & Penas, M. F. (2015). Market size structure and small business lending: Are crisis times different from normal times? *Review of Finance, 19*(5), 1965–1995.

Berger, A. N., Makaew, T., & Roman, R. A. (2019). Do business borrowers benefit from bank bailouts?: The effects of TARP on loan contract terms. *Financial Management, 48*(2), 575–639.

Berger, A. N., & Roman, R. A. (2017). Did saving wall street really save main street? The real effects of TARP on local economic conditions. *Journal of Financial and Quantitative Analysis, 52*(5), 1827–1867.

Berger, A. N., Saunders, A., Scalise, J. M., & Udell, G. F. (1998). The effects of bank mergers and acquisitions on small business lending. *Journal of Financial Economics, 50*(2), 187–229.

Berrospide, J. M., & Edge, R. M. (2010). The effects of bank capital on lending: What do we know, and what does it mean? (Working paper).

Black, L. K., & Hazelwood, L. N. (2013). The effect of TARP on bank risk-taking. *Journal of Financial Stability, 9*(4), 790–803.

Boot, A. W. A., & Thakor, A. V. (2000). Can relationship banking survive competition? *The Journal of Finance, 55*(2), 679–713.

Cao-Alvira, J. J., & Núñez-Torres, A. (2019). On TARP and agency securitization. *International Finance, 22*(2), 186–200.

Carbo-Valverde, S., Rodriguez-Fernandez, F., & Udell, G. F. (2009). Bank market power and SME financing constraints. *Review of Finance, 13*(2), 309–340.

Carpenter, S., Demiralp, S., & Eisenschmidt, J. (2014). The effectiveness of non-standard monetary policy in addressing liquidity risk during the financial crisis: The experiences of the federal reserve and the European Central Bank. *Journal of Economic Dynamics and Control, 43*, 107–129.

Cetorelli, N., & Strahan, P. E. (2006). Finance as a barrier to entry: Bank competition and industry structure in local US markets. *The Journal of Finance, 61*(1), 437–461.

Chang, S.-H., Contessi, S., & Francis, J. L. (2014). Understanding the accumulation of bank and thrift reserves during the US financial crisis. *Journal of Economic Dynamics and Control, 43*, 78–106.

Chavaz, M., & Rose, A. K. (2019). Political borders and bank lending in post-crisis America. *Review of Finance, 23*(5), 935–959.

Chu, Y., Zhang, D., & Zhao, Y. E. (2019). Bank capital and lending: Evidence from syndicated loans. *Journal of Financial and Quantitative Analysis, 54*(2), 667–694.

Contessi, S., & Francis, J. L. (2011). TARP beneficiaries and their lending patterns during the financial crisis. *Federal Reserve Bank of St. Louis Review, 93*(2), 105–125.

Cornett, M. M., McNutt, J. J., Strahan, P. E., & Tehranian, H. (2011). Liquidity risk management and credit supply in the financial crisis. *Journal of Financial Economics, 101*(2), 297–312.

Cortés, K. R., Demyanyk, Y., Li, L., Loutskina, E., & Strahan, P. E. (2020). Stress tests and small business lending. *Journal of Financial Economics, 136*(1), 260–279.

Degryse, H., Morales-Acevedo, P., & Ongena, S. (2019). Competition in the banking sector. In *The Oxford handbook of banking*. Oxford: OUP.

Duchin, R., & Sosyura, D. (2014). Safer ratios, riskier portfolios: Banks' response to government aid. *Journal of Financial Economics, 113*(1), 1–28.

Ivashina, V., & Scharfstein, D. (2010). Bank lending during the financial crisis of 2008. *Journal of Financial Economics, 97*(3), 319–338.

Jang, K. Y. (2017). The effect of TARP on the propagation of real estate shocks: Evidence from geographically diversified banks. *Journal of Banking and Finance, 83*, 173–192.

Koetter, M., & Noth, F. (2016). Did tarp distort competition among sound unsupported banks? *Economic Inquiry, 54*(2), 994–1020.

Li, L. (2013). TARP funds distribution and bank loan supply. *Journal of Banking and Finance, 37*(12), 4777–4792.

Lin, Y., Liu, X., & Srinivasan, A. (2017). Unintended consequences of government bailouts, evidence from bank-dependent borrowers of large banks (Working Paper).

Montgomery, H., & Takahashi, Y. (2014). The economic consequences of the TARP: The effectiveness of bank recapitalization policies in the US. *Japan and the World Economy, 32,* 49–64.

Petersen, M. A., & Rajan, R. G. (1995). The effect of credit market competition on lending relationships. *The Quarterly Journal of Economics, 110*(2), 407–443.

Puddu, S., & Waelchli, A. (2015). TARP effect on bank lending behaviour: Evidence from the last financial crisis (Working Paper).

Sheng, J. (2017). *The real effects of government intervention: Firm-level evidence from TARP.* Working Paper.

Taliaferro, R. (2009). How do banks use bailout money? Optimal capital structure, new equity, and the TARP (Working Paper).

Wu, D. (2015). The effects of government capital and liquidity support programs on bank lending: Evidence from the syndicated corporate credit market. *Journal of Financial Stability, 21,* 13–25.

Zheng, C. (2017). Three essays on bank liquidity (Ph.D. dissertation). Curtin University.

Effects of TARP on bank portfolio risk

As already discussed, reducing systemic risk is a key ultimate goal of TARP. We address one component of this in Chapter 9, the leverage risk of the TARP banks. This chapter investigates another factor affecting systemic risk, the portfolio risk of the TARP banks.

The research in Chapter 11 strongly suggests that bank credit supplies increased as a result of TARP, which should have a first-order effect on portfolio risk. More loans on the balance sheet and more loan commitments off the balance sheet likely increase the risks of TARP banks' portfolios unless the new credits are relatively low risk and/or their returns are negatively correlated with returns of existing loans. Credit risk from commercial credit, particularly the commercial real estate (CRE) credit that was increased by TARP, is generally acknowledged as a key source of bank portfolio risk and significantly contributes to observed bank failures. As shown below, the evidence suggests that TARP banks shifted into relatively riskier commercial credits.

In this chapter, we go beyond the effects of credit quantities and focus on three additional ways in which TARP banks may have changed their portfolio risk. Section 12.1 discusses the extent to which TARP banks may have shifted into safer versus riskier credits. Section 12.2 describes the effects on portfolio risk of changing the contract terms of the loans and loan commitments issued, and Section 12.3 deals with how these contract term changes differed between safer and riskier borrowers. Section 12.4 provides conclusions and caveats from this research. Notably, many of the research papers reviewed in this portfolio risk chapter are also reviewed in Chapter 11 on credit supply, as these papers investigate both credit supply and the risks of the borrowers to which the credits were supplied.

12.1 Effects of TARP on shifting into safer versus riskier credits

The studies of TARP banks shifting into safer or riskier credits mostly come from the research on credit supply at the *extensive margin*. Duchin and Sosyura (2014) use the Home Mortgage Disclosure Act (HMDA) dataset and find that large, publicly-traded TARP banks approve riskier residential mortgages. Specifically, using the difference-in-difference (DID) approach, they find that mortgages with high loan-to-income ratios are more likely to be approved by TARP banks after the program was in effect. Duchin and Sosyura (2014) similarly find that these TARP banks approve riskier large corporate loans by employing the DealScan dataset. In this case, the credit risk measures are the borrowers' cash flow volatility, intangible assets, and interest coverage, which are shown in prior research to be related to corporate default risk.[1] Consistent with these findings, Duchin and Sosyura (2014) also find increased loan charge-offs for TARP banks after the capital injections. Black and Hazelwood (2013) use the banks' internal risk ratings of individual commercial loans from the Survey of Terms of Business Lending (STBL) dataset to see whether riskier or safer loans are issued by TARP banks. They find mixed results—higher-risk loans for large banks and lower-risk loans for small banks—suggesting again that large banks tend to shift into riskier credits, but *vice versa* for small banks. As discussed in Chapter 11, Berger and Roman (2017) use bank Call Reports and find the increases in commercial loans for TARP banks are mostly in the CRE category and most of the loan commitments are for real estate loans (not broken out in the Call Report data by commercial vs. residential). CRE loans are widely acknowledged to be very risky and are strongly associated with bank failures (e.g., Cole and White, 2012; Berger, Imbierowicz, and Rauch, 2016).

Two papers examine *ex post facto* loan performance issues of loans made by TARP and non-TARP banks. Chavaz and Rose (2019) find higher nonperforming loans two years later for TARP banks with increased home-district lending, consistent with a shift into lending to riskier borrowers. Agarwal and Zhang (2018) study residential mortgages, and find more modifications of these mortgages (e.g., interest rate reductions, term extensions, and principal write-downs) by TARP than non-TARP banks. However, the authors attribute this finding to the *ex post facto* behavior of the TARP banks due to their increased liquidity, rather than the *ex ante*

---

[1] Duchin and Sosyura (2014) also use Call Report data and find weakly significantly higher interest plus fee income per dollar of total loans and leases. They interpret this finding as indicative of shifting to higher-risk borrowers. However, they do not control for loan type (mortgages, C&I, CRE, loans to governments, etc.) or borrower risk (no borrower characteristics are controlled for) in this regression, so a shift in loan type or a reduction in credit supply to some types of borrowers cannot be ruled out.

riskiness of the mortgages. That is, the TARP preferred equity injections cause the TARP banks to more often modify the mortgages instead of foreclosing on them.

Finally, two other papers study credit risk consequences for TARP banks by looking at either changes in these banks' transparency or CEO retention practices. Kim, Kim, and Lee (2019) test whether TARP affected recipient banks' transparency. A number of theories suggest that risky banks may reduce transparency in order to engage in moral hazard behavior (e.g., Cordella and Yeyati, 1998; Acharya and Ryan, 2016; Jungherr, 2018). Kim, Kim, and Lee (2019) find that TARP banks significantly reduced their transparency relative to non-TARP banks after the injection of government funds by recognizing smaller and less timely loan loss provisions (LLP) relative to actual changes in current and future nonperforming loans. TARP banks also increased discretionary provisions relative to non-TARP banks. Their results are mainly driven by TARP banks that did not repay their funds early. These findings suggest that TARP banks may have increased their credit risks as a result of the program, consistent with the earlier results. Bunkanwanicha, Di Giuli, and Salvadè (2019) find that TARP banks that retained their high risk taking CEOs rather than firing them exacerbated their moral hazard problems. These banks' risks were augmented, as measured by both accounting measures, such as loan loss provision ratios and market risk measures, such as the stock return volatility.

Thus, the evidence overwhelmingly suggests that large banks shifted toward riskier credits. Only the study by Black and Hazelwood finds that small banks may have reduced their portfolio risks by shifting to safer commercial borrowers.

12.2 Effects of TARP on easing or tightening credit contract terms

There are only two studies to our knowledge of the extent to which TARP banks eased or tightened their credit contract terms - Berger, Makaew, and Roman (2019) and Cao-Alvira and Núñez-Torres (2019). The DealScan dataset used by Berger, Makaew, and Roman (2019) mainly covers loans by large banks to large borrowers. Their study of credit supply at the *intensive margin* discussed in Chapter 11 finds that TARP banks eased loan contract terms for large business borrowers relative to non-TARP banks, even after controlling for borrower risk. That is, borrowers of given credit risks from large TARP banks had lower interest rate spreads, larger amounts of credit, longer maturities, less frequency of collateral, and less restrictive covenants. These findings suggest increases in portfolio risks because the bank is less protected from risks by the contract terms. There is less interest income on successful loans to cover losses of problem loans, larger credit exposures for longer maturities, and less protection against losses by collateral and covenants. Again, the findings point toward higher portfolio risk for large TARP banks.

Cao-Alvira and Núñez-Torres (2019) similarly find lower spreads on conforming residential mortgages securitized by Fannie Mae, suggesting higher risk on these loans. However, an important difference here is that a significant portion of the credit risk from the DealScan C&I loans ends up in the TARP bank portfolio (lead banks typically keep part of the loans in their portfolios), while the credit risk on mortgages securitized by Fannie Mae is virtually all borne by Fannie Mae and does not significantly affect TARP banks' portfolio risks.

12.3 Effects of TARP on changing credit contract terms to safer and riskier borrowers

Berger, Makaew, and Roman (2019) also find that loan contract terms of TARP banks improved more for riskier borrowers than for safer borrowers. This evidence at the *intensive margin* is consistent with the findings in Section 12.1 at the *extensive margin* that large TARP banks shifted their increased credit supply toward riskier borrowers, increasing TARP bank portfolio risk.

In contrast, Cao-Alvira and Núñez-Torres (2019) find that residential mortgage spreads on securitized mortgages decreased more for borrowers with higher FICO credit scores, suggesting a shift in credit supply toward safer mortgages. As above, this has little effect on TARP bank portfolio risks, since the credit risk on these securitized mortgages is largely borne by Fannie Mae.

12.4 Conclusions and caveats from the portfolio risk research

The research summarized here, as well as the credit supply findings from Chapter 11, strongly suggest that large TARP banks increased their portfolio risks significantly. This is based on findings indicating increased credit supply, shifting of credit toward riskier borrowers, easing of credit terms for borrowers, and easing them more for riskier borrowers. There is much less information on small banks, and it is more mixed.

However, similar caveats to those discussed in earlier chapters apply here as well. The DID studies measure differences between TARP and non-TARP banks, and we cannot be sure how non-TARP banks may have changed their portfolio risks. We also note that increases in large bank portfolio risks do not necessarily mean that these banks became riskier or increased their contributions to systemic risk. As shown in Chapter 9, TARP banks appear to have decreased their leverage risk, and as discussed earlier, contributions to systemic risk depend on the effects on other banks as well. A more complete analysis of the effects of TARP on systemic risk is provided in Chapter 15.

References

Acharya, V. V., & Ryan, S. G. (2016). Banks' financial reporting and financial system stability. *Journal of Accounting Research, 54*(2), 277–340.

Agarwal, S., & Zhang, Y. (2018). Effects of government bailouts on mortgage modification. *Journal of Banking and Finance, 93*, 54–70.

Berger, A. N., Imbierowicz, B., & Rauch, C. (2016). The roles of corporate governance in bank failures during the recent financial crisis. *Journal of Money, Credit, and Banking, 48*(4), 729–770.

Berger, A. N., Makaew, T., & Roman, R. A. (2019). Do business borrowers benefit from bank bailouts?: The effects of TARP on loan contract terms. *Financial Management, 48*(2), 575–639.

Berger, A. N., & Roman, R. A. (2017). Did saving Wall Street really save Main Street? The real effects of TARP on local economic conditions. *Journal of Financial and Quantitative Analysis, 52*(5), 1827–1867.

Black, L. K., & Hazelwood, L. N. (2013). The effect of TARP on bank risk-taking. *Journal of Financial Stability, 9*(4), 790–803.

Bunkanwanicha, P., Di Giuli, A., & Salvadè, F. (2019). *The effect of bank bailouts on CEO careers* (Working Paper).

Cao-Alvira, J. J., & Núñez-Torres, A. (2019). On TARP and agency securitization. *International Finance, 22*(2), 186–200.

Chavaz, M., & Rose, A. K. (2019). Political borders and bank lending in post-crisis America. *Review of Finance, 23*(5), 935–959.

Cole, R. A., & White, L. J. (2012). Déjà vu all over again: Che causes of US commercial bank failures this time around. *Journal of Financial Services Research, 42*(1–2), 5–29.

Cordella, T., & Yeyati, E. L. (1998). Public disclosure and bank failures. *Staff Papers, 45*(1), 110–131.

Duchin, R., & Sosyura, D. (2014). Safer ratios, riskier portfolios: Banks' response to government aid. *Journal of Financial Economics, 113*(1), 1–28.

Jungherr, J. (2018). Bank opacity and financial crises. *Journal of Banking & Finance, 97*, 157–176.

Kim, J., Kim, M., & Lee, J. H. (2019). The effect of TARP on loan loss provisions and bank transparency. *Journal of Banking and Finance, 102*, 79–99.

13

Effects of TARP on recipient banks' credit customers

This chapter covers the key issue of the effects of TARP on the credit customers of the recipient banks that obtain loans and/or loan commitments from these banks. This is important because these customers are primary conduits through which TARP may affect the real economy. As discussed in Chapter 4, TARP can only significantly improve the real economy if the credit supplies of TARP and/or non-TARP banks are increased, and the borrowers that receive the extra credit increase their positive net present value (NPV) investments, employment, and/or other spending on goods and services.

There is much less evidence on the effects of TARP on credit customers than there is on the credit supply implications of TARP. That is, there is much more evidence about the loans and off-balance sheet commitments than about the effects of this credit on the recipients. Moreover, only a part of the research on the credit customers gives information on their expenditures on investments, employment, or other goods and services that may help the real economy. This stands in sharp contrast to other literatures on the effects of banks on the real economy, such as the research on the geographic deregulation of the US banking industry (see Berger, Molyneux, and Wilson, 2020 for a survey).

In line with the rest of Part II of the book, we begin this chapter by briefly revisiting some direct evidence from an earlier chapter on the issue at hand in this chapter. Specifically, Section 13.1 briefly discusses the consequences for credit customers of the results on the effects of TARP on credit supply in Chapter 11. Section 13.2 discusses two research studies on the effects of TARP on the stock market returns to investors in publicly traded relationship corporate borrowers, as well as one paper on credit default swap (CDS) spreads on such borrowers. Section 13.3 reviews a small number of studies on the effects of TARP on expenditures and trade credit issued by corporate borrowers of TARP banks. Finally, Section 13.4 wraps up the chapter by discussing caveats and conclusions.

239

13.1 Consequences for TARP banks' credit customers from changes in credit supply

Most of the literature on the effects of TARP on credit supply in Chapter 11 suggests that credit supply increased at both the *extensive* and *intensive margins* for TARP banks relative to non-TARP banks, which would seem to suggest benefits for at least some borrowers. However, there are at least three reasons why these results may not imply that credit customers as a whole are significantly better off as a result of TARP. First, as discussed in Chapter 11, the difference-in-difference (DID) methodology of most of the studies does not measure the total credit supply of TARP plus non-TARP banks, which may not have increased because non-TARP banks may have reduced their credit supplies. As discussed, this may be less of an issue for the studies of credit supply at the *intensive margin*, but we still cannot be sure that bank credit supply increased significantly overall. Second, it is possible that any increase in bank credit supply may have been offset by less external finance provided by the capital markets, such as the bond and stock markets. That is, firms may have substituted bank credit for other funding.[1] Third, any increase in overall funding does not necessarily imply a significant welfare increase for the borrowing firms, as some may have simply borrowed to increase their liquidity during very uncertain times, with relatively little benefits.

13.2 Effects of TARP on the stock market returns and CDS spreads of publicly traded relationship corporate borrowers

The two papers on the consequences of TARP on the market valuations of the stocks of publicly traded relationship corporate borrowers document opposing results. Norden, Roosenboom, and Wang (2013) measure firms' exposures to TARP with intervention scores based on their pre-crisis banking relationships, using DealScan data and their relationship banks' TARP participation. The authors find positive abnormal stock returns around intervention events in the firms' relationship banks, and a positive association between the firms' intervention scores and their average daily stock returns. The results hold whether or not their relationship banks are voluntary or involuntary TARP participants. Consistent with the shift in lending toward riskier borrowers documented in Chapter 12, Norden, Roosenboom, and Wang (2013) also find stronger stock return gains for riskier firms.

[1] Sheng (2016) finds that the corporate investment, employment, and R&D expenditures of corporate borrowers from TARP banks remained essentially unchanged.

Lin, Liu, and Srinivasan (2017) find sharply conflicting results to those of Norden, Roosenboom, and Wang (2013). Similar to the earlier paper, Lin, Liu, and Srinivasan (2017) identify each firm's main relationship bank using DealScan data and whether that bank received a TARP bailout. The authors find a significant stock market valuation loss for firms with main relationships with TARP banks relative to firms related to non-TARP banks around the time of the TARP approval announcements. Their results are consistent with their finding of reduced lending to these borrowers documented in Chapter 11, and with some findings on the borrowers' cash flow sensitivities and investments summarized in Section 13.3 below.

Song and Uzmanoglu (2016) examine the CDS spreads of large corporate borrowers from 11 largest TARP lenders around the initial announcement of the program. CDS spreads are widely used indicators of market perceptions of the credit risks of corporations. The authors test a number of hypotheses about how the reactions of these spreads of 280 large corporations that borrow from the largest TARP banks should vary with the health of their relationship banks (measured by asset write-downs), as well as with their own financial health (proxied by leverage, interest expense, and stock returns). For example, the authors predict that borrowers from healthy banks should gain and see their CDS spreads decline, while borrowers from unhealthy banks may see the opposite effect, consistent with healthier banks being more effective in providing liquidity relief to their borrowers, especially the most vulnerable ones. Their empirical findings confirm their expectations, again leaving us with mixed results for whether investors in large corporate borrowers gained or lost from TARP.

13.3 Effects of TARP on the expenditures and trade credit issued by relationship corporate borrowers

The small number of studies on the effects of TARP on expenditures and trade credit behavior of corporate borrowers of TARP banks also yield conflicting conclusions. One finds significant negative effects, one finds essentially no significant effects, and one finds positive effects.

Specifically, Lin, Liu, and Srinivasan (2017) find that the borrowers become more financially constrained, with increased cash flow sensitivity to cash. These firms also reduce their capital investment expenditures, with potentially negative consequences for the real economy. In contrast, Sheng (2016) finds that TARP banks' corporate borrowers did not have any real activity differences in terms of investment, employment, or R&D from non-TARP banks' borrowers, suggesting no important consequences for the real economy. Finally, Norden, Udell, and Wang (2020) consider the influence of TARP on the provision of trade credit granted to the customers of commercial borrowers of US banks. The authors find that corporate borrowers of TARP banks increased their supply of trade credit, while those borrowing from non-TARP banks did not. It seems likely that most of these counterparties spent at least some of the funds on real economic goods and services. Thus, contrary to the first two studies, the third study suggests that TARP likely helped boost the real economy.

13.4 Conclusions and caveats regarding the effects of TARP on recipient banks' credit customers

The research summarized in this chapter is obviously mixed. It is also largely subject to the caveats in Chapter 11 about drawing conclusions from DID studies. One other key limitation is that the evidence presented is for large corporate borrowers from the largest banks. We are not aware of any direct evidence for unlisted small business borrowers or for any borrowers from small and medium banks. Thus, it is very difficult to draw any significant conclusions for the overall effects of TARP on credit customers or their spending that may impact the real economy. However, some evidence provided in Chapter 14 on the real economy suggests that at least some loan customers benefitted and increased their real expenditures.

References

Berger, A. N., Molyneux, P., & Wilson, J. O. S. (2020). Banks and the real economy: An assessment of the research. *Journal of Corporate Finance, 62.*

Lin, Y., Liu, X., & Srinivasan, A. (2017). *Unintended consequences of government bailouts, evidence from bank-dependent borrowers of large banks* (Working Paper).

Norden, L., Roosenboom, P., & Wang, T. (2013). The impact of government intervention in banks on corporate borrowers' stock returns. *Journal of Financial and Quantitative Analysis, 48*(5), 1635—1662.

Norden, L., Udell, G. F., & Wang, T. (2020). Do bank bailouts affect the provision of trade credit? *Journal of Corporate Finance, 60,* 101522.

Sheng, J. (2016). *The real effects of government intervention: Firm-level evidence from TARP.* Working Paper.

Song, W.-L., & Uzmanoglu, C. (2016). TARP announcement, bank health, and borrowers' credit risk. *Journal of Financial Stability, 22,* 22—32.

14

Effects of TARP on the real economy

We next turn to our final two chapters on the empirical research on the effects of TARP on the two main goals and ultimate desired outcomes of the program. This chapter and Chapter 15 cover the very limited research on improving the real economy and reducing systemic risk, respectively. At first blush, it might seem surprising that these are also the two least directly researched TARP topics, with only one paper each that directly measures and tests the effects of TARP on the real economy and systemic risk. On the other hand, this may not be so surprising, given that we cannot observe the counterfactuals of what would have happened to the whole economy and the entire financial system in the absence of TARP. Thus, some changes in methodology are needed to directly address these questions, which are discussed in these chapters, along with the results of these studies.

We begin this chapter on TARP and the real economy by revisiting the two paths through which TARP might improve the real economy. Both involve increasing credit supply, which in turn may help credit customers increase their real spending and boost the real economy. The direct path begins with the primary channels through which TARP banks may increase their credit supply, followed by increased spending by the recipients of this credit on investment, employment, and/or other real goods and services. The indirect path begins with reducing systemic risk by bailing out banks that might otherwise fail or threaten the financial system. The safer financial system with healthier, better capitalized banks may increase credit supply by both TARP and non-TARP banks, which may, in turn, result in increased real spending by the borrowers from both types of banks. The remainder of this chapter reviews the evidence on the success of the program through both paths.

Section 14.1 briefly reviews the implications for the real economy from the evidence on the credit supply of TARP banks and their credit customers from Chapters 11 and 13. Section 14.2 discusses the methodology

243

and results of the research paper that directly measures and tests the effects of TARP on real economic outcomes. Section 14.3 briefly reviews two other relevant research papers on the effects of bank failures on real outcomes that have some secondary findings on the effects of TARP. Section 14.4 draws conclusions and briefly looks ahead to the implications of the systemic risk findings in Chapter 15.

14.1 Implications for the real economy from the effects of TARP on recipient banks' credit supply and credit customers

Most of the research summarized in Chapter 11 suggests increased credit supply by TARP banks relative to non-TARP banks for both large and small banks, and for both large and small loan customers, but little information is available about the credit supply effects of TARP for non-TARP banks. The much smaller research literature summarized in Chapter 13 on TARP banks' credit customers is mostly limited to the large corporate customers of largebanks. The results of the different studies are conflicting as to whether and which customers were better off or not and whether their real spending increased or decreased.

Thus, the findings summarized in these earlier chapters are quite limited in any potential implications about the effects of TARP on the real economy. They provide essentially no information about the second path through which TARP may have boosted the real economy through improving lending conditions for non-TARP banks. They give little information about the effects of TARP on small businesses that are widely acknowledged as being economic engines of growth and employment. The findings are also subject to a number of caveats and have conflicting implications.. As a result of these deficiencies, we conclude that the only way to assess the effects of TARP on the real economy is to skip the analyses of credit supply and of the borrowing firms and proceed directly to estimating a reduced form model of the effects of the local presence of TARP banks on local real economy, which we turn to in Section 14.2.

14.2 Methodology and results of direct measurement of the effects of TARP on the real economic outcomes

As indicated above, directly measuring the effects of TARP on the real economy requires a different methodology than is employed in the earlier difference-in-difference (DID) analyses that focus on the treatment effects of TARP on the recipient banks relative to the untreated non-TARP banks for two main reasons. First, the outcome of the real economy cannot be linked to an individual bank, as can the other TARP outcomes studied earlier in Part II of the book, such as the lending of an individual bank. Second, the real economy is affected by the credit supply of both TARP and non-TARP banks through the direct and indirect paths outlined above, so differences between these two sets of banks are not very revealing for the question of the real economy.

Berger and Roman (2017) address these issues using a DID approach that investigates the effects of TARP on local market economic conditions as functions of the proportions of TARP banks in these localities. This contrasts with the DID analyses reviewed above that analyze individual banks' outcomes as functions of whether the bank received TARP. If TARP improved the real economy, then local markets in which more banks received TARP should have improved significantly relative to local markets in which fewer or no banks received TARP. This methodology directly links TARP to the real economy and includes the effects of both TARP and non-TARP banks in these local areas. As discussed in the caveats at the end of this chapter, this methodology still understates the effects of TARP on the real economy to the extent that TARP also helped save the financial system, which is investigated in Chapter 15.

Berger and Roman (2017) use economic outcomes at the state level in their main analysis because more data are available at the state level than at the county level, but a county-level analysis with different dependent variables provides consistent results. In order to capture whether "Saving Wall Street Saved Main Street," a key goal of TARP espoused by Henry Paulson, the US Treasury Secretary that initially implemented the program, the authors choose variables reflecting the welfare of average Americans as the outcome variables. In particular, they choose net job creation, net hiring establishments, and business and personal bankruptcies, each measured on a per-capita basis.

The authors find strong statistically and economically significant and robust results for all variables, suggesting that TARP resulted in an improved real economy that benefited average Americans. The data suggest that the average state had 8.09 new jobs, 1.60 more establishments creating jobs, and 0.052 fewer business bankruptcies and 1.08 fewer personal bankruptcies, all per 1000 people due to TARP. All of these magnitudes are large relative to their sample means. Berger and Roman (2017) also study the dynamics of the effects and find that most of the job creation and hiring establishment results are concentrated in 2009 and 2010, when the economy needed them the most, while the bankruptcy results are more long-lasting.

The authors also provide ancillary results that may help explain why the real economic effects may not be well reflected in the results regarding large corporations in Chapter 13. Berger and Roman (2017) find that the main mechanisms driving the results appear to be increases in commercial real estate lending and off-balance sheet real estate guarantees, most of which are likely for small businesses, rather than large corporations. Commercial and industrial (C&I) loans and financial letters of credit were also positively affected. In addition, when the results are broken down by bank size class, the findings are strongest for medium-sized banks with between $1 billion and $3 billion in assets that typically are too small to make large syndicated corporate loans. Thus, the benefits to the real economy from TARP may have gone mainly through small business credit, rather than through large corporations, although much more research is needed to draw definitive conclusions in this regard. We return to this discussion of necessary research in Chapter 29.

14.3 Other relevant research on the real economic effects of TARP

Two additional research papers that focus on the negative real economic effects of bank failures also include some secondary findings on the effects of TARP in cushioning these negative effects. Contreras, Delis, Ghosh, and Hasan (2019) examine the impacts of bank failures on business formation and net job creation at the local level, and find negative effects on both measures. Contreras, Ghosh, and Kong (2019) estimate the effects of bank failures on corporate innovation, as proxied by patents and citations. In both studies, they include interactions with the local presence of TARP banks, and in both cases, they find mitigating effects. Thus, TARP appears to lessen the negative real economic effects of bank failures.

14.4 Conclusions and caveats regarding the effects of TARP on the real economy

The research reported here has statistically and economically significant results that suggest positive economic effects from TARP that may operate mainly through small business lending, but strong caveats are in order. Clearly, more research is needed before drawing strong conclusions. In addition, to the extent that the findings are correct, they may understate the full positive effects on the real economy because of the limitations of the DID framework. The findings suggest that localities with more TARP bank presence had better economic performance than those with fewer banks receiving TARP. However, to the extent that the financial system was saved, banks in all localities may have been able to lend more and improve the real economy. In Chapter 15, which comes next, we explore this question by examining the effects of TARP on systemic risk.

References

Berger, A. N., & Roman, R. A. (2017). Did saving Wall Street really save Main Street? The real effects of TARP on local economic conditions. *Journal of Financial and Quantitative Analysis, 52*(5), 1827–1867.

Contreras, S., Delis, M., Ghosh, A., & Hasan, I. (2019). *Bank failures, Local business dynamics, and government policy* (Working Paper).

Contreras, S., Ghosh, A., & Kong, J. H. (2019). *Financial crisis, bank failures, and corporate innovation* (Working Paper).

15

Effects of TARP on systemic risk

Our final TARP chapter covers the effects of the program on systemic risk. Ideally, we would like to know if TARP rescued the financial system from collapse or at least prevented the system from further substantial deterioration, but events that did not occur are fundamentally unobservable. However, as we show in this chapter, the research can provide consistent and highly statistically and economically significant results suggesting whether or not the TARP program reduced the systemic risk contributions of the publicly traded TARP banks. As discussed in Chapter 14, only one paper directly measures these systemic risk contributions. However, as will become clear, a number of other studies provide useful additional information on this important issue.

Starting with the fundamentals, as discussed in Chapter 4 and shown in Table 4.3, systemic risk is reduced by higher bank stock valuations, and systemic risk is exacerbated by increases in bank leverage risk, credit supply, portfolio risk, and systemic importance. We discuss each of these effects in this chapter.[1] Table 4.4 also illustrates that an improving real economy during a recession likely helps reduce systemic risk.

Section 15.1 discusses empirical research on the fundamental effects of TARP on systemic risk. The main part of this process is reviewing the implications of the empirical findings from Chapter 7 on bank leverage risk, Chapter 11 on bank credit supply, Chapter 12 on bank portfolio risk, and Chapter 14 on the real economy. Section 15.2 reviews some additional relevant research on the effects of TARP on more complete measures of bank risks as well as market risks that contribute to systemic risk. Section 15.3 discusses the methodology and results of the research paper that directly measures the effects of TARP on the systemic risk contributions of

---

[1] The effects of the other intermediate outcomes of TARP—market discipline, competition, and loan customer valuations and behavior—which have ambiguous effects on bank systemic risk contributions—are not covered here.

TARP banks. Section 15.4 draws conclusions and gives caveats, as well as briefly revisits the findings on the effects of systemic risk on the real economy.

15.1 Empirical research on the fundamental effects of TARP on systemic risk

Starting with bank leverage risk, we briefly review the findings from Chapter 7 on the effects of TARP on publicly traded banks' market valuations. These valuations directly affect bank leverage risk—higher valuations reduce leverage risk. As discussed in Chapter 7, most of the studies find positive stock returns associated with the announcement of the program and the preferred equity injections into the involuntary participants. These findings suggest that TARP reduced systemic risk. Note that these studies generally do not differentiate between TARP and non-TARP banks, given that most of the decisions to obtain TARP funds had not been made at the announcement date.

In contrast, most of the studies of TARP banks' valuation around the time of individual capital injections are either insignificant or significantly negative. As well, nonparticipation or declining TARP funds have measured insignificant valuation effects. Early repayment of TARP generally had positive effects, which may reflect the ability to repay or removal of TARP restrictions, rather than the risk implications of the program.

Taken together, the valuation research suggests that the financial system may have reduced risk by TARP, but the individual TARP banks may not have benefited as much. However, we caution against drawing strong conclusions from these event studies due to the limitations espoused at the end of Chapter 7 about valuation changes around TARP events potentially being partially driven by other confounding bank characteristics or macroeconomic conditions or other effects of TARP. As earlier indicated, few of the studies include regression analyses that control for other bank and market characteristics.

The research on TARP banks' credit supply and portfolio risk in Chapters 11 and 12, respectively, more clearly suggests that TARP banks increased their portfolio risks relative to non-TARP banks. Most of the Chapter 11 studies find increased credit supply for TARP banks relative to non-TARP banks, which almost surely increases their portfolio credit risk. Most of the Chapter 12 papers find that large TARP banks shifted credit toward riskier borrowers and eased credit terms more for riskier borrowers. Information on small banks is sparser and more mixed, but we note that the large banks are generally more important for systemic risk. Large banks generally have greater numbers of counterparties exposed to credit losses from their impairment. In terms of implications for systemic risk, a clear limitation of these studies is that they measure the difference between TARP and non-TARP banks, rather than the systemic risk contributions of both sets of banks.

As indicated in Chapter 4, systemic risk also increases as banks become more systemically important, but we have not devoted a research chapter to this issue because there is little empirical research attention paid to it. As discussed in Chapter 3, and shown in Table 3.9, the US Treasury Annual Use of Capital Survey for the TARP indicates that 82 of the 664 survey respondents in 2009, or 12.4%, report that they used TARP capital to purchase another financial institution or purchase assets from another financial institution. One difference-in-difference (DID) research analysis on the effects of TARP on bank size by Berger, Roman, and Sedunov (2020) suggests that TARP banks increased gross total assets (GTA) relative to non-TARP banks after the implementation of TARP.

During the financial crisis, many other large financial institutions became larger and more systemically important with government approval, although not necessarily linked with TARP. Bank of America's former CEO Kenneth D. Lewis claimed to be pressured by the US Treasury into completing the merger with Merrill Lynch after receiving an additional $20 billion in capital from the US Treasury from the Targeted Investment Program (TIP) of TARP.[2] During the crisis, the Federal Reserve also expedited a number of large bank mergers with other large financial institutions, such as Bank of America with Countywide, JP Morgan Chase with both Bear Stearns and Washington Mutual, and Wells Fargo with Wachovia. The Federal Reserve also quickly approved conversions of large investment banks, including Goldman Sachs and Morgan Stanley, into financial holding companies, a special type of bank holding company.

Thus, a number of large, systemically important banks became larger and more systemically important, which by itself may imply more systemic risk. However, there is more to these actions than just the increases in size and systemic importance. By placing weak and failing institutions under the control of healthier organizations and giving better access to liquidity to large investment banks, the financial system may have been made safer.

The research reviewed in Chapter 14 suggests that the real economy was improved as a result of TARP. As discussed in Chapter 4, Section 4.4 and shown in Table 4.4, improvements in the real economy can reduce systemic risk during recessions. A better economy reduces credit problems for the banks—lowering their portfolio risks—and helps banks earn higher profits—increasing their capital and reducing their leverage risks. Safer individual banks almost certainly result in lower systemic risk except under very unusual interconnections.

---

[2] https://www.nytimes.com/2009/06/12/business/12bank.html.

Overall, the evidence on the fundamental determinants of systemic risk is mixed. The portfolio risks of individual banks appear to have increased, raising systemic risk, and the real economy appears to have improved, decreasing systemic risk. The other findings on leverage risk and systemic importance have less clear implications for systemic risk. We turn to research on more complete measures of bank risk and market risks in Section 15.2, and then to direct measures of contributions to systemic risk in Section 15.3.

15.2 Empirical research on more complete measures of bank risk and market risk

A number of research papers use more complete measures of individual bank risk and market risks. This research may shed additional light on the issue of whether TARP decreased or increased financial system risks, but does not employ direct measures of systemic risk.

Duchin and Sosyura (2014) find a marked increase in the overall risk of individual TARP banks compared to observably similar non-TARP banks. They use several different measures based on both accounting and market data. These are bank Z-Score (an inverse of financial insolvency), earnings volatility, stock volatility, and stock market beta. Del Viva, Kasanen, Saunders, and Trigeorgis (2017) also find higher bank risk from TARP using the likelihood of bank stock "lotteryness" and risk-shifting as a measure of bank risk. Their measure takes into account the bank stocks' idiosyncratic volatility and skewness. They find that lottery-type bank equities are riskier after TARP and exhibit fatter right to left tails. Semaan and Drake (2016) provide evidence suggesting that the perceived risk of TARP recipients, most notable idiosyncratic risk, remained higher than that of banks that did not receive TARP funds for up to 4 years following disbursements, consistent with persistent long-term moral hazard behavior due to TARP. Farruggio, Michalak, and Uhde (2013) use event studies around TARP key events and document decreases in banks' systematic risk around TARP announcement and capital repayments but not around capital injections. Decomposing banks' systematic risk into its components reveals increases in the correlation component of the banks' stocks with the market around the TARP announcement and capital injections (but not around capital repayments), suggesting increased risk from TARP. In contrast to these studies suggesting higher overall bank risk associated with TARP, Berger, Roman, and Sedunov (2020) conduct DID analyses of the effects of TARP on several overall bank risk measures—Merton Expected Default Probability, Z-Score, and Sharpe Ratio—and find that TARP banks reduced risk relative to non-TARP banks after implementation of the program.

Turning to measures of market risks, Coffey, Hrung, and Sarkar (2009) find that covered interest rate parity deviations decreased after the TARP announcement, suggesting that arbitrage transactions in international capital markets decreased due to less counterparty credit risk. Nguyen and Enomoto (2009) use a GARCH(1,1) model and find evidence that the volatility in stock index returns was reduced after October 14, 2008 when TARP was announced. Huerta, Perez-Liston, and Jackson (2011) use event study methodology and examine the effect of TARP on measures of stock market volatility and "fear indices," including the Chicago Board Options Exchange Volatility Index (VIX). They find significant decreases in both types of indicators. While their indicators are not direct measures of systemic risk, their evidence supports the view that TARP calmed financial markets and investor fears, and thus may have reduced systemic risk in the short term. The mixed results for individual bank risks and lower market risks discussed here do not suggest a clear conclusion as to whether the entire financial system was made safer or riskier by TARP. We next turn to more direct evidence on this issue using direct measures of contributions to systemic risk.

15.3 Methodology and results of the measurement of the effects of TARP on bank contributions to systemic risk

Berger, Roman, and Sedunov (2020) use essentially the same DID methodologies as in most of the other TARP studies, but use the relatively newly developed systemic risk contributions of the TARP banks as the dependent variables. Thus, while one cannot observe the counterfactual of how the financial system might have collapsed in the absence of TARP, this study allows us to observe whether the banks that received TARP funds decreased or increased their contributions to the risk of a systemic collapse.

The authors primarily examine the effects of TARP on two measures: normalized conditional capital shortfall, or normalized *SRISK* (*NSRISK*), and Systemic Expected Shortfall (*SES*). *SRISK* measures the amount of capital a bank would need to raise in a crisis to maintain a given capital-to-assets ratio. It is measured using market data on equities and balance sheet information on liabilities (Acharya, Engle, and Richardson, 2012; Brownlees and Engle, 2017). *NSRISK* normalizes *SRISK* by bank market capitalization, so it measures the proportional capital increase that would be needed in a crisis.

SES measures the bank's propensity to be undercapitalized when the system is undercapitalized (Acharya, Pedersen, Philippon, and Richardson, 2017). *SES* is a linear combination of Marginal Expected Shortfall (*MES*) and Leverage (*LVG*). *MES* estimates how individual institutions' stock returns co-move with the entire market (including nonfinancials) when aggregate returns are low. *LVG* is approximated by: (book value of liabilities plus the market value of equity) divided by the book value of equity.

Berger, Roman, and Sedunov (2020) find statistically and economically significant average reductions of 76.4% in *NSRISK* and 43.0% in *SES* relative to sample means as a result of TARP. They also find consistent results for another systemic risk measure, *ΔCoVaR*, which estimates the contribution of a single institution to the overall losses suffered by the financial system, given a crisis event (Adrian and Brunnermeier, 2016).

The authors' findings of reduced contributions to systemic risk are also robust to a number of different specifications, including, but not limited to, an instrumental variable analysis, alternative measures of TARP, and controlling for systematic risk. The results appear to be driven primarily by TARP banks that were larger, safer, and in locations with better economic conditions *ex ante*, consistent with the theoretical model of Choi (2014), which finds that recapitalization of stronger rather than weaker banks more effectively reduces systemic risk.

Examination of dynamics suggests that the benefits covered the heart of the financial crisis and may be reversed in the long run. That is, using DID terms for each of the years before and after the TARP suggests very strong beneficial effects in terms of reducing systemic risk contributions in 2009, which fade away and eventually go in the opposite direction in the last sample year, 2012. The latter finding is consistent with moral hazard incentives taking greater hold after the crisis.

Berger, Roman, and Sedunov (2020) also conduct a number of additional analyses to better identify the sources of the results. They run the tests separately for the *MES* and *LVG* components of *SES* and find that almost all of the effect flows through reductions in *LVG*, suggesting large increases in market values of the common equity of these banks relative to what they otherwise would have been. These increases in market value do not include any direct or mechanical effects of the preferred equity injected by the Treasury, which is not part of *LVG*. Further analysis reveals that the source of the increase in market values is an increase in the share prices for TARP banks relative to non-TARP banks, rather than any new issuance or change in dividends. This finding suggests that TARP increased market confidence in these banks, which is crucial to financial stability.

These findings may appear to conflict with some of the event study findings that market returns for TARP banks were either insignificant or significantly negative for TARP banks around the time of the injections. However, the different methodologies make the findings difficult to compare. The event study methodology typically covers only a few days, often does not control for other bank and market characteristics, and does not compare TARP banks with comparable non-TARP banks. In contrast,

Berger, Roman, and Sedunov (2020) use quarterly data, control for many bank and market characteristics, and compare TARP and non-TARP banks.

15.4 Conclusions and caveats regarding the effects of TARP on systemic risk

Many of the research results reported in this chapter related to individual TARP bank risk have mixed or contradictory results. However, the market risk studies and studies of the overall announcement of the program suggest that TARP may have calmed financial markets. Moreover, the one study discussed here using direct measures of contributions to systemic risk suggests that TARP banks reduced these contributions very significantly relative to non-TARP banks. To the extent that this last study is correct, it may significantly understate the reduction to systemic risk from TARP. The DID framework employed measures only reduced contributions to systemic risk of the TARP banks relative to non-TARP banks, but the non-TARP banks were almost surely made safer as well.

We close Chapter 15 and Part II of the book on the empirical research on TARP with a reminder that any reductions in systemic risk from the program also imply that the findings in Chapter 14 on the effects of TARP in boosting the real economy may also be understated. Berger and Roman's (2017) findings summarized in Chapter 14 comparing states with more or less TARP bank presence exclude the systemic risk benefits to states with little or no TARP bank presence. Saving the financial system implies that banks in all states can supply more credit and boost their real economies.

References

Acharya, V. V., Engle, R., & Richardson, M. (2012). Capital shortfall: A new approach to ranking and regulating systemic risks. *The American Economic Review, 102*(3), 59−64.

Acharya, V. V., Pedersen, L. H., Philippon, T., & Richardson, M. (2017). Measuring systemic risk. *The Review of Financial Studies, 30*(1), 2−47.

Adrian, T., & Brunnermeier, M. K. (2016). CoVaR. *The American Economic Review, 106*(7), 1705.

Berger, A. N., & Roman, R. A. (2017). Did saving Wall street really save Main street? The real effects of TARP on local economic conditions. *Journal of Financial and Quantitative Analysis, 52*(5), 1827−1867.

Berger, A. N., Roman, R. A., & Sedunov, J. (2020). Did TARP reduce or increase systemic risk? The effects of government aid on financial system stability. *Journal of Financial Intermediation.* forthcoming.

Brownlees, C., & Engle, R. F. (2017). SRISK: A conditional capital shortfall measure of systemic risk. *The Review of Financial Studies, 30*(1), 48−79.

Choi, D. B. (2014). Heterogeneity and stability: Bolster the strong, not the weak. *The Review of Financial Studies, 27*(6), 1830−1867.

Coffey, N., Hrung, W. B., & Sarkar, A. (2009). *Capital constraints, counterparty risk, and deviations from covered interest rate parity* (Working Paper).

Del Viva, L., Kasanen, E., Saunders, A., & Trigeorgis, L. (2017). *Bank lottery behavior and regulatory bailouts* (Working Paper).

Duchin, R., & Sosyura, D. (2014). Safer ratios, riskier portfolios: Banks' response to government aid. *Journal of Financial Economics, 113*(1), 1–28.

Farruggio, C., Michalak, T. C., & Uhde, A. (2013). The light and dark side of TARP. *Journal of Banking and Finance, 37*(7), 2586–2604.

Huerta, D., Perez-Liston, D., & Jackson, D. (2011). The impact of TARP bailouts on stock market volatility and investor fear. *Banking and Finance Review, 3*(1), 45–54.

Nguyen, A. P., & Enomoto, C. E. (2009). The Troubled Asset Relief Program (TARP) and the financial crisis of 2007-2008. *Journal of Business and Economics Research, 7*(12).

Semaan, E., & Drake, P. P. (2016). TARP and the long-term perception of risk. *Journal of Banking and Finance, 68*, 216–235.

Empirical evidence on bank bailouts other than TARP, bail-ins, and other resolution approaches

Introduction to Part III

Part III reviews empirical evidence on methods other than TARP of resolving financially distressed banking organizations. This part of the book comprises three chapters. Chapter 16 presents empirical research on bank bailouts other than TARP, Chapter 17 reviews empirical findings on bail-ins, and Chapter 18 summarizes the findings on other resolution approaches. The material here covers research results and excludes institutional details of these resolution methods, which are provided earlier in Chapter 3.

The tree of knowledge for Part III shows leaves with the fruits of all the references for the three chapters. As for other parts of the book, each leaf shows the topic of the corresponding chapter with the references for that chapter, which bear the "fruits" of knowledge about the topic.

As a guide to Part III, Chapter 16's discussion of empirical research on bailouts other than TARP covers findings for several other US bailouts during the Global Financial Crisis, including the Federal Reserve's Expanded Discount Window (DW) and Term Auction Facilities (TAF) liquidity programs, the FDIC Temporary Debt Guarantee Program (TDGP), the Small Business Lending Fund (SBLF), Federal Home Loan Bank (FHLB) advances, and the Federal Reserve's Quantitative Easing (QE) programs. For the non-US evidence, we cover research on bailouts in other nations, including political determinants, competition, credit supply, bank risk, real economy, and systemic risk. The empirical research on bail-ins in Chapter 17 focuses on the Orderly Liquidation Authority (OLA) bail-in program in the US and bail-ins in other countries such as the BRRD Directive in the European Union. It also covers other bail-in instruments, such as contingent convertible bonds (CoCos) and double liability, as well as the 1998 resolution of the hedge fund Long-Term Capital Management (LTCM), which involved a mix of bailout and bail-in. Finally, Chapter 18 on other resolution approaches covers research related to bankruptcy/failure resolution, living wills, regulatory forbearance, and breaking up the large, systemically important institutions by size or by activities. Each chapter ends with a short conclusions-and-caveats section.

16. Empirical research on bailouts other than TARP

Acharya, Drechsler, and Schnabl, 2014; Acrey, Lee, and Yeager, 2019; Ali, 2019; Amel and Mach, 2017; Armantier, Ghysels, Sarkar, and Shrader, 2015; Ashcraft, Bech, and Frame, 2010; Barro and Lee, 2005; Bassett, Demiralp, and Lloyd, 2020; Behn, Haselmann, Kick, and Vig, 2016; Berger, Black, Bouwman, and Dlugosz, 2017; Berger, Bouwman, Kick, and Schaeck, 2016; Berger, Li, Morris, and Roman, forthcoming; Bernal, Oosterlinck, and Szafarz, 2010; Bersch, Degryse, Kick, and Stein, 2016; Blau, Hein, and Whitby, 2016; Bowe, Kolokolova, and Michalski, 2019; Brandao-Marques, Correa, and Sapriza, 2016; Buch, Krause, and Tonzer, 2019; Calderon and Schaeck, 2016; Carbó-Valverde, Cuadros-Solas, and Rodríguez-Fernández, 2019; Carpenter, Demiralp, and Eisenschmidt, 2014; Chakraborty, Goldstein, and MacKinley, 2020; Correa, Lee, Sapriza, and Suarez, 2014; Cortés and Millington, 2014; Cyree, Griffiths, and Winters, 2013; Dam and Koetter, 2012; Davidson and Simpson, 2014; Dell'Ariccia, Schnabel, and Zettelmeyer, 2002; Drechsler, Marquez-Ibanez, and Schnabl, 2016; Eichengreen and Mody, 2001; Fischer, Hainz, Rocholl, and Steffen, 2014; Gerhardt and Vander Vennet, 2017; Giannetti and Simonov, 2013; Gropp, Gruendl, and Guettler, 2014; Gropp, Gruendl, and Saadi, 2018; Gropp, Hakenes, and Schnabel, 2011; Helwege, Boyson, and Jindra, 2017; Homar, 2016; Homar and van Wijnbergen, 2017; Hryckiewicz, 2014; Kandrac and Schlusche, 2017; King, 2013; Kleymenova, 2018; Körner and Schnabel, 2013; Lee and Shin, 2008; McAndrews, Sarkar, and Wang, 2017; Nistor Mutu and Ongena, 2019; Puddu and Wälchli, 2015; Rodnyansky and Darmouni, 2017; Sedunov, 2019; Stojanovic, Vaughan, and Yeager, 2008; Thornton, 2010; Wang, 2014; Wei, Zhang, and Du, 2010; Wu, 2011; Wu, 2015.

17. Empirical research on bail-ins

Allen and Tang, 2016; Ammann, Blickle and Ehmann, 2017; Anderson, Barra, and Choi, 2018; Avdjiev, Bolton, Jiang, Kartasheva, and Bogdanova, 2017; Avdjiev, Kartasheva, and Bogdanova, 2013; Bai, Cabanilla, and Middeldorp, 2012; Beck, 2011; Beck, Da-Rocha-Lopes, and Silva, 2019; Berger, Himmelberg, Roman, and Tsyplakov, 2020; Boccuzzi and De Lisa, 2017; Bodenhorn, 2016; Bonfim and Santos, 2018; Brown, Evangelou, Stix, 2018; Conlon and Cotter, 2015; De Spiegeleer, Hoecht, and Schoutens, 2015; Duhou and Swertson, 2016; Eisen, 2016; Eszy, 1998; Evans and Quigley, 1995; Fajardo and Mendes, 2017; Flannery, 2016; Furfine, 2001; Giuliana, 2017; Grodecka and Kotidis, 2016; Grossman, 2001; Grossman and Imai, 2013; Hesse, 2016; Hickson and Turner, 2003; Iseklint and Bengtsson, 2014; Kabir and Hassan, 2004; Kho, Lee, and Stulz, 2000; Koudijs, Salisbury, and Sran, 2018; Leone, Porretta, and Riccetti, 2017; Lindner and Redak, 2017; Macey and Miller, 1992; Mutchener and Richardson, 2013; Moody's Investor Services, 2013, 2015; Neuberg, Glasserman, Kay, and Rajan, 2019; Pigrum, Reininger and Stern, 20 6; Salter, Veetil, and White, 2017; Schäfer, Schnabel, and Weder, 2016; Schmidt and Azarmi, 2015; Standard & Poor's Rating Services, 2015; Tel ah, Hassan, and Kilic, 2001; U.S. Government Accountability Office, 2014.

Part III: Empirical evidence on bank bailouts other than TARP, bail-ins, and other resolution approaches

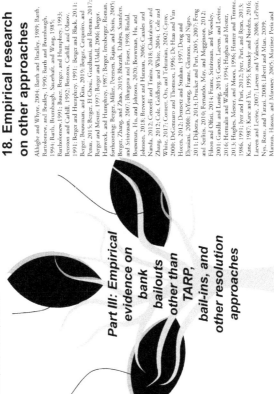

18. Empirical research on other approaches

Akhigbe and Whyte, 2004; Barth and Bradley, 1989; Barth, Bartolomew, and Bradley, 1990; Barth and Brumbaugh, 1994; Barth, Brumbaugh, Sauerhaft, and Wang, 1985; Bartholomew, 1991; Bauer, Berger, and Humphrey, 1993; Benston and Carhill, 1992; Benston, Carhill, and Olasov, 1991; Berger and Humphrey, 1991; Berger and Black, 2011; Berger, Bouwman, and Kim, 2019; Berger, Cerqueiro, and Penas, 2015; Berger, El Ghou, Guedhami, and Roman, 2017; Berger and Mester, 1997; Berger and Udell, 2006; Berger, Hanweck, and Humphrey, 1987; Berger, Irresberger, Roman, forthcoming; Berger, Miller, Petersen, Rajan, and Stein, 2005; Berger, Zhang, and Zhao, 2019; Bharath, Dahiya, Saunders, and Srinivasan, 2007; Bhargava and Fraser, 1998; Bindal, Bouwman, Hu, and Johnson, 2020; Bouwman, Hu, and Johnson, 2018; Brewoot and Hannan, 2006; Canales and Nanda, 2012; Cetorelli and Traina, 2018; Chakrabarty and Zhang, 2012; Cole, Goldberg, and White, 2004; Cole and White, 2017; Cornet, Ors, and Tehranian, 2002; Cyree, 2000; DeGennaro and Thomson, 1996; De Haas and Van Horen, 2012; Demsetz and Strahan, 1997; Deng and Elyasiani, 2008; DeYoung, Frame, Glennon, and Nigro, 2011; Dijkstra, 2013; Drucker and Puri, 2005, 2007; Feng and Serfeis, 2010; Fernando, May, and Megginson, 2012; Filson and Olfati, 2014; Frame, Srinivasan, and Woosley, 2001; Gandhi and Lustig, 2015; Goetz, Laeven, and Levine, 2016; Hermalin and Wallace, 1994; Hughes and Mester, 2013; Hughes, Mester, and Moon, 1996; Hunter and Timme, 1986, 1991; Iyer and Puri, 2012; Iyer, Puri, and Ryan, 2013; Kane, 1987; Kane and Yu, 1995; Kysucky and Norden, 2016; Laeven and Levine, 2007; Laeven and Valencia, 2008; LePetit, Nys, Rous, and Tarazi, 2008; Liberti and Mian, 2009; Mamun, Hassan, and Maroney, 2005; Mariner, Peria and Schmukler, 2001; Mester, 2018; O'Hara and Shaw, 1990; Oliveira, Schiozer, and Barros, 2015; Osili and Paulson, 2014; Petersen and Rajan, 2002; Pozso, Fricker, and Muolo, 1989; Pyle, 1995; Santos, 2014; Stein, 2002; Stiroh and Rumble, 2006; Wheelock and Wilson, 2012, 2016; White, 1991.

16

Empirical research on bailouts other than TARP

This chapter reviews empirical research on the effects of bailouts in the US other than TARP, as well as bailouts in other countries. All of these programs are described in Chapter 3. All of these bailouts have the same ultimate goals as TARP—restoring financial stability and limiting damage to the real economy. As in Part II for the TARP research, the research on these other bailouts covers a number of determinants and consequences of the programs. Section 16.1 reviews research on other bailouts in the US, and Section 16.2 discusses research on bailouts in other countries. Because there are so many bailouts over time, we limit ourselves to research on relatively recent bailouts. For the reasons discussed below, we organize Sections 16.1 and 16.2 in different fashions. Section 16.3 gives conclusions and caveats from the research summarized in this chapter.

16.1 Empirical research on bailouts other than TARP in the US

In this section, we focus on US bailouts other than TARP during the Global Financial Crisis. Most of these bailouts focused on providing liquidity to the banks, as opposed to the preferred equity injections under TARP. We organize these bailouts here into subsections by program. We discuss all of the determinants and consequences for each program for which empirical research is available in the subsection for that program. Specifically, we concentrate on the empirical research on the Federal Reserve's Discount Window and Term Auction Facilities in Section 16.1.1, the FDIC Temporary Debt Guarantee Program in Section 16.1.2, the Small Business Lending Fund in Section 16.1.3, Federal Home Loan Bank advances in Section 16.1.4, and the Federal Reserve's Quantitative Easing in Section 16.1.5.

16.1.1 Research on the Federal Reserve's expanded Discount Window and Term Auction Facilities liquidity programs

We first cover the evidence on the prevalence and usage of the Federal Reserve's liquidity provision through the expanded Discount Window (DW) and Term Auction Facilities (TAF). We then summarize research findings on the effects of these liquidity injections on bank stigma, risks, and lending.

Berger, Black, Bouwman, and Dlugosz (2017) find that the usage of DW and TAF was extraordinary during the Global Financial Crisis. About 62% of large US banks with assets over $1 billion and 20% of smaller banks took part in the programs and borrowed an average of $221 billion per day over the crisis. Several of the largest institutions accessed over $30 billion on some days. The authors also find that for both large and small banks, DW and TAF programs neither substantially substituted for nor complemented other funding sources, suggesting that these programs generally enhanced the funding of the recipient banks. Bui (2019) finds that the DW and TAF and the other Federal Reserve liquidity programs were *ex ante* efficient in that they targeted illiquid banks with low core stable funding. They also show that large banks and those with greater pre-crisis undrawn commitments were more likely to participate. In contrast to these findings, Helwege, Boyson, and Jindra (2017) conclude that the DW and TAF programs provided relatively more liquidity relief to foreign banks than to US institutions.

As briefly mentioned in Chapter 3, borrowing from the lender of last resort (LOLR) through the DW was historically associated with stigma. Such stigma can offset the benefits of the extra liquidity by harming the reputation of the participating banks and driving away other market participants. TAF was created largely for the purpose of avoiding such stigma and encouraging bank participation. A number of papers address the extent to which such stigma persisted versus was eliminated by investigating changes in bank valuation associated with these programs. Blau, Hein, and Whitby (2016) find that there were no significant stock market reactions when the details of which banks accessed DW and TAF were finally made public by the Federal Reserve after the financial crisis. However, further investigation suggests that the publicly traded banks experienced significant stock price declines and negative cumulative abnormal returns around the time that the DW and TAF borrowings were initiated, with the largest effects for banks with the greatest funds borrowed. This suggests that investors were able to trade on timely information about the Federal Reserve's programs despite the Federal Reserve trying to keep the information private, and that the programs did stigmatize the borrowers. In contrast, Kleymenova (2018) finds that DW disclosures yielded positive incremental market information and decreased banks' cost of equity and debt capital. Nevertheless, banks avoided accessing the DW facility following the disclosures, consistent with the presence of stigma. Also consistent with stigma, Armantier, Ghysels, Sarkar, and Shrader (2015) show that banks were willing to pay relatively large premia to borrow from other sources in order to avoid borrowing from the DW program during the crisis. They also uncover evidence suggesting decreases in stock prices relative to banks that did not access the DW. Cyree, Griffiths, and Winters (2013) estimate the wealth effects during the financial crisis of DW and TAF and other Federal Reserve liquidity programs for a variety of financial institutions. The authors find negative wealth effects of TAF during the height of the crisis for publicly traded banks, consistent with stigma. For the largest banks, DW was initially viewed positively, but continued use was mostly viewed negatively. Consistent with these papers, Helwege, Boyson, and Jindra (2017) find that most healthy US banks tend to avoid DW and TAF when they need liquidity.

There is also research on whether TAF announcements and operations mitigated liquidity problems in the interbank funding market, which might have reduced bank liquidity risk. The findings are mixed. Most of these studies employ a market-based liquidity risk measure, the spread between the term and overnight interbank lending rates, i.e., LIBOR-OIS (Overnight Index Swaps) spread. Thornton (2010) finds that the TAF announcement increased the risk premium and other bond rates, suggesting that market participants interpreted the announcement as a signal that the crisis was worse than previously thought. In contrast, Wu (2011) and McAndrews, Sarkar, and Wang (2017) find that TAF was associated with downward shifts of the LIBOR-OIS spread, consistent with the program easing strains in the interbank funding market. Puddu and Wälchli (2015) assess the impact of the TAF program on bank liquidity risk and find that TAF bank participants had drastically reduced funding liquidity risk after first accessing TAF funds. Bui (2019) finds that the DW and TAF programs increased moral hazard incentives and crash risk due to the stigma discussed earlier. Sedunov (2019) analyzes the effects of these liquidity programs as well as other Federal Reserve emergency actions during the crisis on systemic risk measures. The author finds that DW and TAF had mixed and inconsistent effects on systemic risk.

We finally turn to the research on the credit supply implications of DW and TAF, which is crucial to the issue of whether these programs boosted the real economy. Berger, Black, Bouwman, and Dlugosz (2017) find that banks using DW and TAF increased their lending overall, both short- and long-term, and in most loan categories. Small banks increased small business lending while large banks enhanced large business lending. Bui (2019) also finds that the participants in DW and TAF programs significantly increased lending and liquidity creation following the program, using the funds to extend loans and off-balance sheet guarantees to borrowers. Three other papers combine DW and TAF data with other programs and investigate lending. Carpenter, Demiralp, and Eisenschmidt (2014) include TAF and TARP and find that both programs were successful in increasing the supply of commercial and industrial (C&I) loans. As discussed in Chapter 11, Bassett, Demiralp, and Lloyd (2020) use combined data on a number of different government programs, including DW and TAF, and find no increases in lending at institutions receiving government support. Finally, Wu (2015) evaluates the effects of three government programs, including DW and TAF, on bank syndicated lending using the Federal Reserve Shared National Credit (SNC) data and finds only small increases in bank syndicated lending as a result of these programs.

16.1.2 Research on the FDIC Temporary Debt Guarantee Program

Ali (2019) researches the effects of the FDIC Temporary Debt Guarantee Program (TDGP). The author distinguishes between the participant and nonparticipant institutions in the program and examines the evolution of loan supply before and after the program. The paper finds that TDGP increased the liquidity available to participants, but their loan supplies declined, suggesting that the TDGP intervention may have helped banks repay other programs such as TARP.

16.1.3 Research on the Small Business Lending Fund

There is also research looking at the effects of the Small Business Lending Fund (SBLF), created as part of the Small Business Jobs Act in 2010, to address the perceived lack of credit supply to small businesses. As of 2019:Q2, the US Department of the Treasury reports that SBLF participants increased their small business lending every year between $1.0 and $15.1 billion since 2011 relative to the baseline numbers reported by current and former SBLF participants.[1] Cortes and Millington (2014) also show that aggregate small business lending has increased in every quarter since the banks received SBLF funds. As of 2014:Q1, mean lending was 142% higher than mean baseline lending for the whole sample, and the increases were experienced in all US regions. Amel and Mach (2017) use Call Report data from community banks and thrift institutions and also find that participants in the SBLF program increased their small business lending by about 10% more than their nonparticipating counterparts. However, estimates that control for the ongoing growth path in

---

[1] https://www.treasury.gov/=resource-center/=sb-programs/DocumentsSBLFTrans actions/LGR%20Oct%202019%20Final%2010-01-2019%20Clean%20v6.pdf.

small business lending indicate no statistically significant impact of SBLF participation on small business lending, leaving more questions than answers.

16.1.4 Research on Federal Home Loan Bank advances

Several research papers address issues regarding Federal Home Loan Bank (FHLB) advances during the Global Financial Crisis. Ashcraft, Bech, and Frame (2010) find that the liquidity facilities of the Federal Reserve and the FHLB System both complemented and competed with each other during the crisis. Several papers find mixed results for the risk effects of the FHLB advances. Stojanovic, Vaughan, and Yeager (2008) find that the FHLB membership induced modest increases in bank liquidity and leverage risks, while interest rate risk declined somewhat, and credit risk and overall bank failure risk were largely unaffected. Davidson and Simpson (2014) find that for banks with relatively normal default probabilities, FHLB advances were associated with decreased bank interest rate risk. However, for banks with high default probabilities, FHLB advances were related to higher bank risk. Finally, Acrey, Lee, and Yeager (2019) find that several large banks that received advances eventually failed.

16.1.5 Research on the Federal Reserve's Quantitative Easing (QE) programs

Finally, a few papers investigate the effects of the Quantitative Easing (QE) programs during and after the crisis. Recall that we treat these as bank bailouts because they involve massive purchases of toxic mortgage-backed securities (MBS) in part to help improve the conditions of banks holding these securities. This was an original plan of TARP that the US Treasury did not follow.

Several papers look at the effects of the QE programs on bank lending and the real economy. Kandrac and Schlusche (2017) find that in response to increases in reserves from the QE programs, banks increased lending and shifted toward riskier loans, such as commercial real estate, construction, C&I, and consumer loans, analogous to some of the findings for the effects of TARP shown in Chapters 11 and 12. Chakraborty, Goldstein, and MacKinlay (2020) find that banks benefiting from MBS purchases under the QE programs increased mortgage originations. However, they also find that these banks reduced commercial lending, and firms borrowing from these banks decreased their investments. The effects of the US Treasury purchases showed either positive or insignificant effects. Their findings suggest distortions caused by the mix of purchases.

Rodnyansky and Darmouni (2017) also find that banks responded heterogeneously to the different QE programs and the type of asset being targeted under each QE program. They find strong credit supply effects for QE3 for commercial banks with the most concentrated holdings of MBS on their books.

One paper looks at the effects of the monetary stimulus provided by the QE programs on liquidity creation. Bowe, Kolokolova, and Michalski (2019) find that the QE programs were ineffective in encouraging bank liquidity creation in all bank size categories.[2]

16.2 Empirical research on bailouts in other nations

As described in Chapter 3, bank bailouts outside the US are in many countries, and there are numerous different programs across these countries. These facts require a different organizational form for this section than the prior section on non-TARP US bailouts. In the interest of simplicity, we organize the discussion here into a small number of subsections based on a few key determinants and consequences of the bailouts, rather than arranging it by country or type of bailout. We arrange these subsections in as closely as possible the same order as the TARP chapters in Part II, but there are some different determinants and consequences categories covered here. We occasionally go beyond the Global Financial Crisis and the European Sovereign Debt Crisis because bailouts in some countries occurred during crises specific to those nations. Specifically, we focus on empirical research on the political determinants of non-US bailouts in Section 16.2.1, competition in Section 16.2.2, credit supply in Section 16.2.3, bank risk in Section 16.2.4, the real economy in Section 16.2.5, and systemic risk in Section 16.2.6.

16.2.1 Political and other determinants of bailouts in other nations

Behn, Haselmann, Kick, and Vig (2016) analyze bailout regimes within the German savings bank sector, including those in which local politicians involved with the banks have the power to influence bailouts. They find that decisions by local politicians who are close to the bank are distorted by personal considerations. The performance of the banks that are bailed

---

[2] Wang (2014) examines the impact of the QE programs, Operation Twist, and Forward Guidance on corporate credit markets rather than the effects on banks. The author finds mixed results, including favorable effects of QE1 in reducing risk premia for nonfinancial corporations, and unfavorable effects of QE2 on the Chicago Board Options Exchange (CBOE) VIX "fear index."

out by local politicians is also considerably worse than banks that are supported by the savings bank association. Berger, Li, Morris, and Roman (forthcoming) use an international sample covering banks in 92 countries over 2000-2014 and find that banks' government bailout support is significantly influenced by national culture values. They find that masculine nations — which emphasize competitiveness, achievements, material success, and less sympathy for the weak — are less likely to bail out their institutions in distress.

16.2.2 Bailouts in other nations and competition

Several papers look at the impacts of bailouts on competition. Gropp, Hakenes, and Schnabel (2011) use data for banks from OECD countries and find that bailouts give rise to market distortions by encouraging competitors of bailed-out institutions to take on more risk and become more aggressive. Calderon and Schaeck (2016) use country-level data for 124 countries and find that government interventions such as liquidity support, recapitalizations, and nationalizations trigger large increases in competition (lower Lerner indices and lower net interest margins) in the banking systems. In addition, higher frequencies of interventions coincide with larger market shares of "zombie banks" with negative economic net worth, suggesting an unfavorable social distortion that also increases risk. King (2013) investigates contagion and competition effects of bank bailouts announced in October 2008 by five countries, and finds that government bailouts are associated with competitive advantages for recipient banks as reflected in stock price reactions. Carbó-Valverde, Cuadros-Solas, and Rodríguez-Fernández (2019) use a sample of 121 underwriters that issue fixed corporate bonds from the Dealogic Debt Capital Markets database to explore the effects of bank bailouts on competition in the underwriting business. Using all the bailout measures on underwriters active in the European corporate bond markets from 2006 to 2013, they find that banks with large market shares (reputable banks) suffer market share losses after being bailed out, while capital infusions have positive impacts on the market share of those with smaller market shares (nonreputable underwriters).

16.2.3 Bailouts in other nations and credit supply

Homar (2016) analyzes the effects of European bank recapitalizations on lending, funding, and asset quality over 2000–2013, and finds that banks that receive large enough capital injections boost the supply of credit, access supplementary deposits, and improve their balance sheets, while banks with small recapitalization amounts show opposite effects.

His results highlight that both the banks' eligibility for bailouts and the actual injection amounts are important to credit supply outcomes.

Giannetti and Simonov (2013) investigate the effects of bank bailouts on credit supply during the Japanese banking crisis in the 1990s. They find that results differ dramatically depending on the size of capital injections. Large capital injections result in larger loans to creditworthy relationship borrowers and reduced exposure to low-quality or "zombie" firms, while small capital injections yield more credit to the zombie firms.

16.2.4 Bailouts in other nations and bank risk

A number of studies suggest that bailouts result in higher risk-taking. Dam and Koetter (2012) focus on German bailouts in which banks receive capital injections from their responsible banking association's insurance fund.[3] The authors find that a higher probability of bailout increases banks' risk-taking significantly, consistent with increased moral hazard. Their effects are primarily due to mutually owned cooperative banks in Germany. Hryckiewicz (2014) investigates the effects of bailouts on bank risk using data on banks rescued during 23 financial crises in 23 countries. The author finds that bailouts increase bank risk significantly, and that blanket guarantees, nationalizations, and asset management companies contribute the most to increased risk. Using a sample for 53 countries, Brandao-Marques, Correa, and Sapriza (2016) also find that more government support is associated with more risk-taking, consistent with strong moral hazard effects from bailouts. The authors also suggest that restricting banks' range of activities can ameliorate the moral hazard problems induced by government support. Gerhardt and Vander Vennet (2017) compare 114 European banks before and after receiving state support during the Global Financial Crisis. They find that the bailed-out banks hardly improve their performance indicators in the years following government aid, suggesting that bailouts may not be able to restore bank health. Drechsler, Drechsel, Marquez-Ibanez, and Schnabl (2016) analyze LOLR lending during the European sovereign debt crisis. Their results suggest that the LOLR funds resulted in a reallocation of risky assets, such as distressed sovereign debt, from strongly to weakly capitalized banks, making the financial system riskier.

Other studies suggest lower bank risk from bailouts or have mixed results. Berger, Bouwman, Kick, and Schaeck (2016) use German data and

---

[3] As discussed in Chapter 3, such capital injections could be considered either bailouts because the funds are from a mutual organization rather than individual bank counterparties, or bail-ins because they are not provided by a government entity or organization supported by government. We simply choose to treat them as bailouts, as they are typically referred to in the literature.

a variety of government interventions in banks as well as capital injections by both the government and bankers associations. The authors find that both regulatory interventions and capital support are associated with significant reductions in risk-taking. They also find that regulatory interventions are linked to significant reductions in liquidity creation. Homar and van Wijnbergen (2017) analyze recessions after 69 systemic banking crises from 1980 to 2014. They find positive and highly significant effects of bank recapitalizations on the probability of recovery, but not for other bailout measures. Three studies, Körner and Schnabel (2013), Fischer, Hainz, Rocholl, and Steffen (2014), and Gropp, Gruendl, and Guettler (2014), use the same quasi-natural experiment in Germany under which bailouts were effectively rescinded. Public guarantees which protected creditors of German savings banks were removed by the government for eight German banks. The first two studies find that these banks increase lending to risky borrowers. This may suggest the franchise value associated with the bailouts may have resulted in the banks choosing safer portfolios. In contrast, Gropp, Gruendl, and Guettler (2014) use the same experiment and find that the banks reduce portfolio risks, suggesting that the bailouts are associated with more risk, rather than less risk.

We next turn to some research on the issue of sovereign risk, which feeds back to bank risk. When governments spend large sums bailing out their banks, they can create large deficits that increase the risks of their sovereign debt. Many banks invest heavily in such debt, so that bank risks may be significantly increased by these sovereign risk problems. As discussed briefly in Chapter 20, the Basel I and II international capital agreements in effect before and during the Global Financial Crisis required little or no capital to be held against risky sovereign debt, encouraging banks to take on these risks.

Acharya, Drechsler, and Schnabl (2014) use bank-level and country-level data from the Eurozone between 2007 and 2011 to examine the links between bank bailouts and sovereign credit risk. They find that greater financial sector distress predicts larger bank bailouts, higher sovereign credit risk, and greater debt-to-GDP ratios across countries. They also discover that bank bailouts triggered the rise in sovereign credit risk in Eurozone countries in 2008, as measured by credit default swap (CDS) rates on European sovereigns, and in turn weakened the financial sector. They also document that the post-bailout changes in sovereign CDS explain the changes in bank CDS even after controlling for aggregate and bank-level determinants of credit spreads, confirming the existence of a bank-sovereign feedback loop. Consistent with these findings, Correa, Lee, Sapriza, and Suarez (2014) use data for banks in 37 countries from 1995 to 2011 and find that sovereign credit downgrades result in greater negative shocks to stock returns for banks that have higher expected government support.[4]

16.2.5 Bailouts in other nations and the real economy

Gropp, Gruendl, and Saadi (2018) exploit the same quasi-natural experiment of guarantees removal in Germany discussed earlier and employ bank-firm matches to examine the real effects of government guarantees. They find that these guarantees effectively direct bank credit to low-productivity, inefficient firms, and keep unproductive firms in business for too long, resulting in inefficient allocation of financial resources.

Bersch, Degryse, Kick, and Stein (2020) analyze real effects of bailouts using German firms and their banks from 2000 to 2013. They find potentially unproductive lending that increases in the connected firms' probability of default. They also find that relationship and transaction banks that are bailed out generate very different bank-induced risk effects. While transaction banks lead to an increase in the probability of defaults for firms with above-median riskiness, relationship banks seem to shield high-risk firms from increases in the probability of default, while leading to a somewhat higher probability of default for higher quality firms. Thus, distressed relationship banks are likely to evergreen their lower quality customers and are less able to perform relationship lending for higher quality firms.

16.2.6 Bailouts in other nations and systemic risk

Finally, two studies analyze the effects of bailouts on systemic risk. Buch, Krause, and Tonzer (2019) use market data for about 80 public European banks from 15 EU countries over 2005—13 to measure each bank's contribution to systemic risk ($SRISK$) at the national and EU levels. They find that European banks that received bailouts are associated with increased contributions to systemic risk at both national and EU levels,

---

[4] Emerging countries during financial crises often rely for financial support on country bailouts from international authorities such as the International Monetary Fund (IMF). Some of these funds are likely channeled to the banking sector. Similar to US bailout evidence on TARP, a country's political connections positively affect the probability and size of the IMF bailout (Barro and Lee, 2005), and IMF bailouts have typically restored rather than reduced investor confidence during country financial crises (Wei, Zhang, and Du, 2010). However, effects of IMF bailouts on moral hazard are mixed, with some papers finding reduced moral hazard (e.g., Eichengreen and Mody, 2001; Dell'Ariccia, Zettelmeyer, and Schnabel, 2002) , while others find increased moral hazard (e.g., Dell'Ariccia, Zettelmeyer, and Schnabel, 2002; Lee and Shin (2008); Bernal, Oosterlinck, and Szafarz, 2010).

but there is considerable heterogeneity across countries and banks. Nistor Mutu and Ongena (2019) analyze a sample of 110 banking institutions from 22 European countries and bank-specific bailout events over 2008–2014. They distinguish among different types of bailouts. They find that guarantees, which account for most of the EU bailouts, have limited effects in reducing systemic risk. In contrast, recapitalizations immediately decrease the banks' contributions to systemic risk. However, the effect is generally short-lived, consistent with the TARP evidence provided in Chapter 15.

16.3 Conclusions and caveats from the research on bailouts other than TARP

The research on the non-TARP bailouts in the US and around the world summarized in this chapter leaves a mixed and incomplete picture. Much of the research suggests that some types of bailouts are successful in increasing bank lending, but this is often at a cost. Bailouts often appear to stigmatize the banks, increase their risk, and their lending may often prop up unproductive borrowing firms that do not help the real economy. The findings on systemic risk are mixed at best, and some of the bailouts may have resulted in distressed sovereign debt.

We return to these issues when we tote up social costs and benefits in Chapter 27 and address policy implications in Chapter 28. There is also clearly much less research on these other bailouts than on TARP. This suggests more future research is needed, particularly targeted at the most important issues of the real economy and systemic risk, as discussed further in Chapter 29.

References

Acharya, V. V., Drechsler, I., & Schnabl, P. (2014). A pyrrhic victory?: Bank bailouts and sovereign credit risk. *The Journal of Finance, 69*(6), 2689–2739.

Acrey, J. C., Lee, W. Y., & Yeager, T. J. (2019). Can Federal Home Loan Banks effectively self-regulate lending to influential banks? *Journal of Banking Regulation, 20*(2), 197–210.

Ali, M. (2019). *Three essays on banking policy and government intervention in the US banking sector* (Ph.D. dissertation). Bangor University.

Amel, D., & Mach, T. (2017). The impact of the small business lending fund on community bank lending to small businesses. *Economic Notes, Review of Banking, Finance and Monetary Economics, 46*(2), 307–328.

Armantier, O., Ghysels, E., Sarkar, A., & Shrader, J. (2015). Discount window stigma during the 2007–2008 financial crisis. *Journal of Financial Economics, 118*(2), 317–335.

Ashcraft, A., Bech, M. L., & Frame, W. S. (2010). The Federal Home Loan Bank system: The lender of next-to-last resort? *Journal of Money, Credit, and Banking, 42*(4), 551–583.

Barro, R. J., & Lee, J.-W. (2005). IMF programs: Who is chosen and what are the effects? *Journal of Monetary Economics, 52*(7), 1245–1269.

Bassett, W., Demiralp, S., & Lloyd, N. (2020). Government support of banks and bank lending. *Journal of Banking and Finance, 112*, 105177.

Behn, M., Haselmann, R., Kick, T., & Vig, V. (2016). *The political economy of bank bailouts* (Working Paper).

Berger, A. N., Black, L. K., Bouwman, C. H. S., & Dlugosz, J. (2017). Bank loan supply responses to Federal Reserve emergency liquidity facilities. *Journal of Financial Intermediation, 32*, 1−15.

Berger, A. N., Bouwman, C. H. S., Kick, T., & Schaeck, K. (2016). Bank liquidity creation following regulatory interventions and capital support. *Journal of Financial Intermediation, 26*, 115−141.

Berger A.N., Li X., Morris C. and Roman R.A. The effects of cultural values on bank failures around the world. Journal of Financial and Quantitative Analysis, Forthcoming.

Bernal, O., Oosterlinck, K., & Szafarz, A. (2010). Observing bailout expectations during a total eclipse of the sun. *Journal of International Money and Finance, 29*(7), 1193−1205.

Bersch, J., Degryse, H., Kick, T., & Stein, I. (2020). The real effects of bank distress: Evidence from bank bailouts in Germany. *Journal of Corporate Finance, 60*, 101521.

Blau, B. M., Hein, S. E., & Whitby, R. J. (2016). The financial impact of lender-of-last-resort borrowing from the Federal Reserve during the financial crisis. *Journal of Financial Research, 39*(2), 179−206.

Bowe, M., Kolokolova, O., & Michalski, M. (2019). *Too big to care, too small to matter: Macro-financial policy and bank liquidity creation* (Working Paper).

Brandao-Marques, L., Correa, M. R., & Sapriza, M. H. (2016). *International evidence on government support and risk taking in the banking sector* (Working Paper).

Buch, C. M., Krause, T., & Tonzer, L. (2019). Drivers of systemic risk: Do national and European perspectives differ? *Journal of International Money and Finance, 91*, 160−176.

Bui, C. (2019). *Bank regulation and financial stability. Doctoral dissertation.* Sydney: University of Technology.

Calderon, C., & Schaeck, K. (2016). The effects of government interventions in the financial sector on banking competition and the evolution of zombie banks. *Journal of Financial and Quantitative Analysis, 51*(4), 1391−1436.

Carbó-Valverde, S., Cuadros-Solas, P., & Rodríguez-Fernández, F. (2019). *Do bank bailouts have an impact on the underwriting business?* (Working Paper).

Carpenter, S., Demiralp, S., & Eisenschmidt, J. (2014). The effectiveness of non-standard monetary policy in addressing liquidity risk during the financial crisis: The experiences of the Federal Reserve and the European Central Bank. *Journal of Economic Dynamics and Control, 43*, 107−129.

Chakraborty, I., Goldstein, I., & MacKinlay, A. (2020). Monetary stimulus and bank lending. *Journal of Financial Economics, 136*(1), 189−218.

Correa, R., Lee, K.-H., Sapriza, H., & Suarez, G. A. (2014). Sovereign credit risk, banks' government support, and bank stock returns around the world. *Journal of Money, Credit, and Banking, 46*(s1), 93−121.

Cortés, K., & Millington, S. (2014). *Gauging the impact of the small business lending fund.* Federal Reserve Bank of Cleveland. Economic Trends.

Cyree, K. B., Griffiths, M. D., & Winters, D. B. (2013). Federal Reserve financial crisis lending programs and bank stock returns. *Journal of Banking and Finance, 37*(10), 3819−3829.

Dam, L., & Koetter, M. (2012). Bank bailouts and moral hazard: Evidence from Germany. *The Review of Financial Studies, 25*(8), 2343−2380.

Davidson, T., & Simpson, W. G. (2016). Federal Home Loan Bank advances and bank risk. *Journal of Economics and Finance, 40*(1), 137−156.

Dell'Ariccia, G., Mr, Zettelmeyer, J., Mr, & Schnabel, I., Ms (2002). *Moral hazard and international crisis lending: A test.* International Monetary Fund.

Drechsler, I., Drechsel, T., Marques-Ibanez, D., & Schnabl, P. (2016). Who borrows from the lender of last resort? *The Journal of Finance, 71*(5), 1933–1974.

Eichengreen, B., & Mody, A. (2001). *Bail-ins, bailouts, and borrowing costs* (Working Paper).

Fischer, M., Hainz, C., Rocholl, J., & Steffen, S. (2014). *Government guarantees and bank risk taking incentives* (Working Paper).

Gerhardt, M., & Vander Vennet, R. (2017). Bank bailouts in Europe and bank performance. *Finance Research Letters, 22*, 74–80.

Giannetti, M., & Simonov, A. (2013). On the real effects of bank bailouts: Micro evidence from Japan. *American Economic Journal: Macroeconomics, 5*(1), 135–167.

Gropp, R., Gruendl, C., & Guettler, A. (2014). The impact of public guarantees on bank risk-taking: Evidence from a natural experiment. *Review of Finance, 18*(2), 457–488.

Gropp R., Guettler A. and Saadi V., Public bank guarantees and allocative efficiency. Journal of Monetary Economics, Forthcoming.

Gropp, R., Hakenes, H., & Schnabel, I. (2011). Competition, risk-shifting, and public bail-out policies. *The Review of Financial Studies, 24*(6), 2084–2120.

Helwege, J., Boyson, N. M., & Jindra, J. (2017). Thawing frozen capital markets and backdoor bailouts: Evidence from the fed's liquidity programs. *Journal of Banking and Finance, 76*, 92–119.

Homar, T. (2016). *Bank recapitalizations and lending: A little is not enough* (ESRB Working Paper).

Homar, T., & van Wijnbergen, S. J. G. (2017). Bank recapitalization and economic recovery after financial crises. *Journal of Financial Intermediation, 32*, 16–28.

Hryckiewicz, A. (2014). What do we know about the impact of government interventions in the banking sector? An assessment of various bailout programs on bank behavior. *Journal of Banking and Finance, 46*, 246–265.

Kandrac, J., & Schlusche, B. (2017). *Quantitative easing and bank risk taking: Evidence from lending* (Working Paper).

King, M. R. (2013). *The contagion and competition effects of bank bailouts announced in October 2008* (Working Paper).

Kleymenova, A. (2018). Consequences of mandated bank liquidity disclosures. In *Chicago Booth Research Paper, no. 16–04*.

Körner, T., & Schnabel, I. (2013). *Abolishing public guarantees in the absence of market discipline* (Working Paper).

Lee, J. W., & Shin, K. (2008). IMF bailouts and moral hazard. *Journal of International Money and Finance, 27*(5), 816–830.

McAndrews, J., Sarkar, A., & Wang, Z. (2017). The effect of the Term Auction Facility on the London Interbank Offered Rate. *Journal of Banking and Finance, 83*, 135–152.

Nistor Mutu, S., & Ongena, S. (2019). *The impact of policy interventions on systemic risk across banks* (Working Paper).

Puddu, S., & Wälchli, A. (2015). *TARP effect on bank lending behaviour: Evidence from the last financial crisis* (Working Paper).

Rodnyansky, A., & Darmouni, O. M. (2017). The effects of Quantitative Easing on bank lending behavior. *The Review of Financial Studies, 30*(11), 3858–3887.

Sedunov, J. (2019). *The Federal Reserve's impact on systemic risk during the financial crisis* (Working Paper).

Stojanovic, D., Vaughan, M. D., & Yeager, T. J. (2008). Do Federal Home Loan Bank membership and advances increase bank risk-taking? *Journal of Banking and Finance, 32*(5), 680–698.

Thornton, M. (2010). Hoover, Bush, and great depressions. *Quarterly Journal of Austrian Economics, 13*(3), 86.

Wang, L. (2014). *The impact of unconventional monetary policies: Evidence from corporate credit markets* (Working Paper).

Wei, S.-J., Zhang, Z., & Du, Q. (2010). Does the global fireman inadvertently add fuel to the fire? New evidence from institutional investors' response to IMF program announcements. *Journal of International Money and Finance, 29*(4), 728–741.

Wu, T. (2011). The U.S. money market and the Term Auction Facility in the financial crisis of 2007–2009. *The Review of Economics and Statistics, 93*, 617–31.

Wu, D. (2015). The effects of government capital and liquidity support programs on bank lending: Evidence from the syndicated corporate credit market. *Journal of Financial Stability, 21*, 13–25.

Empirical research on bail-ins

Chapter 17 discusses empirical research on the effects of bank bail-ins, in which the aid to distressed banks is provided by the private sector. Section 17.1 reviews the research on the bail-ins in the US via the Orderly Liquidation Authority (OLA). Section 17.2 reviews the research on the bail-ins in several European countries via the Bank Recovery and Resolution Directive (BRRD). Section 17.3 covers contingent convertibles (CoCos) that are used in some European nations. Sections 17.4 and 17.5 discuss other historical episodes of bail-in-like tools such as the double liability on shareholders used by US regulators prior to the Great Depression (17.4), and the resolution case of the hedge fund Long-Term Capital Management (LTCM) in 1998 (17.5). Section 17.6 provides some concluding remarks.

17.1 Research on the OLA bail-in program in the US

While there have been substantial policy debates on OLA resolution, there is little empirical research on it because bail-ins under OLA have not been triggered as of this date. We first discuss some evidence on whether the OLA bail-in framework affected the bank behavior, and then we review evidence on the market perception of OLA.

Investigating effects of OLA bail-in expectations on bank capital structure behavior, Berger, Himmelberg, Roman, and Tsyplakov (2020) conduct empirical tests using data on the top 50 publicly traded US BHCs for the bailout period prior to the Global Financial Crisis (2000:Q3-2007:Q2)—when bailouts of large institutions were most likely expected, and the bail-in period (2010:Q3-2017:Q2)—after the 2010 Dodd−Frank Act introduced OLA and bail-ins were most likely expected for the largest institutions. They consider the eight very large, complex US BHCs designated as Global Systemically Important Banks (G-SIBs) as the treatment group most likely to be subject to bailouts and bail-ins. They show that switching from *expectations* of bailouts pre-crisis to *expectations* of bail-ins post-crisis results in

275

improved BHC capital incentives. They find that G-SIBs increased their capital ratios statistically and economically significantly more than the control group when moving from the bailout period to the bail-in period. In addition, G-SIBs more than doubled their adjustment speeds toward target capital ratios when changing from the bailout to the bail-in period, while those in the control group did not significantly change their adjustment speeds, consistent with predictions that the bail-in regime provided incentives to recapitalize.

Other studies investigate market perceptions of OLA. While traditionally, the biggest banks and their stakeholders enjoyed TBTF government protections, part of the intention of OLA is to remove perceptions of these protections and encourage market participants to monitor and discipline banks more intensively (e.g., Eisen, 2016). While opinions are mixed, one initial market reaction is demonstrated by the acknowledgment of the regime change by the major credit rating agencies. These agencies have removed the "uplift" from the expectations of government support from the ratings of US G-SIBs after the Dodd–Frank Act OLA resolution implementation.[1] S&P and Moody's precisely cited the Federal Reserve's OLA resolution regulation as a basis for doing so (Moody's Investor Service, 2013, 2015; Standard and Poor's Rating Services, 2015). In addition, a study by the U.S. Government Accountability Office (2014) suggests that the competitive advantages of the largest banks of lower costs during the 2007–2009 financial crisis have declined or reversed in more recent years after the Dodd–Frank Act OLA implementation, again consistent with reduced government support expectations for these banks.

Bai, Cabanilla, and Middeldorp (2012) find that the OLA resolution regime has increased the CDS market's expectations of default for G-SIBs by approximately 20 basis points, or by about a fifth of the average CDS-implied default probability for these institutions. This finding is consistent with the CDS market taking into account that senior bondholders may take more losses in bank resolution. However, Afonso, Blank, and Santos (2018) find that bond and CDS market participants have different opinions on the credibility and effectiveness of OLA from credit rating agencies.

---

[1] See page 19 from https://home.treasury.gov/sites/default/files/2018-02/OLA_REPORT.pdf, https://www.capitaliq.com/CIQDotNet/CreditResearch/RenderArticle.aspx?articleId=1490452&SctArtId=357868&from=CM&nsl_code=LIME&source ObjectId=9438258&sourceRevId=1&fee_ind=N&exp_date=20251202-14:59:54, and https://libertystreeteconomics.newyorkfed.org/2015/06/what-do-rating-agencies-think-about-too-big-to-fail-since-dodd-frank.html. For example, Moody's notes that "Today's rating actions reflect strengthened US bank resolution tools, prompted by the Dodd–Frank Act, which affect Moody's assumptions about US government support."

17.2 Research on bail-ins in other countries

Most of the existing empirical research on bail-ins in countries other than the US focuses on the effects of bail-ins on market discipline. Recapitalizing banks using bail-ins may encourage bank creditors and other stakeholders to better monitor and assess risk, while also improving the *ex ante* behavior of bank management in order to avoid bail-ins. All of these may ultimately help decrease moral hazard at large institutions and reduce systemic risk. The literature finds improvements in market discipline by several sets of stakeholders—depositors, bondholders, shareholders, and CDS holders—as a result of bail-ins, as discussed next.

Brown, Evangelou, and Stix (2018) examine household depositor behavior changes following the 2013 banking crisis in Cyprus. As mentioned in Chapter 3, during this crisis, the two largest banks in the country were resolved involving a bail-in of uninsured depositors and other debtholders. The authors use anonymized survey data comprising households with differential exposures to the bailed-in banks: uninsured depositors, subordinated debtholders, and shareholders. They find that after the crisis, households significantly reduce their various holdings in the resolved banks and increase their cash holdings. This behavior is stronger for households that experienced a bail-in of deposits or subordinated debt than for households that held equity or did not suffer any loss.

Bonfim and Santos (2018) also use the same Cyprus bail-in event in 2013 as a quasi-natural experiment and show that bail-in events can have non-negligible spillover effects and increase market discipline even among depositors in other unaffected EU countries. In response to the Cyprus crisis, on March 16th, 2013, European authorities announced losses on all Cypriot bank deposits, including those insured by the Cyprus deposit insurance scheme (haircuts of 6.7% for insured and 9.9% for uninsured over €100,000). The decision was later reversed on March 25th, and only uninsured depositors suffered losses, but the initial announcement set off panic and contagion across not only in Cyprus, but also in other EU countries, questioning the credibility of the deposit insurance in Europe. The authors find that depositors in Portugal reacted to this event by withdrawing deposits, even though there was no strong direct economic or financial link. The reaction was stronger for deposits held at weaker banks with less capital and lower profitability that may be more likely to fail, suggesting that depositors reacted based on bank health characteristics.

Boccuzzi and De Lisa (2017) document depositors' and creditors' discipline in reaction to the first application of the BRRD bail-ins in Italy in 2015 of four small failing banks. Using proprietary data from the Italian Deposit Guarantee Scheme, they find that since the start of the banks' bail-in resolution, depositors and other creditors take flight dramatically, while resolved banks incur a significant loss of total funding. The run-off is stronger for uninsured deposits than for insured deposits. Market discipline also extends to deposits of banks that are solvent but send signals of weakness (capital shortfalls), which become infected as well.

Giuliana (2017) focuses on the discipline of bondholders. The author uses bond data for financial institutions in six major European countries—Italy, Spain, UK, Germany, Austria, and France—and finds increased market discipline on banks by bondholders around events related to the legislative process of bail-ins as well as events of actual impositions of bail-ins. First, events indicating an increased commitment toward the bail-ins regime increased the difference in yield between unsecured (i.e., subject to bail-ins) and secured (i.e., not subject to bail-ins) bonds, consistent with authorities' commitment to the bail-in principle being credible. Second, actual bail-ins increase investors' incentives to incorporate the default probability of a specific bank into the price of its securities, consistent again with an improvement in market discipline.

Schafer, Schnabel, and Weder (2016) provide evidence on discipline by shareholders. These authors exploit cases of European banks being restructured where creditors were bailed-in. They document falling bank stock prices after the bail-in event in Cyprus, consistent with market discipline by shareholders.

Two papers test market discipline to bail-in events using credit default swap (CDS) data. Schafer, Schnabel, and Weder (2016) mentioned above find evidence of increased CDS spreads after bail-in events, most notably after the bail-in in Cyprus. They find that reactions are stronger for banks in countries with low fiscal capacity, which may be more likely to use bail-ins rather than bailouts to resolve banks. Also, as expected, actual bail-ins lead to stronger market reactions than the legal implementation of the bail-in resolution regime. Somewhat in contrast, Neuberg, Glasserman, Kay, and Rajan (2019) use the CDS premium to extract the market-implied probability of government support. They find that despite the fact that market expectations of government support initially decreased and market discipline increased, expectations have increased again since 2016 to pre-reform levels. This indicates that the introduction of BRRD may not have reduced expectations of government support for distressed banks as intended, raising doubts about the credibility of bail-ins.

Closely related to market reactions to bail-ins, two papers study the composition and ownership of EU banks' bail-inable creditors that are likely the most affected ones in bail-in episodes, and report opposing results. Lindner and Redak (2017) focus on the potential impact of bail-ins on households in the EU. Using the Eurosystem Household Finance and Consumption Survey (HFCS), they find that the participation rate of households in bail-inable instruments, in particular bank bonds, is rather low, between 0.2% and 5.5%. The authors suggest that such households may generally earn higher incomes, so their resilience to shocks from asset devaluation is quite high. In contrast, Pigrum, Reininger, and Stern (2016) analyze the structure of the demand and supply side of bail-in-able bank debt securities in each euro-area country, drawing on the Securities Holdings Statistics of the ECB for evidence. They find that the euro household sector holds a significant share of bail-inable bank debt securities, accounting for about one-fourth of the total. This implies that bail-in applications may have some negative impacts on households, with potential implications for financial stability and consumer protection.

Finally, an effective bank resolution approach needs to solve the trade-off between imposing market discipline and minimizing the effects of a bank failure on the rest of the financial system and the real economy (e.g., Beck, 2011). Bail-ins are supposed to minimize this trade-off because part of the bank continues to operate while moral hazard is reduced due to creditors' increased expectations of being bailed-in in case of distress (e.g., Giuliana, 2019). However, whether this is achieved is an empirical question. There is very little empirical evidence on the effects of bail-ins on the broader systemic risk and the real economy. Focusing on systemic risk effects, Conlon and Cotter (2014) apply a bail-in framework retrospectively in the context of failed European banks during the Global Financial Crisis. They argue that bail-in can be effective in reducing systemic risk by limiting the impact of bank runs by depositors and making bank debt more risk-sensitive. Their analysis suggests that if bail-ins were utilized in the last crisis, shareholders and subordinated bondholders would have been the main losers from the large impairment losses realized by failed European banks. Losses to senior debtholders would have been small, and depositors would have suffered no losses. Boccuzzi and De Lisa (2017) (cited above) find that bail-ins may work best when the crisis is not systemic. However, in the presence of a systemic crisis, funding outflows can be very large, weaken market confidence, and affect other creditors with adverse effects on financial system stability. Also related to systemic risk, Leone, Porretta, and Riccetti (2017) use panel data analysis on a sample of large European banks and find that in 2016, there was an increase in stock market volatility around the introduction of the BRRD bail-in regime. The stock volatility was more pronounced for Italy, likely due to the strong presence of retail investors owning bank shares in that country, who might have understood the risk related to BRRD only after the burden-sharing of the four Italian banks in November 2015.

Focusing on the real economic effects of bail-ins, Beck, Da-Rocha-Lopes, and Silva (2019) find some less favorable consequences. They use a quasi-natural experiment involving the unexpected failure and bail-in of a major bank in Portugal—Banco de Espirito Santo—and a unique dataset of matched firm-bank data on credit exposures from the Portuguese credit register. They find that banks more exposed to the bail-in significantly reduced credit supply after the shock, and firms more exposed to the intervention (particularly small to mid-size enterprises (SMEs)) register a tightening of credit conditions as well as lower investment and employment due to the increased uncertainty induced by the bail-in. However, these firms were subsequently able to compensate for the credit crunch with funding offered by other institutions. They argue that the negative real effects uncovered suggest that the bail-in mechanism is not a silver bullet that can solve all the problems.

17.3 Other bail-in instruments: Contingent convertible bonds

As mentioned in Part I, CoCos are special hybrid bonds with loss-absorbing capacity. These instruments have been proposed as bail-in instruments. When the issuing bank's capital falls below a certain level, the bond can be written down or can be converted into equity. Since the first issuance of CoCo bonds in 2009, this market has continued to grow and had a size of over €120 billion in 2015 (De Spiegeleer, Hocht, and Schoutens, 2015).

Some research on CoCos investigates which investors and banks use these instruments. Avdjiev, Kartasheva, and Bogdanova (2013) find that the bulk of the demand for CoCos is from small investors, while the spreads of CoCos over other subordinated debt greatly depend on the trigger level and the loss absorption mechanism. CoCo spreads are more correlated with the spreads of other subordinated debt than with CDS spreads and equity prices. Fajardo and Mendes (2017) find that banks that issue CoCo bonds are typically large and have high leverage, aiming to meet the Basel III rules and replace debt with equity funding. Avdjiev, Bogdanova, Bolton, Jiang, and Kartasheva (2017) also find that large banks with relatively adequate core capital bases are among the early adopters of CoCos.

Similar to the other bail-in research, the literature on CoCos finds that these instruments can also be associated with increased market discipline (e.g., Iseklint and Bengtsson, 2014; Duhonj and Sivertsen, 2016; Flannery, 2016; Hesse, 2016). For example, Iseklint and Bengtsson (2014) analyze the CoCo market from the first issues during 2009-2014, covering a sample of 118 CoCos. They find evidence of market discipline, suggesting that investors are sensitive to the risk profile of the issuing bank, and several contract features prove to have significant relationships with the spread of these instruments. Avdjiev, Bogdanova, Bolton, Jiang, and Kartasheva (2017) also analyze banks' securities pricing post-CoCo issuance and show that investors in CoCos regard these instruments as risky and place a significant likelihood on conversion. Similarly, Hesse (2016) finds that investors are aware of the incentive problem created in writing down CoCo bonds, and demand a yield premium for bonds with this feature.

Nevertheless, similar to the other bail-ins, the effects of CoCos on risk are ambiguous. Some papers find increased stability effects (e.g., Allen and Tang, 2016; Ammann, Blickle, and Ehmann, 2017; Avdjiev, Bogdanova, Bolton, Jiang, and Kartasheva, 2017). For example, Allen and Tang (2016) find evidence that CoCos can lead to reduced systemic risk by automatically recapitalizing banks during financial crises if the trigger mechanism is properly designed. They propose a dual trigger mechanism based on the aggregate systemic risk in the banking system (CATFIN) and the individual bank's contribution to overall systemic risk ($\Delta CoVaR$). The dual trigger is highly correlated with system-wide insolvency risk and prices systemic risk. Using a 99% trigger cut-off, systemic CoCos issued by Lehman Brothers and Bear Stearns would have been triggered in November 2007, well prior to their actual takeover and bankruptcy, respectively. Consistently, Avdjiev, Bogdanova, Bolton, Jiang, and Kartasheva (2017) find that CoCo issuance reduces bank credit risk, leading to a decline in the issuers' CDS spreads. Ammann, Blickle, and Ehmann (2017) investigate the effects of CoCo bond issuances by 34 global banks between January 2009 and June 2014. They find positive abnormal stock returns and negative CDS spread changes in the immediate post-announcement period, which they interpret as evidence of a lower probability of costly bankruptcy proceedings.

Other papers find that CoCos may lower financial stability. For example, Schmidt and Azarmi (2015) analyze the effects of the revolutionary use of CoCos in Europe by Lloyds Banking Group in 2009. They document a reduction in the bank's market value and an increase in the bank's CDS spread following the announcement of the bank's intention to issue CoCos.

17.4 Other historical bail-ins: Double liability

As mentioned in Part I, double liability was common in the US before the introduction of the federal deposit guarantees in 1933. Many US states imposed such double or even greater liability on bank shareholders as a feature of their banking charters to constrain moral hazard and protect depositors. Similar systems were in place in other parts of the world in the 18th century, such as in Scotland after the Banking Copartnership Regulation Act of 1825 and in the UK after the passage of the Banking Copartnership Act of 1826.[2] The Global Financial Crisis brought this mechanism back into attention as a potential way to increase the bank owners' skin into the game.

---

[2] See Salter, Veetil, and White (2017) for more details on the international experience with double liability in banking.

A number of studies investigate whether double liability can make banks safer and find mixed results. Some studies find that double liability helps reduce bank risk. Based on cross-sectional studies that compare single with extended liability systems, Grossman (2001) investigates US bank failures over 1892–1930 and finds that extended liability reduced the risk of bank failure. Mitchener and Richardson (2013) find that banks operating in multiple-liability states were safer because they used less leverage and converted each dollar of capital into fewer loans, and thus could survive larger loan losses (as a fraction of their portfolio) than banks in limited liability states. Esty (1998) investigates 27 banks in California that switched from unlimited liability to double liability and finds that banks in states with stricter liability rules had balance sheets with lower equity and asset volatilities, held a lower fraction of risky assets, and were less likely to increase their investments in risky assets when their net worth declined. These findings are consistent with the idea that stricter liability discouraged bank risk-taking. Evans and Quigley (1995) study the capital ratios of a set of Scottish banks after the free banking period. They find that in 1885, the four largest unlimited liability banks had capital ratios three times as large as the limited liability banks. This suggested that the large unlimited-liability banks responded strongly to the incentive created by the obligation to cover liabilities fully in case of a bank failure. Koudijs, Salisbury, and Sran (2018) find that banks with managers that had more exposure to their bank's downside risk reduced bank risk-taking. Exploiting the varying levels of extended liability of British banks before the First World War, Grossman and Imai (2013) conclude that stricter liability rules were associated with less risky bank behavior. Finally, Hickson and Turner (2003) test the Walter Bagehot's hypothesis that shareholders in an unlimited liability bank would find it profitable to extract rents by transferring stock ownership to poor individuals, turning the bank into *de facto* limited liability. Investigating the banking system in the 19th century in Ireland, they find no evidence of such transfers, even in times of increased probability of bank distress.

Conversely, some studies find that double liability can increase bank risk. For instance, Macey and Miller (1992) show that banks with double liability were able to operate with lower capital ratios than banks without double liability. Bodenhorn (2016) also finds that banks increased their leverage after they adopted double-liability rules, which he attributes to the fact that bank creditors were content with this change due to the additional off-balance sheet guarantees provided by the double-liability provision. Grodecka and Kotidis (2016) investigate the effects of the abolition of the double-liability requirement in the years 1934–1950 in Canada on bank risk-taking and find that this abolition was not accompanied by increased bank risk taking. Finally, Anderson, Barth, and Choi (2018) use a novel identification strategy that compares state Federal

Reserve member banks and national banks in New York (which operated under double liability) and New Jersey (which operated under single or limited liability) to examine whether double liability was effective at moderating bank risk. They find no evidence that double liability reduced risk prior to the Great Depression. However, they find that deposits in double-liability banks were stickier during the Great Depression, suggesting that shareholders of double-liability banks faced less risk of bank runs. Their results are consistent with the shifting of losses from depositors to shareholders, weakening market discipline, and attenuating the effects of increased skin in the game.

17.5 Other historical bail-ins: Long-Term Capital Management

Also mentioned in Part I, another historical bail-in case involved the world's largest hedge fund LTCM in 1998. Its resolution involved a combination of bailout and bail-in in which the Federal Reserve Bank of New York helped arrange financing by a group of 14 private-sector banks and brokerage institutions, some of which took heavy losses.[3]

The extant empirical evidence on LTCM does not distinguish between the bailout and bail-in phases of the LTCM near-collapse, but we try to extrapolate as much as possible from the few studies that investigate this episode. Due to the large size of LTCM, and its leverage positions with commercial and investment banks, the near-collapse or unwinding of LTCM's positions may have affected its counterparties or other banks with LTCM exposure. Several papers evaluate bank valuation effects around the LTCM near-collapse events and almost unanimously find significantly negative market reactions among different types of institutions.

Kho, Lee, and Stulz (2000) examine the impact of the LTCM crisis and its bailout on US bank stock returns, based on banks' exposures or participation in the rescue of the fund. Their event study results show that on the three days surrounding September 2, 1998, the banks exposed to LTCM underperformed the non-exposed banks by 14.24%. The findings imply that the market was capable of distinguishing between exposed and non-exposed banks.

Telfah, Hassan, and Kilic (2001) examine the effects of the LTCM near-collapse on the financial institutions' stock returns during September 1998 using a market model framework. They find that the LTCM near-collapse affected all types of financial institutions negatively, but the banking industry was affected the most. They further find that the Federal Reserve's

---

[3] For more details see: https://www.federalreservehistory.org/essays/ltcm_near_failure.

involvement succeeded in reducing the negative effects of the crisis and then in containing the expected hyper-volatility after the near-collapse.

Kabir and Hassan (2005) show that commercial and investment banks that were exposed to LTCM lost market values significantly around important events surrounding the near-collapse of LTCM. The losses experienced by investment banks were much higher than the losses faced by commercial banks. Smaller S&L institutions and bigger insurance companies were also affected by the crisis, implying a form of contagion effect in the financial sector. However, around the involvement of the Federal Reserve in LTCM, they find that the market reaction turned positive, although not statistically significant for all but the investment banks. This latter result is consistent with a TBTF resolution view as perceived by the markets.

Finally, Furfine (2001) uses data on 164 borrowing and lending banks, including nine commercial banks that partially rescued LTCM in the federal funds market. The author finds that the creditor banks that partially rescued LTCM reduced their borrowing during the peak period of the crisis, but this reduction was not supply-induced, but rather a voluntary reduction in net borrowing by the creditor banks. The author also finds no significant increase in borrowing from uninformed banks immediately before the bailouts, suggesting that the market did not perceive that the creditor banks were in danger of default. However, after the bailout, creditor banks did not change their level of borrowing while very large banks reduced their borrowing. This suggests a different market treatment by lenders in the interbank market that demanded a risk premium to lend to LTCM creditor banks.

17.6 Concluding remarks regarding the empirical research on bail-ins

Most of the bail-in programs, events, and instruments are relatively recent. Because of the relatively few observations to study, the bail-in research is significantly underdeveloped relative to the bailout literature. Nonetheless, one strong, consistent research result is that bail-ins appear to promote market discipline by a variety of stakeholders including depositors, bondholders, stockholders, and CDS holders. Bail-in regimes may also provide much better incentives for banks to build capital than bailouts. There is insufficient evidence on the effects of this resolution on the real economy.

The research on the effects of bail-ins on systemic risk is mixed, with some papers reporting lower systemic risk, while other papers reporting increased stock market volatility from bail-ins. Bail-ins may also result in harm to other stakeholders through reduced credit supply to connected borrowers and losses to debtholders and depositor households that do not understand their exposures well and are ill-prepared to monitor and provide market discipline. CoCo instruments confirm the market discipline effects from bail-ins and also report mixed effects on bank risk. However, their benefits and effectiveness may depend on their design and method of implementation. Usage of historical bail-in-like instruments also report a mixed picture. Research on double liability of shareholders finds mixed results on financial stability. The resolution of the hedge fund LTCM, which involved a mix of bailout and bail-in, may have exacerbated contagion effects to connected parties.

References

Afonso, G., Blank, M., & Santos, J. A. C. (2018). *Did the Dodd-Frank Act end 'Too Big to Fail'?* Federal Reserve Bank of New York, Liberty Street Economics. Available at: http://libertystreeteconomics.newyorkfed.org/2018/03/did-the-dodd-frank-act-end-too-big-to-fail.html.

Allen, L., & Tang, Y. (2016). What's the contingency? A proposal for bank contingent capital triggered by systemic risk. *Journal of Financial Stability, 26,* 1–14.

Ammann, M., Blickle, K., & Ehmann, C. (2017). Announcement effects of contingent convertible securities: Evidence from the global banking industry. *European Financial Management, 23*(1), 127–152.

Anderson, H., Barth, D., & Choi, D. B. (2018). *Reducing moral hazard at the expense of market discipline: The effectiveness of double liability before and during the great depression.* Office of Financial Research Research Paper, no. 18–06.

Avdjiev, S., Bogdanova, B., Bolton, P., Jiang, W., & Kartasheva, A. (2017). *CoCo issuance and bank fragility.* Working Paper National Bureau of Economic Research No. w23999.

Avdjiev, S., Kartasheva, A. V., & Bogdanova, B. (2013). *CoCos: A primer* (Working Paper).

Bai, J., Cabanilla, C., & Middeldorp, M. (2012). *The new bank resolution regimes and "too big to fail".* Liberty Street Economics. Available at https://libertystreeteconomics.newyorkfed.org/2012/10/the-new-bank-resolution-regimes-and-too-big-to-fail.html.

Beck, T. (2011). Chapter 3 Bank resolution: A conceptual framework. In *Financial regulation at the crossroads, implications for supervision, institutional design and trade. Kluwer law international B.V.*

Beck, T., Da-Rocha-Lopes, S., & Silva, A. (2019). Sharing the Pain? In *Credit Supply and Real Effects of Bank Bail-ins* (Working Paper).

Berger, A. N., Himmelberg, C. P., Roman, R. A., & Tsyplakov, S. (2020). Bank bailouts, bail-ins, or no regulatory intervention? In *A dynamic model and empirical tests of optimal regulation* (Working Paper).

Boccuzzi, G., & De Lisa, R. (2017). Does bail-in definitely rule out bailout? *Journal of Financial Management, Markets and Institutions,* (1), 93–110.

Bodenhorn, H. (2016). *Double liability at early American banks* (Working Paper).

Bonfim, D., & Santos, J. A. C. (2018). *The importance of deposit insurance credibility* (Working Paper).

Brown, M., Evangelou, I., & Stix, H. (2018). *Banking crises, bail-ins and money holdings.* Central Bank of Cyprus Working Paper, no. 2017–2.

Conlon, T., & Cotter, J. (2014). Anatomy of a bail-in. *Journal of Financial Stability, 15,* 257–263.

De Spiegeleer, J., Höcht, S., & Schoutens, W. (2015). *Are banks now safer? What can we learn from the CoCo markets?* (Working Paper).

Duhonj, B., & Sivertsen, T. R. (2016). *Design matters, an event study of CoCo bond offering announcements: How does design affect equity and credit markets perception of CoCo's?* (Working Paper).

Eisen, B. (2016). A new worry for bank investors: Bail-in risk. *Wall Street Journal*.

Esty, B. C. (1998). The impact of contingent liability on commercial bank risk taking. *Journal of Financial Economics, 47*(2), 189–218.

Evans, L. T., & Quigley, N. C. (1995). Shareholder liability regimes, principal-agent relationships, and banking industry performance. *The Journal of Law and Economics, 38*(2), 497–520.

Fajardo, J., & Mendes, L. (2017). *On the propensity to issue Contingent Convertible (CoCo) Bonds* (Working Paper).

Flannery, M. J. (2016). Stabilizing large financial institutions with contingent capital certificates. Quarterly Journal of Finance, 6(2), 1650006.

Furfine, C. (2001). *The costs and benefits of moral suasion: Evidence from the rescue of LTCM*. BIS Working Paper No. 103, Bank of International Settlements.

Giuliana, R. (2017). *Bail-in's effects on banks' bond yields and market discipline. A natural experiment* (Working Paper).

Grodecka, A., & Kotidis, A. (2016). *Double liability in a branch banking system: Historical evidence from Canada*. Sveriges Riksbank Working Paper Series No. 316.

Grossman, R. S. (2001). Double liability and bank risk taking. *Journal of Money, Credit, and Banking, 33*(2), 143–159.

Grossman, R. S., & Imai, M. (2013). Contingent capital and bank risk-taking among British banks before the First World War. *The Economic History Review, 66*(1), 132–155.

Hesse, H. (2016). *CoCo bonds and risk: The market view* (Working Paper).

Hickson, C. R., & Turner, J. D. (2003). The trading of unlimited liability bank shares in nineteenth-century Ireland: The Bagehot hypothesis. *The Journal of Economic History, 63*(4), 931–958.

Iseklint, D., & Bengtsson, D. (2014). *Global evaluation of contingent convertibles: Testing for evidence of market discipline in the CoCo market* (Working Paper).

Kabir, M. H., & Hassan, M. K. (2005). The near-collapse of LTCM, US financial stock returns, and the Fed. *Journal of Banking & Finance, 29*(2), 441–460.

Kho, B. C., Lee, D., & Stulz, R. M. (2000). US banks, crises, and bailouts: From Mexico to LTCM. *The American Economic Review, 90*(2), 28–31.

Koudijs, P., Salisbury, L., & Sran, G. (2018). *For richer, for poorer: Bankers' liability and risk-taking in New England, 1867-1880*. National Bureau of Economic Research.

Leone, P., Porretta, P. P., & Riccetti, L. (2017). *Determinants of European large bank stock market volatility: Is there a bail-in effect?* (Working Paper).

Lindner, P., & Redak, V. (2017). *The resilience of households in bank bail-ins*. OeNB Financial Stability Report 33 (pp. 88–101).

Macey, J. R., & Miller, G. P. (1992). *Double liability of bank shareholders: History and implications* (Working Paper).

Mitchener, K. J., & Richardson, G. (2013). Shadowy banks and financial contagion during the Great Depression: A retrospective on Friedman and Schwartz. *The American Economic Review, 103*(3), 73–78.

Moody's Investor Service. (November 14, 2013). *Rating action: Moody's concludes review of eight large US banks*. Available online at https://www.moodys.com/credit-ratings.

Moody's Investor Service, U.S. (November 9, 2015). U.S. TLAC Proposal Falls Within Expectations; Banks Able to Comply. Available online at https://www.moodys.com/credit-ratings.

Neuberg, R., Glasserman, P., Kay, B., & Rajan, S. (2019). *The market-implied probability of government support for distressed European banks* (Working Paper).

Pigrum, C., Reininger, T., & Stern, C. (2016). *Bail-in: Who invests in noncovered debt securities issued by euro area banks*. Financial Stability Report 32 (pp. 101–119).

Salter, A. W., Veetil, V., & White, L. H. (2017). Extended shareholder liability as a means to constrain moral hazard in insured banks. *The Quarterly Review of Economics and Finance, 63*, 153–160.

Schäfer, A., Schnabel, I., & Weder, B. (2016). *Bail-in expectations for European banks: Actions speak louder than words* (Working Paper).

Schmidt, C., & Azarmi, T. (2015). The impact of CoCo bonds on bank value and perceived default risk: Insights and evidence from their pioneering use in Europe. *Journal of Applied Business Research, 31*(6), 2297–2306.

Standard and Poor's Rating Services. (December 2, 2015). *U.S. global systemically important bank holding companies downgraded based on uncertain likelihood of government support*. Available at https://emma.msrb.org/ER933061-ER728601-ER1130090.pdf.

Telfah, A., Hassan, K., & Kilic, O. (2001). *The near collapse of long-term management (LTCM) and its bail out effect on the US financial institutions* (Working Paper).

U.S. Government Accountability Office. (July 2014). *Report to Congressional Requesters. Large Bank Holding Companies: Expectations of Government Support*. Available online at: https://www.gao.gov/assets/670/665162.pdf.

Empirical research on other resolution approaches

Chapter 18 reviews the empirical research on the effects of resolution approaches other than bailouts and bail-ins. Section 18.1 covers the effects of bankruptcy/failure resolution (the BHC goes bankrupt and the systemically important bank fails). Section 18.2 discusses the effects of the reorganization of the BHC using living wills as directed by the Dodd—Frank Act. Section 18.3 reviews research on the effects of regulatory forbearance (keeping the banks operating with little or no capital), and focuses on the example of the US Savings and Loan (S&L) crisis. Section 18.4 discusses the effects of breaking up the large systemically important institutions, either by size or by activities. Section 18.5 provides some concluding remarks.

18.1 Research on bankruptcy/failure resolution

As mentioned in Part I, the bankruptcy/failure resolution implies that the systemically important BHC goes bankrupt and its commercial bank fails as described under the Financial CHOICE Act that was passed by the US House of Representatives in 2017. While there have been long policy debates on this type of resolution, this has not been enacted yet, and thus there is no direct evidence and research on it. The closest to this experience and resolution would be the failure of Lehman Brothers in September 2008, with the caveat that this institution did not own commercial banks. This was the fourth largest investment bank with over $600 billion in total assets and the largest bankruptcy filing in US history. The research on the Lehman Brothers bankruptcy finds significantly negative contagion effects to other parties connected to the institution.

Chakrabarty and Zhang (2012) test credit contagion channels through which Lehman Brothers' bankruptcy affected other firms. Using market microstructure variables to measure the various dimensions of contagion effects, they provide evidence supporting the counterparty risk channel, under which exposed firms suffer from deterioration of their liquidity. They find that firms with exposure to Lehman suffered more severe negative effects—wider bid—ask spreads, higher price impacts, greater information asymmetry, and greater selling pressure—than unexposed firms.

Fernando, May, and Megginson (2012) examine the long-standing question of whether firms derive value from investment bank relationships by studying how the Lehman collapse affected industrial firms that received underwriting, advisory, analyst, and market-making services from Lehman Brothers. They find that equity underwriting customers experienced a significantly negative abnormal return of about-5% on average in the seven days surrounding Lehman's bankruptcy, totaling $23 billion in overall risk-adjusted losses. Losses were especially severe for companies that had stronger and broader security underwriting relationships with Lehman or were smaller, younger, and more financially constrained, while other customer groups were not harmfully affected.

De Haas and Van Horen (2012) find that after Lehman Brothers filed for bankruptcy in September 2008, cross-border bank lending contracted sharply. To explain the severity and variation in this credit contraction, they analyze detailed data on cross-border syndicated lending by 75 banks in 59 countries. They find that banks that had to write down subprime assets refinanced large amounts of long-term debt, experienced sharp declines in their market-to-book ratios, and transmitted these shocks across borders by curtailing their lending abroad. The authors further find that the most exposed or shocked banks restricted their lending more to smaller rather than larger borrowers.

Berger, Zhang, and Zhao (2019) also find damage in the secondary market for syndicated loans from the Lehman collapse. They investigate the market for institutional term loans (ITLs), syndicated loans that are mainly funded by institutional investors. They find that ITLs bundled with credit lines from Lehman Brothers exhibited significant increases in secondary market bid—ask spreads after the Lehman collapse relative to ITLs bundled with credit lines issued by other lead banks.

18.1.1 Research on living wills

We next discuss the empirical research on the effects of the reorganization of the BHC using living wills as directed by the Dodd—Frank Act of 2010. As a reminder from Part I, a living will is a resolution plan that is designed *ex ante* by the organizations to restore financial strength and viability in cases of material distress and failure. There is only one paper to our knowledge addressing the effects of bank living wills in the US. Cetorelli and Traina (2018) use a synthetic control research design to investigate the effects of the living will regulation on banks' cost of capital. They find that the "living will" regulation statistically and economically significantly increased banks' annual costs of capital. This effect is stronger in banks that were deemed as systemically important before the regulation's announcement. This finding is consistent with "living will" regulation reducing the value of subsidies from TBTF guarantees. When decomposing the cost of capital into its equity and debt components, authors find that it is the impact on equity costs driving the main effect, while the impact on deposit costs is statistically indistinguishable from zero.

18.2 Research on regulatory forbearance

Next, we review research on regulatory forbearance. We focus most of our attention on the S&L crisis in the US, which was described in Part I of the book, but we also discuss one paper looking at forbearance around the Global Financial Crisis, and one looking at forbearance in an international context.

As mentioned in Part I, the main causes of the S&L debacle of the 1980s were the extensive use of long-term fixed rate mortgages (adjustable rates were not allowed by law) that were encouraged by the thrift rules at the time, coupled with the extreme increase in short-term interest rates caused by monetary policy. The S&Ls were stuck in financing long-term, low interest rate mortgages with short-term high interest rate deposits. These circumstances ended up devastating much of the S&L industry, as S&Ls depleted their capital ratios and lost most or all of their net worth.

During the S&L crisis in the 1980s, regulators delayed closing large numbers of insolvent S&Ls exhibiting regulatory forbearance. This made the resolution costs potentially higher as they allowed institutions with little or no capital and high moral hazard incentives plenty of time to gamble for resurrection, pushing the problems off into the future.[1] Barth and Bradley (1989) identify three distinct phases of the S&L crisis: 1980–1982, 1983–1984, and 1985–1988. Focusing on these three periods, Barth, Bartholomew, and Bradley (1990) provide empirical evidence on supervisory forbearance in the S&L crisis. Their data suggest that supervisory treatment changed substantially over the 1980s, with forbearance becoming significantly worse in the 1985–1988 period, just before the FIRREA resolution in 1989. Specifically, they find that many more institutions, 564 or 18.2% of the 3097 thrifts, were operating with

[1] See Pyle (1995) for a review of the S&L crisis.

negative regulatory net worth in this period than earlier in the 1980s, clear evidence of regulatory forbearance. These authors also provide evidence that this regulatory net worth substantially understated the magnitude of the negative market value net worth.

A number of papers focus on the effects of this regulatory forbearance on the ultimate costs of resolution to the taxpayers compared to alternatively employing prompt resolutions, and find mixed results. White (1991) and Benston and Carhill (1992) find that the costs due to regulatory forbearance were not increased, while Kane (1987), Bartholomew (1991), Kane and Yu (1995), Barth and Brumbaugh (1994), and DeGennaro and Thomson (1996) find that costs substantially increased. Kane (1987) finds that both *ex ante* and *ex post*, the forbearance strategy rewarded managers and owners of a few lucky institutions, while increasing the expected bill to taxpayers for resolving the thrifts that ultimately failed. Bartholomew (1991) finds that for 1130 thrifts closed from 1980 to 1990 and thrifts likely to be closed in 1991, forbearance increased resolution costs by $66 billion (in 1990 dollars). Kane and Yu (1995) define forbearance using insolvency by a mark-to-market rule and find that over the second half of the 1980s, each year of forbearance added about $8 billion to the ultimate cleanup costs. DeGennaro and Thompson (1996) also use the synthetic market value approach from Kane and Yu (1995) to compute estimates of the embedded losses on the books of insured thrifts that failed to meet accounting-based minimum capital standards. They compare the estimated cost of resolving the insolvencies of S&Ls in 1980 with the actual failure-resolution costs for those that were closed by August 31, 1994. Looking at direct costs associated with the delayed closure of the 372 thrifts that were subsequently closed as independent institutions, they find that regulatory forbearance was a bad bet for taxpayers and that ultimate costs exceeded estimates of the cost of prompt resolution by over $16 billion (1979 dollars).

There are also papers that focus on the individual-level causes of the massive insolvencies other than legislative and regulatory failure, although many of the individual factors may still be products of the regulatory environment. For example, Benston and Carhill (1992), Pizzo, Fricker, and Muolo (1989), and Barth, Brumbaugh, Sauerhaft, and Wang (1985) all argue that S&Ls' reliance on brokered deposits was an important factor for the S&L problems. Benston and Carhill (1992), Benston, Carhill, and Olasov (1991), and Barth and Bradley (1989) further find that some S&Ls faced insolvency problems following deregulation because they grew large too quickly.

Hermalin and Wallace (1994) conduct a careful investigation of the S&L insolvency causes and seek to explain first the efficiency of the S&Ls, and then use measures of efficiency as predictors of the S&L insolvency in their analysis. They have several important findings. They first reveal that the lines of business and investments that S&Ls were engaging in— particularly new deregulated lines of business like investments in service corporations, commercial real estate mortgages, and real capital such as offices and land—were significantly negatively related to their efficiency and this inefficiency contributed to their insolvency. However, investments in residential real estate which were their traditional line of business were found to be positively rather than negatively associated with their efficiency. Looking at the types of assets held by the S&Ls, they find that S&Ls that experienced rapid growth were stock corporations, used more brokered deposits, and had lower tangible net worth. In addition, S&Ls located in California, Florida, and Texas (which allowed the broadest use of deregulated assets) were more likely to engage in the less efficient deregulated line of business. The authors further show that less efficient S&Ls were more likely to fail.

One paper looks at forbearance during the last Global Financial Crisis. Cole and White (2017) estimate the costs of delay in the FDIC's closures of 433 commercial banks between 2007 and 2014 based upon a counterfactual closure regime. They find that bank regulators acted too slowly to close financially troubled banks. The FDIC could have saved as much as 37% of its estimated closure costs—or about $18.5 billion—by earlier closures of banks that were failing.

Finally, in an international context, Laeven and Valencia (2008) find that regulatory forbearance is a common crisis management approach in the 42 cross-country crisis episodes that they analyze. They find prolonged forbearance in about two-thirds of the crises analyzed. The authors also discuss that forbearance leads to a decline in the net worth of banks, cripples tax burdens to finance bank bailouts, and can lead to a more acute credit contraction and economic decline.

18.3 Research on breaking up the large systemically important institutions by size and by activity

Finally, another frequently proposed resolution for large systemically important institutions is to break up these institutions. One set of proposals calls for breaking up large institutions into several smaller organizations. Another set of proposals calls for breaking up different types of activities of banks or repealing the Gramm—Leach—Bliley Act of 1999 and going back to Glass—Steagall Act restrictions on combinations of commercial and investment banks.

Starting with the first set of proposals, we do not have any research on what the breakup of such a large institution would mean for the bank behavior, financial system, and the economy, as this type of resolution was never applied. However, we can infer some of the potential effects from the banking research that evaluates the relative comparative advantages of large versus small banks to understand if reducing the sizes of the institutions would yield positive or negative outcomes. Large banks are often considered to have comparative advantages relative to small banks due to their scale economies and perceived safety, while small banks tend to be better at relationship lending and may be more often trusted by the households (e.g., Berger, Irresberger, Roman, 2020). The overall net benefits or costs from having smaller versus larger institutions can indicate whether such resolution is desirable or not.

We first review some research on large bank comparative advantages that might be lost from such breakups. Studies on bank scale economies using data from the 1980s and early 1990s find moderate scale economies for small banks and moderate scale diseconomies for large banks (e.g., Hunter and Timme, 1986, 1991; Berger, Hanweck, and Humphrey, 1987; Berger and Humphrey, 1991; Bauer, Berger, and Humphrey, 1993). But research starting in the mid-1990s up to current times shows scale economies exist even the largest US banks (e.g., Berger and Mester, 1997; Feng and Serlitis, 2010; Wheelock and Wilson, 2012, 2016; Dijkstra, 2013; Hughes and Mester, 2013). These changes may be mainly due to technological progress in information and lending technologies and/or regulatory changes like branching deregulation that may have permitted banks to operate more efficiently at larger scales. To the extent that breaking up the banks reduces their efficiency during normal times, the research cited in Chapter 2 by Assaf, Berger, Roman, and Tsonias (2019) suggests that a consequence may be increased performance problems and failure during subsequent financial crises.

Second, Berger, Irresberger, Roman (2020) suggest that large banks are likely to be safer than small banks due to better diversification, more prudential regulation and supervision, and greater access to implicit government bailout guarantees. Literature on the effects of US geographic diversification on bank risk is mixed, with some finding no effects on risk (e.g., Hughes, Lang, Mester, and Moon, 1996; Demsetz and Strahan, 1997), and others finding reductions in risk (e.g., Deng and Elyasiani, 2008; Goetz, Laeven, and Levine, 2016). Furthermore, international diversification by US banks is found to increase rather than decrease bank risk (e.g., Berger, El Ghoul, Guedhami, and Roman, 2017). Large banks are also subject to more prudential regulation and supervision than small banks. For example, the Dodd—Frank Act has imposed more strict requirements for large banks. Thus, banks having over $10 billion in assets are subject to the Consumer Financial Protection Bureau enforcement and examinations and are also subject to annual, self-administered stress tests. Banks having over $50 billion in assets have been subject to semi-annual self-administered stress tests and also subject to Federal Reserve–administered stress tests up to 2018 (e.g., Bouwman, Hu, and Johnson, 2018; Bindal, Bouwman, Hu, and Johnson, 2020).[2] The size threshold for stress tests has been raised to $250 billion upon passage of the Economic Growth, Regulatory Relief, and Consumer Protection Act (aka Crapo Bill) in May 2018, which provided immediate regulatory relief for BHCs with assets less than $250 billion and nonbank assets less than $75 billion. Chapter 22 provides more details on these regulatory changes.

Lastly, large banks are often perceived as TBTF and more likely to be covered by government guarantees, so breaking them up may reduce some of the social costs of providing the TBTF guarantees. Some literature finds positive stock and bond effects for the TBTF banks (e.g., O'Hara and Shaw, 1990; Santos, 2014; Gandhi and Lustig, 2015). Other literature shows that large banks are less subject to deposit withdrawals and bank runs and may benefit from inflows of deposits during financial crises (e.g., Martinez Peria and Schmuckler, 2001; Iyer and Puri, 2012; Iyer, Puri, and Ryan, 2013; Osili and Paulson, 2014; Oliveira, Schiozer, and Barros, 2015).

We next review research suggesting that both large and small banks have some unique comparative advantages. These may translate into important economic benefits with implications for the proposals to break up the large banks. Large banks tend to specialize in hard technologies, being better at serving less opaque and larger firms. In contrast, small banks tend to be better at using soft, qualitative information technologies, such as relationship lending, and thus are better at serving more opaque and smaller firms. A large literature supports these views (e.g., Stein, 2002; Cole, Goldberg, and White, 2004; Berger, Miller, Petersen, Rajan, and Stein, 2005; Liberti and Mian, 2009; Canales and Nanda, 2012; Berger, Cerqueiro, and Penas, 2015; Kysucky and Norden, 2016). Thus, breaking up the large banks may reduce credit supply to more transparent large firms, but could increase the supply to small firms. However, other research suggests that technological progress in hard information technologies in recent years such as credit scoring and fixed-asset lending helped large banks improve their competitiveness and made it easier to serve small, opaque firms using hard information (e.g., Frame, Srinivasan, and Woosley, 2001; Petersen and Rajan, 2002; Berger and Udell, 2006; Brevoort and Hannan, 2006; Berger and Black, 2011; DeYoung, Frame, Glennon, and Nigro, 2011). Two studies suggest that despite the technological advances, small banks continue to have comparative advantages

---

[2] More details about the 2010 Dodd–Frank Act changes on BHCs of different sizes can be found at: https://corpgov.law.harvard.edu/2010/07/07/summary-of-dodd-frank-financial-regulation-legislation/

in serving small businesses. Berger, Cerqueiro, and Penas (2015) find that greater small bank presence leads to significantly more credit to recent start-ups and slightly lower firm failure rates during normal times. Berger, Bouwman, and Kim (2017) use small business managerial perceptions of financial constraints and find that small banks still have comparative advantages in mitigating these constraints.[3]

Finally, we discuss research on the second set of proposals for separating commercial and investment activities or going back to the Glass—Steagall Act. There is no direct evidence on the effects of breaking up institutions this way. But research exists on the benefits and costs of having them together or allowing commercial banks to diversify operations into nontraditional activities. This diversification was permitted via several consequent regulatory changes, which are detailed in Chapter 23. We discuss research below on two of these changes. Section 20 subsidiaries allowed banks to conduct investment banking activities starting in 1987, while the Gramm—Leach—Bliley Act of 1999 allowed commercial banks, investment banks, securities firms, and insurance companies to consolidate. The evidence reviewed below generally suggests increases in competition and efficiency with benefits for the customers, welfare value increases for the banks, and mixed effects on bank risk.

Drucker and Puri (2005, 2007) find that since banks entered the securities underwriting business, there has been an increase in competition and efficiency gains due to informational economies of scope, with significant benefits for the customers. Particularly, they find increased capital access for the small firms, lower underwriting fees and discounted loan yield spreads for customers, and reductions in the degree of underpricing of new issues. Finally, they find that concurrent lending and underwriting help underwriters build relationships, increasing the probability of receiving current and future business.

Bharath, Dahiya, Saunders, and Srinivasan (2007) find evidence of a different type of scope economy between commercial and investment banking. Their results suggest that relationship lenders are slightly more likely to be chosen to provide debt and equity underwriting services.

Three papers find clear value gains from activities deregulation. Cyree (2000) finds that BHC share prices register positive increases at the adoption of the increased Section 20 affiliates powers, and effects are stronger for money center banks, banks with prior Section 20 subsidiaries, and large regional commercial banks as compared to small regional banks. Cornett, Ors, and Tehranian (2002) examine the performance of

---

[3] Other small bank comparative advantages are highlighted by the *Chicago Booth/Kellogg School Financial Trust Index Survey*—Wave 24, which suggests that small banks may be trusted more by households than large banks (Mester, 2018; Berger, Irresberger, Roman, 2020). Wave 24 is available at http://www.financialtrustindex.org/resultswave24.htm

commercial banks around their establishment of a Section 20 subsidiary, and find that Section 20 activities undertaken by these banks result in increased operating cash flow and return on assets, due mainly to revenues from noncommercial banking activities. At the same time, they find that risk measures for the sample banks do not change significantly. Filson and Olfati (2014) also find positive abnormal returns from US BHC acquisitions over the period 2001—2011, suggesting that diversification into investment banking, securities brokerage, and insurance under the Gramm—Leach—Bliley Act of 1999 created market value. Their effects are strongest for large acquirers with negative returns over the prior year.

One paper finds mixed results on market value. Bhargava and Fraser (1998) investigate market returns and risk effects of four Federal Reserve Board decisions to allow BHCs to engage in investment banking through Section 20 subsidiaries. They find positive abnormal returns for commercial banks around the initial limited powers granted by the Federal Reserve, but negative effects around the authorization to engage in underwriting corporate debt and equity and subsequent expansion of potential revenues from the underwriting business.

Regarding effects on risk, two papers find decreases or no effects on bank risk after the Gramm—Leach—Bliley Act of 1999. Mamun, Hassan, and Maroney (2005) find that the Act led to value gains for the banking industry, with money center and superregional banks benefiting the most. They also find that the exposure to systematic risk for different categories of banks decreased after the passage of this law, which implies that the Act was successful in containing the risk and creating diversification opportunities. Cornett, Ors, and Tehranian (2002) find that Section 20 activities undertaken by these banks result in increased operating cash flows and return on assets that did not change risk measures for the sample banks significantly.

In contrast, two other papers report increases in risk after the Gramm—Leach—Bliley Act. Akhigbe and Whyte (2004) find that commercial banks experienced an increase in risk regardless of whether they have taken steps to participate actively in the investment banking business, insurance companies also experience an increase in risk, whereas securities firms experience a decrease in risk. They argue that the increase in risk for commercial banks and insurance companies is due to their involvement in the securities business which is relatively more risky, while the decline in risk for securities firms is due to expanded diversification opportunities into relatively less risky commercial banking and insurance businesses. Filson and Olfati (2014) find that acquirer characteristics of size and past performance from US BHC acquisitions after 1999 may have some adverse consequences. Large size is associated with increasing systematic risk, and falling acquirer values are associated with increasing idiosyncratic risk. Finally, several papers focus more broadly on bank product diversification also find mixed effects on risk (e.g., Stiroh and Rumble, 2006; Laeven and Levine, 2007; LePetit, Nys, Rous, and Tarazi, 2008).

Many opine that the Global Financial Crisis was caused by the combined commercial and investment activities of banks, although in fact combining them may have been part of the solution to the crisis. The main firms causing the crisis were likely stand-alone investment banks like Lehman Brothers, Bear Stearns, and Merrill Lynch, thrifts like Countrywide and IndyMac, and the insurance giant AIG. The stand-alone large investment banks appeared to be unable to survive a severe liquidity crisis, and thus making them parts of Financial Holding Companies with commercial banks, as allowed by Gramm—Leach—Bliley Act, may have helped them weather such a crisis. Thus, breaking up large systemically important institutions may exacerbate systemic risk and could lead to future financial disasters similar to the failure of Lehman Brothers.

18.4 Concluding remarks

This chapter reviews five alternative resolution approaches to bailouts and bail-ins for large systemically important institutions—bankruptcy/ failure, living wills, regulatory forbearance, and breaking up the large organizations into either smaller or more specialized institutions. The experience for each of these is limited, and so is the corresponding empirical research about their potential effectiveness and consequences. Clearly, more research is needed, as we echo in Chapter 29.

So far, this research seems to suggest that bankruptcy/failure, regulatory forbearance, and breaking up large institutions may more often exacerbate contagion problems and systemic risk in the financial sector and/or result in reduced bank efficiency. These effects may have potentially undesirable real economic effects for bank customers. As regards living wills, the only existing research seems to suggest that this may be a potentially useful approach by preparing large institutions to be resolved in case of failure. This may also increase banks' transparency and may reduce TBTF subsidies and moral hazard incentives that some other resolution approaches such as bailouts and forbearance tend to engender or accentuate. However, it is uncertain if this alone or in conjunction with other approaches may be sufficient for a successful resolution that does not endanger the financial system and the real economy. In sum, more experience and empirical evidence are needed to evaluate these alternative approaches to bailouts and bail-ins.

References

Akhigbe, A., & Whyte, A. M. (2004). The Gramm-Leach-Bliley Act of 1999: Risk implications for the financial services industry. *Journal of Financial Research, 27*(3), 435–446.

Barth, J. R., Bartholomew, P. F., & Bradley, M. G. (1990). Determinants of thrift institution resolution costs. *The Journal of Finance, 45,* 731–745.

Barth, J. R., & Bradley, M. D. (1989). Evidence of the real interest rate effects on money, debt, and government spending. *Quarterly Review of Economics and Business, 29*(1), 49–58.

Barth, J. R., & Brumbaugh, R. D., Jr. (1994). Moral-hazard and agency problems: Understanding depository institution failure costs. *Research in Financial Services, 6,* 61–102.

Barth, J. R., Brumbaugh, R. D., Sauerhaft, D., & Wang, G. (1985). Thrift institution failures: Causes and policy issues. In Federal Reserve Bank *of Chicago proceedings.*

Bartholomew, P. F. (1991). *The cost of forbearance during the thrift crisis* (Staff memorandum). Washington D.C: Congressional Budget Office.

Bauer, P. W., Berger, A. N., & Humphrey, D. B. (1993). Efficiency and productivity growth in US banking. In Harold O. Fried, C. A. Knox Lovell, & Shelton S. Schmidt (Eds.), *The Measurement of Productive Efficiency: Techniques and Applications* (pp. 386–413). Oxford University Press.

Benston, G., & Carhill, M. (1992). *The thrift disaster: Tests of the moral-hazard, deregulation, and other hypotheses.* Atlanta: Emory University.

Benston, G. J., Carhill, M., & Olasov, B. (1991). The failure and survival of thrifts: Evidence from the southeast. In *Financial markets and financial crises.* University of Chicago Press, 305–84.

Berger, A. N., & Black, L. K. (2011). Bank size, lending technologies, and small business finance. *Journal of Banking and Finance, 35*(3), 724–735.

Berger, A. N., Bouwman, C. H., & Kim, D. (2017). Small bank comparative advantages in alleviating financial constraints and providing liquidity insurance over time. *The Review of Financial Studies, 30*(10), 3416–3454.

Berger, A. N., Cerqueiro, G., & Penas, M. F. (2015). Market size structure and small business lending: Are crisis times different from normal times? *Review of Finance, 19*(5), 1965–1995.

Berger, A. N., El Ghoul, S., Guedhami, O., & Roman, R. A. (2017). Internationalization and bank risk. *Management Science, 63*(7), 2283–2301.

Berger, A. N., Hanweck, G. A., & Humphrey, D. B. (1987). Competitive viability in banking: Scale, scope, and product mix economies. *Journal of Monetary Economics, 20*(3), 501–520.

Berger, A. N., & Humphrey, D. B. (1991). The dominance of inefficiencies over scale and product mix economies in banking. *Journal of Monetary Economics, 28*(1), 117–148.

Berger, A. N., Irresberger, F., & Roman, R. A. (2020). Bank size and household financial sentiment: Surprising evidence from the University of Michigan Surveys of Consumers. *Journal of Money, Credit, and Banking.* Forthcoming.

Berger, A. N., & Mester, L. J. (1997). Inside the black box: What explains differences in the efficiencies of financial institutions? *Journal of Banking and Finance, 21,* 895–947.

Berger, A. N., Miller, N. H., Petersen, M. A., Rajan, R. G., & Stein, J. C. (2005). Does function follow organizational form? Evidence from the lending practices of large and small banks. *Journal of Financial Economics, 76*(2), 237–269.

Berger, A. N., & Udell, G. F. (2006). A more complete conceptual framework for SME finance. *Journal of Banking and Finance, 30*(11), 2945–2966.

Berger, A. N., Zhang, D., & Zhao, Y. E. (2019). *Bank specialness, credit lines, and loan structure* (Working Paper).

Bharath, S., Dahiya, S., Saunders, A., & Srinivasan, A. (2007). So what do I get?: The bank's view of lending relationships. *Journal of Financial Economics, 85*(2), 368–419.

Bhargava, R., & Fraser, D. R. (1998). On the wealth and risk effects of commercial bank expansion into securities underwriting: An analysis of section 20 subsidiaries. *Journal of Banking and Finance, 22*(4), 447–465.

Bindal, S., Bouwman, C. H. S., Hu, S., & Johnson, S. A. (2020). Bank regulatory size thresholds, merger and acquisition behavior, and small business lending. *Journal of Corporate Finance*, 101519.

Bouwman, C. H. S., Hu, S., & Johnson, S. A. (2018). Differential bank behaviors around the Dodd–Frank Act size thresholds. *Journal of Financial Intermediation, 34*, 47–57.

Brevoort, K. P., & Hannan, T. H. (2006). Commercial lending and distance: Evidence from Community Reinvestment Act data. *Journal of Money, Credit, and Banking*, 1991–2012.

Canales, R., & Nanda, R. (2012). A darker side to decentralized banks: Market power and credit rationing in SME lending. *Journal of Financial Economics, 105*(2), 353–366.

Cetorelli, N., & Traina, J. (2018). *Resolving 'too big to fail'* (Working Paper).

Chakrabarty, B., & Zhang, G. (2012). Credit contagion channels: Market microstructure evidence from Lehman Brothers' bankruptcy. *Financial Management, 41*(2), 320–343.

Cole, R. A., Goldberg, L. G., & White, L. J. (2004). Cookie cutter vs. character: The micro structure of small business lending by large and small banks. *Journal of Financial and Quantitative Analysis, 39*(2), 227–251.

Cole, R. A., & White, L. J. (2017). When time is not on our side: The costs of regulatory forbearance in the closure of insolvent banks. *Journal of Banking and Finance, 80*, 235–249.

Cornett, M. M., Ors, E., & Tehranian, H. (2002). Bank performance around the introduction of a Section 20 subsidiary. *The Journal of Finance, 57*(1), 501–521.

Cyree, K. B. (2000). The erosion of the Glass–Steagall Ac: Wtinners and losers in the banking industry. *Journal of Economics and Business, 52*(4), 343–363.

DeGennaro, R. P., & Thomson, J. B. (1996). Capital forbearance and thrifts: Examining the costs of regulatory gambling. *Journal of Financial Services Research, 10*(3), 199–211.

De Haas, R., & Van Horen, N. (2012). International shock transmission after the Lehman Brothers collapse: Evidence from syndicated lending. *The American Economic Review, 102*(3), 231–237.

Demsetz, R. S., & Strahan, P. E. (1997). Diversification, size, and risk at bank holding companies. *Journal of Money, Credit, and Banking*, 300–313.

Deng, S., & Elyasiani, E. (2008). Geographic diversification, bank holding company value, and risk. *Journal of Money, Credit, and Banking, 40*(6), 1217–1238.

DeYoung, R., Frame, W. S., Glennon, D., & Peter, N. (2011). The information revolution and small business lending: The missing evidence. *Journal of Financial Services Research, 39*(1–2), 19–33.

Dijkstra, M. (2013). *Economies of scale and scope in the European banking sector 2002–2011*. University of Amsterdam (Working Paper).

Drucker, S., & Puri, M. (2005). On the benefits of concurrent lending and underwriting. *The Journal of Finance, 60*(6), 2763–2799.

Drucker, S., & Puri, M. (2007). Banks in capital markets. In *Handbook of empirical corporate finance*. Elsevier, 189–232.

Feng, G., & Serletis, A. (2010). Efficiency, technical change, and returns to scale in large US banks: Panel data evidence from an output distance function satisfying theoretical regularity. *Journal of Banking and Finance, 34*(1), 127–138.

Fernando, C. S., May, A. D., & Megginson, W. L. (2012). The value of investment banking relationships: Evidence from the collapse of Lehman Brothers. *The Journal of Finance, 67*(1), 235–270.

Filson, D., & Olfati, S. (2014). The impacts of Gramm–Leach–Bliley bank diversification on value and risk. *Journal of Banking and Finance, 41*, 209–221.

Frame, W. S., Srinivasan, A., & Woosley, L. (2001). The effect of credit scoring on small-business lending. *Journal of Money, Credit, and Banking*, 813–825.

Gandhi, P., & Lustig, H. (2015). Size anomalies in US bank stock returns. *The Journal of Finance, 70*(2), 733–768.

Goetz, M. R., Laeven, L., & Levine, R. (2016). Does the geographic expansion of banks reduce risk? *Journal of Financial Economics, 120*(2), 346–362.

Hermalin, B. E., & Wallace, N. E. (1994). The determinants of efficiency and solvency in savings and loans. *The RAND Journal of Economics,* 361–381.

Hughes, J. P., Lang, W., Mester, L. J., & Moon, C.-G. (1996). Efficient banking under interstate branching. *Journal of Money, Credit, and Banking, 28*(4), 1045–1071.

Hughes, J. P., & Mester, L. J. (2013). Who said large banks don't experience scale economies? Evidence from a risk-return-driven cost function. *Journal of Financial Intermediation, 22*(4), 559–585.

Hunter, W. C., & Timme, S. G. (1986). Technical change, organizational form, and the structure of bank production. *Journal of Money, Credit, and Banking, 18*(2), 152–166.

Hunter, W. C., & Timme, S. G. (1991). Technological change in large US commercial banks. *Journal of Business,* 339–362.

Iyer, R., & Puri, M. (2012). Understanding bank runs: The importance of depositor-bank relationships and networks. *The American Economic Review, 102*(4), 1414–1445.

Iyer, R., Puri, M., & Ryan, N. (2013). *Do depositors monitor banks?* National Bureau of Economic Research.

Kane, E. J. (1987). Dangers of capital forbearance: The case of the FSLIC and 'Zombie' S&Ls. *Contemporary Economic Policy, 5*(1), 77–83.

Kane, E. J., & Yu, M. T. (1995). Measuring the true profile of taxpayer losses in the S&L insurance mess. *Journal of Banking & Finance, 19*(8), 1459–1477.

Kysucky, V., & Norden, L. (2016). The benefits of relationship lending in a cross-country context: A meta-analysis. *Management Science, 62*(1), 90–110.

Laeven, L., & Levine, R. (2007). Is there a diversification discount in financial conglomerates? *Journal of Financial Economics, 85*(2), 331–367.

Laeven, M. L., & Valencia, F. (2008). *The use of blanket guarantees in banking crises.* International Monetary Fund.

Lepetit, L., Nys, E., Rous, P., & Amine, T. (2008). Bank income structure and risk: An empirical analysis of European banks. *Journal of Banking and Finance, 32*(8), 1452–1467.

Liberti, J. M., & Mian, A. R. (2009). Estimating the effect of hierarchies on information use. *Review of Financial Studies, 22*(10), 4057–4090.

Mamun, A., Hassan, M. K., & Maroney, N. (2005). The wealth and risk effects of the Gramm-Leach-Bliley Act (GLBA) on the US banking industry. *Journal of Business Finance and Accounting, 32*(1-2), 351–388.

Martinez Peria, M. S., & Schmuckler, S. L. (2001). Do depositors punish banks for bad behavior? Market discipline, deposit insurance, and banking crises. *The Journal of Finance, 56*(3), 1029–1051.

Mester, L. J. (2018). *A practical viewpoint on financial system resiliency and monetary policy* (Working Paper).

O'Hara, M., & Shaw, W. (1990). Deposit insurance and wealth effects: The value of being 'too big to fail. *The Journal of Finance, 45*(5), 1587–1600.

Oliveira, R. D. F., Schiozer, R. F., & Barros, L. A. D. C. (2015). Depositors' perception of "too-big-to-fail". *Review of Finance, 19*(1), 191–227.

Osili, U. O., & Paulson, A. (2014). Crises and confidence, systemic banking crises and depositor behavior. *Journal of Financial Economics, 111*(3), 646–660.

Petersen, M. A., & Rajan, R. G. (2002). Does distance still matter?: The information revolution in small business lending. *The Journal of Finance, 57*(6), 2533–2570.

Pizzo, S., Fricker, M., & Muolo, P. (1989). *Inside job: The looting of America's savings and loans.* New York: McGraw-Hill.

Pyle, D. H. (1995). The US savings and loan crisis. *Handbook in Operations Research and Management Science, 9,* 1105–1125.

III. Empirical Evidence On Bailouts and Bail-Ins

Santos, J. A. (2014). *Evidence from the bond market on banks' 'too big to fail' subsidy'*. Federal Reserve Bank of New York. Economic Policy Review.

Stein, J. C. (2002). Information production and capital allocation: Decentralized versus hierarchical firms. *The Journal of Finance, 57*(5), 1891–1921.

Stiroh, K. J., & Rumble, A. (2006). The dark side of diversification: The case of US financial holding companies. *Journal of Banking and Finance, 30*(8), 2131–2161.

Wheelock, D. C., & Wilson, P. W. (2012). Do large banks have lower costs? New estimates of returns to scale for US banks. *Journal of Money, Credit, and Banking, 44*(1), 171–199.

Wheelock, D. C., & Wilson, P. W. (2016). *The evolution of scale economies in U.S. banking*. Federal Reserve Bank of St Louis. Paper No. FEDLWP2015-021.

White, L. J. (1991). *The S&L debacle: Public policy lessons for bank and thrift regulation*. USA: Oxford University Press, 1991.

First lines of defense to help avoid bailouts, bail-ins, and other resolutions

Introduction to Part IV

Part IV summarizes the concepts, mechanisms, and research on the "first lines of defense"—tools that governments may be able to use to reduce the likelihood of bank financial distress that might otherwise result in bailouts, bail-ins, and other resolution methods. First lines of defense are quite important because of the very high social costs of the resolutions that they help to avoid. However, as discussed in the chapters below, they differ significantly from one another in how well they work, and in some cases may not work. As indicated in the introduction to the book, Part IV may be considered to be a relatively comprehensive review of prudential banking theory, practice, and policies around the world, and may serve as a primer or mini-textbook on this topic for interested readers.

The Part IV tree of knowledge shows leaves with the references or "fruits" for the eight chapters. As shown in the tree, this part of the book is heavy with references, given that we aim for a relatively inclusive primer on prudential banking regulation and supervision.

By way of preview of Part IV, Chapter 19 describes the three mechanisms through which the first lines of defense operate to lessen the chances of bank financial distress. These are the *Prudential*, *Certification*, and *Subsidy Mechanisms*. We use the term "mechanisms" to avoid confusion with the "channels" employed above for the effects of bailouts, bail-ins, and other resolution methods. Each line of defense uses a different combination of these mechanisms. The remaining seven chapters cover the individual first lines of defense, the mechanisms through which they primarily work, practical examples of the lines of defense used around the world, and empirical research on how well they function through the three mechanisms to the extent that such research is available.

The seven lines of defense that we cover here are capital requirements (Chapter 20), liquidity requirements (Chapter 21), stress tests (Chapter 22), prudential regulatory activity restrictions (Chapter 23), prudential supervision (Chapter 24), deposit insurance (Chapter 25), and direct government ownership of banks (Chapter 26). We acknowledge that governments engage in other activities to keep banks safe as well, but we focus on these major ones in the interest of brevity.

26. Direct government ownership

Adrianova, Demetriades, and Shortland, 2012; Banerjee, 1997; Beck, Hesse, Kick and von Westernhagen, 2009; Berger, DeYoung, Genay, and Udell, 2000; Berger, Hasan, and Zhou, 2009; Berger, Klapper, Peria, and Zaidi, 2008; Berger, Molyneux, and Wilson, 2020; Berray, Demirgüç-Kunt, and Huizinga, 2015; Bresan and Saka, 2018; Bonin, Hasan, and Wachtel, 2005; Borisova and Megginson, 2011; Boubakri, Cosset, Fischer, and Guedhami, 2005; Brown and Dinc, 2011; Caprio and Martinez Peria, 2002; Cornett, Guo, Khaksari, and Tehranian, 2010; Cull and Martinez Peria, 2012; Cull, Peria, and Verrier, 2019; Dinç, 2005; Davydov, 2016; De Bonis, Pozzolo, and Stacchini, 2012; Demirgüç-Kunt and Detragiache, 1999; Faccio, Masulis, and McConnell, 2006; Fernandez, Fonseca, and Gonzalez, 2006; Gerschenkron, 1962; Hart, Shleifer, and Vishny, 1997; Hossain, Jain, and Mitra, 2013; Iannotta, Nocera, and Sironi, 2013; Jakko and Massoc, 2012; La Porta, Lopez-de-Silanes, and Schleifer, 2002; Lassoued, Sassi, and Attia, 2016; Megginson, 2005; Micco, Panizza, and Yanez, 2007; Nakane and Weintraub, 2005; Pennathur, Subrahmanyam, and Vishwasrao, 2012; Piatkowski, 2011; Rubaszkii and Yoshino, 2008; Sapienza, 2002; Schmidt, 1996; Shen and Lin, 2012; Shleifer, 1998; Stiglitz, 1993; Yeyati and Micco, 2007.

25. Deposit insurance

Acharya, Anginer, and Warburton, 2016; Allen and Gale, 1998, 2000; Anginer, Demirgüç-Kunt and Zhu, 2014; Anginand, 2009; Barth, Caprio, and Levine, 2013; Berger and Turk-Ariss, 2015; Berger, Herring, and Szegö, 1995; Berlin, Saunders, and Udell, 1991; Bhattacharya, Boot, and Thakor, 1998; Bonfim and Santos, 2017; Calomiris, 1996; Calomiris and Chen, 2016; Chari and Jagannathan, 1988; Chernykh and Cole, 2011; Cooper and Ross, 2002; Cornett, Mehran, and Tehranian, 1998; DeLong and Saunders, 2011; Demirgüç-Kunt and Detragiache, 2002; Demirgüç-Kunt, Kane, and Laeven, 2014; Demirgüç-Kunt, Kane, Karacaovali, and Laeven, 2008; Diamond and Dybvig, 1983; European Union, 1994; Flannery and Bliss, 2019.; Flannery and Sorescu, 1996; Gropp and Vesala, 2004; Ioannidou and Penas, 2010; Iyer and Puri, 2012; Jacklin and Bhattacharya, 1988; John, John, and Senbet, 1991; Kane, 1995, 2000; Kareis and McClatchey, 1999; Laeven, 2002; Lambert, Noth, and Schüwer, 2017; Martin, Puri, and Ufier, 2017; Merton, 1977; Ngalawa, Tchana, and Viegi, 2016; Nier and Baumann, 2006; Roini and Verma, 1986; Wagster, 2007; Wheelock and Wilson, 1994.

24. Prudential supervision

Barth, Caprio, and Levine, 2006; Berger, Cai, Roman, and Sedunov, 2020; Berger and Davies, 1998; Berger, Davies, and Flannery, 2000; Berger, Kyle, and Scalise, 2001; Board of Governors of the Federal Reserve System, 2012; Cole and Gunther, 1998; Collier, Forbush, Nuxoll, and O'Keefe, 2003; Commercial Bank Examination Manual Supplement 45, 2016; Corsetti, Pesenti, and Roubini, 1998; DeYoung, Flannery, Lang, and Sorescu, 2001; DeYoung, Hughes, and Moon, 2001; Gunther and Moore, 2003; Jordan, Peek, and Rosengren, 1999; Kiser, Prager, and Scot, 2012; Mishkin, 2001; O'Keefe and Dahl, 1997; Quinyun and Taylor, 2003; Roman, 2020; Shleifer and Vishny, 2002; Sinkey, 1978; Wahlen, 2010; Whalen and Thompson, 1988; Wheelock and Wilson, 2005.

23. Regulatory activity restrictions

Berger, El Ghoul, Guedhami, and Roman, 2017; Claessens and Klingebiel, 2001; Cyree, 2000; Godlewski and Weill, 2008; Keeley, 1990; Kim, Plosser, and Santos, 2018; Laeven and Levine, 2009; Schenck and Shi, 2017; Simons, 1993; Turk and Swecgood, 2012.

22. Stress tests

Acharya, Engle, and Pierret, 2014; Acharya, Berger, and Roman, 2018; Berrospide and Edge, 2019; Choi, 2014; Connolly, 2017; Cornett, Minnick, Schorno, and Tehranian, 2018; Cortés, Demyanyk, Li, Loutskina, and Strahan, 2020; Covas, 2017; Flannery, Hirtle, and Kovner, 2017; Georgescu, Gross, Kapp, and Kok, 2017; Peristiani, Morgan, and Savino, 2014; Petrella and Resti, 2013; Schuermann, 2014.

Part IV: First lines of defense

20. Capital requirements

Acharya and Thakor, 2016; Admati, DeMarzo, Hellwig, and Pfleiderer 2013; Aiyar, Calomiris, and Wieladek, 2012; Allen and Santomero, 1998; Avery and Berger, 1991; Baker and Wurgler, 2015; Berger and Bouwman, 2009, 2013; Berger and Sedunov, 2017; Berger and Udell 1994; Berger, DeYoung, Flannery, Lee, and Öztecan, 2008; Berger, Herring, and Szegö, 1995; Berger, Zhang, and Zhao, 2019; Berrospide and Edge, 2010; Bhattacharya and Thakor, 1993; Blum, 1999; Bouwman, Kim, and Shin, 2218; Calem and Rob, 1999; Calomiris and Wilson, 2004; Carlson, Shan, and Warusawitharana, 2013; Chu, Zhang, and Zhao, 2014; De Jonghe, Dewachter, and Ongena, 2220; Deli and Hasan, 2017; Diamond and Rajan, 2000, 2001; Distinguin, Roulet, and Tarazi, 2013; Donaldson, Piacentino, and Thakor, 2018; Farhi and Tirole, 2012; Ferrari, Pirovano, and Kalwasser, 2016; Francis and Osborne, 2012; Franklin, Carletti, and Marquez, 2011; Freixas and Rochet, 2008; Fungáčová, Weill, and Zhou, 2017; Gorton and Winton, 2017; Hakenes and Schnabel, 2011; Hancock, Lang, and Wilcox, 1995; Haubrich and Wachtel, 1993; Horváth, Seidler, and Weill, 2014; Kim and Santomero, 1988; Kein and Turk-Ariss, 2018; Koehn and Santomero, 1980; Mehran and Thakor, 2011; Morrison, 1995; Mishkin, 2000; Modigliani and Miller, 1958; Nguyen, 2015; Osborne, Fuertes, and Milne, 2012; Peek and Rosengren, 1994, 1995; Thakor, 1996, 2014, 2018, 2019; Van den Heuvel, 2008; Von Thadden, 2004.

21. Liquidity requirements

Adrian and Boyarchenko, 2018; Bai, Krishnamurthy, and Weymuller, 2018; Banerjee and Ho,..014; Basel Committee on Bank Supervision, 2013, 2013, 2014; Berger and Bouwman, 2009, 2016; Bouwman, 2019; Calomiris, Heider, and Hoerova, 201.; Campello, Giambona, Graham, and Harvey, 201..; Diamond and Dybvig, 1983; Duijn and Wierts, 2013; Friedman, 1948; Hong, Huang, and Wu, 2014; Ivashina and Scharfstein, 2010; Lee, 2013; Malherbe, 2014; Rowers, Sarkar, and Shachat, 2018; Thakor, 2018.

19. Mechanisms

Keeley, 1980.

Mechanisms for the first lines of defense

Here, we briefly describe the three mechanisms through which the first lines of defense operate to reduce the chances of bank financial distress that may trigger bailouts, bail-ins, or other resolution methods. We also clarify that these mechanisms are not entirely independent of one another by describing some of the interdependencies among them.

To help guide the reader through Part IV, Table 19.1 illustrates the three mechanisms and indicates which are functional and which do not work for each of the seven first lines of defense. Similar to the treatment of channels for bailouts and bail-ins in Chapter 4 above, the columns of Table 19.1 show the seven first lines of defense, and the rows indicate the three mechanisms through which they may operate to reduce financial distress. In each row in the table, a "+" indicates that the line of defense may operate through the mechanism, a "−" signifies the effects may go in the opposite direction, a "?" signals an ambiguous effect, and an "N/A" rules out any effect. The signs in Panel A indicate the directions of the mechanisms predicted by theory, while Panel B shows the results found by the preponderance of the *empirical studies* reviewed in the subsequent chapters in Part IV, Chapters 20 − 26. The overwhelming number of "?s" in Panel A reveal that in most cases, the theories give contradictory predictions for the *Prudential* and *Certification Mechanisms*. In contrast, the empirical research summarized in Panel B indicates that most of the first lines of defense operate successfully through these two mechanisms, as shown by " +s". In Chapters 20 − 26, we briefly refer back to the appropriate columns of Table 19.1 Panels A and B.

TABLE 19.1 Mechanisms for the First Lines of Defense

Panel A: Theory

No	Mechanisms for the First Lines of Defense	Capital Requirements	Liquidity Requirements	Stress Tests	Prudential Regulatory Activity Restrictions	Prudential Supervision	Deposit Insurance	Government Ownership
1	*Prudential mechanism*	?	?	?	?	?	-/+	-/+
2	*Certification mechanism*	?	?	?	?	?	+	+
3	*Subsidy mechanism*	N/A	N/A	N/A	N/A	-	+	+

Panel B: Empirical Results

No	Mechanisms for the First Lines of Defense	Capital Requirements	Liquidity Requirements	Stress Tests	Prudential Regulatory Activity Restrictions	Prudential Supervision	Deposit Insurance	Government Ownership
1	*Prudential mechanism*	+	+	+	+	+	?	-/+
2	*Certification mechanism*	+	?	+	?	+	+	+
3	*Subsidy mechanism*	N/A	N/A	N/A	N/A	-	+	+

This table shows the seven first lines of defense, and the rows indicate the three mechanisms through which they may operate to reduce financial distress. A "+" indicates that the line of defense may operate through the mechanism, a "−" signifies the effects may go in the opposite direction, a "?" signals an ambiguous effect, and an "N/A" rules out any effect.

19.1 The *Prudential Mechanism*

The most straightforward way to reduce the likelihood of bank financial distress is through reducing bank risk via the *Prudential Mechanism*. Under this mechanism, most of the lines of defense directly target the mitigation of a bank's idiosyncratic risks that are primarily under the bank management's control, such as leverage risk, liquidity risk, and credit risk.[1] As a result of these risk reductions, banks may become less likely to experience financial distress and may also reduce their contribution to the systemic risk.

As will become clear in the chapters that follow, capital requirements are primarily designed to reduce leverage risk, liquidity requirements are mostly intended to decrease liquidity risk, and regulatory activity restrictions and prudential supervision are largely focused on limiting credit risk. These first lines of defense also often have secondary effects on other types of risk as well. For example, some capital requirements specify the ratios of capital to risk-weighted assets, where the weights are mostly based on credit risks, so these requirements also target credit risk reductions.

19.2 The *Certification Mechanism*

Under the *Certification Mechanism*, some of the lines of defense assure the public of the safety of their investments in the banks. This reduces the risks of banks that are primarily driven by members of the nonbank public. Such risks include those from runs by depositors, other liability holders, and off-balance sheet loan commitment and derivative counterparties. Such runs can result in bank financial distress because even a well-functioning bank has fewer liquid assets than liquid claims against it and would suffer devastating losses in the event of a full run. In addition, a run on one bank may spread to other institutions and create systemic risk.

The *Certification Mechanism* also works by loosening the likelihood of rapid sales by shareholders or short sales by others that might reduce the market values of the banks and/or make it difficult for the banks to raise

---

[1] Banks take a number of other types of risks, some of which are also targeted by the first lines of defense. These include interest rate risk, market risk, off-balance sheet risk, foreign exchange risk, country or sovereign risk, operational risk, technology risk, compliance and legal risks, and reputational risk. We recognize that these risks are not all mutually exclusive. For example, interest rate risk and some types of off-balance sheet risk from derivatives are types of market risk, while country or sovereign risk generally involves credit risk.

equity capital during distress. As discussed in Chapter 14 above regarding the effects of TARP on systemic risk, declines in market values of banks increase their market leverage, exacerbating their contributions to systemic risk. Thus, first lines of defense can avoid market valuation declines through the *Certification Mechanism,* and they can make the entire financial system safer and reduce the likelihood of widespread bailouts, bail-ins, or other resolutions.

A line of defense that operates through the *Certification Mechanism* is stress tests. A passing grade on a stress test may raise the public's perception of the safety of the bank—reducing the likelihood of runs on the bank or significant drops in their market values. However, a failing stress test grade may have the opposite effects. Deposit insurance and direct government ownership of banks also clearly certify the safety of the banks and reduce the likelihood of bank runs.

19.3 The *Subsidy Mechanism*

Under the *Subsidy Mechanism* associated with some of the first lines of defense, the government subsidizes banks in various ways. These subsidies may prop up the bank and deter financial distress. They can increase the bank's capital and reduce its leverage risk.

Two lines of defense that operate through the *Subsidy Mechanism* are deposit insurance and direct government ownership. Deposit insurance supports the banks by allowing them to borrow at close to the risk-free rate due to the government protection. As discussed below, this is a subsidy even if the insurance is actuarially fairly priced. The subsidies from direct government ownership of banks come from direct access to government funds and/or implicit guarantees of taxpayer funds which can be used to cover credit losses.

19.4 Interactions among the mechanisms

There are also interdependencies in which one mechanism can have effects that complement the others. This is best illustrated with examples.

First, the *Prudential Mechanism* may have secondary effects in terms of certifying the quality of banks or the banking system, complementing the *Certification Mechanism.* That is, to the extent that capital requirements, liquidity requirements, regulatory activity restrictions, and prudential supervision make banks safer through the *Prudential Mechanism,* the public may gain confidence in individual banks and/or the banking system. This reduces runs by depositors, other liability holders, and off-balance sheetoff-balance-sheet counterparties, as well as stock sales that would otherwise depress the market value of the bank.

Second, the increases in bank market valuations from the *Certification* and *Subsidy Mechanism*s may have additional prudential benefits. As discussed in some of the later chapters in Part IV, higher bank valuations may be associated with increases in bank charter value. Higher charter values may encourage prudential behavior by banks, such as reducing portfolio risks to protect the charter value (e.g., Keeley, 1990). Thus, the *Certification* and *Subsidy Mechanism*s may encourage banks to reduce their risks, complementing the *Prudential Mechanism*.

Reference

Keeley, M. C. (1990). Deposit insurance, risk, and market power in banking. *The American Economic Review, 80*(5), 1183–1200.

Capital requirements

This chapter discusses capital requirements, also referred to as capital standards, which are key tools employed to keep banks from falling into financial distress that might otherwise result in bank bailouts, bail-ins, or other resolutions. Section 20.1 discusses the concepts of capital requirements, and Section 20.2 summarizes how capital requirements may or may not from a theoretical standpoint function through the three mechanisms for avoiding bank financial distress. Section 20.3 gives a brief history of internationally agreed-upon bank capital requirements and some key deviations from these agreements for some individual nations. Section 20.4 compiles the empirical evidence regarding the effectiveness of capital requirements in terms of the mechanisms for avoiding bank financial distress. Finally, Section 20.5 reviews the evidence on two other controversial issues regarding capital requirements—their effects on bank liquidity creation and profitability. Although these issues are not necessarily tightly linked to the incidence of bank financial distress, these issues are key because they embody the main arguments against high capital requirements.

Importantly, while we couch the discussion in this chapter in terms of formal bank regulatory capital requirements, bank capital ratios are also primary targets of bank supervisors. Supervisors not only enforce the minimum ratios that are required by regulations, but also frequently go further for individual banks. Supervisors often mandate much higher capital ratios than the regulatory minimums for individual banks that are deemed to be particularly risky on an individual basis or those that pose outsized systemic risks.

The effects of formal regulatory capital requirements and informal supervisory requirements that capital ratios be maintained or increased are essentially the same. Therefore, the discussion in this chapter about the effects of capital requirements should be interpreted as reflecting the effects of both regulatory and supervisory actions with regard to capital ratios.

20.1 What are capital requirements?

Capital requirements generally specify regulatory minimums for certain capital ratios. The ratios are generally based on accounting information and may be leverage ratios or risk-based ratios.[1] The numerators of both types of ratios are accounting values of equity, and in some cases other hybrid and debt financial instruments with low priorities of repayment in the event of bank failure. The numerators are intended to measure cushions available to absorb losses associated with bank risk-taking activities before these losses can result in financial distress. The denominators of the leverage ratios are usually unweighted assets and sometimes off-balance-sheet activities. The denominators of the risk-based ratios are risk-weighted assets and off-balance sheet activities, in which the weights are intended to roughly proxy for the risk imposed by the financial instruments, primarily credit risk. The capital cushions in the numerators are intended to protect the banks from the risks proxied by the denominators.

Banks often have to meet multiple different capital requirements simultaneously. For example, under the US version of the Basel III capital requirements discussed below, US banks have to meet at least four different minimum capital ratio requirements with varying numerators and denominators. The application of multiple ratios may reduce the likelihood of regulatory arbitrage or "gaming" the requirements. Capital requirements are sometimes applied differently based on bank systemic importance. For example, 30 banks worldwide that are considered to be most systematically important are called Global Systemically Important Banks (G-SIBs), and are given some of the highest requirements.[2]

Before proceeding, it is important to recognize that bank capital ratios are determined by market forces as well as capital regulation and supervision. Berger, Herring, and Szegö (1995) define a bank's "market capital requirement" as the capital ratio that maximizes the value of the

---

[1] In principle, regulators and supervisors could also target market capital ratios for publicly listed banks, but this is not normally done.

[2] As of 2019, the G-SIBs and their corresponding additional G-SIB capital surcharge buffers on top of other capital requirements to become effective on January 1, 2021, are as follows: JP Morgan Chase (2.5% G-SIB buffer), Citigroup and HSBC (2.0% G-SIB buffer), Bank of America, Bank of China, Barclays, BNP Paribas, Deutsche Bank, Goldman Sachs, Industrial and Commercial Bank of China, Mitsubishi UFJ FG, and Wells Fargo (1.5% G-SIB buffer), and Agricultural Bank of China, The Bank of New York Mellon, China Construction Bank, Credit Suisse, Groupe BPCE, Groupe Crédit Agricole, ING Bank, Mizuho FG, Morgan Stanley, Royal Bank of Canada, Santander, Société Générale, Standard Chartered, State Street, Sumitomo Mitsui FG, Toronto-Dominion Bank, UBS, and UniCredit (1.0% G-SIB buffer). For details, please see https://www.fsb.org/wp-content/uploads/P221119-1.pdf.

bank in the absence of capital regulation and supervision. It is determined largely by weighing the value effects of different deviations from Modigliani and Miller's (1958) frictionless world of full information and complete markets, in which a firm's capital structure cannot affect its value. Such deviations include taxes, costs of financial distress, transactions costs, asymmetric information, and non-capital regulation and supervision. Miller (1995) argues that these imperfections may not be important enough to overturn the Modigliani and Miller proposition that capital structure is irrelevant.

The minimum capital requirements required by regulators and supervisors may be above or below "market requirements" for individual banks and may increase the ratios that are optimal for the banks to hold. Banks may also hold capital buffers slightly above the minimum regulatory requirements to guard against unexpected losses that could push capital ratios below the minimums and generate unfavorable supervisory responses, such as those discussed in Chapter 24 below. In practice, however, banks typically hold capital buffers well in excess of regulatory capital requirements and manage them carefully. This applies to even the largest banks that often rail against these capital requirements most vociferously (e.g., Berger, DeYoung, Flannery, Lee, and Öztekin, 2008). However, these large buffers do not mean that the regulatory requirements do not influence capital ratios—but rather that market forces also play important roles.

20.2 Capital requirements and the three mechanisms for avoiding bank financial distress

Capital requirements are designed to reduce the likelihood of bank financial distress through the *Prudential* and *Certification Mechanisms*, but the theory below suggests that they may have the opposite effects. Capital requirements do not function through the *Subsidy Mechanism*. These effects are reflected in the capital requirements column in Table 19.1 Panel A with "?s" for both the *Prudential* and *Certification Mechanisms* and "N/A" for the *Subsidy Mechanism*.

20.2.1 The *Prudential Mechanism* of capital requirements

While capital requirements are essentially used worldwide, not all agree on the efficacy of these requirements. A key issue is whether capital requirements succeed in making banks significantly safer through the *Prudential Mechanism*. As discussed in Chapter 19, this mechanism involves reducing banks' idiosyncratic risks that are primarily under the bank management's control.

Economists often argue that capital requirements make banks safer for several reasons. First, higher capital serves as a cushion to absorb expected and unexpected losses, reducing leverage risks. Second, higher capital may also reduce the moral hazard incentives to take on excessive credit risk and other types of risk created by policies that shield shareholders from the negative consequences of their actions, such as limited liability, deposit insurance, TBTF, TITF, and TMTF policies, and other government guarantees and bailouts. These moral hazard incentives can be blunted by forcing shareholders to bear more of the losses from such risk -taking (e.g., Admati, DeMarzo, Hellwig, and Pfleiderer, 2013; Thakor, 2014, 2018, 2019; Nguyen, 2015). A third reason why the *Prudential Mechanism* may reduce bank risks is that banks may choose to at least partially satisfy the risk-based capital ratios by choosing assets and off-balance sheet activities with low credit risk weights in the capital ratio denominators. The extent to which this is effective depends on how well the risk weights correspond to actual credit risks.[3] Higher capital ratios may also reduce systemic risks (e.g., Farhi and Tirole, 2012; Acharya and Thakor, 2016).

However, others argue that banks may react to higher capital standards by taking on more portfolio risk to counteract the forced reduction in leverage risk (e.g., Koehn and Santomero, 1980; Kim and Santomero, 1988; Calem and Rob, 1999). One author finds a similar result in a dynamic model—the expectation of future capital requirements raises the portfolio risk chosen at the present time (Blum, 1999). Capital requirements could also increase bank risk by increasing bank market power, which could increase loan rates and encourage more borrower risk-taking (e.g., Hakenes and Schnabel, 2011). Finally, to the extent that capital requirements harm bank profitability, such requirements may also decrease bank charter value and increase risk. A review of the theories suggests that the former view that capital requirements reduce risk generally dominates (Freixas and Rochet, 2008), but we reserve judgment on the *Prudential Mechanism* until we review the empirical evidence in Section 20.4 below.

20.2.2 The *Certification Mechanism* of capital requirements

Capital requirements may also operate through the *Certification Mechanism*, which reduces the likelihood of bank financial distress by assuring the public of bank safety. This reduces risks from the nonbank public by lessening the incidence of destructive runs by risk-sensitive counterparties and declines in bank value that exacerbate systemic risk.

---

[3] An analysis of the risk-based capital ratios by Avery and Berger (1991) suggests that these ratios do contain valuable information that is not in the simple leverage ratios. This study uses data from before the risk-based ratios took effect, avoiding the potentially confounding effects of the banks' risk reactions to the ratios.

To the extent that the *Prudential Mechanism* of capital requirement is functional, and more capital reduces bank risk, the *Certification Mechanism* is also likely to work. In this case, the public is likely to reward banks for the higher capital ratios with fewer runs and better access to the markets for debt, equity, and other risk-sensitive financial instruments (e.g., off-balance-sheet guarantees and derivatives), as well as lower costs for all of these instruments. Alternatively, to the extent that the *Prudential Mechanism* of capital requirements make banks riskier, the *Certification Mechanism* may also make banks riskier by encouraging more runs and worsening access to risk-sensitive instruments. As above, we reserve judgment on this mechanism until we review the empirical evidence in Section 20.4 below.

20.3 Descriptions of different capital requirements

Capital requirements have a long history, but we start here with the evolution of international capital requirements that started in the late 1980s and continue through this day. At that time, three basic problems were recognized with conventional capital requirements, simple leverage ratio restrictions based on unweighted asset denominators. First, the capital requirements were not risk-based—all assets from very safe US treasuries to very risky subprime loans required the same amount of capital. Second, no capital was required against off-balance sheet activities, despite the obvious and growing risks from off-balance sheet guarantees and derivatives. Third, there was an uneven playing field for banks headquartered in different nations, with banks from lower-capital-requirement countries having regulation-based competitive advantages over others.

The Basel Accord international capital requirements described below were designed to address these issues among others. Banks in most developed and many developing nations must abide by some form of these requirements. In the interest of brevity, we keep the descriptions concise and only discuss implementation in the US—more details may be found in virtually any banking textbook. We also include a brief discussion of countercyclical capital standards.

20.3.1 Basel Accord international capital requirements

The Basel Committee on Banking Supervision (BCBS) was established in 1974 by central banks from the G10 countries, which wanted to build new international financial structures to replace the Bretton Woods system. BCBS was headquartered in the offices of the Bank for International Settlements (BIS) in Basel, Switzerland. As of 2019, BCBS consists of central banks and other banking regulatory authorities from 28 different jurisdictions and has 45 members.[4]

The BCBS developed a series of influential policies known as the Basel Accords, which formed the basis for the banks' capital requirements in countries represented by the committee and beyond. The first Basel Accord, known as Basel I and discussed below, was finalized in 1988 and implemented in the G10 countries at least to some degree by 1992. At that time, there was no legal force to implement these regulations, so those member countries operated solely on moral incentives to implement these standards in their countries. Basel I was followed by several other series of capital requirements changes intended to further mitigate bank risks as outlined by the law. These are known as Basel II, III, and IV, and all are discussed below. While not every country has signed on to the Basel Accords, most countries with international banks still follow the Basel capital standards.

20.3.1.1 Basel I

Basel I addresses the three problems associated with applying the leverage ratio alone by requiring more capital against assets of higher perceived credit risk, by applying it to off-balance sheet activities as well as assets, and by applying the requirements to all countries with a BIS membership and to the many others without a BIS membership who adopt them as well.

Among the agreements that were settled during the first Basel Accord was a Tier 1 capital ratio that required to Tier 1 capital $\geq$ 4% of risk-weighted assets. Basel I also required a Total capital ratio of [Tier 1 capital plus Tier 2 capital] $\geq$ 8% of risk-weighted assets. Tier 1 capital in the numerator includes book value of common equity, plus perpetual preferred stock, plus minority interests of the bank held in subsidiaries, minus goodwill, while Tier 2 capital includes loan loss reserves (up to maximum of 1.25% of risk-adjusted assets) plus various convertible and subordinated debt instruments with maximum caps. Risk-weighted assets in the denominator is a weighted sum of both assets and off-balance sheet activities, with higher weights assigned to items perceived to be associated with greater credit risks. When considering the on-balance-sheet assets, each asset was assigned to one of four different risk-weighted percentages of 0%, 20%, 50%, and 100%. As examples, US treasuries were assigned a 0% weight, reflecting essentially no credit risk, while

---

[4] Committee members come from Argentina, Australia, Belgium, Brazil, Canada, China, France, Germany, Hong Kong, India, Indonesia, Italy, Japan, Korea, Luxembourg, Mexico, the Netherlands, Russia, Saudi Arabia, Singapore, South Africa, Spain, Sweden, Switzerland, Turkey, the United Kingdom, and the United States.

commercial loans were assigned to the 100% category. Residential mortgages were given a 50% weight, reflecting an implicit assumption that they posed half as much credit risk as commercial loans. For off-balance sheet activities, there was a conversion factor used to convert the activity to credit equivalent amounts and they would then multiply the credit amounts by their appropriate risk weights.

In the US, Basel I was partially implemented in 1990 and fully implemented in 1992. There was also a Tier 1 leverage ratio, using Tier 1 for the numerator and unweighted assets in the denominator.

20.3.1.2 Basel II

Basel II was created to supersede Basel I with several revisions that were published in 2004, along with further updated rules published in 2005. Basel II comprised three pillars which rely on each other to be most effective. The first pillar calculated the regulatory minimum capital requirements based on credit risk, market risk, and operational risk. The second pillar specified the importance of regulatory review to ensure sound internal processes to manage capital adequacy. The last pillar specified detailed guidance on disclosure of capital adequacy of banks, with the goal of improving market discipline.

Pillar 1 had three different forms of capital standards: a standardized approach, a foundation internal rating based (F-IRB) approach, and an advanced internal rating based (A-IRB) approach. The standardized approach is similar to Basel I, but with slightly different risk weights. The standardized approach widened differentiation of credit risks by redefining Basel I to incorporate credit rating agency assessments, including a 150% category for those with the worst credit ratings. F-IRB and A-IRB refer to credit risk measurement techniques under which banks developed their own empirical risk models.

As discussed in Subsection 2.4.1 of Chapter 2, European nations transitioned to Basel II before the Global Financial Crisis, and Basel II was blamed in part for the spread of the crisis to Europe. The low-capital weights on AAA-rated tranches of mortgage-based securities based on subprime mortgages encouraged investments in very risky securities, as well as the high ratings on the sovereign debt of some risky national governments.

A-IRB was to be applied to large, internationally active US banks, but was never fully implemented. It was expected to result in significantly lower average capital ratios for these institutions. It was in the process of parallel runs when the Global Financial Crisis struck. It was essentially invalidated by the Dodd−Frank Act, which prohibited the use of credit ratings in financial regulation.

20.3.1.3 Basel III

Basel III, which is now fully implemented, requires banks to meet four different capital ratios: Common Equity Tier 1 risk-based capital ratio, Tier 1 risk-based capital ratio, Total risk-based capital ratio, and Tier 1 leverage ratio. Tier 1 and Total risk-based ratios are the same as those defined in Basel I, with slightly different risk weights. The Tier 1 risk-based ratio has a requirement of 6%, which is slightly higher from that in Basel I, while the Total risk-based ratio has a requirement of 8%, the same as in Basel I. Common Equity Tier 1 risk-based capital ratio is similar to the Tier 1 risk-based capital ratio, except that it excludes some items as capital and has a minimum requirement of 4.5%. The Tier 1 leverage ratio is Tier 1 capital divided by total exposure, which is total assets (except for the few banks using the advanced approach, which requires adjusted off-balance sheet activities as well), and has a minimum capital requirement of 4%. Basel III also changes the risk weights for mortgages and sovereigns. All US banks and all bank holding companies with over $500 million in assets must meet Basel III requirements, which were phased in by January 2019.

20.3.1.4 Basel IV

Basel IV was agreed upon in 2017 and is meant to complement the changes in Basel III and to limit the reduction in capital that can result from the IRB models from Basel II. Basel IV implements a standardized floor, which means that capital requirements must be at least 72.5% of the requirement under the standardized approach that was implemented in Basel II. It also implements a simultaneous reduction in standardized risk weights for low-risk mortgage loans. In addition, Basel IV requires banks to comply with change in several capital ratios, including an increase in the leverage ratio, an increase of 50% in the risk-adjusted capital for the G-SIBs, as well as more detailed disclosure of reserves and other financial statistics. The BCBS has proposed a nine-year window to implement the Basel IV requirements, which allows for four years of preparation and a five-year phase-in period from January 2022 to January 2027.

20.3.2 US changes to capital requirements

In October 2018 and April 2019, the Federal Reserve Board proposed changes to the bank regulatory requirements including stringency of capital requirements, consistent with the 2018 Economic Growth, Regulatory Relief, and Consumer Protection Act. The changes would apply capital requirements to large banking organizations based on four risk-based categories, while considering the stability of the financial system. Banks would be assigned to risk and complexity categories based on their size, cross-jurisdictional activity, reliance on short-term wholesale funding, nonbank assets, and off-balance sheet activities, among other factors.

The new rules would divide large US banks into the following four categories based on the factors outlined above. Category I, that would apply to US GSIBs, would remain subject to the most stringent standards. Category II capital standards would apply stringent prudential standards to US intermediate holding companies (and any depository institution subsidiaries thereof) that have $700 billion or more in assets or $75 billion or more in cross-jurisdictional activity. Category III capital standards would apply prudential standards appropriate for elevated risk profiles to US intermediate holding companies (and any depository institution subsidiaries thereof) that are not subject to Category II standards and that have $250 billion or more in assets or $75 billion or more in any of the following indicators: nonbank assets, weighted short-term wholesale funding, or off-balance sheet exposure. Finally, Category IV capital standards would apply reduced capital, liquidity, and risk management requirements to US intermediate holding companies (and any depository institution subsidiaries thereof) that have at least $100 billion in total consolidated assets and do not meet any of the thresholds specified for Category II or III capital standards.

The estimated changes of these Federal Reserve final rules would lower capital requirements modestly by about 0.6% or about $11.5 billion. The capital tailoring rule was approved by the Federal Reserve Board on October 10, 2019.[5]

20.3.3 Countercyclical capital buffers

As mentioned earlier, countercyclical capital buffers (CCyBs) can be used by regulators as additional capital buffers. Specifically, CCyB was added as part of Basel III. This buffer can be built up during seemingly good economic times, so that it can be run down during poor economic times. The CCyB is set between 0% and 2.5% of total risk-weighted assets, and will apply to each bank to reflect its portfolio geographic composition and jurisdictional credit exposures. Banks must meet this buffer with CET1 or be subject to restrictions on distributions. While currently the US does not require any addition to this buffer, 12 countries in Europe, including the Czech Republic, Iceland, UK, and Sweden,have already imposed such requirements with rates ranging from 0.25% to 2.5% [6].

---

[5] For more information, see https://www.federalreserve.gov/newsevents/pressreleas es/brainard-statement-20191010.htm, https://www.federalreserve.gov/newsevents/ pressreleases/bcreg20191010a.htm, and https://www.nytimes.com/2019/10/10/bus iness/economy/federal-reserve-bank-regulations.html.

[6] For details see https://www.esrb.europa.eu/national_policy/ccb/html/index.en.html

20.4 Empirical evidence on the mechanisms of capital requirements

Next, we review the empirical evidence on how well capital requirements work through the *Prudential* and *Certification Mechanisms*. As discussed above, capital requirements do not work through the *Subsidy Mechanism*. This section is extraordinarily brief and has very few references. This is not because there is little research, but rather because the references are covered elsewhere in the book, and we wish to avoid unnecessary repetition.

20.4.1 Empirical evidence on the *Prudential Mechanism* of capital requirements

The most important empirical evidence on the *Prudential Mechanism* is the evidence already reviewed in Chapter 2, Subsection 2.4 on bank failures. As we report there, virtually all of the empirical studies find that low capital ratios raise the probability of bank failure. This is strong evidence favoring the *Prudential Mechanism* of capital requirements, and we know of no counterevidence showing a positive relation between capital and bank risk. These findings are reflected in the "+" shown in the Capital Requirements column in Table 19.1 Panel B for the *Prudential Mechanism*.

20.4.2 Empirical evidence on the *Certification Mechanism* of capital requirements

To the extent that the *Certification Mechanism* of capital requirements is operative, bank creditors, shareholders, and other counterparties that are sensitive to risk would reward higher capital requirements with more funding at lower costs. We are not aware of empirical evidence on the effects of capital requirements, but there is evidence on how market participants treat banks with higher capital ratios. To the extent that higher capital is rewarded by market participants, we view this as evidence favoring the *Certification Mechanism*, and *vice versa* if participants punish banks with more capital.

As is the case for the *Prudential Mechanism* above, the empirical evidence on the *Certification Mechanism* is essentially one-sided supporting the mechanism. The many papers on bank market discipline by depositors and other creditors reviewed in Subsection 25.4.2 in Chapter 25 below include bank capital and find that it either has significant favorable or insignificant effects on creditors. No studies of which we are aware find that creditors punish banks for more capital. For these reasons, we show a

" + " for the *Certification Mechanism* in the Capital Requirements column in Table 19.1 Panel B.

In terms of shareholder discipline, Mehran and Thakor (2011) find positive relations between equity capital and bank value using data on bank acquisitions, again suggesting that market participants reward banks that have more capital. Additional findings that banks with more capital earn higher market returns are provided in Subsection 20.5.2 below.

20.5 Additional issues of bank capital requirements and liquidity creation and profitability

Any serious discussion of capital requirements requires confrontation of the additional issues of bank liquidity creation and profitability. As discussed above, there is relatively little issue with the benefits of capital requirements in terms of reducing the incidence of bank financial distress through the *Prudential* and *Certification Mechanisms*. Thus, unless there are other costs of capital requirements, there is little to argue against 100% minimum capital requirements, which essentially make bank financial distress impossible. If capital is very costly in terms of harming the ability of banks to create liquidity for the public or to perform in terms of earning profits for shareholders, then it may be sensible from a social viewpoint to keep capital requirements relatively low and bear more risks of bank failures and systemic crises in order to maintain higher levels of liquidity creation and profits. We investigate these issues here.

20.5.1 Bank capital requirements and liquidity creation

One of the essential functions of banks is liquidity creation, as briefly discussed in Chapter 2. Liquidity creation is a comprehensive measure of the liquidity that banks provide to the public on the asset and liability sides of the balance sheet, as well as off the balance sheet (Berger and Bouwman, 2009). Its main components include deposits, loans, and loan commitments. Bank liquidity creation is also a relatively complete measure of bank output that is shown to have positive effects on the real economy (Berger and Sedunov, 2017). Thus, to the extent that capital requirements may reduce bank liquidity creation, they would create trade-offs between the benefits of these requirements in terms of greater financial stability and the costs of reduced bank output and corresponding negative effects on the real economy. While we discuss the broad topic of bank liquidity creation, many authors focus more narrowly on the lending component of bank liquidity creation.

The theories give mixed predictions about the effects of capital requirements on liquidity creation. Some argue that more capital reduces the financial fragility needed to compel banks to commit to monitoring borrowers, and so reduces on- and off-balance sheet credit supply (e.g., Diamond and Rajan, 2000, 2001). Others argue that more capital crowds out deposits (e.g., Van den Heuvel, 2008; Gorton and Winton, 2017). Both arguments predict negative effects of capital requirements on bank liquidity creation. In contrast, some researchers argue that banks with more capital work harder to screen and monitor credits, resulting in more liquidity creation (e.g., Franklin, Carletti, and Marquez, 2011; Donaldson, Piacentino, and Thakor, 2018). Others suggest that more capital results in greater liquidity creation for another reason—more capital provides greater capacity to absorb the risks associated with increased liquidity creation (e.g., Bhattacharya and Thakor, 1993; Allen and Santomero, 1998; Von Thadden, 2004). This argument is based on market forces—bank creditors and shareholders want banks to have sufficient capital to support their risk taking or else they may charge higher rates or ration funds to these institutions.

Of course, the real world is much more complicated than the theoretical one, making empirical research on bank capital and liquidity creation quite complex. The effects on bank liquidity creation may differ between (a) capital requirements and capital ratios that are determined by market forces, (b) the short run and the long run, (c) on- and off-balance sheet liquidity creation, and (d) large and small banks, among other dimensions.

The empirical research to date provides meaningful results on some of these issues, although more research is needed, as noted in Chapter 29. One relatively clear result in the empirical literature is that increasing capital requirements reduces the lending component of bank liquidity creation in the short run. Studies of the causes of the credit crunch in the US in the early 1990s generally find that the increases in capital requirements during those times reduced the supply of credit. However, it is difficult to disentangle the effects of the higher explicit or implicit regulatory capital standards based on leverage ratios from those based on implementation of the Basel I risk-based capital standards (e.g., Haubrich and Wachtel, 1993; Berger and Udell 1994; Peek and Rosengren, 1994, 1995; Hancock, Laing, and Wilcox, 1995; Thakor, 1996). Similarly, Aiyar, Calomiris, and Wieladek (2012) find that increases in minimum capital requirements in the UK are associated with reduced lending by most banks, although subsidiaries of foreign banks made up some of this lending. Deli and Hasan (2017) compare capital regulations across countries. Their findings suggest only a modest negative effect on lending of greater capital stringency. Ferrari, Pirovano, and Kaltwasser (2016) find modest reductions in mortgage credit supply in Belgium from increased capital requirements using lending spreads, rather than loan quantities. De Jonghe, Dewachter, and Ongena (2020) study changes in capital requirements in Belgium using detailed data on corporate borrowers and also find that higher capital requirements reduce credit supply.

A large number of studies using US and international datasets also suggest that changes in capital due to market forces, such as negative shocks from loan losses, yield a positive relation between capital and lending (e.g., Peek and Rosengren, 1995; Calomiris and Wilson, 2004; Berrospide and Edge, 2010; Francis and Osborne, 2012; Carlson, Shan, and Warusawitharana, 2013; Klein and Turk-Ariss, 2018; Chu, Zhang, and Zhao, 2019). Putting these two sets of strong findings together suggests that capital requirements likely reduce bank lending in the short run, but that the higher capital ratios that result from these requirements might result in higher lending in the long run, as the higher capital provides a cushion to absorb future loan losses.

There is also a smaller empirical literature on bank capital and the more comprehensive measure of liquidity creation, although this literature does not generally deal directly with capital requirements. Using US data, Berger and Bouwman (2009) find a positive relation between bank capital and liquidity creation for large banks, which create most of the liquidity, driven primarily by off-balance sheet loan commitments. However, the relation is negative for small US banks. Studies of European banks, which typically have much fewer off-balance sheet activities, also typically find negative relations between bank capital and liquidity creation (e.g., Distinguin, Roulet, and Tarazi, 2013; Horvath, Seidler, and Weill, 2014; Fungácová, Weill, and Zhou, 2017). These findings suggest that any conclusions regarding the long-run impact of bank capital requirements on liquidity creation be nuanced and consider the types of banks and components of liquidity creation.

20.5.2 Bank capital requirements and profitability

As briefly noted above, bankers often argue that high capital requirements harm bank profitability and market returns. This is despite the fact that these bankers generally choose to hold capital well above the requirements (e.g., Mishkin, 2000). We first discuss research on accounting or book-value profitability, followed by some findings for market returns.

As discussed in Berger (1995), the relation between a bank's capital to asset ratio and its after-tax return on equity (ROE)—a common accounting measure of profitability—should be negative according to standard one-period models of perfect capital markets with symmetric information, as being as well consistent with conventional wisdom. Higher capital reduces the risk of equity, which lowers the expected ROE required by investors. Higher capital also reduces the tax shield from the deductibility of interest payments and lowers the value of access to government deposit insurance and other government protections that tend to subsidize risk taking.

Despite these arguments, much of the US data show positive relations between capital and earnings, and the author provides some additional arguments and empirical analysis that support these findings. Relaxation of the one-period assumption allows an increase in earnings to raise the capital ratio, provided that the higher earnings are not fully paid out in dividends. Relaxation of the perfect capital markets assumption allows for higher capital to raise expected earnings by reducing the expected costs of financial distress and bankruptcy that are built into the costs of uninsured debt. Relaxing the symmetric-information assumption allows banks that expect to have better profitability to signal this information through higher capital. We add here the argument that higher capital can alleviate some of the costs of dealing with supervisory discipline described in Chapter 24 below. Berger (1995) also argues that individual banks may have optimal capital levels that maximize value by balancing the benefits and costs. The capital-earnings relation may be positive when capital is below optimal and negative when capital is above the optimal level.

The author runs Granger causality tests between capital ratios and ROE, controlling for a number of other factors as well as bank and time fixed effects, and finds positive Granger causality in both directions for most of the sample. The positive Granger causality from earnings to capital is unsurprising and consistent with banks retaining some of their marginal earnings. More important for the arguments about capital requirements is the positive Granger causality from capital to earnings, which more directly challenges conventional wisdom. Further evidence suggests that higher capital is followed by higher earnings primarily through reduced interest rates on uninsured purchased funds. These findings are strongest for banks with low capital and high portfolio risk, which decreased their portfolio risks as well as increased their capital positions relative to what they otherwise would have been. This is consistent with the arguments above that these banks had below-optimal capital. The results do not appear to hold when banks have above-optimal capital ratios. These findings suggest that capital requirements may improve bank profitability for individual banks specifically and during time periods generally in which bank risks are high relative to their capital positions, and *vice versa* when risks are low relative to capital.

Osborne, Fuertes, and Milne (2012) study a longer time period and differentiate banks by their target capital ratios and find results that are consistent with the arguments in Berger (1995). Specifically, they find negative effects of capital for banks with high capital ratios relative to targets, but less negative or positive effects when banks are below their target capital.

Berger and Bouwman (2013) examine the effects of capital ratios on performance, differentiating by bank size and by different types of financial crises and normal times. These authors analyze performance in terms of both profitability and market share (as well as survival, covered elsewhere in the book). They find that higher capital results in increased profitability and market share for small banks at all times, while large banks experience positive performance effects of higher capital mostly during banking crises, which are defined as financial crises originating in the banking sector. These authors offer a potential interpretation—small banks may be essentially endangered at all times and therefore generally benefit from higher capital. This is consistent with the shrinking numbers of small banks during both financial crises and normal times. Large banks, in contrast, tend to significantly benefit from higher capital in terms of better performance solely during banking crises, the only times these institutions are typically imperiled.

Regarding stock market returns for shareholders, the research is mostly confined to large banks, given that small banks are generally not publicly traded. Bouwman, Kim, and Shin (2018) find that more highly capitalized banks earn greater risk-adjusted returns during bad times than low-capital banks, while earning similar returns during other times. This is quite consistent with the better accounting performance of large banks only during banking crises, as reported in Berger and Bouwman (2013). Beltratti and Stulz (2012) similarly find that banks with higher Tier 1 capital ratios prior to the Global Financial Crisis had better stock performance during the crisis. Baker and Wurgler (2015) find that over 40 years, publicly traded banks with higher capital have lower betas and higher stock returns. Finally, Berger, Zhang, and Zhao (2019) find that higher capital has additional performance benefits in terms of greater secondary market liquidity for syndicated loans initiated by lead banks with higher capital ratios.

Overall, the research summarized here does not appear to be consistent with the argument that higher capital requirements generally impair bank profitability. Higher capital is often, but not always, associated with improved profitability, and there is no evidence that it has severe negative effects during other times.

References

Acharya, V. V., & Thakor, A. V. (2016). The dark side of liquidity creation: Leverage and systemic risk. *Journal of Financial Intermediation, 28,* 4–21.

Admati, A. R., DeMarzo, P. M., Hellwig, M. F., & Pfleiderer, P. C. (2013). *Fallacies, irrelevant facts, and myths in the discussion of capital regulation: Why bank equity is not socially expensive* (Working Paper).

Aiyar, S., Calomiris, C. W., & Wieladek, T. (2012). *Does macro-pru leak? Evidence from a UK policy experiment*. National Bureau of Economic Research.

Allen, F., & Santomero, A. M. (1998). The theory of financial intermediation. *Journal of Banking and Finance, 21*, 1461–1485.

Avery, R. B., & Berger, A. N. (1991). Risk-based capital and deposit insurance reform. *Journal of Banking and Finance, 15*(4–5), 847–874.

Baker, M., & Wurgler, J. (2015). Do strict capital requirements raise the cost of capital? Bank regulation, capital structure, and the low-risk anomaly. *The American Economic Review, 105*(5), 315–320.

Beltratti, A., & Stulz, R. M. (2012). The credit crisis around the globe: Why did some banks perform better? *Journal of Financial Economics, 105*(1), 1–17.

Berger, A. N. (1995). The relationship between capital and earnings in banking. *Journal of Money, Credit and Banking, 27*, 432–456.

Berger, A. N., & Bouwman, C. H. S. (2009). Bank liquidity creation. *The Review of Financial Studies, 22*(9), 3779–3837.

Berger, A. N., & Bouwman, C. H. S. (2013). How does capital affect bank performance during financial crises? *Journal of Financial Economics, 109*(1), 146–176.

Berger, A. N., DeYoung, R., Flannery, M. J., Lee, D., & Öztekin, Ö. (2008). How do large banking organizations manage their capital ratios? *Journal of Financial Services Research, 34*(2–3), 123–149.

Berger, A. N., Herring, R. J., & Szegö, G. P. (1995). The role of capital in financial institutions. *Journal of Banking and Finance, 19*(3–4), 393–430.

Berger, A. N., & Sedunov, J. (2017). Bank liquidity creation and real economic output. *Journal of Banking and Finance, 81*, 1–19.

Berger, A. N., & Udell, G. F. (1994). Did risk-based capital allocate bank credit and cause a "credit crunch" in the United States? *Journal of Money, Credit, and Banking, 26*(3), 585–628.

Berger, A. N., Zhang, D., & Zhao, Y. E. (2019). *Bank specialness, credit lines, and loan structure* (Working Paper).

Berrospide, J. M., & Edge, R. M. (2010). *The effects of bank capital on lending: What do we know, and what does it mean?* (Working Paper).

Bhattacharya, S., & Thakor, A. V. (1993). Contemporary banking theory. *Journal of Financial Intermediation, 3*(1), 2–50.

Blum, J. (1999). Do capital adequacy requirements reduce risks in banking? *Journal of Banking and Finance, 23*(5), 755–771.

Bouwman, C. H. S., Kim, H., & Shin, S.-O. S. (2018). *Bank capital and bank stock performance* (Working Paper).

Calem, P., & Rob, R. (1999). The impact of capital-based regulation on bank risk-taking. *Journal of Financial Intermediation, 8*(4), 317–352.

Calomiris, C. W., & Wilson, B. (2004). Bank capital and portfolio management: The 1930's capital crunch and scramble to shed risk. *The Journal of Business, 77*, 421–455.

Carlson, M., Shan, H., & Warusawitharana, M. (2013). Capital ratios and bank lending: A matched bank approach. *Journal of Financial Intermediation, 22*(4), 663–687.

Chu, Y., Zhang, D., & Zhao, Y. E. (2019). Bank capital and lending: Evidence from syndicated loans. *Journal of Financial and Quantitative Analysis, 54*(2), 667–694.

De Jonghe, O., Dewachter, H., & Ongena, S. (2020). Bank capital (requirements) and credit supply: Evidence from pillar 2 decisions. *Journal of Corporate Finance, 60*, 101518.

Deli, Y. D., & Hasan, I. (2017). Real effects of bank capital regulations: Global evidence. *Journal of Banking and Finance, 82*, 217–228.

Diamond, D. W., & Rajan, R. G. (2000). A theory of bank capital. *The Journal of Finance, 55*(6), 2431–2465.

Diamond, D. W., & Rajan, R. G. (2001). Banks and liquidity. *The American Economic Review, 91*(2), 422–425.

Distinguin, I., Roulet, C., & Tarazi, A. (2013). Bank regulatory capital and liquidity: Evidence from US and European publicly traded banks. *Journal of Banking and Finance, 37*(9), 3295–3317.

Donaldson, J. R., Piacentino, G., & Thakor, A. (2018). Warehouse banking. *Journal of Financial Economics, 129*(2), 250–267.

Farhi, E., & Tirole, J. (2012). Collective moral hazard, maturity mismatch, and systemic bailouts. *The American Economic Review, 102*(1), 60–93.

Ferrari, S., Pirovano, M., & Kaltwasser, P. R. (2016). *The impact of sectoral macroprudential capital requirements on mortgage loan pricing: Evidence from the Belgian risk weight Add-on* (Working Paper).

Francis, W. B., & Osborne, M. (2012). Capital requirements and bank behavior in the UK, are there lessons for international capital standards? *Journal of Banking and Finance, 36*(3), 803–816.

Franklin, A., Carletti, E., & Marquez, R. (2011). Credit market competition and capital regulation. *The Review of Financial Studies, 24*(4), 983–1018.

Freixas, X., & Rochet, J.-C. (2008). *Microeconomics of banking.* MIT press.

Fungácová, Z., Weill, L., & Zhou, M. (2017). Bank Capital, Liquidity Creation and Deposit Insurance. *Journal of Financial Services Research, 51*, 97–123.

Gorton, G., & Winton, A. (2017). Liquidity provision, bank capital, and the macroeconomy. *Journal of Money, Credit, and Banking, 49*(1), 5–37.

Hakenes, H., & Schnabel, I. (2011). Bank size and risk-taking under Basel II. *Journal of Banking and Finance, 35*(6), 1436–1449.

Hancock, D., Laing, A. J., & Wilcox, J. A. (1995). Bank capital shocks: Dynamic effects on securities, loans, and capital. *Journal of Banking and Finance, 19*(3–4), 661–677.

Haubrich, J. G., & Wachtel, P. (1993). *Capital requirements and shifts in commercial bank portfolios.* New York University Salomon Center, Leonard N. Stern School of Business.

Horváth, R., Seidler, J., & Weill, L. (2014). Bank capital and liquidity creation: Granger-causality evidence. *Journal of Financial Services Research, 45*(3), 341–361.

Kim, D., & Santomero, A. M. (1988). Risk in banking and capital regulation. *The Journal of Finance, 43*(5), 1219–1233.

Klein, P.-O., & Turk-Ariss, R. (2018). *Is the cost of a safer banking system lower economic activity?* (Working Paper).

Koehn, M., & Santomero, A. M. (1980). Regulation of bank capital and portfolio risk. *The Journal of Finance, 35*(5), 1235–1244.

Mehran, H., & Thakor, A. (2011). Bank capital and value in the cross-section. *The Review of Financial Studies, 24*(4), 1019–1067.

Merton, M. H. (1995). Do the M & M propositions apply to banks? *Journal of Banking and Finance, 19*, 483–489.

Mishkin, F. S. (2000). Inflation targeting in emerging-market countries. *The American Economic Review, 90*(2), 105–109.

Modigliani, F., & Miller, M. (1958). The cost of capital, corporation finance and the theory of finance. *The American Economic Review, 48*(3), 291–297.

Nguyen, T. T. (2015). *Bank capital requirements: A quantitative analysis* (Working Paper).

Osborne, M., Fuertes, A., & Milne, A. (2012). *Capital and profitability in banking: Evidence from US banks* (Working Paper).

Peek, J., & Rosengren, E. S. (1994). Bank real estate lending and the New England capital crunch. *Real Estate Economics, 22*(1), 33–58.

Peek, J., & Rosengren, E. (1995). Bank regulation and the credit crunch. *Journal of Banking and Finance, 19*(3–4), 679–692.

Thakor, A. V. (1996). The design of financial systems, an overview. *Journal of Banking and Finance, 20*(5), 917–948.

Thakor, A. V. (2014). Bank capital and financial stability: An economic trade-off or a faustian bargain? *Annual Review of Financial Economics, 6*(1), 185–223.

Thakor, A. V. (2018). Post-crisis regulatory reform in banking: Address insolvency risk, not illiquidity! *Journal of Financial Stability, 37*, 107–111.

Thakor, A. V. (2019). *The purpose of banking: Transforming banking for stability and economic growth* (1st ed.). Oxford University Press.

Van den Heuvel, S. J. (2008). The welfare cost of bank capital requirements. *Journal of Monetary Economics, 55*(2), 298–320.

Von Thadden, E.-L. (2004). Asymmetric information, bank lending and implicit contracts: The winner's curse. *Finance Research Letters, 1*(1), 11–23.

Liquidity requirements

Liquidity requirements are another set of supervisory tools to avoid bank distress and reduce the likelihood that bailouts, bail-ins, or other resolutions are needed. Section 21.1 reviews the concepts and goals of liquidity requirements. Section 21.2 discusses how liquidity requirements may function through the three mechanisms to avoid bank financial distress. Section 21.3 describes liquidity requirements in Basel III and other liquidity requirements that have been implemented in the US, EU, and other nations. Section 21.4 gives empirical evidence on the effectiveness of the liquidity requirements mechanisms.

21.1 What are liquidity requirements?

Liquidity requirements are imposed by regulators to reduce liquidity risk and lessen the likelihood that liquidity shocks result in financial distress of the banks. Liquidity risk is the risk of a sudden surge in demand for liquid funds by customers, which may require a bank to engage in "fire sales," liquidating assets in a very short period at less than fair market prices, or forego profitable investments such as commercial loans or loan commitments. The demand for liquid funds may come from the liability side of the bank's balance sheet, such as a run by depositors or refusal to roll over other debt by capital market participants. Alternatively, the demand for liquid funds may be from off-balance sheet customers who may draw down loan commitments or similar claims to liquid funds.

The most significant bank liquidity risk comes when bank customers suspect or know that the bank is in financial distress from liquidity, credit, or any other source of problems or rumors of problems, and they "run" on the bank—trying to obtain liquid funds before the liquidity dries up (Diamond and Dybvig, 1983). During the the Great Depression in the 1930s, many depositors ran on US banks when they suspected financial distress, turning illiquidity problems into insolvency and failure. There was no deposit insurance at that time, so the "sequential service constraint"—under which

331

depositors that are first in line obtain their funds and later depositors do not—meant that it was rational for depositors to run on a bank based solely on the knowledge that others were running on it. During the Global Financial Crisis, most US depositors were fully insured and did not run, and FDIC deposit insurance coverage was raised from $100,000 to $250,000 per account to help prevent runs by depositors who were partially uninsured. Nonetheless, many loan commitment customers, whose access to funds was not government-insured, drew down their loan commitments, draining liquidity from the banks, in a type of run (e.g., Ivashina and Scharfstein, 2010; Campello, Giambona, Graham, and Harvey, 2011).

Banks are especially prone to liquidity risk because one of their core functions is liquidity creation, which they do on the asset and liability sides of the balance sheet as well as off the balance sheet. Creating more liquidity for the nonbank public generally makes banks more illiquid (Berger and Bouwman, 2009). To illustrate, banks can create more liquidity on the asset side by holding more illiquid loans, on the liability side by issuing more transactions deposits, and on the off-balance sheet side by making more loan commitments. More transactions deposits and more loan commitments increase potential demands for liquid funds, and more illiquid loans imply fewer liquid assets to meet those demands. No well-functioning bank that is creating liquidity for the nonbank public can withstand a full run because banks almost always have fewer liquid assets than liabilities and off-balance sheet claims.[1]

Liquidity requirements are usually imposed by central banks in the form of minimum ratios, whose numerators have liquid assets such as cash and government securities, and the denominator is a measure of deposits or other proxies for the potential need for liquid funds. Historically, the most common requirements were reserve requirements of cash or reserves held at the central bank relative to some subset of deposits. The reliance on reserve requirements declined over the years leading up to the Global Financial Crisis because these requirements are costly as a tool of prudential regulations and rather blunt as tools of monetary policy (Bouwman, 2019).

However, the rapid drying out of liquidity in the financial system during the Global Financial Crisis provided momentum for bank regulators in the US and other nations to impose much more comprehensive bank liquidity requirements for banks. As discussed in Section 21.3 below, the Basel III Accord introduces international liquidity requirements for the first time.

---

[1] Friedman's (1948) proposal of 100% reserve requirements on demand deposits, which was primarily intended to give more perfect control over monetary policy to the central bank, would come close to eliminating bank liquidity risk. However, it would also largely destroy the ability of banks to create liquidity for the nonbank public.

Before proceeding with the details of liquidity requirements, we raise two important issues. The first is the interaction between capital requirements discussed in Chapter 20 with liquidity requirements reviewed in this chapter. Adrian and Boyarchenko (2018) analyze a dynamic stochastic general equilibrium model in which capital and liquidity regulations interact with the supply of risk-free assets. In their model, the endogenously time-varying tightness of the capital and liquidity constraints generates intermediaries' leverage cycles, affecting the pricing and the level of risk in the economy. Their model suggests that liquidity requirements are preferable to capital requirements, as tightening liquidity requirements lowers the likelihood of systemic distress without impairing consumption growth.

Second, we address whether it is appropriate to have liquidity requirements that are strict enough to guard against large aggregate liquidity shocks like financial crises, given the existence of central banks' lender of last resort (LOLR) function. That is, while liquidity requirements may be useful for preventing idiosyncratic liquidity shocks from turning into financial distress or failure of individual banks, for major liquidity shocks, it may be more efficient to mitigate the liquidity problems through the LOLR. Having each bank store enough liquidity to mitigate a major shock may be quite costly in terms of foregone income from not investing in profitable loans, commitments, and other investments, whereas central banks can create essentially any amount of liquidity at virtually no cost, and may be able to distribute it to banks at relatively low cost through the LOLR function during a financial crisis. As discussed in Chapter 16, the Federal Reserve distributed trillions of dollars of liquidity through the expanded discount window (DW) and Term Auction Facilities (TAF) during the Global Financial Crisis, and these programs were highly successful in increasing bank lending. In addition, evidence reviewed in Thakor (2018) suggests that the Global Financial Crisis was essentially an insolvency risk crisis, not a liquidity crisis. If this conclusion is correct, strict liquidity requirements would not have even significantly contained a very severe financial crisis, furthering the case against liquidity requirements to guard against large aggregate liquidity shocks.

21.2 Liquidity requirements and the three mechanisms for avoiding bank financial distress

This section provides arguments about how liquidity requirements may affect the probability of bank financial distress. From a theoretical standpoint, liquidity requirements can work through the *Prudential*

Mechanism by limiting liquidity risk, and through the *Certification Mechanism* by assuring the public about the safety of the banks. However, as discussed above for capital requirements, both mechanisms may also go in the opposite direction and make banks riskier. Liquidity requirements do not work through the *Subsidy Mechanism*. These effects are reflected in the Liquidity Requirements column in Table 19.1 Panel A with "?s" for both the *Prudential* and *Certification Mechanisms* and "N/A" for the *Subsidy Mechanism*.

21.2.1 The *Prudential Mechanism* of liquidity requirements

Liquidity requirements may reduce liquidity risk and the probability of financial distress by ensuring that banks have enough liquid assets to withstand unexpected liquidity shocks. Liquidity requirements can encourage banks to hold more liquid assets, and fewer liquid liabilities and off-balance sheet claims on liquidity. Liquidity requirements can also potentially reduce risks other than liquidity risk and encourage safer bank risk management practices. Holding more liquid assets may reduce credit risk and mitigate banks' risk-shifting activities, since cash and other liquid assets generally have little or no credit risk (Calomiris, Heider, and Hoerova, 2013).

In contrast, banks may react to higher liquidity standards by taking on more portfolio risk or other types of risk to counteract the forced reductions in liquidity risk from liquidity requirements. These requirements may also increase bank risk by harming profitability and charter value. These arguments are analogous to those made in the capital requirements literature reviewed in Chapter 20. We are not aware of these arguments in the literature on liquidity requirements, which is much sparser than the capital requirements literature. An additional theoretical argument made by Malherbe (2014) is that liquidity requirements can backfire, as holding cash worsens future adverse selection in markets for long-term assets, impairing their role for liquidity provision, and thus can become a source of liquidity crises.

21.2.2 The *Certification Mechanism* of liquidity requirements

Liquidity requirements may also work through the *Certification Mechanism* by assuring the public of the safety of both individual banks and the banking sector. The requirements can reduce liquidity risk and possibly credit risk or other risk management problems as described above, and lessen the chances that such risks devolve into financial distress through runs by depositors, other liability holders, and off-balance sheet loan commitment customers and other connected counterparties. In contrast, to the extent that liquidity requirements make banks riskier through the *Prudential Mechanism*, the *Certification Mechanism* may also make banks riskier, encouraging runs and damaging access to risk-sensitive instruments.

21.3 Descriptions of the different liquidity requirements

In this section, we explain the liquidity requirements implemented by central banks or other regulators in the US, Europe, and to a lesser extent, other nations. We begin with the liquidity requirements introduced in the Basel III Accords, which are agreed upon and enforced by central banks in most developed nations and mimicked by many other developed and developing nations.

21.3.1 Basel III liquidity requirements

The Basel Committee on Banking Supervision included in the Basel III Accords two explicit liquidity requirements as part of the effort to reform the liquidity risk framework (Basel Committee on Bank Supervision, 2013, 2014). The new requirements take into consideration the overall expected and unexpected cash outflows that the bank is subject to over a given period. The Liquidity Coverage Ratio (LCR) and the Net Stable Funding Ratio (NSFR) aim to improve the resilience of the liquidity risk profile of banks.

LCR is a short-term ratio that requires banks to hold sufficient high-quality liquid assets (*HQLA*) to meet liquidity needs over a 30-day stress period. The *LCR* is defined as follows:

$$LCR_{it} = \frac{High\ quality\ liquid\ assets_{it}}{Outflows_{it} - \min(Inflows_{it},\ 0.75\ Outflows_{it})} \qquad (21.1)$$

where i indexes the banks and t indicates the time period. The *HQLA* in the numerator include Level 1 and Level 2 assets. Level 1 assets are cash, central bank reserves, and certain debt securities backed by high-rated sovereigns and corresponding central banks. Level 2 assets are considered of slightly lower liquidity and include certain government securities, certain qualifying corporate bonds, covered bonds, and some securitized residential mortgages. The denominator of the *LCR* is the net cash outflow, calculated as the difference between the expected cash outflows and the expected cash inflows over a 30-day period. The cash inflows are bounded at 75% of the cash outflows to be conservative and encourage banks to hold more *HQLA*. The *LCR* is required by the Basel Committee to exceed one, so that under most circumstances, the bank's holding of *HQLA* is greater than the realized net cash outflows. The *LCR* was phased in between January 1, 2015 and January 1, 2019.

In contrast to the short-term orientation of the *LCR* requirement, the *NSFR* requirement aims to "promote resiliency over longer-term time horizons by creating additional incentives for banks to fund their activities with more stable sources of funding on an ongoing basis" (Basel Committee on Bank Supervision, 2010). It is expressed as the following ratio:

$$NSFR_{it} = \frac{Available\ stable\ funding_{it}}{Required\ stable\ funding_{it}} \qquad (21.2)$$

where banks are required to maintain an *NSFR* ratio of at least one. The Available Stable Funding (*ASF*) in the numerator is determined by assigning weights to the value of each element of stable funding that the bank has. Stable funding consists of a bank's capital, liabilities with maturities greater than 1 year, and liabilities with maturities less 1 year that are expected to remain within the institution during a crisis. An *ASF* factor of 100% means that the funding from this source is expected to be fully available for more than 1 year and an *ASF* factor of 0% reflects the expectation that the funding source is unreliable.

The Required Stable Funding (*RSF*) in the denominator is calculated as the sum of the amount of stable funding required to be held for each element of the bank's assets and off-balance sheet activities based on their liquidity characteristics. To determine the *RSF* amounts for each item, an *RSF* factor is assigned to the carrying value of the bank's liquidity risk exposure. *RSF* factors range from 100%, meaning that the asset or exposure is illiquid and needs to be fully financed by a stable source of funding, to 0%, applying to assets that are fully liquid.

21.3.2 US liquidity requirements

The Federal Reserve, the FDIC, and the Office of the Comptroller of the Currency (OCC) in September 2014 finalized a rule to implement the LCR in the US. The following US bank organizations are subject to the LCR: (a) banking organizations with consolidated assets of over $250 billion; (b) on-balance sheet foreign exposure exceeding $10 billion; and (c) subsidiary depository institutions of bank organizations in (b). For BHCs and savings and loan holding companies that do not meet these thresholds, but have total assets greater than $50 billion, a less stringent, modified LCR is applied. With regard to the NSFR, the Federal Reserve proposed a rule in May 2016 that was supposed to become effective on January 1, 2018, but was not finalized.[2] On October 31, 2018, US regulators issued proposals to modify the enhanced prudential liquidity requirements for large banks. The proposals

[2] https://www.federalreserve.gov/newsevents/pressreleases/bcreg20160503a.htm

exempt domestic US banks with total assets between $100 billion and $250 billion from the LCR and NSFR, and cut the LCR and NSFR requirements for banks with assets between $250 and $750 billion to a level between 70% and 75%. As of this writing, the NSFR has not yet been implemented.

The Federal Reserve also uses the Comprehensive Liquidity Analysis and Review (CLAR) for the largest and most systemically important institutions under the Large Institution Supervision Coordinating Committee (LISCC) framework, a process composed of multiple dimensions rather than a single quantitative ratio. The CLAR includes a detailed bank-run liquidity stress test, an independent Federal Reserve review of the bank's analysis, and an evaluation of the banks' liquidity planning and governance. The CLAR is intended to reflect more accurately bank-specific circumstances during a liquidity crisis. The Federal Reserve's independent review enables it to alter any results if it detects any biases in the bank's calculations. The CLAR was first introduced in late 2012 and applied to a few systemically important banks.[3] The results of the CLAR exercise are confidential.

Prior to Basel III and CLAR, US liquidity requirements generally took the form of minimum ratios of cash reserves to a subset of deposits. That is, banks were required to maintain as reserves a fraction of their depository liabilities. Cash reserve requirements have been reduced several times, but are still in effect.

Vault cash reserve requirements were launched at the national level in 1863 with the passage of the National Banking Act. Banks with a national charter were required to hold a 25% reserve against national bank notes and deposits. The requirement was reduced to 15% for banks located outside the largest cities. An Act of 1874 replaced reserve requirements on bank notes with a required redemption fund which counted toward fulfilling reserve requirements on deposits.

Various bank runs and panics in the late 19th and early 20th centuries led to the establishment of the Federal Reserve as LOLR in 1913. As discussed above, LOLR at least somewhat substitutes for liquidity requirements, but reserve requirements continued to be imposed on transaction and time deposits.

In the 1970s, rising interest rates increased the cost that banks incurred for satisfying reserve requirements, since the Federal Reserve paid no interest on reserves. This caused banks to leave the Federal Reserve system. In part to stop this trend, the Depository Institutions Deregulation and Monetary Control Act (DIDMCA) of 1980 mandated that all depository institutions be subject to reserve requirements. Initially, the

---

[3] Currently, the LISCC firms are: Bank of America, The Bank of New York Mellon, Barclays, Citigroup, Credit Suisse Group, Deutsche Bank, Goldman Sachs, JPMorgan Chase, Morgan Stanley, State Street, UBS, and Wells Fargo.

IV. First lines of defense to help avoid bailouts and bail-ins

reserve requirements were set at 3% on the first $25 million of transaction deposits and 12% on the remainder, and 3% on nontransaction deposits. Over time, these percentages have declined, possibly to avoid disintermediation due to nonpayment of interest on reserves.

Under reserve requirements for US banks as of this writing, last updated on January 17, 2019, there is no minimum reserve requirement for the first $16.3 million in net transactions accounts (NTAs), a minimum reserve requirement ratio of 3% in terms of reserves held at Federal Reserve Banks plus vault cash for NTAs between $16.3 million and $124.2 million, and a minimum ratio of 10% of NTAs that exceeds $124.2 million. These cutoffs are generally adjusted upward each January. The Federal Reserve uses a lagged reserve accounting system in which required reserves are calculated by a 14-day computation period, and then must be held over a later 14-day maintenance period.[4]

However, these minimum ratios have little cost for most banks. Since December 2008, the Federal Reserve has paid interest on both required and excess reserves. At least in part as a result of these interest payments, many banks hold very large amounts of excess reserves, which may be a significant factor in deterring bank credit supplies.

US bank regulators also grade the banks on their liquidity risks in bank examinations. It is part of their overall evaluation of the banks (liquidity is the "L" in CAMELS supervisory ratings). These ratings are confidential, and little is known about their effectiveness.

21.3.3 European liquidity requirements

Most European nations adhere to the Basel III liquidity requirements. Prior to the introduction of the LCR, regulators in several European nations applied quantitative liquidity requirements. German institutions are required to maintain liquid assets equal to or greater than their total liabilities coming due within one month. Liquid assets are calculated as the sum of expected cash inflows from high-quality, liquid assets such as assets coming due within one month and marketable securities. The calculation and underlying assumptions of the German liquidity requirements are very similar to the LCR in Basel III.

In France, banks are similarly required to maintain a minimum ratio of the market liquid assets plus expected cash inflows to the assumed cash outflows over one month of at least one.

The Irish requirement mandates that institutions maintain the ratio of liquid assets to total borrowing of 25% or more. The definition of liquid assets includes cash, government securities, and balances with central banks.

---

[4] https://www.federalreserve.gov/monetarypolicy/reserve-maintenance-manual-calculation-of-reserve-balance-requirements.htm

The Luxembourgian liquidity requirement is based on liquid assets relative to a fraction of current liabilities. Banks are expected to maintain a ratio of at least 30%.

The Dutch requirement is defined as the difference between banks' Actual Liquidity (AL) and their Required Liquidity (RL) over seven- and 30-day stress periods. AL is defined as the sum of liquid assets and assumed cash inflows. RL includes moderate retail and substantial wholesale outflows as well as significant calls on contingent liquidity lines.

In the United Kingdom (UK), the liquidity requirement mainly aims at dealing with maturity mismatches. The Prudential Regulatory Authority (PRA) sets the maximum netcumulative mismatch limits, which are reflected as an institution-specific percentage of total deposits over 8- and 30-day horizons. Banks are also required to hold a minimum amount of *HQLA* such as cash, central bank reserves, or UK government bonds.

21.3.4 Liquidity requirements in other nations

South Korean banks are required to have enough liquid assets to cover liabilities within a three-month horizon. Liquid assets include the stock of marketable securities as well as assumed inflows from maturing assets. The regulatory liquidity ratio in South Korea is sometimes revised to send warning signals in case many banks fall below regulatory or precautionary levels (Lee, 2013).

21.4 Empirical evidence on the mechanisms of liquidity requirements

We next review the empirical research regarding how well liquidity requirements perform through the mechanisms. The empirical findings suggest mostly favorable effects in terms of liquidity requirements reducing bank risk through the *Prudential Mechanisms*. However, we are not aware of any academic research on the *Certification Mechanism* for these requirements. Thus, Table 19.1 Panel B shows a "+" for the *Prudential Mechanism* and a "?" for the *Certification Mechanism*.

21.4.1 Empirical evidence on the *Prudential Mechanism* of liquidity requirements

A key goal of the LCR and NSFR restrictions under Basel III is to ensure that the banks have adequate liquidity, so a key issue is the extent to which the LCR and NSFR actually measure bank liquidity. Berger and Bouwman (2016) measure correlations of the LCR and NSFR provided by

Hong, Huang, and Wu (2014) with the liquidity creation measure of Berger and Bouwman (2009) normalized by GTA, an inverse indicator of bank liquidity. They find that the correlations are often weak and sometimes go in the unexpected direction, particularly for LCR, especially during the Global Financial Crisis. While there is no perfect measure of bank liquidity, these results suggest that the Basel Accord measures, particularly, LCR, may have room for improvement. Consistent with this, Hong, Huang, and Wu (2014) estimate a bank failure model and find that banks below the LCR and NSFR thresholds have only marginally higher probabilities of failure.

Other research suggests that the Basel III measures may be effective in encouraging banks to become more liquid. Roberts, Sarkar, and Shachar (2018) find results suggesting that the implementation of the LCR for larger banks improved their liquidity using both the Liquidity Mismatch Index (LMI) of Bai, Krishnamurthy, and Weymuller (2018) and Berger and Bouwman's (2009) liquidity creation measure normalized by assets. Specifically, they find a decline in LMI and liquidity creation by LCR banks relative to non-LCR banks since 2013. This reduction in liquidity creation was primarily driven by a decrease in holdings of illiquid assets and an increase in holdings of liquid assets. Duijm and Wierts (2016) investigate the effects of LCR on bank liquid assets and liabilities. They find that banks adjust both liquid assets and liabilities to meet the minimum requirement of short-term liquidity buffer, with most of the changes occurring on the liability side of the balance sheet. Their results are based on a dataset for Dutch banks that have been subject to similar liquidity requirements before the introduction of the Basel III LCR. Banerjee and Hio (2014) find UK banks significantly increase their stocks of liquid assets and reduce their holdings of financial assets and reliance on short-term wholesale funding once they become subject to the requirement.

21.4.2 Empirical evidence on the *Certification Mechanism* of liquidity requirements

We are not aware of any direct empirical evidence on the *Certification Mechanism* of liquidity requirements. However, we note that to the extent that the public is aware of the evidence in the prior section that the requirements encourage banks to become more liquid, it seems likely that this would discourage runs on the banks.

References

Adrian, T., & Boyarchenko, N. (2018). Liquidity policies and systemic risk. *Journal of Financial Intermediation, 35*, 45—60.
Bai, J., Krishnamurthy, A., & Weymuller, C.-H. (2018). Measuaring liquidity mismatch in the banking sector. *The Journal of Finance, 73*(1), 51—93.

Banerjee, R., & Hio, M. (2014). *The impact of liquidity regulation on bank behaviour: Evidence from the UK* (Working Paper).

Basel Committee on Bank Supervision. (2010). *Basel III: International framework for liquidity risk measurement, standards and monitoring.* Available at https://www.bis.org/publ/bcbs188.pdf.

Basel Committee on Bank Supervision. (2013). *Basel III: The liquidity coverage ratio and liquidity risk monitoring tools.* Basel Committee on Banking Supervision. Available at https://www.bis.org/publ/bcbs238.pdf.

Basel Committee on Bank Supervision. (2014). *Liquidity coverage ratio disclosure standards.* Basel Committee on Banking Supervision. Available at https://www.bis.org/publ/bcbs272.pdf.

Berger, A. N., & Bouwman, C. H. S. (2009). Bank liquidity creation. *The Review of Financial Studies, 22*(9), 3779–3837.

Berger, A. N., & Bouwman, C. H. S. (2016). *Bank Liquidity Creation and Financial Crises.* Elsevier – North Holland.

Bouwman, C. H. S. (2019). In A. N. Berger, P. Molyneux, & J. O. S. Wilson (Eds.), *Oxford Handbook of Banking* (Third Ed., pp. 181–228). Oxford: Oxford University Press.

Calomiris, C. W., Heider, F., & Hoerova, M. (2013). *A theory of liquidity requirements.* Mimeo.

Campello, M., Giambona, E., Graham, J. R., & Harvey, C. R. (2011). Liquidity management and corporate investment during a financial crisis. *The Review of Financial Studies, 24*(6), 1944–1979.

Diamond, D. W., & Dybvig, P. H. (1983). Bank runs, deposit insurance, and liquidity. *Journal of Political Economy, 91*(3), 401–419.

Duijm, P., & Wierts, P. (2016). The Effects of Liquidity Regulation on Bank Assets and Liabilities. (Working Paper).

Friedman, M. (1948). Monetary and Fiscal Framework for Economic Stability. *The American Economic Review, 38*, 245–264.

Hong, H., Huang, J.-Z., & Wu, D. (2014). The information content of Basel III liquidity risk measures. *Journal of Financial Stability, 15*, 91–111.

Ivashina, V., & Scharfstein, D. (2010). Bank lending during the financial crisis of 2008. *Journal of Financial Economics, 97*(3), 319–338.

Lee, S. H. (2013). Systemic liquidity shortages and interbank network structures. *Journal of Financial Stability, 9*(1), 1–12.

Malherbe, F. (2014). Self-fulfilling liquidity dry-ups. *The Journal of Finance, 69*(2), 947–970.

Roberts, D., Sarkar, A., & Shachar, O. (2018). *Bank liquidity provision and Basel liquidity regulations.* FRB of New York Staff Report, no. 852.

Thakor, A. V. (2018). Post-crisis regulatory reform in banking: Address insolvency risk, not illiquidity! *Journal of Financial Stability, 37*, 107–111.

Stress tests

In this chapter, we discuss bank stress tests. Section 22.1 reviews the concepts and goals of the stress tests. Section 22.2 discusses how stress tests may function through the three mechanisms for avoiding bank financial distress. Section 22.3 describes the bank stress tests that have been performed in the US and EU, and Section 22.4 gives empirical evidence on the how well the tests worked through the mechanisms.

22.1 What are stress tests?

Stress tests generally refer to simulation exercises designed to determine how a given individual, institution, or system would perform under unusually stressful situations. Stress tests estimate the degree to which banking organizations would be able to lend and perform other normal banking functions in simulated adverse scenarios that emulate possible future financial crises or difficult periods. These tests are conducted by government agencies, and the banks are given either pass or fail grades. Stress test failures may come with restrictions on capital payouts through dividends and share buybacks, as well as requirements he banks failing the tests must implement plans to improve risk management processes and raise capital ratios.

These tests are essentially forward looking capital requirements that mandate sufficient capital to absorb future risks. This contrasts with conventional capital requirements reviewed in Chapter 20 that mandate minimum capital ratios based on perceptions of portfolio risks that are derived from past experiences.

22.2 Stress tests and the three mechanisms for avoiding bank financial distress

Similar to capital requirements, stress tests may prevent or deter bank financial distress through both the *Prudential Mechanism* and the *Certification Mechanism*, but not through the *Subsidy Mechanism*. Also similar to capital requirements, the *Prudential* and *Certification Mechanisms* may alternatively go the opposite way and make banks riskier. The Stress Tests column in Table 19.1 Panel A mirrors that of the Capital Requirements column with "?s" for both the *Prudential* and *Certification Mechanisms* and "N/A" for the *Subsidy Mechanism*.

22.2.1 The *Prudential Mechanism* of stress tests

Stress tests may have prudential benefits in reducing the likelihood of future bailouts or bail-ins by requiring banks to have sufficient capital to withstand at least some form of adverse future scenarios. Similar to capital requirements discussed in Chapter 20, this extra capital may reduce future distress by providing a cushion to absorb losses and by reducing moral hazard incentives to take on excessive portfolio risks.

From a theoretical viewpoint, stress tests may be more effective than conventional capital standards in lowering the need for future bailouts or bail-ins due to the forward-looking nature of stress tests. Stress tests may also have an advantage over standard capital requirements because the capital is targeted toward providing capital cushions when they are most needed to avoid bank financial distress. In addition, stress tests have prudential benefits by forcing the banks to be more forward-looking and to develop loss models that help them predict the effects of future financial crises.

As previously argued, theory also allows for the possibility that higher capital can result in higher portfolio risk. As a result, stress tests may also increase bank risk in opposition to the *Prudential Mechanism*.

22.2.2 The *Certification Mechanism* of stress tests

Stress tests may work through the *Certification Mechanism* by assuring the public about the safety of banks that pass the stress tests. They can additionally help certify the safety of the banking industry more generally and reduce contagion risks by letting the public know that some of the banks that help stabilize the financial system are relatively safe (Choi, 2014). In contrast, to the extent that the *Prudential Mechanism* makes banks riskier, the *Certification Mechanism* may also increase runs and contagion risks for the industry.

At the individual bank level, the effects of the *Certification Mechanism* are ambiguous as well. Banks that pass the stress tests may have positive reputational effects from the tests. For banks that fail the stress tests, the *Certification Mechanism* is less clear. The stigma of failure may reduce public confidence in the banks that fail the tests. Alternatively, to the extent that the stress tests require these banks to adhere to a capital plan that brings them up to standards, the *Certification Mechanism* may play a positive role for these banks.

A potential downside of the *Certification Mechanism* of the stress tests is that they may confer TBTF status on the participant banks. That is, the stress tests are generally only applied to the largest banks and may make the managers and other stakeholders in these banks believe that they are more likely to get future bailouts and other safety net benefits, creating moral hazard incentives to take on more portfolio risks.

22.3 Descriptions of the different stress tests

This section discusses US and EU stress tests and the empirical research on their effectiveness. These tests are typically targeted toward the most systemically important institutions that often cover the majority of the banking industry assets in their nations.

22.3.1 US stress tests

There have been three different US stress test programs since the Global Financial Crisis of the late 2000s—the Supervisory Capital Assessment Program (SCAP), the Comprehensive Capital Analysis and Review (CCAR), and the Dodd–Frank Act Stress Tests (DFAST). As discussed below, the SCAP was a one-time test during the Global Financial Crisis in 2009, and the CCAR and DFAST are annual events that started in 2011 and 2013, respectively.

22.3.1.1 Supervisory Capital Assessment Program

The first US stress test program was the SCAP of 2009, in which stress tests were conducted simultaneously on he nation's 19 largest BHCs with consolidated assets exceeding $100 billion.[1] The main purposes of SCAP were to measure the strength of these BHCs and their ability to withstand

---

[1] The 19 BHCs tested were Bank of America, JPMorgan Chase, Citigroup, Wells Fargo, Goldman Sachs, Morgan Stanley, Metropolitan Life Insurance, PNC Financial Services, U.S. Bancorp, the Bank of New York Mellon, GMAC, SunTrust Banks, Capital One, BB&T, Regions Financial Corporation, State Street Corporation, American Express, Fifth Third Bank, and KeyCorp.

more adverse scenarios, and to require them to have or raise sufficient capital to continue lending in such scenarios (*Prudential Mechanism*). SCAP was also viewed as helpful in reducing investor fears during the Global Financial Crisis and getting more capital invested back into these BHCs (*Certification Mechanism*).

SCAP involved two macroeconomic scenarios. The "baseline" scenario was intended to be representative of the poor economic climate brought on by the Global Financial Crisis. The more "adverse" scenario included the unemployment rate above 10%, and home prices dropping another 25%. The BHCs would have to calculate how much more capital they would need to have Tier 1 capital $\geq$ 6% and Tier 1 common capital $\geq$ 4%, with the estimates reviewed by bank supervisors. These organizations had to have or raise enough capital to meet capital requirements under the more adverse scenario, or the US Treasury would provide the capital. The results showed that 10 of the 19 BHCs did not immediately meet the capital ratio targets under the more adverse scenario, but they raised the funds privately within a seven-month period afterward because of the confidence that the disclosure of the results gave investors (Schuermann, 2014). Thus, the *Certification Mechanism* appeared to work quite well for SCAP.

22.3.1.2 Comprehensive Capital Analysis and Review

The CCAR started in 2011 and made stress testing a permanent part of capital adequacy review processes in order to quantify any gaps that might exist at banks. CCAR started with the $100 billion BHCs in 2011, but in 2014, this changed to cover any bank with consolidated assets more than $50 billion, 30 institutions at that time. CCAR allows for the Federal Reserve to evaluate capital adequacy, internal capital adequacy assessment processes, and plans for dividends and stock buybacks. These banks have to submit annual capital plans to the Federal Reserve, which decides if these plans are sufficient to provide enough capital to weather economic and financial stress. If they are not sufficient, the bank is restricted in its capital payouts and must submit an amended plan. Banks can fail the stress tests for insufficient capital (quantitative assessment), inadequate risk management (qualitative assessment), or both.[2] As of 2019, the

---

[2] In 2018, government regulators decided to give a conditional nonobjection to three BHCs: Goldman Sachs Group, Inc., Morgan Stanley, and State Street Corp. These BHCs were about to fail a portion of the exam, so regulators proposed that if they decided to limit their capital distributions to their stakeholders, they would be given the opportunity for a second chance to retake the tests for a passing grade. This was decided on grounds of the harsher scenario by design leading to higher projected losses and the new tax reform that impacted projections as well. A negotiation of this stature had not been heard of before this 2018 testing cycle, which was considered one of the harshest yet, in which scenarios included skyrocketing unemployment, crashing markets, and large loan losses.

Federal Reserve issued a final rule to exempt from the qualitative portion large firms that have participated in CCAR for four consecutive years and have passed the final year's qualitative component without objection.[3] The qualitative part of a bank's capital plan would remain for "large and complex" institutions. In addition, the Federal Reserve more recently proposed replacing the quantitative portion of CCAR with stress capital buffer requirements tailored to individual banks as well as enhanced transparency of the stress testing program. Under this proposal, the banks would have to keep year-round capital ratios above the stress buffer requirements in order to avoid restrictions on capital distributions and bonuses.[4]

22.3.1.3 Dodd–Frank Act stress tests

A provision of the Dodd–Frank Act of 2010 is the DFAST, which are supplementary to CCAR. DFAST requires state nonmember banks and state savings associations with more than $10 billion in consolidated assets to perform internal stress tests. While DFAST was released in 2010 when the Dodd–Frank Wall Street Reform Act was signed into law, it was only from 2013 onwards that banks were mandated to participate in this stress testing exercise. There are three scenarios that are used in this examination: "baseline," "adverse," and "severely adverse." While the "adverse" and "severely adverse" scenarios are not representative forecasts of the future of the economy, they are used as hypothetical situations to assess the strength and resilience of these financial institutions. These institutions had to turn in their financial results so that their risk profiles may be analyzed. The institutions were required to publish a summary of their results by October 15th of that year.

While DFAST and CCAR are complementary, they differ in their goals and structures. While CCAR is a capital plan, DFAST is different in that it is a mandated-by-law stress test rule per the Dodd–Frank Act. It includes only quantitative information in both the micro (firm-specific) and macro (industry-wide) capital ratio perspectives. One of the biggest differences between CCAR and DFAST is the capital actions assumed in generating the post-stress capital ratios. CCAR has planned capital actions based on the firm's capital plan, while DFAST has stylized capital actions, which use assumptions about dividends based on each BHC's recent behavior. There are also differences between the two when it comes to what happens should a bank fail the stress tests. If a bank fails DFAST, this puts a restriction on dividends, while failing CCAR results in restrictions on

---

[3] https://www.federalreserve.gov/newsevents/pressreleases/bcreg20190306b.htm

[4] https://www.federalreserve.gov/newsevents/pressreleases/files/bcreg20180410a1.pdf

both planned dividends and capital repurchases and enhanced supervisory review of BHC risk management processes.

22.3.1.4 Recent changes in US stress testing

On May 14, 2018, the Congress passed, and President Trump signed into law the Economic Growth, Regulatory Relief, and Consumer Protection Act (aka Crapo Bill) that made changes to DFAST. This is the first major legislation to change the financial regulatory landscape since the Dodd–Frank Act in 2010.[5] The Act provides immediate regulatory relief from DFAST for BHCs with total consolidated assets less than $250 billion and nonbank assets less than $75 billion by rolling back some of the provisions in DFAST (not CCAR).[6] Thus, banks with less than $100 billion would no longer be subject to the DFAST oversight,[7] while banks between $100–$250 billion would no longer be subject to these tougher regulations 18 months after the enactment of the bill.[8] Finally, BHCs with assets greater than $250 billion[9] remain subject to CCAR/DFAST requirements and all enhanced prudential standards such as G-SIB capital surcharges, enhanced supervisory leverage ratio (eSLR), and total loss absorbing capacity (TLAC). For both DFAST and CCAR stress tests, the Bill also reduces the number of stress test scenarios from three to two ("baseline" and "severely adverse"), removing the "adverse" scenario.

In 2018, the Federal Reserve put forward a proposal to create an integrated framework linking large banks' CCAR quantitative stress test results with their current capital buffer requirements using new "stress capital buffers." Thus, the new large bank capital requirements would reflect both the erosion of the firm's capital in a severely adverse scenario (the stress capital buffer requirement) and the risk due to their potential distress to the broader financial system (any GSIB surcharge and countercyclical capital buffer amount). In late 2018, Randal Quarles, Vice Chairman for Supervision of the Federal Reserve, mentioned that due to

[5] https://www.congress.gov/bill/115th-congress/senate-bill/2155

[6] https://www.federalreserve.gov/newsevents/pressreleases/bcreg20190205b.htm

[7] There are eight institutions no longer subject to public CCAR/DFAST stress tests: BB&T, BBVA Compass, BMO Financial, BNP Paribas, MUFG Americas, RBC USA, Santander, and SunTrust Banks.

[8] There are nine institutions in the $100–$250 billion category: American Express, Ally Financial, Citizens Financial, Fifth Third Bancorp, KeyCorp, Regions Financial, M&T Bank, Huntington Bancshares, and Discover Financial.

[9] There are 18 institutions with $250 billion and more in assets: Bank of America, Credit Suisse, The Bank of New York Mellon, Barclays US, Capital One Financial, Citigroup, Deutsche Bank, Goldman Sachs, HSBC North America, JPMorgan Chase, Morgan Stanley, Northern Trust, PNC Financial, State Street, TD Group US Holdings, U.S. Bancorp, UBS Americas, and Wells Fargo.

numerous comments received from the industry, this stress capital buffer rule is not likely to take effect before 2020.[10] In late June 2019, all 18 stress-tested banks passed the Federal Reserve's examination and were allowed to distribute excess funds to shareholders. Compared to 2018, the 2019 stress test weighted credit card exposures more than commercial loan exposures and examined foreign banks' operations, specifically the US arm of Deutsche Bank AG, which failed the exam three times before passing in 2019.

22.3.2 EU stress tests

The EU stress testing experience is quite different from that in the US. EU stress tests also comprised a "baseline" scenario and an "adverse" scenario, similar to that of the US stress tests. The first EU-wide stress test took place in 2009, the purpose of which was to assess the EU banking industry in aggregate. After the disclosure of the results, investors did not find the results to be sufficiently transparent. During the European Sovereign Debt Crisis in 2010, the Committee of European Bank Supervisors (CEBS) implemented stress tests for the second time on 91 EU banks in 20 EU member states which represented 65% of the total assets of the EU banking sector at that time. Of the 91 banks that participated, only seven did not meet the Tier 1 capital adequacy ratio and were required to raise extra capital. However, after having to bail out Irish banks that had previously passed the stress tests, the tests began to receive significant scrutiny.

The 2011 EU stress tests were conducted on 90 EU banks. The tests contained two scenarios, a "baseline" and an "adverse" scenario. Of the 90 banks that participated, eight of the banks failed, five of which were Spanish banks, demonstrating a clear disconnect in the strength of the Spanish banking system compared to that of the rest of the EU. This time around, the stress tests results were more transparent, but were also tarnished after Dexia N.V./S.A, a Franco-Belgian bank, received €6 billion in taxpayer bailouts after also having passed the stress tests. That year, IMF's head was also quoted mentioning that EU banks were in desperate need of more capital, estimated at €200 billion, which led to more scrutiny of the stress tests.

22.4 Empirical evidence on the mechanisms of the stress tests

We next review the empirical research regarding how well the stress tests performed through the *Prudential* and *Certification Mechanisms*.

---

[10] https://www.federalreserve.gov/newsevents/speech/quarles20181109a.htm

The empirical findings are consistent with those for capital requirements, with favorable effects for stress tests in terms of reducing bank risk for both the *Prudential* and *Certification Mechanisms*. These are shown as "+s" in Table 19.1 Panel B.

22.4.1 Empirical evidence on the *Prudential Mechanism* of stress tests

We evaluate research on the prudential effects of stress tests. We first note some difficulties in analyzing these tests. First, for the US in particular, actual financial conditions have only improved since the onset of the stress tests, so it is not possible to directly observe whether the tests met their goals of enabling banks to withstand adverse scenarios that never materialized. A second problem is that many other factors that also affect bank risk occurred over the same time period. A third complication is that stress tests are intended to work through changing banks' behaviors, such as their willingness to supply credit, which must be disentangled from the choices of their customers, their demand for credit.

There are several ways to assess whether stress tests made the tested institutions safer. One way is to examine whether the loan portfolios of stress-tested banks became safer relative to peers after the tests went into effect. Acharya, Berger, and Roman (2018) find that the BHCs with over $100 billion in assets subject to the 2009–2013 SCAP and CCAR stress tests reduced their credit risks. The BHCs did so by increasing interest rate spreads on commercial loans—particularly to relatively risky borrowers. The authors' tests use loan characteristics from DealScan, borrower characteristics from Compustat, and bank characteristics from Call Reports. Three other sets of tests analyzing credit supply at the extensive margin use broad credit categories, small business loans, and bank risk measures based on Call Report data, and provide consistent results. Covas (2017) and Cortés, Demyanyk, Li, Loutskina, and Strahan (2019) also find that stress-tested institutions reduce their willingness to supply loans to small businesses, which are typically relatively risky credits. Berrospide and Edge (2019) find that CCAR stress tests significantly reduce commercial and industrial (C&I) lending to large firms by the stress-tested banks. However, the economic effects are inconsequential, and firms are generally able to borrow elsewhere and do not reduce their investments or hiring. Connolly (2018) similarly finds that credit reductions in the syndicated loan market by stress-tested banks in the 2009 SCAP were largely offset by credits from other institutions. Thus, stress-tested banks reduced their risks, but such risks may have been transferred to other banks not subject to stress tests. This may have reduced systemic risk, given that the other banks are generally less systemically important.

Another method to gauge bank safety is to examine the capital ratios of the stress-tested banks. Cornett, Minnick, Schorno, and Tehranian (2018) examine bank behavior from 2009 to 2016 and find several inconsistencies that suggest banks may be window dressing or managing financial performance to look more attractive to regulators and investors. They find that stress-tested banks have higher capital ratios than their peers in the CCAR starting quarter, which are reversed in later quarters.

Another way to evaluate the prudential effects of the stress tests is to assess the stress test models themselves. Acharya, Engle, and Pierret (2014) compare projected losses from stress tests to the contributions to systemic risk such as the SRISK of the institutions, which represent the capital shortfall a financial institution would need to raise during a crisis. They evaluate stress tests in both the US and the EU and conclude that the projected losses of both stress tests and systemic risk match well, suggesting that stress tests are helpful in preparing banks for actual losses.

22.4.2 Empirical evidence on the *Certification Mechanism* of stress tests

There is a considerable research agenda showing that the *Certification Mechanism* of stress tests works at the individual banking organization level. The evidence strongly suggests that stress tests other than the first EU test in 2009 improve transparency and allow investors to distinguish better among banking organizations with different risk profiles.

Morgan, Peristiani, and Savino (2014) compare how stock prices reacted to the announcement of the 2009 SCAP stress test, the clarification of the motives behind it, the release of the white paper detailing the methodologies of the exam, and the release of the actual results. They find that the clarification and results disclosure were informative to the public in terms of stock prices. Investors were fairly informed on which banks have capital deficiencies, as the stress tests allowed them to better quantify the banks' capital gap and revalue banks via stock prices.

Petrella and Resti (2013) review the 2011 EU stress test and find that the disclosure of the results created abnormal price and volume movements, signaling the creation of new information. Flannery, Hirtle, and Kovner (2017) examine US stress tests and find consistent results. They find that US stress test disclosures are associated with significantly higher absolute abnormal returns, as well as higher abnormal trading volume, indicating information improvements, while finding no reduction in private information collection by analysts.

Finally, Georgescu, Gross, Kapp, and Kok (2017) show that for both the US and EU, after the release of stress test results, poorly capitalized banks under the "adverse" scenario report higher negative returns compared to banks with higher capital ratios.

References

Acharya, V. V., Berger, A. N., & Roman, R. A. (2018). Lending implications of US bank stress tests: Costs or benefits? *Journal of Financial Intermediation, 34,* 58—90.

Acharya, V. V., Engle, R., & Pierret, D. (2014). Testing macroprudentialstress tests: The risk of regulatory risk weights. *Journal of Monetary Economics, 65,* 36—53.

Berrospide, J. M., & Edge, R. M. (2019). *The effects of bank capital buffers on bank lending and firm activity, what can we learn from five years of stress-test results?* (Working Paper).

Choi, D. B. (2014). Heterogeneity and stability: Bolster the strong, not the weak. *The Review of Financial Studies, 27*(6), 1830—1867.

Connolly, M. (2018). *The real effects of stress testing* (Working Paper).

Cornett, M. M., Minnick, K., Schorno, P. J., & Tehranian, H. (2018). An examination of bank behavior around Federal Reserve stress tests. *Journal of Financial Intermediation,* 100789.

Cortés, K. R., Demyanyk, Y., Li, L., Loutskina, E., & Strahan, P. E. (2020). Stress tests and small business lending. *Journal of Financial Economics, 136*(1), 260—279.

Covas, F. (2017). *The capital allocation inherent in the Federal Reserve's capital stress test* (Working Paper).

Flannery, M., Hirtle, B., & Kovner, A. (2017). Evaluating the information in the federal Reserve stress tests. *Journal of Financial Intermediation, 29,* 1—18.

Georgescu, O. M., Gross, M., Kapp, D., & Kok, C. (2017). *Do stress tests matter? Evidence from the 2014 and 2016 stress tests* (Working Paper).

Morgan, D. P., Peristiani, S., & Savino, V. (2014). The information value of the stress test. *Journal of Money, Credit and Banking, 46*(7), 1479—1500.

Petrella, G., & Resti, A. (2013). Supervisors as information producers: Do stress tests reduce bank opaqueness? *Journal of Banking and Finance, 37*(12), 5406—5420.

Schuermann, T. (2014). Stress testing banks. *International Journal of Forecasting, 30*(3), 717—728.

CHAPTER

23

Prudential regulatory activity restrictions

In this chapter, we discuss prudential regulatory activity restrictions, which are designed to keep banks safe and sound and avoid financial distress that may otherwise trigger bailouts, bail-ins, or other resolution methods. Section 23.1 defines the concepts and goals of prudential regulatory activity restrictions. Section 23.2 describes how these restrictions may function through the three mechanisms for avoiding bank financial distress. Section 23.3 reviews a few important prudential regulatory activity restrictions that have been imposed in the US and EU. Finally, Section 23.4 summarizes the empirical evidence on the mechanisms through which the restrictions may reduce the likelihood of bank financial distress and the need for resolutions.

23.1 What are prudential regulatory activity restrictions?

Prudential regulatory activity restrictions are limits or prohibitions on bank behaviors that are designed to reduce risks. They include limits on how much banks may engage in some activities, such as legal lending limits on credit exposures to a counterparty, as well as outright bans on other activities that are considered to be too risky, such as investments in junk-grade bonds.

Prudential regulatory activity restrictions generally apply industry-wide or to a size class or other group of banks. We distinguish them from activity restrictions brought about by prudential supervision, which usually target specific banks that are deemed to be particularly risky or engaging in some problem behavior. The 1933 Glass—Steagall Act prohibition on combining commercial and investment banking and the 2010 Dodd—Frank Wall Street Reform and Consumer Protection Act's Volcker Rule forbidding proprietary trading are examples of prudential regulatory activity restrictions. Activity restrictions by prudential supervisors,

353

in contrast, include enforcement actions (EAs), such as cease-and-desist orders applied to individual banks overengaging in risky activities. Prudential supervisory activity restrictions are discussed further in Chapter 24 on prudential supervision.

23.2 Prudential regulatory activity restrictions and the three mechanisms for avoiding bank financial distress

As discussed below, prudential regulatory activity restrictions may or may not reduce the likelihood of financial distress through the *Prudential* and *Certification Mechanism*s. These restrictions do not involve government subsidies, so the *Subsidy Mechanism* is not in effect. Reflecting these effects, the Prudential Regulatory Activity Restrictions column in Table 19.1 Panel A shows "?s" for the *Prudential Mechanism* and the *Certification Mechanism* and "N/A" for the *Subsidy Mechanism*.

23.2.1 The *Prudential Mechanism* of prudential regulatory activity restrictions

The argument that prohibiting or restricting the amount that a bank can engage in a relatively risky activity reduces bank risk is intuitive. Doing less of something that is relatively risky would seem to reduce bank risk, so prudential regulatory activity restrictions that prohibit or limit relatively risky activities seemingly would work through the *Prudential Mechanism*.

However, this simple argument ignores at least three well-reasoned theoretical arguments to the contrary—diversification, charter value, and shadow banking. We briefly review these alternatives next.

First, basic finance theory demonstrates that diversification into other assets can reduce portfolio risk, even if the other assets are riskier, provided that the correlations between the returns are relatively low or negative. This same argument applies to activities as well as assets. Berger, El Ghoul, Guedhami, and Roman (2017) investigate this issue in terms of international diversification. They present a simple model of how diversification may increase or decrease the traditional Z-score measure of bank risk, the number of standard deviations of returns away from wiping out bank capital. Using numerical simulation methods, they find cases in which more diversification does and does not reduce overall risk. Their model yields the intuitive findings that diversification generally reduces overall portfolio risk when the correlations of returns are negative and the additional asset or activity is relatively safe, and generally increases overall risk when correlations of returns are positive and the additional asset or activity is relatively risky.

Second, regulatory restrictions may reduce bank franchise value by lowering bank profits that otherwise might be made by engaging in the prohibited activity. The bank might otherwise profit from the risky activity because of either generally higher expected returns on relatively risky activities or exploiting economies of scale and/or scope by engaging in the restricted activity (e.g., Claessens and Klingebiel, 2001). The profit losses from the prudential regulatory activity restrictions may encourage banks to take on more risk elsewhere in their activities because there is less franchise value to protect by acting prudently (e.g., Keeley, 1990).[1]

Third, when there is significant market demand for the financial services that banks are restricted from providing, it is likely that these services may be alternatively provided by "shadow banks." Shadow banks are financial institutions that provide financial services that compete with or are similar to those of banks, but are less regulated and supervised because they do not have insured deposits. The risks associated with the restricted services do not go away when they move to shadow banks, and may in fact be intensified because of the lighter regulation and supervision. Thus, prudential regulatory activity restrictions on banks may actually increase systemic risk by shifting risky activities to parts of the financial system that are less monitored and controlled.

23.2.2 The *Certification Mechanism* of prudential regulatory activity restrictions

If prudential regulatory activity restrictions make the banking industry safer through the *Prudential Mechanism*—which is uncertain as discussed above—they may also make the banking industry safer through the *Certification Mechanism*. That is, by assuring the public about the safety of the banking industry, they may reduce the likelihood of public panics, runs that might otherwise create liquidity problems or make it difficult for the banks to raise funds. Of course, the opposite holds if prudential regulatory activity restrictions increase banks' risks.

---

[1] The response of the banks to prudential restrictions from either regulators or supervisors may also depend on the corporate governance of the banks because of the different risk preferences of bank shareholders and managers. Shareholders may more often wish to take more risk to exploit protections from limited liability, deposit insurance, TBTF, TITF, or TMTF status, etc., while bank managers may be more worried about their potential human capital losses associated with bank distress and failure. Thus, the effects of prudential activity restrictions on bank risk may depend crucially on the extent to which the corporate governance of the bank gives shareholders versus managers more control (e.g., Laeven and Levine, 2009).

23.3 Prudential regulatory activity restrictions in practice

There are far too many prudential regulatory activity restrictions in practice to describe here, so we briefly sample a few important restrictions in the US and EU.

23.3.1 US

US regulators directly impose prudential regulatory activity restrictions on both bank holding companies (BHCs)—which own banks and other financial firms—and on the banks and sometimes other financial firms. Generally speaking, US prudential regulatory activity restrictions are tightened immediately following financial crises that create significant real economic harm. Examples include the 1933 Glass–Steagall Act and the 2010 Dodd–Frank Act. They followed the 1929 financial crash and bank failures that caused the Great Depression and the Global Financial Crisis that caused the Great Recession, respectively. Such restrictions are typically rolled back or loosened when some time has passed since these events. Examples of such deregulation include the 1980 Depository Institutions Deregulation and Monetary Control Act (DIDMCA), the 1994 Riegle-Neal Act, the 1999 Gramm–Leach–Bliley Act (aka Financial Services Modernization Act), and the 2018 Economic Growth, Regulatory Relief, and Consumer Protection Act. Parts of some of these changes in prudential regulatory activity restrictions are covered below.

23.3.1.1 The separation and reintegration of commercial and investment banking—including the 1933 Glass–Steagall Act and the 1999 Gramm–Leach–Bliley Act

The 1933 Glass–Steagall Act had three main functions. First, it created the FDIC, which provides deposit insurance in order to reduce the frequency of bank runs, which were common in the Great Depression, protect small depositors who were often wiped out in these runs, and achieve other goals. Second, it imposed upper limits on deposit interest rates, including zero on demand deposits (Regulation Q), to offset what was thought to be ruinous competition that destroyed banks during the Great Depression. Third, it separated commercial and investment banking activities as well as insurance underwriting, which we discuss further in this subsection.

A key purpose of the separation of commercial and investment banking was to prevent the use of insured deposits for risky investment bank activities. These "improper banking activities" were thought to be among the important causes of the financial crash that created the Great

Depression. As discussed above, even if investment banking is riskier, restricting commercial banks from engaging in such activities may or may not reduce bank risk because such restrictions may limit the possibilities for risk diversification, charter value enhancement from scale and scope economies, or profitable investments that may reduce overall bank risks. This restriction may also increase systemic risk by pushing risky activities into less regulated and monitored "shadow banks."

After various challenges, the Federal Reserve in 1987 allowed BHCs to establish Section 20 affiliates as investment banks to underwrite commercial debt and equity. The revenues from restricted securities underwriting activities had to be less than 5% of the total revenue of the Section 20 affiliates, later raised to 10% in 1989, and then to 25% in 1997. The permissible activities of BHCs were expanded further by the Federal Reserve and the OCC later in 1997, allowing them to acquire existing investment banks, rather than establishing Section 20 subsidiaries. This resulted in a number of M&As between commercial and investment banks from 1997 through 2000.

An important M&A was the 1998 combination of Citicorp and Travelers into Citigroup. Citicorp was a very large and diversified BHC that owned one of the largest US banks, Citibank, and Travelers was a diversified financial conglomerate that owned Travelers Insurance, as well as the investment bank Salomon Brothers and other firms.

Despite the fact that Travelers was spun off in 2002, the 1998 M&A was a catalyst for the 1999 Gramm–Leach–Bliley Act. The inclusion of insurance underwriting in a BHC was prohibited by the Glass–Steagall Act, but CEOs Sanford Weill and John Reed received assurances for exemptions for five years from the Federal Reserve to give time for the US Congress and President to enact legislation to make the combination legal.

It only took one year to enact the 1999 Gramm–Leach–Bliley Act, which allows Financial Holding Companies (FHCs), a type of BHC, to own commercial banks, investment banks, and insurance underwriters. Notably, the corporate governance form, in which the different functional entities may be owned by the same FHC, but must be separately chartered and capitalized, reduces the possibility of economies of scale and scope benefits. In contrast, the full universal structure in Germany and other countries allows for commercial banking, investment banking, and insurance underwriting to be provided by the same financial institution.

23.3.1.2 The 2010 Dodd–Frank Act's Volcker Rule and the 2018 Economic Growth, Regulatory Relief, and Consumer Protection Act

The Volcker Rule, Section 619 of the 2010 Dodd–Frank Act, prohibits banks and BHCs from proprietary trading and limits investments in hedge fund/private equity fund sponsorship to a total of 3% of capital.

Key exceptions to the proprietary trading restrictions are "risk-mitigating hedging activity" and "underwriting and market-making activities," which make the rule difficult to enforce.

As above for investment banking in the 1930s, the argument was made that proprietary trading, hedge funds, and private equity activities are inherently riskier than traditional commercial bank activities and should not be funded by insured deposits. Former Federal Reserve Chairman Paul Volcker, after whom the Rule is named, went further and claimed that such speculative activity played a key role in the Global Financial Crisis.

It is quite possible that the enforcement of the Volcker rule makes banks safer, but there are several issues with these arguments. First, it is also possible that these restrictions make banking organizations riskier by cutting off sources of profit that would otherwise boost charter value and capital and possibly diversify bank risk. Second, banks and BHCs are not the only institutions that are bailed out during financial crises, so it might not make sense to push risky activities to other financial institutions that may also be protected by the government. As examples, hedge fund Long-Term Capital Management (LTCM) was rescued during the Russian debt crisis of 1998, and investment bank Bear Stearns and insurance company American International Group (AIG) were bailed out during the Global Financial Crisis in 2008. Third, we are not aware of evidence that proprietary trading by banking organizations played a key role in the Global Financial Crisis. Rather, bad investments in mortgage-backed securities (MBSs), which are not restricted by the Volcker Rule, seem to have driven the crisis.

The 2018 Economic Growth, Regulatory Relief, and Consumer Protection Act, also known as the Economic Growth Act, scales back certain requirements of the 2010 Dodd—Frank Act and provides other regulatory relief. For our purposes here, we note that banking organizations with less than $10 billion in assets are exempt from the Volcker Rule and its proprietary trading prohibitions under the 2018 Act.

23.3.1.3 Interagency guidance on leveraged lending

A leveraged loan usually means a loan to a company with a high leverage ratio, often for the purpose of an M&A or leveraged buyout. They have high credit risk and typically carry high rates of interest to compensate for that risk. Such loans are also often syndicated, passing much of the risk from the originating bank to investors. In 2001, the Federal Reserve, OCC, and FDIC collectively issued leveraged lending guidance, highlighting the need for comprehensive screening and monitoring to control the risk.[2]

In March 2013, the agencies issued explicit guidelines that updated and replaced the 2001 guidance regarding loans that should not be made by banks.[3] The guidance states that banks should not make loans to firms that would leave the companies with a debt of at least six times their earnings. Although the Leveraged Lending Guidelines were not formal rules traditional lenders who do not comply with the Guidelines could be subjected to a broad range of potential informal and formal enforcement measures. However, some of the banks essentially ignored these rules after the 2013 issuance. Later on, the examiners cracked down in examinations and regulatory officials, including the then-Federal Reserve Chair Janet Yellen, issued warnings. In 2016, Federal Reserve examiners cracked down by questioning the calculations of earnings in the ratio. Apparently, some firms had misrepresented their earnings to get around the restrictions.

The consequences of the regulatory pressure include some loans that banks would have made going through shadow banks. However, many others may not have been made with potentially significant macroeconomic impacts. As with the earlier examples, the effects of the restrictions are not known, in part because it is not known whether the profits from the high rates on these loans fully compensate for the risks, nor are the diversification benefits of these loans well understood.

23.3.2 European Union

Prudential regulatory activity restrictions in EU largely mimic those in the US We briefly mention two of these.

23.3.2.1 *ECB Guidance on Leveraged Transactions*

On May 18, 2017, the European Central Bank (ECB) published its final Guidance on Leveraged Transactions.[4] The ECB Guidance is aligned with the 2013 Leveraged Lending Guidance published by the US bank regulators It states that transactions presenting total leverage in excess of six times should remain exceptional. Similarly, the ECB Guidance recommends that borrowers should show the cash-flow ability to repay all of their senior debt or at least half of their total debt in five to seven years (or "deliver to a sustainable level").

---

[2] https://www.federalreserve.gov/boarddocs/press/general/2001/20010409/default.htm

[3] https://www.federalreserve.gov/supervisionreg/srletters/sr1303a1.pdf

[4] https://www.bankingsupervision.europa.eu/ecb/pub/pdf/ssm.leveraged_transactions_guidance_201705.en.pdf

23.3.2.2 Liikanen Report

In response to European banking problems during the Global Financial Crisis and European Sovereign Debt Crisis, the EU set up its high-level expert group on reforming the structure of the EU banking sector. It was chaired by Erkki Liikanen, governor of the Bank of Finland. In October 2012, it issued the Liikanen Report,[5] which contained a number of recommendations. Most of the recommendations concern bail-ins, capital standards, and corporate governance of banking organizations. However, some fall in the category here of prudential regulatory activity restrictions. These include mandatory separation of proprietary trading and other high-risk trading activities, similar to the US Volcker Rule.

23.4 Empirical evidence on the mechanisms of the prudential regulatory activity restrictions

We next review the empirical research regarding how well prudential regulatory activity restrictions perform through the three mechanisms. There is little empirical research supporting or contradicting the *Prudential and Certification Mechanisms*. These findings are shown as a "+" and a"?," respectively in Table 19.1 Panel B.

23.4.1 Empirical evidence on the *Prudential Mechanism* of prudential regulatory activity restrictions

In the interest of brevity, we restrict attention here to two sets of research evidence on the bank risk effects of prudential regulatory activity restrictions. The first set assesses the effects of legal lending limits, which were only briefly noted above. These limits typically restrict credit exposure to any one counterparty as a function of bank capital. US banks are generally limited to loans plus other exposures to a single borrower of no more than 15% of the institution's capital, with additional 10 percentage points if the credits are very well collateralized. Some research suggests that these limits may be effective in the syndicated loan market, forcing banks to diversify credit risks by selling off parts of bigger loans. Simons (1993) finds that the loan-to-capital ratio is one of the primary factors that drive loan syndication. Similarly, Godlewski and Weill (2008) focus on emerging markets, such as Asia, the Middle East, Central and Eastern Europe, and Latin America, and find that lending limits motivate the syndication of the largest loans.

---

[5] https://ec.europa.eu/info/publications/liikanen-report_en

The second set of research focuses on the leveraged lending guidance discussed above. Schenck and Shi (2017) find that the leveraged lending guidance is effective in reducing the risky syndicated lending of the largest banks. However, Kim, Plosser, and Santos (2018) find that the guidance did not reduce overall system-wide leveraged lending, but rather shifted it to less-regulated lenders.

23.4.2 Empirical evidence on the *Certification Mechanism* of prudential regulatory activity restrictions

There is very sparse research on the *Certification Mechanism* of prudential regulatory activity restrictions and the results differ for different activity restrictions analyzed. As noted above, these restrictions generally apply industry-wide or to a size class or other group of banks, rather than individual institutions, making it difficult to perform such research.

Cyree (2000) studies stock price reactions to the December 20, 1996 announcement of the 1997 increase from 10% to 25% of the total revenue of Section 20 affiliates in the restricted securities underwriting activities noted above. The author finds that BHC share prices react favorably to the adoption of the increased Section 20 powers. Abnormal returns are significantly higher for money center banks, banks with prior Section 20 subsidiaries, and large regional commercial banks as compared to small regional banks. These findings of a positive effect of lifting activity restrictions suggest that markets perceived activity restrictions negatively, inconsistent with the *Certification Mechanism*.

Turk and Swicegood (2012) measure the market's reaction to the emergence of the Dodd—Frank Act, focusing on various events surrounding it, including the announcement and endorsement of the Volcker Rule in January 2010. Authors find a significantly positive stock market reaction around the announcement of the Volcker Rule, consistent with the *Certification Mechanism* for these activity restrictions for banks.

References

Berger, A. N., El Ghoul, S., Guedhami, O., & Roman, R. A. (2017). Internationalization and bank risk. *Management Science, 63*(7), 2283—2301.

Claessens, S., & Klingebiel, D. (2001). Competition and scope of activities in financial services. *The World Bank Research Observer, 16*(1), 19—40.

Cyree, K. B. (2000). The erosion of the Glass—Steagall Act: Winners and losers in the banking industry. *Journal of Economics and Business, 52*(4), 343—363.

Godlewski, C. J., & Weill, L. (2008). Syndicated loans in emerging markets. *Emerging Markets Review, 9*(3), 206—219.

Keeley, M. C. (1990). Deposit insurance, risk, and market power in banking. *The American Economic Review, 80*(5), 1183—1200.

Kim, S., Plosser, M. C., & Santos, J. A. C. (2018). Macroprudential policy and the revolving door of risk: Lessons from leveraged lending guidance. *Journal of Financial Intermediation, 34,* 17–31.

Laeven, L., & Levine, R. (2009). Bank governance, regulation and risk taking. *Journal of Financial Economics, 93*(2), 259–275.

Schenck, N., & Shi, L. (2017). *Leveraged lending regulation and loan syndicate structure: A shift to shadow banking?* (Working Paper).

Simons, K. (1993). Why do banks syndicate loans? *New England Economic Review,* (January), 45–52.

Turk, G., & Swicegood, P. (2012). Assessing the markets reaction to the Dodd-Frank Act. *Journal of Business and Economics Research, 10*(10), 569–578.

24

Prudential supervision

In this chapter, we review prudential supervision, a key tool designed to keep banks safe and sound and deter financial distress that may otherwise trigger costly bailouts, bail-ins, or other resolution approaches. Section 24.1 defines the concept and goals of prudential supervision. Section 24.2 describes how supervision may function through the three mechanisms for avoiding bank financial distress. Section 24.3 discusses the prudential supervision structures that have been implemented in the US and EU. Finally, Section 24.4 presents the empirical evidence on how well prudential supervision functions in reducing the likelihood of financial distress through the mechanisms. To avoid unnecessary repetition, we exclude specific discussions of bank capital, stress tests, and other supervisory topics covered in earlier chapters.

24.1 What is prudential supervision?

The central goal of prudential supervision is risk identification and management that enable financial institutions to have operational and financial stability under potential financial crises or various other hazardous circumstances (Board of Governors of the Federal Reserve System, 2012). This supervision may also be viewed as types of delegated monitoring. Government supervisors collect private information on bank risk that depositors, debtholders, shareholders, and other market participants cannot access from public sources, and help keep that risk under control on their behalves.

We distinguish between microprudential and macroprudential supervision. The former focuses on the safety and soundness of individual banks, while the latter is concerned with overall financial stability and the prevention or dampening of financial crises. Both types of supervision are intended to help offset the effects of moral hazard incentives created by deposit insurance, TBTF, TITF, TMTF, and other aspects of explicit and implicit safety nets and bailout expectations for banks (e.g., Mishkin,

363

2001). Since the financial and economic devastation brought about by the Global Financial Crisis, both types of supervision have received more attention, but attention to macroprudential supervision has been amplified much more. Note that the microprudential versus macroprudential distinction applies to regulation as well as supervision, but in the interest of brevity, we discuss it here only, rather than in all of the regulation chapters.

In practice, microprudential supervision consists of three basic activities. The first involves assessing if the banks are complying with legal rules and regulations related to bank safety and soundness. The second is monitoring whether banks are taking excessive risks independent of whether or not they are in compliance with rules and regulations. Both of these activities are accomplished in large part through off-site and on-site examinations of individual banks, as discussed below. The off- and on-site examinations also require significant efforts on the parts of the supervised banks. They must file periodic reports with information on their activities (e.g., US quarterly Call Reports) to facilitate off-site monitoring, as well as prepare detailed records for on-site bank examinations. The third basic activity of supervisors is taking actions against banks that are assessed to be either out of compliance with rules and regulations or excessively risky. These actions include formal supervisory enforcement actions (EAs), discussed below.

Macroprudential supervision also requires monitoring on but a broader scale, using tools like financial stability reports. This type of supervision may also involve national and international coordinating organizations like the Financial Stability Oversight Council (FSOC) in the US created by the Dodd–Frank Act and the Basel Committee on Banking and Supervision (BCBS) discussed in Chapter 20. It is sometimes argued that inadequate supervision in the past may have resulted in currency crises or financial crises in various countries (e.g., Corsetti, Pesenti, and Roubini, 1998), making quality prudential supervision all the more important.

24.2 Prudential supervision and the three mechanisms for avoiding bank financial distress

Theoretically, prudential supervision may or may not reduce the likelihood of financial distress through the *Prudential* and *Certification Mechanisms*. These activities do not involve government subsidies, so the *Subsidy Mechanism* does not work for prudential supervision, and in fact generally goes the other way as supervisors impose costs on and collect funds from the banks. Thus, the Prudential Supervision column in Table 19.1 Panel A shows "?s" for both the *Prudential* and *Certification Mechanisms* and "−" for the *Subsidy Mechanism*.

24.2.1 The *Prudential Mechanism* of prudential supervision

Prudential supervision may function through the *Prudential Mechanism* by incentivizing or forcing banks to adjust their financial and operational deficiencies that are identified through the supervisory process. Barth, Caprio, and Levine (2006), among others, discuss the importance of official supervision in promoting efficient banking and alleviating the market failure of having too little monitoring. Since bank monitoring is difficult and costly, if left in the hands of the market alone, banks would face suboptimal stability. Prudential supervision may work as a socially efficient device in producing value-relevant information and applying prudential discipline that may partially substitute for market discipline of bank performance and stability (e.g., DeYoung, Flannery, Lang, and Sorescu, 2001).

In contrast, some literature alternatively suggests that supervision may have the unintended effects of impeding bank efficiency and stability if supervisors use their power to cater to the politically connected constituents, extract bribes, and/or attract donations to their campaigns (e.g., Shleifer and Vishny, 2002; Quintyn and Taylor, 2003; Barth, Caprio, and Levine, 2006). Under these circumstances, supervision may not function well in improving bank performance, but instead may be more focused on directing bank resources to these private parties.

24.2.2 The *Certification Mechanism* of prudential supervision

If prudential supervision makes the banks and the banking system safer through the *Prudential Mechanism*, it may also make the banks safer through the *Certification Mechanism*. That is, if prudential supervision assures the public about the safety of the banking system, it may reduce the likelihood of panic runs that might trigger bailouts or bail-ins. However, analogous to our stress test discussion in Chapter 22, the *Certification Mechanism* may also have *unfavorable* effects on the individual banks that receive downgrades of examination ratings or enforcement actions. The market may impose negative consequences on these institutions when the unfavorable private information of supervisors is revealed.

24.2.3 The *Subsidy Mechanism* of prudential supervision

Prudential supervision does not generally involve any government subsidies, so there is no *Subsidy Mechanism* for it. In fact, it often goes the other way with the supervisors directly imposing costs on banks, such as operational costs of dealing with examinations and EAs. Supervisors also often charge the banks for their supervisory services (e.g., the OCC charges national banks), or make the banks pay fines or civil money penalties for violating rules or regulations or exhibiting various illicit behaviors.

24.3 Prudential supervision in practice

There are far too many prudential supervisory agencies and procedures to describe here, so we briefly sample a few important practices in the US and EU.

24.3.1 US

In the US, nationally chartered banks are supervised by the Office of the Comptroller of the Currency (OCC). There are relatively few nationally chartered banks, but they include most of the largest banks. State-chartered banks are generally smaller and are supervised at both the state level by state supervisors and at the federal level. Their federal supervisor is the Federal Reserve if the banks choose to be members of the Federal Reserve and is the FDIC otherwise. All BHCs are also supervised by the Federal Reserve.

In the US, we briefly discuss on-site examinations, off-site examinations, and enforcement actions.

24.3.1.1 On-site examinations

Under the rules outlined in the Federal Deposit Insurance Corporation Improvement Act of 1991 (FDICIA), all US banks must comply with thorough, regularly scheduled federal or state on-site examinations. For most US banks, on-site full scope examinations are performed every 12 months, while for most BHCs, one full scope and one limited scope inspection (essentially the BHC equivalent of an examination) occur every year. However, there are exceptions. Examinations and inspections are more frequent for troubled banks and BHCs, based on off-site monitoring and past ratings. Supervisors also examine early when there are indications of fraud, embezzlement, or other criminal activity (e.g., Berger, Kyle, and Scalise, 2001). Small banking institutions with less than $3 billion in total assets with top examination ratings can be examined every 18 months. The largest and most complex banks and BHCs are essentially examined continuously with permanent on-site staff, although some of the supervisory agencies are moving some of the examiners of the large institutions to other locations to avoid supervisory capture. For commercial banks, the on-site examinations focus on the six components of bank safety and soundness, evaluated based on the CAMELS rating criteria. This consists of capital adequacy (C), asset quality (A), management (M), earnings (E), liquidity (L), and sensitivity to market risk (S). Supervisory examiners evaluate the banks and award an integer grade of one (best) through five (worst) for each of the components. The five component ratings are weighted subjectively by the examiners who must also report a composite CAMELS rating that also ranges from one to five. Most banks have composite CAMELS ratings of one (strong) or two (satisfactory). Banks with ratings of three, four, or five (fair, marginal, and unsatisfactory) are generally encouraged or required to take actions to improve their conditions. Bank holding companies (including financial holding companies) are evaluated using the RFI/C(D) rating system. This includes the components of risk management (R) covering both management and internal risk controls, financial condition (F) covering capital, asset quality, earnings, and liquidity subcomponents, impact (I) analyzing the potential negative impact that issues within the parent company and nonbank subsidiaries may have on the bank subsidiaries. It also includes composite (C), which provides an overall evaluation on a scale of one to five (from strong to unsatisfactory) based on the prior RFI components, and depository institution (D), which reflects the overall condition of the subsidiary banks and thrifts as determined by their primary supervisor.[1]

A key component of on-site examinations is the evaluation of the bank's loan portfolio. Examiners typically review bank's loan policies, read the minutes of the bank's loan committee meetings, internal reports on problem loans, and similar documents. They also evaluate a certain proportion of the loan portfolio, depending on the bank's most recent composite and asset quality ratings. Examiners assign ratings of pass, special mention, substandard, doubtful, or loss or split ratings to each loan sampled, and compare these to the bank's own internal ratings to check for the bank's risk management competence. Importantly, more loans classified into the most serious categories may force a bank to shift funds from equity to its allocation for loan and lease losses (ALLL). If the bank is close to its minimum capital requirements, the unfavorable assessment of its loan portfolio may force the bank to raise equity or reduce its risk-weighted assets to meet capital requirements (Berger, Kyle, and Scalise, 2001).

24.3.1.2 Off-site examinations

Because on-site examinations are costly for both supervisors and banks, bank supervisors complement on-site examinations with off-site surveillance, which involves utilizing banks' quarterly balance sheet and income statement data from quarterly Call Reports and other

---

[1] There is also a new rating system—LFI—for BHCs exceeding $50 billion in assets. See https://www.federalreserve.gov/publications/files/bhc.pdf

information. Supervisors use surveillance tools including screens and econometric models to assess the financial health of banks from these reports. Supervisory screens entail using financial ratios derived from quarterly Call Reports for commercial banks and Y-9C reports for BHCs, and often supervisors may focus on the information that has been unsatisfactory in the past to weigh any changes in content or bank behavior. Econometric models also utilize quarterly Call Report data to summarize the banks' financial conditions.

Analysis of these data provides initial evaluations of the individual components of the CAMELS and RFI/C(D) ratings other than management, which may be changed during the on-site examination if conditions are not consistent with what was reported or expected (e.g., Commercial Bank Examination Manual Supplement 45, 2016, Section 1020.1).[2] Off-site examinations help supervisors to schedule examinations and set priorities on which area of risk exposure to focus when warning signs from these assessments are triggered at specific institutions.

24.3.1.3 Enforcement actions (EAs)

During their on-site and off-site examinations, the three main federal bank supervisors in the U S, the Federal Reserve, the FDIC, and the OCC, may uncover a variety of problems at the supervised institutions and hence can issue supervisory enforcement actions (EAs) against BHCs, banks, and their institution-affiliated parties (IAPs, i.e., management officials) to address the issues identified. The most common reasons for issuing EAs are violations of bank laws, rules, or regulations, breaches of fiduciary duty, and unsafe or unsound banking practices. The main purposes of these actions are to strengthen the financial institutions and the financial system and/or prevent further financial aggravation and/or minimize losses at the subject institutions and the FDIC deposit insurance funds.

Many of the EAs fall into the category of prudential supervision, the topic of this chapter. Based on the severity of the violation, supervisors can issue EAs that are either informal or formal (publicly announced). The informal actions (e.g., commitment letters, board resolutions, moral suasion, and memoranda of understanding) are written documents through which supervisors give banks recommendations to remedy problems and improve their behavior, but are not legally binding and are not disclosed to the public. For example, supervisors may use moral suasion to try to convince the bank to refrain from a certain action in the best interest of the institution. A memorandum of understanding is similar to a private formal agreement between the bank and the supervisor outlining all the issues that need to be addressed, but unlike formal actions it is not legally

---

[2] https://www.federalreserve.gov/publications/files/cbem.pdf

binding. Banks cannot be taken to court if they do not follow the recommendations outlined.

If the informal actions do not produce the expected results, supervisors
can issue formal enforcement actions (e.g., written agreements, cease and
desist orders, deposit insurance termination, termination of Federal
Reserve membership, prohibitions from banking, prompt corrective action, civil money penalties, etc.) which are legally binding. These can
impose some relatively high costs on the institutions, as they need to
spend resources to correct the issues identified in the actions, pay fines
and/or provide monetary remedies to aggrieved parties, and face some
potentially severe reputational losses as these actions are released to the
public.

For example, a cease and desist order (one of the most severe actions) is
an order issued against a banking organization that engages in a severe
violation of a law, rule, or regulation or engages in an unsafe or unsound
practice. This is enforceable in the federal court system. Such an order
may require the institution to stop engaging in the specific practices or
violations and/or may include corrective actions, including restrictions
on growth, debt, and dividends, orders to get rid of problem assets, increase capital, directives to make restitutions for unjust gains or reckless
behavior, and other actions that supervisors deem appropriate.

Another example of an EA is a prompt corrective action. This is an
order against a bank which is significantly or critically undercapitalized
or fails to remain at least adequately capitalized. This may require the
institution to inject additional capital to raise its capital to an acceptable
level and can also prompt dismissals of management, restrictions on executive pay, asset growth, and prohibition of acquisitions or new branch
establishments, selling company shares, and disposing assets, among
others. There are many other types of EAs across the three types of
banking supervisors. A full list of public EA types is available on the
supervisory websites.[3]

24.3.2 EU

The Global Financial Crisis and European Sovereign Debt Crisis
revealed serious problems in the financial system and the structure of the
supervision mechanisms in the EU. Because of the integrated nature of
the EU, many of the financial institutions operate across countries, so the
existing supervisory mechanisms that operated at the national level
proved insufficient. As a remedy, the European Commission proposed a
number of reforms that create a new supervisory system, the European

---

[3] Links for the enforcement actions webpage of each banking regulatory agency can be
found on the FFIEC website at: https://www.ffiec.gov/enforcement.htm

System of Financial Supervision (ESFS), which became effective in January 2011. The ESFS consists of the European Systemic Risk Board (ESRB) to oversee macroprudential supervision, three European Supervisory Authorities (ESAs) and Joint Committee of the European Supervisory Authorities (JCESA) to conduct supervision, in addition to all the national supervisory authorities. The ESFS combines supervisory bodies to operate in both across the EU and within each nation. The ECB mainly oversees supervision for larger banks that impose systemic risk, more of a macroprudential bent, while the microprudential supervision for smaller banks is more concentrated within national authorities.

24.4 Empirical evidence on the mechanisms of the prudential supervision

We next review the empirical research regarding how well prudential supervisions perform through the three mechanisms of defense. The empirical findings suggest positive effects in terms of prudential supervision reducing bank risk through both the *Prudential* and *Certification Mechanisms.* There is no academic research on the *Subsidy Mechanism*, but the fees paid the banks from enforcement actions are established facts. Thus, Table 19.1 Panel B shows " +s" for the *Prudential* and *Certification Mechanisms*, and " − " for the *Subsidy Mechanism*.

24.4.1 Empirical evidence on the *Prudential Mechanism* of supervision

A large body of research examines the relation between the ability of supervisors and supervisory models to monitor the banks and their financial conditions. The literature generally finds that balance-sheet–based risk measures alone do not perform well (e.g., Cole and Gunther, 1998; Berger, Kyle, and Scalise, 2001; Collier, Forbush, Nuxoll, and O'Keefe, 2003; Whalen, 2010; Kiser, Prager, and Scott, 2012), but several studies find that regular examinations and CAMELS ratings may serve as good predictors of bank financial health. For instance, using proportional hazard models with time-varying covariates, Wheelock and Wilson (2005) show that composite CAMEL ratings (the predecessor of CAMELS without market risk sensitivity) and their components contain information about bank failure hazards. Similarly, Gunther and Moore (2003) find that while subperforming banks are more likely to understate losses, supervisory examinations may effectively detect these financial problems and play an auditing role in ensuring that bank accounting statements are restated to reflect the underlying performance. DeYoung,

Hughes, and Moon (2001) find that supervisory CAMELS ratings reflect risk-taking levels and that supervisors are able to distinguish the risk-taking of efficient banks from that of inefficient banks.

Some of the research compares the information in supervisory ratings versus the assessments of market participants. Berger, Davies, and Flannery (2000) use quarterly data from inspections of large BHCs (inspections are the equivalents of examinations on the holding company level) and find that BHC supervisors and bond rating agencies both have some timely prior information that is useful to the other. Both Cole and Gunther (1998) and Berger, Davies, and Flannery (2000) find evidence that supervisory ratings may get "stale" and have less predictive power after a few quarters.

Studies of bank "early warning" systems test how well supervisory ratings can be predicted from publicly available information, such as Call Report data (e.g., Sinkey, 1978, Whalen and Thompson, 1988, O'Keefe and Dahl, 1997). They generally find that the supervisory ratings are not well predicted from the public information, consistent with the supervisors adding timely private information.

A final article of evidence suggests that EAs against banks may make the financial system safer. Berger, Cai, Roman, and Sedunov (2020) analyze how supervisory EAs affect bank systemic risk and find that over time, the systemic risk contributions of banks receiving these actions decline significantly, consistent with the risk disciplining effects of the EAs. They further find that the reductions are stronger for the more severe actions and those issued against banking organizations rather than their management officials.

24.4.2 Empirical evidence on the *Certification Mechanism* of prudential supervision

It is not possible to test the *Certification Mechanism* effect at the system level of having prudential supervision because the counterfactual of how depositors, creditors, shareholders, and other bank stakeholders would react to the removal of such supervision is not observable. However, there are tests of the potential negative *Certification Mechanism* effects of the revelation of unfavorable private information of supervisors, and the research evidence supports these negative effects.

Berger and Davies (1998) find that examination downgrades appear to reveal unfavorable private information about bank condition that is later reflected in stock market performance. There is also evidence of negative effects of EAs. Jordan, Peek, and Rosengren (1999) find statistically significant and economically large negative abnormal returns on the stock prices of banking organizations receiving EAs around the time when the details of the actions appear in the press. Roman (2020) also finds negative short-term valuation effects for the relationship borrowers of banks that are subjected to these actions.

References

Barth, J. R., Caprio, G., & Levine, R. (2006). *Rethinking bank regulation. Till angels govern*. Cambridge University Press.

Berger, A. N., Cai, J., Roman, R. A., & Sedunov, J. (2020). Enforcement actions and systemic risk (Working Paper).

Berger, A. N., & Davies, S. M. (1998). The information content of bank examinations. *Journal of Financial Services Research, 14*(2), 117−144.

Berger, A. N., Davies, S. M., & Flannery, M. J. (2000). Comparing market and supervisory assessments of bank performance: Who knows what when? *Journal of Money, Credit, and Banking*, 641−667.

Berger, A. N., Kyle, M. K., & Scalise, J. M. (2001). Did US bank supervisors get tougher during the credit crunch? Did they get easier during the banking boom? Did it matter to bank lending?. In *Prudential supervision, what works and what doesn't, 301−56*. University of Chicago Press.

Board of Governors of the Federal Reserve System. (December 17, 2012). *Consolidated supervision framework for large financial institutions. SR 12-17*. http://www.federalreserve.gov/bankinforeg/srletters/sr1217.htm.

Cole, R. A., & Gunther, J. W. (1998). Predicting bank failures: A comparison of on-and off-site monitoring systems. *Journal of Financial Services Research, 13*(2), 103−117.

Collier, C., Forbush, S., Nuxoll, D. A., & O'Keefe, J. (2003). *The SCOR system of off-site monitoring, its objectives, functioning, and performance* (Working Paper).

Commercial Bank Examination Manual, Supplement 45, (2016). Available at https://www.federalreserve.gov/publications/files/cbem.pdf.

Corsetti, G., Pesenti, P., & Roubini, N. (1998). *What caused the Asian currency and financial crisis? Part II, the policy debate*. National Bureau of Economic Research.

DeYoung, R., Flannery, M. J., Lang, W. W., & Sorescu, S. M. (2001). The information content of bank exam ratings and subordinated debt prices. *Journal of Money, Credit, and Banking*, 900−925.

DeYoung, R. E., Hughes, J. P., & Moon, C.-G. (2001b). Efficient risk-taking and regulatory covenant enforcement in a deregulated banking industry. *Journal of Economics and Business, 53*(2−3), 255−282.

Gunther, J. W., & Moore, R. R. (2003). Loss underreporting and the auditing role of bank exams. *Journal of Financial Intermediation, 12*(2), 153−177.

Jordan, J. S., Peek, J., & Rosengren, E. S. (1999). *The impact of greater bank disclosure amidst a banking Crisis* (Vol. 2). Federal Reserve Bank of Boston.

Kiser, E. K., Prager, R. A., & Scott, J. (2012). *Supervisor ratings and the contraction of bank lending to small businesses* (Working Paper).

Mishkin, F. S. (2001). *Financial policies and the prevention of financial crises in emerging market economies*. The World Bank.

O'Keefe, J., & Dahl, D. (1997). *Scheduling bank examinations* (Working Paper).

Quintyn, M., & Taylor, M. W. (2003). Regulatory and supervisory independence and financial stability. *CESifo Economic Studies, 49*(2), 259−294.

Roman, R. A. (2020). Winners and losers from supervisory enforcement actions against banks. *Journal of Corporate Finance, 62*.

Shleifer, A., & Vishny, R. W. (2002). *The grabbing hand: Government pathologies and their cures*. Harvard University Press.

Sinkey, J. F. (1978). Identifying "problem" banks: How do the banking authorities measure a bank's risk exposure? *Journal of Money, Credit, and Banking, 10*(2), 184−193.

Whalen, G. (2010). Are early warning models still useful tools for bank supervisors? (Working Paper).

Whalen, G., & Thomson, J. B. (1988). *Using financial data to identify changes in bank condition*, (pp. 17−26). Federal Reserve Bank of Cleveland Economic Review, (Second Quarter).

Wheelock, D. C., & Wilson, P. W. (2005). The contribution of on-site examination ratings to an empirical model of bank failures. *Review of Accounting and Finance, 4*(4), 110−133.

Deposit insurance

In this chapter, we assess deposit insurance as a tool to prevent and/or deter financial distress that might otherwise require costly bailouts, bail-ins, or other resolution methods. Section 25.1 discusses the concepts and goals of deposit insurance, as well as its economic benefits and costs. Section 25.2 examines the extent to which deposit insurance may function through the three mechanisms for preventing financial distress. Section 25.3 reports on the use of this safety net scheme around the world. Section 25.4 presents empirical evidence on the extent to which the mechanisms are effective in preventing bank financial distress.

25.1 What is deposit insurance?

Deposit insurance refers to government guarantees that assure that depositors will get their funds back in full or in part should their banks fail and/or are unable to pay their creditors. Rather than directly paying insured depositors, deposit insurers often pay other banks to take over failing institutions to preserve more of the franchise value of the institutions, but the key for the insured depositors is that they are protected. The classic work of Diamond and Dybvig (1983) reveals that by providing such protections, deposit insurance brings about market confidence and serves as a financial safety net that prevents contagious bank runs and helps restore stability in the banking sector. Extensive later theoretical work examines the benefits and costs of deposit insurance and explores optimal deposit insurance designs that balance these benefits and costs (e.g., Ronn and Verma, 1986; Chari and Jagannathan, 1988; Kane, 1995, 2000; Calomiris, 1996; Allen and Gale, 1998; Bhattacharya, Boot, and Thakor, 1998). For explicit or *de jure* deposit insurance schemes, countries may vary in terms of the categories of institutions covered, the types of deposits that are insured, the cap or maximum amount of deposits that are eligible for reimbursement, and whether there are deductibles or copayments required (e.g., Demirgüç-Kunt, Kane, and Laeven, 2014). Even without explicit insurance in place, the possibility of government intervention in the event of a financial crisis or the financial distress of TBTF, TITF, or TMTF banks can serve as implicit or *de facto* deposit insurance. For instance, TBTF banks benefit from the implicit deposit insurance as risk is not fully incorporated into the pricing of unsecured funding for these banks (e.g., Acharya, Anginer, and Warburton, 2016). In some cases, implementation of an explicit insurance scheme can mean that there is *less* insurance in total, since the added structure may make explicit the extent and boundaries of previously existing implicit deposit insurance.

It is often the case that both *de jure* and *de facto* insurance are in place simultaneously. Insured depositors are essentially fully protected against losses by *de jure* insurance, while uninsured depositors and other creditors are at least partially protected by *de facto* protection. For example, as discussed in more detail below, US depositors with accounts up to $250,000 are covered by *de jure* insurance from the Federal Deposit Insurance Corporation (FDIC), but uninsured depositors with larger accounts, as well as some other uninsured liability holders in TBTF banks may feel at least partially protected by *de facto* insurance provided by the expectations of bailouts and other government protections.

There are significant economic benefits of deposit insurance in reducing destructive bank runs on fundamentally solvent banks due to contagion or other information problems. In the absence of this insurance, depositors have incentives to withdraw when there is a real, rumored, or suspected significant decline in the value of assets held by banks, or there is a real, rumored, or suspected significant run by other bank creditors. The first-come, first-serve nature of transaction deposits—also called the "sequential service constraint"—makes it rational for depositors to get in line to withdraw once a run has started for any reason. No bank can easily liquefy all its assets and may end up facing costly liquidation of long-term assets and default (e.g., Jacklin and Bhattacharya, 1988; Allen and Gale, 2000). Because of incomplete information and interbank claims, a liquidity shock to one bank may spread to other banks that are fundamentally solvent but illiquid (e.g., Allen and Gale, 2000). Deposit insurance provides assurance to the depositors that they are covered in the event of default, and thereby prevents unnecessary economic losses from bank runs. The same assurance, however, may also produce unintended economic costs. In particular, moral hazard problems may distort the incentives of both the banks and depositors, as discussed further below.

25.2 Deposit insurance and the three mechanisms avoiding bank financial distress

The theory does not suggest that deposit insurance prevents or deters financial distress at the individual bank level through the *Prudential Mechanism*, but rather may make bank portfolios riskier due to moral hazard incentives. However, deposit insurance could reduce systemic risk during recessions — which often coincide with financial crises — because it allows for continued lending and support for the real economy during these times that may improve stability of the financial system. Deposit insurance does likely function through the *Certification* and the *Subsidy Mechanisms* at all times. Reflecting these, Table 19.1 Panel A shows " + / − " under Deposit Insurance for the *Prudential Mechanism* and " + " for the *Certification* and *Subsidy Mechanisms*.

25.2.1 The *Prudential Mechanism* of deposit insurance

The *Prudential Mechanism* for reducing the likelihood of financial distress is inoperative for deposit insurance at the individual bank level. In fact, deposit insurance may exacerbate moral hazard problems and encourage banks to take excessive risks that increase the likelihood of future bailouts, bail-ins, or other resolution methods. For instance, a number of theoretical works extend the Diamond–Dybvig model to include investment in risky assets and analyze the impact of deposit insurance on banks' risk-taking behavior and market incentives to monitor the banks (e.g., Kane, 1995; Calomiris, 1996; Cooper and Ross, 2002). Deposit insurance gives banks incentives to take on additional risks because the potential losses from taking more risks are shared with the deposit insurance funds, while the upside profits are captured by the bank. As long as the expected profits from risk-taking are greater than the sum of explicit costs of insurance premiums and implicit insurance regulation costs, banks have incentives to engage in excessive risk-taking. Merton (1977) is the first to evaluate deposit insurance as a put option. In the event that the value of the assets falls to the point of default, the bank can "put" its assets to the deposit insurer. As long as insurance premiums are unrelated or imperfectly related to the expected cost of bank insolvency and the deposit insurer bears the losses in case of bank insolvency, the guarantee may give banks incentives to take on excessive risks. These arguments apply to both *de jure* and *de facto* deposit insurance and imply that a well-designed deposit insurance policy must be implemented in conjunction with effective capital, liquidity, and other regulations and supervisory policies as described in earlier chapters on first lines of defense to keep these moral hazard incentives in check (e.g., Berlin, Saunders, and Udell, 1991).

Notably, some of the moral hazard incentives to take on excessive risks due to deposit insurance may also be offset through risk-based pricing of the premiums paid to the insurers. To the extent that banks have to pay higher premiums for taking on higher risks, the moral hazard incentives may be blunted. In some cases, deposit insurers do charge risk-based premiums. For example, the FDIC began a crude system of risk-based pricing in 1993 based on a 3×3 matrix of risk categories using capital ratios and supervisory ratings (Cornett, Mehran, and Tehranian, 1998).[1] Since then, FDIC has significantly improved the risk modeling behind the risk-based premiums. However, it is not possible to entirely offset the moral hazard incentives through risk-based pricing alone for many reasons, including the difficulties of reacting to risk-taking precisely enough and fast enough (e.g., John, John, and Senbet, 1991).

However, deposit insurance may work through the *Prudential Mechanism* at the system level during problematic economic times. Deposit insurance may allow banks to continue supplying credit during recessions, propping up the real economy. As illustrated in Table 4.4 above, boosting the real economy during recessions may reduce systemic risk as it helps borrowers repay their loans on an aggregate basis, helping the entire banking system.

Before proceeding to the *Certification Mechanism* of deposit insurance in the following subsection, we note that the *Certification Mechanism* may also worsen the prudential behavior of problem banks, making the system riskier. The main goal of *Certification Mechanism* is to reduce the likelihood of destructive bank runs of solvent but illiquid banks. To the extent that depositors and other bank counterparties also reduce healthy market discipline of problem banks because of deposit insurance, these banks may have more incentives to take on excessive risks. Such healthy market discipline includes requiring risky banks to pay higher rates or accept lower quantities of deposits and other risk-sensitive instruments (e.g., Flannery and Sorescu, 1996; Flannery and Bliss, 2019).

25.2.2 The *Certification Mechanism* of deposit insurance

In sharp contrast to the *Prudential Mechanism*, deposit insurance does function through the *Certification Mechanism* by assuring the market that their bank deposits are safe. Foundational studies, including Diamond and Dybvig (1983), provide a framework where the existence of deposit insurance works as an equilibrium selection device that eliminates the

---

[1] Cornett, Mehran, and Tehranian (1998) find that the announcements of the matrix resulted in positive and negative stock market reactions of publicly traded banks assigned to low and high premium categories, respectively.

need for depositors to run. In their model, deposit insurance essentially eliminates the incentives of depositors to run and withdraw their funds because the insurance guarantees that depositors will get their funds back, regardless of whether they are the last in line to withdraw funds and regardless of whether banks become insolvent. Thus, the "sequential service constraint" is no longer binding, reducing the incentives to run on banks. By guaranteeing that depositors will get their money back from the insurance fund, the deposit insurance scheme also helps certify the safety of the entire banking sector and prevent contagious bank runs that may lead to bailouts, bail-ins, or other types of resolution.

25.2.3 The *Subsidy Mechanism* of deposit insurance

Deposit insurance may also work through the *Subsidy Mechanism* by allowing banks to borrow at close to the risk-free rate because of the government protection. The government guarantees give creditors the perception that the government will intervene in case of insolvency, and thus reduces the interest rates they demand for bearing the bank's risks. Such an implicit subsidy boosts bank capital through higher earnings and awards insured banks and other depositories competitive advantages over uninsured nondepository institutions. Thus, even if the risk-based deposit insurance premiums discussed above could be perfectly actuarially priced, access to deposit insurance would still be a subsidy because of the competitive advantages it bestows to the banks and other depositories relative to other firms without such access. The government guarantee is especially beneficial to smaller banks because it enables them to attract deposits without incurring excessive risk premiums. Essentially, it offsets some of the competitive advantages that large banks have due to TBTF protections.

25.2.4 Descriptions of deposit insurance in practice

This section discusses how deposit insurance schemes operate in practice in the US, Europe, and other nations.

25.2.5 US Deposit insurance

The US is the first nation in the world to adopt explicit deposit insurance. The failure of thousands of banks during the Great Depression led to the Glass—Steagall Act of 1933, which established the FDIC that guaranteed deposits of commercial banks and thrift institutions up to a certain limit. Prior to the establishment of the FDIC, similar insurance was provided by state-sponsored deposit insurance schemes, but such schemes were not capable of handling the very significant financial distress during the Great Depression. The FDIC aims to maintain financial stability and restore public confidence by insuring deposits and regulating and supervising the financial institutions along with the other US regulatory and supervisory authorities. In the event of bank insolvency, the FDIC insures deposits covered by commercial banks and thrift institutions to prevent bank runs. The original coverage insured by the FDIC amounted to $2,500, which was raised gradually over time to $100,000 in 1980, then temporarily for 5 years to $250,000 during the financial crisis in 2008. Through the Dodd—Frank Act, the amount later became permanently extended to $250,000. The coverage is per depositor, per insured bank, and for each account ownership category, and families can get multiple accounts using different combinations of family member names. The insurance coverage by FDIC spans all deposit accounts, including checking accounts, savings accounts, money market deposit accounts, and certificates of deposit.

25.2.6 European deposit insurance

Prior to the mid-1990s, deposit insurance in Europe was largely limited to high-income countries, but since 1995, lower- and middle-income countries that joined the European Union (EU) started introducing explicit deposit insurance systems (Demirgüç-Kunt, Kane, Karacaovali, and Laeven, 2008). The 1994 EU directive on the deposit guarantee scheme (Directive 94/19/EC) required all member countries to have a minimum guarantee on deposits of 20,000 euros per person (European Union, 1994). This directive, however, only set a minimum level requirement and failed to harmonize domestic deposit insurance among member countries. This left much scope for competition, and proved to be detrimental to financial stability, especially during the Global Financial Crisis. After the crisis, the original scheme was amended to increase the protection to a minimum of 50,000 euros, and then to a uniform coverage of 100,000 euros by 2010. In 2014, the EU adopted a system of national Deposit Guarantee Schemes (DGSs) regulated by Directive 2014/49/EU, which required member countries to introduce at least one DGS that all banks must join. DGSs must guarantee all deposits up to 100,000 euros at all branches of member banks in other EU countries. Building on Directive 2014/49/EU, European Deposit Insurance Scheme (EDIS) was proposed in 2015 as the third pillar of the banking union and aimed to provide a stronger and more uniform insurance coverage within the EU.

25.2.7 Other nations

By 1980, only around 20 countries had explicit deposit insurance schemes (Demirgüç-Kunt, Kane, Karacaovali, and Laeven, 2008).

The banking crises in the 1980s and 1990s spurred many countries to adopt explicit deposit insurance systems as a way to stabilize the markets. By 2011, the cross-country survey on bank regulation and supervision by Barth, Caprio, and Levine (2013) shows that 98 of 143 responding countries had explicit deposit insurance schemes in place. Today, the International Association of Deposit Insurers (IADI) reports that as many as 146 countries have explicit deposit insurance.[2] It is reasonable to presume that other countries have implicit deposit insurance during times of systemic banking distress due to political pressure (Demirgüç-Kunt, Kane, Karacaovali, and Laeven, 2008).

25.3 Empirical evidence on the mechanisms of deposit insurance

We next review the empirical research regarding how well the insurance deposit scheme functions through the three mechanisms first lines of defense. The results in the empirical literature are mixed with respect to the *Prudential Mechanism* of deposit insurance, but suggest that deposit insurance may make banks safer through the *Certification* and *Subsidy Mechanisms*. Thus, Table 19.1 Panel B shows a "?" for the *Prudential Mechanism* and " +s" for the *Certification* and *Subsidy Mechanisms*.

25.3.1 Empirical evidence on the *Prudential Mechanism* of deposit insurance

We first discuss empirical research on deposit insurance and risk-taking. As explained above, deposit insurance likely encourages risk-taking, contrary to the *Prudential Mechanism*. Consistent with the theory, a number of empirical studies find that deposit insurance comes with an unintended consequence of encouraging moral hazard behavior that results in excessive risk-taking. In their comprehensive study examining 61 countries, Demirgüç-Kunt and Detragiache (2002) find that the implementation of explicit deposit insurance has an adverse impact on financial stability. The effect is more pronounced when the insurance coverage is more extensive, where the scheme is funded, and if the insurance is operated by the government. Their results suggest that explicit legal insurance commitment by the government may serve as an important source of moral hazard.

Berger, Herring, and Szegö (1995, Fig. 1) show that bank capital ratios dropped precipitously following the 1933 Glass–Steagall Act that created the FDIC in the United States, although there were many other regulatory and market changes at that time. Other studies similarly show that deposit

[2] https://www.iadi.org/en/=deposit-insurance-systems/=dis-worldwide/

insurance results in lower bank capital buffers for a sample of 32 countries (e.g., Nier and Baumann, 2006) and increases loan-to-asset and debt-to-equity ratios for a sample spanning 69 countries (e.g., Calomiris and Chen, 2016). Ioannidou and Penas (2010) also find that the post-deposit insurance period in Bolivia is associated with the origination of riskier loans.

Other studies, however, report mixed results. Wheelock and Wilson (1994) do not find a relation between deposit insurance and bank failures in the US. The authors compare insured and uninsured banks' likelihood of failure, drawing on historical data between 1909 and 1929 during which membership in the Kansas deposit insurance system was voluntary. Karels and McClatchey (1999) fail to establish a relation between the adoption of deposit insurance and risk-taking of US credit unions. Wagster (2007) shows that deposit insurance led to declines in overall risk in Canadian banks and trust companies, although idiosyncratic risks increased.

25.3.2 Empirical evidence on the *Certification Mechanism* of deposit insurance

A number of empirical studies document the benefits of deposit insurance in ensuring depositor confidence, supporting the *Certification Mechanism* of deposit insurance. DeLong and Saunders (2011) find that after the introduction of fixed-rate federal deposit insurance in the US, overall stability increased as depositors had fewer incentives to discriminate between weaker and stronger banks. Using account-level data, Martin, Puri, and Ufier (2017) find corroborating evidence that the insurance guarantees were effective in increasing deposit stability by reducing the outflow of deposits and creating additional inflows.

Gropp and Vesala (2004) find that the establishment of the deposit insurance scheme in the EU is associated with a reduction in bank risk-taking. This effect largely comes from monitoring by uninsured subordinated debtholders believing that deposit insurance credibly leaves them out. Chernykh and Cole (2011) also show that the adoption of deposit insurance in Russia is associated with increased deposits and decreased reliance on state-owned banks by retail depositors. In a study examining 47 crises in 35 countries, Angkinand (2009) also finds that countries enforcing more comprehensive insurance coverage experienced smaller output losses.

As discussed above, the *Certification Mechanism* of deposit insurance may also have a downside. It may reduce beneficial market discipline that would otherwise help keep bank risk-taking in check. That is, the *Certification Mechanism* may make the system safer by eliminating destructive runs on banks that are otherwise solvent but illiquid, but it may also protect problem banks and encourage them to take more risks. A number of empirical papers investigate the issue of reduced market discipline.

Lambert, Noth, and Schüwer (2017) find that banks that increased deposits due to the temporary increase in US deposit insurance cap from $100,000 to $250,000 in 2008 increased their investments in risky commercial real estate loans and became riskier relative to other banks, consistent with exacerbated moral hazard. Ioannidou and Penas (2010) also find that the post-deposit insurance period in Bolivia is associated with the origination of riskier loans, while removing deposit insurance subjects the banks to more market discipline. Using both US and EU data, Berger and Turk-Ariss (2015) find significant depositor discipline prior to the recent financial crisis. However, they also find that the implementation of government actions during the crisis, such as expanding insurance coverage limits, reducing coinsurance, and rescuing troubled institutions may have resulted in the erosion of depositor discipline, except for among smaller US banks.

Some empirical research also shows that the effect of deposit insurance on bank risk-taking interacts with various factors. Iyer and Puri (2012) study an Indian bank and find nuanced results that deposit insurance does not fully mitigate depositors' propensity to run. The authors identify the length and depth of bank-depositor relationships, as well as social networks, as important factors in curbing incentives to run. Bonfim and Santos (2017) provide evidence that the credibility of deposit insurance affects depositors' reactions in Portugal, including the movement and pricing of insured liabilities. The authors use a policy announcement that insured depositors in Cyprus may have had to share the losses in their banks an exogenous shock to deposit insurance credibility in the whole EU.

Other papers attempt to examine the net effect of deposit insurance by comparing the stabilization benefits with the moral hazard effects. Ngalawa, Tchana, and Viegi (2016) distinguish banking instability caused by panic withdrawals of deposits from instability caused by insolvency problems. They find that the moral hazard costs dominate the benefit of deposit insurance in preventing bank runs. Anginer, Demirgüç-Kunt, and Zhu (2014) find that the effect of deposit insurance depends on the state of the economy and type of risks. While more generous deposit insurance increases individual bank risk and reduces systemic risk during non-crisis years, the effect reverses during financial crises. The authors find that over the 1997–2009 period, deposit insurance increased systemic risk.

25.3.3 Empirical evidence on the *Subsidy Mechanism* of deposit insurance

Empirical research confirms that deposit insurance also functions through the *Subsidy Mechanism* by allowing banks to borrow at lower rates. Laeven (2002) estimates the value of annual implicit subsidies banks receive from stock price information and finds that explicit deposit insurance increases subsidies to the banks. However, he also finds that in the presence of a strong regulatory environment, this relation is curbed, suggesting that deposit insurance may be especially valuable in countries with effective regulatory frameworks.

References

Acharya, V. V., Anginer, D., & Warburton, A. J. (2016). *The end of market discipline? Investor expectations of implicit government guarantees* (Working Paper).

Allen, F., & Gale, D. (1998). Optimal financial crises. *The Journal of Finance, 53*(4), 1245–1284.

Allen, F., & Gale, D. (2000). Financial contagion. *Journal of Political Economy, 108*(1), 1–33.

Anginer, D., Demirguc-Kunt, A., & Zhu, M. (2014). How does competition affect bank systemic risk? *Journal of Financial Intermediation, 23*(1), 1–26.

Angkinand, A. P. (2009). Banking regulation and the output cost of banking crises. *Journal of International Financial Markets, Institutions and Money, 19*(2), 240–257.

Barth, J. R., Caprio, G., Jr., & Levine, R. (2013). Bank regulation and supervision in 180 countries from 1999 to 2011. *Journal of Financial Economic Policy, 5*(2), 111–219.

Berger, A. N., Herring, R. J., & Szegö, G. P. (1995). The role of capital in financial institutions. *Journal of Banking and Finance, 19*(3–4), 393–430.

Berger, A. N., & Turk-Ariss, R. (2015). Do depositors discipline banks and did government actions during the recent crisis reduce this discipline? An international perspective. *Journal of Financial Services Research, 48*(2), 103–126.

Berlin, M., Saunders, A., & Udell, G. F. (1991). Deposit insurance reform: What are the issues and what needs to be fixed? *Journal of Banking and Finance, 15*(4–5), 735–752.

Bhattacharya, S., Boot, A. W. A., & Thakor, A. V. (1998). The economics of bank regulation. *Journal of Money, Credit, and Banking*, 745–770.

Bonfim, D., & Santos, J. A. C. (2017). *The importance of deposit insurance credibility* (Working Paper).

Calomiris, C. W. (1996). *Building an incentive-compatible safety net: Special problems for developing countries.* Columbia University.

Calomiris, C. W., & Chen, S. (2016). *The spread of deposit insurance and the global rise in bank leverage since the 1970s* (Working Paper).

Chari, V. V., & Jagannathan, R. (1988). Banking panics, information, and rational expectations equilibrium. *The Journal of Finance, 43*(3), 749–761.

Chernykh, L., & Cole, R. A. (2011). Does deposit insurance improve financial intermediation? Evidence from the Russian experiment. *Journal of Banking and Finance, 35*(2), 388–402.

Cooper, R., & Ross, T. W. (2002). Bank runs, deposit insurance and capital requirements. *International Economic Review, 43*(1), 55–72.

Cornett, M. M., Mehran, H., & Tehranian, H. (1998). Are financial markets overly optimistic about the prospects of firms that issue equity? Evidence from voluntary versus involuntary equity issuances by banks. *The Journal of Finance, 53*(6), 2139–2159.

DeLong, G., & Saunders, A. (2011). Did the introduction of fixed-rate federal deposit insurance increase long-term bank risk-taking? *Journal of Financial Stability, 7*(1), 19–25.

Demirgüç-Kunt, A., & Detragiache, E. (2002). Does deposit insurance increase banking system stability? An empirical investigation. *Journal of Monetary Economics, 49*(7), 1373–1406.

Demirgüç-Kunt, A., Kane, E., Karacaovali, B., & Laeven, L. (2008). Deposit insurance around the world : A comprehensive database. In *Deposit insurance around the world, issues of design and implementation.* MIT Press.

Demirgüç-Kunt, A., Kane, E., & Laeven, L. (2014). *Deposit insurance database.* The World Bank.

Diamond, D. W., & Dybvig, P. H. (1983). Bank runs, deposit insurance, and liquidity. *Journal of Political Economy, 91*(3), 401–419.

European Union. (1994). *Directive 94/19/EC of the European Parliament and the Council of the European Union.* Retrieved from EurLex: http://eur-lex.europa.eu/.

Flannery, M. J., & Bliss, R. R. (2019). Market discipline in regulation: Pre- and post-crisis. In *The Oxford Handbook of banking.* Oxford: OUP.

Flannery, M. J., & Sorescu, S. M. (1996). Evidence of bank market discipline in subordinated debenture yields: 1983–1991. *The Journal of Finance, 51*, 1347–1377.

Gropp, R., & Vesala, J. (2004). Deposit insurance, moral hazard and market monitoring. *Review of Finance, 8*(4), 571–602.

Ioannidou, V. P., & Penas, M. F. (2010). Deposit insurance and bank risk-taking: Evidence from internal loan ratings. *Journal of Financial Intermediation, 19*(1), 95–115.

Iyer, R., & Puri, M. (2012). Understanding bank runs: The importance of depositor-bank relationships and networks. *The American Economic Review, 102*(4), 1414–1445.

Jacklin, C. J., & Bhattacharya, S. (1988). Distinguishing panics and information-based bank runs: Welfare and policy implications. *Journal of Political Economy, 96*(3), 568–592.

John, K., John, T. A., & Senbet, L. W. (1991). Risk-shifting incentives of depository institutions: A new perspective on federal deposit insurance reform. *Journal of Banking and Finance, 15*(4–5), 895–915.

Kane, E. J. (1995). Three paradigms for the role of capitalization requirements in insured financial institutions. *Journal of Banking and Finance, 19*, 431–459.

Kane, E. J. (2000). *Designing financial safety nets to fit country circumstances.* The World Bank.

Karels, G. V., & McClatchey, C. A. (1999). Deposit insurance and risk-taking behavior in the credit union industry. *Journal of Banking and Finance, 23*(1), 105–134.

Laeven, L. (2002). *Pricing of deposit insurance.* The World Bank.

Lambert, C., Noth, F., & Schüwer, U. (2017). How do insured deposits affect bank risk? Evidence from the 2008 Emergency Economic Stabilization Act. *Journal of Financial Intermediation, 29*, 81–102.

Martin, C., Puri, M., & Ufier, A. (2017). *On deposit stability in failing banks* (Working Paper).

Merton, R. C. (1977). An analytic derivation of the cost of deposit insurance and loan guarantees: An application of modern option pricing theory. *Journal of Banking and Finance, 1*(1), 3–11.

Ngalawa, H., Tchana, F. T., & Viegi, N. (2016). Banking instability and deposit insurance: The role of moral hazard. *Journal of Applied Economics, 19*(2), 323–350.

Nier, E., & Baumann, U. (2006). Market discipline, disclosure and moral hazard in banking. *Journal of Financial Intermediation, 15*(3), 332–361.

Ronn, E. I., & Verma, A. K. (1986). Pricing risk-adjusted deposit insurance: An option-based model. *The Journal of Finance, 41*(4), 871–895.

Wagster, J. D. (2007). Wealth and risk effects of adopting deposit insurance in Canada: Evidence of risk shifting by banks and trust companies. *Journal of Money, Credit, and Banking, 39*(7), 1651–1681.

Wheelock, D. C., & Wilson, P. W. (1994). Can deposit insurance increase the risk of bank failure? Some historical evidence. *Federal Reserve Bank of St. Louis Review, 76*(3), 57.

IV. First lines of defense to help avoid bailouts and bail-ins

26

Direct government ownership of banks

This chapter discusses direct government ownership of banks, a tool employed in many countries at least in part to try to achieve financial system stability. Section 26.1 briefly describes this ownership and reviews the economic concepts behind it. Section 26.2 discusses how direct government bank ownership may function through the three mechanisms for avoiding bank financial distress. As will become clear, direct ownership operates through these mechanisms in a similar fashion as deposit insurance described in Chapter 25. Section 26.3 describes the practice of direct government ownership in various nations. Section 26.4 gives empirical evidence on how well direct government ownership works in preventing bank financial distress through the three mechanisms.

26.1 What is direct government ownership?

Direct government ownership of banks means that the government holds majority stakes or controlling interest in banks either directly or indirectly through some government-controlled agencies. The shares held by the government can be in the form of common stock, preferred stock, or other securities that give the government the option to purchase common stocks. Direct government ownership generally implies public resources will be used to bail out the institution in the event of distress. When the government directly controls a bank's assets, the scope of government's influence over the bank's finances is much wider than the regulation and supervision functions described in the earlier first lines of defense chapters.

Before proceeding to the three mechanisms, we briefly discuss here the basic economic concepts behind government ownership of banks. There are two benign views in the literature. The "development view" stresses the critical role that government-owned banks play in allocating resources to strategic economic sectors that may not be fully valued by privately-owned banks (e.g., Gerschenkron, 1962; Cull, Martinez Peria, and Verrier, 2019). The "social view" underscores that government-owned banks can promote social welfare by enhancing investment and overcoming externalities of financial disruption. The failures of financial institutions often have public consequences beyond the private interests of the institutions' owners, and government ownership can help avoid bank failure and stabilize the economy through the continuation of lending during financial crises (e.g., Stiglitz, 1993).

There are also two pejorative views of government bank ownership that may be more widely held by economists. According to the "agency view," government-owned banks are associated with higher agency costs, which leads to operational inefficiencies and misallocations of resources. Under this view, government-owned banks are likely to be both cost-inefficient and misallocate funding to inefficient or negative net present value (NPV) projects (e.g., Banerjee, 1997; Hart, Shleifer, and Vishny, 1997). According to the "political view," government-owned banks are vehicles for politicians to realize their own objectives and are influenced by political bureaucrats to finance unprofitable projects, often through forced lending to state-owned enterprises (SOEs) (e.g., Shleifer, 1998).

In discussing the three mechanisms below, we incorporate these "views" to the extent possible. That is, we include them when they are relevant to financial distress at the bank level or at the financial system level.

26.2 Direct government ownership and the three mechanisms for avoiding bank financial distress

As briefly noted above, direct bank ownership operates through the three mechanisms for avoiding bank distress similarly to deposit insurance described in Chapter 25. Given the similar logic, we keep most of the discussions here relatively short. Consistent with the Deposit Insurance column of Table 19.1 Panel A, the Direct Government Ownership column shows "$+s$" for the theoretical prediction for the *Certification* and *Subsidy Mechanisms*. However, unlike Deposit Insurance, Direct Government Ownership displays "$-$ / $+$" for the *Prudential Mechanism* because such ownership could make individual banks behave in a riskier fashion, but also help reduce systemic risk as described below.

26.2.1 The *Prudential Mechanism* of direct government ownership

Similar to for deposit insurance, government ownership does not make banks safer at the bank level through the *Prudential Mechanism*, but rather more likely increases banks' risk-taking even more than deposit insurance. To the extent that government ownership provides banks with access to government funds and backstops almost unlimited portfolio losses, it acts as insurance to both depositors and other creditors in the extreme. Such protections may provide very strong moral hazard incentives to take on more risks or fail to monitor and control risks. The inefficiency of operations because of weak incentives to control costs or maximize profits, as well as the pressures to pursue noneconomic objectives under the "agency" and "political views" above may also contribute to higher individual bank risks.

However, analogous to the arguments made about deposit insurance in Chapter 25, there is also the possibility that the *Prudential Mechanism* may operate at the system level during recessions, which often coincide with financial crises. To the extent that government banks continue to provide credit during tough times as under the "social view" above, this may provide a countercyclical boost to the economy (e.g., Cull and Martinez Peria, 2012), which in turn helps keep other banks and nonbank institutions in the financial system functioning.

26.2.2 The *Certification Mechanism* of direct government ownership

Similar to deposit insurance, government ownership reduces risks through the *Certification Mechanism* by deterring runs by depositors and other liability holders, both of whose claims are almost as safe as the government treasury. That is, the presence of government stakes helps mitigate depositors' and other liability holders' fears that the banks may fail (e.g., Brown and Dinç, 2011), giving these creditors little reason to ration credit to the banks (e.g., Faccio, Masulis, and McConnell, 2006). Government ownership may be more effective in this regard than deposit insurance, which typically has caps or other limitations on payments, whereas government ownership may provide almost limitless guarantees on all deposits and other bank liabilities.

26.2.3 The *Subsidy Mechanism* of direct government ownership

Also similar to deposit insurance, government ownership makes banks safer by giving them access to more steady streams of funds at close to risk-free rates, thanks to the confidence of depositors and other creditors of access to government funds in the event of bank distress (e.g., Borisova and Megginson, 2011). As with deposit insurance, the superior access to credit is a type of subsidy that helps keep the banks afloat. Banks with government ownership may receive other preferential treatments from the government, especially in developing countries.

26.3 Descriptions of direct government ownership

It is very common across the world that governments own shares in banks. The amount of government ownership varies from insignificant minority to majority or even full ownership. The size of government ownership is generally inversely related to the development level of the country's financial market. For example, governments in transition countries in which the financial markets are less developed tend to own more shares in their banks. As discussed below, direct government ownership is essentially nonexistent except for TARP in the US, the nation with the most developed financial markets. However, it does exist in other developed nations such as Germany.

Prior to the Global Financial Crisis, total assets held by government-owned banks worldwide were on a downward trend. Over the prior decades, governments of many developed countries rapidly transferred their ownership rights in the banking system to the private investors. The underlying rationale was the generally accepted view that state ownership is associated with inefficiency, bad financial performance, and slower economic growth (e.g., Cull, Martinez Peria, and Verrier, 2019). Many emerging countries were actively developing privatization programs to reduce their high levels of state bank ownership (e.g., Megginson, 2005).

The crisis disrupted these trends. Several countries took large stakes in major private banks or even nationalized failing banks during the crisis. Consequently, the average share of bank assets held by the government increased from 7.3% in 2007 to 10.8% in 2009 in high-income countries (e.g., Cull, Martinez Peria, and Verrier, 2019).

We next discuss how direct ownership differs around the world.

26.3.1 US direct government ownership

As noted above, the US government does not directly own commercial banks except under the TARP program. Even so, most of the TARP ownership is through preferred, rather than common shares, and there is no direct control by the government over the bank's operations other than the restrictions discussed in Chapter 3.

26.3.2 Direct government bank ownership in Europe

In Germany and some other European countries, direct government ownership of banks is long-term public policy. The German banking system consists of three pillars: private banks based on private law, government-owned banks based on public law, and cooperative banks based on cooperative law (Robaschik and Yoshino, 2000). While these three pillars are broadly equally sized (e.g., Beck, Hesse, Kick, and von Westernhagen, 2009), federal or state governments have ownership rights in some banks based on private law (e.g., Robaschik and Yoshino, 2000).

In France, there were significant privatization initiatives during the 1980s and 1990s, moving the French economy from highly state-controlled to more market-oriented (e.g., Schmidt, 1996). During this process, formal institutional ties between the state and the banks were weakened. The French central bank became independent in 1993 and Crédit Lyonnais, the last large public bank, became privatized in 1999 (e.g., Jabko and Massoc, 2012).

There are three main groups of banks in the Spanish banking system—private banks, savings banks, and official credit institutions. In 1985, the 31/1985 national law, or LORCA law, unified the governance systems of savings banks under which local and regional governments were assigned 40% governance representation.[1] The LORCA law also empowered regional parliaments to modify the representation percentages for depositors, employees, founders, and governments (e.g., Fernandez, Fonseca, and Gonzalez, 2006).

In Greece, Alpha Bank, Eurobank, National Bank of Greece (NBG), and Piraeus Bank are the four largest banks by assets, and hold about 90% market share.[2] The Greek government owns significant with shares in these biggest four through the Hellenic Financial Stability Fund (HFSF), created in 2010. As of the last disclosed data on each bank, HFSF holds 10.9%, 1.4%, 40.4%, and 26%, respectively, in Alpha Bank, Eurobank, NBG, and Piraeus Bank.[3]

In Italy, state-owned banks held about 70% market share by assets for nearly six decades starting at the end of the 1930s. In the 1990s, privatization got off to a fast start, and the public banks were transformed into

---

[1] LORCA stands for "Ley de regulación de normas básicas sobre órganos rectores de las cajas de ahorros."

[2] https://capx.co/six-things-you-need-to-know-about-greek-banks/

[3] https://www.alpha.gr/en/group/investor-relations/share-information/shareholder-structure, https://www.eurobank.gr/en/group/investor-relations/shareholders/shareholding-structure, https://www.marketscreener.com/NATIONAL-BANK-OF-GREECE-1408785/company/, https://www.piraeusbankgroup.com/en/investors/share/shareholder-structure

limited companies. The transition to private ownership ended public ownership of banks in Italy (e.g., De Bonis, Pozzolo, and Stacchini, 2012).

In contrast to some of the continental countries, the UK generally found it an unfamiliar territory taking government stakes in banks until the Global Financial Crisis and the European Sovereign Debt Crisis (e.g., Andrianova, Demetriades, and Shortland, 2012). The UK government injected a total of £45.5 billion into the Royal Bank of Scotland (RBS) between October 2008 and December 2009 to maintain financial stability during the turbulent times. The UK government's ownership stake reached 84.4% after further share purchases. However, the government initiated the selling process of the shares to the private sector in August 2015 and reduced its ownership of ordinary shares to 62.4% as of June 2018.[4] The UK government also took stakes in Lloyds TSB and Halifax Bank of Scotland to stabilize the banking system during the crisis. Lloyds become fully private again after the UK government sold its 43% ownership in 2017.[5]

26.3.3 Direct government ownership in other nations

In China, before 1978, there was a mono-bank model, where the Peoples' Bank of China (PBOC) combined the roles of central and commercial banking. The banks—which were taken over or restructured into the PBOC system or under administration by PBOC or the Ministry of Finance—were just part of the hierarchy to ensure that national production plans would be fulfilled, with no incentives to compete with one another. Under reforms that began in 1978, the banking system expanded by establishing several large state-owned commercial banks and splitting the Big Four state-owned banks and the lending functions from the PBOC. The Bank of China (BOC, established 1912), China Construction Bank (CCB, 1954), Agricultural Bank of China (ABC, 1979), and Industrial and Commercial Bank of China (ICBC, 1984) were initially limited to serve only their designated sector of the economy (i.e., foreign trade and exchange; construction; agriculture; industrial and commercial lending, respectively). In 1985, the Big Four were allowed to compete in all sectors. Nonetheless, competition among them was very limited until the mid-1990s because they served mainly as policy-lending conduits for the government and lacked incentives to compete (e.g., Berger, Hasan, and Zhou, 2009).

After China entered the World Trade Organization (WTO) in 2001, the four largest state-owned banks reached agreements to take on minority foreign ownership, up to 25%. Besides the Big Four, other smaller

---

[4] https://uk.reuters.com/article/uk-britain-economy-rbs/uk-government-plans-to-sell-remaining-rbs-stake-by-2024-idUKKCN1N32E7

[5] https://www.nytimes.com/2017/05/17/business/dealbook/lloyds-britain-bank.html

domestic commercial banks have the state as the largest shareholder. Today, the Big Four are the largest banks in the world. Along with almost all other largest commercial banks in China, they are listed at stock exchanges in mainland China or Hong Kong. Despite the foreign bank participation and the shares held by the public, the Chinese government remains the largest shareholder of the Big Four and has true control over the banks' managerial appointments.

In India, there are two types of state-owned banks: the state-owned State Bank of India (SBI) and its associates and nationalized banks that were formerly private large banks and became state-owned in two waves, 1969 and 1980. Following independence in 1945, the Reserve Bank of India (RBI) was established as the central bank, and high priority was given to increasing credit to rural areas and small businesses. In 1955, the government took over the largest bank, the Imperial Bank of India, to form SBI. The State Bank of India Act in 1959 directed SBI to take over regional banks that were associated with local governments and make them subsidiaries of SBI, which were later named "associates." SBI is now the largest commercial banking organization in the country. SBI and its seven regional associates have a substantial rural branching footprint of about 14,000 branches of these banks, 74% of which are in rural and semi-urban areas (e.g., Berger, Klapper, Martinez Peria, and Zaidi, 2008).

The Indian government nationalized 14 large banks in 1969 and another six banks in 1980 to redirect credit to "underserved" sectors and populations. Unlike SBI, nationalized banks remained corporate entities and retained most of their management and staff. Although their boards of directors were replaced by the state, appointees included representatives from both the government and the private industry (e.g., Berger, Klapper, Martinez Peria, and Zaidi, 2008).

South Asia has the highest share of government-owned banks among all regions across all years, while the share of assets held by government-owned banks has fallen prior to the Global Financial Crisis from 23% in 1995 to 13% by 2008 (e.g., Cull, Martinez Peria, and Verrier, 2019).

26.4 Empirical evidence on the mechanisms of direct government ownership

In this section, we summarize the empirical research regarding how well direct government ownership reduces bank-level and systemic risks through the three mechanisms of the first lines of defense. The empirical literature finds that government ownership may make banks safer through the Certification and Subsidy Mechanisms. However, the results are split for the Prudential Mechanism, as this first line of defense may encourage individual banks to operate in a riskier fashion, but may make the banking system safer. Thus, Table 19.1 Panel B shows "+s" for the

Certification and Subsidy Mechanisms, and "- / +" for the Prudential Mechanism.

26.4.1 Empirical evidence on the *Prudential Mechanism* of direct government ownership

Our discussion of the empirical evidence on the *Prudential Mechanism* of government ownership proceeds in two subsections that follow from the discussion of the concepts above. In the first subsection, we review empirical evidence on the risks and efficiencies of state-owned banks that follow from the arguments about the negative effects of government ownership on individual bank performance. In the second, we discuss research on beneficial effects on financial system stability from their countercyclical credit supply responses to overall financial distress and their own stability from their government connections during times of financial distress.

26.4.1.1 *Evidence on direct government ownership and individual bank performance*

The empirical research often, but not always, finds that government ownership in banks is associated with inefficiency and poor performance. Cross-country research almost always finds that in developing countries, state-owned banks have lower profitability and higher costs than private banks, although some of the evidence for banks in developed countries is more mixed. For example, Cornett, Guo, Khaksari, and Tehranian (2010) examine the performance differences between private and state-owned banks in 16 Far East countries and find that bank performance is negatively related to the extent of state ownership. Yeyati, and Micco (2007) focus on the Latin American banking sector and find that the relative efficiency of government-owned banks is particularly low in Colombia and Honduras. Boubakri, Cosset, Fischer, and Guedhami (2005) examine the post-privatization performance of 81 banks located in 22 developing countries, and suggest that privatization improves bank performance. Shen and Lin (2012) use bank data from 65 countries over the period of 2003–2007 and document evidence that government banks underperform private banks due to political interference. Iannotta, Nocera, and Sironi (2013) examine large European banks and find that government-owned banks have higher operating risk. Micco, Panizza, and Yanez (2007) show that state-owned banks in developing countries tend to be less profitable and have higher costs than domestic private banks, but the relation between ownership and performance for banks in industrial countries is not significant. Bonin, Hasan, and Wachtel (2005) use a dataset of 225 banks from 11 transition countries and also find that government-owned banks are not significantly less efficient than domestic private banks.

Some research provides country-specific evidence, which more consistently finds that state-owned banks are relatively poor performers. Berger, Hasan, and Zhou (2009) study the Chinese banking system and find that the largest state-owned banks are the least efficient ones, and also suffered significant credit losses requiring bailouts. Nakane and Weintraub (2005) examine Brazilian banks over the period 1990–2001 and find that state-owned banks are less productive relative to private banks. Lassoued, Sassi, and Attia (2016) investigate the impact of ownership on banking in the Middle East and North Africa (MENA) and find that government ownership encourages more bank risk-taking. Using data on Turkish banks, Bircan and Saka (2018) find that the lending behavior of state-owned banks is affected by local elections, as opposed to economic incentives. Sapienza (2002) similarly finds evidence of credit misallocation by Italian banks.

Thus, the individual country evidence is essentially unanimous that state ownership is associated with poor individual bank performance. Most of the international evidence also suggests poor state-owned bank performance, but some results disagree. It is sometimes argued that within-nation comparisons of bank performance may be more convincing because international comparisons may be confounded by differences in language, culture, law, currency, and other important disparities, while domestic studies are able to compare institutions operating side-by-side in similar environments (e.g., Berger, DeYoung, Genay, and Udell, 2000; Berger, Molyneux, and Wilson, 2020).

26.4.1.2 Evidence on direct government ownership and the beneficial systemic effects

A number of studies find evidence consistent with the *Prudential Mechanism* working at the systemic level through countercyclical credit supply effects and government safety effects. Bertay, Demirgüç-Kunt, and Huizinga (2015) investigate the lending behavior of state-owned banks over the business cycle and find stabilizing effects of state banks during financial turmoil. Countercyclical lending behavior is especially strong for banks located in countries with good governance and high-income countries. Demirguc-Kunt and Detragiache (1999) also use a panel data of 53 countries for 1980-1995 and find an increase in the number of banking crises after the financial liberalization that reduces the role of government ownership.

Studies of individual nations also suggest beneficial systemic effects. Davydov (2016) studies Russian banks during the Global Financial Crisis and finds that state-supported banks demonstrated countercyclical credit supply effects during the crisis. Fully state-controlled banks in Russia increased lending and charged lower interest rates during this time period. A study of banks in Brazil also finds evidence consistent with the view that government ownership in banks can help mitigate a recession through countercyclical lending behavior (e.g., Coleman and Feler, 2012). A study of Poland finds that lending by PKO Bank Polski (PKO BP), a state-controlled bank that is also the largest bank in Poland, provided critical lending that helped the country be the only EU economy that avoided recession in 2009 (e.g., Piatkowski, 2011).[6]

26.4.2 Empirical evidence on the *Certification Mechanism* of direct government ownership

A few studies find that government-owned banks have lower default risk than other banks, consistent with the reduced market discipline under the *Certification Mechanism* of government ownership, lessening risks of runs and assuring access to financing. Pennathur, Subrahmanyam, and Vishwasrao (2012) examine the impact of ownership on Indian banking. They find that state-owned banks have lower default risk than private banks. Iannotta, Nocera, and Sironi (2013) present similar findings for large European banks. They show that government-owned banks have higher operating risk, but lower default risk than private banks. On the other hand, the benefit of certification may be offset or even overweighed by the increasing effects of government ownership on banks' risk taking. For example, Caprio and Martinez Peria (2002) find a positive relation between government ownership and the likelihood of banking crises. La Porta, Lopez-de-Silanes, Shleifer, and Vishny (2002) also study the correlation between government ownership and banking crises but find no significant results.

26.4.3 Empirical evidence on the *Subsidy Mechanism* of direct government ownership

Finally, some empirical research finds that government-owned banks have easier access to credit and often experience lower costs of capital,

---

[6] Although slightly off the topic of financial stability, we also note that there is an issue of whether state-owned banks hurt or help economic growth. The famous findings by La Porta, Lopez-de-Silanes, Shleifer, and Vishny (2002) are that government ownership has a negative and almost always significant relations with economic growth. We note that Adrianova, Demetriades, and Shortland (2012) find evidence to the contrary using a cross-country dataset over the period 1995–2007 that include some variables omitted by previous studies.

consistent with the *Subsidy Mechanism* supporting these banks. Borisova and Megginson (2011) find that credit spreads are negatively associated with government ownership, consistent with higher confidence in repayment associated with implicit government guarantees. Hossain, Jain, and Mitra (2013) examine the stock performance of banks from 107 countries over the period of 1999–2009, and find that greater state ownership contributes to improved stock performance during the Global Financial Crisis. Their findings suggest that at least partially state-controlled banks have advantages over privately-owned banks in terms of enhanced ability to raise equity capital during financial crisis periods.

References

Andrianova, S., Demetriades, P., & Shortland, A. (2012). Government ownership of banks, institutions and economic growth. *Economica, 79*(315), 449–469.

Banerjee, A. V. (1997). A theory of misgovernance. *The Quarterly Journal of Economics, 112*(4), 1289–1332.

Beck, T., Hesse, H., Kick, T., & von Westernhagen, N. (2009). *Bank ownership and stability: Evidence from Germany* (Working Paper).

Berger, A. N., DeYoung, R., Genay, H., & Udell, G. F. (2000). Globalization of financial institutions: Evidence from cross-border banking performance. *Brookings-Wharton Papers on Financial Services, 2000*(1), 23–120.

Berger, A. N., Hasan, I., & Zhou, M. (2009). Bank ownership and efficiency in China: What will happen in the world's largest nation? *Journal of Banking and Finance, 33*(1), 113–130.

Berger, A. N., Klapper, L. F., Martinez Peria, M. S., & Zaidi, R. (2008). Bank ownership type and banking relationships. *Journal of Financial Intermediation, 17*(1), 37–62.

Berger, A. N., Molyneux, P., & Wilson, J. O. S. (2020). Banks and the real economy: An assessment of the research. *Journal of Corporate Finance, 62*.

Bertay, A. C., Demirgüç-Kunt, A., & Huizinga, H. (2015). Bank ownership and credit over the business cycle: Is lending by state banks less procyclical? *Journal of Banking and Finance, 50*, 326–339.

Bircan, Ç., & Saka, O. (2018). *Political lending cycles and real outcomes: Evidence from Turkey* (Working Paper).

Bonin, J. P., Hasan, I., & Wachtel, P. (2005). Bank performance, efficiency and ownership in transition countries. *Journal of Banking and Finance, 29*(1), 31–53.

Borisova, G., & Megginson, W. L. (2011). Does government ownership affect the cost of debt? Evidence from privatization. *The Review of Financial Studies, 24*(8), 2693–2737.

Boubakri, N., Cosset, J.-C., Fischer, K., & Guedhami, O. (2005). Privatization and bank performance in developing countries. *Journal of Banking and Finance, 29*(8–9), 2015–2041.

Brown, C. O., & Dinç, I. S. (2011). Too many to fail? Evidence of regulatory forbearance when the banking sector is weak. *The Review of Financial Studies, 24*(4), 1378–1405.

Caprio, G., & Martinez Peria, M. S. (2002). *Avoiding disaster, policies to reduce the risk of banking crises* (pp. 193–230). Monetary Policy and Exchange Rate Regimes, Options for the Middle East.

Coleman, N. S., & Feler, L. (2012). *Bank ownership, lending, and local economic performance during the 2008-2010 financial crisis*. Mimeo: Johns Hopkins University, 1099.

Cornett, M. M., Guo, L., Khaksari, S., & Tehranian, H. (2010). The impact of state ownership on performance differences in privately-owned versus state-owned banks: An international comparison. *Journal of Financial Intermediation, 19*(1), 74–94.

Cull, R., & Martinez Peria, M. S. (2012). *Bank ownership and lending patterns during the 2008-2009 financial crisis. Evidence from Eastern Europe and Latin America.* World Bank, Mimeo.

Cull, R., Martinez Peria, M. S., & Verrier, J. (2019). *Bank ownership, trends and implications.* The World Bank.

Davydov, D. (2016). Does state ownership of banks matter? Russian evidence from the financial crisis. *Journal of Emerging Market Finance, 17*(2), 1–38.

De Bonis, R., Pozzolo, A. F., & Stacchini, M. (2012). *The Italian banking system: Facts and interpretations* (Working Paper).

Demirgüç-Kunt, A., & Detragiache, E. (1999). *Financial liberalization and financial fragility.* The World Bank.

Faccio, M., Masulis, R. W., & McConnell, J. J. (2006). Political connections and corporate bailouts. *The Journal of Finance, 61*(6), 2597–2635.

Fernández, A. I., Fonseca, A. R., & González, F. (2006). The effect of government ownership on bank profitability and risk: The Spanish experiment. *Working Paper, 33*(3), 224–229.

Gerschenkron, A. (1962). *Economic backwardness in historical perspective: A book of essays.* MA: Belknap Press of Harvard University Press Cambridge.

Hart, O., Shleifer, A., & Vishny, R. W. (1997). The proper scope of government: Theory and an application to prisons. *The Quarterly Journal of Economics, 112*(4), 1127–1161.

Hossain, M., Jain, P. K., & Mitra, S. (2013). State ownership and bank equity in the Asia-Pacific region. *Pacific Basin Finance Journal, 21*(1), 914–931.

Iannotta, G., Nocera, G., & Sironi, A. (2013). The impact of government ownership on bank risk. *Journal of Financial Intermediation, 22*(2), 152–176.

Jabko, N., & Massoc, E. (2012). French capitalism under stress: How Nicolas Sarkozy rescued the banks. *Review of International Political Economy, 19*(4), 562–585.

La Porta, R., Lopez-de-Silanes, F., Shleifer, A., & Vishny, R. (2002). Investor protection and corporate valuation. *The Journal of Finance, 57*(3), 1147–1170.

Lassoued, N., Sassi, H., & Attia, M. B. R. (2016). The impact of state and foreign ownership on banking risk: Evidence from the MENA countries. *Research in International Business and Finance, 36,* 167–178.

Megginson, W. L. (2005). The economics of bank privatization. *Journal of Banking and Finance, 29*(8–9), 1931–1980.

Micco, A., Panizza, U., & Yanez, M. (2007). Bank ownership and performance. Does politics matter? *Journal of Banking and Finance, 31*(1), 219–241.

Nakane, M. I., & Weintraub, D. B. (2005). *Bank privatization and productivity: Evidence for Brazil.* The World Bank.

Pennathur, A. K., Subrahmanyam, V., & Vishwasrao, S. (2012). Income diversification and risk: Does ownership matter? An empirical examination of Indian banks. *Journal of Banking and Finance, 36*(8), 2203–2215.

Piatkowski, B. M. (2011). *Positive GDP growth, relatively low increase in unemployment, and growing real wages helped sustain demand for loans, particularly among households. On the supply side, growth in lending* (Working Paper).

Robaschik, F., & Yoshino, N. (2000). *Public banking in Germany and Japan's fiscal investment and loan program: A comparison.* Fachbereich Wirtschaftswiss.

Sapienza, P. (2002). The effects of banking mergers on loan contracts. *The Journal of Finance, 57*(1), 329–367.

Schmidt, V. (1996). The Transformation of French Business and Government. In *From the State to Market?.* Cambridge: Cambridge University Press.

Shen, C. H., & Lin, C. Y. (2012). Why government banks underperform: A political interference view. *Journal of Financial Intermediation, 21*(2), 181–202.

Shleifer, A. (1998). State versus private ownership. *The Journal of Economic Perspectives, 12*(4), 133–150.

Stiglitz, J. E. (1993). The role of the state in financial markets. *The World Bank Economic Review, 7*(Suppl. l), 19–52.

Yeyati, E. L., & Micco, A. (2007). Concentration and foreign penetration in Latin American banking sectors: Impact on competition and risk. *Journal of Banking and Finance, 31*(6), 1633–1647.

Looking toward the future

Introduction to Part V

Parts I, II, III, and IV summarize a very large amount of research on a number of related topics and lead us to Part V. Here, we finally digest and integrate the research, draw the larger meanings from it, and look forward toward its implications for the future. Since the three chapters in Part V digest the research as a whole, the only references in the Part V tree of knowledge are a small number of papers in Chapter 27 on some topics that were not covered in the earlier parts of the book. Each of these three final chapters tries to paint a different big picture from the body of research.

As noted in the Introduction to Part I of the book, we take a holistic approach that considers many policy choices, including bailouts, bail-ins, and other approaches to resolving systemically important banks in financial distress. Additional choices include the "first lines of defense" that may help keep individual banks out of financial distress in the first place, as well as countercyclical policies that lean against lending booms and excessive aggregate bank liquidity creation. Both of the latter sets of policies may help lessen the likelihood and severity of financial crises that bring about most of the resolutions of distressed banks.

Some readers may be tempted to skip most of the text of the book and proceed quickly to these concluding chapters to view our opinions. However, we recommend against this behavior because these final chapters are not simply our opinions. Rather, they are the logical conclusions drawn from the research reviewed in the earlier chapters. Chapter 27 assesses the social costs and benefits of the 16 different major programs and approaches researched in the book to dealing with and preventing bank financial distress based on the research. This chapter also reviews some additional research evidence that is relevant for drawing conclusions, but does not match the topics of the earlier chapters. Chapter 28 draws the logical implications for policymakers and bank managers from the extant research, and Chapter 29 discusses the open questions and gaps in the extant research to be addressed by future researchers. Although these topics are written as separate chapters, they are highly interrelated. For example, we can only draw strong implications for policymakers and bank managers in cases in which the costs and benefits are relatively clear, and these costs and benefits can only be seriously analyzed where the relevant research questions have already been sufficiently addressed and there is less need for future research.

Before proceeding, we note that the different approaches for coping with bank financial distress are not treated equally here because some of the approaches have much more research than others. Thus, in discussing social costs and benefits and implications for policymakers and bank managers from the research in Chapters 27 and 28, respectively, we focus more on the materials from Part II on Troubled Asset Relief Program (TARP) and Part IV on first lines of defense because there is much more research on these topics. In contrast, in asking the profession for more future research in Chapter 29, we focus more on the book topics with less extant research available—bailouts other than TARP, bail-ins, other resolution approaches, and countercyclical policies—which are more starved for research-based knowledge.

27. Social costs and benefits

Akin, Coleman, Fons-Rosen, and Peydro. Forthcoming; Ashcraft, 2006; Barofsky, 2013; Benes and Kumhof, 2015; Berger, 2018; Berger and Bouwman, 2017; Berger, Curti, Mihov, and Sedunov, 2020; Bernanke, 2015; Bernanke and Blinder, 1992; Bunkanwanicha, Di Giuli, and Salvade, 2019; Bush, 2008; Caballero and Simsek, 2013; Calomiris and Khan, 2015; Diamond and Rajan, 2011; Drehmann and Gambacorta, 2012; Driscoll, 2004; Edge and Liang, 2019; Ehrmann, Gambacorta, Martinez-Pages, Silvestre, and Worms, 2003; Faria-e-Castro, 2020; Fischer, Hainz, and Steffen, 2014; Friedman, 1968; Harris, Huerta, and Ngo, 2013; Issac, 2010; Jagolinzer, Larcker, Ormazabal, and Taylor, 2017; Jiménez, Ongena, Peydró, and Saurina, 2017; Kashyap and Stein, 1997, 2000; Liang, 2013; Lown and Morgan, 2006; Lucas, 2019; Massad, 2011; Mester, 2018; N'Diaye, 2009; Paulson, 2013; Repullo and Salas, 2011; Roman, 2019; Thakor, 2005; Yellen, 2011; Zingales, 2011.

Part V: Looking toward the future

28. Implications for bank policymakers and bank managers

No references applicable.

29. Open research questions

No references applicable.

Social costs and benefits

The assessments of social costs and benefits discussed in this chapter follow as logically as possible from the research summarized earlier in the book. We do not attempt to put precise dollar figures on the costs and benefits of the various approaches for dealing with the financial distress of banking organizations that are researched in the book. This would require a level of accuracy far beyond what is available from the extant research. Rather, we make reasoned judgments about which social costs and benefits are relatively large and small based on the research.

From these judgments, we form rough assessments of whether the many different approaches have net social benefits—benefits that quite clearly outweigh the costs—versus net social costs—costs that plainly dominate the benefits. In some cases, neither social benefits nor costs dominate, or the research evidence is insufficient to draw either conclusion. We also differentiate some of our conclusions by financial stability conditions and by short- versus long-run orientations. Thus, whether social benefits versus social costs dominate often depends on the financial circumstances under which they are considered and whether the short-run or long-run consequences are weighted more heavily in the social welfare function. For example, bail-ins may provide excellent long-run incentives that reduce bank risk taking during relatively tranquil financial times. However, bail-ins may also have unfavorable short-run consequences in terms of imposing heavy losses on market participants and dragging down other financial institutions during severe financial crises and TMTF circumstances when many institutions are in danger of failing simultaneously.

Readers are also encouraged to read other surveys of TARP research that tote up its costs and benefits by Calomiris and Khan (2015), Berger (2018), and Roman (2019) that are noted in Chapter 6. In addition, we provide pros and cons of bailouts and bail-ins in Box 1.6 in Chapter 1. Readers may also find useful the many books, congressional testimonials, and presidential statements with opinions on TARP by prominent economic and political figures, including Bush (2008), Issac (2010), Massad (2011), Zingales (2011), Barofsky (2013), Paulson (2013), and

Bernanke (2015), that are displayed in Chapter 3, Table 3.3, Panel A. Panel B of that table also shows the results of public opinion polls by the Pew Research Center, Bloomberg, *USA Today*/Gallup, and ABC. The availability of all these prior analyses and conclusions allows us to focus more on the "big picture" conclusions from the entirety of the research covered in this book.

Section 27.1 briefly summarizes a few TARP research articles that are not covered in Part II above because they do not fit neatly into the topics of Part II. Section 27.2 summarizes a modest amount of research on countercyclical prudential and conventional monetary policies that might reduce the likelihood and severity of financial crises that is not adequately reviewed earlier in the book. As discussed further below, Section 27.2 excludes unconventional monetary policy, which is covered under bailouts in Chapter 16 and excludes fiscal policies that do not directly affect banks. The evidence in Sections 27.1 and 27.2 is necessary for drawing comprehensive conclusions in our final three chapters. Finally, Section 27.3 addresses the main mission of the chapter. This section gives our rough assessments based on the research of whether the different approaches of dealing with bank financial distress have net social benefits, net social costs, or neither under different financial stability conditions in the short run and long run. We cover bailouts (including TARP, unconventional monetary policies, and other bailouts), bail-ins, five other resolution approaches, seven different first lines of defense, and countercyclical prudential and conventional monetary policies.

27.1 Additional TARP research articles not covered in Part II

We briefly discuss a few additional research papers on TARP that did not fit neatly into the TARP literature review in Part II. Harrisa, Huertab, and Ngo (2013) examine the impact of TARP bailouts on bank efficiency using the nonparametric Data Envelopment Analysis (DEA) methodology. They find that bank operating efficiency declined as a result of the crisis, and this decline is significantly worse for TARP banks than non-TARP banks. The authors attribute this to bailout-related moral hazard incentives—the operating efficiency of the TARP banks deteriorated because TARP reduced incentives of bank managers to adopt best practices.

Bunkanwanicha, Di Giuli, and Salvadè (2019) address how TARP affected CEO careers. They find that during the financial crisis, CEOs of TARP banks were shielded and had an 18% higher probability of retaining their jobs relative to CEOs of non-TARP banks. However, after the crisis, the situation reverted as TARP CEOs were less likely to be employed, consistent with the idea that in the long run, the labor market may have punished the CEOs of bailed-out banks. They also find that TARP banks that did keep their CEOs tended to increase their risk-taking behavior and changed their CEOs once losing their political connections.

Two papers examine the relation between political connections and informed trading by corporate insiders of TARP banks. Akin, Coleman, Fons-Rosen, and Peydro (forthcoming) find different insider trading behaviors for politically connected and unconnected TARP banks. For politically connected banks, they find that buying during the pre-TARP period is associated with increases in abnormal returns around TARP, while for unconnected TARP banks, insider trading and returns are uncorrelated. They also find that the ratio of requested to received funds by TARP participants strongly correlates with abnormal returns, and is also a predictor of buying behavior for the connected banks.

Jagolinzer, Larcker, Ormazabal, and Taylor (2017) also document a strong relation between political connections and the informativeness of corporate insiders' trades around TARP. This is consistent with political connections conferring corporate insiders an information advantage related to the government bailouts. They find that the relation is strongest during the period in which TARP funds are disbursed, and among politically connected insiders at banks that received TARP capital injections. They also find significant insider trading in the 30 days before the announcement, and that these trades predict the stock market reaction to the announcement and are present only for the trades of politically connected insiders. These findings suggest that politically connected insiders of TARP banks had an information advantage and traded to exploit this advantage.

Lucas (2019) develops a theoretical framework that pinpoints the principles governing economically meaningful estimates of the cost of bailouts and derives actual cost estimates for all of the US bailouts, during the Global Financial Crisis, including TARP. Other bailouts considered include the Federal Reserve's emergency facilities, the FDIC programs and expanded coverage, the SBLF program, as well as rescue measures and guarantees for Fannie Mae and Freddie Mac after being taken in conservatorship, federal student loan programs, and the Federal Housing Administration (FHA). The author estimates that the total direct cost of the crisis-related bailouts in the US was on the order of $500 billion, or 3.5% of GDP in 2009. The author cautions that the estimate rests on many uncertain assumptions and the estimates should be viewed as having a wide error band. Nonetheless, Lucas (2019) argues that the derived cost is large enough to conclude that the bailouts were not a free lunch for policymakers, and may raise serious questions about whether taxpayers could have been better protected. The author also finds that the unsecured creditors rather than shareholders of large financial institutions were the largest direct beneficiaries at the time of the bailouts.

27.2 Countercyclical prudential and conventional monetary policies

We next briefly discuss research on countercyclical prudential and conventional monetary policies, which are designed at least in part to temper excessive bank credit supply and liquidity creation booms. As discussed in Chapter 2, these bank credit booms and liquidity build-ups may result in financial bubbles or excessive risk taking that can create future financial crises. Such crises, in turn, may result in the distress of large financial institutions that need to be resolved via bailouts, bail-ins, or any of the other resolution approaches. These policies also are intended to boost the supplies of bank credit and liquidity creation during downturns and help the real economy recover from recessions. We next introduce the concepts, review some existing practices, and then discuss some research evidence.

Notably, we exclude countercyclical unconventional monetary policies that are typically conducted during stressful periods, such as greatly expanded lender of last resort (LOLR) measures such as the Federal Reserve's Expanded Discount Window (DW) and Term Auction Facilities (TAF) Liquidity Programs as well as the Federal Reserve's quantitative easing (QE) programs. For the purposes of this book, these unconventional policies are considered bailouts, and the research on them is covered in Chapter 16.

We also exclude countercyclical fiscal policies, such as taxation and public spending designed to counter economic cycles. The reason is that our book is primarily concerned with approaches to resolving or preventing the financial distress and failure of systemically important banks which would otherwise significantly damage the financial system and real economy. Countercyclical prudential and monetary policies function directly through adjusting the banks' supplies of credit and liquidity (although monetary policy also affects credit and liquidity demands). In contrast, fiscal policies affect banks only indirectly as firms and consumers may demand more bank credit and liquidity creation.

27.2.1 Countercyclical prudential and conventional monetary policies

Countercyclical prudential policy tools cover a variety of measures and are generally intended to reduce build-ups of systemic risk by slowing credit growth during good times and boosting it during bad times (e.g., Yellen, 2011). As discussed in Part IV, bank capital requirements have historically been crucial prudential tools. More recently, under Basel III, regulators agreed to vary minimum capital requirements over the business cycle through countercyclical bank capital buffers. The Basel III countercyclical capital buffer (CCyB) increases the minimum capital requirements when cyclical risks begin to build to ensure banks have enough capital to absorb losses that may arise in any subsequent downturn. During a stress period, the buffer can be released, helping maintain bank credit and liquidity supply to the economy.[1] As a reminder, a brief description of the CCyB and some research about it is included in Chapter 20. We provide more details below.

The main countercyclical conventional monetary policy tools are open market operations (OMO), repurchase agreements of government securities, and setting interest rates on reserves to target interbank funding rates.

27.2.2 Countercyclical macroprudential policy in practice

The US Federal Reserve Board released a policy statement providing details about how the Board will set CCyB for private-sector credit exposures located in the US. The Board views CCyB as a macroprudential tool that can improve the resilience of the financial system and will be activated when systemic vulnerabilities are meaningfully above normal. The Board intends to increase the CCyB gradually and expects to remove or reduce the CCyB when the conditions that led to its activation abate or lessen and when the release of CCyB capital would promote financial stability. The CCyB applies to banking organizations subject to the advanced approaches capital rules, generally those with more than $250 billion in assets or $10 billion in on-balance sheet foreign exposures, and to any depository institution subsidiary of such banking organizations. The US CCyB rate is currently set at 0%.[2]

The CCyB has already been adopted by many countries. In a study of macroprudential authorities, Edge and Liang (2019) find that 53 of 58 countries in their sample established an authority to set the CCyB. This type of authority resides mostly with central banks and independent prudential regulators, in only two countries, the UK and France, and the financial stability committee has the authority on its own to implement the CCyB. In the UK, the Bank of England's Financial Policy Committee (FPC) is in charge of the CCyB implementation, and the UK CCyB rate is currently set at 1%. The FPC increases the CCyB when it judges that risks

---

[1] Countries other than US have also used as countercyclical prudential tools limits on loan-to-value ratios and debt-to-income ratios that vary over the cycle and are targeted to particular sectors like housing or household credit to control leverage (e.g., Liang, 2013; Fischer, 2014; Mester, 2018).

[2] https://www.federalreserve.gov/newsevents/pressreleases/bcreg20190306c.htm

are building up. This means that banks are required to have an additional cushion of capital with which to absorb potential losses caused by cyclical systemic risks, enhancing their resilience and contributing to a stable financial system. Edge and Liang (2019) also find that eight countries[3] have raised the CCyB above zero at least once, mainly to respond to rapidly rising house prices and high mortgage debt in their countries.

27.2.3 Research evidence on countercyclical prudential policies

Several papers analyze the effects of CCyB. The results in all of these papers suggest that the CCyB requirements tend to work as intended, smoothing credit supply cycles and making the financial system more resilient. Drehmann and Gambacorta (2012) find that the Basel III CCyB could help to reduce credit growth during booms and attenuate the credit contraction once it is released. Jiménez, Ongena, Peydró, and Saurina (2017) analyze the impact of the CCyBs held by banks on the supply of credit to firms and their subsequent performance in Spain using dynamic provisioning experiments and a comprehensive bank-, firm-, loan-, and loan application-level dataset. They find that CCyBs help smooth credit supply cycles and in bad times uphold firm credit availability and performance. N'Diaye (2009) finds that binding countercyclical prudential regulations can help reduce output fluctuations and lessen the risk of financial instability. The countercyclical capital adequacy rules allow monetary authorities to achieve the same output and inflation objectives, but with smaller adjustments in interest rates. The countercyclical rules can help stem swings in asset prices, lean against a financial accelerator process, and thereby help to lower risks of macroeconomic and financial instability. Benes and Kumhof (2015) find CCyBs can create a precautionary motive for banks when the creditworthiness (or riskiness) of borrowers depreciates and thus lead to a significant increase in social welfare and reduce the need for countercyclical adjustments in policy interest rates. Faria-e-Castro (2020) investigates quantitative macroeconomic effects of the CCyB and finds that raising the capital buffer during leverage expansions can reduce the frequency of crises by more than half. The author's quantitative application to the 2007–08 financial crisis indicates that the CCyB in the 2.5% range could have greatly allayed the financial panic of 2008, for a cumulative gain of 29% in total consumption. In contrast to all of this research, Repullo and Saurina Salas (2011) assess

---

[3] These countries are UK, Hong Kong, Iceland, Norway, Sweden, Switzerland, The Czech Republic, and Slovakia. For more information on Basel Committee member jurisdictions that used CCyB, see https://www.bis.org/bcbs/ccyb/

the countercyclical capital buffer in Basel III, and find that the buffer tends to decrease capital requirements when GDP growth is high and increase them when GDP growth is low.

27.2.4 Research evidence on the countercyclical conventional monetary policy

We next discuss research on countercyclical conventional monetary policy. Prior to the 1980s, monetary economists generally focused on the effects of the money supply on aggregate credit demand by the nonbank public and its effects on the business cycle, as opposed to credit supply by individual banks and the financial system. For example, Friedman (1968) contended that monetary policy overreactions to the business cycle exacerbated the cycle and advocated using simple rules for money supply growth in place of discretion.

Later research suggests that conventional monetary policy largely works through the bank lending channel, affecting bank lending supply (e.g., Bernanke and Blinder, 1992; Kashyap and Stein, 1997). Kashyap and Stein (2000) provide empirical support for the existence of a bank lending channel of monetary transmission. Using a very large data set of quarterly observations covering all US banks, they find that monetary policy shocks have greater effects on lending for banks with low ratios of securities to total assets. They also find that the result is largely attributable to the smaller banks, those in the bottom 95% of the size distribution, which have the fewest alternatives to raise funds to offset the deposit outflows induced by a monetary policy contraction. Ehrmann, Gambacorta, Martinez-Pages, Silvestre, and Worms (2003) summarize results for EU nations. They find that for most of the euro area nations, the effects of monetary policy on bank lending are consistent with the findings in Kashyap and Stein (2000), but they are not found to be strongly related to bank size as in the US.

However, there is not much evidence on whether the effectiveness of monetary policy in changing bank lending behavior differs during financial crises and normal times. During financial crises, banks may hoard loanable funds due to the difficulty of accessing liquidity in the market and be less responsive to incentives to lend (Diamond and Rajan, 2011; Caballero and Simsek, 2013). The demand for and supply of loan commitments and other off-balance sheet guarantees may also be affected by financial crises (e.g., Thakor, 2005). Berger and Bouwman (2017) investigate the effects of monetary policy on bank liquidity creation using US data and differentiate between normal times and financial crises, and between on- and off-balance sheet liquidity creation. These authors find that conventional monetary policy has statistically significant, but economically minor effects on liquidity creation by small banks during normal times, consistent with Kashyap and Stein (2000), and these effects are even weaker during financial crises. In addition, monetary policy has very little effects on medium and large bank liquidity creation during both normal times and crises.

Some other research focuses on whether bank lending due to monetary policy has significant effects on the real economy and finds mixed effects. Ashcraft (2006) finds that the change in bank lending owing to a monetary policy shock does not have an important effect on state income. Using a structural VAR, the author estimates that about 25% of the response of bank lending to monetary policy can be attributed to frictions related to the bank lending channel, but less than about 5% of the response of real GDP to monetary policy may be attributed to this conduit of monetary policy. Consistent with these results, Driscoll (2004) also finds that bank loans in a state have small, often statistically insignificant effects on that state's output. Conversely, Lown and Morgan (2006) proxy for changes in bank credit supply using information on lending standards from the Federal Reserve's Senior Loan Officer Opinion Survey. The authors find that monetary shocks to banks' credit standards have substantial effects on both C&I loan growth and GDP after controlling for a variety of factors. They also find a close link between bank credit standards and some measures of inventory investment in a structural model, suggesting a relatively strong effect of bank loan supply on real activity.

27.3 Rough assessments of net social benefits and costs

Table 27.1 summarizes our rough assessments based on the research of 16 different approaches to dealing with bank financial distress in tabular form for the reader's convenience. The table shows a "+" to indicate net social benefits, i.e., that social benefits exceed social costs. A "−" designates net social costs, that social costs dominate social benefits. When neither conclusion can be drawn, the table shows a "?," signifying that neither benefits nor costs dominate, or that there is insufficient research evidence to draw conclusions.

The table shows the assessments by two sets of financial stability conditions—severe financial crises and TMTF versus other financial conditions, i.e., when there are and are not significant risks of short-run serious damage to the financial system. The table also shows the assessments by two orientations of the social welfare function—relatively high weights for the short run versus the long run. Thus, there are four different boxes with signs for each approach in the table row that corresponds to that approach.

TABLE 27.1 Rough assessments of net social benefits and costs of approaches for dealing with the financial distress of banking organizations under different financial conditions in the short run and long run.

Approaches		Severe Financial Crises and/or TMTF		Other Financial Conditions	
		Short Run	Long Run	Short Run	Long Run
Bailouts		+	?	−	−
Bail-ins		?	?	+	+
Other Resolution Approaches	Bankruptcy/Failure	−	−	−	−
	Living Wills	−	−	?	?
	Regulatory Forbearance	−	−	−	−
	Breaking Up TBTF	−	?	?	?
	Breaking Up Types of Activities	−	−	−	−
First Lines of Defense	Capital Requirements	−	−	+	+
	Liquidity Requirements	−	−	?	?
	Stress Tests	−	−	+	+
	Prudential Regulatory Activity Restrictions	?	?	?	?
	Prudential Supervision	+	+	+	+
	Deposit Insurance	+	+	+	+
	Direct Government Ownership	?	?	−	−
Countercyclical Policies	Countercyclical Prudential Policy	+	+	+	+
	Countercyclical Conventional Monetary Policy	?	?	?	?

This table summarizes our rough assessments based on the research of 16 different approaches (7 resolution approaches (7 lines of defense, and 2 countercyclical policies) to dealing with bank financial distress in tabular form for the reader's convenience. "+" indicates net social benefits, "−" designates net social costs, and "?" signifies that neither social benefits nor costs dominate, or that we do not have enough evidence.

We recognize that this simple method of analysis neglects some significant differences across financial conditions and orientations, but it allows us to give a relatively complete picture in one table that can be relatively concisely described. As shown in more detail below, the conclusions differ across financial conditions and orientation for only some of the approaches like bailouts and bail-ins. For other approaches, such as forbearance, prudential supervision, and deposit insurance, our conclusions hold in all cases, as indicated by a consistent sign across all four boxes in a row. We also note in advance that the last two columns—short- and long-run assessments during other financial conditions—have identical signs in every row. That is, net social benefits are consistent between the short run and long run when there are no significant risks of short-run financial system collapse.

Given the large size of Table 27.1, we devote more attention to bailouts and bail-ins, the main topics of the book, and keep the discussions of the other approaches shorter in the interest of brevity.

27.3.1 Assessments of bailouts

Starting with the first conclusion in the first column of Table 27.1, we assign a "+," indicating that the short-run social benefits very likely exceed the social costs of bailouts when there are significant risks of serious damage to the financial system. This conclusion is largely based on the research shown in Part II that suggests that TARP largely achieved the two ultimate goals of the program—boosting the real economy and reducing the risks to the financial system in the short run during the heart of the Global Financial Crisis. In a severe financial crisis, such as the Global Financial Crisis, or in a TMTF situation in which many financial institutions may become distressed and/or fail at roughly the same time, bailouts can help save the real economy and financial system from near-term disasters. During these times, the failure of even one very large and/or highly interconnected financial institution can exacerbate financial system conditions, such as occurred when Lehman Brothers failed.

While there are relatively few research papers that directly address the issues of the real economy and systemic risk in Chapters 14 and 15, respectively, these conclusions are bolstered by significant additional evidence in the other chapters of Part II. The research findings that TARP resulted in increased credit supply is consistent with short-run improvements in the real economy, and the research results that TARP generally increased stock market values of banks and reduced their leverage risk augment the case for reduced systemic risk in the short run. The research on non-TARP bailouts in Chapter 16 also generally shows increases in credit supply from some of the programs that may have boosted the real economy in the short run.

As also noted in Part II, the estimates of the short-run improvements in the real economy may also be significantly understated. This occurs in part because the difference-in-difference (DID) methodology only measures differences rather than total improvements in real economic outcomes. The understatement may also occur because saving the financial system through reductions in systemic risk almost surely helped the real economy further by increasing credit supply by banks that were not bailed out and in states with relatively few bailed-out banks.

We recognize the short-term social costs of TARP created by many distortions and dislocations of the program. These include the allocations of funds to banks with political and regulatory connections, the increases in TARP bank market shares and market power that distorted banking competition, and the shift of these banks into riskier loan portfolios due to moral hazard incentives. Another social cost of TARP and other bailouts is the opportunity cost associated with tying up government funds in bank preferred equity. The financial returns on investment in TARP to the US Treasury were positive, but far below market-required returns for very risky investments like preferred equity of banks during the financial crisis. It is reasonable to assume that similar distortions, dislocations, and taxpayer costs may often occur for other bailouts as well.

We also recognize the short-run social costs of the moral hazard incentives to take on excessive risks created by TARP and other bailouts. The research summarized in Part II clearly suggests increases in portfolio risks from TARP due to the increased credit supplies and shifts toward riskier borrowers. Nonetheless, we argue that the short-run social costs created by the increases in portfolio risk may be relatively small for two reasons. First, some of the other research in Part II suggests that the increased portfolio risks from TARP are more than offset by the increases in common equity from TARP, leaving the TARP banks contributing less to systemic risk in the short run than non-TARP banks, other things equal. Potential increases in systemic risk from moral hazard appear to be more of a long-run issue, as discussed below. Second, in dire situations such as the Global Financial Crisis, even risky lending may have short-run benefits from helping to offset the real economic losses from the recession created by the crisis.

More generally, the short-run social benefits from bailouts during severe financial crises and TMTF circumstances of keeping the economy from falling into a deeper recession and preserving the safety of the financial system are likely much larger in magnitude than all of the short-run social costs. These social benefits may total in the tens of trillions of dollars. As discussed in Chapter 1, the value of lost output and financial wealth in the US from the Global Financial Crisis is estimated to be $12 trillion–$22 trillion. These losses might have been several times higher without TARP and the other bailouts, although a precise estimate for such a counterfactual is not possible. As discussed above, Lucas (2019) estimates the total direct cost of all bailout programs in the United States during the financial crisis at about $500 billion. These bailout costs amount to a relatively small percentage of the trillions of dollars of lost output and financial wealth from the crisis, which might have been much higher without the bailouts.

We acknowledge as well that most of the research behind our conclusions is from one preferred equity injection program in one nation during one financial crisis. There are many other types of bank bailouts, they occur in almost every other nation, and they happen during nearly every financial crisis. These other bailouts may be either more or less effective than TARP. Nonetheless, the very large number of high-quality research studies on TARP covering more than a decade, as well as the more limited number of excellent research papers on the other bailouts covered in this book, jointly provide reasonably strong evidence that allows us to draw relatively firm conclusions.

Before moving on to the other social consequences of bailouts in the remainder of the first row of Table 27.1, we observe that bailouts may be the only viable options to prevent substantial damage in the short run to the financial system and real economy during severe financial crises and/ or TMTF circumstances. When financial conditions are dire and the pending collapse of TBTF, TITF, and/or TMTF institutions are threatening the safety of the financial system and a potentially costly severe economic downturn, none of the other approaches shown in the table may be sufficiently powerful to prevent such problems. There are only two other "+s" in the remainder of the first column of the table. These are for prudential supervision and deposit insurance, which have social benefits during all financial conditions and in both the short run and long run ("+s" for all columns). However, these two approaches alone are unlikely to offset the short-run financial and economic damages of the failures of TBTF, TITF, and/or TMTF institutions.

As a reminder, the discussion to this point takes a short-run orientation. Thus, the "+" assigned in the first column of the first row of Table 27.1 only suggests that bailouts are desirable in relatively dire financial circumstances if the social welfare function places a relatively high weight on short-run relative to long-run consequences. We turn next to the relative costs and benefits of bailouts in the long run.

In the second column of the first row of the table, we assign a "?" to the long-run social consequences of bailouts that occur during severe financial crises and/or TBTF circumstances, indicating uncertainty as to whether long-run social benefits versus costs dominate. On the one hand, some of the research using the DID methodology summarized in Part II suggests long-run social costs from TARP. This research is consistent with exploitation of moral hazard incentives that resulted in increased portfolio risks due to increased expectations of future bailouts, real economic benefits from TARP that are mostly limited to the short run, and possible increases in systemic risk in the long run. On the other hand, the research using the DID methodology may not fully capture the counterfactual of what would have happened in the absence of TARP and other bailouts. The DID approach—which mostly compares TARP banks to non-TARP banks or local markets with more TARP banks to those with fewer or no TARP banks—may miss some of the long-term benefits. If the bailouts had not occurred during the crisis, the real economy and the financial system may not have recovered for a long time. Such consequences occurred in the Great Depression of the US in the 1930s and in Japan in the Lost Decade of the 1990s when bank bailouts were not quickly applied. The existing research is simply not able to accurately weigh the long-run costs and benefits.

Turning to bailouts during other financial conditions—when the financial system is not at significant risk of serious damage—we assign "−s" for both the short run and long run. We argue that the social costs from encouraging excessive risk taking due to exacerbating moral hazard incentives, as well as the distortions, dislocations, and taxpayer costs documented above for TARP would likely dominate the economic and financial social benefits when the financial system is healthy and not at significant risk of damage. As noted above, the distinction in costs and benefits between the short run and the long run is not consequential during these relatively tranquil financial conditions. As discussed below, bail-ins may be a more appropriate resolution approach than bailouts during these times.

27.3.2 Assessments of bail-ins

We next discuss the social costs and benefits of bail-ins, as illustrated in the second row of Table 27.1. We first assign a "?" to bail-ins in the first column of the table, reflecting doubts about the short-run consequences of this approach during adverse financial circumstances. As discussed in Chapters 4 and 17, the theoretical and empirical research literatures, respectively, suggest that bail-ins may provide excellent long-run incentives that reduce bank risk taking when the financial system is not in significant danger. Bail-ins protect taxpayer funds and reduce moral hazard incentives for financial institutions to engage in excessive risk taking. This is because shareholders are wiped out and managers lose their jobs in the event of a bail-in and because those that stand to pay for the bail-in may impose market discipline. The research suggests that bail-ins encourage banks to hold higher capital ratios and to recapitalize preemptively before distress becomes severe. Bail-ins may also improve market discipline and reduce the competitive advantages given to TBTF,

TITF, and TMTF financial institutions over other institutions provided by the expectations of bailouts.

Despite these long-run beneficial consequences of bail-ins, in the short run during severe financial crises or TMTF circumstances, bail-ins may also drag down some of the other important financial institutions that provide the bail-inable debt and are forced to pay for the bail-ins or transfer risks to other parts of the financial system that may also be fragile. The financial distress or failure of these other institutions at such times may significantly harm the financial system and real economy by acting slowly to reestablish market confidence in the bailed-in institution and potentially increasing contagion and causing runs by creditors, worsening credit supply and economic outcomes for connected borrowers. It may also result in bailouts of these other institutions. These potential adverse consequences, balanced against the beneficial consequences discussed above, result in the "?" assigned above. While not a perfect match, the closest real-world analogy to these relative short-run social benefits and costs of bailouts and bail-ins during dire circumstances may be the bailout of American International Group (AIG) Insurance. This firm was bailed out by the US Treasury and Federal Reserve Bank of New York on September 16, 2008, the day after the Lehman Brothers collapse. As discussed earlier in the book, AIG provided CDS contracts on mortgage-backed securities to some large banks, which required significant payments that might have bankrupted AIG without the bailout. In effect, AIG was doing something similar to bailing-in the large banks by paying off on its CDS contracts, and received a bailout to ensure that the banks got their full payments and AIG did not fail.

Bail-ins may be a more appropriate resolution approach than bailouts under more tranquil financial conditions, as illustrated by "+s" for bail-ins in the last two columns of Table 27.1. Bail-ins are less likely to drag down many other financial institutions when there is neither a severe financial crisis nor a TMTF circumstance. Thus, the socially beneficial effects discussed above likely dominate during these other financial conditions.

27.3.3 Assessments of other resolution approaches

Focusing next on the five other resolution approaches for large, distressed banking organizations, we assign "−s" for all of them in the first column of Table 27.1. Thus, bankruptcy/failure, living wills, regulatory forbearance, and breaking up the large, systemically important institutions either by size (i.e., into smaller institutions) or by activity types (i.e., separating commercial and investment banks) during dire financial conditions would likely do more harm than good in the short run.

Enforcing bankruptcy/failure resolution or living wills during problematic times may significantly reduce bank credit supply, substantially harming the real economy, and may disrupt financial markets as well. Regulatory forbearance is likely to result in significant moral hazard-induced behavior by undercapitalized institutions, such as occurred in the S&L crisis discussed in Part III, and may make any financial crisis worse. Breaking up the banks by size into smaller institutions might reduce systemic risk in the long run by imposing less risk on other interconnected institutions, but may create short-run chaos in credit markets, reducing credit supply and harming the real economy. Separating commercial and investment banks during a crisis would risk a repeat of the exacerbation of the Global Financial Crisis caused by the Lehman Brothers bankruptcy. As discussed in Part III, large standalone investment banks may not be able to withstand liquidity crises. All of the large US investment banks other than Lehman Brothers were either merged into BHCs (Bear Stearns merged into JPMorgan Chase, Merrill Lynch merged into Bank of America) or became BHCs with approval from the Federal Reserve (Goldman Sachs and Morgan Stanley) during the financial crisis to improve their access to liquidity.[4]

In the last three columns of the table, we continue to assign "−s" to bankruptcy/failure, regulatory forbearance, and break-ups by activities. We are not aware of any strong evidence suggesting that these approaches generate significant social benefits that offset the social costs detailed in the prior paragraph. For living wills and break-ups by size, we assign "?s" in the last three columns, allowing for the possibility of significant social benefits that offset the social costs, but the research is not sufficiently rich to draw strong conclusions. Living wills might have benefits in terms of preparing bank managers for the worst, increasing transparency that might improve market discipline, and reducing TBTF subsidies. Break-ups of large banks might reduce systemic risk and TBTF subsidies to be weighed against the efficiency losses and other costs of these break-ups.

---

[4] Goldman Sachs and Morgan Stanley converted to BHC status as of January 1, 2010 and participated in TARP. They became subject to the "Hotel California" provision of the Dodd−Frank Act. This provision stipulates that even if the institutions dropped their banks and ceased to be BHCs, they would remain under the supervision and regulation of the Federal Reserve as nonbank Systemically Important Financial Institutions (SIFIs). See https://www.wallstreetprep.com/knowledge/investment-banking-after-the-2008-financial-crisis/

27.3.4 Assessments of first lines of defense

Turning our attention to the first lines of defense, we focus first on the social costs and benefits during less distressed financial times on the right hand side of Table 27.1. The reason for this focus is that these times are when these first lines are primarily intended to work. As explained in Part IV, first lines are primarily designed to keep banks from becoming financially distressed in the first place through the *Prudential, Certification,* and *Subsidy Mechanisms,* and the empirical research in Part IV suggests that these mechanisms often work. A secondary benefit of the first lines that is less researched is that they may also help prevent severe financial crises and TMTF circumstances from occurring or lessen their severity by strengthening the health of the banking sector. Thus, they may help prevent or reduce the impacts of banking crises (crises that originate in the banking sector) and may lessen the impacts of market crises (those that originate in financial markets) or risk events to individual banks, such as large operational losses that may have systemic risk implications.[5]

As shown in the table, we give "+s" to capital requirements, stress tests, prudential supervision, and deposit insurance during relatively tranquil times. As discussed in Part IV, the predictions of the theoretical research on capital requirements, stress tests, and prudential supervision are ambiguous, but the empirical research is clear. Capital requirements have been well documented in the empirical research literature as making banks safer and reducing the likelihood of failure without significantly harming bank performance, strongly supporting the positive net social benefits. The empirical research on stress tests also suggests that they make banks safer, although this research is much less well developed than that on capital requirements. In principle, stress tests could potentially provide even more benefits than traditional capital requirements because of their forward-looking nature, but more empirical research is needed to investigate this. As discussed in Part IV, prudential supervision is essential to keep banks financially sound by monitoring them to keep excessive risk taking under control. The theory on deposit insurance is somewhat mixed for the *Prudential Mechanism,* but the *Certification Mechanism* of deposit insurance is vital to maintaining public confidence in the financial system and to prevent destructive runs that can turn illiquidity into insolvency. Thus, these first lines also have positive net social benefits outside of turbulent financial circumstances.

---

[5] Berger, Curti, Mihov, and Sedunov (2020) find that losses from operational risk events can increase systemic risk both by impairing the bank experiencing the events and related institutions through spillover channels.

For two of the other first lines of defense, liquidity requirements and prudential regulatory activity restrictions, we allocate "?s" during relatively tranquil financial times, suggesting that we are uncertain of the net social benefits even when financial markets are relatively calm. The evidence suggests that liquidity requirements may make banks safer, but we do not know if they are more efficient than the central bank providing liquidity when it is needed. As discussed in Part IV, central banks can create liquidity and distribute it to banks at relatively low cost through the LOLR function or through OMO. In addition, liquidity requirements may come at a significant cost of reduced bank liquidity creation, although we are not aware of any research on this topic. Regulatory activity restrictions also receive a "?" during these other financial conditions because it is unclear if they reduce risks or help certify bank safety.

For the final first line of defense, we assign "−s" to direct government bank ownership during relatively calm financial conditions. As discussed in Part IV, this ownership generally makes the financial system safer, these benefits are likely outweighed by its other social costs in terms of efficiency losses, destructive lending to state-owned enterprises, more risk taking, and taxpayer losses due to subsidies.

We turn next to the social costs and benefits of the first lines of defense during severe financial crises and TMTF circumstances on the left hand side of the table. We give "−s" on the left hand side of the table in place of "+s" on the right hand side of the table to capital requirements and stress tests because enforcing these requirements during stressful times may result in significant reductions in bank credit supply and harm the real economy and possibly disrupt financial markets as well. As discussed in Part IV, studies of one particular episode of financial distress—the early 1990s US credit crunch—find that increases in capital requirements contributed significantly to the decline in the supply of credit. As well, as we discuss below, the research evidence on counter-cyclical capital requirements suggests that running down capital buffers during dire financial circumstances is effective in boosting bank credit supply. Thus, we expect that allowing banks to run down normal capital buffers and less strict enforcement of forward-looking capital buffers under stress tests may have similar beneficial effects. For essentially the same reasons, we switch to "−s" on the left hand side in place of "?s" on the right hand side for liquidity requirements. We keep consistent "+s" for prudential supervision and deposit insurance, which are needed at all times. Finally, for direct government ownership, we switch to "?s" on the left hand side in place of "−s" on the right hand side because of the argument given in Part IV that such ownership may result in less contractions in aggregate credit supply during stressful times, helping the real economy.

27.3.5 Assessments of countercyclical prudential and conventional monetary policies

Consistent with our discussion in Section 27.2, we focus here on countercyclical prudential and conventional monetary policy because we consider unconventional monetary policy as bailouts and fiscal policies as not directly affecting banks.

We assign "+s" under all financial conditions and time orientations for countercyclical prudential policies. These assessments are based on the research reviewed above in Section 27.2 that suggests that these policies work at all times as intended, smoothing the effects of business cycles and increasing the resilience of the financial system. In contrast, we assign "? s" across the board for countercyclical conventional monetary policy. The research literature mostly suggests that this policy only significantly affects the credit and liquidity supplies of small banks. While such effects may help the real economy somewhat by changing the credit supply to bank-dependent small businesses, they do little for overall financial stability that depends primarily on the financial status of large banks.

References

Akin, Ozlem, Nicholas S. Coleman, Christian Fons-Rosen, and Jose-Luis Peydro. forthcoming. Political Connections and Informed Trading: Evidence from TARP. Financial Management forthcoming.

Ashcraft, A. B. (2006). New evidence on the lending channel. *Journal of Money, Credit, and Banking, 38*, 751–775.

Barofsky, N. (2013). *Bailout: How Washington abandoned Main Street while rescuing Wall Street*. Simon and Schuster.

Benes, J., & Kumhof, M. (2015). Risky bank lending and countercyclical capital buffers. *Journal of Economic Dynamics and Control, 58*, 58–80.

Berger, A. N. (2018). The benefits and costs of the TARP bailouts: A critical assessment. *Quarterly Journal of Finance, 8*(02), 1–29.

Berger, A. N., & Bouwman, C. H. S. (2017). Bank liquidity creation, monetary policy, and financial crises. *Journal of Financial Stability, 30*, 139–155.

Berger, A. N., Curti, F., Mihov, A., & Sedunov, J. (2020). *Operational risk is more systemic than you think: Evidence from US bank holding companies* (Working Paper).

Bernanke, B. S. (2015). *The courage to act: A memoir of a crisis and its aftermath*. WW Norton & Company.

Bernanke, B. S., & Blinder, A. S. (1992). The federal funds rate and the channels of monetary policy transmission. *The American Economic Review, 82*, 901–921.

Bunkanwanicha, P., Di Giuli, A., & Salvadè, F. (2019). *The effect of bank bailouts on CEO careers* (Working Paper).

Bush, G. W. (2008). *President Bush discusses Emergency Economic Stabilization Act of 2008*. White House Press Release. Available at https://georgewbush-whitehouse.archives.gov/news/releases/2008/10/20081003-11.html.

Caballero, R., & Simsek, A. (2013). Fire sales in a model of complexity. *The Journal of Finance, 68*, 2549–2587.

Calomiris, C. W., & Khan, U. (2015). An assessment of TARP assistance to financial institutions. *The Journal of Economic Perspectives, 29*(2), 53–80.

Diamond, D. W., & Rajan, R. G. (2011). Fear of fire sales, illiquidity seeking, and credit freezes. *Quarterly Journal of Economics, 126*, 557–591.

Drehmann, M., & Gambacorta, L. (2012). The effects of countercyclical capital buffers on bank lending. *Applied Economics Letters, 19*(7), 603–608.

Driscoll, J. C. (2004). Does bank lending affect output? Evidence from the U.S. States. *Journal of Monetary Economics, 51*, 451–471.

Edge, R., & Liang, N. (2019). *New financial stability governance structures and central banks* (Working Paper).

Ehrmann, M., Gambacorta, L., Martínez-Pagés, J., Sevestre, P., & Worms, A. (2003). Financial systems and the role of banks in monetary policy transmission in the euro area. In I. Angeloni, A. K. Kashyap, & B. Mojon (Eds.), *Monetary policy transmission in the euro area: A study by the Eurosystem monetary transmission network*. Cambridge; New York and Melbourne: Cambridge University Press.

Faria-e-Castro, M. (2020). *A quantitative analysis of countercyclical capital buffers*. Federal Reserve Bank of St. Louis (Working Paper).

Fischer, M., Hainz, C., Rocholl, J., & Steffen, S. (2014). *Government guarantees and bank risk taking incentives* (Working Paper).

Friedman, M. (1968). The role of monetary policy. *The American Economic Review, 58*(1), 1–17.

Harris, O., Huerta, D., & Ngo, T. (2013). The impact of TARP on bank efficiency. *Journal of International Financial Markets, Institutions and Money, 24*, 85–104.

Isaac, W. M. (2010). *Senseless panic: How Washington failed America*. John Wiley and Sons.

Jagolinzer, A. D., Larcker, D. F., Ormazabal, G., & Taylor, D. J. (2017). *Political connections and the informativeness of insider trades*. Rock Center for Corporate Governance at Stanford University. Working Paper 222.

Jiménez, G., Ongena, S., Peydró, J.-L., & Saurina, J. (2017). Macroprudential policy, countercyclical bank capital buffers, and credit supply: Evidence from the Spanish dynamic provisioning experiments. *Journal of Political Economy, 125*(6), 2126–2177.

Kashyap, A. K., & Stein, J. C. (1997). The role of banks in monetary policy: A survey with implications for the European Monetary Union. In *Economic perspectives*. Federal Reserve Bank of Chicago. September/October, 3–18.

Kashyap, A. K., & Stein, J. C. (2000). What do a million observations on banks say about the transmission of monetary policy? *The American Economic Review, 90*, 407–428.

Liang, N. (2013). Systemic risk monitoring and financial stability. *Journal of Money, Credit and Banking, 45*(s1), 129–135.

Lown, C., & Morgan, D. P. (2006). The credit cycle and the business cycle: New findings using the Loan Officer Opinion Survey. *Journal of Money, Credit, and Banking, 38*, 1575–1597.

Lucas, D. (2019). Measuring the cost of bailouts. *Annual Review of Financial Economics, 11*, 85–108.

Massad, T. G. (2011). *Written testimony before the Senate Committee on Banking, Housing and Urban Affairs*. Available at https://www.treasury.gov/press-center/press-releases/Pages/tg1108.aspx.

Mester, L. J. (2018). *A practical viewpoint on financial system resiliency and monetary policy* (Working Paper).

N'Diaye, P. M.'B. P. (2009). *Countercyclical macro prudential policies in a supporting role to monetary policy*. International Monetary Fund. Working Paper No. 9-257.

Paulson, H. M. (2013). *On the brink: Inside the race to stop the collapse of the global financial system with original new material on the five year anniversary of the financial crisis*. Business Plus.

Repullo, R., & Saurina Salas, J. (2011). *The countercyclical capital buffer of Basel III: A critical assessment* (Working paper).

Roman, R. A. (2019). Bank Bailouts and Bail-Ins. Oxford Handbook of Banking, 3rd Edition, Oxford University Press, Oxford, 630-684.

Thakor, A. V. (2005). Do loan commitments cause overlending? *Journal of Money, Credit, and Banking, 37*, 1067–1099.

Yellen, J. L. (2011). Macroprudential supervision and monetary policy in the post-crisis world. *Business Economics, 46*, 3–12.

Zingales, L. (2011). *Oral testimony of Luigi Zingales on overall impact of TARP on financial stability.* Congressional Oversight Panel.

Implications for bank policymakers and bank managers

In this chapter, we discuss implications for both bank policymakers and bank managers. As above for the social costs and benefits, we emphasize that these are logical implications from the extant research, rather than simply our opinions. Our goals are not to preach to policymakers and managers about how to behave. In any situation, these individuals will make their own best judgments based on their personal information sets, skills, and training. Rather, our goals are to summarize the implications of the many research papers referenced in the book to help augment their information sets so that they might make better informed judgments.

Analogous to our assessments of social costs and benefits in Chapter 27, we tailor our suggestions in this chapter to the stability conditions of the financial system for both bank policymakers and bank managers. The recommendations for bank managers also differ by the individual financial conditions of their banks. We also recognize that the short-run versus long-run orientations of the decision makers depend on these conditions. Thus, during a severe financial crisis in which the financial system is in danger of collapse and the real economy is in peril of a deep recession, we expect bank policymakers to put more weight on short-run outcomes to prevent worst-case outcomes. In contrast, policymakers are likely to focus more on long-run optimization during other financial conditions. Similarly, when a bank is in significant financial distress and in danger of failing, we expect its managers to try their best to save the bank in the short run, whereas they are more likely to maximize shareholder value by taking the best long-run decisions when the bank is not in short-run danger.[1] Section 28.1 focuses on

---

[1] We recognize that bank managers often have long-run objectives other than maximizing shareholder value, but in the interest of simplicity and brevity, we maintain the value maximization assumption for our discussions of the implications of the research for bank managers.

423

implications under different conditions for bank policymakers, and Section 28.2 gives analogous implications for bank managers.

28.1 Implications for bank policymakers

As indicated above, the implications of the research for bank policymakers vary with financial system stability conditions. We use the same simplified bifurcation of conditions as in Chapter 27—severe financial crises and TMTF versus other financial conditions. We recognize that bank policymakers are not a uniform group. They include legislators, who generally set broad guidelines for regulations that last for a number of years; regulators, who fill in the details of these regulations as well as design their own rules; supervisors, who conduct on- and off-site examinations to determine adherence to the regulations, assess bank safety and soundness, and take actions against banking organizations and managers that violate the regulations and/or behave in unsafe or unsound fashions; and central bankers, who conduct monetary policy, as well as often serve as regulators and/or supervisors. Despite this significant heterogeneity, in the interest of brevity, we lump the implications for these different policymakers together in this section under the assumption that readers and policymakers can sort out relatively easily which policymaker implements each of the policies.

28.1.1 Implications for bank policymakers under tranquil financial system conditions

Our implications for bank policymakers follow directly from our evaluations of net social benefits and costs in Chapter 27. We start with the implications under other financial conditions—that is, when there is neither a severe financial crisis nor a TMTF situation. As noted above, we expect policymakers to focus on long-run optimization under these tranquil conditions.

At first blush, it seems rather clear that policymakers would be best off choosing the approaches with the "+s" in the final column of Table 27.1 and avoid those with "−s." That is, choose policies in which long-run social benefits appear to exceed social costs under nonstressful or more tranquil financial conditions and eschew pursuit of policies for which social costs are assessed to exceed social benefits. However, it is more complicated than this because not all "+s" and "−s" imply the same magnitudes of relative benefits and costs, respectively, nor is there a uniformity of certainty about these effects.

We argue that under circumstances in which the financial system is not in near-term significant danger, there are three main priorities and corresponding policy choices that help achieve these prioritized goals. The first priority is keeping the current financial system from degrading into a severe financial crisis that might impose serious damage to the financial system and real economy. The most important policy tool to achieve this during tranquil systemic conditions is applying bail-ins to resolve any TBTF or TITF banks that are in individual financial distress and/or pose a danger of dragging down other connected institutions that might endanger the financial system or the real economy. The discussion in Chapter 27 made it clear that bail-ins dominate the other resolution approaches in terms of protecting taxpayer funds and providing better capital and risk managerial incentives, and bail-ins is the only one of them with a " + " for these financial conditions.

The second priority during tranquil times is to reduce the long-run likelihood that individual banks, particularly TBTF, TITF, and TMTF banks, become financially distressed and potentially in need of resolution. This is the primary role of the first lines of defense. The research supports the efficacy of capital requirements, stress tests, prudential supervision, and deposit insurance, as shown with "+s" on the right hand side of Table 27.1. In addition, the research suggests that bail-in policies also help keep banks out of future distress by incentivizing them to voluntarily choose higher capital ratios and to recapitalize prior to financial distress. We recommend that policymakers use all of these tools, as opposed to choosing among them, although we note that the research showing prudential benefits is strongest for capital requirements.

The third priority under these circumstances is to reduce the long-run likelihood and severity of future financial crises that bring about most of the resolutions of distressed banks. This is the primary role of countercyclical policies as well as a secondary role for the first lines of defense. We acknowledge that countercyclical prudential policies such as countercyclical capital requirements are supported by the limited extant research, and some of the first lines of defense such as capital requirements are supported by more extensive research. Nevertheless, it is not clear from the research how much can be done to reduce the long-run likelihood and severity of future financial crises.

In the interest of brevity, we refrain from discussion of the extent to which the "−s" differ in their inabilities to achieve these priorities.

28.1.2 Implications for bank policymakers during severe financial crises and/or TMTF circumstances

We next discuss implications for policymakers under stressful financial conditions when there is a severe financial crisis and/or a TMTF circumstance. Policymakers are expected to optimize over the short run in such a situation to save the financial system from collapse and the economy from a deep recession or depression.

Analogously to the case of tranquil conditions above, policymakers would optimally choose approaches with the "+s" and avoid those with "−s" in the first column of Table 27.1. Again, it is more complicated because not all approaches with the same signs have the same relative benefits and costs with the same degree of certainty.

In this particular case, we argue that there is really only one goal with a high priority and that is to minimize the damage to the financial system and real economy. The only resolution approach with a "+" in the first column of Table 27.1 is bailouts. The research discussed in Chapter 27, particularly the TARP research in Part II, made it clear that bailouts of highly distressed TBTF, TITF, and TMTF banks tend to reduce systemic risk and improve the real economy. In contrast, none of the other resolution methods is established as working well during stressful intervals. While bail-ins may be superior in more tranquil times, during stressful times, bail-ins run the risk of imposing distress and failure on other important financial institutions that can also drag down the financial system and real economy. Of the first lines of defense, only prudential supervision and deposit insurance appear to have favorable effects during these times. Countercyclical prudential policies can also help keep the banks supplying credit and liquidity to the economy.

28.2 Implications for bank managers

The research reported on earlier in the book as well as the social costs and benefits analysis in Chapter 27 also result in some implications for bank managers. As above for policymakers, our goal here is to inform these managers so that they might make better decisions for their banks.

We begin with the recognition that bank managers do not have control over any of the approaches shown in Table 27.1. They cannot choose their own resolution approach among bailouts, bail-ins, and the other resolution approaches in the event of their severe financial distress and impending failure. They also have no ability to set their own capital requirements, liquidity requirements, or other first lines of defense applied by regulators and supervisors. As well, countercyclical government policies are out of bank managers' control.

However, we argue that they can still learn from our analysis how to better apply their own first lines of defense. While it does not work in every case, a number of the regulatory and supervisory tools to keep banks safe and sound can also be applied by bank managers to their own banks to reduce their risks. For example, the research finding that higher bank capital significantly reduces the likelihood of bank failure strongly suggests that bank managers can make their banks safer by holding more capital.

28.2.1 Implications for managers of healthy banks under tranquil financial system conditions

As indicated above, the implications for bank managers depend on the financial conditions of both the individual banks and the financial system. We start here by assuming that neither the bank nor the financial system is in distress. We expect bank managers in this situation to adopt a long-term orientation and maximize shareholder wealth conditional on the constraints imposed by policymakers, i.e., resolution approaches, first lines of defense, countercyclical policies, etc. While the findings in the book do not provide advice for conducting day-to-day asset, liability, and off-balance sheet activities, we note that reducing the expected costs of financial distress and resolution are quite important to maximize shareholder wealth.

As noted above, we recommend that bank managers apply their own first lines of defense to reduce the expected costs of financial distress and resolution based on the research on some of the regulatory and supervisory first lines of defense. That is, bank managers can increase their capital and liquidity buffers, conduct their own stress tests, avoid risky activities outside their core expertise, and make prudent risk management decisions such as avoiding very risky loans and off-balance sheet activities. These are based on the first lines of defense research findings regarding capital and liquidity requirements, stress tests, regulatory activity restrictions, and prudential supervision, although the research does not uniformly support all of these approaches.

At first blush, it might seem that these steps to protect the bank against the expected costs of financial distress and resolution would be relatively unimportant during times when neither the bank nor the financial system is troubled. However, the research suggests that just the opposite is true. As discussed in Part I, the worst risk decisions are typically made during the best of times, and these risks are then only revealed during the worst of times. For many reasons discussed in Part I, bankers tend to make bad decisions during lending and liquidity booms that hurt them later. In addition, the research on countercyclical capital standards clearly suggests that build-ups of capital buffers during good times are helpful in troubled times when these buffers can be run down.

Moreover, large banks can reasonably expect harsher resolution treatment during periods of aggregate tranquility. As illustrated in Table 27.1, it seems more likely during such times that bail-ins that wipe out shareholder value would occur, whereas bailouts might be more likely during severe financial crises and/or situations when many banks are on the brink of failure (i.e., TMTF).

28.2.2 Implications for managers of distressed banks under tranquil financial system conditions

We next consider the situation where the financial system remains tranquil, but the individual bank is significantly distressed. The manager of a distressed bank is expected to optimize over the short run in this situation to keep the bank from failure or preempt some other resolution.

The most important difference is that the steps to reduce risk must be larger, must be taken more quickly, and must be taken almost irrespective of their costs. That is, bank managers likely need to quickly increase their capital and liquidity buffers, avoid risky activities outside their core expertise, and make risk management decisions to reduce risks quickly (e.g., cutting risky loans and off-balance sheet activities). Conducting their own stress tests is not likely helpful when they are already stressed. The tougher expected resolution policies during tranquil times increase the speed at which managers need to act.

28.2.3 Implications for managers of both healthy and distressed banks during severe financial crises and/or TMTF circumstances

Finally, for both healthy and distressed banks, there are two important differences under stressful aggregate financial conditions. First, as noted above, policymakers are likely to be easier on the banks in terms of their resolution decisions during severe financial crises and/or TMTF circumstances. For example, the banks may be more likely to be bailed out during these conditions, reducing some of the incentives for bank managers to bolster their own lines of defense. Thus, bank managers may be expected to be more modest in their recapitalization plans if bailouts are expected to provide the capital for them.

Second, bank managers need to be much more aware of aggregate financial conditions as well as the individual conditions of their counterparties during stressful times for the financial system. The managers need to be wary of taking on significant risk exposures to other institutions that are distressed or likely to become distressed.

29

Open research questions to be addressed by future research

The earlier chapters of this book contain over 500 references, providing powerful and convincing evidence about some of the key topics in the book, but many important open research questions remain. The goal of this final chapter is to identify the important unresearched and under-researched questions that need the most attention and provide some guidance as to how future researchers might proceed to address them. Section 29.1 first provides some general suggestions for the future research on the larger issues of the financial distress and potential failure of TBTF, TITF, or TMTF financial institutions that endanger the financial system and real economy. Section 29.2 then systematically goes through the approaches identified earlier for dealing with these issues—bailouts, bail-ins, and other resolution approaches; first lines of defense, and countercyclical policies—and discusses the open research questions regarding each of them to be addressed by future researchers.

29.1 General suggestions for future research

Much remains to be done to keep the financial system and real economy safe from the distress and potential failure of important financial institutions. The research that informs policymakers, bank managers, and other researchers needs to be an important part of the solution. In this subsection, we provide five general suggestions for the directions of this research.

First, we recommend that more of the research be directed toward reducing the likelihood and severity of financial crises. As discussed earlier, financial crises bring about most of the bailouts, bail-ins, and other resolutions of important financial institutions, as well as cause massive damage to the financial system and real economy. This suggested research effort involves more study of the causes and predictors of these crises and

429

the macroprudential tools to combat them. We also strongly suggest more research on some of the less-researched first lines of defense, such as liquidity requirements and stress tests, that may also reduce the likelihood and severity of financial crises. Better first lines of defense also have social benefits in terms of better preparing banks for avoiding financial distress and failure, reducing their contributions to systemic risk, and allowing the banks to continue supplying the credit that fuels the real economy when financial crises occur.

Second, we recommend that more research be undertaken on the more ambitious goal of directly comparing two or more methods or approaches for dealing with the same problem or issue, rather than just studying one particular method or approach at a time. For example, most bailout research papers examine just one bailout program or lump several bailout programs together without differentiating among them. These practices make it difficult to draw conclusions as to which programs might be best. In the research summarized in earlier chapters, we only find one European paper that compares bailout types and one US paper that compares bailouts and bail-ins. We argue that such comparisons may actually provide the most value in terms of policy recommendations, given that policymakers have limited resources and can usually only afford to pursue the best policies.

We strongly suggest that future researchers directly compare different bailout programs; different bail-in types; bailouts with bail-ins; bailouts and bail-ins with the other resolution approaches of bankruptcy/failure, living wills, and/or breakups of large complex financial institutions by size or activity type; different first lines of defense with each other; and different countercyclical policies with one another, etc. Future researchers are also encouraged to use their imaginations and research skills to pursue innovative new policies and policy comparisons not covered in this book as well.

Third, we suggest that researchers endeavor as much as possible to measure the total effects of the approach that they are studying. For approaches in which some banks, loans, states, etc. are treated—i.e., bailed out, bailed-in, stress tested, etc—and others are not; this includes investigating both the direct effects on the treated group and indirect effects on the untreated group. As discussed extensively in Part II, most of the TARP studies use the difference-in-difference (DID) methodology which focuses on the differences between the treated and untreated groups, essentially assuming that there are no indirect effects on the untreated group. For example, most studies of the effects of TARP on credit supply measure the difference between loans of TARP and non-TARP banks, effectively assuming that the lending of non-TARP banks is unaffected by the program. While this may be a reasonable assumption or the only way to proceed in some cases, we recommend trying to measure the indirect effects whenever possible.

Fourth, we suggest that researchers examine more of the long-term effects of the approaches they study to protect the financial system and the real economy. In most cases, the research on bailouts, bail-ins, and other topics covered in the over 500 references in the book focus on the short-run effects of the program or policy they study. In a minority of cases, the researchers extend their results to the following few years. As discussed in detail in Chapters 27 and 28, the conclusions of which policies to follow and the implications for bank policymakers and bank managers often vary considerably with weights that the decision maker places on short-run versus long-run outcomes. It is quite clear that the researchers up to this point in time, the authors of this book included, have provided insufficient research results to assist the decision makers with long-term orientations. We, therefore, urge future researchers to provide more long-run outcomes.

Finally, we recommend that more of the research focus on developing nations. As noted earlier, the research on most of the topics is highly US- and Euro-centric, likely due to the better availability of data on US and European nations as well as the locations of many of the researchers. Nonetheless, financial crises, costly resolutions of distressed financial institutions, and damages to the financial system and real economy are not just first-world problems. It is likely that these problems are worse in developing nations, but we need more research to find out more about the problems in these nations. An important additional question to be addressed is whether the best approaches to deal with the financial distress and potential failure of important financial institutions differ between developed and developing nations. It is quite likely that some of the approaches that work well in one group of nations may not be as beneficial in the other group.

29.2 Open research questions to be addressed by future researchers on all of the approaches

As indicated above, we systematically proceed through all of the approaches discussed in the book, and identify open questions on each to be addressed by future researchers. Subsection 29.2.1 discusses bailouts, 29.2.2 examines bail-ins, 29.2.3 covers other resolution approaches, 29.2.4 goes over first lines of defense, and 29.2.5 considers countercyclical policies.

29.2.1 Bailouts

Our first and most important research suggestion regarding bailouts is to use the extant TARP research to motivate similar research on other bailouts, which are very much understudied relative to TARP. Part II provides a relatively complete primer or mini-textbook on empirical research on TARP, with one chapter on methodologies and 10 chapters addressing different important questions. The same methodologies and questions could be applied to other bailouts for which the research literature is less developed. Thus, we suggest that future researchers use methodologies like DID, instrumental variables (IV), propensity score matching (PSM), Heckman sample selection correction, and placebo tests from Chapter 5 to address the determinants of receiving and exiting other bailout programs as in Chapter 6; the effects of other bailouts on the recipient banks' valuations as in Chapter 7; the results of other bailouts on market discipline as in Chapter 8; the impacts of other bailouts on banks' leverage risk as in Chapter 9; the influences of other bailouts on bank competition as in Chapter 10; the consequences of other bailouts on banks' credit supply and portfolio risks as in Chapters 11 and 12, respectively; the results of other bailouts on recipient banks' credit customers as in Chapter 13; and the influences of other bailouts on the real economy and systemic risk as in Chapters 14 and 15, respectively. We especially encourage more research on the effects of the other bailouts on the most important goals of bailouts—improving the real economy and reducing risks to the financial system. Such a research program would greatly deepen the available knowledge about bank bailouts and allow for improved comparisons of different types of bailouts.

For the other US bailouts during the Global Financial Crisis—the Federal Reserve's Expanded Discount Window (DW) and Term Auction Facilities (TAF) liquidity programs; the FDIC Temporary Debt Guarantee Program (TDGP); the Small Business Lending Fund (SBLF); Federal Home Loan Bank (FHLB) Advances; and the Federal Reserve's Quantitative Easing (QE) Programs—the research summarized in Part III reveals that there are much fewer articles that address a much more restricted set of research questions compared to the TARP research. For the bank bailouts outside of the US, more of these questions are already addressed by the research, but generally with fewer research papers than the TARP literature.

The TARP research summarized in Part II could also be made more complete by adding more research studies on the relatively understudied questions. As alluded to in Part II, more investigations are needed on the questions of market discipline effects of TARP; the market and accounting leverage impacts of the program; and whether TARP may have given large TBTF banks competitive advantages over small banks. There is also very little information on the channels through which TARP works, the effects of TARP on other banks that did not receive the bailouts, and whether the beneficial effects of TARP on the real economy were primarily through large versus small business activities. Other important questions regarding TARP about which we are unaware of any research include the stigma effects of the program and the extent to which it may have resulted in "zombie" lending to unproductive firms.

29.2.2 Bail-ins

The bail-in literature summarized in Part III covers the US Orderly Liquidity Authority (OLA) bail-in program, the Bank Recovery and Resolution Directive (BRRD) in the European Union, contingent convertibles (CoCos), double liability, and the combination bailout–bail-in resolution of Long-Term Capital Management (LTCM). Most of these topics are covered by much fewer research papers addressing a very limited number of questions relative to the empirical literature on TARP. Our key recommendation is again to borrow the methodologies and 10 sets of questions from the empirical TARP literature—particularly the questions regarding the real economy and the financial system—and apply them to the different types of bail-ins. If bail-in data are unavailable, theoretical work can also help inform bank policymakers and bank managers about the expected effects.

29.2.3 Other resolution approaches

The research literature on the other resolution approaches in Part III covers bankruptcy/failure, living wills, and breakups of large complex financial institutions by size or activity type. Most of these topics are covered by much fewer research papers addressing a very limited number of questions relative to the empirical literature on TARP. To the extent that the data allow, our key recommendation is again to borrow the methodologies and 10 sets of questions from the empirical TARP literature and apply them to these different resolution approaches. Theoretical work on these topics may also prove useful.

29.2.4 First lines of defense

The research on the first lines of defense summarized in Part IV includes capital requirements, liquidity requirements, stress tests, regulatory activity restrictions, prudential supervision, deposit insurance, and direct government ownership. For some of these lines—stress tests, prudential supervision, and direct government ownership—there are treated and untreated banks, so many of the techniques and questions raised in the TARP literature are appropriately applied. For other lines—capital requirements, liquidity requirements, and direct government ownership—the most compelling new questions concern how the net social benefits and costs differ between tranquil stressful and financial conditions, as shown in Table 27.1. That is, it may be helpful to policymakers to go beyond our simple " + ," " − ," and "?" marks and quantify the circumstances under which these approaches are helpful or not. For the remaining line, deposit insurance, the strong benefits are relatively clear, so the most helpful future research may involve the optimal setting of deposit insurance premiums and caps.

29.2.5 Countercyclical policies

The extant research on countercyclical policies summarized in several places in the book suggests that countercyclical capital requirements function well in smoothing out the cycle, but that the benefits of conventional monetary policy may be limited. As discussed in Chapter 28, a key priority for policymakers is to reduce the long-run likelihood and severity of future financial crises. Given this priority as well as the extant research, we suggest that future researchers focus on finding additional countercyclical policies that may further smooth out the cycle and reduce the social costs of severe financial crises. We also recommend further research on how the effectiveness of countercyclical policies varies across nations' different formal and informal institutions, different stages of economic and banking sector development, and different regulatory and market structures.

Author Index

Subject Index